RUDYARD KIPLING

RUDYARD KIPLING
Martin Seymour-Smith

St. Martin's Press
New York

Library of Congress Cataloging-in-Publication Data

Seymour-Smith, Martin.
    Rudyard Kipling / Martin Seymour-Smith.
        p.   cm.
    "A Thomas Dunne book."
    ISBN 0-312-03925-5
    1. Kipling, Rudyard, 1865-1936—Biography.   2. Authors,
English—19th century—Biography.   3. Authors, English—20th
century—Biography.   I. Title.
PR4856.S39   1990
828'.809—dc20
    [B]   89-27048
                                                                            CIP

First published in Great Britain by Queen Anne Press, a division of Macdonald &
Co. (Publishers) Limited.

First U.S. Edition

10 9 8 7 6 5 4 3 2 1

To David and Oonagh Wright,
and in memory of Philippa Wright and Patrick Swift

Contents

Acknowledgments

I am deeply grateful to Alan Samson and Sara Wheeler of Queen Anne Press
for all their interest in and concentration on this book and its various earlier
versions – and for their constructive and always sensitive suggestions. It
was a pleasure to work on the details with Sara Wheeler. My warmest
and most appreciative thanks to both. Errors and deficiencies remain, of
course, entirely my own.

Nann du Sautoy, who originally suggested that I write on Kipling, later
proved a loyal and encouraging ally when difficulties arose.

To my friend Shena Mackay I owe the kind of debt that can only be
owed by one writer to another with whom he is in sympathy: she helped
keep me going at a time when circumstances might well have forced me
to give up.

It is a great pleasure to record my debt to my near neighbour Walter
Frizell, who was once in the employ of Mr and Mrs Rudyard Kipling: I
thank him for his shrewd and candid reminiscences, and for showing me
a farming handbook annotated by Kipling which is in his possession. I am
also grateful to David Arscott, Senior Producer of BBC Radio Sussex, for
allowing me to listen to tapes of broadcasts relating to Kipling.

As always, I am grateful to the invaluable and wonderful London Library,
and to the East Sussex County Library (particularly to Richard Acam).
Others who helped are Colin Britt, C.H. Sisson (for a characteristic single
remark which put me on the track of an important feature of Kipling),
Brigadier-General (Own Imperialist Army) Basil de Petúlo-Gregerson, Giles
Gordon and, above all, my wife.

Thanks are due to the following authors and publishers for the use of
quotations from their work: Charles Carrington and Macmillan Publishing
Ltd for passages from *Rudyard Kipling: His Life and Work*; Sir Angus Wilson
and Secker and Warburg Ltd for passages from *The Strange Ride of Rudyard
Kipling*; the Estate of the late Lord Birkenhead and Weidenfeld and
Nicolson Ltd for passages from *Rudyard Kipling*; Philip Mason and Jonathan
Cape Ltd for passages from *Kipling: The Glass, the Shadow and the Fire*.

Foreword to the Second Edition

I take the opportunity presented by the publication of the second edition of this biography to make some comments on its initial reception, and thus to illuminate the principles upon which it was written. The text does not differ substantially from that of the first edition; but I have made many changes, and added some new information.

When *Rudyard Kipling* was published in February 1989 there was an immediate reaction from both ends of the press, and from two classes of reviewer: from those who were not authors of serious books, who thought themselves angry at what they wrongly took to be an unwarranted attack on an eminent person; and from those who were authors of serious books, who were more considered in their approach. It was stated in a television programme that the 'critics' had universally decided that in the matter of Kipling, 'Mr Seymour-Smith was out to lunch', but this was not the case. Apart from the fact that reviewers are only occasionally critics, *Rudyard Kipling* got, even in the places where it is supposed to count, as many respectful, and even 'good', reviews as it got indignant ones — the more the writers knew about Kipling the more they tended to take the book seriously. But any author can tell a similar tale.

More important, the reactions, ranging from the ignorant through the casual to the intelligent, cast light on the curious nature of Kipling's reputation. By far the larger part of this is anchored in assumptions about Great Britain that are so uncritical as to be wholly emotional. It is not commonplace enough to say that such assumptions are patriotic only in name. This is so not only amongst tabloid journalists but also amongst some who pose as their betters. One of the latter found it necessary (perhaps in an oblique attempt at 'defence of the realm') to describe the book in terms so palpably false that, when I dealt with his misrepresentations in a long letter to the press, he did not even try to deny it. But since those more immediate reactions I have received many letters, of which there have been enough to confirm my belief that this book, whatever else it may be, is the first biography of the real Rudyard Kipling, for whose best work — as, for example, John Bayley noticed — I feel 'a real love'. There are useful biographies of him, but even the more enlightened leave him as the stuffed dummy of the popular imagination, rather than as a human being. The more realistic approach has its penalties, even though it led to one tabloid exclaiming 'SEX-SLUR ON PATRIOT "LUDICROUS NONSENSE"', quoting Dr A. L. Rowse, who had not read it. But all that can only be expected.

This is the point at which I should explain what I tried to do in writing the book and the circumstances in which it had to be done. I can now be more explicit than, initially, I perhaps over-politely was.

Given the job of writing a critical biography of Rudyard Kipling, I discovered that the 'definitive' work had been postponed by his daughter until a 'trusted' writer could be found. Then Charles Carrington was procured, but the resultant book cannot be called definitive. Perhaps I am rather too affable, if one can be too affable, about it in my introduction. It is based on ideas about literature that might have been taught in a good school in 1900, and on a Victorian psychological model. Some of this is still pertinent; but water has passed under the bridge. Carrington's biography, though, was very satisfying to those who dislike psychological enquiry but who want something that looks as though it writes off the need for it (this is the *raison d'être* of 'official biographies'); it was invaluable but, in the main, because some of the material upon which it was based was afterwards destroyed. Exactly how much, you may ask? Who took the decision to destroy Carrie Kipling's diary and to replace it with 'selections' made by Carrington himself? I cannot, yet, quite answer these questions. A functionary of the Kipling Society pronounced, in lieu of reading it, that this book by me should be destroyed, like those diaries. Some of my readers will understand why I do not want to get into arguments with people like that. Of course I do not question their right to do whatever they like with the material. What I have announced is their motivation. What you eventually get when you act from such motivation is some public nuisance such as myself; I am not ashamed of that.

With Carrington's biography safely published, it seemed, to those whom I define (in my introduction) as *ardent Kiplingites,* that the job had been done; now whatever might 'mislead the public' could be dispensed with (indeed, destroyed). The time for speculation had been officially ended. The great patriot was no more than he seemed to be. Indeed, like any other 'great man', he had been divested of his inner life, dusted off in Carlylean fashion, and put on a shelf. He now had the status of, say, the subject of H. V. Marrot's 'standard life' of Galsworthy; but that, and its like, ought to be entitled *The Standard Death.*

One simply cannot imagine Carrington (in his capacity as writer) being able to deal, at any level, with such cynical pragmatism as Kipling's public heroes, for example Rhodes or Milner, displayed when off the record. Milner talked (as the reader will discover) of 'excellent simple-minded fellows', amongst imperialists, and also of 'fully initiated augurs'. There is certainly room for a biography of Kipling's much admired Milner, the friend at Oxford of Oscar Wilde; but the matter is not urgent because Milner left nothing valuable behind. If we remember him at all, it is as the half-German, and German-educated, architect of the Boer War, and as the administrator who raised no serious objection to importing young slaves from China to work in the mines of the Rand, meanwhile depriving them of all freedom in their 'spare time', by confining them to camps. If the shrewd and entertaining Milner did not think of Kipling as 'simple-minded', I doubt if he accepted him as 'fully initiated'.

Surely a writer of Kipling's literary, if not political, calibre eventually deserves more sophisticated treatment than this? His fiction fell into critical disfavour because his politics became unfashionable. But the critical disfavour arose from a wrong assumption: that his creative work must be generated by his repulsive ideology — an ideology that was confused, egoistic (racism is extended egoism), bloodthirsty and ungenerous. In fact the best of Kipling's fiction, deeply humane, transcended all such 'ideas': it arose from self-critical impulses that are so profound as to be, at times, breathtaking. The rest of his work (most of it) veers uneasily, one way or the other, between the two extremes, without achieving the grand imaginative objectivity of the best.

Let me be explicit about my own assumptions: that art of the kind Kipling could sometimes practise is associated with virtue (if this be defined as something of the nature of Thomas Hardy's 'loving kindness'), or, more accurately, with the pursuit of it; that human beings have a vigorous and indeed incessant inner life, part of it of a horrible or at least disingenuous nature; that they are neither consistent or rational; that they do not consist of one but of many disparate selves. Since this is a biography, I should say a little more about the nature of this multi-selved inner life (it is in no way a new notion). True, we have a ghostly single self, which corresponds to what is often called our 'type', behind that; but we seldom want to learn about it. Anyone may verify this for themselves; most care not to. Inner life may, too, be described as 'stream-of-consciousness'. More precisely, though, it consists of a mixture of three mental activities: such actual perception of reality as we are capable of exercising; our more or less distorted and sometimes violently conflicting interpretations of those perceptions; and fantasy. Such biographers as Carrington thus assume qualities of consistency and rationality which do not even exist in their subjects. So that in ascribing what certain commentators called 'bad feelings' to Kipling, I do no more than tell *his* story as distinct from anyone else's. Such commentators, who do not have bad feelings, or who prefer to write as if they did not, assumed that I must therefore 'hate' Kipling.

So tabloid-minded people, when they were not pretending to have 'known all along' that Kipling was 'queer', tried to make out that I was simply attempting—in their own horribly false and simplistic manner—to change the 'image' of Kipling from one of 'patriot' to one of 'sodomite'. 'Kipling said that the female of the species was more deadly than the male; he did not know Martin Seymour-Smith', an evening newspaper commented. 'I don't *care*, Kipling gives such pleasure!' cried a columnist.

Care about what? The 'sex-slur'? There is no 'sex-slur'. There is in this book no more than confident psychological speculation that Kipling experienced powerful homosexual desires, and was for a time conscious of them. After all, there is no such thing as *a homosexual*, or *a heterosexual.* There are people who engage in exclusively homosexual behaviour, there are people who engage in exclusively heterosexual behaviour, there are people who engage in both types of behaviour. There are people who experience desires of both kinds, and engage in no sexual behaviour at all with others. There are people who experience homosexual desires but who engage in and enjoy heterosexual behaviour, from which children are sometimes born. And so on. That is all. The rest is abstraction, labelling, wishful thinking, egoism.

Yet John Bayley (a good critic of fiction, whose fair-minded and comprehensive review affords me the best opportunity of making the more serious points I need to make in this foreword) declared that I had brought in the matter of Kipling's sexuality only in order 'to affront the conservative Kipling lobby': 'the author's real purpose was to display his own principles, as an *honnête homme* of our day, against Kipling's flashy, dishonest authoritarianism'. Yes, but he has not considered the predicament of a biographer who finds himself confronted with the *truth.* Must this biographer alter it in order to avoid being accused of trying to affront reactionary opinion in order to gain publicity, or, even worse, of being an *honnête homme?* More charitably, Bayley believes that I have been led astray by a failure to understand the nature of Victorian friendship. But the reader will discover that it is Bayley, not I, who is over-confident in that matter.

For it is not as simple. The world of Victorian friendship (of the Tennyson-Hallam kind, explains Bayley) demonstrably overlapped very closely indeed with that of wholly self-conscious paedophilia, the necessarily furtive manifestations of which varied from excessively pure to excessively depraved. There is after all some evidence that Kipling himself, though closely guarded in everything by his wife (I have suggested why), was in fact on the extreme fringe of that world. Reggie Turner, one of its doyens, assured Gide that it was so. Max Beerbohm assumed it. It seems, too, that Kipling viewed a famous collection of provocative photographs of boys, while his wife languished at a hotel. There is more of this sort of thing, although only a little of it suggests that he 'did' much about these tastes.

All the now mounting evidence for Kipling's homoerotic predilections is of more interest to contributors to tabloid newspapers than it is to me; it is being collected by those fascinated by such matters. I was simply looking for the likely explanation of his naive and ferocious politics in the light of artistic achievements which contradict them. Only to that extent did it matter to me. Everyone who has read *Kim* knows very well that Kipling was sexually aroused by 'beautiful boys'; it has in any case been noted by those who do not pretend not to know about such matters. Nor is he the only married 'heterosexual' to whom that (or many other feelings held by our culture to be discreditable) applies. There is nothing surprising about it. We cannot afford to be moral until we have freed ourselves from certain illusions, by fuller psychological descriptions than have ever been publicly fashionable. Besides, Bayley's view of Victorian male friendship as wholly separate from homosexual desires won't stand up to close psychological scrutiny: it is neither subtle nor complete enough, and it wilfully ignores how the human mind works. He says that Proust 'thought homosexuality a matter of fashion'. In view of Proust's actual and agonised confusions over the matter, and in view of the other things he said about it, that really is evasive.

As for *honnête homme:* it is clearly, in Bayley's mouth, a slightly pejorative term. If he means, 'on impossibly high moral ground', then I can sympathise, although without accepting the label. One thinks of the frustrations in regard to that latest phenomenon of our times, the too exquisite Green Party. But because I simply wonder what stance Kipling would take on the matter of nuclear power, were he alive today, and because (with necessary brevity) I trace many present Irish troubles to mistakes made by governments in London, he assumes that I 'leave . . . no doubt' as to where I stand. He then gravely corrects me: Kipling would have 'believed' in what he describes as 'the nuclear deterrent'; my 'passion for current affairs' leads me to fail to understand the complex difficulties facing Britain as an imperial power; I am 'short on history'. Here Bayley, as perhaps too much of a 'fully initiated augur' of the latest status quo, whatever that now is, is mistaken. He isn't able to correct any of my historical accounts. He just doesn't like what he takes to be my nasty tone: the criminal actions of eminent statesmen and others are (he feels) so eminently excusable, in the frightful circumstances, as to require total suppression. History is too 'complicated'. But political views are in the same case as moral judgements: they have to be withheld (as in fact I withhold mine, since I do not pretend that criminal actions are the province of only certain parties: they are the province of history) until the fullest possible description of the circumstances has been made. And it is my too vivid descriptions that Bayley does not like. Human beings, he feels, ought to be easier on themselves: don't let's be so intense, it's like serious religion, and surely we've dispensed with *that*. Let's just all push along being as nice as we can to each other until the certain end.

The trouble is that none of this vague atheist humanism in the least applies to Kipling, and to try to view him from that particular slot-out-onto-the-world is quite useless in gaining an understanding of him. You cannot thus get even closer to him. To view from that particular slot, indeed, entails the suppression of self-critical impulses and the stifling of a certain sort of inner conscience, as well as the allaying of fear that is the real object of the exercise. And so in this book I had to describe, as best I could, some part of Kipling's inner life. It is the only means of reaching some sense of the conscience in him from which his finest work arose. No, he was not 'worse' than anyone else. But he was famous, and so his confusions became famous.

I here deal, therefore, in psychological realities as uncomfortable to me as to my reader. I assume that Kipling's political ideas really were particularly grotesque, perhaps lunatic. I then ask: How is it that such art as Kipling's could arise from such a bizarre and apparently undistinguished mixture? Some have said that they already knew the answer, others (such as Peter Ackroyd, in a generous review) have said that it does not matter, that it is irrelevant in any case; still others that they remain unconvinced. But how else, at least for the person of good will (a better term, perhaps, than Bayley's *honnête homme*), can it be explained?

Ah! What avails the classic bent
And what the cultured word,
Against the undoctored incident
That actually occurred?

RUDYARD KIPLING

Introduction

Until her death in 1976, Mrs George Bambridge, Rudyard Kipling's daughter, held control over the material needed for a definitive account of his life. Some of this material, including the diary of Kipling's wife, Caroline – it is not at all clear what or how much else – has since been destroyed. What remains that is not restricted has now for the most part been published or incorporated in other works. Soon after Kipling's death in 1936 the task of writing the definitive account was entrusted to the New Zealand novelist and biographer Hector Bolitho. Perhaps Bolitho was initially approached because it was felt that he could be trusted: Kipling had been on good terms with the late King George V, and Bolitho had written insipid but approved royal biographies – for example, a polite one of King Edward VII. A grateful Palace had allowed him to work on his books in the library of Windsor Castle. Bolitho's habit was to grumble about whatever restrictions were imposed upon him, but to carry on regardless. However, even he could not manage Mrs Bambridge. He gave up. He wrote a brief account of the affair in his autobiography.

Next came Taprell Dorling, author of popular and respectable sea-stories under the name of 'Taffrail'; he also gave up.

Then the Scottish novelist and writer Eric Linklater, more distinguished than either Bolitho or Taffrail, was asked to have a try; but he, too, could not agree to terms with Mrs Bambridge, although he did not quarrel with her.

Next was Frederick Winston Furneaux Smith, son of F.E. Smith. Having succeeded to his father's title in 1930, he had long been the second Earl of Birkenhead. An encounter with Mrs Bambridge's husband, Captain George Bambridge, led him to seek permission to undertake the work. Although he had already written two books, he was ambitious to become a more seriously considered writer.

The good-hearted Birkenhead had himself been Principal Private Secretary to Lord Halifax at the time of Munich, and was for some reason never anxious to conceal it. Mrs Bambridge was familiar with her father's feelings about the Germans. The first Earl of Birkenhead had initially been against Home Rule for Ireland (anathema to Kipling), but he had then turned to compromise. He had also been Secretary for India from 1924 until 1928, and had offended Kipling in that capacity (as any other person filling the post would have done). Kipling also spoke of F.E. contemptuously in a letter to Rider Haggard after he had attended a dinner at which Birkenhead gave a drunken speech, which was broadcast by the BBC. The first Earl, a wily and persuasive lawyer, had also been the smooth spokesman for those involved in the Marconi scandal, which called forth one of Kipling's most celebrated hate-poems, 'Gehazi', about the crooked and successful politician Sir Rufus Isaacs (later Lord Reading). The omens were not good.

In about 1943, Birkenhead entered into an agreement with Mrs Bambridge so self-punitive that his eagerness to establish himself as an imperialist historian, biographer pleasing to Mrs Bambridge, independent psychological analyst, and solver of the Kipling enigma, must have been desperate. He undertook to visit the United States to inspect the Brattleboro property, should Mrs Bambridge deem it necessary for him to do so, at his own expense. He was not allowed to visit India or South Africa unless Mrs Bambridge 'consented' – but if she did, then she would, on those occasions, pay two-thirds of his expenses. He was instructed to visit Stanley Baldwin (Kipling's cousin) and 'Trix' (Mrs Fleming, Kipling's sister) 'at an early stage', and also such other persons as Mrs Bambridge might 'indicate'. The copyright in the work was to be Mrs Bambridge's property. He must submit it to her as he went along, although at his own convenience; he agreed to omit any passages or quotations from documents which she might desire him to omit. Mrs Bambridge would have 'entire' control of the work. As author, Birkenhead was to have one-third of her receipts, less her costs, from the 'publication, exploitation and sale'. He did in fact visit America and was well remembered for the many enquiries he made there.

This was a hard, even bizarre, agreement. It might seem to tell us something about Mrs Bambridge, whose opinion of biographers by then could not have been far from her father's of journalists. She never trusted Birkenhead, and became increasingly nervous about the project. Not many biographers would have found it attractive at that time. Kipling's works sold, but neither he nor his achievements were fashionable.

Mrs Bambridge felt herself to be the sole guardian of her father's honour. His stock had been falling for many years. Like most esteemed people, he had been subject to many outrageous and malevolent rumours, amongst them that he was a bastard and a half-caste and that he had, before leaving India, begotten many children. Elsie Bambridge accepted that she could not write the book herself, but needed to trust whoever did. If she could not trust, then she must exercise full control. This is understandable in a person largely ignorant of literary matters. Her limitations were no greater than anyone else's who might have been in her position. She was as jealous of her father's privacy as he had been, and clearly resented psychological speculation of any kind; she even confused this with what she called 'amateur psychoanalysis'. But she had no wish to suppress any of the external facts of his life so far as she felt that these were respectable. She probably felt that all of them were respectable, and thus susceptible only to speculative contamination of a kind hateful to her. Alas, it was all too likely that a man like the second Earl, the son of his father and servant of Halifax (betrayer, in Kipling's eyes, of India), had heard of Freud.

Nonetheless, while she felt it her duty to reveal facts, she demanded that they be aired in ways approved by herself. Her mother Caroline had tried to erase all trace of Kipling's relationship with Mrs Edmonia Hill, and with Mrs Hill's family; when she succeeded in buying up his letters to them, she destroyed them. Mrs Bambridge, who was critical of her mother's jealousy and possessiveness (as those who have read her Epilogue to Charles Carrington's biography will know), discovered that copies had been made before the sale: she bought these at a high cost and put them in the Wimpole Archive (so named after her residence, a large Georgian mansion near Cambridge). The character of Carrie Kipling is well known; its effect on her husband has been largely suppressed – by means, however, of skating (Carrington) or pleasantly smoothing (Wilson) the matter over, rather than totally ignoring it.

Birkenhead did not like the terms of the contract he had signed. But, as his son and heir tells us, he felt secure in the early stages. George Bambridge assured him that when the time came to submit some actual work he would himself 'see that everything was all right', and relations with Mrs Bambridge seemed, at least to Birkenhead, to be good. Doubtless Captain Bambridge, thinking him to be a fundamentally sound man, told him that he ought not to take much notice of his wife's severity. But, she later told Carrington, she never liked Birkenhead. Probably she felt it would have been indelicate to question her husband's judgement, and probably George felt that the sooner this biography was out of the way the better.

Mrs Bambridge told Carrington that when Birkenhead was working at Wimpole he had not been 'a welcome guest'. Clearly she initially gave way only for her husband's sake. At the least Birkenhead lacked the necessary tact to get round her. She continued to be polite to him only for so long as she had not seen anything of his book. He must surely eventually have blinded himself to her dislike of him. Many writers would have given up in the light of that dislike – whether it was just, or unjust and hurtful, or not. To lack the trust of so important a witness would be crippling for any biographer. If he really was unaware of it then this may even account for a certain insensitivity in him. Writing definitive biographies of people recently deceased, as of those still alive, is inevitably partly a matter of tact and of steering one's way through minefields; the more interesting the life of the subject, the more, perhaps, this is so. Sometimes the biographer has to make a decision as to who ought to be offended least – when someone is bound to be – if his book is not to be reduced to a simple deceitful encomium. Birkenhead was just not up to that kind of thing. Where the smooth, deceitful, practised professional Hector Bolitho, privately embittered and complaining, but always publicly obedient, had failed, he was not likely to succeed.

By 1948, when Birkenhead handed Mrs Bambridge his first draft, her husband had been dead for five years. Now the restraining influence upon her dislike of him was removed. She would not even discuss the matter with him: 'I consider it so bad as a book that any attempt at palliative measures such as you describe, rewriting here and altering there is not feasible.' T.S. Eliot pronounced it 'too slight', but Birkenhead's friends John Betjeman and Robert Blake (now Lord Blake) could not see what was so wrong. It was with great reluctance that Mrs Bambridge eventually paid £5000 compensation in return for Birkenhead's undertaking never to publish or 'cause to be published' any biography of her father. That contract was binding upon him alone, so the book was posthumously published, in revised form, by his son and heir Robin in 1978 under the title *Rudyard Kipling*. It shows that he was not up to the job, but only to the extent that it is disjointed and does not cohere. It is amateurish by the side of Carrington – and, it must be added, by the side of much other Kipling criticism.

However, there have been worse books about eminent people, and Mrs Bambridge's hostility was not on the face of it justified, especially as what she saw was only a draft. What we now have of the book is a finished version worked on, presumably, in the light of Carrington's biography and, I suppose, of what had been published on Kipling since. Carrington says that he is convinced that the passages to which Mrs Bambridge objected were excised; I am not sure that quite all of them were. There is something of a mystery as to what Elsie Bambridge could have objected to. Carrington does not enlighten us on this point, and perhaps could not allow himself to do so. No doubt it was a very sensitive subject, especially as Mrs Bambridge was aware that not a few felt her to have behaved outrageously. She told Carrington, revealingly, that Birkenhead's book was 'riddled with the amateur psychoanalysis that had become fashionable in the 1930s' and that the author was 'allied to the Bright Young Things' (perhaps she meant 'short skirts and Freud'). There is no sign of this in the book as we have it. Clearly she was too embarrassed or frightened to voice her specific objections. I am not sure that Birkenhead himself ever knew, for his son tells us unequivocally that he, himself, did not. Perhaps Mrs Bambridge was right: perhaps Birkenhead's original draft did contain clumsy analysis of a 'psychoanalytical' type, or ineffectual speculations about Kipling's sexuality. But it is clear that Mrs Bambridge objected to all psychological speculation in itself.

The matter of Kipling's sexual orientation was not something I had wanted to labour more than necessary: as it is, I have treated it only in order to explain certain hitherto inexplicable things. Yet it explains much. Sir Angus Wilson in his book is clearly aware of it, and seems to agree with the view I take, though he chooses to make nothing of it. Philip Mason also mentions it, but nervously and obliquely. Leon Edel, a 'Freudian' biographer who has dealt with a big homosexual subject and made it his own (Kipling's friend Henry James), has mentioned it; but he then dismisses it in far too over-confident a fashion.

It is often stated in conversations that Wilson is 'good' on the subject of 'Kipling's sexual ambivalence'. But that is just what Wilson is determined not to discuss. He has one sentence on it (and some hints in his discussion of Kim), even though that is straightforward enough. Were the matter well known and well discussed, I could understand – even defend – a reluctance to go into it. But the complete failure to discuss it – I think the ardent Kiplingites, those who love Kipling for what they believe are his ideas, have played a major role here – misses an opportunity to clarify unexplained factors not only in Kipling the man, but, more importantly, in his writings. Were this not so, I should have thought not twice but at least three times about mentioning the matter at all. It is enough to say at this stage that the manner in which all people's sexuality leaks into and thus distorts their thinking and their emotion tells us a great deal about them. It is foolish and dishonest to invent arguments against this.

Birkenhead is the only man except Carrington to have been allowed full use of material that has since been destroyed. Even had he been inept and unintelligent, his use of this material would be of some interest. In fact, to any post-Carrington commentator, the book is invaluable. After all, admirably though Carrington performed his task, he was undoubtedly inhibited by Elsie Bambridge. He had to be; probably he wanted to be. Birkenhead in the end was not.

Carrington was well suited to be the author of the official biography. He is an imperial historian, but reasonably well informed on the general outlines of literary history. He is sympathetic to Kipling's politics; indeed, his own politics were formed partly under Kipling's influence. But he did not admire Kipling only because his political attitude attracted him: he loved his writing. Such a sympathy cannot be a bad thing in a biographer. Carrington clearly loves Kipling, though never wholly uncritically. That again is an advantage: hatred is a much more dubious aid to the production of a good book. His *Rudyard Kipling* appeared in 1955.

But any truly successful biographer has to recognise that Kipling has been much hated, and has to try to understand why. It is not of any use to tell people off for hating him, as Carrington irately does. Kipling's extremist polemic has long been the easiest target for this dislike: it has been broken off from the whole man, as though it actually were the whole man, and railed at for its awfulness. It is not an unreasonable attitude, but ultimately it has proved unhelpful. Much of Kipling's polemic *is* horrible and absurd, in terms both human and historical. Imperialism generated little that was virtuous, except blind courage and a sense of duty – inasmuch as these may be taken as virtues. Full account of the hatred and distaste that Kipling has attracted must be taken. This is what Carrington could not manage. He could not begin to understand it. Philip Mason and Angus Wilson, in major books that have succeeded his, have gone further in that direction; but much more remains to be said – if only because so few critics have bothered, or have wanted, to take up the challenge.

Carrington is a conventional literary critic without being a clever or 'professional' one; we should not have wanted cleverness in the definitive work. If the style is pedestrian, no page is without its interest. Kipling's fame, though never strictly literary in the sense that his friend Henry James's was, was far greater during his lifetime than that of any other author. Carrington was just the kind of writer needed in the circumstances, and his politics were close to those of Kipling. Imperialism, of all the political crazes that have arisen in the past century and a half, is the most nakedly egocentric and subjective. Yet literature, the real thing, always tries to be about (among other things) the few means available to human beings *not* to be nakedly egocentric, *not* to wish to be ruled by power and money, *not* to lie, to be objective. Therefore we have, here, a subject who was both a crude imperialist and a writer of the real thing.

Carrington's continuously implied 'defence' of his subject's views operates in his biography as a simple assumption of rectitude. Doubtless echoing Kipling's fears, he believes that the Empire has been dispersed by evil powers. He is at his least effective on this subject: evidently he cannot understand or, possibly, even excuse anyone's bad or critical feelings about the Empire. That distorting factor has to be allowed for. Good imaginative writing and active empire-building are no more compatible than good imaginative writing and the pretence of, for example, practising 'communism'. If good writing comes into existence, then it is always in spite of, and never because of, political fantasy. Politics, as we have to understand it, is based on the pretence that people want to live together in harmony. Its result is to ensure that they do not. This is pertinent to Kipling, for we often feel in his writings the religious power of one who has the courage to take that apparently 'élitist' view. Yet equally often we detect, although at a less exalted level, the whining voice of the extremist. For, of all the articulate imperialists, Kipling was the most offensive. A clear and in no wise political look at the phenomenon reveals a stunning paradox.

Such obvious imperialistic dogmatism as Carrington's is not, however, understandable to people of a younger generation. Such episodes as the Falklands War are very quickly forgotten. People are just as dogmatic as they ever were, but they are (in general) even more ignorant and even less well informed than were the imperialists (who must not be confused with the Tories). The prejudices of the post-Carrington generations lie in not owning to any views at all. We are dogmatic about not being dogmatic. We know nothing; and so we do not like to be embarrassed by having views about what we do not know. To have a view would mean effort, and effort is unfashionable unless it consists of depriving others of their money to one's own advantage, or becoming famous, or being on television just once, or being in politics. I do not pretend that any set of contemporary political views is superior to imperialism. Imperialism is, indeed, more coherent than any contemporary set of views that I can think of. But at the time of the imperialist hysteria, which began to build up in the 1880s and then died off after the Boer War, there were some less coarse and less stupid sets of ideas in existence – and, better than ideas, practice.

The imperialist question has by now been dealt with by certain critics, including Americans, not in sympathy with Kipling. Lionel Trilling did so woodenly, and nothing beside the odd brilliant insight is really enlightening in his account. It was dealt with nobly and with an attempt at true objectivity, but not in much detail, by George Orwell – and this from a humane rather than a socialist point of view. The Leavis-inspired essay by Boris Ford was influential when it was written in 1942, and is still useful as a paradigm of the 'orthodox' 'case against Kipling'; but it is too simplistic to count for much now.

I have often dealt with the matter of Kipling's politics in this book by, initially, basing my discussion on the remarks of those who, writing in an unequivocally post-imperial age, have been able to see more impartially than Carrington either could or wished to: on Philip Mason in his sensible *Kipling: The Glass, the Shadow and the Fire*, and on Angus Wilson's *The Strange Ride of Rudyard Kipling*. Mason understands India from the inside and is an acknowledged expert on it; he is critical but sympathetic. Wilson is a lifelong liberal, too determined not to hold Kipling's imperialism against him. He chooses to treat the matter as politics; but literature demands something better. However, these two books are so valuable that I have frequently used their judgements as jumping-off points for my own. That applies, also, to several good shorter works such as those collected in Andrew Rutherford's *Kipling's Mind and Art*. Well-known essays by Edmund Wilson and Noel Annan are important, too, though perhaps more (especially the latter) for their misstatements. Still, it was Edmund Wilson more than anyone else who made the way for sensible criticism of Kipling, even if he was in some respects (as his namesake calls him) 'somewhat naïvely Freudian'.

I must also mention John A. Maclure's *Kipling and Conrad* (1981). Before it came to hand, I had decided that a useful reference point for the consideration of Kipling would be Adorno's (and others') pioneer study, *The Authoritarian Personality*. I then found that Maclure had anticipated me. My use of the concept has been sceptical rather than triumphantly demonstrative, as is the case with Maclure; but I have picked up a few points he makes in his book, which presents Kipling as an 'imperialist spy' (this seems to me to be absurd), and am glad to acknowledge this.

Kipling was not one of the writers that we are in the habit of calling 'very great'; nor was he an admirable man. His best work was written in spite of and not because of himself. He has been as much a scourge to humane Tories as a butt of the cruelly dogmatic left, which has been interested in him only as the inventor of 'The White Man's Burden'. He has almost invariably been seen through the veil of his politics, as though, in terms of his art, these were anything more than a defensive superstructure. Or as though his best work was his best work because it made political points. My approach is, broadly, that his politics have no value whatsoever.

Kipling lacked kindness of heart. He tried to compensate for this by turning himself into a universal uncle, a writer for children. In personal terms, as an actual storyteller to children, he did cast a spell. But as a children's writer pure and simple, except in *Kim*, the least flawed and the most concentrated of his longer books (is it really just a children's book?), there is something not quite right. As much of a slight ingratiating touch of Blyton as of Stevenson, perhaps ... A touch, at the least, of cheap dogmatism: a sly settling of some score against life that is beyond the innocence of his rapt audience? Sales of these books are declining. Children do not like them so much any more.

He was not altogether good to his own son: he used him as an instrument, a thing, and was initially happy to sacrifice him for what he saw as his own politics. He continually gave in to a wife who could be, and frequently was, almost pathological in her hatefulness, meanness and pettiness; he was not good to or about other people. True, he could be gracious; but he was more often vulgar and unpleasant, speaking openly of 'yids', for example, at dinner parties or in clubs, taking shameless advantage of his fame. When he was gracious, it was only gracious as a celebrity is gracious. He understood, fully, that to be a celebrity is very frightening to a sensitive person – or even to a person who has not lost all sensitivity. Such people are either wholly dead, hypnotised, or, in fleeting moments of consciousness, desperately unhappy, afraid and desirous of escape. But Kipling, despite his own fame, was aware of all this. He needed to be realistic about the nature of fame in order to stay alive and satisfy what he would come to call his daimon.

The celebrities to whom this lonely man chose to be gracious had, for the most part, to share his beliefs. He had family connections with Stanley Baldwin, so he kept up with him; but he regarded him as dangerously left-wing, and said so. He had none of his hero Joe Chamberlain's compassion for the poor; he shared only his savage and misguided imperialism. Men such as Milner, Jameson, Rhodes, Roberts – these were the apple of his eye. Yet as a public man he did not see the cynicism and the cruelty that existed in such men. He remained naïve. One wonders how he would have reacted if any of his heroes had stated that Rhodes was untrustworthy – which of course, among themselves, they all did, since treachery, as well as rhetoric, was one of Rhodes's famously strong suits. Kipling was the innocent one always. He liked Beaverbrook, but only until he disagreed with him. Friendship, for all the conventional value he put on it, was hardly known to him: a person only had to give utterance to views different from his to be dismissed out of hand.

The warmth we know he possessed scarcely ever came across: only in a few scattered and oblique phrases (such as to Hugh Walpole), in which he expressed his own needless sense of guilt and despair. His guardianship of his privacy was fierce and not pleasant in nature; he did not like the quality of mercy because he did not believe, despite his enormous success, that it had ever been shown to him. His letters to Rider Haggard, whom he regarded as an intimate, are lacking in true warmth, inasmuch as the little that is intimate in them is cast in formal terms, almost in clichés. They show that he kept a strict distance from all men, and that he would not and could not talk to anyone about his own darkness of soul and loneliness. His pronouncements of his feelings of 'unworthiness' are invariably generalised. For the meaning of it all one has to search his work. In his lectures to young people, given in his capacity as a famous and successful man, he talks just like the pompous and insincere speechifiers whom he specifically despised and mocked. His bitterness about killing in war, expressed capably (his capability is one of the keys to him), but with little power, arose very largely from his own bereavement, about which he occasionally complained (if only to his friends) in an unseemly manner. His philosophy of life, judged simply by how he expressed it as a public man, was cheap, shoddy, cruel, unworthy and impractical. *Stalky* is fluent and readable – again, highly capable – but, had we only that to judge him by, is disgraceful fantasy in its ethics and its lack of realism. As an intellectual, a thinker, a public man making public utterances, Kipling is grotesque, merciless and insensitive.

And yet, and yet. The history of the cruelty that developed in him has a great poignancy. And at his very best, when he was directing his imagination as distinct from imagining that he was thinking, he displays genius of the very highest order. There is not, proportionately, much of this: some of the very early and therefore immature work, before he had gained experience; and then such stories as 'The Disturber of Traffic' or, later, 'Wireless', and, still later, 'Dayspring Mishandled'. Perhaps there are a dozen such stories in all. He continued to produce stories of that calibre as long as he wrote, simultaneously producing abjectly pseudo-comic farces dealing crudely with his feelings of hatred and revenge, trying to justify his absurd 'political position'.

But how can one not love the author of the best work, comparatively rare though it may be? From the brilliantly observed early sketches through the cryptic middle tales to such compassionate masterpieces as 'The Wish House' and 'The Gardener'? His technique was, to say the least, unusual: that it was based on concealment (cutting and paring down) is surely significant, a reflection of his own pathological secrecy. This work, the best, is not simply minor – minor in the sense that the work of such a certainly good and not-to-be neglected writer as, say, A.E. Coppard is minor. 'The Disturber of Traffic', in its complexity and power and inevitability, is positively Shakespearean; it has supreme poetic force; every single word and phrase and sentence and paragraph in it is right. 'Wireless', too, has a strangeness and uniqueness about its atmosphere that transcends the slight clumsiness of conception.

Kipling cannot say as much as Hardy or Conrad or James (I take these writers as examples, as men known to Kipling, and as admirers of his) were able to say. His range is necessarily more limited. All of them in their own way reached his heights; but they could also sustain them. Their off-days were just off-days. Kipling's off-days can hardly be thus described: his poorer works – and this includes the flaws that distort some good material – are suffused with hatred, bad thinking, rage and cruelty. One does not call the failures of James 'misguided', as he very properly called *Stalky & Co.*, nor Conrad's last weaker novels, nor the lighter of Hardy's romances. They are just inferior work. But 'The Brushwood Boy'! The feeble and loathsome farces of revenge! What can one call them? Not simply the result of off-days, or things that don't come off. There is something seriously wrong. Yet does the story 'Mrs Postgate', once so notorious as a piece of unadulterated war-hate, really reflect hatred? Or is it self-criticism? The poem 'Neighbours', which prefaces 'Beauty Spots' (1932), an enigmatic revenge tale with a twist, reads:

> But he that is costive of soul toward his fellow,
> Through the ways, and the works, and the woes of this life,
> Him food shall not fatten, him drink shall not mellow;
> And his innards shall brew him perpetual strife.

One of the few well-known facts about the last twenty years of Rudyard Kipling's life is that his 'innards' brewed him perpetual strife! He would double over in agony and ask to be left alone. It killed him in the end. He could never ignore it, or not be aware of it.

It is certainly a paradox, and is made more of one by the fact that Kipling's extreme subtlety of technique was intellectually naïve, 'unliterary' – and unique. So I have not tried to defend what is hateful in him, as some have done. But, as any critic should, where the subject is not unworthy, I have tried to give emphasis to the love, the good impressions, that the common reader directs towards Kipling's highest achievements, which involved a terrifyingly lonely questioning of himself.

I must repeat that I hope that no one will mistake my approach as being in any sense political. If I have emphasised how peculiarly short-sighted and mistaken imperialism was – an accidental accretion of alien territory metamorphosed for a few years into a hysterical and meaningless passion – then that is only because it relates so intimately to my subject.

So far as pure literary criticism is concerned, the best and most comprehensive work on Kipling the artist is *The Art of Rudyard Kipling* (1959) by the late Joyce M.S. Tompkins. This admirable book has little to say of Kipling's life, but there are few of his works which it leaves undiscussed. Tompkins' pioneer judgements are so generally subtle and enlightening that I felt it would be wrong to disguise my indebtedness to them even though they are sometimes used only as starting points for my own. This remains, for all its 'old-fashioned' point of view (criticism does not change much, but the ways of presenting it do – and these get increasingly ambitious), one of the best critical books on any modern author. Joyce Tompkins dealt with some of the difficulties others had almost studiously ignored, and provided

the first real basis for critical discussion. But she, too, wished to see the
work and the public man in one piece. No human being is one piece, but
Kipling is such least of all. His selves, greatly at variance with each other,
at times ignorant of each other, were particularly well defined.

Philip Mason does not like to say much about Kipling's psychology.
Angus Wilson's book is fascinating; but, for reasons of his own, possibly
partly connected with the fact that Carrington generously aided him in
his work, he eschews detailed psychological speculation. I frequently
and gratefully refer to him. I will say now only that I believe his remark
'Freudianism is too easy' begs the question. Certainly any old-fashioned
attempt to see Kipling in terms of some over-rigid application of 'classical'
Freudian tenets, such as one used to see in some biographies of fifty
and even less years ago, would be absurd. I suspect him, here, of
uncharacteristically fudging the issue: he is not using 'Freudianism'
in its proper sense. All too often it is used to mean, simply, 'intimate
psychological exploration', even if that exploration be along Adlerian,
Jungian or even Reichian lines! There are now two distinct senses of the
word, anyway: one is 'along the lines of official psychoanalytical dogma',
and the other is the rich sort of speculation practised by Freud himself in
some of his own investigations. Yes, the latter is sometimes infected by the
former, and the same man was responsible for both; but surely everyone
now knows that they are two different things? Surely Wilson simply means
'probing psychological investigation', with a slight overtone of 'unseemly'.
I too am sure that any probing psychological investigation is thoroughly
unseemly, but then so, in a way (which Kipling himself understood and
often defined), is any naked bid for fame. Those who blindly seek fame,
as Kipling did when he was a young man, eventually discover what it
is like, and then cover their tracks as best they can (or become entirely
self-absorbed, in the manner of contemporary media celebrities). But
whereas such celebrities, almost by definition, have nothing to them and
are soon forgotten, Kipling was something, and can never be forgotten.

It is clear that no famous man – media fame was still being invented when
Kipling achieved it, and he was one of its first victims – endeavoured to be
more conscientious about his fame than Kipling. Or was at the same time
so humanly irresponsible! I should add, at this stage, that I am not in any
way a dogmatic Freudian – or, indeed, a Freudian at all, or anything else
like that – and that I do not think psychoanalysis itself is of much use to
anyone except as self-fulfilling fantasy or as a means of passing time or
spending money, or both.

There will, in any case, always be phenomenological speculation. I
use the word 'phenomenological' in its sense of 'what actually happens
psychologically, in full detail'. Those who hold back, for whatever reason,
from speculation still speculate; but they are not open about it. Doubtless
they cannot bear to think of their own natures being exposed, even to
themselves. I suspect that the commentators who congratulate themselves
upon their reticence, their observation of Kipling's own famous bid for
silence about his private self, are glad to do so not so much because
they are observing Kipling's wishes, but, rather, because they don't
know what to make of him. Everyone agrees that he is an enigma, just
as some of his own stories very deliberately are. He was a man who took
pleasure – pleasure that was necessary and precious to him – in covering

his tracks, in setting puzzles, in being enigmatic. He invented, as T.S. Eliot long ago pointed out, a new form (or adapted it from Indian models): a story sandwiched between two poems, or prefaced by a poem. This too was to set puzzles, to add to the enigma. So, while eschewing any simplistic solution of a problem which could not in any case be solved in a simple manner, I have been boldly speculative. I have spent time on the public man, of course. But the story I have tried to tell, so far as it can be told, is that of the recluse who lived all those hours and days and weeks and months, and, finally, years, in Bateman's, buried within himself, of the lonely self-hater who could not keep his nose out of affairs he had long ago given up. And I have ended, not with the pomp of his death, but with his later art, the latter being by far the more important. If the part of the book dealing with the first half of his life is much longer than its successor, then this is simply because so much less actually happened to him in the second.

About any writer of the calibre of Kipling at his best, there is an element of mystery. His best works exist not because of but in spite of the problems which afflicted him. They cannot ultimately be explained by reference to those problems, but only by how each of you reads and responds to them within your own mind, uninstructed by any ambitious critic anxious to force his view down your throat. Already criticism is patronising art, although it is curious that its stars do not trouble to produce it, and curious, too, that they state that it no longer really exists. Perhaps they do not like it all that much! Or perhaps, after all, things are not as terribly complicated and impossible as they would wish.

But the nature of Kipling's best works can at least be illuminated: we are able, by looking at him more closely, to understand better what subjects he is really trying to deal with (perhaps not imperial ones), so that we can read him better. More can now decently be said than has been said.

India I

Kipling's ambivalence about women, not unique but more uneasily and frequently articulated in him than in most men, may have stemmed from an early emotional reservation about his mother. But whether that is the case or not, it tells us more about him than about her. She was in his account suspiciously exemplary. But then his father, by all the known accounts (only Angus Wilson is a little sceptical), was actually a paragon, and a person all too demonstrably ('I know I look like a holy-holy, but I'm not,' he once said) admirable and naturally to be lived up to. Or is this just a fantasy invented by Kipling and then perpetuated by Carrington? Was he really a silly and opinionated little man, insignificant and full of himself?

It seems not, although there are falsehoods connected with his very early professional status. John Lockwood Kipling's qualities as a man stand up to what scrutiny we are able to give them; but of course we are mostly in the dark. Many high reputations of that age have turned out to be founded on worse than nothing; but there is not a jot of evidence to suggest that he was not, as his brother-in-law Fred Macdonald wrote, gentle, unselfish and lovable.

If Rudyard's mother, too, was a paragon of similar proportions, so far as near-perfection of external character is concerned, then it is not quite as evident. So, if the Father (as Kipling called him) was admittedly exemplary, then was the Mother always a trifle wanting in the esteem, if only by comparison, of that appalling and astonishingly powerful little emperor who was the tiny boy? Certainly it must have been Alice Kipling who received most of the emotional blame from her son when she and her husband 'abandoned' him to what he and his sister always thereafter called the 'House of Desolation'. Did he instantly sublimate this blame, or did he rail against her in his mind and then later suppress it? If he did have such a reservation before he was 'abandoned', then certainly his mother cannot be blamed for it. Such reservations are by no means always the result of neglect. In any case, even if the wound was very deep, it healed right over: Mothers were very high up, sometimes nauseatingly so, in Kipling's list of life's official priorities. Yet the female of the species was always more deadly than the male.

John Kipling, born in Pickering, Yorkshire on 6 July 1837, was the eldest son of a Wesleyan minister, Joseph Kipling, and his dark-eyed, raven-haired wife, Frances, née Lockwood. During the later part of his engagement to Alice Macdonald, John added his mother's maiden name to his own, and people – except his family and his wife, who always called him by his proper name – referred to him by it. Frances was felt, by her architect father from Cleveland, to have married a little beneath her: the Kiplings were of Yorkshire farming stock, 'plain, simple, lowly folk'. Rudyard Kipling in his old age told an enquirer, with characteristic bitterness, that he did not know much about them, and that he wasn't really interested anyway, as he had no son to whom he could pass the information. The fact is that delving into his ancestry seemed to Kipling like unhealthily delving into himself, and this was something that he consistently tried not to do, since he was fearful of what he might find. Angus Wilson is absolutely right to insist on this feature in Kipling. But he sees it as a weakness: 'he should have sought to find himself', because 'this persistent evasion of introspection, of further questioning of the source of the despair and anxiety and guilt that enmesh so many of his best characters in his best stories, does keep him out of the very first class of writing'. I agree that Kipling is out of the first class except in a few stories, but good writing, especially of the first class, can arise as much from ignorant evil as from good, even though the latter, in its capacity as the imagination's natural drive for truthfulness, must finally transcend all else.

On the contrary, then, it is one of Kipling's incidental strengths that he did practise evasion: the more thoroughly and painstakingly he practised it, the more surely he revealed his nature in its essence, if not in all its less important details and particulars. But Kipling was nevertheless very frightened of what he would find if he probed into himself, and of the possibility that it might turn out to be nothing.

It was, at least until Carrington's book was published, supposed that John Kipling received an excellent and, sometimes by implication, even a happy education at the Northern Connexional School, Woodhouse Grove, near Bradford. Certainly, as Carrington states, it would have been better than anything he could have had from one of the then unreformed public schools. The curriculum included Latin and French. The school had been founded for the purpose of taking in, as boarders, the eight- to fifteen-year-old sons of Wesleyan ministers, who were both poor and liable to be moved around at short notice. Mr James Craig has discovered that, whether the school was 'nobly built' (A.W. Baldwin) or not, it was rough, demoralised and staffed with bad teachers. John Kipling was not happy at it, and it may even be that his subsequent turning away from Wesleyanism was due, in the main, to his experiences there. However, a year before he left the school in 1852 he went to London to see the Great Exhibition. This visit gave his life its direction.

'The Great Exhibition of the Works of Industry of all Nations 1851' has been described as 'one of the most outstanding success stories of the nineteenth century'; its benefits were incalculable. What was shown there led to the development of the Arts and Crafts Movement, and to a more general awareness of the deadness and tastelessness of machine-produced objects. It made fertile the field within which John Ruskin (another imperialist) would soon begin to preach his gospel of anti-commercialism, and that within which William Morris (who, unlike Ruskin, allowed discreet machinery) would work.

John Kipling attended an art school at Stoke, and then studied in London. He worked on the building of what is now the Victoria and Albert Museum. But the only evidence of his participation, curiously enough, is his appearance (already balding) in a terracotta mosaic designed in 1910 by Godfrey Sykes, who supervised the original building. He is one of seven figures, and is included, it seems, simply as a gesture of courtesy to an assistant – and, presumably, because they remembered and liked him. But his work there must have been very subordinate, and could not then have gained him much credit: he had to earn a living by giving French lessons for a time. Doubtless he was incorporated into the 1910 mosaic because he was the father of Rudyard Kipling.

It was as the employee of a Burslem pottery (which was eventually to be absorbed by Doulton) that Lockwood met Fred Macdonald, a recently appointed Wesleyan minister of twenty years old. Fred became President of Conference in 1899, and did not die until 1928. He wrote a valuable book of reminiscences in 1921. John's firm, a Wesleyan one, gave a spring picnic at a reservoir, a beauty spot just outside the Staffordshire town of Leek, which took its name from a nearby village – Rudyard. John had no notion that he would within a few years be offered a position in India; it is therefore entirely a coincidence that Rudra should be the celebrated malevolent Hindu tempest god of wildness and danger, the 'howler' or 'ruddy one', and father of all the Rudras and Maruts. John and Alice Macdonald, the elder sister of Fred, met at the picnic and soon understood one another – mainly, it is said, via a mutual pleasure in the poetry of Mr Robert Browning. They became engaged in the summer of 1863.

Alice Macdonald was one of the eleven children (seven survived to majority) of a Methodist minister, George Macdonald, who was descended from a Scot who fled to Ireland after the defeat at Culloden. George's grandfather James had been one of the original Methodists; his father was yet another preacher. The family was entirely Celtic: Irish, Welsh, Scottish. Alice's sister Georgiana, to be much loved by Rudyard despite her political views, married (1860) Edward Burne-Jones, a High-Church inclined painter from Birmingham who had once shared a studio with William Morris. Her brother Henry was a noted scholar. Her sister Louisa married Sir Alfred Baldwin, the ironmaster and later the Chairman of the Great Western Railway; she became the mother of Stanley Baldwin. Another sister, Agnes, married Edward John Poynter, a draughtsman and painter who became Director of the National Gallery in 1894 and President of the Royal Academy in 1896. Poynter never understood what was going on in the art world, but was a Distinguished Man.

Alice does not appear to us quite as clearly as Lockwood. She was high spirited, 'talented' in witty conversation, music and creative writing, in the manner in which young girls were able to be in those days when children made all their own entertainment. She had considerable reserves of malice; but these have been played down by biographers. The family was not Calvinist, or even puritanical, and all the children were married in the Church of England. Alice's father called her and her sisters flirts, but did so only humorously. Nonetheless, he had quite strict views. She had once been engaged for a short time to the English but Donegal-born poet William Allingham ('Up the airy mountain,/Down the rushy glen,/We daren't go a-hunting/For fear of little men'), a customs official who settled in England in 1863 and who became editor of *Fraser's Magazine* in 1874 in succession to J.A. Froude. Allingham was certainly a skilful poet, and Alice's involvement with him indicates that she had some interest in and taste for real intellectual quality in men. Allingham eventually married Helen Patterson, a talented painter. One would like to know more about this affair, and about Alice's other suitors – she had two other broken engagements; but details are not forthcoming. She was forthright, impetuous, 'sharp-tongued', 'nimble-minded', witty and probably careless, which her husband, with his painstakingness and attention to detail, was not. She saw things so quickly (her brother Fred wrote) that she could not find the words to express her insights quickly enough; thus in speaking she tumbled over herself.

Apropos of that, there is a splendid story about her. Before she got married, she is said to have thrown into the fire a treasured family relic with the remark, 'See, a hair of the dog that bit us!' It was a lock of John Wesley's hair. She surely must have got into trouble for that, if she really did it. But her family was not in practice a very severe one. That this story was told at all is testimony to her high spirits, wit, impetuosity and readiness to risk disrespect to her elders. Clearly her son inherited much of his defiant spirit from her.

She and Lockwood were married on 18 March 1865, and Swinburne and the Rossetti brothers – friends of her sister – were at the reception. The wedding, which was at St Mary Abbots' Church, was managed by Georgiana Burne-Jones from 41 Kensington Square. Was the couple, prompted perhaps by the impulsive Alice, in a hurry to get away from the immediate past? If they were, and probably it is the case, then they had little to which to look forward. The family was afraid for them. True, Lockwood had been lucky: he had been offered a menial but welcome post at the Jeejeebhoy School of Art in Bombay. If Burne-Jones did obtain it for him, as has usually been supposed, then it was the very best he could have done at the time. Norman Page in his useful *A Kipling Companion* (1986) chides Angus Wilson for 'some occasional errors of detail', but states that the Jeejeebhoy School of Art was 'new' (it was not) and implies that John Lockwood Kipling went there as 'Principal'. This is badly to miss the point. As the allegedly careless Wilson writes, Lockwood was one of three subordinate teachers appointed 'to instruct pupils in utilitarian crafts'. He taught architectural sculpture and terracotta pottery to about a score of pupils, and his pay – which he was allowed to supplement by private teaching if he wished to – was acknowledged to be poor by his employers. The social position of the Kiplings in Bombay was therefore difficult. As Wilson says, this 'genteelising of their past' by Victorian middle-class people is 'sad': it diminishes the credit due to them for their determination. No more so than in the case of the Kiplings: when Lockwood went to Lahore sixteen years after his first arrival he had achieved the reputation that he deserved, although his social position in India was never easy.

The Kiplings complemented each other ideally for people much in love, and were ambitious for themselves and the children they planned to have. It was through their determination and industry that they made (almost) a social silk purse for themselves out of the sow's ear that India might have been. Lockwood's position was lowly, but he did have an assistant. He eked out his living by acting as Bombay correspondent to a leading Indian newspaper, by teaching, and by carrying out such artistic commissions as he could obtain. As is often remarked, neither of their families could have been much pleased by their Indian adventure, and this may have made them sensitive to criticism within the family; they showed courage and independence in making a good thing out of it.

Their extraordinary son Joseph Rudyard Kipling (he never used the Joseph, and tried to suppress it at school by changing it to John, since, according to his schoolchum Beresford, Joseph 'invited ridicule') was born on 30 December 1865.

Southsea

Like other children of British people living in India in those times, Rudyard learned to talk in the vernacular with his *ayah* and with other Indian servants. He had, as he tells us, to be reminded to speak English when sent in to his parents. The vernacular he picked up was what Philip Mason calls 'kitchen Hindi', and he would have forgotten most of it while in England: his grasp of Indian languages has been exaggerated. Again like other such children, Kipling was inordinately spoiled by comparison with his English counterparts. His parents' position was then so insecure that they were forced, being ambitious, to be 'social climbers'; but none of that rubbed off on him. He lived in a bungalow adjacent to the school in which his father tried to inculcate the artistic principles of William Morris into Indians. A portrait of him in a sailor suit taken some time shortly before he was sent to Southsea shows an insidiously imperious little creature; and so he came to be known when he went home to England. Alice became pregnant again, and, because her life had been despaired of while she was bearing Rudyard, it was decided that she should have this new child back in England. She took little Rudyard, at the age of two-and-a-half, with her. He claimed to remember some details of this journey, including the town of Zagazig near the Suez Canal; but these memories may well have been fanciful, or he may have confused it with a later journey. He acted so spoiled on the ship that Birkenhead, relying on information in the now destroyed papers, says Alice was relieved to get him on shore. But he continued to embarrass her, and may even thus have sealed his fate a few years later, when she sent him to strangers instead of to someone in the family.

While Mrs Kipling spent her confinement in her sister Georgiana's house, Rudyard was left at Bewdley with his aunt Louisa and her husband Alfred Baldwin. There were two houses, the smaller one being occupied by the now aged Macdonald parents, who were being cared for by Alfred and Louisa. Kipling's one maiden aunt, Edith (she survived him), with whom he had to share a bed, used to say that Ruddy's noise had 'hastened and embittered' the old man's end. He died that autumn. So might any loud grandson's; only Ruddy really was very noisy, waking up everyone at all hours, kicking Edith in her bed all night, and going around the village of Bewdley shouting, 'Ruddy is coming!' or 'An angry Ruddy is coming!' There was little room, Stanley Baldwin was present at the difficult age of only one, his mother Louisa was unwell, and Ruddy made himself memorable in the wrong way.

Fred wrote to his brother: 'Ruddy aged three is a power and a problem with strange gifts of upsetting any household . . . I hope John will be very firm with him for dear Alice is as wax in his hands.' Clearly the boy's power over his mother, and his own reputation as a holy terror, were already

being discussed and reticently criticised. Rudyard's sister Alice (called
'Trix' because her shy father called her 'tricksy' when he first saw her),
whose life was to be clouded by periods of mental instability, was born in
June 1868 in the Burne-Jones's house in North End Road, Fulham. Louisa
wrote of Alice on her return with Trix that 'her children turned the house
into such a bear-garden, and Ruddy's screaming tempers made Papa so ill,
we were thankful to see them on their way. The wretched disturbances one
ill-ordered child can make is a lesson for all time to me.' Her mother was
deeply relieved, when Alice next came to England (to leave her children
at Southsea), not to have one sharp word with her.

On 15 April 1871 Alice, with Lockwood this time, set out again with
the two children to spend six months in England. When they returned
they left Rudyard and Trix in Southsea. This was normal enough practice:
India was very hot in the summer, and health suffered (Alice had just lost
a third baby); the children who did stay went to cheap Indian schools and
mixed with 'inferiors'. Anglo-Indians felt that the children who did stay
might, owing to their exposure to native ways, become more Indian than
British. It was well understood that all the children of English parents
born in India were spoiled – and none was more so than the insufferable
Ruddy. But Ruddy's awfulness may have been one of his parents' chief
motivations. He at least had not endeared himself to any of his family,
and the parents doubtless dared not ask any of them to take him, so it
may have been felt that the two children would be best together in the
house of respectable strangers. Alfred Baldwin did gallantly offer to take
Trix and to share Ruddy with others in the family; but Alice, remembering
the rows earlier, declined. There is, however, one other possible reason for
the Kiplings' much discussed decision: Alice Kipling may have feared that
if she left her son with a member of the family she would be supplanted.
Kipling's attitude towards his mother – and mothers in general – was
always intense; perhaps she, too, was a little intense.

But one very serious mistake was made, even if it was only in the nature
of a tactical error. In December, when the two children were left with a
Southsea couple who had advertised in a newspaper, the parents departed
without informing them. *That* was the 'shock', I think, which Kipling never
got over. The new guardians were given fictional status as relatives, as was
the custom of that time: they were Uncle Harry and Aunty Rosa. Alice
Kipling later explained – doubtless she felt obliged to, in view of her son's
famous tale of an unhappy childhood – that she had left them in England
chiefly because she needed to be able to help her husband with his work.
And indeed she did help him: socially, and by becoming a writer of stories
and other items for Indian magazines. One may guess that she made her
mistake because both she and her husband went in some fear of the rows
that young Ruddy was wont to make when he did not get his way. He was
as peculiarly horrible as a child, one is led to believe, as he was peculiarly
interesting as a man. Anyhow, the Kiplings did mishandle the parting. Trix
wrote, admittedly with the advantage of knowing what her elder brother
had made of it, that a

> simple reiteration of the necessity of leaving us in England would easily
> have been understood by a six-year-old boy of my brother's intelligence,

and he would have made it clear to me. As it was, we felt that we had been deserted, 'almost as much as on the doorstep', and what was the reason? They had seen the horrible little house before they left us there, they knew how far it was from the sea and the Common, with the garden the size of a pocket handkerchief, too small even for the battledore and shuttlecock. They had seen Harry's crafty eyes, they had heard Aunty's false voice: they must have known that she was of the seaside landlady's type, and yet they let her be my only teacher and companion till I was ten years old.

Kipling's abandonment has now gained the status of a myth. He wrote three accounts of his time at the so-called 'House of Desolation'. The first and most substantial is in the famous early story 'Baa, Baa, Black Sheep', published in 1888; the second, and shortest, where more obvious but slight alterations are made, is in the novel *The Light that Failed*, where Mrs Holloway is Mrs Jennett; the third is in the work of his old age, the autobiography (or what passes for it), *Something of Myself*, where she is the Woman. His sister Trix came to believe in this myth, perhaps in part because of her own resentment of her parents and of Rudyard, and even herself embroidered it.

Rudyard's myth, like most myths of that kind, was based pretty securely on fact, since 'Aunty Rosa' was clearly a narrow woman. Many might have come to feel sorry for her, but not Rudyard. She turns up in his fiction again and again in various guises. But, in the way in which clever and revengeful people often do, he carefully selected the facts of the case in order to conceal what was not, retrospectively, so much severe suffering as a profound chagrin, a grievance against his mother, or possibly just a sense that he had been badly used by life. This was his first reaction to being crossed, as one might put it. His representations of this much vaunted episode were not based on a strictly truthful, and certainly not an objective, view of the circumstances at Southsea. If later in life he occasionally came to the reluctant conclusion that life at Aunty's might not have been quite so awful had he not contributed to Aunty's dislike for him by being so horrible to her, then he must quickly have suppressed it. Carrington takes this view of the matter. But Rudyard must have known that his account of his time at Southsea was unfair to Aunty Rosa.

Captain Pryse Agar Holloway and his wife Sarah (known as Rosa) lived with their son Harry, four or five years older than Rudyard, in Lorne Lodge, Havelock Park (later Campbell Road), Southsea, just along the coast east of Portsmouth, but virtually the same place. The captain, an old tar who used to exclaim 'Shiver my timbers!' to please the boy, was all right, and Rudyard liked him. Then he died, and, according to Rudyard and to Trix, Aunty Rosa and her Harry came into their own. It is not known if the Captain had married beneath him or not. But he had known better days, and clearly his wife felt it. He had transferred from the Navy to the Merchant Marine, a step in the wrong direction. He knew the Provost of Oriel. His eldest brother was a General, and another brother was a Lieutenant-Colonel. He had seen service at the Battle of Navarino (1827), and had been wounded in an accident with a harpoon-line. Rudyard used to look at the purplish scar on his ankle with horror. His wife, once perhaps thrown upwards in the social scale, cannot have liked being forced to take in lodgers, or the cut in income when the Captain died. It may be that the young Kiplings were the first lodgers she took; this is not known. The General seems to have promised to remember his nephew Harry in his will, but when he died in 1875 was found to have cut him out of it. Perhaps he thought he was a horrid boy, which he seems to have been.

But let us compare what is likely to have been the truth (so far as we are able to know it) with the picture Kipling gives us. And let us first of all admit that, on the face of it, the picture he gives in 'Baa, Baa, Black Sheep' is fairly scrupulous, so far as it goes. The narrator is under no illusion that Punch was not a spoiled and imperious little boy, used to having his own way. But the picture of Aunty Rosa is not only unflattering (particularly when it is implied that she was drunk in the afternoon after taking wine 'for her stomach'): it also has the elements of her as some special Evangelical demon. The special demon, if there was one, seems actually to have been her son, although he may not have been much more than an ordinary nasty and hypocritical boy, who might well have grown out of his unpleasantness. What is surprising is that Kipling did not, some years afterwards, make allowances for Mrs Holloway's weaknesses, and for the difficulties with which he presented her. Could she not, had she been a writer, have given us a story about a religious woman sorely tried by God by being sent such a villainous little charge? Evangelicals, such as she was, got themselves a bad name because they were tiresome, and worse, in their conversation; but they could be and usually were humane.

Carrington's sceptical account of this period of Rudyard's life is by far the most sensible. As he writes, Mrs Holloway 'must' have been a 'good woman and a good housewife', since Trix stayed there for three more years after Rudyard left in 1877. In *Something of Myself* Kipling grudgingly admits that he was 'adequately fed', although he adds a gratuitous sneer about boiled tomatoes and string-boiled mutton. As Carrington suggests, the boy was unlikely to have been responsive to any affection Mrs Holloway might initially have shown him, and his hostility would not have brought out the best in her. Knowing what we do about Kipling, and about how 'powerful' he was even when very young, there is every reason to suppose that he decided to take out his rage against his absent mother, or against fate ('someone is going to pay for this') on Mrs Holloway. Alice and John Kipling were well aware of how difficult their little son was. Mrs Holloway liked Trix, and the Kiplings saw no reason for her not to continue there for a further three years.

In all three of his accounts his parents are carefully protected, and he does criticise himself as an unruly little boy; but no real quarter is shown to the Woman, or of course to her son. Surely the two fictional accounts – or at least 'Baa, Baa, Black Sheep', since in the novel Mrs Jennett is merely incidental – might have been improved had some attention been given to the motivations and personality of the Woman, apart from how she happened to appear to the young Rudyard? His technique is to recall the outrage he felt at the time, an outrage that any little boy in his position may be expected to have felt, but not to modify it in the light of retrospective reason, or compassion. One suspects, and has reason for suspecting, that Mrs Holloway did try to make some or even many gestures of affection towards him, but that every one of these was rebuffed. Natural enough, or at the least understandable. In his accounts she is an Evangelical monster, and that is that: and so she has gone down into the history of guardians as an Evangelical monster, a cruel and misguided woman, in the words of a pre-Carrington biographer, a 'type of religious sadist with many of the attributes of a prison wardress'. Perhaps such descriptions gave Kipling satisfaction. But there have been plenty of Evangelical women, and men, who have been tiresome or even misguided but not at the same time cruel. This sort of Evangelicism, even when not specifically Calvinistic, was a habit of the age. So were the beating and caning of both boys and girls. Kipling always wholeheartedly approved of this, and in 'Baa, Baa, Black Sheep' he goes almost out of his way to make it clear that Punch's father gives him the slipper. Few besides Carrington have had a good word to say for Mrs Holloway, although Birkenhead remarks that she might have been 'over-abused'. Angus Wilson believes that she may have been an Anglican Calvinist, of whom there were then a few. Certainly she seems to have threatened young Rudyard with hell; but there are many ways of doing that, and it seems likely that he drove her to that unwise or nasty course.

But was he really getting at Mrs Holloway in the revenge story 'Baa, Baa, Black Sheep'? He certainly thought he was. It is more likely, however, that he was getting at his mother in spite of himself: settling an emotional score with her. That he should have felt those emotions while in Southsea is one thing. That he should pretend to see his parents' point of view eleven years later, and in old age too, but still need obliquely to revenge himself on them (on his mother, to be more precise), is more peculiar. In that story Mrs Holloway, an 'Evangelical' fact of life such as is supposed in the famous Kipling philosophy to be good and hardening to the soul, stands for the mother he cannot allow himself openly to attack.

Imperious and spoiled little boys are either cured of their imperiousness and spoiltness or they are not. They can even sometimes preach simple-minded stoical philosophies that prescribe hardship as indispensable in the formation of fine characters – and still not be cured. The early story, the slightly changed account given in the novel *The Light that Failed*, and the late version given in *Something of Myself*, all undoubtedly stand for a protest: without its being stated, there is a complaint that, despite the famous philosophy, the young boy suffered a terrible experience at the hands of a terrible woman and her devilish son. The arrangements at United Services College are later expressly presented as utterly suitable for the operation of the philosophy. Indeed, as we shall see, those arrangements, where they did not fit in with the philosophy, were considerably altered by Kipling, who chose to put a very much greater emphasis on corporal punishment than his school had itself done. The philosophy, as everyone knows, involves not complaining, which is represented as no more than a form of unmanly whining. Yet when the propounder of the philosophy has a grievance, his complaint has special status! This may demonstrate something about the philosophy that renders it as specious as what Edmund Wilson called the 'Polonius precept' advice given in the notorious poem 'If'. And writing about Kipling the man and Kipling the writer must necessarily entail a full consideration of that.

What certainly happened at Southsea, though, was that Rudyard did not get on with his new guardian, who, being quite unable to cope with him, began to characterise him as a liar, a 'black sheep' (by contrast to his virtuous sister) and wicked boy whom she may have sincerely believed would go to hell if she did not punish him to prevent it. Better women than her have made such rationalisations. When he came to her he could not read (it is not rare for those who turn to literature to start reading late), and that frustrated her, perhaps because he was so ingeniously clever and dumbly insolent in other respects. She must have felt his resentment deeply, and must, too, have been jealous of her husband's capacity to make a friend of him. But we may fairly infer that she was, as I have suggested, a narrow woman, out of her depth with the beastly little future genius (a genius at expressing his dislike of people already?). She saw or intuited how much cleverer than her own son he was going to be, and must have resented that, too. And Harry himself must have been jealous, if only of his father's attentions to the stranger, whose side he evidently took in at least two disputes, when Harry got a thrashing. Did anyone bother to discover if he became an avid Kipling reader in later life? He never came forward, even in a local newspaper, and no one else from Southsea did, either. Perhaps no one there remembered Rudyard as at all likeable, but did not want to have the embarrassment of putting their memories on record. According to Trix, Harry put both the boy and the girl to various childish torments, tried to trap them by feigning sympathy and then reporting their complaints to his mother, and was no friend to them. Apparently he professed to share his mother's beliefs, but was not above being two-faced. But it must be remembered that his mother's having lodgers who needed to be treated at least as well as her own child would have put him out of countenance. Doubtless also he wanted to revenge himself on Rudyard and Trix for the thrashings from his father after the latter died. Kipling later called him the 'Devil Boy'. Whether he taunted Rudyard, who·slept in his room (Trix slept with Mrs Holloway), with various aspects of the sexual disturbances of adolescence is not known. If the accusation that he provided 'calculated torture' at breakfast is partly exaggerated, perhaps he really did in the bedroom at night. Perhaps this is the origin of Kipling's sense of 'swinishness' in respect of homosexual activities?

The house was narrow but had three storeys; it had a tiny garden and a waste lot at the end of the street where Trix was sometimes sent to play. It was not what these children were used to. But it was very typical of that kind of house at that time; the house of, as Angus Wilson has suggested, 'poor relations', even down to its admonition to CONSIDER THE LILIES. The Kipling parents, however, had seen it and knew all about it, if not perhaps the detail of Harry's crafty eyes. Aunty Rosa, defeated by Rudyard's hostility, took to caning him to save him from himself, and to putting him in 'solitary confinement' (a nasty cellar with a fireplace which never saw a fire). When at seven he finally learned to read – she taught him by the most mechanical method possible, ab being ab because she 'said it was' – she then jealously punished him by forbidding him to read (or so he asserted, perhaps basing this on one instance). Since by 1876 or at the least 1877 he was writing astonishingly accomplished verses, she may well have envied his prowess. One so wicked did not *deserve* to be so gifted, she might have decided. There is little doubt that Mrs Holloway did some unattractive things. It is alleged by Kipling that she beat her wretched girl servants for stealing food when they were hungry. But how often and how consistently she did such things is in doubt; these nasty things were by no means out of the ordinary, in any case. Difficult little people usually were treated in that way by their guardians, religious or otherwise, and no doubt more especially if the little charges let them know that they were of 'lower caste', which Rudyard did. Even at only six years old, he knew how to lay it on, and Mrs Holloway was made to be keenly aware that in his estimation she was a *kuchnay*: 'of such low caste as not to matter'. As readers will recall, Punch does wonder (and it was scrupulous of Kipling to make him do so) why Aunty Rosa does not call him Sahib. An adult would have needed, if he or she were not to be wax in his hands, more than a sense of Christian righteousness to withstand giving such a boy a box on the ears. Certainly we can sympathise with the boy who within only a year or two would begin to display signs of his subtle genius: it must have been hard for one of such sensitivity and sophistication to put up with the crudities of Mrs Holloway and her smarmy son. Rudyard's method of keeping out of trouble at school was going to be sarcasm, and there is really no doubt that he got in some excellent practice with Mrs Holloway. One can feel a certain pity for her.

Unreligious and unscrupulous guardians, in it for the money (and many who took in such children as the Kipling brother and sister were in it for just that), treated little people much worse than Mrs Holloway ever did, and neglected them too. A person with a sense of duty, however narrow and hateful that sense may be, is sometimes preferable to a person without one. 'I have heard of some,' wrote the missionary W. J. Wilkins in 1887, 'for whose education and comfort large fees have been paid, being half starved . . . and made little better than domestic drudges . . . and all this time the children were compelled to write to their parents elaborately false statements speaking of the kindness they received . . .' We must have leave to doubt the extremes of Mrs Holloway's narrowness. Certainly she could not have compelled the children to write home false letters. Yet she is presented by Kipling and Trix as a person not at all unlike one of the many evil foster-parents alluded to by Wilkins.

When Rudyard was sent to Hope Lodge School, a local day school which Harry also attended, he refused to work at his lessons, and, as he tells us, learned to lie. He claimed that on one occasion, when he tried to conceal a bad report, he was sent by Aunty Rosa through the street to school, with a placard bearing the words KIPLING THE LIAR on it. Trix corroborated this claim by asserting, in old age, that she had herself rushed into the street to tear it off, and had been threatened with the cane by Aunty Rosa, but managed to intimidate her by counter-threats to the effect that she would tell everyone. Carrington thinks that Kipling might have taken this from a scene in *David Copperfield* in which David is made to carry a similar placard saying THE BOY BITES (it is interesting that he can bring himself to infer such dishonesty in his subject). Birkenhead, being much indebted to Trix, does not question it. Angus Wilson is inclined to believe it, saying that he thinks it was a bit of surviving 'puritan fire' of the sort Dickens had so objected to. I find it hard to believe that Mrs Holloway, however fired by righteousness, would have dared to resort to this, which would have been unusual even then, as well as reminiscent of a notorious scene of injustice and cruelty in a very famous book. It would certainly have caused her to be condemned by some neighbours, and possibly have discredited her as a fit guardian for any children; but it is hard to accuse Kipling *and* Trix of making it up. Rudyard was always a truthful man, except when writing fiction or deceiving Mrs Holloway.

I mean that he was an enemy of the downright lie, and preferred to keep silence rather than indulge in that direct type of falsehood. His many errors in his writings of reminiscence were less lies as such, more suppressions, misrecollections or carelessness – or, at worst, self-deceit in the form of rationalisations.

It seems to me most likely that Mrs Holloway stated, in the most savage terms, that Kipling *ought* to undergo that punishment, and that later he persuaded himself that he had actually endured it. But this conclusion lays Trix open to the charge of having a very vivid imagination indeed. However, we know that she had, or developed, great resentments of her own over the Southsea episode; and doubtless she had unconscious resentments of Rudyard, too. He had resentments of her, generated partly by normal sibling rivalry but also by the fact that she had put him to shame by learning to read before he did. He would tell her that he had much more brain than her, and he told his parents at the time of her leaving Southsea that making plans for her eduction would be 'difficult': 'in high falutin' she beats me, but in solid learning, she can't spell "shut".' Also she did live in the shadow of mental illness or hysteria from a quite early age, and perhaps succumbed to some element of fantasy in the matter of childhood memories. She wrote two Anglo-Indian novels herself, and must have hoped that they would do well. The first, *The Heart of a Maid*, appeared in 1891, and was largely autobiographical. Her lack of success must have caused her to feel some resentment of Rudyard. It creeps out in her reminiscences of old age, in which she accuses her brother of inaccuracy in his autobiography and yet, so to speak, corroborates the essence of it because it is established. Here she is enjoying the limelight, literary and otherwise, she felt she was denied in his lifetime: she is riding on his reputation, but resentfully. Thus she expresses her own resentment against her parents for leaving her at Southsea for three more years by reinforcing his; and in the fictitious KIPLING THE LIAR episode gives herself a dramatic role ('I am ashamed to say I reduced her to tears'). Males were then even more privileged in families than they are now: in part her feelings reflect the undoubted injustice of this.

Once every year for a whole month, while Trix stayed at 'home' with Mrs Holloway, Rudyard visited his aunt ('the Beloved Aunt') and uncle (Ned Burne-Jones) at their house, The Grange. He never said a single word about his alleged ill treatment at Southsea on those joyous occasions. Much later, in his autobiography, he felt obliged to account for this failure of communication:

> Often and often afterwards, the beloved aunt would ask me why I had never told anyone how I was being treated. Children tell little more than animals, for what comes to them they accept as eternally established. Also, badly-treated children have a clear notion of what they are likely to get if they betray the secrets of the prison-house before they are clear of it.

This cannot be true. Had any boy, let alone one with the powers Rudyard early possessed, wished to convey to a kindly and indulgent aunt – and, moreover, one very much *in loco parentis* – that he was suffering where he was, he would have found a means to do it. At the very least he would have told all as soon as he had safely left the clutches of the Woman. But

he never did until he published 'Baa, Baa, Black Sheep' – at a time when
his mother had annoyed him. Only after that did he put himself into a
position where he would be expected to answer such questions from his
aunt. It is not conceivable that the Kiplings would have kept Trix on with
Mrs Holloway had Rudyard then represented the place as he did in the
story. Either he said nothing much, or they did not believe him, or they
even privately believed that he had been deserving of such treatment.
There were perhaps two 'monsters' in Southsea during those years.

There really is a mystery here, unless Kipling deliberately manufactured
by far the larger part, if not all, of his sufferings expressly in order to appeal
to his mother's conscience, or perhaps for some other reason. In that
case he must already have held very dark secrets indeed in the recesses
of his mind. But then his fiction abounds in examples of such darkness.
He would, in such a case, have been so keen on a subtle sort of revenge
that he was prepared to sacrifice his own happiness in order to enjoy it.
And, as we shall see, that is possible. It was the sort of thing people would
do to one another in some of his fiction. The other alternative is that Mrs
Holloway really was a mistress of subtle terror. That is possible; but, as we
have seen, there are serious objections. He had had enough of his parents'
indulgence of him to be fairly sure that Mrs Holloway's hell did not exist.
It is doubtful that, with such parents, he ever took any serious notice of
such threats. The point is important because pretty well every account of
Kipling, despite Carrington, assumes that the 'severity' of Mrs Holloway
in some way itself actually 'stunted' Rudyard.

In the end his eyes went wrong. They must have been bad for years;
it is even possible that his eyesight affected his earlier failure to learn to
read. Short sight such as he had does not develop in a child in a matter
of months. Probably he had needed glasses since at least the time of his
arrival at Southsea. While on holiday at The Grange he was found beating
an apple-tree: 'I thought it was grandmama, and I had to beat it to see!' So
he was in a bad state. But this state need not have been induced in him by
Mrs Holloway's secret sadistic cruelty. One can hardly believe that she
could really have deceived everyone.

His aunt immediately wrote to her sister, who came post haste from
India. She descended upon Lorne Lodge without warning, but found
nothing untoward except a son now terrified of blindness. Rudyard
suffered similar delusions in later life when he was overworked; clearly,
from the account of such a one in 'The End of the Passage', they were
psychological in origin. Alice Kipling wrote to her husband that she had
felt a pang that the *two* children clung round Mrs Holloway rather than
round her. Does that suggest an out-and-out sadist? Trix, writing after
Kipling's death, echoed him rather too closely in explaining this: 'She
did not know that well-trained animals watch their tamer's eye, and the
familiar danger signals of "Aunty's" rising temper had set us both fawning
upon her.' That does not ring true, although it does suggest indignant
conversations about the 'House of Desolation' held between brother and
sister, during which they doubtless indulged themselves in semi-fantasies
ever after. It was Trix who declared that none of her relations had ever
visited her while she was at Southsea. Yet certainly her grandmother did,
and several times. She found them 'well and happy'. Is it likely that Mrs
Holloway would have shown any sign at all of such 'temper' in view of

Alice Kipling's trust in her, and in view of her three sisters' similar trust? Birkenhead says that Georgiana Burne-Jones told Stanley Baldwin that she regretted that she had never been to Lorne Lodge; but Wilson says that she, too, made visits. That not one of these bright and intelligent women saw anything at all wrong between her and the boy suggests strongly that he, both at the time and later, made use of Mrs Holloway's faults for his own emotional ends. After all, his sufferings would have been even greater had he been abandoned to a strict, cheap boarding establishment for little boys. Now who does that 'scar for life' (Ms Tompkins)?

Rudyard was very secretive by nature, and perhaps, in his original consternation at being so suddenly left by his parents, preferred to indulge himself emotionally from within in a complex and self-torturing game. And perhaps by the time his eyes became worse he had more than he could bear of tension, and so experienced the first of his breakdowns. Kipling as a writer had an uncanny knowledge of hysteria, as a careful reading of, for example, 'Mary Postgate', with its differing versions of reality, demonstrates. After his aunt took him to an eye specialist he went back to Southsea, where Mrs Holloway seems to have shown enough understanding to know that he was ill as well as wicked. Or so Carrington carefully adjudges. But Birkenhead, relying on Trix's recollections in old age, goes so far as to suggest that the KIPLING THE LIAR episode took place during this period. Rudyard in his autobiography says that he was then shut away from Trix for being a 'moral leper'; she added that she was told to sit at the piano and not move from the stool for forty-five minutes, that there was a 'bitter wind blowing', and that Harry, when she asked to see her brother, told her 'perhaps you'll never see him again, and a good job too'. Then, in this version of events, followed the placard incident. But wouldn't Harry have been getting ready for the bank? And wouldn't Mrs Holloway, whether a cunning sadist or a concerned woman, have known that Alice Kipling was on her way? The story is not credible.

Furthermore, Rudyard visited Trix and Mrs Holloway from his school on at least the occasion that he met Flo Garrard, his first love. Would a boy as damaged as he claimed he had been by this woman ('misused and forlorn' he later told his wife, who noted it) have made, or been expected to make, such a visit? He had nothing to fear by then. The reason for the visit was to pick up Trix, and it seems to have been quite casual.

It is difficult not to suspect that Mrs Holloway might even have been as kind a woman, at times, as she was severe at others. The notion of the special cunning act of a 'seaside landlady's type', before the boy's parents and several relatives, as well as before some of her own relatives, such as Trix implied in her account, is unconvincing: it suggests a degree of wickedness and insincerity which would have failed to pass the scrutiny of so many watchful people.

But Rudyard had to feel that *his* mother, the Mother, as he would come to call her, could not be disloyal. His security had been suddenly destroyed at a very early age. But he must survive. Therefore, as an author of fiction and fantasy, he unconsciously groped around for a scheme in which all the betrayal and inhumanity could be ascribed to one evil woman and her equally evil son. Clearly it was this early shock that launched him into that form of lying that is fiction. It had little to do with Mrs Holloway, but everything to do with his mother (the Mother). Equally clearly he had a bad conscience about leaving out, because it suited him, many pleasant aspects of the character of Mrs Holloway. He was not going to be a romancer, simply making his living out of fiction. What he would call his daimon, the inspiration – external to him – that was solely responsible for his achievement and which he unworthily served, was already asserting itself. So he lied about Mrs Holloway, attacking his mother in the guise of her; but another force was already manifest in him, seeking desperately to compensate for that lie.

So Rudyard at the age of twelve had already been profoundly influenced. First and foremost, by the paradise of his early childhood, in which he was an emperor both fully loved and fully in command. Being from birth a character of more power and determination than most, he was not going to allow that situation to change. Whatever price he was going to have to pay for it, he would pay. If this included a feeling of unworthiness, or of selling his soul, then so be it. He must have his power. This is what Alan Sandison means in his thoughtful essay, 'Kipling: The Artist and the Empire', when he calls Rudyard 'solipsist'. Rudyard was not born with a natural care for others. But those born with the lust for personal power are not denied the rage for virtue, mercy and justice. Kipling's insistence upon his unworthiness by the side of his daimon has to be explained somewhere. And this is the point at which we can begin to explain it.

After this early childhood he became influenced by what seemed to him to be catastrophe. Desertion. The end of his power. A sudden and temporary revulsion against him on the part of his mother, his father for once unable to counter her impulsiveness? He did not really get over it, and eventually collapsed with eye trouble, and was taken away. In those desolate years he struggled with absolute defeat – but not with Mrs Holloway, only with what he made Mrs Holloway in his mind. Then he began to manufacture the legend. The evil mother, so tart about Evangelicals ('a hair of the dog that bit us!'), is transformed into an evil Evangelical. Never mind the real character of Mrs Holloway, with its mixed emotions, mixed motivations and sadnesses and shames and disappointments and guilty cruelty and patches of good-heartedness and despair at such savage rejection by a nasty little boy. After all, no one is going to go to Rudyard Kipling because of his wholesale mastery of human psychology; one of his main obsessions is going to be revenge. So that the cause of his distress and loss of power may remain spotless, his mother, the Mother, Mrs Holloway must bear the burden of it all, to the extent that in the last year of his life he was still writing of her as a totally evil woman.

But there were other smaller influences upon him, too. Enormous power had been conferred upon him, and his parents had even called him, unwittingly of course, after a very powerful god of the country in which he was born – as well as after the peaceful lake at which they had met. His power, as we have seen, did not make him an easy person to deal with. Every child undergoes a change as it leaves its essence and becomes a personality in its own right; one of the things it starts to do when it realises that the entire world is not simply a part of it, is to say 'I'. Rudyard's 'I' was very loud indeed, so loud that before very long the world would hear it, and Mrs Holloway would hear it, and Harry would hear it, and above all Mrs Alice Kipling would hear it and know in her heart that she had sinned. But another part of Rudyard's power, unfortunately for the comfort of the many-peopled confusion that he described as 'I', was to create his daimon, to seek after mercy, truth, justice, kindness, detachment from ill feeling and hatred. He had registered other influences, then, too.

First there was the kindly old captain, a man with enough sense of justice to punish his own son when he saw that he had been untruthful, bullying, spiteful and cruel. A man who would gently correct his wife when she told the children that they had been sent to her because they had 'been wicked', and that she had taken them out of pity. I think she meant to be kindly, and that she did not say such things with a hell-fire thrust: she just did not understand that she was expressing her sense of bitterness and disappointment, and she did not understand how children take remarks.

The dear old salt, for such he seems to have been, was the first man in Rudyard's life who told him true tales of action, and of how things (ships, mostly) worked. Doubtless there were also tales of the action at Navarino. In his later life Kipling would continually seek out such men, whom he would remorselessly pump for information. When he got himself a son he delightedly compared him to a form of ship. Perhaps Mrs Holloway's insensitive jokes had a small influence on him, too.

Then there was his uncle Ned Burne-Jones, who was responsible for much of the real and rare pleasure he obtained in the unhappy Southsea years. He came, in time, to disapprove of Burne-Jones's politics – not that these were very alarming – as of the beloved aunt's; but even he could never deny the strong appeal and high spirits of those wholesome and kindly people at The Grange. He owed to Uncle Ned much of his own understanding of, and his appeal to, children. Indeed, he owed more to Pre-Raphaelitism than he would later wish to acknowledge. He spent months away from Southsea at The Grange, and he was able to forget his misery and betrayal and fear of what that meant.

He would arrive at The Grange (his cousin Margaret remembered), stout and cheerful and showing no signs of ill-treatment. Birkenhead, who falls hook, line and sinker for the 'ill-treatment' story, notes that Margaret already thought him exceedingly imaginative. When Aunt Georgie made a joke about wishing she could be cut into half so that one part of her could be with the children and the other downstairs he dramatised the remark: 'I have just seen her cut in half', and Margaret spoke of 'horrible glimpses of lacerated internal organs'. Meanwhile he picked up a great deal about art from his Uncle Ned and his friend William Morris, who used to drop in from time to time, and who had a genius for amusing children.

As for Harry and Mrs Holloway, he learned from them, he said, how to lie: 'It made me give attention to the lies I soon found it necessary to tell: and this, I presume, is the foundation of literary effort.' Well, lying of a certain kind is certainly one of the foundations of literary effort. But a propensity to lying for convenience is not in itself conducive to literary effort. Rudyard, I think, treated this offensive stranger who was his guardian from the beginning as someone of lower caste who could automatically be lied to. I do not think that she taught him to lie. He began to lie when he saw that he could not have his own way. Perhaps the upbringing of Anglo-Indian boys had undesirable elements: this is what their wiser parents thought, and this is why they were in the habit of sending them to England. How were the Kipling parents to know that they should not have tried this with

Rudyard? They knew enough, however, to know that they daren't tell him what they were going to do. They were afraid, and slunk off. So what he wrote in his autobiography is exceedingly bitter:

> These things, and many more of the like, drained me of any capacity for real, personal hate for the rest of my days. So close must any life-filling passion lie to its opposite. 'Who having known the Diamond will concern himself with glass?'

Since so many of his stories deal with hatred of various kinds, and since he was a man so very clearly full of hate – the love in him, although it was there, is harder to find – this cannot be taken as anything but defensive and disingenuous. He of all people was certainly not 'drained' of the capacity for real, personal hate, although overtly his hate seems to have been directed towards those groups whom he found it convenient to regard as the enemies of England and its Empire: Germans, Irish, Jews sometimes (although he was ambiguous about Jews), socialists, liberals. What he says here about love ('its opposite') is really, although frequently quoted, somewhat obscure. Is the second of the sentences quoted above offered as some kind of explanation of the first? Does he mean, or is he hinting, that in some way he was drained of the capacity for love, too? What he thinks he is saying is that he had known (in early childhood) the 'opposite' of hate, and so – he asks rhetorically – why would anyone who has known such love, the diamond, be concerned with any sort of glass? But the question follows uneasily upon the sentences preceding it. The confused remark betrays a profound unease about the myth of Mrs Holloway's severity. Is he not, a terrified being, pretending to himself that the Mother loved him always and did not abandon him? It may well be that he embarrassed himself from the time when he burst out with 'Baa, Baa, Black Sheep', and thus felt that he had to justify the myth. It points to a deep-seated, temperamental resentment and bitterness in him. Perhaps he nursed his sense of grievance about his mother's betrayal of him for many years: throughout his schooldays and most of his Indian journalistic apprenticeship. Perhaps his mother upset him with one of her tart remarks (for which she was well known); perhaps he then retaliated with the story, a violent exaggeration of the sufferings he underwent. At all events, he soon manipulated himself into a position in which it would be very hard to challenge his veracity. Who of all those who had reason to know would wish to come forward to say that Rudyard Kipling was a liar? Harry? Mrs Holloway? Aunt Georgie? Lockwood? Alice herself? He had won, and he had been revenged.

One of the most famous of all the incidents of 'Baa, Baa, Black Sheep' is when Punch's mother comes to kiss him good night. He puts up an arm as if to ward off a blow. Did Rudyard really do that? It seems hard to imagine that, if Alice's little boy was prompted by the behaviour of Mrs Holloway to make such a terrible gesture, she would still have left his sister to her mercies. Did he imagine, after he invented it, that this incident really had taken place? Some have said that his mother told him of this. But did he tell her that she had told him? Was Mrs Holloway in the habit of seeing him off to sleep with a blow? This gesture, or the imagination of it, may be interpreted as no doubt Kipling wished us to interpret it – or as a calculated reproach. Whether he did it or thought of doing it, he was soon out of the care of Mrs Holloway. Whatever the exact nature of his unhappiness at Southsea, he was never to be as unhappy in that way again. As he so often said, he learned a great deal from the interlude.

Young Rudyard, now twelve years old, was consoled by his parents for his unhappy state, even if they may have felt that he didn't altogether deserve it. First they all went to the family house of Mr Pinder, who had been his father's last English employer, in the Staffordshire potteries. The daughter of that house long afterwards told Birkenhead, perhaps wonderingly, that Rudyard was then 'like an oyster' and would say nothing of 'what he had endured'. But by that time she would have read the famous story and the piece of autobiography, and have absorbed the myth in other ways. Perhaps at this time Rudyard had nothing much of account to tell anyone: just a few isolated incidents, which he had provoked, upon which he later imposed a complete mythology.

Then, with his mother and Trix, he went to Goldring's Farm, at Loughton, near Epping Forest, a district at that time completely rural. His cousin Stanley Baldwin came to visit him, and together they roamed the district so memorably that many years later they almost collapsed with laughter recalling the wild times they had had together. This interlude in Essex provided Rudyard with valuable and enjoyed experience. He records that his mother did not like it when he and Stanley came in red with blood from their regular attendances at pig-slaughtering sessions.

Soon after the Loughton visit, Rudyard, again with his mother and Trix, went to a lodging-house at 227 Brompton Road. He thought that London would not agree with him, but found to his delight that it interested him almost as much as the country had. In this house he may have performed his first experiment in a sort of audience-manipulation, inasmuch as writing for a large public is a matter of manipulating an audience. He and Trix would make up little parcels containing coal, stones, and so forth, and then drop them into the street. Then he would delight in seeing passers-by eagerly open them up, only to discard their contents with disgust. When he was not doing this he was mostly at what was then the South Kensington Museum. On one occasion he tried, in his mother's bedroom, to give a drink to a toad he had brought from Loughton; he broke the water-jug.

Then he went to the house where he would spend almost all his school vacations: in Warwick Gardens, near Addison Road. Here lived the Misses Craik and a Miss Winnard, the 'three dear ladies' of his autobiography. They were well connected so far as literature and the arts were concerned: they had a pipe Carlyle had smoked, and knew Christina Rossetti, Jean Ingelow, and many others from the world of what Kipling, summing it up in *Something of Myself*, said 'would today be called culture'. It was, he added, a 'natural atmosphere'. One of these ladies, mistakenly called by Birkenhead Georgiana Craik (her name was the same as Kipling's aunt's), 'wrote novels on her knee'. But she should not be confused with the better known novelist Mrs Craik, author of *John Halifax Gentleman*, or, I think, with the Georgiana Craik who wrote *Lost and Won* (1859) and was a quite popular domestic novelist from 1857 – that Georgiana married a man called A.W. May, and must surely have done so by 1877.

It was by now the spring of 1888 and high time for Rudyard to go to school. His parents may have been even wiser than we think in arranging that he attend an institution whose headmaster was both an unusual man and a personal friend of theirs. Possibly they were worried about him, and believed that they detected a tendency towards untruth in him. If Rudyard did feel a sense of privilege in having Cormell Price, headmaster of United Services College, stand *in loco parentis* to him, then he never once took advantage of it. He seems, in the nine months between leaving Lorne Lodge and going to Westward Ho!, to have grown up in many ways. Possibly his sight 'chose' to play up badly in just the nick of time, so as to summon back the Mother and to gain reassurance. It takes time for even a clever mother to recognise that her son is no ordinary boy. In any case the Mother and the Father surely made up for any previous lapse by their decision to put the boy in the charge of Price.

School I

The most attractive, if acidulous, description of the foundation of United Services College, Westward Ho!, Devonshire, came from the pen of the 'M'Turk' of *Stalky & Co.*, G.C. Beresford, in his *Schooldays with Kipling* (1936):

> It was started by some Army and Navy Service people who, through the niggardliness of fortune, had to look on both sides of a shilling. They wished to call into being a school or college, on public-school lines, for the sons of officers – but a school completely without frills, bare of Gothic pinnacles, encaustic tiles and the other superfluities beloved of 'pious founders'.
>
> Our founders, in casting round for a box or a pack of boxes in which to nest their idea, hit upon a row of what seemed promising lodging-houses at Westward Ho!, near the middle of the curve of Bideford Bay. These were twelve file of fine, upstanding terrace houses of five storeys. They were all of equal height and perfect dressing by the right: very well drilled, but without side-arms. This it was that took the eye or eyes of the officer founders.
>
> The generals and admirals built a corporal to take the right of line, in command. This non-com took the form of a gymnasium whose internals comprised only three or four pieces of apparatus. Being thus fairly empty, it could act as a large hall in which the whole school could be assembled at 'call-over' or for any purpose when it was necessary to parade the full strength, so that it could have a good look at itself. Later on, one half of the floor space of this gym was filled with plank desks and forms for large classes.

Some Kipling commentators, particularly Birkenhead, have misunderstood Beresford's aloof and facetious manner, imagining him to have been jealous of Kipling and anxious, as one who had done less well in life, to do him down. They have missed a point they could have grasped from *Stalky & Co.* as well as from *Something of Myself*. 'Stalky' himself, General L.C. Dunsterville, had contributed an irritated foreword to Beresford's book, and had also written (to Kipling's annoyance) a less shrewd though lively book, *Stalky's Reminiscences*, in 1928. A year before he died, in 1946 (Beresford had died in 1938), Dunsterville told Birkenhead that his old schoolchum was 'quite the type of stage Irishman who is agin anybody and everybody, and he kept this up until the day of his death. He was then a swank photographer in Yeoman's Row, but filled with hatred and contempt for his fellow men.' Beresford was born acidulous, and needed no contempt or hatred to make him so. Rudyard himself recognised this with tolerant amusement.

But Dunsterville was then eighty, and in any case Birkenhead missed his tone of amused, contemptuous, knowing tolerance for a person of very long acquaintance. Beresford, as Rudyard said, had a 'tongue dipped in some Irish-blue acid'. His front was, and always had been, one of facetious superciliousness, and his friends liked him for it. His book is well written, and, although it very occasionally sinks under the weight of its own facetiousness, is amusing, perceptive and sometimes funny. The dislike he has incurred from ardent Kiplingites is on account of his acerbic candour rather than of any malice, which he did not possess.

Beresford, who went out to India at the time Kipling did, and became a civil engineer, was an enterprising man, and a sharper and more intelligent observer of human nature than Dunsterville. Those after the more accurate picture should therefore go to Beresford, who remembered more and who quite lacked a rigid, authoritarian mentality. The commentators who deplore his 'patronising and embittered disparagement of his brilliant contemporary Kipling, who had so far outstripped him in the race of life' (Birkenhead), over-dutifully confuse a deliberately off-putting, amused and imperturbable manner, with envious malice. *Schooldays with Kipling* is far too relaxed to be malicious. It is affectionate, but always sceptical and truthful; not perhaps a book suitable for those who like a spade called a silver spoon. Kipling knew his M'Turk, who would, he also tells us, speak of his teachers as 'ushers'. His attitude, says Kipling, was far beyond 'mere insolence'. One more reason for the failure of the ardent Kiplingite to appreciate Beresford may be discovered in his membership of the Fabian Society. It is clear that he was a careful and wide reader. His championship of Ruskin is made into a feature of *Stalky*.

The United Services College was founded in 1874. It was one of the most peculiar of public schools, and it had a headmaster very peculiar in an institution whose purpose was to cater for boys destined for the army or navy. As their advertisement in the *Illustrated London News* for 23 January 1875 puts it:

> The object of the United Services Proprietary College at Westward Ho is to provide for the sons of the officers of the Army and Navy an inexpensive education of the highest class and of a general nature. It is also to prepare them for the military, naval and civil examinations, or for the universities, or for the liberal professions, or for mercantile and general pursuits.

The headmaster in *Stalky* is not at all like Cormell Price, who in the book is idealised by Kipling as 'that amazing man': wise enough to flog three boys and 'perpetrate a howling injustice' because 'when you find a variation from the normal – this will be useful to you in later life – always meet him in an abnormal way'. Although in *Stalky* Kipling set out to demonstrate how perfect a place United Services had been for the formation of the sort of characters who would maintain an empire, Price hardly ever flogged any boy, and was anti-imperialist. Yet Rudyard was so personally fond of him (*Stalky* is dedicated to him) that he could not resist doing him the honour of making him what he was not. In fact Price belonged very securely to the Pre-Raphaelite aspect of Kipling's early life, that aspect which he deeply valued but also took care to condemn as politically misguided and degenerate.

Cormell Price was born in 1835 and went, not to a public school, but to King Edward's School, Birmingham. One of his schoolfellows was

Kipling's uncle Henry Macdonald. Another was Ned Burne-Jones. He went up to Brasenose College, Oxford, and became friendly there with William Morris. Beresford implies that he received a bad degree: he took it in 1858, 'without frills', and he 'took no honours at Oxford, either with his head, or his arms, or his legs'. He was one of those who took part in the famous painting of the Union walls with Pre-Raphaelite frescoes.

Then he was a medical student in London for two years. He gave that up and went as an English tutor to a Russian family for two more. 'On the artistic career he made no attempt', Beresford says: perhaps he was initially frustrated. But Pre-Raphaelitism, and its specifically anti-military attitude, had got into his blood. He was the kind of man who becomes a schoolmaster because there is really nothing else he can do. But, unusually, he happened to be a good teacher. In 1863 he got a mastership at Haileybury College, and in time became head of the 'modern side'. He was near London, and kept in touch with all his old friends, among them Kipling's parents. To Rudyard he was always 'Uncle Crom'.

At Haileybury he was a success at teaching languages. This must have been as great a surprise to him as it was to everyone else. The founders of USC, a number of them from Haileybury, cannot have known too much about his politics (Angus Wilson goes as far as to call him a political extremist), for they unanimously selected him as Head of the new United Services College. He took with him a select few from Haileybury: boys whose parents were anxious to get them through the Army Entrance examination. These parents were less bothered about the Empire than about this obstacle to the military success of their offspring, and that is presumably why a blind eye was turned to Price's politics.

Haileybury charged £73.10s a year. If boys there or at similar schools failed the Examination they had to go to crammers, 'shops' run by dubious persons who might charge anything up to £300. United Services charged about £60, possibly even less. The place was cheap – and there was thus, ironically, no room for military trimmings. They must have had great faith in Price: a quarter of the two hundred boys were taken on to make the project pay, and these boys were not destined to become officers – they were hopeless cases who had been expelled from other public schools. It was a bold and wholly pragmatic venture. Kipling, Dunsterville and Beresford are all agreed in their view of the majority of the masters there: a 'job lot', with few men of real ability. Yet the school was successful and got boys into the army. Indeed, it was badly set back when, after Rudyard's time there, the Army Exam was simplified and made less formidable. Price was the star so far as the Army Exam was concerned; but there must have been others with some ability. One of these was the more traditional William Crofts, of whom 'King' in Stalky is a partial portrait. Crofts apparently lamented that the school was not more traditional; but Rudyard never really liked him, although the antagonism that sprang up between them was a fruitful one, and it is obvious that he admired him.

A single corridor ran through all the buildings, and the gym was used as an assembly hall and place of worship. The atmosphere was not religiose, and there were few high-toned sermons. Boys and masters (but not Price: 'Was there enough of him for this performance? . . . he could not afford to lose everything', comments Beresford) bathed naked either in the salt-water baths or, sometimes, in the sea. Rudyard claimed that he had some small distinction as a swimmer, although deficient in other games; Beresford says he had no distinction even as a swimmer.

The food would 'now raise a mutiny on Dartmoor', Rudyard wrote in 1936. Beresford writes amusingly of the headmaster's experiment in giving breakfasts: he never could get any answers to his questions from the visitors, who were too busy taking advantage of the 'unaccustomed viands'. 'Let the other three boys, one's fellow guests, perform the necessary social duties if the Head was to receive a feast of reason and flow of the soul during the repast. Why spoil bacon and eggs with attempts at verbal essays or intellectual fireworks?' The meat was cooked in primitive ovens with naked flames, and always had a scorched taste. There was beer at the tables, but no one took much notice of it. Since those at the crammers' shops were able to smoke, United Services became the first public school at which senior boys were allowed to smoke. (This may really have been a ploy to keep the rejects quiet: they were only there to provide more cash.) This became the subject of one of Rudyard's oddest late stories, 'The United Idolaters', in which the smoking is in some way equated with the persistently alleged fact that the school was a uniquely 'clean' one. It was a theme he found irresistible, and I shall return to it.

A few days before Rudyard was brought down to the school, by Price himself, in January 1878, the Head, with his friends Burne-Jones and Morris, had organised an anti-jingoist protest against Disraeli's policy of intervention in the Russo-Turkish war – an event some historians equate with the beginning of imperialism as a real issue in British politics. This protest was the Workmen's Neutrality Demonstration, at Islington and at Exeter Hall. Thus Price, after four years at USC, was not inhibited about expressing his views. The irony of this has often been commented on. But Kipling did not form his imperialistic philosophy until he was in India, and might just as well have been a Gladstone as a Disraeli man at this point in his history. His father and therefore his mother would both have been Disraeli people, but he would not yet have heard much talk about this. Rudyard was, in the words of H.M. Swanwick, a fellow pupil at United Services, 'a bookworm, entirely absorbed in the life of books, unathletic, unsociable, and, sad to say – decidedly fat'. Beresford said exactly the same.

In *Stalky* Rudyard held up his old school as the perfect training ground for soldiers of the Empire. The majority of commentators therefore feel it incongruous to suggest that while he was actually there he may have well have been, inasmuch as boys and girls of that age are anything, a Gladstonian liberal and a Pre-Raphaelite sympathiser. Swanwick also said that it 'always amused us that he should have *become* so fervidly the prophet of Action and the laureate of the Deed' (my italics). Because of the peculiar nature of Kipling studies, and the fact that even critics of a liberal cast of mind are forced onto the defensive when wishing to draw attention to his virtues, it has become almost *infra dig* to point out the compensatory nature of Kipling's devotion to action. The fact is, Rudyard felt a strong sense of humiliation in the fact that he was not and could not be a man of action. It is yet another of the keys to an understanding of him.

Rudyard's desperate bid for success was tightly bound up with a sense of what it would feel like to fail, to have nothing, to have no power. 'Failure', in the Kipling sense, is to be *without power*. Others less strong, less

determined, more kindly, more concerned with others, less pressured by
a sense of inadequacy, may find contemplation of the state of this sort of
powerlessness less horrible. But for Rudyard it was a matter of humiliation.
The repulsive and childish scene of the punishment, by Dick Heldar, of
the cardiac publisher who has an unfair control over his pictures in *The
Light that Failed* is an indication of how its author felt about others who
might have power over him. It is explained by his immense will to power.
He had been unusually powerful since babyhood. As I have suggested,
he had been born like that, just as Beresford had been born acidulous and
provocatively sarcastic.

Wherever he was, Rudyard was going to make himself felt. So long as he
could first establish himself as the chief feature in his environment, then
secondly, but always secondly, he would see about moderating his attitude
towards others. Indeed, that attitude was throughout his life much, and
conscientiously, tempered, even though he lacked what is ordinarily
called an intellect. Right from the start, though, dominance of the environment had to be established, and he demanded support – support from his
family and all his relatives. Ruddy is coming. An angry Ruddy is coming.
This is the temperament with which Kipling was born, and throughout his
life it was only his very active literary and imaginative conscience that
countered its natural and savage egocentricity. But he was also, like his
early mentor the crippled W.E. Henley, a man of action who was denied
action. He had very poor sight, he was so hopelessly bad at games that
he had discreetly to be excused them by his friend Price, he was clumsy,
and he lacked coordination. He had the sensibility and the sense to know
that, at this school, he was teacher's pet, and that without being teacher's
pet he could not have endured. Price was watching his young charge like
a hawk; but he possessed a remarkable sense of tact. It was not his fault
that, just as Rudyard's mother, whatever she may really have done, had to
be spotless, so he, Rudyard's headmaster, had eventually to be spotlessly
cruel, imperialistic, and so forth. He managed the school by being what
we should today call 'laid back'. Beresford mistook it for inferiority. Yet in a
way Beresford was not wrong: he was, in the context of successful, tough,
outspoken headmasters who would plunge into the waters alongside their
staff and pupils, inferior. Price had to be unobtrusive to succeed, and he
knew it, and Beresford alone spotted it. It is ironic, in view of his false
reputation as the headmaster in the fantasy *Stalky*, that Price should have
been so successful at his job by being so very inconspicuous. But it was
through this unsung inconspicuousness that he was able to show favour
to the ever-so-vulnerable Rudyard, who had not yet learned to use his
verbal facilities to defend himself. Nor did Kipling ever fully believe in
verbal power. He preferred, like his hero Teddy Roosevelt, the big stick.

At Lorne Lodge, as we have seen, Rudyard fought off his hatred of
his absent mother by fighting; and he had thus aroused the hostility of an
adversary who could do much to make his life miserable. He may have
learned from that. His parents certainly did. Although without means, they
managed to put him into the hands of a personal friend.

What did he do in the potentially very much more adverse circumstances of a new boy at what must have been a tough school? Not enough
attention, perhaps, has been given to this, although it has been assumed
that he was initially utterly miserable and that he was badly bullied. He

tells us so in *Something of Myself*. And he must have been bullied to a certain extent. But how much? Angus Wilson says that 'as a new boy he had been horribly bullied', and I should certainly not dismiss anything Wilson says lightly. But I can find no evidence for it, and, rather, evidence to the contrary. He was bullied, I think, to about the same degree as Mrs Holloway was really cruel to him: sometimes, but not much, and not out of the way. Kipling tells us in the official chronicle of his life that he was bullied because it would not have done for the apostle of Empire to have failed to go through this character-forming ritual. That is one of the intentions of the 'parable', as he himself called it, of *Stalky*.

There are difficulties involved in Kipling's preaching of the gospel of bullying and flagrantly unjust flogging for boys: it is a gospel which relies greatly on Social Darwinist assumptions, and it therefore suggests that any victim of such a system who is unresourceful is worthless and dysgenic trash in any case. The author of *Stalky* is careful to ascribe brilliantly calculated injustices to an all-wise Head – but Price was not in fact at all like that, even if he was quite wise. What Price clearly did was to see that Rudyard was not in fact bullied. He owed it to his friends, and it was well within his powers.

Rudyard had learned from Lorne Lodge that straightforward lofty antagonism does not necessarily lead to the best results. The manner in which a boy survives – if he does survive – at a boarding school in his early years there can offer valuable clues to his character; and, while we know comparatively little about Kipling's private life as an adult, we know more about his school life.

He wrote intensely miserable letters to his mother during his first term at Westward Ho! They contained the usual complaints of small boys during their first weeks at boarding school: how unhappy they are and how much they want to be taken away. Rudyard himself more than once alludes, in his writings, to this epistolary habit in the very young. It is not often pointed out that Rudyard wrote letters to his mother, not to far-off India, but to England. She did not leave England until the autumn of 1880, and in 1878 she was joined by her husband, who spent eight months there and in France. She must have stayed in order to keep an eye on her son. Lockwood took Rudyard on a visit to France to compensate him for having had to spend the Easter holidays at the school. These parents were beginning to listen to what their son wanted. He was now getting most of what he wanted. He was lucky, and he was spoiled. How many real empire-builders had a headmaster who was his father's personal friend? But perhaps all that is untypical of the proper sort of suffering in youth recommended for future bearers of the white man's burden. Later perhaps this history of spoiling could all be changed, by a process sometimes described – although in another context – as 'retrospective falsification'.

Therefore, though feeling forlorn, Rudyard would have felt quite different in 1878 from how he felt in 1871, besides which he was older (twelve), more experienced and more resourceful. Beresford mentions his special relationship with the Head, although he goes out of his way to make it clear that Rudyard was not openly favoured by Price. Boys would have known that Rudyard had turned up at the beginning of term with the Head. The masters knew it, too. They would have kept a discreet eye on him. By 1881 he had got himself made a special case: 'released from formal studies', as Angus Wilson puts it. Price was indeed able to favour him, without appearing to. It is astonishing at what a young age Rudyard got himself into such a special position. His only real problem lay in the future, when he would have to invent a different sort of childhood.

Beresford says that Rudyard avoided being bullied from the start. He was smiling, he was diplomatic, he gave an air of being 'rather more formidable than he was'. That is a shrewd observation, and has been criticised by ardent Kiplingites as a manifestation of Beresford's envy because it is true, rather than because it is envious. Unlike a Kiplingite, Beresford does not believe that it is wonderful to be Kipling. He has his own existence, and rather likes it. After all, anything can be put down to envy. Birkenhead admits that Rudyard was not 'particularly unhappy' in his first year. He was befriended by Beresford himself, from about his second day at the school. Dunsterville, who had been there longer than the others, says that the worst of the bullying was over by 1878. Before then boys were hung out of the high windows by their ankles, or were made to put their ear to a keyhole while someone hammered it from the other side.

Kipling and Dunsterville, echoed by many an approving commentator, also insist that USC was unusually 'clean' – but we shall come to that. Beresford is wiser and says nothing so po-faced. He saw what he saw and was able to remember it because it didn't bother him that much – nor did he need to keep any secrets about his sexuality.

Amongst all those who wrote of Kipling from direct knowledge, it is Beresford who shows the most shrewdness in getting to the heart of the matter of Kipling's politics while he was still a schoolboy. Discussions of this, as of Kipling's politics as a whole, tend to be robbed of their usefulness by the amount of political bias displayed by the majority of Kipling's admirers. These admirers like Kipling less for his creative writings than for his opinions, which they wrongly believe to be firmly embedded in his work. This is what I mean by an 'ardent Kiplingite'.

The properly directed imagination of an artist, a writer, a composer – of a reader above all – is not of any political party, even if the owner of it is. This pressure of the imagination, which involves seeing cases on their objective merits rather than in the theory-bound terms of politics, proved a great strain on the apostle of Empire. Sometimes it all but vanished, obscured in great clouds of fury and rage. But it was never destroyed. Kipling's obstinacy may have been childish, but it operated on what was best in him, as well as on what was worst. Carrington prints a revealing story about him, recounted by one of Fred Macdonald's children, relating to the year 1880 when he was fourteen.

> He came in one day tense with anger – rolled on the nursery floor in fury. 'Why Ruddy! What's the matter?!' 'The porter at the station boxed my ears.' 'But what made him box your ears?' 'Oh, I expect I cheeked him.' His manner changed; he smiled, and went towards the door with a purposeful look. 'Where are you going, Ruddy?' 'Back to the station to cheek that porter again.'

He did not in the least change in this respect, although he liked to look as though he had.

School II

Price made Rudyard the editor of a revived school magazine, the *United Services College Chronicle*, which had been abandoned after three earlier issues. The boy produced only an average school magazine, writing most of it himself, and overseeing it at a Bideford printer.

One says 'boy' but, with his precocious moustache, his heavy smoking, his thickly hirsute chest, arms and legs, he was more like a fully formed little man, and a formidable one. When his parents' friend Miss Pinder reproved him for smoking so heavily, during a vacation in 1881, he replied, 'I know my birth certificate gives my age as sixteen, but you know as well as I do that I am twenty-six in everything else.' Such was his authority that he could get away with this kind of remark. A school photograph of him in a group helps us to understand why. His small head close to his shoulders earned him his nickname of 'Beetle', though this was used only by his intimates. His more general nickname was Giggers, a reference to his glasses: a local drunk called Rabbits Eggs, well known to the schoolboys, and figuring in *Stalky*, one day looked at Rudyard and asked 'Who's old giglamps?' The name stuck, but was shortened to Giggers.

His studiedly romantic attitude to his chosen intimates, mainly but not exclusively Lionel Dunsterville and George Beresford, is well expressed in one of his earliest poems, 'The Dusky Crew'. He had read and imbibed enough poetry to feel in this way:

Our heads were rough and our hands were black
  With the ink-stain's midnight hue;
We scouted all, both great and small –
  We were a dusky crew;
And each boy's hand was against us raised –
  'Gainst me and the Other Two.

This is exceedingly well accomplished for a boy of thirteen (it was written before August 1879, when it was refused by an American magazine); it appeared with other of his poems in the family magazine *Scribbler* (November 1878–March 1880), devoted to the work of the young Morrises and Burne-Joneses, and Rudyard authorised its publication in later life, though not in the *Definitive Edition of Rudyard Kipling's Verse*. Each boy's hand was by no means raised against Stalky and Co., but here we have the clue to Kipling's predominant attitude: rebel and outcast, but without the inconvenience of actually being so. He was even then somewhat of a pragmatist (even if the budding writer in him wasn't): Beresford explains how mature his attitude to the editorship of the *Chronicle* was. He was full of importance 'really, but not showing it'; he said that he well understood that the magazine could contain no complaints about the way the school was run, 'they knew that was all rot . . . the Head . . . would have nothing of that sort . . .'; he put a stop to suggestions that he was caricaturing the masters by pretending that the caricatures were of other masters at schools 'one had been at'. He managed to keep his private poems, as distinct from the ones he wrote for exhibition, intact from inspection by telling his friends that they were 'letters to the mater'.

Beresford maintains that Rudyard was the only boy at USC who wore glasses. Even in this Rudyard made the best of it: one fancies that he well knew that the eyes without the glasses were of a brilliant and piercing blue. He was so well known for his sarcasm and wit that his teacher Crofts told him that he would 'die in a garret a scurrilous pamphleteer' (what a compliment to a schoolboy, and of course clearly intended as one: the same master threw a volume of Browning's poems at his head in class, calling him 'Gigadibs the literary man').

Rudyard had another and quite distinct life in his vacations. But there was one link between these two lives, and that was Crom Price. Rudyard (undoubtedly the leading light and inspirer) and Stalky and M'Turk decorated their study in an almost luridly Pre-Raphaelite manner, and that they got away with this piece of (in its context) preciosity must have been due to the power Price exerted in the school. Price's own quarters were similarly decorated, if more expensively and less defiantly. Whenever the boys entered these precincts the face of Janie Morris would look out at them from various frames: the 'daughter of Oxford', as the knowing and sardonic Beresford put it (she was originally picked up in the theatre by Morris), who seemed more lifelike than anyone else around, and no wonder. Price would, during Rudyard's last year at the school, invite the boy to these quarters for long talks and pipes and brandy until well into the night: Beresford says that he returned befuddled with drink.

The picture we gain is one of a well protected and authoritative boy. But a couple of subalterns who had been at USC with Kipling told Edmonia ('Ted') Hill in 1888 that he had been 'so brilliant and cynical that he was most cordially hated by his fellow students'. That, one may guess, was the view the school as a whole had of him, although it changed when they heard that he was a genius. But their hands were not exactly against him. Kipling's knowingness ('cynicism'), then, existed well before his imperialism. Indeed, the two are somewhat contradictory, although he – exactly like his hero Rhodes – was able to reconcile them. It is predictable that he should have enthused over and contributed much to Baden-Powell's scout movement; but there was also that in him which could laugh at its goody-goody intentions, just as he and his friends laughed at *Eric, or Little by Little* and even at the *Boy's Own Paper*. This subversiveness became more and more deeply buried as he got older, but it surfaced in unexpected places. While one cannot see Price very enthusiastically flogging anyone in the officially merciless and sexually delighted Kipling manner, one can see him being sympathetic to laughter at the *Boy's Own Paper*.

It is worth noting, too, that Rudyard already had a highly developed intuitive power in his choice of companion: Dunsterville actually became a minor military hero, and Beresford could look after enemies with his sarcastic tongue.

On the matter of flogging: Kipling untruthfully told Trix that he had often been beaten and had richly deserved it. But Beresford says that apart from some mild attentions from a sadistic chaplain, Campbell, who was there for only two of Rudyard's years, he did not get beaten – he knew, as one might have guessed, how to avoid it: 'Gigger showed laudable skill in safe-guarding in every respect his epidermis.' As for Campbell's capacity to inflict pain: 'Not that any bodily pain worth mentioning resulted'. Yet that Kipling was early fond of the idea is evident from a poem written before January 1880:

> . . . That echoing loud caused a master's ire.
> The heavy stripes, the long-drawn gasping sob,
> Repentant vows wrung from the chastened soul,
> The victim's anguish, and the after-glow . . .

Could Price on any of those nights with brandy and pipes have shown him any of the pornographic and unpublished lines ('Swish, swish, swish! Oh how I wish . . .', and so on) written in honour of the rod by his admired Swinburne? That seems unlikely, enlightened though Price was. In the story called 'The Impressionists' in *Stalky*, the three boys go to the lavatory to inspect the 'damage' after a beating from the fictitiously savage Head, and this damage is described as characterised by 'thoroughness, efficiency, and a certain clarity of outline that stamps the work of the artist'. Kipling might just as well have been openly addressing his fellow flagellants, especially as he goes on to draw attention to a copious flow of blood, which the boys are supposed to wash off. But according to Beresford the cane was applied only to the hands 'or on the garmented person'. It seems that Kipling's debt in the matter of flagellation was owed solely to Aunty Rosa: at least that is one interest they always shared.

Stalky is not a good guide to the details of Kipling's schooldays or to those who taught him; but there is one famous passage that rings true. It describes the time when Price opened up his library to Rudyard:

> He gave Beetle the run of his brown-bound, tobacco-scented library; prohibiting nothing, recommending nothing. There Beetle found a fat armchair, a silver inkstand, and unlimited pens and paper. There were scores and scores of ancient dramatists; there were Hakluyt, his voyages; French translations of Muscovite authors called Pushkin and Lermontoff; little tales of a heady and bewildering nature, interspersed with unusual songs – Peacock was that writer's name; there was Borrow's *Lavengro* . . .

And he goes on to describe the world with which this brought him into touch, and how Price would sometimes read from one of the poets, and tell tales of them from his youth. So, little monster though he was in most ways, conscience began to grow in him: that interest in the status of one's inner being which makes one immune from, or even horrified by, the crasser world of the senses.

Price was quite as remarkable as he was unobtrusive; one is led to wonder whether he really liked being a schoolmaster or was one *faute de mieux*. He seems to have been one who was not formidable but who managed to appear so when it mattered. Beresford sensed some 'reservation' in him, observing that when he went off to London (doubtless on business as Pre-Raphaelite as it was official), and the more conventional though literary Crofts took charge, the school 'sprang smartly to attention and threw out its chest ... When Price returned this beauty and romance vanished and the dream was shattered.'

Price, Beresford thought, owed his position 'to a single hair, or at most two hairs'. This was an allusion to his beard, the 'trump card', since a beard 'is a great help to a retreating chin'. 'A hair or two less, and the game would have been up. Price would have been withstood on many occasions – or ignored, which is worse.' His eyeglass, too, which looked to Beresford like plain glass and probably was, 'was as potent as an "order" ... it brought a metropolitan air to the sodden pastures of Devonshire'. Yet Beresford pays tribute to his achievement. It seems as though Price was a little like Kipling in that he manipulated the environment by cunning rather than real strength.

He was by no means as aggressive as Rudyard, and anger seems not to have been one of his methods, although he is said to have terrified a boy out of an inconvenient sleepwalking habit by threatening him with a terrible caning. One may most easily imagine this incident as having taken place before a highly appreciative audience of boys, all more sophisticated than, or senior to, the sleepwalker. Price's influence on Rudyard was considerable and altogether benign; he certainly contributed nothing to his imperialism. And Kipling admired him so much that on the occasion of his retirement in 1894 he paid him the tribute of calling him what he certainly was not (but had, as Kipling's hero, necessarily to be): all that he had 'ever arrived at', he said in a speech, 'was to make men able to make and keep empires'. Price was fond of Kipling, but can hardly have been flattered; at the same time, he had long been in the habit of never disagreeing. That was not how you handled Rudyard. He knew, however, what his most distinguished pupil never learned in the matter of political opinion: how to keep his own counsel. Angus Wilson suggests that the two men were so fond of one another that a 'wry smile' may have passed between them even as Kipling made the absurd misrepresentation. This is quite possible, although I do not believe it; even if it were the case, it implies a certain arrogance and failure to respect the views of others on Kipling's part. If he could not help but feel gratitude and admiration for Price (as human being, as man-to-be-kept-quiet-and-from-writing reminiscences, above all as headmaster), then he must change the object of it into something acceptable to him. However, when Price died in 1911 and left his son and daughter badly provided for, Kipling showed his gratitude in unequivocal form: he looked after their education and befriended them.

Before we can examine some of the original poetry, both private and public, that Rudyard wrote during his adolescence, we need to know that he 'fell in love'. This happened in 1880, two months before his mother returned to India.

It was at Lorne Lodge, in July 1880. He had been entrusted with the task of bringing Trix away from Mrs Holloway's for her summer holiday. The girl was called Florence Garrard, and she was at Southsea because her parents were abroad. Carrington tells us that she was a little older than Rudyard – about fifteen, possibly sixteen – and that though beautiful she had been 'badly brought up in continental hotels' and was very 'ill educated'. She sat as the original for Maisie in *The Light that Failed*, because, as we shall see, Kipling ran into her again ten years later. Carrington further says that she had a 'shrewd sophisticated manner', was 'self-centered and elusive' and 'lacking in sympathy and affection'. The sources for this view of Flo are the Kipling family, though; and one wonders how far a 'shrewd and sophisticated manner' at fifteen can go with an altogether bad education. Trix had the job of supervising Flo's reading, and at that time 'adored' her. She dutifully wrote:

> Flo was very slender with a long plait of brown hair, as thick as your arm, and the same thickness all the way down, swinging below her knees. Her head was too small for her body, her hair too heavy for her head, hair like Rapunzel; her eyes too big for her face, of the true grey with no hint of blue or hazel, and the thickest straightest black lashes I have ever seen. An ivory pallor that never flushed or changed but always looked healthy. The mouth in repose was a straight line, and the small features as delicate as a cameo. She gave most of her dress allowance to her sister, who always looked like a rag-bag, and fluttered out of doors like a worrycrow, or bird-scarer, while she wore old Holland dresses or the simplest blue serge.

At Mrs Holloway's she owned a goat called Becquot, which, it amused Rudyard to observe, butted Aunty Rosa (but would such a cruel Evangelical as Rudyard's Mrs Holloway have submitted to this indignity without bringing out her cane and threats of hell fire?). No doubt it also nuzzled her lap embarrassingly. The goat is yet another character in *The Light that Failed*, where it functions uneasily as a symbol of lust, as well of as itself. 'Where and how often Flo and Rudyard met was their own secret,' says Carrington. It does seem, though, as if it were as often as Rudyard could get away during his vacations. By now he regarded himself as something of a senior romantic.

When Rudyard went off to India in September 1882 Carrington says that he considered himself engaged to Flo; but it is not known if she agreed to this, and some may prefer to take Rudyard's word lightly in such matters. On the other hand there is record of a breach with her in May 1882: on the 22nd and then again on the 28th of that month he wrote to one of the mother-substitutes he kept in reserve, Mrs Tavenor Perry (wife of an architect friend of his parents, to whom he wrote while at school and addressed as 'Mater'), speaking of the end of the relationship ('*entirely at an end,*' he said) and enclosing a poem on that theme called 'Discovery'. Either that was a purely temporary quarrel or, when he spoke of being 'engaged', he had other motives, possibly ones of self-protection against romantic involvement. Certainly Flo wrote disabusing him of any notion of an engagement in 1884 – which makes it the more likely that the May breach was a passing one, but also that any idea of an engagement had been no more than a characteristically bullying assumption on his part.

Perhaps he was not 'swept away' by Flo herself. He had by now certainly decided to become a writer. A writer, as he then thought of a writer, would necessarily be swept away by so romantic a person. She certainly was something of a find for a boy brought up so firmly in the Pre-Raphaelite tradition, and she must have had at least as powerful an influence on him as had Swinburne, Wilde, Rossetti, Morris, Poe and the other writers who meant most to him as a schoolboy. She told him that she 'came from a hopeless family', that both her parents were drunkards, and that 'her sister suffered from curvature of the spine, incipient sex mania and a hungry gushing manner'. It is quite possible that she considered herself to be an abandoned or doomed woman, and that Rudyard, being just that much younger, was deeply over-impressed. She went to art school in France and then to the Slade; Trix said that she died in 1902 of tuberculosis ('neglected lungs'). Birkenhead calls her a 'dreamy *allumeuse*', but there is no independent evidence for that. Birkenhead also says that 'her background had certain romantic drawbacks': I do not know what this means except that, in its vagueness, it may represent what attracted Rudyard. Like Mrs Holloway, she has ended up in history as a monster: a woman incapable of love because she wanted to do her own work, which (naturally) was no good. The tiny bit that survives of it (drawings in a sketch-book owned by Kipling in America) is neither here nor there – 'art-school stuff', as they say. Whether anything else she did showed promise or not, it has to be said that she wanted to devote herself to it, and that had she not turned Kipling down she would have had a less bad reputation – if only in the sense that no reputation at all is preferable to being the 'coldly indifferent' Maisie of *The Light that Failed*, who made Ronald Colman so unhappy. We shall return to her when we come to that novel.

It must be mentioned here that Carrington obtained evidence that Flo Garrard and her lifelong companion, Mabel Price, survived long after 1902. He discovered that both 'indignantly repudiated' the reality of the motivations attributed to them in *The Light that Failed*. This is correct information, as many people were well aware that Florence Garrard, in the 1920s, was exceedingly sceptical about Rudyard–Dick's motives in the novel that made her famous. Did Kipling hear a very vague rumour that she was dead and then quickly take advantage of it to kill her off: 'That was the end of Maisie', as he wrote in his novel? Trix conspired almost fully in all his legends of his early life, and may have been doing so when she declared that Florence had died in 1902.

Many, although not all, of Rudyard's early, more private poems are in an elaborately presented notebook called *Sundry Phansies* which he gave to Flo when he sailed for India in 1882. This has survived in the Berg Collection in the New York Public Library, and has now been printed in its entirety by Andrew Rutherford in his *Early Verse by Rudyard Kipling* (1986). Rudyard gave it a title-page with a scroll announcing '1882 FEBRUARY SUNDRY PHANSIES WRIT BY ONE KIPLING'. The focus, the real excellence, in his early verse is upon high technical accomplishment. There is a great feeling for the manner of other poets, and, as 'The *Mary Gloster*' and other narrative poems show, he was learning from Browning, even if Browning (whom he had met at Ned Burne-Jones's house) was not then his favourite poet. But there is no feeling for Florence Garrard as a person: everything in that region has been learned from his masters. There is not even much sense of her as a person, any more than there is of Maisie in *The Light that Failed*.

However, Rudyard was only ever *in love* with one person, though he may have loved several, and without doubt he loved his wife. That one love, as we shall see, was shatteringly reluctant, self-shocking and agonised. But there is nothing in the early poetry to Florence to suggest that his feelings for her were anything but, in essence, a cluster of self-protective devices. His shrewd and sharp-tongued mother felt that such an 'unrewarded devotion' kept him (says Birkenhead) from 'lesser loves' (by which she may have meant women of loose morals). It is probable that this is what he intended: such engagement elsewhere would serve to save him from temptation, if he was tempted, and it would also save him from further idealistic attachments, these all sharing a quality of sameness. In that way one big attachment was economical of his poetical efforts. But he certainly thought that he suffered, and was just as certainly quite unconscious of his underlying motives. However, the evidence for the existence of these mostly comes from his later attitude to Florence.

'Discovery', one of the best accomplished and smoothest of these poems, and a product of the May 'breach' already referred to, was the subject of a dispute between Trix and the three ladies at Warwick Gardens, to whom he read and sent much of his verse.

> We found him in the woodlands – she and I –
>   Dead was our Teacher of the silver tongue,
> Dead, whom we thought so strong he could not die,
>   Dead, with no arrow loosed, with bow unstrung.
> And round the great, grey blade that all men dread
>   There crept the waxen white convulvulus,
> And the keen edge, that once fell hard on us,
>   Was blunt and notched and rusted yellow red.
> And he, our Master, the unconquered one,
>   Lay in the nettles of the forest place,
> With dreadful open eyes and changeless face
>   Turned upward – gazing at the noonday sun.
> Then we two bent above our old, dead king,
> Loosed hands and gave back heart and troth and ring.

Trix, who always ostensibly supported her brother's intentions, maintained that this was a 'kind of allegory': 'it means dead love – Cupid you know'. The ladies, in the person of Miss Winnard (who later became Mrs Hooper), a little lacking in deference to what was after all a pretty good exercise for a boy, thought the king was a dead canary. Rudyard confided to a notebook, probably before February 1884, that Miss Winnard's mistake, though genuine, was one for which he found it 'hard to forgive her'. She erred, we may feel, not so much in failing to ascribe to Rudyard feelings of lost love, as in being deprecatory. It was just the kind of thing he did find hard to forgive, and little or no self-criticism is ever apparent in him on that score; but his daimon did not leave that tendency alone, either.

Rudyard's more public poetry, the stuff he passed around at school, ranges from the ceremonial to the satirical. There is no cockney or other dialect, but plenty of hints as to his future strengths. One poem relegated all his enemies to hell in the manner of Dante; this has not survived. His later comments on it all, printed by Rutherford in his excellent edition, are shrewd and often comic. He called 'Discovery' 'cheap'. He was even then very ambitiously trying to place these poems in various adult magazines, but he did not let many people know about it: he needed to be seen as a success, not as one trying for success.

'The Story of Paul Vaugel' is typical of what he was at this time trying for: a Pre-Raphaelite melancholy very much in the style of Uncle Topsy (William Morris), whose socialist politics he had not yet learned to dislike. One of the books he must have read most carefully, and absorbed, is Morris's *The Defence of Guenevere* (1858); 'Paul Vaugel' much resembles 'The Haystack in the Floods'. But that highly original, desolating mode – expressing sexual defeat and despair – was not, well though he imitated its manner, to be available to him. Topsy was racked by feelings of his shortcomings and failures. So was Rudyard, but he was made of sterner, more aggressive stuff.

It is sometimes asserted that Rudyard first showed his patriotic and imperial feelings in an early school poem (which he published in the *College Chronicle*) called 'Ave Imperatrix'. Beresford, however, tells us that it was not written in earnest; Dunsterville was indignant about this opinion. In fact it was simply an exercise, inspired by the Queen's escape from an attempted assassination by a madman, and by one of Rudyard's favourite poets of that time, Oscar Wilde. Wilde's 'Ave Imperatrix' is simply routine. He, for example, wrote:

> For some are by the Delhi walls,
>   And many in the Afghan land,
> And many where the Ganges falls
>   Through seven months of shifting sand.
> And some in Russian waters lie . . .

Whereas Kipling wrote:

> Such greeting as should come from those
>   Whose fathers faced the Sepoy hordes,
> Or served you in the Russian snows,
>   And, dying, left their sons their swords.
> And some of us have fought for you
>   Already in the Afghan pass . . .

But whereas Wilde ended:

> Yet when this fiery web is spun,
>   Her watchmen shall descry from far
> The young Republic like a sun
>   Rise from these crimson seas of war.

Kipling was happy with:

> Trust us if need arise, O Queen,
>   We shall not tarry with the blow.

That he was content to use Wilde's poem as a source, however, suggests that he was not offended by its sentiments. What we see here is the schoolboy Pre-Raphaelite swept away by Wilde.

Although there are a number of points of resemblance between Rudyard's life at United Services College and *Stalky*, it is more logical to discuss the latter against the background of his mental state at the time he wrote it. Since it is a series of school stories rather than an attempt at autobiography it might be objected that this is being too hard on him. So it would be if he had not offered the book as being in the nature of a tract, which is what he actually called it (as well as a 'parable'). It has hardly been judged as a tract by its readers, or not by many of them; but what Kipling made of his schooldays long after they were over is revealing.

One matter, however, calls for some discussion at this point: that of the peculiar 'cleanliness' of United Services College. Dunsterville refers to this feature of the school; Beresford does not. Kipling mentioned it often. In his autobiography he writes:

> Setting aside the foul speech that a boy ought to learn early and put behind him by his seventeenth year, it was clean with a cleanliness that I have never heard of in any other school. I remember no cases of even suspected perversion, and am inclined to the theory that if masters did not suspect them, and show that they suspected, there would not be quite so many elsewhere. Talking things over with Cormell Price afterwards, he confessed that his one prophylactic against certain unclean microbes was 'to send us to bed dead tired'. Hence the wideness of our bounds, and his deaf ear towards our incessant riots and wars between the Houses.

As we shall discover, this is, strictly speaking, a lie – or a lapse in memory. Since Kipling refers to 'perversion', it must be assumed that he means by 'clean' an absence of that temporary homosexual behaviour which is a normal manifestation, and always has been, in all schools – and in particular, of course, boarding schools. The phrase 'certain unclean microbes' must mean, in view of the alleged preventative weariness, 'natural temptation to perversion'. In statistical terms this is not, at that stage of life, a 'perversion' at all: it is in fact (statistically) perverse not to be, to use Kipling's knowing word, 'unclean'. However, the Victorians did not take that attitude. They were eminently justified in it, because the subject of sex is very difficult, indeed impossible, to handle satisfactorily for more than a few seconds of our time. The Victorians failed to handle it by putting it out of the way, and so made themselves look ridiculous; and we now fail to handle it by putting it in the way, and so make ourselves look even more ridiculous. As Malinowski said: 'Sex is regarded as dangerous . . . for the reason that *sex really is dangerous.*' Kipling knew that, all right, but he nonetheless maintains an odd and paradoxical attitude. It was one case in which he learned not to take his usual knowing line of being privy to the very best information, being fully aware of what the real thing really consisted, and so forth. But that knowingness, as usual, was his initial impulse. Beresford writes:

> That baffling entity, Woman, which includes Girl, was no mystery to Gigger. He could smilingly turn in all directions and answer all questions, however abstruse, that were postulated concerning this occult phenomenon.
>
> How complacently and kindly he could enlighten a dull intelligence, or enlarge theoretically a limited experience! The procedure to be adopted in all cases and to meet every crisis in the relation of the sexes was laid down by him as surely and certainly as the Queen's Regulations. No quandary or fix but had its cure, or at least its mitigation, and its most hopeful line of action. One would never be checkmated or get into inextricable difficulties in this internecine war of the sexes if only one had Gigger at one's elbow for counsel and guidance. But, as this was impossible, one's

best chance was to propound all possible dilemmas and complications and get advice, to be stored in the memory, so that one's feeble wits would be armed and armoured with Gigger's prescience and invincible astuteness, when the time came.

Gigger liked people to believe he had had a vast romantic experience. He wouldn't enter into details about it; the business gained by being left cloudy. But if it was a question of writing another *Don Juan*, well, we knew whom to come to. If a publisher would give a commission, we should see what we should see; but he wouldn't do that sort of thing without definite terms and a payment in advance.

He said it was not gentlemanly to boast of conquests. The motto was 'Never Tell', even when the other side went more than half way – though that was terrible when it was a road you didn't want to travel. A reputation was rather a burden sometimes. It laid you open to so much aggressive action, and you were plenteously eyed, both by good and bad, by nice and un-nice. We said Gigger was eyed because his specs were thought odd. He said the sex didn't care a snap for a fellow's phiz. They looked to other qualities; and if he hadn't as many qualities as we had, he would be sorry . . .

But in dealing with this subject of Gigger we are on delicate ground – very delicate ground indeed. In some circles it would be considered very bad form, outrageous behaviour, to tell tales of this kind out of school. All I wish to make clear is that it would not be fair to assert, as he has himself implied, that our Gigger posed as a monk, painted himself as an anchorite; nor to make him state that bright eyes were of all things those that he most avoided.

Had he taken this attitude, what influence could Gigger have had with roaring youth? If he had declared that Woman was a topic forbidden to boys, not to be discussed till later in life, when a full and sufficient income had been attained; if he had held up a warning hand or cast his eyes up to heaven when ladies . . . were mentioned . . . how, then, could his knowledge of the world have been deferred to . . . Would he have been pointed out as the local Solon, compact of wisdom and of vast experience?

Our Gigger was not one to jettison his career over a trifle, over a seeming delicacy on the subject of the fair. It would be more in his manner to pose as an authority, to bear others down . . . His interminable reading might supply instances; and if he should say they were personal experiences, who was there to check his statements? . . . in listening to his expositions one had an idea that not all the charming anecdotes that were shadowed forth had actually transpired on the planetary sphere . . .

This description (Rudyard was only after all, showing off, as most boys do on this subject) makes it clear that in Beresford's estimation Rudyard had no knowledge at all of girls at this time. There is also a sly although unmalicious hint that, if he wished, Beresford could tell us more. But it is also clear that Rudyard did not regard heterosexual inclinations among boys – indeed, heterosexual activity on their part – as 'immoral', or, to stick to his own terminology, partaking of the nature of bacteria. This is confirmed by a letter, quoted by Birkenhead but not by Carrington, he wrote from India to his teacher Crofts in 1886, when he had just had a meeting with Dunsterville. The master with whom he is so angry, M.H. Pugh in real life, appears as the well-meaning near-idiot Prout, the butt of many jokes, in *Stalky*. Kipling remembered that Pugh, his housemaster, had moved him from a dormitory. Now he understood why.

Dunsterville pointed out a little fact to me which has made me rabidly furious against M.H.P. You will not recollect that he once changed my dormitory – just before I left – and insisted upon the change with an unreasoning violence that astonished me. Thereafter followed a row, I think. I objected to be transferred ... About this time M.H.P, who must be a very Stead in his morals and virtuous knowledge of impurity and bestiality, transferred me to my old room ... It never struck me that the step was anything beyond an averagely lunatic one on the part of M.H.P. – I was not innocent in some respects, as the fish girls of Appledore could have testified had they chosen – but I certainly didn't suspect anything. Dunsterville told me on Wednesday, in the plain ungarnished tongue of youth the why and wherefore of my removal according to M.H.P., and by the light of later knowledge I see very clearly what that moral but absolutely tactless Malthusian must have suspected. It's childish and ludicrous, I know, but at the present moment I am conscious of a deep and personal hatred against the man which I would give a good deal to satisfy. I knew he thought me a liar but I did not know that he suspected me of being anything much worse. However, I have my consolation. He shall be put into my novel ... to finish the revenge I'll marry him to a woman who shall give him something else to think about! But 'tis an unsavoury subject and a *most* unsavoury man. Let us drop him off the pen point and burn incense to cleanse the room.

If Pugh, painted in *Stalky* as a ridiculous person, could suspect Kipling of what Birkenhead calls 'homosexual behaviour', then such behaviour could hardly have been as rare as Kipling boasted. When in *Something of Myself* he claimed never to have heard of a case of even suspected 'perversion', he had conveniently put out of his mind the case in which he was himself the suspect! He seems to have wanted there to have been no 'vice'. And if he wanted it to be so, then it was that much easier to turn a blind eye to any hints of it. The environs of Westward Ho! were boundless for the boys there; they were far freer than most boys at such schools, and they were no more likely than any other boys to talk about what they knew very well to be forbidden. In such a place the 'homosexual behaviour' does not need to be dormitory-bound. Yet when in July 1917 Kipling heard of some sexual incident having taken place at USC, he wrote to a friend (whose identity Birkenhead, who quotes the letter, does not specify):

> This is perfectly sickening – specially when one knows, as you and I do, what the conditions have been – and *above all* the sort of atmosphere that, mainly through the Masters' carelessness and neglect, must have been allowed to grow up. It makes me furious when I am told of cases of this sort by men, without, as far as one can see, any memory of their own youth and boyhood. You can imagine for yourself what the old Coll would have been with a system of cubicles instead of the open dormitories and the Masters moving at all times through 'em – which is what saved us. But I don't think that as the world is today – and people are getting more reasonable than they were – that the thing will count against him in the future. And yet – how many men do we know who have risen to all sorts of positions, who when they were kids were – not found out!

Risen to all sorts of positions, indeed! Perhaps Birkenhead did not specify the recipient of this letter because it involved a son, or a nephew: otherwise Kipling need hardly have given the opinion that the 'thing' would not 'count against' the offender in later life. But we learn much from this and from the preceding quotation. There may have been more of this sort in the original draft Birkenhead submitted to Elsie Bambridge. This may well have been the reason why she hated the book so much, but could not allow herself to be exact as to why. It is said that eventually she claimed that 'she could not remember' why she had condemned it so roundly. Certainly she used to say, whenever the unpleasant subject was brought up, that 'Birkenhead did not like Kipling'. This is not true. She here mistook the recording of unpalatable facts for dislike. Probably Birkenhead, himself unworried by this theme, had little idea of what he was getting into.

There is a confusion, though, in Kipling's attitude. On the one hand he believes homosexuality (even its manifestation in adolescence) is 'bacterial', i.e. diseased, 'wrong'. He shares the Victorian fear of it. But it is also clear that he shares a view of it earlier than the Victorian: that it is a 'temptation', i.e. that it is 'natural', which should be avoided. There is some contrast here between the '"guilt" culture' of the Victorians and the earlier '"shame" cultures'. That guilt–shame distinction, made by Ruth Benedict in order to clarify some of her notions about Japanese society, has largely been discarded on account of its lack of explanatory potential. Indeed, it does not explain societies or cultures; but it is descriptively useful. Societies or cultures do tend (or have tended) to rely either on external sanctions (shame) or internal sanctions (guilt). But they contain elements of both, because individuals do. An individual can be either mostly ashamed or mostly guilty, or very ashamed and very guilty. In the person of Rudyard Kipling himself we see a confusion of both intense shame and intense guilt. The famous 'sense of unworthiness', taken no doubt by the ardent Kiplingite as just a noble modesty, is a mixture of shame and guilt: fear of both outer and inner sanctions fuelled his imagination.

Charles Allen, in the introduction to a recent anthology of Kipling's Indian stories, has naively suggested that 'young Kipling' could not have written 'so feelingly about the young Sahibs . . . and their forbidden loves' had he not 'shared their agonies and delights in some measure'. But there is nothing whatever in those stories that could not have been gathered from careful listening, and Kipling was throughout his life a careful listener. Of course there is no way of knowing whether and/or how Kipling dealt with his sexual frustrations during the years of his apprenticeship in India, or indeed whether he did not yield to the temptations of other boys (or Price – or even another master?) at Westward Ho! This is the sort of thing that does not usually get found out. However, from what he says that has been quoted above, and elsewhere, we do know that he regarded homosexual activity in adolescence as, simultaneously, natural and undesirable. It was the staff and the arrangements of *his* school that were supposed to make it impossible. Price was no doubt mollifying him when he answered his question about how he had kept USC 'so clean': as he told Sidney Cockerell, 'Kipling remembers things that I have forgotten, and I remember some things that he would like me to forget.' This was said in relation to some of the alleged Stalky escapades, but may well have included other matters. When Cockerell told Kipling this much later, Kipling commented that the dear fellow never had given him away. Nor, doubtless, had he given away the dear fellow.

'Homosexual' behaviour in adolescence is 'natural' in at least this sense: it is not an indicator of adult homosexuality (nor is it one of adult heterosexuality). But Rudyard clearly believed – and laboured the point by going on so insistently about the 'cleanliness' of USC – that this was an example of man's natural wickedness manifesting itself in boyhood. This view of the matter, besides having its roots in conventional Victorian morality, fits in neatly with his mature views about the human condition. A moral order was seen by him as something necessary to oppose the dark forces of chaos and disorder. As Shamsul Islam puts it in an able summary of Kipling's *Weltanschaung*: 'At every turn Kipling sees nameless, shapeless Powers of Darkness which throw him deep into the abyss of nothingness.' Homosexuality he rationalised as something anarchic, dark, powerful and evil. The man who sees himself and his friends as *saved* by open dormitories is a man who would have remembered himself as being tempted, and one who feels that he would have succumbed in the terrible evil of cubicles. Had he been 'guilty' in the cubicle-like dormitory from which the vigilant Pugh moved him? No one can know the answer to such questions.

Rudyard was 'in love', simply as a protective exercise, with Florence Garrard, who may in fact have been rather an unusual girl for her time. He was able to keep fiercely aloof from the nature of his own sexuality, even perhaps to avoid self-questioning – but at the same time to let it be known to his audience that he knew all about 'wenching', but did not, as he once said, do this in public. He did not do it in private either. And he could explain this to himself by saying that was keeping himself pure for Flo.

India II

It has not until recently been fully acknowledged that Rudyard's school performance was exceedingly erratic. He was deficient in the subjects in which he was not interested – or in those which he felt might defeat him. When Price reported to his parents he must have had something to say about that. (His performance in literature was brilliant.) Problems arose when it came to a choice of career. All that he had so far done outside his school was to contribute a few news items to a Bideford newspaper. He had long been excused games, and no one, least of all himself, had thought him destined for the army. He had been a special case from the start – and had enjoyed quite different treatment from that which he was soon to prescribe for other boys.

In the spring of 1882 Rudyard received a visit from a man he was to know, within the year, as the Amber Toad. Probably he (or Lockwood) invented the opprobrious term. But when Stephen Wheeler, editor of the *Civil and Military Gazette* of Lahore, called upon him while in England he could only make an intelligent guess as to what was afoot. His parents, both occasional contributors to the *Civil and Military*, were very worried about him, and had used all their influence in India to obtain him an appointment. Cormell Price had excited and encouraged him with tales of the great poets he had known, and doubtless of his own wild young days. A part of him wanted to go to London and become a young Pre-Raphaelite poet, living the bohemian life and 'being in love'; London, Beresford tells us, was what he then felt to be his 'natural socket'. But while he was telling his schoolmates this, he was writing to his English mater-substitute Mrs Perry that he could not wait to get out of England. He was divided, but knew very well that he would have to do what his mother and father wanted. However, the music halls – which he had already begun to haunt – and the notion of the bohemian life did hold its attractions. But by the time he did go to London, to conquer it, he had developed a very different set of ideas about bohemia. He toyed with the notion of becoming a doctor; this was probably from a mixture of motives. First, he wanted to do something for other people. Secondly, a medical career would keep him in England, and his parents might not be able to object. Thirdly, he seems to have been morbidly attracted by death and surgery.

In 1875 Lockwood had left Bombay for Lahore: as curator of the Lahore Museum and as Principal of the new Mayo School of Industrial Art. He had certainly gone up in the world, and gone up in the 'Order of Precedence', which was like holy writ in the India of that time. This 'order' was actually printed, at the end of the *Civil List* 'which everyone had on his desk' (Mason), and 'did not include reporters'. This fearsome document showed everyone's pay and exact place in the hierarchy. Such a list is not in any way a good thing, even amongst people who were – as we have often been reminded by those who know about the India of the time – by and large better educated and better read than their equivalents at home. It was a narrow world in Lahore, and Lockwood and Alice Kipling's social position was still difficult. She had attracted attention by attending a dinner without jewellery – and the couple might, if they did anything at all to annoy or offend, be reckoned 'arty' and 'above their station' (there was no lack of intelligence or nastiness at Lahore). The Bombay of Rudyard's boyhood was cosmopolitan and dominated by business interests, mostly British. In Lahore there were only some seventy civilians. It was a community living, and feeling that it lived, in exile. The general practice was not to remain in India on retirement, but to return to the mother country. It was therefore a very closed community, with strict rules and rituals. Not an easy one for a young man to settle into.

Kipling wrote (in an anonymous 'tourist's letter') of these Lahore people in January 1887 in the *Civil and Military Gazette*:

> There are no books, no pictures, no conversation worth listening to . . . no one talks lightly or amusingly . . . They call the Himalaya mountains 'the hills' . . . when a man dies he 'pegs out' . . . They have a high opinion of themselves, and I think they have a right to, so far as work goes. But they don't seem to realise the beauties of life . . .

This displays, as late as 1887, lurking 'Pre-Raphaelite' criticisms of the society he lived in. Throughout the piece – written though it is in the guise of an enlightened stranger – one can see the conceptions of life, the 'artistic' and the 'dutiful', struggling. But the dutiful wins hands down, and we can see that Kipling the young journalist, now writing stories of quite a different hue, was determined to please and to ingratiate. He had imagined, he says, that there must be 'a solid foundation of brutality' to account for the 'domineering and arrogant' habits of the Anglo-Indians. But

> my first notions were altogether wrong . . . Anglo-Indians of any experience resent at once any attempt to establish caste scruples where the position of the man does not entitle him to it . . . This letter has been full of Anglo-Indians – not natives – and you wanted to hear about natives. I'll tell you frankly, I can't get on with them, and I'm not going to support any people that turn out work as bad as the samples I have sent you. My private belief is, that nothing short of a new Deluge and a new Creation could improve them – at least the ones I've seen. They talk too much and do too little.

One self in him believed this absolutely. But another knew it to be untrue. The insecure, snobbish and deliberately ill-informed, yet on the whole comparatively well-educated lot for whom he wrote, were the ones with whom Kipling had to come to terms. As is natural anywhere, human virtues and vices blossomed and flourished amongst them. Kipling's need to please them for the first few years of his writing life may be one reason why he never purged his work of vulgarity and philistinism (but that was not altogether a loss). What is now called 'prejudice' – but was, in fact, more than prejudice: a convenient narrowness of outlook and lack of imagination and a refusal to speculate – tended often to form the structure of his work.

This audience, too, was the one he set out – with due care – to shock, if only in order to wake them up to what he took to be their responsibilities. The anonymous 'tourist' praised army men, as he was soon to do consistently, but he never consciously wrote *for* them. The reason for that is simple: he knew that they knew better than he did. However, if he could not be one of them, then he was certainly going to be their laureate and representative. Like his near-contemporary Knut Hamsun, although in an entirely different and more conventional-looking manner, he was one of the very few major European authors to question the value of writers. But where Hamsun extolled the virtues of farmers, and became a Norwegian Nazi, Kipling extolled the virtues of the 'doers', the army men and the engineers and the people who really ran things, and became an exponent of the ideas of the extreme right, an excited supporter of Mussolini, but not a British Nazi.

The civilians in Lahore, like their fellow-exiles elsewhere in India, had not been taught the pleasures of bounty or tolerance; instead, they worshipped the 'virtues' of powerful authority and domination. It spilled over into their family life, and in the way they treated their servants. Kind men were kind. Cruel men were cruel. But, as Kipling told them in a little story concerning caste which he inserted into the 'letter' from which I have just quoted, they always knew best. They looked after the 'welfare' of their servants. One man's servant's wife was ill; the master said that she should go into the hospital. The servant, although of low caste, wanted to 'swank' about his stature, and so refused to let her go. The wise master, who had known his servant's father, swore at him and threatened him with a good thrashing. The wife went into hospital, and recovered. The masters know best. Don't question them.

Not one of Kipling's audience could publicly question his or her ethnocentricity, or regard it as anything but absolutely right. They could not imagine that their servants themselves had any such ethnocentric feeling. To be British was God-given. In their depths they doubtless suffered from various guilts; but a sense of how awful it was to be *shamed*, especially within their own tiny but dominant circle, was stronger in their consciousness.

They, or at least the men amongst them – and one may guess also most of the women – were people of what has come to be known, since 1950 when the classic study *The Authoritarian Personality* (by Theodor Adorno and others) was published, as authoritarian mentality.

Readers will be relieved that I am not going to put Kipling forward as 'an authoritarian personality'. Far from it. He was more subtle than that – and more subtle and complex than those amongst whom he found himself at the verge of such maturity as he chose to experience. Nor do I think that these people could have been anything other than genuinely 'authoritarian' in mentality without failing in their mission in life – without suddenly abandoning their place in history. Their history is a complex one, but they were certainly a part of the legacy reaped by the acute authoritarianism of the twentieth century. They were 'forced' to be of that type, although they did not always, initially, go to the work they did because it attracted them. If they could not develop into people of authoritarian outlook, they became high eccentrics who survived – or they quit and returned home. The ironic and intelligent Beresford, 'always a bit of a socialist', soon went

home. The general political views and world-view of Kipling's agreeable
father may well have been changed as he grew older through the nature of
his work and his position: he does not seem to have been an authoritarian
when he was young. But he eventually developed into a conventional
imperialist. This authoritarian mentality had been developing in Europe,
and then in America, since the Reformation.

Kipling can be explained most fruitfully as a man of acute sensibility
who was forced to come to terms with this mentality; in doing so certain
parts of that sensibility became strained. There were, as we shall soon see,
personal factors, too. But, unless he were to leave India and his first job
and risk becoming a writer too soon to be certain of success (which he
must have), he had no alternative but to adapt himself to these ways. I
think that, like his hero and friend Cecil Rhodes, he was both corrupted
by, and then in turn corrupted, these ways. Unlike Rhodes, though, he had
his daimon. Rhodes when he died had nothing except a mad will which he
managed to make seem a little sane, as if in the reluctant knowledge that his
greatness could only be seen by posterity and no longer, alas, by himself.
In 1877 Rhodes wrote a paper which he subsequently sent to W.T. Stead
– also half-mad – in which he said:

> I contend that we are the first race in the world, and that the more of
> the world we inhabit, the better it is for the human race. I contend that
> every acre added to our territory provides for the birth of more of the
> English race, who otherwise would not be brought into existence. Added
> to which, the absorption of the greater part of the world under our rule
> simply means the end of all wars.

Lockwood and Alice Kipling, then, were concerned about their son's
future, and Cormell Price must have felt a keen sense of responsibility
because of his encouragement of the boy's interest in literature and
therefore in the bohemian life. What passed in the way of confidences
between master and boy on those nights when they stayed up smoking
and drinking cannot be known. But I speculate that Rudyard might have
been as close to Price, then, as he ever was able to be to anyone in
his life – except one.

Ned Burne-Jones and his wife told Alice that Rudyard was 'seeing too
much of life about town'. They could not control him, of course: he was
to demonstrate, insofar as he had not already demonstrated, that he would
control himself and that no one else would. This freedom that he had taken
upon himself was remarked upon when his future had already been decided, and he was staying with them at their new home at Rottingdean near
Brighton. But similar warnings must have been delivered earlier, arising
from his too eager anticipation of adulthood in his school vacations.

At one point, after he had been told by Price that he would be
leaving for India in August, Kipling wrote testily to his father that he
might well say, when the time came, that he 'had married a wife' and
could not come. This declaration would have made the Kipling parents
anxious: they knew as well any parents can that their son was unusually
gifted, but also that he was difficult, aggressive and in some ways even
considered to be an obnoxious cub and a know-all. Price would have
told them all this. They would have remembered the attitude he had
cultivated towards the wretched Aunty Rosa. Suppose he proposed and

the unpredictable Flo accepted him! Lockwood must have felt relieved that he had fixed up with the Lahore barrister and half-owner of the *Civil and Military Gazette*, William Rattigan, for Kipling to work there as Assistant Editor for the salary of 150 rupees a month. Rattigan founded this paper in 1872 with James Walker, an Anglo-Indian transport merchant. They also owned the greater part of the *Pioneer*, which in time became an all-India paper operating out of Allahabad under the editorship of George Allen, whom Kipling would in time also come to know. It is said that George Allen came to England on furlough in the summer of 1882, saw Kipling, and wired back 'KIPLING WILL DO'.

It must now have seemed to Kipling that he had indeed only to learn to play the cards that were dealt him. Although he had to work exceedingly hard (sometimes up to fifteen hours a day, often in intense heat) and was driven by his editor, he suddenly found himself treated like a man. His mother begged him to shave off his side-whiskers, which he did; but he was allowed to keep his moustache (or grow it again – a photograph of him in the summer of 1882 shows him without it). He lived in his parents' bungalow in his own quarters, had his own servant (the son of his father's), his own horse and trap, and his own groom. He had his place of work (it is now the Shalimar Supermarket), the Gymkhana Club, Montgomery Hall, where all the British, and even some of the Eurasians, met three times a week, and the Punjab Club, which was exclusively for officers and 'picked men at their definite work', but which accepted him as an honorary member. The white fox terrier called Vixen slept with him in his little bed, its head on the pillow like his. He was one of those people who prefer animals, in this case dogs, to human beings, although he did not usually put it quite like that. He had this (and other features) in common with his counterpart in music, Edward Elgar, a gentler man whose hatred of war was unequivocal.

He said that his life in what his mother called 'the Family Square' was perfect:

> My English years fell away, nor ever, I think, came back in full strength . . . I had returned to a father and mother of whom I had seen but little since my sixth year. I might have found my mother 'the sort of woman I don't care for' . . . and my father intolerable. But the mother proved more delightful than all my imaginings or memories . . . I do not remember the smallest friction in any detail of our lives.

There *were* frictions, though. In what lives are there not? One was Kipling's discovery, a few days after he came to Lahore, and while he was helping his father in the museum before going to work for the ill-tempered Wheeler, that his mother had, the previous year, collected together his schoolboy poems and published them in a small edition under the title *Schoolboy Lyrics*. Lockwood had been against it, but both parents had kept this from him, although Price was probably in the secret. According to Trix he flew into a rage and sulked for three days (Alice must have told her daughter this, either in a letter or later, for Trix was not brought back from England until January 1884). There were probably many more such exhibitions, both on the part of Alice Kipling and of her son. She is said to have found him 'strangely moody'. It is clear that these two fought each other, in various oblique ways, as well as loved each other – and clear, too, that Alice, however generally perceptive, was not always able to curb her possessiveness. 'I am sure his Mother will know less of him than any other woman of his acquaintance,' she had written anxiously and nervously a couple of years earlier to a friend. That the relationships in that household were 'perfect' is yet another myth. Lockwood was quiet; one has doubts about Alice Kipling, who could create distinctly thick atmospheres if she felt displeased or thwarted in her possessiveness. Mason makes the shrewd point that Kipling was, 'in the cold months' (October to April), under her eye.

The work at the paper was hard, and Wheeler thought that Kipling was too 'literary'. He did everything he could to knock it out of him. But he was often away with fever, and then Kipling had the run of the whole paper. That he could conform when he wanted to is shown by the fact that, of all his known offences while in Lahore (and at first there were many), making over-bold with the paper while the boss was away was not one of them. Kay Robinson, who edited the paper later, and who encouraged Kipling, spoke highly of him as a journalist. But he did this retrospectively: it was part of the process of the making of the myth that began to take place immediately Kipling took London by storm. However, the son of the Rattigan from whom he had, through Lockwood, got his first chance, remembered quite otherwise:

As a journalist Rudyard Kipling was far from being a great success. His father had induced my own father and the other proprietors of the two papers to give the young Rudyard a post on the Lahore paper. But in the day-to-day business of journalism Kipling did not by any means shine. He had little taste for mere routine duties; he was apt to neglect the rather tedious assignments that inevitably fell to the lot of the junior members of a very small staff.

Well, the early journalism as collected in *Kipling's India* (edited by Thomas Pinney, 1986), is good – but it is not that good, and certainly not as good as the early stories. Whatever the truth, Lockwood was pleased, and from a letter he wrote to a friend we can gather what he feared might have happened to Rudyard had he not been found this useful employment: 'I am sure he is better here, where there are no music hall ditties to pick up, no young persons to philander about with, and a great many other negatives of the most wholesome description. All that makes Lahore profoundly dull makes it safe for young persons.'

Wheeler, the Amber Toad, 'tetchy and irritable', broke him in very gradually. The line the paper had to take was laid down, and Kipling never tried to change it, although he chafed under the restrictions. Much of it was simply rehashing the news in an acceptable form. Price had trained him especially in précis-writing, and now 'this stood him in good stead: his main job, when the Amber Toad was there, was to knock the telegrams from the news agencies together ready for the press at midnight. He must have showed much shrewd self-discipline. But his innate independence and dislike of working under or for anyone else did not fail to break through, as is evidenced by his frequent social gaffes. He did not much like it, and he suffered for it: he was hissed by the members of the Punjab Club when the paper switched sides on the question of Indian country magistrates being given the right to hear cases against British accused. The paper had been vociferous against this liberal measure, but then switched: one of the proprietors, as Kipling hints in his autobiography, was after a knighthood (they all got them, though at different times). The noise against Kipling would have been even louder had a senior officer not reminded the company that the boy was doing what he was paid to do.

Unused to the heat and the hard work, he could not sleep easily, and took to wandering around the city at night, linking his imaginary adventures with one of the poems which had made the most forceful impression on him at USC: James Thomson's decadent but powerful *The City of Dreadful Night*. (He never in his life did learn to sleep; he usually had horrible dreams when he fitfully did. He also suffered the bad stomachs and malarias everyone in India suffered from.) There was not yet much of the professional imperialist about him. He tried to master his horse, Joe, but was often thrown while on his morning canter. He reported sports meetings and court cases, and hung around barracks as much as he could. The subaltern-worship from which he always suffered now began to set in: always the officer, the administrator, would seem to him to be superior to the long-haired artist. That was one of the features that would make him so original when he went to London at the beginning of the next decade. The people he mixed with did not much like him: he was uncouth and ill-mannered, and bored everyone with his immature swearing (his 'caddishly dirty tongue'). But these people knew, too, that he was bright and one to be reckoned with. Three incidents in which he incurred unpopularity are well known – there were probably many more.

On one occasion Sir Henry MacMahon was, he told Birkenhead, on a military exercise near Lahore. He repaired to the Club, where he saw a bumptious young moustached man in civilian clothes, to whom someone said: 'Kipling, I want you to meet MacMahon.' 'Why should *I* want to meet MacMahon,' was the answer, and Kipling turned away. The soldier offered to thrash him, but the others dissuaded him. When word of this got back to his parents, which it must certainly have done, it can hardly have pleased them. It is a good example of Kipling's excited over-estimation of himself, and ready eagerness to show his scorn for everyone.

On another occasion he made rude remarks about the Indian Civil Service, and was put firmly in his place. In the third incident he was not so lucky. He intruded into a conversation between two lawyers, let it be known that he was 'seeking a new experience' – and was kicked downstairs and out of the building. No wonder revenge was one of his chief preoccupations: one speculates as to how he repaid those two lawyers – perhaps through something he was able to put about them in the paper later. But all the time he was learning: learning from common soldiers (not from the officers he worshipped and envied, as was well remembered by those who knew him then), from his nocturnal wanderings, from his work, from the bazaar, from his father. By the beginning of 1884 he had learned the values of modesty, for he began a speech to the Club (the first public speech he ever made) on the occasion of the Honorary Secretary's marriage, 'So far as a youngster of my position and inexperience . . .' Everyone admires a bright boy of spirit, even if he is brash, who is willing to learn; and Kipling knew that, too. He was already writing long letters to his Aunt Edith, and some of these show the promise that was to distinguish the first short stories.

In his informative book *Kipling in India* Louis L. Cornell tries to counter what he calls the 'old theory that Kipling wrote about men of action because he wished he had been one himself': 'The more we learn about Kipling's dedication to the art of literature, the less tenable it becomes.' Cornell seems to assume that it is discreditable, if you are not a man of action, to want to be a man of action. It might from certain viewpoints be so, but is any case irrelevant. You would hardly get a person writing about the sort of action in which they did not participate unless they were in some way interested in participating in it – and so what? No writer of 'action adventures' (Robert Louis Stevenson?) would have the least effectiveness if he did not imagine himself 'in them'. So much of the phenomenological life of human beings, of idle speculation, fantasy and desire, seems discreditable that we do best to regard it as inevitable, and try to be aware of it: our defences of our heroes are earnestly foolish if they seek to pretend that they were not human and corrupt. Would Cornell protest if a critic stated that Kipling wrote about corruption because he felt himself to be corrupt? He said he was corrupt. The enigma has always been that he would not directly say why.

Of course Kipling was *first*, and *partly*, drawn to writing about action not just because he wanted to be a man of action but because he was envious of those who were – and because he knew very well in his heart that he was far too clumsy and ineffectual and quite possibly cowardly, quite apart from having bad eyes, to make a man of action. This is neither creditable nor discreditable, but a fact. Achievement rarely stems, initially, from virtue; it usually stems from vice. All we can say for certain about Kipling is that he disliked scenes, outside his own fiction, and that when, much later in his life, he was put to the test on a lonely road in Vermont he did not display physical courage. The important thing, for us, is what he made of his envy of physically brave fellows, and here the nature of his dedication to literature is pertinent. It is also true, and has been conceded by the majority of his critics, that one of the outstanding flaws of his writing is the taking up of the mantle of the man of action: he is not entitled to it, and many of his texts are strained because of it.

One of the really strange things about Kipling, however, is that he is a writer who does not like the role of the writer: like Knut Hamsun, he rejects it even while taking it upon himself. Unlike a number of twentieth-century writers, he does not question it in a guilty manner, worrying if he should not become a doctor or serve humanity (this very problem troubled Rilke, Broch, Joyce, Mann and many others; Rudyard rejected the medical solution before he reached seventeen). He just pours Hamsun-like scorn on it: his seriousness about it is hard to find.

As Kipling wrote in his old age, his 'English years fell away' when he returned to India, never fully to return. This happened during the short period in India before he took up writing professionally – which was as soon as he had discovered and made certain of an audience. What he meant by this was that his schoolboy Pre-Raphaelitism never self-acknowledgedly returned: Anglo-Indian values seemed to take its place. Those Anglo-Indian values therefore always secretly contained the sort of romantic, even subversive, appeal that Pre-Raphaelitism had had, and in truth still had, for him. A queer mixture, since the overt values are, in themselves, quite specifically against *all* forms of subversion. In any case he did not subscribe to the Anglo-Indian set of values because they appealed to his intellect (he was not an intellectual writer, as Henry James was careful to note), but because they suited him emotionally, and because he simply had to conform to them if he was to distinguish himself where he was right then. That he had to do. Yet he was not a conforming type, and always had it in for anyone to whom he was obliged to conform. The early bumptiousness demonstrated that. But to distinguish himself took precedence even over the need for independence and non-conformity. However, the way in which he conformed was eventually ideological, rather than social. John A. Maclure quotes Leslie Stephen's brother, James Fitzjames Stephen, a high official in the administration of India, on the subject of the sort of government the British had founded in India:

> . . . an absolute government, founded not on consent, but on conquest. It does not represent the native principles of life or of government, and it can never do so until it represents heathenism and barbarism. It represents a belligerent civilisation, and no anomaly can be more striking or so dangerous, as its administration by men, who being at the head of a Government founded upon conquest, implying at every point the superiority of the conquering race, of their ideas, their institutions, their opinions and their principles, and having no justification for its existence except that superiority, shrink from the open, uncompromising, straightforward assertion of it.

Stephen wrote this in a letter to *The Times* on 1 March 1883. Nearly five years before that, at a time when Disraeli was Prime Minister, Gladstone commented, in the magazine *Nineteenth Century* (September 1878), on the 'terrible dismemberment' created by the peace with the former American colonies, and then continued:

> But England was England still: and one of the damning signs of the politics cf the school is their total blindness to the fact, that the central strength of England lies in England. Their eye travels in satisfaction over the wide space upon the map covered by the huge ice-bound deserts of North America or the unpenetrated wastes of Australasia, but rests with mortification on the narrow bounds of latitude and longitude marked by nature for the United Kingdom. They are the materialists of politics: their faith is in acres and leagues, in . . . long lists of territories. They forget that the entire fabric of the British Empire was reared and consolidated by the energies of a people which was . . . insignificant in numbers . . . In the sphere of personal life, most men are misled through the medium of the dominant faculty of their nature. It is round that dominant faculty that folly and flattery are wont to buzz . . . The dominant passion of England is extended empire . . . and the most essential or the noblest among all the duties of government, the exercise of moral control over ambition and cupidity, have been left to the intermittent and feeble handling of those who do not govern.

This latter was a point of view with which Kipling soon violently disagreed (or so it appears). Where he was in 1883, still a boy posing as man, no one around him agreed with it – or, if they did, kept quiet about it. It is worth remembering, however, that the admired Cormell Price would, without doubt, have agreed with every word of it. The Kipling parents, being Anglo-Indian, did not. (Plenty of Lockwood's stereotyped imperialistic utterances have been recorded.) Stephen's statement of the issues involved is admirably pragmatic. There is, deliberately, none of the humbug about it that is sometimes found in imperial apologetics. It is forthright in its description, and no imperialistic administrator could have disagreed with it: the Indians are inferior heathens, they have been conquered by a superior race by force of arms, and any softness shown towards them would become a most dangerous thing. But would the Kipling parents have chosen to put it quite like that, as the Kipling son would very soon come to do – and even more strongly? It is an interesting question. Just possibly there were some arguments about the likely future of India in the bungalow where Kipling and his parents lived. Or were they all of one accord? There is no evidence, it has to be stressed, of the sort of political ferocity exhibited by Kipling in his parents, although we do know that they took the imperialistic side over the Indian question – it would be surprising if they had not. Virtually all the servants of the Crown in India did so, even if their practice of their duties differed in emphasis, and was more or less humane.

The Kiplings would certainly have approved of Disraeli's Crystal Palace speech of 1872, when he spoke of the issue not being

> a mean one. It is whether you will be content to be a comfortable England, modelled and moulded on Continental principles and meeting in due course an inevitable fate, or whether you will be a great country, an Imperial country, a country where your sons, when they rise, rise to paramount positions, and obtain not merely the esteem of their country-men but command the respect of the world.

This, and the philosophy of Empire set forth by such as Froude, and Seeley in his influential *The Expansion of England,* formed the background for Kipling's imperialism. There was a moral as well as – even rather than – a mercenary motive: the Empire was necessary for (as Alfred Milner put it) 'the maintenance of civilised conditions of existence' amongst peoples who, it was assumed, lacked the faculties for maintaining these conditions themselves. Anthropology in the contemporary sense of the word was only just about then being invented, and it began as a study of subject peoples.

The fact is, though, that for all Kipling's extremism in the matter of expressing his political views, his fiction is much more ambivalent. As a schoolboy I always wondered why the 'East is East . . .' quotation was so notorious: it struck me from the beginning as being obvious that Kipling was by no means saying what most people still suppose he was saying:

> Oh, East is East, and West is West, and never the twain shall meet,
> Till Earth and Sky stand presently at God's great Judgement Seat;
> But there is neither East nor West, Border, nor Breed, nor Birth,
> When two strong men stand face to face, though they come from the ends
> of the earth!

This – rhetorical, self-righteous and gnomic – may not be 'true', and is in any case ambiguous because it is not clear what is meant by 'strong'; I do not want to put it forward as good poetry because it is not, it is merely effective rhetorical swagger; but the unmistakable message is that

'strength', whatever it is, is above race, social degree and country. It is
odd how these lines and other writings in which Kipling's message is
unequivocal, have been taken to be ambiguous. How many people who
hold those lines against Kipling even know their context? 'The Ballad of
East and West' is a silly but spirited and vigorous poem about the mutual
high respect felt between a British soldier and the noble horse-thief whom
he chases. It is good schoolboy stuff, with knowing observations about
breech-bolts snicking unseen. This context makes the non-, indeed,
apodictically anti-racist message of the refrain perfectly clear. It actually
goes against what Stephen and so many others declared, although at the
same time it is careful *not* to go against any idea of being 'soft' on the
heathen, or any nonsense like that. The two men respect each other so
much because they are prepared to chase and slaughter each other in the
interests of their upbringing. But while it is all for the slaughter, it does
allow that the horse-thief's son must not be shot as he enters the gate of
the colonel. That is precisely because this boy and his father are 'strong'.
Kamal, the thief of the poem, is not 'inferior' in any sense to those who are
after him – indeed, since the Englishman could have been killed at any
moment by him, it is the Englishman who is, if not actually inferior, then
at least not so experienced.

No doubt those who would have agreed with Stephen in his *Times* letter
would nevertheless have conceded that certain Indians could achieve
nobility in this way. But that, in their estimation, would have been by
accident, or owing to a keen imitation of British ways. Would an imperialist
really even have approved of, had he thought about it, the ultimate honour
offered by the French to their colonials: *assimilation*? That concept went
so far as to concede that there was a potentiality in the 'native' to achieve
perfection: to become no less than actually French! This is the extremity
of patronage, and it is easy to see how tempting it could be to the
emotions of a good colonial. I do not think, however, that in this poem
of Kipling's, or in a number of his writings like it, there can be said to be
any of that sort of patronage. He does here question his ethnocentricity,
as he does when he allows a narrator to speak of the much and properly
flogged Gunga Din as nonetheless being 'a better man'. But the worship
of *strength*, while 'intellectually' based in the dubious precepts of Social
Darwinism, is even more strongly based in an emotional worship of it. But
that is another story.

If you did not know anything of Kipling's writing and were told that
this ballad had been written by a young man eager to correct current
imperialistic ideas of British superiority, you could believe it. It is only
because we know about Kipling's overt views that we also know that
he is writing in an assumption that Indians are generally inferior. But
is he doing even that? He says, in this particular simple-minded mood
of his about bravery and 'strength' and honour: 'They are uncivilised
but they're as good as you at heart.' His tone is not such as to offend,
so he is not being anti-imperialistic; but he is being subversive in the
guise of writing a stirring adventure piece. Those who agreed with the
sentiments described by Stephen in his *Times* letter were convinced that
their government could serve 'native' interests only when it surrendered
to 'heathenism' and 'barbarism'. Kipling, though, is at least asserting that
the Indian is capable of sterling British virtues: therefore, if someone in

the administration was stirred by such a poem, it could have been argued that Kipling was guilty of subversion in suggesting that the Indian could even assimilate such values. What is important is that, while Kipling's attitudes were not worked out (they never were at a conscious and uncreative level), they undermined each other. His belief that Indians were inferior was undermined by his belief that they were not, and his belief that they were not was undermined by his belief that they were. But which belief was a conviction, at an imaginative level, and which was an abstraction that he needed for his peace of mind? No one ever expressed such sentiments as that Gunga Din is a better man than his British master so forcefully as Kipling. There is a clash here between Kipling's admiration for the amoral, mysterious and 'strong', and his respect for the 'civilised'. Certainly he wondered how peoples with religions such as Hinduism and Buddhism could really be so 'heathenish'; his own religious feelings were always more Eastern than Western.

So it is not as simple as Maclure, after he has quoted the Stephen passage, suggests:

> Stephen's description clarifies Kipling's situation. The India to which he returned in 1882 was a country under occupation, and the kind of communication he sought at first to establish with the Indian people would have involved real physical and social risks. Instead of taking those risks, Kipling retreated, not only from the reality of India but from the painfully exposed social and psychological position most modern artists have endured. Perhaps because his own early experience of isolation and hostility had been so great, he chose to enlist his energies in the service of that 'belligerent civilisation' celebrated by Stephen, and to project its values and vision in his work. As an artist, then, Kipling assumes the same relation to the Indian people that he celebrates in his hero Strickland. He infiltrates the Indian community as a secret agent of imperialism, exposing himself just enough to gain the knowledge needed to give his reductive and distorted portraits of the Indians the semblance of adequacy and authenticity.

There is certainly something in this – if that is what a self-consciously enlightened person wishes to make of it – so far as Kipling's overt politics are concerned. But it is a dangerous over-simplification, cast in the form of an accusation, of the attitude towards the Indians which Kipling expresses in his stories (and in *Kim*); and it is not even accurate.

In any case, are we as interested in what Kipling thought he thought – or to put it more exactly, what he enjoyed feeling he thought – about the true nature of England's greatness, as we are in how and when and why he came to form this set of views, in what he meant by these pseudo-thoughts, in what he (his daimon) would have liked to have meant by it? We are interested in the views themselves mainly because of the contrast with what his imagination has to say. Carrington, and others more half-heartedly, like to think that Kipling is all of a whole. That is absurd. Kipling was seldom troubled by considerations which we should describe as intellectual. He did not 'think', or, if he occasionally did, then his thought processes are not of interest as such. He worked through emotion when he worked badly, and through intuition when he worked well.

Unfortunately, not all of what the admirably liberal Maclure has to say makes sense. It is hardly true that Kipling avoided taking risks and therefore never met the Indian people. It is true that he viewed them from afar, so to say – his tales of fatal mixes with them are entirely speculative. So far as he knew them, in the Lahore of his youth, most Indians spent their time serving, and thus making a livelihood from, the British. He formed his picture of the 'right' Indian, the Indian who knew his place in the world, from a servile set of Indians – ones who would not say what they thought when they allowed themselves to think at all. On the other hand, as a sort of superior tourist rather than a true mingler, he really did get to know them, and took every allowable 'risk', I should think, that could have been taken, by such a tourist. Wandering around the city at night, though he could often use his father's or his paper's name to get him out of trouble, cannot be described as cautious behaviour, as anyone who has made similar explorations can testify. Nor was India 'under occupation' in the sense that France was under occupation in the Second World War. Kipling, as I have already said, was not like Hamsun, a self-confessed crook and liar, delighted to cheat the literary world from the start: he had to have a respectable set of values, and he built that up out of what he imitated from his parents and then from his first newspaper audience. He had more or less to re-invent his experiences at Southsea and Westward Ho!. It is the same process, and it is an entirely egocentric process; but here it takes a different form.

Maclure writes of Kipling's 'portraits'. But as readers we do not turn to Kipling for his skill in creating character. This is another way of saying that all his portraits (like those of Dickens) are 'distorted'; and if they are reductive, then they are so only in the interests of what he is trying to do. It is wrong to say that any Indian in Kipling is more diminished or 'distorted' than any English, or 'white' character. At his worst Kipling will diminish whoever he hates, or feels defensively that he must hate: it is one of his most notorious faults. When in one of his poems ('Loot') he speaks of giving a nigger a dose of cleaning-rod so as to get him to give up his property, he is only demonstrating how diminished that nigger is in the consideration of the British soldier. Yes, he does get pleasure out of this vileness and this vulgarity. Of course he does. But he is not inventing a new attitude. A subversive self in him is taking advantage of an attitude that already exists: the amoral and thievish brutality of the British soldier when he is hunting in a pack. Anyone who has been a soldier knows about this. But most of Kipling's vigour and delight here comes from being able to assert without fear of contradiction: 'Look, you can say what you like, but it is like that, and they are like that.' I do not sense here any pleasure in the nigger getting thrashed (*Stalky* seems to make it clear that Kipling was sexually excited by thrashing, but whether of niggers or white men probably made little difference to him except that it was easier to thrash niggers and feel 'right' about it). The poem as a whole is not about niggers, but about how disgusting British soldiers can be. And Kipling is telling us this in the spirit of their and his enjoyment of their disgustingness. He is using irony. It may not be going very deep to say to readers who despise niggers, 'this is what your superior and so-called civilised Englishman whose force actually controls the niggers is really like: no work for a gent like you, eh?'; but that nevertheless is what he is saying.

Roger Martin du Gard – like Kipling, a winner of the Nobel Prize – was much later to describe French peasants in a very negative manner:

as godawful, horrible and hopeless people. But he was motivated by sheer disgust: there was no naturalist relish in his descriptions. Kipling's relish in 'Loot' partakes of the generally naturalist feeling just then rising in the minds and emotions of unsentimental observers. A literary movement never gets a hold unless there are readers (if only a few at first) ready to respond to it. Gradually a new paradigm of what 'literature ought to be like' becomes created. Naturalism never did get a real hold in Britain except indirectly and to a very small audience, by way of the Vizetelly translations of Zola (for which Vizetelly was eventually prosecuted). Here we are too hypocritical to be able to enjoy disgust, except as something 'foreign'. The French are more openly corrupt, especially in their politics: naturalism flourished there directly. The appearance of an important aspect of naturalism in the work of the Indian Kipling is less often noticed.

However, I am not trying to assert any general, conscious or liberal nicety in Kipling on the subject of race. I am asserting only that when he was in the grip of his imaginative vigour he was not much aware of it, or that (as in 'The Ballad of East and West') he sometimes actually tried to fight it. He came to deplore the Ilbert Bill (for his paper's eventual support of which he had been hissed at the Club), and at no point in his life could he have condoned the idea of an Englishman being judged by an Indian magistrate – but at least in principle he was prepared to allow that a fight to the death on a ride through hostile countryside would be all right.

India III

In the summer of 1886 the editorship of the *Civil and Military Gazette* was taken over from Stephen Wheeler by E. Kay Robinson. Kipling owed a great debt to the Amber Toad: for keeping him at drudgery at just the time he needed it. In time he came to be grateful. But with the advent of Robinson his fortunes on the paper changed: he was encouraged to use his talents within its pages.

He had in the meanwhile been gathering the material for Mulvaney and his other common soldier characters. Not one of these is based on a single model. Just as, *pace* McClure, he could see the Indians he met as they actually were (an important component of naturalist zest was love of fact, even if this was complemented by relish), so too did he see the life of the common soldier in India as it was. He did not idealise it. He thought it absurd delicacy that the prostitutes of Lahore should not be checked for pox and clap, and never preached about the soldiers' exercise of their lusts. It soon led to his being called by readers back at home 'unpleasant'. There has always been a section of the British (and doubtless every other) public glad to countenance suffering at the expense of respectability; Kipling sympathised with the 9000 men who annually lay ill in the Lock Hospital for the sake of this respectability. He did not set out to be falsely delicate.

He also learned, then, how useless he himself was for a life of action. He was for a time in 'B' Company of the Punjab Volunteers as a private; but apparently he could not bring himself to go on parade, and when the Company Commander asked him to 'make good the capitation grant which he had failed to earn', he sent the fee and frankly apologised. As so often, he was afraid of making a fool of himself: there had been, curiously in the circumstances, no Officer Cadet Corps at USC in which he could have practised. Perhaps the founders, being army men, knew the wastefulness and valuelessness of such organisations.

When Trix arrived from England his writing was stimulated, and Mrs Kipling tutored them in at least poetry. The result was a small privately printed – but published by the *Civil and Military*, as the *School Lyrics* had been – book edition of thirty-nine parodies and imitations called *Echoes* (1884). There was also a supplement to the paper, a 'Christmas Annual' of December 1885 called *Quartette*, written by all four Kiplings, 'Four Anglo-Indian Writers'. Both of these publications received excellent reviews, and actually sold out. Although the first of the stories that he later published, 'The Strange Ride of Morrowbie Jukes' and 'The Phantom Rickshaw', were exercises inspired by Poe and other masters of the macabre, Kipling was already observing life. He went to Simla both on vacation and for his paper; there, the residence of the Viceroy, he could find spies, whores, society life and unfaithful grass widows. This was a false, richer world than Lahore, and he had an eye for it.

When he was by himself at home in the autumn of 1884 he had the experience of being in very severe pain with colic, and of being cured with opium by his servant. He now discovered Freemasonry, which attracted him not only because of its schoolboy notion of a secret society but also – *pace* McClure once again – because it was a way of overcoming caste, race and even class. He joined the Lodge 'Hope and Perseverance' in 1885. In his autobiography he proudly described the mix: Hindu, Sikh, Muslim, English, 'Indian Jew'. As Carrington puts it, this was the supposed organisation of the 'Sons of Martha' devoted to the 'burden of the world's work'. Whatever erroneous but convenient assumptions about race that he imitated, this concept was a genuinely romantic one to Kipling, and it took precedence: it was the concept that appealed to his imagination; the imaginative heart of his work embodies it. But it was deeply challenged by his conscious convictions. However, he used Masonry as a framework for many of his later tales, and never lost his affection for or admiration of it. Apparently he found it hard to get into the Lodge. But, having got in, he could feel that it was legitimate and vaguely but respectably 'religious'.

When he was not feeling bad-tempered boredom at the Punjab Club – 'all *connu* and triply *connu* . . . I look forward as I have never looked forward to anything in my life for its ending . . . but as it all fits in with my plans it must be got through' – or doing his work, or writing to England, or wandering sleepless through the city at night, he devoted himself to his great love-agony: Flo. To his confidantes in correspondence he presented himself as one whose life's love was shattered by a careless woman. Birkenhead quotes this sentence: 'There is this strange quality in Love, that it has in common with Death – the curious and unquenchable remorse for carelessness in the past, for pique and misunderstandings that ravaged the golden time.' He was all but copying from books rather than expressing genuine emotion. Birkenhead is surely right in commenting upon his self-delusion, and in adding: 'Among the emotions that were to agitate him so fiercely a capacity for the passionate love of woman never seems to have found a place.' He continually called Flo frigid, but it was his own posturings that were frigid – as frigid as George Bernard Shaw's notorious and nauseating 'love-letters' to Mrs Patrick Campbell. He would write (December 1885, after Flo had officially ended their 'engagement') to his cousin, Margaret Burne-Jones, to ask her if she would try to look out for Flo at the Slade – and at the same time pretend to be 'in love' with someone else, causing his father to write (also to the Burne-Joneses):

We have been immensely amused by his falling in love recently, a most wholesome sign that he is growing to his proper boyhood – which sounds more topsy-turvy than it really is. The Rev Duke . . . has a lovely daughter . . . so the boy for 2 Sundays has driven five miles to attend . . . church . . . He is vastly funny about it and I cannot make out whether there is anything in it.

Rudyard believed in all this, and was not aware that he was striking poses. But no one has ever shown a shred of evidence that he was truly serious, at his wits' end, about any of it. What was it that his father, and his mother, were worried about, so that the father should speak of 'wholesomeness'?

He must have been troubled by sexual desires at this time, and one wonders just what kind of desires were troubling him. He represented himself as cynical about women to his sister (most very young men thrust their preferred self-images onto their sisters, if they have them); and he used them for copy with great and ostentatious ruthlessness. Certainly his 'love' for Flo – it is surprising that anyone has taken this at its face value – protected him. But from the predatory women of whom his mother had such fears? Or from desires he could not and did not want to face? At this stage of life it is possible to experience lusts but somehow to prevent them from entering into consciousness. That could not go on forever with a man as shrewd as Kipling. But in the meantime he convinced others, but chiefly himself, of his romantic interest in Flo – or, if reassurance required it, in other women, too.

When Kay Robinson became editor of the *Civil and Military* Kipling began more seriously to try to express his attitude towards the Anglo-Indian society of which he felt himself to be a part. He was after success, but he understood first and foremost that it was success as a serious writer with something to say, not as a mere purveyor of work that would be popular but would not last. And the attitude that began to emerge was, as we have begun to see, far more complex than McClure's 'imperialist spy' concept will allow. But even Cornell, who is sympathetic to Kipling, is wrong in ascribing to him the exact views of the Anglo-Indian community: it is true that he *thought* he 'never seriously questioned them'; but we have already found that he did. In those early stories and poems Kipling is questioning these values, or at least trying to question them, all the time. There is conflict in him (as in any other fair-minded Anglo-Indian) between the contempt felt for Indian traditions, born out of fear, ignorance and solidarity with other Britishers, and the actual feeling for them. Kipling as a creator was always more influenced by Hinduism than he was by the religion in which he had been brought up. He disliked missionaries, and he never equated the native religions with 'heathenism' or with superstition.

The writer who shared the exact views of his audience could never have written (as he did in a presentation copy of *Echoes*, for Mrs Tavenor Parry):

> Who is the Public I write for?
> 　Men 'neath an Indian sky,
> 　Cynical, seedy and dry,
> Are these then the people I write for?
> 　No, not I.

The focus of Kipling's imperialist views came to be very largely upon his strong, even resentful, notion that people living in England lived in an ignoble comfort: they failed to realise the huge sacrifices that were made for them by the workers of the Empire. Insofar as the Empire was in reality a trading venture, and insofar as everyone benefited from it, this is a justifiable but retrospective view. Kipling was not inspired by this notion of British prosperity owing itself to insufficiently sung imperial servants, whom in any case he frequently mocked and criticised. He was projecting a personal resentment, but generalising it. Whatever the ethical merits of the case, so far as he did not simply invent it, he used it as a repository for his emotions. His parents had to be perfect, whether they were or not, because they were Rudyard Kipling's parents. But he maintained some scrupulosity towards reality: he wanted to entertain and be talked about. His serious purpose overrode even that desire.

The first real stories Kipling wrote appeared in the *Civil and Military* from 1886 onwards. They were collected under the title *Plain Tales from the Hills* in 1888, and published by a firm in Bombay. They became very popular in India almost instantly, but the copies that went to England were for the time being almost unheeded there. Very naturally and properly, they are exceedingly journalistic. But that does not obscure their merit. Kay Robinson, seeing Kipling's talent, gave him the opportunity to write these sketches (which is what they really are) by inaugurating 'turnovers', 'column-and-a-quarters', tales which started on the front page and were then continued further into the paper. They contain much of the later Kipling in embryo. But there is little sign in them, as yet, of what may be called Kipling's 'mature imperialism', the kind of attitude just described. They are certainly brilliant, with some powerful descriptive prose in them. They are essentially hard and cynical little pieces, extraordinarily professional for so young a man, and often over-redolent with worldly wisdom. It is their professionalism, though, that distinguishes them as remarkable. The knowingness is smart. It is not often actually offensive, although it becomes monotonous. Yet his audience is being got at, their assumptions are being questioned. Any serious writer, even a comic one, must question assumptions in order to obtain the 'shock of recognition'. The degree of consciousness of Kipling's use of irony is a matter for speculation; but the irony is irresistibly present. 'Lisbeth', the first tale in the book, is specifically against the sort of Christianity practised amongst the Anglo-Indians, and, in its way, all 'for' primitive innocence and trust and love. But the attitude is strategically detached. The Hill-girl who has taken to Christianity and has not reverted to her own religion ('as do some Hill-girls') finds an injured Englishman. He flirts with her and then, on the advice of the wife of the chaplain who is her mistress, pretends to her that he will return and marry her. She has taken his attentions with the greatest possible seriousness. 'It takes a great deal of Christianity to wipe out uncivilised Eastern instincts, such as falling in love at first sight.' The Englishman does not return and the Hill-girl is then told by the chaplain's wife that she had been assured that he would do so only 'as an excuse to keep you quiet': Englishmen are of 'superior clay'. The patronising unkindness of this is all the more evident for being presented without comment.

Lisbeth now does revert: 'she took to her own unclean people savagely'. The moral is sharp and obvious. These people were liars and not Christians; they made light of her feelings. Whether the worth of Christianity itself is being questioned is not perfectly clear; but there is irony in the use of the word 'unclean'. Thus Kipling is being sharply critical of the Christianity practised by chaplains and their wives in India. And, by contrast, he is presenting the Hill-girl as full of faith: she cannot at first even comprehend how what the chaplain's wife told her could be a lie, such was her trust in the moral superiority of these people – whose actual moral superiority is of course thus called into question. The poignancy of her desertion, though, is kept right back, as is emotion in general: one only knows that the author feels it because it provides him with the vehicle of his satire, or at least of his irony.

Already, in this 'turnover' for his newspaper, Kipling has developed a strategy. Those who like to believe in 'love-at-first-sight' can rejoice with Kipling in his irony. Those who go unmoved by such notions need take no notice. But the youthful romantic message is obvious, even if it was in no way necessary to Kipling at this stage. It is not at all deeply felt – it might just be a value to which Kipling is appealing on behalf of anyone else out there who is young and romantic – but it is there. And when Anglo-Indians talked about Kipling in later years, it was as a young man 'with ideas above his station', even as 'subversive': the impression, one feels, that any writer worth his salt would have to create amongst such people. If Kipling was spying, he was spying for himself. Yet readers even as rigid in their assumptions as the Anglo-Indians do not mind individual exceptions to their rules, provided they have nice mainsprings like love-at-first-sight. Kipling knows what he can get away with. He displays his cunning from the very beginning.

There is already plenty of knowingness in the second story in the book, 'Three and – an Extra'. Thus the twenty-one-year-old author writes, 'Speaking to or crying over a husband never did any good yet', and 'a woman's guess is much more accurate than a man's certainty'. These aphorisms are facile, and are born neither of wisdom nor observation. He had an excellent ear, though, for this kind of thing. He wanted to be liked by the women amongst his readers. In this volume first appears the famous Mrs Hauksbee, certainly modelled on his sharp-tongued mother but also, more precisely, on another woman, Mrs F.C. Burton (to whom *Plain Tales from the Hills* is dedicated: 'the wittiest woman in India'), the wife of a colonel. Mrs Hauksbee, the woman living apart from her husband who is simultaneously an awful unprincipled flirt and a fount of worldly wisdom and even compassion, is certainly essentially modelled on his mother. It is an ambiguous portrait. Kipling managed to make Mrs Hauksbee two things at once: one who knows the rules, and one who is subversive. That was his own lifelong position, and is well and sympathetically illustrated by his presentation of the characters of Mulvaney, Learoyd and Ortheris, the 'soldiers three' who first appear in this prentice volume. Here we already have the amoral, 'all too human' men who are yet the paradoxical backbone of Empire, who are brave but who know when to be cowards (an excellent example of this is provided by Mulvaney's behaviour in the later tale 'Love-O'-Women').

Mrs Hauksbee is also, as one might expect from a writer of Kipling's age, a somewhat shallow conception. But he needed to create a woman with whom he could be on terms. He did not at this stage fall in love with any woman, although he played protectively at it with Flo for as long as he could. He eschewed 'personal' poetry. He did not possess emotional security, and kept himself away from all introspection in the best Victorian tradition, by keeping his thoughts on whatever he was doing at the time. This is what he says Price had told him was the means of preventing 'immorality' at USC. He eased himself successfully into the peculiar society at Lahore, especially after Robinson, who admired and encouraged him, took over the paper. But he eased himself into it largely on his own terms. He was beginning to be read and talked about. His topical verses, later to be collected as *Departmental Ditties*, were soon seen to have an edge quite lacking in the welter of such stuff which filled the columns of the Indian papers in the English language. But he did have what are quite casually described as 'breakdowns'. Presumably they were periods of complete exhaustion and prostration, attended by nightmares and hysterical fears. The work was very hard, and Kipling kept himself at it. It is unlikely that Robinson's description of him at this time is exaggerated: 'Driving or walking home to breakfast in his light attire plentifully besprinkled with ink, his spectacled eyes peering out under an enormous mushroom-shaped hat, Kipling was a quaint looking object.' But he could deal with emergencies: a drunken photographer in the office, a party of people that tried to invade his rooms at night.

By the beginning of 1887 he was known all over India, and critics in other parts began to discuss him. Some, such as Andrew Lang, compared him favourably to Bret Harte, the American writer from whom he learned much, and upon whom he improved so much. Bret Harte was worthy and popular but tended to be monotonous; Kipling was popular but had greater depths. It was all exactly as he had planned it, and this local success – together possibly with his despair about India being handed over to 'nationals' and 'liberals' – led to his departure for London in 1889. But when a young man is emotionally and sexually confused, and possessed of immense energy and powers of self-assertion, a plan is essential. Kipling did have a plan. And in *Plain Tales from the Hills* he sometimes gave away details of it, as when he wrote: 'Next to a requited attachment, one of the most convenient things that a young man can carry about with him at the beginning of his career, is an unrequited attachment . . . he can mourn over his lost love, and be very happy in a tender, twilight fashion.' There is 'much evidence' that he 'shrank from intimacy with women', writes Carrington. Young men frequently do this because they are afraid that they will be found wanting. Sometimes they are 'rescued' by enterprising women of their own age. Kipling made sure that he could be rescued, though, from women of his own age. The new woman friend he made at Simla in 1887, Edmonia ('Ted') Hill, to whom he was to become very close, perhaps so close as for him to consider or to dwell upon the idea of marrying her when she became a widow, was the American wife of a meteorologist in government service; she was about thirty. Young men may also shrink from the intimate company of women of their own age because they are ambitious and do not want to have their strength literally drained from them by Delilahs. There may or may not be a misogynistic element in that state of mind; and the origins of homosexuality sometimes lie in misogyny.

Perhaps there was something Samson-like in Rudyard's shrinking away from 'intimate contact' with women. But perhaps, too, he felt himself to be on the whole unattracted, and frightened, by women. Perhaps, when his thoughts did wander, or when he had night terrors and 'breakdowns' and the old trouble with his eyes threatened, he was aware that his physical desires focused more upon men than upon women. Self-knowledge of

the capacity for full sexual love of one's own sex could more easily be
kept at arm's length in that age, when such matters were considered
beyond the human pale, and were hardly ever discussed; but clues, of
surges of simple sexual desire with their half-dismaying, half-delightful
physiological consequences, of erotic dreams and involuntary emissions,
could hardly be wholly suppressed. A man of acute sensibility, driven
(fundamentally and despite ambitions and even 'bumptiousness') by a
desire for the 'Good' (in Plato's general sense) could not keep such feelings
and physical desires wholly out of consciousness. Such matters could only
be ignored as best as might be. Such a strenuous procedure could lead to
breakdowns, especially when anxious parents were assiduously watching
out for tell-tale signs of 'normal' impulses – unless Alice's intuitions were
even subtler than that. It is not too hard, then, to surmise one of the origins
of a theme that will become one of Kipling's main concerns. This is why
I have suggested that his attitude towards the Empire began to develop as
it did. It was a false attitude, though, and it continued to develop, even in
contradiction to other impulses within him. We are able to trace this false
development until just after the Boer War, when it froze.

The theme is that of the morally reprehensible and irredeemable
('unpleasant', as it was so often called by Kipling's shocked, affronted,
admiring contemporaries) human material upon which the 'system', the
Law, the only means of human survival, depends. This is what comes
across in Kipling with such force and anxiety. In the Christian system
this is called 'original sin' and in other systems by other names. The
'soldiers three', the paradigmatic and initial instance, are simultaneously
praiseworthy and, by frank implication, morally culpable (just as Mrs
Hauksbee is a figure both unprincipled and yet compassionate and
'wise' – if not 'street-wise' then 'Simla-wise'). These soldiers have the sex
they want, that is made clear enough; they do have 'decent' impulses; but
they are never presented as 'admirable' in any conventional sense. Even
at this stage the Kipling universe is shockingly pragmatic. 'No wise man
has a Policy,' says the admired Viceroy in 'A Germ Destroyer': 'A Policy
is the blackmail levied on the Fool by the Unforeseen. I am not the former,
and I do not believe in the latter.' It is shown with naturalistic relish and
romantic energy, as being upheld by 'doers' who are either immoral, in
the exact awful sense of the immorality of the looters in 'Loot', or, at the
best, cynical or wanting in the civilised faculties. What is Kipling's 'Law'?
And is not the apparent keeping of it more important than the law itself?
Officious or foolish characters are 'broken' not according to 'rules' at all,
but according to an amoral pragmatic code known only to a few select
men, who might be described as the 'knowers' and the 'doers', Kipling's
real heroes, as perhaps the symbols of his own heroic conscience, the
guardians of his honour, the preservers of his civilised (and therefore
eventually married) circumstances. These are the ultimately cynical
(although Kipling does not use that word) supervisors of the people with
the power, the 'looters' at worst, the 'soldiers three' at best. To a certain
extent 'knowing' and 'doing' overlap, but the supervisors (knowers) behave
according to agreed civilised standards.

Sometimes Kipling lost sight of his 'knowers' and 'doers'. Those
whom in his stories he demeans and diminishes are shown as getting
their comeuppances through circumstances that are all too obviously

manipulated. There is nothing subtle about it, even when the person who is being demeaned bears more than a passing resemblance to his creator.

This sort of manipulation, although to cruder ends, usually erotic or violent, is one of the chief features of ephemeral fiction. The manipulations are effected by means of 'characters' who are without credibility, and to whom therefore any gratifying set of motives and/or actions may safely be attributed. At a somewhat higher level, certainly at the one Kipling inhabited with such efficiency, characters are established as such only by means of the opinions they hold. They are Dickensian cardboard, but don't have the Dickensian comic energy. They are rather too obviously there to be shot down instantly, and one gets to know that they will be. This is all the worse, really, in view of his capability.

In fact, though, such bad stories do have a serious dimension, quite apart from their skill and craftsmanship, that sets them entirely apart from ephemeral fiction, and even from such worthier novels as those written by Kipling's innocently imperialistic friend, Rider Haggard. This is because the impulse behind them is not impure: the perpetrator is not, for purposes of commercial gain, giving his reader the opportunity to enjoy ignoble emotions and dream ignoble dreams – of lust, violence, power, or at the very best mere fantasies of the unattainable – in the guise of noble or at least acceptable ones. In the bad kind of trash, showing its head in Kipling's time, cold-blooded and psychopathic killers (in the most familiar examples) are carefully set up as human beings possessed by decent and socially necessary impulses. Then the readers may enjoy the trail of mayhem and lust with a good conscience.

Kipling's motives are not essentially commercial or lustful or murderous; although he craved money and the power it confers, felt lust, and was probably sexually stimulated by flogging and hanging (as 'Danny Deever' indicates). But there is a very real indignation, intellectually justified or not, that impels him. It is the sort of indignation that, however distorted or irrational, possesses a moral quality. This is because it is the result of the involuntary reactions of a man of sensibility. It is based on some originally true ideal, which in turn is based on some warm and existentially grasped apprehension of the truth. Where it goes wrong may be only in the way that idealism can become strained and therefore distorted. That is why we still read the 'worst of Kipling', the rather silly revenge stories, the jejune *Stalky & Co.* He is never merely a crude hack. This is why his inferior novel *The Light that Failed* possesses the quality of readability. Always, even at worst, there is evidence of a profound sensibility cruelly puzzled and disturbed, a desperate implication of high concern with why we are and what we ought to do about it. In Kipling there may be ugliness, but there is no terribly limited certainty, such as that of the 'modern scientist' – the certainty that excludes phenomenological reality, and is humanly defeated. Kipling will never be defeated. He will be horrible and stupid, but he will not lie down, or pretend that he has told the whole truth when he knows he lies. That is why the skill of this writer stands up, even in the worst stories. Had there not been this quality of concern, the craftsmanship would early have failed and collapsed. Kipling was eventually ostracised by many good-willed readers because his reputation seemed to them to be based on some of the more dubious qualities of popular hacks: bloody-minded and cruel prejudice, a nasty *frisson* in even the best pieces, such as 'Danny Deever', and insensitivity to violence. Yet how could he achieve, quite late in life, a story with the truly gentle and compassionate qualities of 'The Gardener', if that not incomprehensible verdict were a just one? Such a story as 'The Gardener' belongs to life, is open, is the good-willed reader's, rather than the brilliant possession of the writer.

The fact is that the writer admired by Henry James, no mean judge, did go seriously astray (as James sadly saw). Not because of the nature of his opinions but because he allowed those opinions to intrude, crudely and rawly, into the imaginative texture of his creations. Yet the record his writings provide is one of a delicate sensibility always struggling to free itself from shame or, in certain cases, what he thought of as shame. We know that he thought of homosexual impulses as both 'natural' (in a Freudianly 'Iddish' sense) and yet socially evil. He hardly questioned the 'evil' of the notion at a conscious level. As we have seen, his notion was rather of everyone being 'saved' from such impulses rather than being freed from them.

Kipling, fearing homosexual impulses in himself, attached to them all manner of other characteristics: anything either emotionally or intellectually dubious to him. His sensibility became highly ambivalent. The sweetnesses of love could only be fulfilled 'illegally' within the ambience of chaos and anarchy, against which Kipling, the polemicist, is always warning us. His defence-job against these impulses and therefore, in a way, against his essential being, was both heroic and poignant. It also explains much about those apparently insensitive attitudes which distress so many of his admirers. He really believed that his own erotic impulses were on a level with the amorality of the looters of 'Loot'. Hence the extra relish, the joy, the desire to shock, the need to establish himself as telling the truth, to force readers (those who would disapprove if they 'knew') to acknowledge the truth of shocking facts. Culture very largely determined this fundamental and paradoxical attitude, so that Kipling's inner rage was directed at a society, a system, which could outlaw and send to terrible perdition and disgrace any sexuality which expressed valid love in a way made unacceptable merely by habit.

A.E. Housman, now famously, felt the bitterness of this fate secretly, but fully consciously; sometimes he smuggled the bleak message through in public. It is easy now to see exactly what he meant. The critic John Addington Symonds married, but led a secret homosexual life, buying Italian men (and others) for himself. E.M. Forster and many of those with whom he was associated led similarly secret lives. Forster once denounced homosexuality in the *New Statesman and Nation*, on the grounds that it was against the continuation of the race. John Maynard Keynes was another who married. There were countless such men, who dealt with the problem as best they could. Homosexuality was Henry James's great cross: he was forced to make, and was probably horribly sincere in, a denunciation of Wilde's 'disgusting' behavior. Now the poignant histories of men like James, Forster, Housman and many others, are being written; such unhappy, puzzled memoirs as they left behind them are being published. Even Kipling's friend, the influential Edmund Gosse, respectably married, was looking at photographs of naked boys at Robert Browning's funeral. Such fringe ambisexuals were able lightly to relieve their guilts and hypocrisies in smoking-rooms. Kipling could never have been one of those. No one ever called him a hypocrite. The sense of decency he always recommended, even if he occasionally broke his own rules, may sometimes have been old-fashioned in its terminology; it may now seem outmoded; but it happened to consist of a humane devotion to decency.

Kipling was one of those sufferers, or victims of fate, who was a homosexual (perhaps an ambisexual, but one whose main orientation was homosexual) at the wrong place and at the wrong time. One must remember that insofar as the guardians of the imperial bliss thought about the dread subject of Sodom (as they wrongly and crudely thought of it), they believed it to be one of the most rottenly unmentionable of all underminings of the power and the glory. But Kipling was different: a different sort of sufferer, a different sort of victim of his own nature: he never spoke about it to anyone, not even to himself. The pressure led him to mix up his creative impulses with politics and with what he, no intellectual, took to be intellectual opinion. The emotional impulse behind his notion of eternal vigilance was a protection and a concealment of what was, at once, most dear and most utterly horrible to him. That was the situation in this man, who had the capacity of a major writer, and who knew it, and who therefore had a sense of his rightful fate. He knew that such fame as ought to be, as would be, his, could never be enjoyed as a homosexual. He knew this, not consciously, but at a very deep level of his being. The knowledge, insistent as only a well-buried need can be, strongly reinforced his plan to succeed. But at this stage he had not fallen in love with anyone, and no doubt he sought to prevent this, too, from ever happening. If it ever did happen, then it would be a catastrophe.

Indian Fiction

Kipling's attitude to India was torn in two: reverence for the ancient, mysterious and wise, which appealed to the religious, sensual, romantic and imaginative side of his personality; and contempt for its political childishness, or childlikeness, and total lack of capacity for self-government. He was always prepared to love the Indians, provided they made no attempts to look after their own destiny. These attitudes were never resolved within him. They ceased to develop after he left India in 1889, and gradually became petrified in him. His imperialistic ideas were founded in part on his notion that he was an expert on India. When he became famous, he had to present a mask, a persona, to the world. One of the penalties of fame is that the famous have to appear to be more consistent than a real person ever can be. Kipling was less consistent than most; reason had little effect on his thinking. It might have had more had his fame been delayed, or (possibly) had his father been able to afford to send him to a university. Kipling's resentment of those educated at universities was liable to come to the surface at any time in his work, especially in his earlier work. This has been well and rightly noted. Thus Angus Wilson draws attention to the influence of this on the dislike of culture, as a beneficial influence, shown in his earlier essays and polemic. He had once said that he would 'give anything' to be in the Sixth at Harrow like his cousin Stan (he did not mention that Stan had been 'asked to leave'), 'with a University Education to follow'. But he was unable to maintain this healthy expression of frank envy.

In 1887, after spending the summer in Simla, he went to work for the *Pioneer* at Allahabad. When he was not travelling he stayed in the house of his friends the Hills. The *Pioneer* was a bigger paper, with a circulation outside India. He remained a Freemason, transferring from the Lahore Lodge to one in Allahabad. He had been 'raised to the Sublime Degree' on 6 December 1886, at Lahore. He was by now turning out an enormous spate of material: poems, some essays, stories (he still contributed to the *Civil and Military Gazette*), and travel sketches, for which he was well supplied with facts, for his job took him all over India – for example, to Benares and Calcutta. He was more secure now, much spoken of, and to an appreciable degree more able to dictate his own terms to his immediate world. His parents, within the limitations imposed by protocol, were moving up the social scale. The new Viceroy, Lord Dufferin, looked in at the Lahore Museum and was bored and critical; but at Simla he soon discovered that the Kiplings were more amusing than most. They could not be invited to the official banquets, but were entertained at more informal ones. Alice Kipling in her capacity as witty woman began to be talked about, too, which caused some annoyance to Trix who made remarks about women of forty pulling the men to the unfair disadvantage of their juniors; Kipling shared in making jokes about that.

There must have been the day when Alice read 'Baa, Baa, Black Sheep' (1888, and included in the first of the collections entitled *Wee Willie Winkie*). She can hardly have been pleased, even if the figure of the mother in that story is well protected from open criticism. Was there some element of competition between mother and son? If so, the son was well ahead on points: in early 1888 *Plain Tales from the Hills* was republished not only in Calcutta but also in London, and in the Indian Railway Library appeared *Soldiers Three, The Story of the Gadbys, In Black and White, Under the Deodars, The Phantom Rickshaw* and *Wee Willie Winkie*. (These were combined into two books published in London in 1890: the first three into *Soldiers Three* and the rest into *Wee Willie Winkie*).

Kipling wrote few more stories about India after the publication of *Life's Handicap* (1891). In its successor *Many Inventions* (1893) he is moving away from the exploitation of Indian themes in the short-story form – the form in which he was surest. The Indian theme is henceforth seen mainly in the books especially devised for children; it culminates in the novel *Kim* (1901), which is partly based on material salvaged from the Indian novel called *Mother Maturin*. Kipling worked on this between March and July of 1885, at Lahore, and it is known that he produced at least 237 foolscap pages of it. It was still in existence in 1899, when his agent Watt sent it down to his home for him to 'ransack ... for notions' (Carrington). Eventually Kipling destroyed it; if he did not then his widow did. He told his Aunt Edith that it was 'not one bit nice or proper', but

> carries a grim sort of moral with it and tries to deal with the unutterable horrors of lower class Eurasian and native life as they exist outside reports ... Trixie says it's awfully horrid; Mother says it's nasty but powerful and I know it to be in large measure true. It is an unfailing delight to me.

What little is known about this text suggests that it was naturalistic (in the sense previously defined). Ted Hill said that it was about an old Irishwoman who kept an opium den in Lahore and who sent her daughter home to be educated in England. The daughter married an Anglo-Indian, came to live in Lahore, and, comments Ted Hill, 'hence a story how Government secrets came to be known in the Bazaar and *viceversa*'. It was his father who condemned it as unsuitable. This might have been for extra-artistic reasons: that it was 'too shocking'. If so, and Lockwood allowed his judgement to be overwhelmed by expediency, then this was a pity. As Angus Wilson suggests, he may not have been without 'holy-holy qualities'. One of the characters in it was inspired by a drunken Oxford drop-out who had 'gone native': his 'account of the life and sins of Mother Maturin' provided the framework of the story. But by 1887 and 1888 Kipling had already put this sort of straightforward romantic ambition behind him.

The faults that spoil the early stories stem mainly from their journalistic origin, for which one can scarcely blame Kipling – unless it is felt that he should later have revised them. But that would have been a mistake. Some of these literary faults, however, are journalistic virtues. In general readers *liked* Kipling's cocky knowingness, his sententious beginnings ('This is not a story exactly. It is a tract . . .' and so forth), his tricks. Most of these tricks could be omitted with advantage, and the tales that lack them are usually the best ones. But Kipling's facetiousness is not so bad that we are not able to get used to it: it is not so obtrusive that it seriously mars the work, and we know that he did it as a snook cocked at university-educated literary gentlemen, who were not (he felt) really as good as the 'knowing' men for whom he wrote. We must never forget that Kipling, as a major writer, is unique in that he refused to be literary, in the sense that he deliberately avoided what he thought of as the habits of literary writers. One or two other European and American writers (I have mentioned Knut Hamsun) could be compared to him in this respect, but no English ones. His refusal is a part of his strange achievement. If it should not be so considered, then he would not be the subject of serious criticism today, and his works would have vanished into oblivion along with those of the other writers of popular fiction of his day.

In the earliest stories, the ones written in India, he is feeling his way. The journalistic effectiveness which he had to cultivate militated against any wholehearted exploration of themes he may really have wanted to pursue. There was no room at all here for self-indulgence in the large-scale manner of the abandoned *Mother Maturin* manuscript. Therefore he brought in what he wanted only when he could. Kipling was not one of those writers who was prepared to struggle with lack of comprehension of his work. His later deliberate riddles were set to a more or less captive audience, inasmuch as he had already established himself as a dominant and highly respected writer.

The view of women in *Plain Tales* is, as we have already seen, knowing; and Kipling's ignorance is well concealed. The almost professional know-ingness of 'Three and – an Extra', in which Mrs Hauksbee's flirtation with a fool is defeated by the fool's wife by the simple expedient of dressing up in a fetching gown at a ball, is soon shattered by examination: it is a triviality, and it is picked up from club-talk.

'Thrown Away' is on a Kipling theme that soon became a familiar one. It begins:

> To rear a boy under what parents call the 'sheltered life' system is, if the boy must go into the world and fend for himself, not wise. Unless he be one in a thousand he has certainly to pass through many unnecessary troubles; and may, possibly, come to extreme grief simply from ignorance of the proper proportions of things.

This ingratiating beginning (especially so when we remember how quickly Rudyard's parents put him under shelter when he let them know how he reacted to being unsheltered) is followed by a short narrative illustrating the fate of one who was brought up under the egregious sheltered life system and was 'killed dead'. The unfortunate 'Boy' came out of Sandhurst 'as high as he went in'. Eventually he is sent to India, where he is 'cut off from the support of his parents'. At this point there is a paragraph of the purest cynicism which is characteristic of Kipling at his most simplistic. Whatever you do, it says with the voice of hardened experience, you must not, above all, take India seriously. You must not work too hard. You can flirt because 'either you or she leave the Station and never return'. 'Good work does not matter', as people judge you on your worst work and others take the credit for your best. Amusements are all right: they are only 'trying to win another person's money'. Sickness 'does not matter': it's 'all in the day's work', and if you die someone else takes over. Nothing matters except furlough and extra allowances – 'and these only because they are scarce'. The best thing is to escape to 'some place where amusement is amusement and a reputation worth the having'.

The Boy (it is an old story, Kipling sagely adds) came out and was too serious. He fretted over women not worth fretting over. He enjoyed the attractions of the subaltern's life in India – more fool him! But his feelings got hurt because he had been sheltered as a child: couldn't understand why they weren't as nice to him there as his mother and father had been. Kipling also smuggles in some pert knowledge, not to impress – that audience would not have been impressed by it, knowing all about such stuff – but to make quite sure everyone knows that he knows everything. Thus:

> He took his losses seriously, and wasted as much energy and interest over a two-goldmohur race for maiden *ekka*-ponies with their manes hogged, as if it had been the Derby. One half of this came from inexperience – much as the puppy squabbles with the corner of the hearthrug – and the other half from the dizziness bred by stumbling out of his quiet life into the glare and excitement of a livelier one.

All through the story The Boy is compared to a puppy – except that the puppy is luckier, having learned for himself what it is like to eat the soap and blacking. So no one told The Boy 'about the soap and blacking, because an average man takes it for granted that an average man is ordinarily careful in regard to them. It was pitiful to watch The Boy knocking himself to pieces . . .' But it was supposed by the people that realisation of what he had done to himself (loss of money, health, laming of his horses) would sober him down and that he 'would stand steady'. It would have happened, too, as in ninety-nine cases out of a hundred it does: but 'this particular case fell through because The Boy was sensitive and took things seriously'. The Boy's trouble was that he thought himself 'beyond redemption'. The cruel words of a woman – the narrator does not think it worth quoting them, 'only a cruel little sentence' – 'kicks the beam' in The Boy, and, after what was really only an 'ordinary' 'Colonel's wigging', which he takes over-seriously, he goes off pretending he is going to 'shoot big game', and shoots himself.

A Major who had taken an interest in him, together with the narrator, reads the three letters he leaves behind him. The one to his parents, containing 'private things . . . too sacred to put into print', would have broken his father's heart and 'killed his mother after killing her belief in her son'. The one to 'the girl at Home' has both men in unashamed tears. They decide to pretend that he has died of cholera. They draft a letter of consolation: 'one of the most grimly comic scenes I have ever taken part in – the concoction of a big, written lie . . .' They want to send a lock of the boy's hair, but The Boy blew his brains out, so the Major sends a lock of his own. By this stage tears have changed to drunken laughter. Afterwards, walking along the river, they feel like murderers. There is jiggery-pokery with the corpse, so as to rig up the right appearances. The Major confesses that he, too, had once considered taking such a way out. 'He also said that youngsters, in their repentent moments, consider sins much more serious and ineffaceable than they are.' The affair soon passes over, with the Major even accused of 'scandalously' not bringing in the body for a regimental funeral.

This tale is not important in its own right; but it is worth looking at in detail because of what it reveals of the later and infinitely more subtle Kipling, when he was not obliged to conform to any but his own rules of writing. For a mere 'turnover' of under 4000 words it mixes together a surprisingly large number of disparate themes: the fate of the over-protected child; the nature of India (where you must not take things seriously) – there is some irony in the would-be cynical and knowing account of how it really is in the army there; the fatal effects on an inexperienced person of taking it too seriously but even then not being able to learn your lesson and continuing to take it all too seriously ('He might be crippled for life financially, and want a little nursing. Still the memory of his performances would wither away in one hot weather, and the bankers would help to tide over the money-troubles. But he must have taken another view altogether . . .'); the dire effect of a woman's cruel words; a slight attempt to convey the effects of all these reverses on the behaviour of young men (it is said that he was 'noisy' and 'offensive' in the Mess, but this is not pursued; probably what Kipling wanted to suggest was that he became 'dissipated', and this is the word used in a number of summaries of the story); the compassionate attitude of the experienced Major as to what must be done; the nature of the ritual (man's stuff, this), including a 'private unofficial prayer for the peace of the soul of The Boy'; there is also an adumbration of a theme common in the later Kipling, that of deception in the general interest; and, finally – this must on no account be missed – the sheer horror, the flies buzzing around the corpse with its head blown to bits and the rest of the details ('I am not going to write about this. It was too horrible').

But the story does not work because these themes are not combined. At the beginning we think we are going to get a forceful illustration of the harm inflicted by the 'sheltered life theory'. But this theme is abandoned: what destroys The Boy is, not, after all, his parents' over-protectiveness, but his sensitivity and taking things too seriously. On this point there is much ironic bitterness, as there is in the description of how cynical you have got to be to survive in India. Because Kipling is uneasy with this sensitivity and seriousness, linking it not so vaguely in his own consciousness with the kind of sensitivity associated with condemned feelings (although there is of course no hint of such specific emotions, unless it be that a *woman's* careless words made The Boy 'kick the beam'), he swamps it in conventional horror, the flies around the bloody corpse and the other grisly details. The verse which heads the tale, as an epigraph, is presented as *Toolungala Stockyard Chorus*:

> And some are sulky, while some will plunge.
> (*So ho! Steady! Stand still, you!*)
> Some you must be gentle, and some you must lunge.
> (*There! There! Who wants to kill you?*)
> Some – there are losses in every trade –
> Will break their hearts ere bitted and made,
> Will fight like fiends as the rope cuts hard,
> And die dumb-mad in the breaking-yard.

There is an immense and open bitterness in this verse, which is incidentally an excellent demonstration of how essential it always is to take the fullest heed of Kipling's verse epigraphs and postludes. The subject of sexuality is hardly hinted at in the text itself, the statement that The Boy was 'pretty and was petted' being in its context merely, once again, worldly-wise. But if any reader doubted whether Kipling was expressing a deep sense of bitterness about the fate of the sensitive and the serious, then he has only to look at the epigraph. What is it there for, what does it say, what is its relevance? Kipling did not invent it and put it there for nothing, but he must have realised that very few of his readers, if any, would bother about its exact relevance. Many of the other epigraphs serve a similar function. The ardent Kiplingite does not discuss this or similar sorts of verse in Kipling: it is too sinister, too bitter – and it is not decently straightforward in the imperial manner.

The focus of bitter pathos in the tale itself is no more nor less than The Boy's tragic sensitivity and seriousness. When Kipling alludes to it as the final cause of his downfall he adds, 'as I may have said some seven times before'. There is actually no reason why parental over-protectiveness, in particular, should cause acute sensitivity. Some sorts might do so, and other sorts might not. But Kipling's point so far as that is concerned is merely brash, on the level of club-talk about not sparing the rod. He would have had to put in some details to illustrate a precisely spoiling type of over-protectiveness, had he really been interested in doing so. But psychology of that immediate kind never did interest him much as a writer. As he knew from his own experience, a boy may be put through the mill of a public school or even an imitation public school, and yet be highly sensitive and serious. So any reading of the story which depended on The Boy's tragedy simply arising from his not being sent through the fire at some such institution as USC, but instead saddled with over-protective parents, won't stand up in the story's own real terms – although that is how it would have been understood and that, too, is how Kipling hoped it would be understood, since he stated at the outset that the 'sheltered life theory' 'killed him dead' because he didn't know the 'proper proportions of things'. But is that cynical set of conditions listed as essential to survival in India really intended by the author to reflect, wholly unironically, the 'proper proportions of things'? Of course not. But there is an ambiguity about the statement of these conditions: Kipling wants the best of both worlds. On the one hand he wants to be cynical and worldly-wise; on the other his conscience obliges him to be ironic. Why, otherwise, would there be any element of pathos in the suicide of The Boy at all? But Kipling might have liked to able to be much more specific, impossible though this would have been. The bitterness in the epigraph, especially in the fourth and last lines, is not at all unlike that found in Housman's famous poem:

Oh who is that young sinner with the handcuffs on his wrists?
And what has he been after that they groan and shake their fists?
And wherefore is he wearing such a conscience-stricken air?
Oh they're taking him to prison for the colour of his hair.

Indeed, although Housman called *The Jungle Book* a 'tract in wolf's clothing' (which it is), he had certain things in common with Kipling, not the least of them an interest in death, execution by hanging, and the military. Hopkins, too, yet another homosexual who could not 'speak out', had this interest in 'our redcoats, our tars'. It goes well beyond the sentiments of the time. One of the personal answers to this question that the tortured Hopkins cannot touch upon is, simply, that he was sexually attracted to soldiers. Like Kipling in his 'Loot' poem, Hopkins, in trying to answer the question as best he can, and in more intellectually conscientious a fashion than Kipling could ever achieve, recognises that both the redcoats and the tars are

                                              the greater part,
But frail clay, nay but foul clay. Here it is: the heart,
Since, proud, it calls the calling manly, gives a guess
That, hopes that, makesbelieve, the men must be no less;
It fancies, feigns, deems, dears the artist after his art;
And fain will find as sterling all as all is smart,
And scarlet wear the spirit of war there express.

Hopkins goes on to bring Christ into the argument:

Mark Christ our King. He knows war, served this soldiering through;
He of all can reeve a rope best. There he bides in bliss
Now, and seeing somewhere some man do all that man can do,
For love he leans forth, needs his neck must fall on, kiss,
And cry 'O Christ-done deed! So God-made-flesh does too:
Were I to come again' cries Christ 'it should be thus'.

Kipling approaches his own interest in pretty soldier boys, subalterns in this case, in a very different and markedly less gnarled manner. In the very early 'Arithmetic on the Frontier' (written in 1885 or '86) he begins:

A great and glorious thing it is
    To learn, for seven years or so,
The Lord knows what of that and this,
    Ere reckoned fit to face the foe –
The flying bullet down the Pass,
    That whistles clear: 'All flesh is grass'.

This goes on to weigh the expensive education in England against the suddenness of death away from Home, and to query the value of such an education in obtaining the skills necessary to avoid such a death. 'No proposition Euclid wrote . . . Will turn the bullet from your coat.' Good old-fashioned stuff likely to appeal to those who appreciate the virtues of strength and who don't count universities for much. It ends:

> With home-bred hordes the hillsides teem.
>   The troopships bring us one by one,
> At vast expense of time and steam,
>   To slay Afridis where they run.
> The 'captives of our bow and spear'
>   Are cheap, alas! as we are dear.

The focus is already all on how the folk at home don't really appreciate the soldiers and their skill; and there is a blow at education itself (which Kipling could not, as a whole, manage). Where Hopkins, with his too extremely developed 'scruples', rationalises his erotic feelings into a complex metaphysic which is even conscientious enough to admit eroticism (if the reader is subtle enough), Kipling simplifies his into an attitude. But there is no true argument in the poem. One of the verses of 'Arithmetic at the Frontier' suggests that a Kurrum Valley scamp who doesn't understand moods and tenses is yet gifted with skill (implied) and 'perfect sight' and so can 'Pick off our messmates left and right'. But what is he really advocating? Euclid is a very good exercise for future precision killers. The poem is written on a crude emotional level, and its sense is not worth pursuing. Does he mean that there should be no education except in soldiering? The notion that struggling with Euclid is of no use in the heat of battle is in any case simply emotional. The poem is not generated by thought, but by two impulses: envy of learning and academic cleverness, and a sentimental identification with the soldiers themselves, which springs from feelings not unlike those of Hopkins or Housman. But Kipling, as the general lightness of the verses in *Departmental Ditties* makes clear, was determined to *try* not to be too 'sensitive' or 'serious' about it. In 'Thrown Away' he was delivering himself a sort of message, too; but it was to no avail. This is a longer story, of the four that he had not previously published; it might have seemed important to him. The very earliest (September 1886) of all the *Plain Tales*, 'The Story of Muhammad Din', is pure pathos, very strongly implying but never directly expressing bitterness: it tells straightforwardly and vividly of a small Indian child who dies needlessly, as so many did, of an infection. One of its oblique morals, incidentally, is that a little Indian boy is quite as delightful as an English or Anglo-Indian one, but more vulnerable to disease.

Another trick that Kipling employed to attract immediate attention to his stories was to make most of them what Cornell calls *contes à clef*. When one of them appeared, all the readers would wonder who was who. Thus, although there could hardly have been an original of The Boy, who has no character to speak of (he is mere vibrating cardboard, a 'type' if ever there was one) readers of the first edition of *Plain Tales* would confidently allude to the 'original', who would be similar to many cases they knew of. Kipling could add spice to all the tales by making people wonder. Was Mrs Hauksbee Mrs Burton? In the comeuppance farce 'A Germ Destroyer', the silly and over-zealous private secretary Wonder 'is' Lord William Beresford, and Mellish, who exhibits his fumigatory to the

Viceroy with such disastrous results, 'is' a certain Major Lucie-Smith who got over-excited when he discovered a vein of coal, and made a conflagration in Government House at Nagpore (really an 'innocuous' man, claims an over-confident Cornell, unused to the annals of contemporary British *grotesquerie*).

Almost all this immediate, delightful, but extra-literary pleasure is denied to us: we cannot be there then. Yet the stories are still highly readable, and, as Randall Jarrell noted, although only about six or seven are 'very good', yet the book as a whole is better even that these. Who were Kipling's masters in this first prose book? There is a superficial influence of Bret Harte, but this counts for little. The real master is Maupassant, although Kipling seldom directly lifts from him. Cornell tries, surprisingly, to play this debt down, pointing out that there is no direct evidence that Kipling had read Maupassant at this stage. This is a pointless exercise. There is nothing wrong with debts, anyway: it is thefts that are sometimes discreditable (but even these hardly matter at such a stage of development). The boy who was made free of Crom Price's French fiction and who was an avid reader of Zola, and who could read French easily, could not have missed Maupassant, and could hardly have missed *Les Soirées de Médan*, the collection in which, effectively, Zola introduced Maupassant. Kipling simply observed how Maupassant gained his effects, of pathos (in, famously, '*Boule-de-suif*', the star contribution to *Les Soirées de Médan*), of terror, and of farce, and then learned to adapt them in his own way, to his own needs. He learned from Maupassant's laconic manner, from his neatness of execution, above all from the manner in which he contrived to make a sharp impact on his readers' emotions. Like Maupassant, he pays little attention to individual details of character: he is more anxious to produce silhouettes, types, minor civil servants, soldiers, society women. He would have approved, had he known of it, Maupassant's dictum that 'psychology should be hidden in a book, as it is hidden in reality under the facts of existence'. He recognised in him (though he could not have known the actual remark) the cast of mind that could ask the question, of bacteria, 'what about *their* diseases?' Kipling seems at this point to be more of a workaday professional than a 'major author': just as Maupassant seemed to be, when compared to his acknowledged masters Flaubert and Zola. When James noted in his sympathetic essay on Maupassant a 'certain absence of love, a sort of bird's-eye view contempt', he might well have been speaking of the early Kipling, in whom the pathos, when it is there, is very much of a *Boule-de-suif*ish sort. What James seems to have missed in this deliberately coarse writer is the yearning of a surprisingly spiritual type, which intensified as he went towards the brink of sanity – the last stage of syphilis.

Later, in 1890, Kipling would affect to find Maupassant's works 'unwholesome'; but the context of this remark is a general baiting of the aesthetes from whom he was then definitively separating himself. Ultimately Kipling discovered himself to be different from Maupassant: he was not as naturally and easily cynical, he was at heart a softer touch, a more sentimental man. He also possessed spiritual yearnings. However, he had no masters such as Flaubert or Zola immediately behind him, to point him on his defiant way. So his way became non-literary. Nor, doubtless, could he have done what Maupassant is supposed to have demonstrated (alas, it was to Frank Harris, so that we can never know if it is true or not) in the street: 'I can have an erection at will: look at my trousers!'. What Kipling had in common always, though, with Maupassant, was an appearance of being a misogynist (both writers were frequently charged with this, and the manner of Kipling's early cynicism about women owed something to Maupassant), and an obsession with primitive fear which is expressed in some discomforting tales of the macabre. The author of Kipling's masterpieces in this genre is unlikely to have been unaware of 'Le Horla', a tale of an unidentifiable haunting presence (although this did not appear in book form until 1887). He would also have appreciated Maupassant's vision of the dead writing the truth about themselves in place of the inscriptions on their tombstones in 'La Morte'.

But Kipling, notwithstanding his special debt to Maupassant, a matter of one fledgling professional's taking advantage of another's highly appropriate mastery, was original. It was not mere imitation. He read the Anglo-Indian literature of his time, but was influenced by it only inasmuch as he did much better with the same material. At the very time that he was turning into the newspaper the stories collected in *Plain Tales*, he was reading Sir Walter Besant's now forgotten sentimental novel of literary life *All in a Garden Fair*, which upset him, yet was (he says in his autobiography) 'a revelation, a hope and strength'. But although it reinforced his determination to leave India eventually (owing, as Carrington says, to remarks made about the East by Besant), and influenced his thinking, it did not influence his work: it was not good enough, and so offered him nothing.

While writing *Plain Tales* Kipling taught himself much about narrative strategy. He was a young man who did not feel himself normal but felt that he must pretend to be normal. He had a terrible thing inside him, which he had to hide from other people – and from himself, so far as possible. It is fitting that the narrator of these tales should be an ambiguous figure. This narrator is by no means Kipling – although he can sometimes be Kipling if that is suitable – but a single invented character common to each tale. His knowingness and his possession of an experience impossible in a man of his creator's age is his least interesting characteristic; Kipling's need to adopt such a pose has been mentioned before, and is, among other things, a sign of his immaturity. But it fulfilled his needs very well: he could feel identified with this observer, this man obliged – like the reporter Kipling actually was – to tell it *as it is*.

This narrator is never initially presented as particularly sensitive. At best rather, his sensitivity is carefully and deliberately restricted to convention, as a list of his personal emotional reactions in 'Thrown Away' makes clear. But even a reporter reveals himself in what he chooses to report upon, and what he chooses to omit. And then again – which is where Kipling's narrative cunning begins to make itself manifest – no reader can claim that the storyteller is not keeping a very stiff upper lip.

Through this narrator, carefully robbed of almost all colour actually personal, Kipling can conduct various experiments with his own various sensitive and vulnerable selves. He felt confident of his powers for the first time in his life, mostly because of Kay Robinson's encouragement, which must have seemed like balm to him after the long apprenticeship under the dour Wheeler, who had believed him 'too literary'. In this new and sudden burst of self-confidence he began, with what would become his first collection of stories, to pursue a lifelong strategy: the incidental working off of personal scores. I use the word 'incidental' advisedly: he kept his art carefully separate from this activity, which, while only a by-product, was precious to him. He was so successful that his best stories depend in no way – unless for the original energy that generated them – on it, so that it really is incidental. He did exploit his audience's liking of gossip, and desire to identify various of his more preposterous characters; but, even if some have commented that scores were paid off, the tales don't depend on that element. Kipling was always careful to obliterate all traces of the person he was really after, usually by giving them positions that they were very far from being able to fill. Therefore what we say along these lines is also incidental: incidental to the stories' literary worth. Kipling brought to literature a unique sort of non-literary thoughtfulness, a kind of oblique intellectuality, no doubt in part originating in his angry envy of 'university men', but also in part in his peculiar defensive mechanisms.

In the farce 'His Wedded Wife' he deals with himself as the clumsy, callow, somewhat feminine young fellow that he feels himself to be whenever he is fatigued, feverish and depressed. But at the same time he both sets himself up above that self (as narrator), and shows it triumphant. A young subaltern, Faizanne, the Worm, a hairless 'pretty' boy, comes out to India to a tough regiment. Besides being physically clumsy, he breaks all the rules, such as refusing to socialise. But he accepts the rough treatment meted out to him because he is 'so anxious to learn'. Eventually he is left alone, except by the Senior Subaltern, whose nature is soured by his being in love (usually this makes people nicer and temporarily more understanding, but we will let that particular piece of pseudo-omniscience pass). The Senior Subaltern doesn't know when to stop. So the Worm calmly and, surprisingly impressively, challenges him in the Mess: he bets him a month's salary that he'll 'work a sell' on him that 'you'll remember for the rest of your days, and the Regiment after you when you're dead or broke'. The Senior Subaltern contemptuously takes him on. This is Kipling showing himself – not to the Mess, but to the world that has so ill used him.

Soon afterwards the Senior Subaltern gets his 'Company and his accept-ance' at the same time. He is holding forth on his girl's merits at a gathering of officers and wives when a woman comes forward, sobbing, to ask for her 'husband', Lionel (the Senior Subaltern's first name). Everyone wonders, and 'the Colonel's face set like the Day of Judgement framed in grey bristles'. (One notes at this point Kipling's use of the trick of giving his victim a slightly stupid name, for the Senior Subaltern here is the Victim, the man who went on with some fine licking-into-shape bullying for too long.) Everyone goes into the ante-room, and the woman pours out an embarrassing story: of how the newly engaged man married her on Home leave eighteen months before, 'we . . . esteemed him a beast of the worst kind'. But, the narrator adds misogynistically, they 'felt sorry for him, though'. Meanwhile the unfortunate Senior Subaltern's terrier was 'hunting for fleas'; it is details like this which an ordinary Anglo-Indian scribbler would have failed to add. Finally the woman is asked for her marriage lines, which she produces from her breast. The document reads: 'This is to certify that I, the Worm, have paid in full my debts to the Senior

Subaltern . . .' The 'woman' was of course the Worm in drag, and he has won an important victory: through an acting ability which no one knew he possessed. There is more of that sort of detail which the ordinary scribbler would not and could not have offered: that everyone was disappointed that it hadn't turned out to be a real tragedy, but 'that is human nature'; and that this joke 'had leaned as near to a nasty tragedy as anything this side of a joke can'. He also says that 'personally' he thinks it 'was in bad taste', since there is 'no sort of use in playing with fire, even for fun'. The only very slight sort of comeuppance the Worm gets for his joke is that, from henceforth, he is known as 'Mrs Senior Subaltern', which is 'sometimes confusing to strangers'. The narrator ends by promising another tale which resembles this one, 'but with all the jest left out and nothing in it but real trouble'.

The promise is kept with 'In the Pride of his Youth'. Here Kipling examines, with a sense of horror that is reflected in the events depicted, what might have happened had he actually married Florence Garrard. In 'Wressley of the Foreign Office' he revenges himself on Flo in the person of the frivolous Tillie Venner (with whom he himself compared Flo, in a letter). 'Pig', a somehow unpleasantly relentless and callous tale of the vendetta pursued by a man against someone who had sold him a bum horse (the revenger is, significantly, a Yorkshireman, the victim a South Devon man 'as soft as a Dartmoor bog'), is another exercise in the revenge theme that was to run through all his work. In so many of these tales someone is made to pay.

Although Kipling could occasionally be venomous about Florence Garrard, his sketch of her as Tillie Venner is cheerful and well under control. But in the more grim 'In the Pride of his Youth' he overdoes his misogyny. Dicky Hatt is 'kidnapped' (Rudyard's Mess word for 'married') just a month before he comes to India to take up a civilian post. The marriage is to be kept secret for a year, then Mrs Hatt is to join him; but the cost of her passage will be seven hundred difficult rupees. During that year Dickie goes without everything in order to remit half (and more) of his salary home. He dreams of his dear wife and their baby, and is made very unhappy when she asks for more and more money – more than he could possible afford. When he tells her that she must wait for more money, her letters grow 'hard'. 'Dicky didn't understand. How could he, poor boy?' The baby dies, and he receives a letter blaming his lack of money for it. It strikes at his 'naked heart'. He overstrains himself, and his senior tells him, 'If a youth would be distinguished in his art, art, art/He must keep the girls away from his heart, heart, heart.' He is then dealt the final blow. His wife writes to tell him that she has gone 'with a handsomer man than you'. Kipling gives us the letter in reported speech, but preserves the lack of stops:

> She was not going to wait for ever and the baby was dead and Dickie was only a boy and he would never set eyes on her again and why hadn't he waved his handkerchief to her when he left Gravesend and God was her judge she was a wicked woman but Dickie was worse enjoying himself in India and this other man loved the ground she trod on and would Dickie ever forgive her for she would never forgive Dickie; and there was no address to write to.

So Dickie gives up: resigns. But he is offered a new post, at a salary high in comparison to his old one. 'And it came then! The seven-hundred-rupee passage, and enough to have saved the wife . . .' Dickie bursts into laughter, and vanishes.

In the more substantial 'Beyond the Pale' Kipling dealt with himself at a more ambiguous level. It is a sickening, genuinely frightening and genuinely poetic story, ostensibly written to illustrate the truth of its opening statement: 'A man should, whatever happens, keep to his own caste, race, and breed.' This, from the author of the later 'Without Benefit of Clergy', is certainly ironic – and, as if to underline it, the epigraph of the story is a 'Hindu Proverb', 'Love heeds not nor caste nor sleep a broken bed. I went in search of love and lost myself.' 'This is a story,' Kipling states blandly, 'of a man who wilfully stepped beyond the safe limits of decent everyday society, and paid for it heavily.' Now all commentators – not simply defenders of Kipling's political attitudes – know very well that there is more in this than meets the eye: a certain irony. Kipling was never a man to deprecate the power of love. Few writers are. It is one of the weapons in their armoury of assertion: this, that, or the other, they will say, is *real* love. Writers almost always flog the enemy, which is whatever state of affairs they deprecate in their world – communism, fascism, democracy – with *real love*. So we know that Christopher Trejago, his protagonist here, has some of his sympathy.

Trejago goes into an alley and has an encounter with a woman through a grating. The next day a message is thrown into his dogcart: a letter written with objects. Trejago, says Kipling, knew 'far too much about these things': he could translate this little bundle of objects. The message is: 'A widow, in the Gully in which is the heap of *bhusa*, desires you to come at eleven o'clock.' That began a 'double life so wild that Trejago today sometimes wonders if it were not a dream'. Bisesa, as she is called, is 'an endless delight' to Trejago. Her relatives discover what is going on, and after three weeks 'without a sign' Trejago again goes down to the Gully to find out what has gone wrong: Bisesa appears, holding out to him her two arms, 'both hands had been cut off at the wrists, and the stumps were nearly healed'. Someone from behind her thrusts 'something sharp' at Trejago: the 'stroke missed his body, but cut into one of the muscles of his groin . . .' The tale ends: 'There is nothing peculiar about him, except a slight stiffness, caused by a riding-strain, in the right leg.'

Cornell says that this wound is reminiscent of the punishment of Abelard (who was castrated). Of course Kipling means that someone tried to castrate Trejago; but there is no parallel with the case of Abelard, who was a priest. However, if this punishment is meted out to those who indulge in forbidden love – people who wilfully step outside the bounds of decent everyday society – then it gains an added significance. 'If you follow your own nature in this world,' Kipling is saying, 'then you will be castrated.'

When Kipling's friend Ian Hamilton sent Andrew Lang the manuscript of the story 'The Mark of the Beast' in 1886 Lang commented: 'I would gladly give Ian a fiver if he had never been the means of my reading this poisonous stuff which has left an extremely disagreeable impression on my mind'; another critic to whom Hamilton sent it thought that Kipling was 'detestable', and that he would die mad before he was thirty. In a month or two Lang would become one of Kipling's champions, introducing *Departmental Ditties*, but he would never really change his mind about the 'disagreeable impression' left by his writing; he would just change his tack, largely because he became aware of Kipling's power. In reviewing a couple of the small Wheeler's Railway Library booklets, in 1889, he suggested that Kipling was not unacquainted with the writings of 'Gyp'. It seems that Kipling may, disingenuously, have denied to Lang, when he met him, that he knew of this French writer; it also seems as though Lang had his doubts about this disclaimer. 'Gyp' was Gabrielle Sibylle Marie Antoinette de Riquetti de Mirabeau, Comtesse de Martel de Janville. In her thirties she wrote *Petit Bob* (1882), sketches about an *enfant terrible* who has the power to satirise the hypocrisy of his elders. Kipling, who had certainly read it, learned to magnify and focus the malice he found in this comedy of manners. Later, when Gyp published *Ces bons Normands* (1895), amused critics excused the malice by pronouncing it 'not altogether serious'. With Kipling they could have no such luxury, and so they had to excuse his 'unpleasantness'. When Kipling had become famous in 1891 Lang published his considered opinion in his *Essays in Little*. But he still did not like the nastiness of the stories about Simla, and thought it 'fortunate' that Kipling had looked elsewhere for his material. He was judicious about the faults, and evidently sympathised with those who could not overcome their antipathy:

> They are curiously visible to some readers who are blind to his merits. There is a false air of hardness (quite in contradiction to the sentiment in his tales of childish life); there is a knowing air; there are mannerisms, such as 'But that is another story'; there is a display of slang; there is the too obtrusive knocking of the nail on the head. Everybody can mark these errors; a few cannot overcome their antipathy, and so lose a great deal of pleasure.

'In the Pride of His Youth' is one of the pieces in which there is too much of the false hardness which Lang noted. It is not a good or an interesting tale, and is marked only by a sullen resentment against woman and the married state. There is no attempt to build up the character of Mrs Hatt, or to demonstrate why she behaves as she does. The clever quotation from her letter reads as though it had been copied from a real letter, and so perhaps it had. The message is simple: 'All women behave like Mrs Hatt: be warned: don't marry.' Kipling was to have a problem for some years in respect to his feelings about women, and these were to bring out the most shallow and superficial elements in his writing. It was apparent in the most guttersnipe, feeble and silly of the verses in *Departmental Ditties*, such as this couplet from 'Certain Maxims of Hafiz': 'Seek not for favour of women. So shall you find it indeed/Does not the board break cover just when you're lighting a weed?' 'In the Pride of his Youth' is not worth more than this other couplet from the 'Maxims': 'Pleasant the snaffle of Courtship, improving the manners and carriages/But the colt who is wise will abstain from the terrible thorn-bit of Marriage.' If its author had not been so extremely youthful, and so evidently ignorant of the subject about which he waxed so wise, this would be no more than contemptible. It is therefore ironic that his own marriage proved to be such a terrible thorn-bit.

Other of the Indian stories express his misogyny in different ways, although it should be emphasised that the best are not vitiated because of it. He had, as I have already mentioned, the knack of making his own affairs incidental to their success.

'False Dawn' is one of the finest of these early stories. It is a cruel account of how a Civilian who is widely regarded as 'strange', and as being interesting to women only because he treated them rudely, proposes to the wrong sister during a dust-storm. He is called Saumarez, and all the nasty observations about him are certainly supposed to be equated with the alleged 'strangeness' of Jews; though there is some cause to wonder if Kipling is not being critical about this attitude. Everyone is returning from a moonlight riding-picnic; the air is charged with electricity. The narrator dramatically chases the disappointed sister, who has overheard the proposal, brings her back, and the mistake is rectified. Saumarez was widely held to prefer the prettier elder sister to whom he made the first proposal; in fact he turns out to be in love with the younger, plainer one.

There is one other story in *Plain Tales* which is certainly a mini-masterpiece. This is 'The Broken-link Handicap'. It is about a jockey, Brunt, whose nerve has been shaken: riding in a race in Melbourne he was involved in a pile-up which he survived – but he heard a fellow-jockey say, as his own mare fell under him, 'God ha' mercy, I'm done for!' Now in India, he has only to ride Shackles (did Kipling feel himself in *shackles*, done for?) in a handicap to win. He is doing that successfully when he hears a whining voice saying 'God ha' mercy, I'm done for!' And he is. For he has confided his story to a gambler, whose evil ruse worked. The moral of this tale might well be said to be: *Don't tell anyone your secrets, ever, or you'll lose everything*!

It is irresistible here, if it is not done too earnestly, to compare the world of racing, pithily characterised by Kipling as 'rotten . . . two-thirds sham . . . looking pretty on paper only . . . immoral, and expensively immoral . . .', with life itself, whose conclusion is death. For Brunt, he tells us, *is* 'done for': he goes off shaking down the road, muttering, 'God ha' mercy, I'm done for!', and 'to the best of my knowledge and belief he spoke the plain truth'. It was a powerful, brief manner of reminding his readers that life could play dirty tricks on a man, even on a mere boy such as Brunt still was. Kipling also shows here his poetic mastery of significant proper names (this Brunt bore the brunt of doom and death, and early; he should not have put his hope in *shackles*), his pithy laconic faculty for suggesting tragedy without needing to state it, his choice of the right phrase: 'God ha' mercy, I'm done for!' – what could be more brutal or more to the terrible point? Or more economically moving?

Indian Fiction II

The group of stories we now know under the general title *Soldiers Three* are, taken together, classics, although minor ones. In 1888 A.G. Wheeler & Co., publishers of the *Pioneer*, decided to start an Indian Railway Library. They issued the first seven volumes, cheap booklets at a rupee each, in paper covers, towards the end of the year. The first six titles were by Kipling: *Soldiers Three*, *The Story of the Gadsbys*, *In Black and White*, *Under the Deodars*, *The Phantom Rickshaw* and *Wee Willie Winkie*. The first three volumes were eventually collected as *Soldiers Three* in 1895. It was Wheeler's senior partner, Emile Edward Moreau, who was responsible for putting Kipling on the international map.

It was Moreau, never acknowledged by Kipling, who proposed that he should publish some of the newspaper stories in book form: he offered him an advance on royalties, a substantial one for those days. Sampson Low published these books, which had designs by Lockwood, in England in 1890. But by that time Kipling could command better terms, and it is likely that he quickly and angrily stifled his gratitude to Moreau, whom he considered ought to have known his popular worth even before it became apparent.

Most readers may enjoy, or, more likely, imagine that they enjoy, the use of dialect – Cockney, Yorkshire and Irish – in *Soldiers Three*. Nowadays Kipling connoisseurs – I will not say ardent Kiplingites in this connection – have their doubts. Philip Mason goes so far as to put most of his quotations from Kipling's dialect passages into English. This use of dialect, in poetry as well as prose, seems initially to be a brilliant tour de force. But it becomes tiresome: as close examination makes immediately apparent, it is not authentic. It is a fictional model bearing little relation to these vernaculars. As such a model it is, doubtless, admirable. But Kipling never did understand Cockney, Yorkshire or Irish, although he came up with a very creditable (and patronising) imitation. However, the necessary effort (which Mason is honest in admitting defeats him; others are less honest) of translating from the pseudo-vernacular into English makes the reader pause. This directs his attention to the sense. In that way it amounts to a useful and clever device. But it becomes too monotonous. What reader, ploughing through the vigorous and interesting narrative detail, has not longed for the writer to move into plain English? The only vernacular Kipling went some way towards successfully capturing was that of East Sussex, where he lived for the last thirty-five years of his life. But the employment of that (he sometimes makes bad mistakes even here) does not act as an impediment to understanding. It is not as dense as Mulvaney's 'Irish'. It is a tribute to his energy, and to the compellingness of his narratives, that readers persisted. Wouldn't 'Love-o'-Women', one of

Kipling's earliest major stories, be improved by the absence of Mulvaney's contorted accents? As Mason says, this 'stage Irish' 'is hard to bear', and it does not sound like any Irish that anyone has ever heard.

In his use of dialect, then, he fails (as Hardy, less ambitious and more sure of what he was doing, did not); he is not Shakespearean in that, and he was clearly trying to be. But there really is a touch of Shakespeare in these fictions of soldierly companionship, and in the dialogue (if not the dialect) that he gives to his characters. Kipling was often vulgar, as Oscar Wilde was one of the earliest to point out, and his vulgarity sometimes let him down; but this particular subject required vulgarity of a bold kind. This was where Kipling's bold separation of himself from literature as it was then variously conceived, paid off. After all, as Michael Edwardes has pointed out, Kipling's critics of the turn-of-the-century, and afterwards, 'found it impossible to reconcile his honesty with his glorification of the military virtues'. Actually the glorification of the military virtues was for the most part confined to the strictly non-fictional persona he put up to the world. The Mulvaney–Learoyd–Ortheris tales can hardly be said to add up to any glorification of anything conventional, but they do glorify human vitality, the ability to bear up against foul conditions – the necessity of being called into action at any time, excessive heat, low pay, mismanagement from on high, ageing, sickness, the presence of death and, above all, boredom. They celebrate the common man, even if he is seen in a uniform.

Kipling believed in the realism of his tales about the other ranks, because his imaginative vision of those people, immediate and subversive and different, came into consciousness as a fact. But he invented what is appropriately called his subaltern-worship out of necessity, and never believed in it with his imagination: that is to say, his daimon did not believe in it. This existed on a grosser emotional plane, as a part of his very elaborate defence mechanism. He was always the sensitive artist beneath the worldly-wise imperialist, although much of his feeling-life was conducted under the aegis of the latter. What he sees in the lower end of military life are comedy, pity and horror. He does not really see much else, and certainly not the stuff of Empire.

For the stuff of Empire he has to turn to the officers who give the orders; but he is less convincing when he is dealing with them. How often, in these tales, the officers come in for it! In 'The God from the Machine', Mulvaney tells of how he stopped an unpleasant captain from eloping with the colonel's daughter. '"Hit a man an' help a woman, an' ye can't be far wrong anyways" – *Maxims of Private Mulvaney*' reads the epigraph, an apparent reverse of Kipling's normal attitude to women. But he saw fit to delete, in all editions after the first one in book form, a dedication, to 'that very strong man, T. ATKINS . . .'. I assume that he deleted this because some reader might infer, 'What! Stronger than officers!' In 'The Big Drunk Draf', in which Mulvaney has left the army and is on the Indian Railways, it is the ex-private who shows the young officer how to deal with a group of undisciplined men. In 'With the Main Guard', although two senior officers are extolled, a 'little orf'cer bhoy' is blooded 'like a young whelp'. And so on. The officers who *count* are invariably seen as having all the attributes of 'men'; but, like Kipling himself, they are gifted with know-how. Mulvaney is a hero but doesn't know it. His 'good' superiors are just like him, but with just that extra attribute. They share Kipling's own authorial arrogance. He is always at his most vital and vigorous when he sees the upper orders through the eyes of the lower, and, although it was his natural bent, he must have learned much from the Jacobean authors of town comedies about how to present it.

Yet the Mulvaney–Learoyd–Ortheris stories do not offer a true, a 'realistic' picture of the army. All three soldiers have qualities that real mercenary soldiers don't have, such as the ability to quote, with elegant variation, from literary sources. However, realism of that precise and necessarily dry sort isn't often the province of literature, because it is too boring, and because it lacks vision: literature is a distillation, through the eyes of the author's genius, of realistic experience. This is the case with even the great realists, George Eliot, Flaubert and Zola among them. The general picture Kipling gives is hugely apt, although its purpose is hardly to extol the virtues of the military. But it is wrong in its particulars, even if the wrongness is artistically right – and inevitable. As Michael Edwardes says, his is the only literary account of the nineteenth-century mercenary army that we have, 'and it is not misleading'. It is essential to separate the two strands, creative and pseudo-intellectual, in Kipling. This has proved difficult for many readers because of his immense influence, and because everyone has, naturally enough, taken him at face value. He took himself at face value for most of the time; but not when he was writing stories, when he contrived to put himself at the mercy of his daimon, which was, he claimed, an outside agency. But to take him at his face value is a mistake: even if it was necessary for him to make it, we do not have to.

Kipling, then, was wrong in his particulars: soldiers did not talk like that. Edwardes quotes Sir George Younghusband: 'I myself had served for many years with soldiers, but had never heard the words or expressions that Rudyard Kipling's soldiers used.' Then, Younghusband continued, 'a few years after, the soldiers thought, and talked, and expressed themselves exactly like Rudyard Kipling had taught them . . .' Well, it was not as direct as that. Robert Graves, who himself had had much more intimate and protracted contact with soldiers than ever Kipling had, suggested in 1923 that officers who had read Kipling accepted the picture, and moulded the men in that image. Was it really like that?

Rather, this demonstrates that Kipling had, after all, got the essence of it right: men, who like to be colourful, found that they could imitate him. But Graves's explanation is not quite correct. Officers don't teach men how to express themselves. The soldiers themselves read Kipling, and saw themselves in that role. And the officers, who had read and believed Kipling, reported them as being more like Ortheris and the rest than perhaps they actually were.

Kipling understood and felt more at home with soldiers than with officers; there were many reasons for this, some of them social. While he tended to idealise officers (as in 'Only a Subaltern'), he could not idealise common soldiers if he tried. One of his most moving poems, which incidentally gives a clue to his true attitude towards women, is 'Follow me 'Ome':

> There was no one like 'im, 'Orse or Foot,
>   Nor any o' the Guns I knew;
> An' because it was so, why, o' course 'e went an' died,
> Which is just what the best men do.

So it's knock out your pipes an' follow me!
An' it's finish up your swipes an' follow me!
  Oh, 'ark to the big drum callin'
    Follow me – follow me 'ome!

'Is mare she neighs the 'ole day long,
  She paws the 'ole night through,
An' she won't take 'er feed cause o' waiting for 'is step,
  Which is just what a beast would do.

'Is girl she goes with a bombadier
  Before 'er month is through;
An' the bans are up in church, for she's got the begger hooked,
  Which is just what a girl would do.

. . .

For it's "Three rounds blank" an' follow me,
An' it's "Thirteen rank" an' follow me;
  Oh, passin' the love o' women,
    Follow me – follow me 'ome!

Kipling had won a battle with Authority. No administrator or officer was going to take up the amorality presented in *Soldiers Three* and base his command on it. He was going to continue to apply conventional, hypocritical morality, even if he delighted privately in Kipling's tales of How Things Really Are. Yet the brash young journalist, not at all secure in his sexual role, envious because he could never lead a life of action, small, already balding, and looking twice his age, had got himself more than merely socially accepted by such people: he was almost lionised by them, even if they questioned his values. That had always been a part of 'the Scheme', as he described his plans for the future to Ted Hill.

One other of the Indian stories written after Kipling had established himself should be mentioned here: 'Without Benefit of Clergy' (1890). It first appeared in *Macmillan's Magazine*, then in two small collections, and finally in *Life's Handicap* (1891).

John Holden, a Civilian clerk, falls in love with a sixteen-year-old Muslim girl called Ameera, establishes her in a house with her mother, and visits her regularly. He keeps this a secret, as he is bound to do. Such affairs were not uncommon. When the story begins Ameera is expecting his child. This is safely born, despite its father's doubts and fears, and becomes the apple of its parents' eyes. But, like poor Muhammad Din, he dies, 'as many things are taken away in India – suddenly and without warning'. Grief unites Holden and Ameera in an even closer bond; but she dies in his arms of cholera, and her dwelling is destroyed by the landlord 'so that no man may say that this house ever stood'.

'Without Benefit of Clergy' is a mixture of Kipling at his best and, so far as the dialogue is concerned, Kipling at his not-so-good. The manner in which Holden's sensibility slowly becomes aware of his own natural pessimism about the universe in which he lives is perfectly done. When his child is about to be born he writes out a telegram to himself, announcing Ameera's death, and hands it to a servant to send on to him while he is away filling in for dying officials in another part of the country. The details of the story all describe ruin, confusion, accident, ugly incongruousness; and they frequently contrast the natural love of these two people of different races with the unnatural but inevitable clash of their upbringings and beliefs. Holden is at one point described as having 'the sensations of a man who has attended his own funeral'. Rushing in to see his new son he steps on and breaks 'a naked dagger' 'laid there to avert ill-luck': he does not really understand this Eastern observance. He is persuaded to offer a 'birth-sacrifice' by killing two goats; this eventually has an effect exactly opposite to what was intended; meanwhile, he is bewildered as the 'raw blood' spurts over his boots, and when this is noticed at his club, pretends it is dew. As he rides away after the killing of the goats, he feels full of 'riotous exultation', which clashes with a 'vast vague tenderness directed towards no particular object'; this makes him 'choke', and his horse is 'uneasy'. He feels a need to 'pull himself together'. The relationship is presented as, simultaneously, a tender and loving one, and a doomed one. When Holden walks into his club, just after observing a superstitious Moslem ritual, he sings 'at the top of his voice', 'In Baltimore a-walking, a lady I did meet!' Told that his boots are covered in blood, he says 'Bosh! . . . It's dew. I've been riding through high crops' – and continues to sing.

Holden's deception of his colleagues at the club should be noted as evidence that Kipling also knew something about this kind of sexual deception: it is much more convincing than his attempts to prove that he was in love with women. Kipling's narrative also continually insists on emphasising the incongruity of the lovers' approaches to their six-week-old baby: '. . . that is auspicious. And he was born on Friday under the sign of the Sun, and it has been told to me that he will outlive us and get wealth. Can we wish for aught better, beloved?' But she is wearing 'all that she valued most', and this includes not only clothes befitting a 'daughter of the Faith', but also 'certain gold bracelets that had no part in her country's ornaments, but, since they were Holden's gift . . . delighted her immensely'. This is certainly, among other things, a tragedy of the barriers raised by differing cultures and creeds against love. The couple discuss what they shall name the baby as it lies in Holden's arms: he

> scarcely dared to breath for fear of crushing it. The caged green parrot that is regarded as a sort of guardian Spirit in most native households moved on its perch and fluttered a drowsy wing.
> 'There is the answer,' said Holden. 'Mian Mittu has spoken. He shall be The Parrot. When he is ready he will talk mightily and run about. Mian Mittu is The Parrot in thy – in the Mussulman tongue, is it not?'
> 'Why put me so far off?' said Ameera fretfully. 'Let it be like unto some English name – but not wholly. For he is mine.'

Neither of their respective customs do them any good: there is a union of love, but not of true human understanding. Ameera wants both worlds, but cannot understand Holden's: she wants that only for love's, not understanding's, sake. Yet while their two worlds are contrasted, they are shown to be much the same, for all that her way is organised apparently more superstitiously than his. Neither is of any use against the cholera. If she has her gods, he has his club. His very secrecy, so necessary if he is to survive as a British official, functions as a kind of ritual custom. But all these observations are much of a muchness against fate: they are all shown to be useless.

But they continue together in happiness so great that the 'delight of that life was too perfect to endure'. The baby boy dies. Yet in their shared sorrow they 'touched happiness again, but this time with caution'. In these sentences are contained two keys to the author's temperament. They hardly require amplification: too much happiness in life cannot last; therefore we must learn to anticipate the end of happiness while enjoying it. All the time private happiness is being enjoyed, the 'Powers', as Kipling puts it, are 'busy on other things'. In the paragraph introducing the Member for Lower Tooting these 'things' are seen to include an allowance for 'thirty million people' of 'four years of plenty', so that the Member may promise 'the establishment of a duly qualified electoral system and a general bestowal of the franchise'. Kipling has been much criticised for this introduction of the Member for Lower Tooting and his liberal plans. Certainly it intrudes into the texture of a tale of tragic love. But it may be argued that it works. We assume perhaps too easily that it is simply a tiresome intrusion of Kipling's anti-liberal politics; that it has no place in the story. No doubt Kipling did, as he wrote it, feel that it would please the audience he was used to pleasing. But let us consider the fuller context. This is the last sentence of the allegedly offending paragraph:

> His long-suffering hosts smiled and made him welcome, and when he paused to admire, with pretty picked words, the blossom of the blood-red *dhak*-tree that had flowered untimely for a sign of what was coming, they smiled more than ever.

This, I suggest, functions as a comment not on the wickedness and stupidity of liberal politicians but on the futility of all politicians, as on the futility of all human plans for happiness. Throughout the story Western values are contrasted with Eastern. The English Holden might well feel that to see the early flowering of a tree as a portent of ill luck suddenly striking is merely superstitious. The fact is that Kipling makes the portent a valid one: cholera does strike. Whether this is a coincidence is not, of course, discussed. His aim is to contrast two different ways of seeing the same phenomena. The Deputy Commissioner tells Holden and other men at the club, of the Member:

> He won't bother any one any more. Never seen a man so astonished in my life. By Jove, I thought he meant to ask a question in the House about it . . . You needn't laugh, you fellows. The member for Lower Tooting is awfully angry about it; but he's more scared. I think he's going to take his enlightened self out of India.

This functions not as a comment on liberalism but as the kind of contemptuous remark about all politicians which seems just and truthful to readers. Literature, under certain circumstances, is one of the few non-pragmatic activities left, and Kipling is in no way actually violating the action of his story, which is one of personal love set against the ruthlessly separating violence of nature and the comic futility of 'progressive' Western political ideas. It may be argued that a man who thus depicts affairs is already forecasting, by implication, that the Empire itself is futile and doomed. And that was indeed the vision of the imaginative writer. But no one can exist, *in propria persona*, just as an imaginative writer. Such a person would certainly have given up writing as useless.

As well as drawing attention to the absurd bases of human happiness, Kipling in this story shows how the death of Ameera is caused by jealousy and doubt. Holden wants her to go to the Hills, where all the English are sending their wives:

> 'Very good talk. Since when hast thou been my husband to tell me what to do? I have but borne thee a son. Thou art only all the desire of my soul to me. How shall I depart when I know that if evil befall thee by the breadth of so much as my littlest fingernail – is that not small? – I should be aware of it though I were in paradise. And here, this summer thou mayest die – *ai, janee*, die! and in dying they might call to tend thee a white woman, and she would rob me in the last of thy love!'

Vainly Holden tells her that love is not born in a moment nor on a death-bed: she insists that his nurse would 'take thy thanks at last', and that, by her God, and by the Prophet and the Prophet's mother, she 'will never endure'. We should be reminded at this point that Ameera has been 'bought with silver' from her mother by Holden, and that she felt this 'slavery' deeply until she became pregnant. Then follow two sentences again characteristic of their author's temperament:

> There are not many happinesses so complete as those that are snatched under the shadow of the sword. They sat together and laughed, calling each other openly by every pet name that could move the wrath of the gods.

Ameera does die of the cholera – just as the rain is starting in the city, from which Holden hears 'shouts of joy'. Even as she dies, she is transfixed by jealousy, and tells Holden to take no hair from her head: '*She* would make thee burn it later on. That flame I should feel.'

Elliot L. Gilbert, in a discussion of this story, points out that the universe as it is pictured here is 'very nearly incapable of supporting human life'; he then says that it is 'through Holden' that we get this sense of human precariousness'. Now although Holden has no character as such, no psychology, he is presented as one who is certain of doom and death. When cholera strikes he is 'absolutely certain that her death would be demanded'. That is making the universe not only blundering but positively hostile: Holden is a pessimist. So Gilbert, who makes the odd error (in so extended a discussion) of referring to the liaison between Holden and Ameera as a 'marriage', has got it the wrong way round: it is Holden's perception of the universe that we are really being shown, not the universe. It may be like that or it may not, and in India it does seem so to foreigners; but we are seeing it through Holden, and we are seeing it because he has entered into a socially forbidden love. A person's own view of the universe can actually degrade it, and that is what we are being shown here.

Where the story falls down is in its stilted dialogue. It is supposed to be a love story, and Kipling had not dared to write many of these. Faced with the need to make the love between Holden and Ameera credible, he chooses to put into both their mouths an ineffective and unconvincing semi-Biblical English, stilted and poetical, and not at all as vigorous as the words he put into the mouths of his private soldiers. There is much unease and possibly ignorance here. How different are the words of the song Ameera sings to her still living child, to the sitar: 'And the wild plums grow in the jungle, only a penny a pound/Only a penny a pound, baba – only . . .' Or the words of Holden's servant Pir Khan when cholera strikes Ameera: 'When there is a cry in the night, and the spirit flutters into the throat, who has a charm that will restore?'

Not much knowledge of femininity is shown, tender though the tale undoubtedly is. Occasionally there is a pseudo-informed note, concealing lack of confidence, which jars, as when Ameera is depicted as growing happier 'when she understood that Holden was more at ease, according to the custom of women'. Is this the custom of women any more than it is the custom of men? It is in the other, non-sexual, details that Kipling is convincing: Ameera hanging up a black jar against the evil eye; Holden losing himself in his work and ritually visiting his club; Pir Khan giving solace to the man bereaved of his lover, 'Eat, sahib, eat. Meat is good against sorrow. I also have known. Moreover the shadows come and go, sahib; the shadows come and go. These be curried eggs'; then the landlord turning up after Ameera's death, 'portly, affable, clothed in white muslin, and driving a Cee-spring buggy'. Ms Tompkins, in her pioneering book, commented on the 'imperfections' in this tale, mentioning Kipling's dwelling for too long on the cholera-stricken city, and on the inappropriate language employed in some of the dialogue; but she could not put her finger on what was wrong. She could hardly have contemplated the fact of Kipling's disturbed sexuality.

Of the erotic actuality of Holden's and Ameera's love Kipling can give us nothing at all. Even an implication of it is absent. Would this have been different if Kipling had been able to depict Ameera as a young man? He would have lost the tragedy of the baby – and the nature of such a loss must have troubled his dreams, as it does those of all conscientious homosexuals – but might have gained something in physical immediacy. It will be remembered that the ambisexual Gide reprimanded Proust for depicting boys as girls. The story first appeared in June 1890, when Kipling had known the publisher Wolcott Balestier for almost a year. How he regarded this young American, who was to play so vital a role in his life, at the time of writing 'Without Benefit of Clergy' cannot be said (as we shall see) with certainty. By the September of that year his health had broken down. But he could not in any case even have begun to contemplate any direct expression of such a theme. Of course the assertion that Ameera, at the deepest level of the author's imagination, was a man, is speculative: to be able to accede to the possibility requires an open-minded judgement of the tone of the tale as whole, and of the depiction of Ameera in particular. The notion gains some strength from Ameera's remark to Holden after their baby boy has died: 'It was because we loved Tota that he died'; and when they feel joined by their sorrow, she says, 'We must make no protestation of delight, but go softly underneath the stars, lest God find us out.' Many of Kipling's readers may feel that they must deny themselves such an open-mindedness: that such a view casts some kind of slur on him. One can only in that case assert that it is not so.

'Passin' the Love O' Women!'

There must have been a reason for Kipling's distrust and fear of women, which is always evident even if frequently undermined. If Ameera of 'Without Benefit of Clergy' is unconvincing as a woman, her femininity being largely based on received ideas about femininity, and perhaps on Kipling's experiences of the older women whom he cultivated, there is still a conscientious attempt to redress the balance. In the earlier 'Beyond the Pale' Bisera's femininity is purely nominal, but the pathos of her amputated hands is supposed to appeal to the reader's sense of compassion as to how women should be treated.

The fear may have been born of a huge resentment towards the fact that he was expected by the world, like all other young men, to fall in love with and to marry a woman. It must have been galling to his considerable pride to have to pose as one of these, as he saw it, *victims*. He compensated for this by making a cult of mothers; this is seen at its worst in the story 'The Brushwood Boy'. But he made sure, especially when he got to London in October 1889, to pose as a healthy and normal young man, and to repudiate what he may have worried that people would take as his Pre-Raphaelite, and therefore suspect, past.

It is not as if Kipling were a coarse, jocular young man who knew no better. He did know better. Yet he had frequently to pose as such a man, and was actually forced into the especially awful and cheap sort of vulgarity about women that is apparent in the 'Maxims' (and occasionally elsewhere) in his early work. But he had chosen not to acknowledge his real sense of himself. Did he, indeed, in that kind of society, where mere survival was a strain anyway, have a choice? But the confusions resulting from his choice, an inevitable one, were to loom large when he came to write a novel. He always tried to question a set of values whose existence threatened his erotic wellbeing; but he employed the finest nuances of irony to do it, since he was ostensibly writing from the former set of values. That is why so many of the Indian tales deal with themes of deception, self-deception and distrust between people. Practical jokes, it must be remembered, involve deception. As Cornell has pointed out, one of the 'unifying themes' of *Plain Tales* is 'the difficulty of distinguishing reality from false appearances'. He 'returns again and again to the theme of deception and fraud'. 'False Dawn' is not about deliberate deception; but it is about falsity. The weakest and most sentimental stories, such as the mawkish 'Only a Subaltern', show him tipping over into conventionalism in high anxiety not to give himself away. He must early on have made a puzzled connection between what he thought 'wrong' about his sexual feelings, and this sensitivity. He did not want anyone else to make such a connection. Carrington approves of Bobby Wicks, the young subaltern, claiming that he is

> the finest specimen of a type which recurs in Kipling's stories . . . They have the public-school virtues of loyalty and common sense, and their absolute standard of honesty is never taken for granted. If they drink a little, the habit never interferes with their duty; if they wench, the weakness is kept decently out of sight. They are the young Anglo-Indians for whom and about whom much of his early work was written.
>
> You might suppose 'Bobby Wicks' crude, a philistine or a prig, but you would be wrong. His inarticulate unexpressiveness is a mask put up against the world to hide an emotional life which may be as strange as that of the 'Brushwood Boy', as rich as that of Holden . . .

This is too good to be true. Carrington doesn't allow for the hypocrisy that lay behind the 'public school virtues' – for all that they were, in isolation, virtues. It ignores the retrospective critical examination of public-school life by ex-public school boys that was conducted between the wars. It is the height of naïvety, in discussing a writer of quasi-naturalist fiction who was never a prude, to talk of 'decently' keeping 'wenching' 'out of sight', when writers are just those persons who have to analyse such 'forbidden' areas if they are to achieve true realism. But Carrington is honest, and so in that passage gives the game away. Bobby Wicks is a failure, for the reason I have given: Kipling in his over-anxiety to be identified with the tough, the righteous and the 'normal', tips over into sentimentality. Yet, as Carrington sees, he does give the otherwise too perfect Bobby an air of hiding some sort of 'strange' 'emotional life'. Carrington sees, too, that none of Kipling's women in the earlier stories 'quite stands alone: they are as they would appear to a very observant dancing-partner'.

But it is a pity that he feels that Kipling has 'fully understood' Bobby Wicks. As Angus Wilson observes, '"Only a Subaltern" is really distinguished by its Sunday-school-prize tone.' And Wilson quotes, tellingly, from the comment of Lord Lugard (soldier and administrator in India, Burma, the Sudan, pioneer of 'indirect rule', and eventually first high commissioner of Northern Nigeria) on an officers' mess tale by Kipling: 'His knowledge of the barrack room is greater than that of the officers' mess.' Yet Kipling so desperately wanted to find rest in somewhere like the officers' mess. He undermined that wish, as he tended to undermine all his most conscious aspirations, by his vivid tales of the barrack room. In his officer stories he is sentimental and false; in his common soldier tales he is vigorous.

In 'The Drums of the Fore and Aft' he partly succeeded in exploding the Victorian legend of child-saints by making his two children disgustingly depraved, and by attributing their rallying of the regiment, when it breaks, to drunkenness rather than to heroism. He is, once again, getting plenty of naturalistic relish out of it. He was coming as near to impropriety as he dared. But this by no means rescues the story from its inherently sentimental appeal.

It has to be added that the ever-resourceful Kipling obtained an advantage from being forced to assume the part of a vulgar misogynist. He managed to get an advantage out of most of his defeats. Oscar Wilde noted, in his remarks on *Plain Tales*, that they made one feel as if one were 'seated under a palm-tree reading life by *superb* flashes of vulgarity' (the italics are mine). He is, Wilde continued, 'a reporter who knows vulgarity better than anyone has known it'.

It was in 1887, after he had left the Allahabad Club for the hospitality of the Hills in their bungalow, that Kipling wrote 'Baa, Baa, Black Sheep'. He probably felt upset and unhappy with his parents because by the time he left their house they were beginning to stifle him, and possibly to make him uneasy. His mother in particular, a sharp woman, a little in competition with him, might well have taunted him, if unconsciously, about his romantic disposition or lack of it. Alice might well have felt anxious: 'a mother knows', as Rudyard himself would certainly have put it. Perhaps he felt that he could best pursue his act of revenge, which would also help serve to justify the persona he would adopt in the next stage of his planned progress, under the aegis of his new confidante Edmonia (Ted) Hill. That he could not suppress the story demonstrates that there was still some buried conflict between him and his mother, doubtless compounded, on both sides, of anxiety as well as competition. Carrington, who always gives the impression of knowing by hearsay more than he will say, remarks that Mrs Hill was 'a kinder critic' than Wheeler and 'Kipling's sharp-tongued mother'. Ted Hill wrote:

> It was pitiful to see Kipling living over the experience, pouring out his soul in the story as if the drab life was worse than he could possibly describe it. He was in a towering rage at the recollection of those days.

Clearly he was determined to be theatrical about the matter, and decided, now away from home, to make a great production out of it. But if he was in a 'towering rage' then it is not hard to conclude against whom it was directed. It seems as if he was prepared to blame all his terrible peculiarities on the Southsea episode, which was in turn the responsibility of his mother. In the vivid little story he combines the nursery rhyme with the notion of the black sheep of a family – and a black sheep, because of his secret tastes and the dangerous and self-threatening tenderness that they generated, he certainly felt himself to be. He may have known that the wool of the black sheep really was less valuable than that of the white, and that this was the origin of the phrase 'black sheep'; perhaps he also knew that the black sheep was the *mauvais sujet*, the thorn in the side, the bitter in the cup, the object of aversion, the *bête noire* who bears the devil's mark. The story, with its savage unstated reprimand of his mother, was something he needed to get off his chest, since it served as justification for his public announcement that such grave damage had been done to him by her (she asks his forgiveness in the story), that henceforth the bitter waters of 'Hate, Suspicion and Despair' can never be wholly washed away by 'all the Love in the World'. In December 1890 he felt impelled to confess in an article that 'Baa, Baa, Black Sheep' was 'not true to life'.

Soon after this he was openly discussing his plan to become a full-time writer in London. He said to Ted Hill, of what he now called 'the Scheme', '*Am* I still for it? You know that, if it is possible, I most assuredly *am* . . . I want rest somehow.' Rest from what? It seems that keeping up a front in India was exhausting him to such an extent that he was getting to the verge of a breakdown. He was soon, at the very height of his phenomenal success in London, to come near to another.

But he kept his end up in this last period in India. He was writing journalism regularly, and travelling a great deal. He was in demand; but there was also hostility to him, which he felt deeply. This is evident in the comment of the Anglo-Indian social historian Dennis Kincaid, who wrote (1939): 'Simla remained cold. The fellow was clearly a bounder; his stories of life in the Hills were informed by the natural envy of a cad who had sought and been refused an entrée into Simla society.' Kipling may have subscribed to the world-view of the wise administrator and the experienced officer, but he resented those whom he regarded as representative of the sort of people who resolutely refused to review his books – and they included the 'spokesmen for Anglo-Indian culture', the *Calcutta Review* and the *Asiatic Quarterly Review*. He was suffering from tachycardia during the summer of his last full year in India, and his condition doubtless heightened the tension between him and his parents when he spent a month at Simla with them. These tensions are implied in a letter he wrote to Mrs Hill at that time, from which Carrington quotes. He has been telling her about his dog and how he knew that he had

> come back to the old life and the ways thereof.
>
> But not wholly, for it is owned that I am no longer ownable and only a visitor in the land. The Mother says that is so and the Sister too and their eyes see far – 'You belong to yourself,' says the Mother, and the Maiden says: – 'You don't belong to us at any rate,' and in the making of this confession we come together after the wreck of the old home on a new and pleasant platform.

Carrington does not record, and perhaps does not know, what Kipling's reaction was to being told that his mother was glad that he was now living with the Hills at their bungalow in Allahabad, called Belvedere, and he records her admonition, 'Living alone has made you so cold and uninterested,' she said. 'You'll have to be civil, Ruddy.'

But, characteristically, he expressed his anxieties and fatigue by getting beyond himself, annoying his editor, provoking the retiring Viceroy (by a set of verses), and being generally, in Carrington's words, 'too ready to assert his views'. There is also evidence to suggest that, at this point (he was now twenty-three) his mother, although she wanted him to go to London to try out his luck there, was pressing various girls on him. As Carrington writes, 'Simla abounded as ever with pretty unattached girls.' He was still torn between love of India and scorn for her backwardness. Emotionally he felt more affinity for Hinduism than for Christianity. But he began to form the notion that the India that *he* loved could be preserved only by British rule. He refused, in effect, to examine the paradox involved. The notion gradually hardened into a dogma. There was an increasing polarisation in him between feeling, creative fiction, and thinking (or what passed, with him, for thinking) journalism. He was at this time doing rather more journalism than fiction.

Some of the journalism was brilliantly descriptive. The rest was uneasy, expressing slightly different views in different short pieces. Writing about it retrospectively in 1890 he expressed – and dogmatised – his dilemma:

'parallel straight lines as everyone does *not* know . . . will never meet'. His own two views of experience would never meet, either. I think he identified his 'forbidden' sexual inclinations with his poor eyesight, his clumsiness, his lack of distinction in active affairs such as sport or riding. Had he not been possessed of the true writer's passion for the truth of things, he might have developed, as so many homosexuals of his generation developed, into a conventional reactionary, particularly hard on homosexuality. We now see more clearly than we used to that the man (I am speaking of male homosexuality here) who is obsessed with the necessity to punish homosexuality is above all most afraid not only of homosexual tendencies in himself, but also of any tenderness or 'femininity' which he may suspect partakes of homosexual feeling. In those harsh days, and especially amongst the Anglo-Indians, all of whom had to pose as worldly-wise and hard, any man who discovered that he had homosexual feelings was likely in fact to touch upon an especial tenderness, precisely because this kind of feeling, while authentic, was so forbidden. It is not only in private, but positively in secret, that most people discover their most delicate and loving emotions. No reader of the mass of Kipling's Indian prose and poetry is possibly going to miss the shafts of tender feelings: they are buried, but they nonetheless shine out of their little graves, as, artistically, they are supposed to do.

All that writing, as some of the writing that came after it, might even be seen as a metaphor for the being of a man convinced that personal love must be denied to him. In the moving poem 'Follow Me 'Ome', more unequivocally homosexual than anything by Hopkins or Housman, Kipling triumphantly pounces on the homosexual element – natural enough, in all conscience – in comradeship. Society and its spokesmen have felt that this is indeed so 'natural' that it must not be described as homosexual at all. But why not? What is more natural than that beneath the hardness, the profligacy, the dishonesty of uneducated men, should lurk the fragile, intuitive awareness and responsiveness that we call feminine – and that is more to the fore in the personalities of Western women than Western men?

> 'E was all that I 'ad in the way of a friend,
>   'An I've 'ad to find one new;
> But I'd give my pay an' stripe for to get the beggar back,
>   Which it's just too late to do!

The poem is a lament for the death of a forbidden love perfectly evoked in the only manner in which it could acceptably be evoked at that time. It is a great triumph of tone and good and decent feeling in a style quite new in English literature. Kipling failed with Bobby Wicks because Bobby was the sort of man with whom he could very easily fall in love. That was too near the bone. He had to kill him off. But in the area of the common soldier, whose vigour he celebrated with natural and joyous gusto, he can locate and exactly define the profound simplicity of love. Also he can, in the extraordinary manner he developed, smuggle in his own private meaning and create a place for it that is artistically not short of perfect: '*Oh, passin' the love o' women!*'

Law and Order

It is easy to see why Rudyard finally lined himself up, in those last months in India, with the forces of Law and Order against those of 'anarchy'. The latter represented all the forbidden tenderness and lawlessness within himself by which he felt threatened; it also represented much that he loved. The daimon, that outside agency to which he would come to attribute his inspiration, continued to see every side of questions, relentlessly exploring paradoxes, doggedly discovering order in chaos. But the artificial yet fiercely determined pseudo-mind of the mask behind which he would confront society was made up. However, because of the peculiarities of his situation and the demands of his daimon, there were odd inconsistencies. These would always puzzle even his admirers, and the ardent Kiplingites who wanted, and who still want, to agree with his views. The mask is not the real Kipling, not the private, living and feeling man. So the inconsistencies are very evident.

For example, he admired the people who ran things, who 'enforced order', 'so long as they rode about on horses' (Mason). Let them sit down at a desk and they instantly became despicable, 'objects of derision'. He really did regard people like himself, bespectacled swots below average height 'who read books and could not play games', with fear and dislike, which he frequently transformed into a facile scorn, and early on developed a trait of self-hatred. Because he liked to be honest with himself in private, he was aware, too, that he was not even much of a swot – his academic record, except in 'artistic' subjects, was poor. Perhaps Price had actually told his parents that – since he was hopeless at games – he could not even guarantee that he could get him into Oxford or Cambridge, whatever the cash situation.

In October 1888 he was seeing much of the 31st East Surreys, stationed at Allahabad; his closest friend of that time was a Captain Bayless. How did he regard this young officer, and others like him, including one who was killed in action on the frontier, in relation to himself? The answer can only be speculative. But writers do leave clues. Everything written, whatever else it is, is inescapably an autobiographical record. If the writer seeks quite deliberately to be non-autobiographical, as Nabokov claimed he did, and as I believe Kipling himself did in certain important respects, he still leaves clues: in what he chooses, in what he selects, in what he omits. But that inevitable autobiographical record is not the chief feature of successful creative work. It is a by-product. The chief feature of any work, as writers of all sorts well understand, is its intellectual and emotional viability. Does it enlighten its readers, expand and enrich insight into life, illumine what were murky or unexplained areas? I have drawn attention to Kipling's capacity, largely intuitive, for satisfying himself as well as his reader in that respect.

He is notorious amongst his more critical readers for occasionally going very badly wrong, for giving us a tale that is all too obviously a clumsy effort at revenge or a strained and unconvincing attempt to ridicule somebody or thing which the author too uncritically hates. He is notorious, in other words, for his lapses. Yet concomittently he is celebrated for his high subtlety, especially notable in a writer who was in so many ways determined to undermine readers' literary expectations. It is easy to understand why his writings were accused of appealing to authoritarian philistines. They did! But his insistent artistic superiority in setting puzzles – in being cryptic – tends to be ignored, 'literary' though that habit is. He envied and wanted to resemble his friend Henry James, whom he met as soon as he reached London, and that influence persisted, and even grew.

Here, in respect of his most intimate thoughts in regard to men like Captain Bayless, a story first printed in the *Civil and Military* of April 1887 is relevant. 'The Conversion of Aurelian McGoggin' was later collected into *Plain Tales*. This 'tract' as Kipling unashamedly (and not to his ultimate advantage) called it in its first sentences ('This is not a story exactly. It is a Tract . . .'), is an anxious study in vanity; but it had the perfectly private function of warning its author of what he might become. It is fearful self-parody: Kipling, when in the company of the young officers with whom he knew he might too easily go over the permitted borderline, saw himself, realistically enough, as just such a creature as the clever McGoggin. That he could do this had the virtue, for him, of demonstrating that he was not. The epigraph is:

> Ride with an idle whip, ride with an unused heel,
> But, once in a way, there will come a day
> When the colt must be taught to feel
> The lash that falls, and the curb that galls, and the sting of the rowelled
> steel.

Thus Kipling hopefully envisages himself as lashed and curbed (he spoke of this, the reader will recollect, in another epigraph). The tale has many implications: McGoggin, being of a type to focus the author's anxieties, is endowed with a set of opinions that also concerned his creator. He is made into an atheist because Kipling wanted to defend himself against the chaos inherent in this tendency. Atheism, whether it is 'true' or not, does notoriously arouse such anxieties. McGoggin's atheism is inspired by Comte and Spencer, as Kipling's (inasmuch as it was atheism and not plain doubt) was not. But it was still atheism. The young author, influenced by the general drift of Darwinism although not deeply read in the controversy, was busy trying to found a new religion against chaos. In this he resembled his contemporaries. Like Dostoievsky, and quite beyond his own personal needs, he felt the terrible weight of the fact that life without God was life without meaning, purpose or order. His nature, like Dostoievsky's (and like Nietzsche's, too, for that matter), felt too intensely the claims of the will to power. But the process of creating a new personal religion that would satisfy him by being nothing less than true for him was only just stirring.

There is some evidence, albeit in as ambiguous a form as he could possibly make it, as to how Kipling felt at this time about religion. Not so long after writing this story, while staying in America on his leisurely return to London, Kipling became engaged to Caroline Taylor, the younger sister of Mrs Hill. Alice Kipling had always been a little jealous of the vital and amusing Mrs Hill, as she must have been of all Kipling's various other maters; certainly she was a little afraid, when Professor Hill died, that Kipling might marry Mrs Hill. However, he had not died by then, and Kipling was doing all he could to get at Mrs Hill as mater-cum-girlfriend. He had left Calcutta on 9 March 1889, but he did not reach England (Liverpool) until 5 October of the same year. He must have felt that he needed some rest before putting the Scheme into effect. Ted Hill had been seriously ill with meningitis, and decided to spend her convalescence at home in America. George Allen asked Kipling to send back travel sketches for the *Pioneer*. It all added together very well: he booked up for Rangoon, Singapore, Hong Kong, Yokohama and then San Francisco; he would travel in the company of the Hills.

Eventually, after over-confidently and brashly alienating himself from as many Americans as possible ('they delude themselves into the belief that they talk English', and the American 'stuffs for ten minutes thrice a day' were just two of his comments), he ended up at the home of the Taylors in Pennsylvania. He was still over-excited and injudicious, but not without resources: when the Hills left him alone in San Francisco for a few days he found another mater for himself, his own mother's friend Mrs Carr, who showed him around. Ted Hill's father was a professor at a small college, and Kipling stayed at his house in Beaver, a town north-west of Pittsburgh, for about eight weeks. Carrington writes:

> 'Ted' must have occasionally been embarrassed by her devoted admirer, though no grain of evidence survives to suggest that Rudyard ever spoke to her as a lover. Almost any happily married woman in her position would have discreetly diverted his attention to her younger sister, unattached and near to Rudyard's age . . .

It is worth bearing in mind that young men who find themselves uncomfortably attracted by their own sex frequently look out for a motherly woman to initiate them into the sorts of mysteries that might release them from their severe embarrassment. Some men, by a successful transference of tender expression from one sex to another, have achieved freedom from a homosexuality which they have not desired. Such looking-out, all of it non-verbal, but giving everything that is said a special nuance, fills the air with tension. Possibly Ted Hill 'diverted' Kipling's attention towards her young unmarried sister in such a way as to make him feel trapped into the necessity of proffering a gesture that was really a surreptitiously reproachful one at herself. Carrington's comment is again appropriate: Kipling was 'now in love', he says, with American girls – but not with the particular specimen which had been laid before him by Mrs Hill. Once again, those who have the most information about Kipling's real state of mind recognise that he was not genuinely in love with Caroline Taylor; but they miss the possibility of the, alas, too impolite alternative. He travelled to Liverpool with Ted and with her sister and thence to London.

After the Hills left for India he wrote several letters to Caroline. The language in which he wrote was that of the too conventional lover. Clearly their author does not know how to go about it, and feels nothing. The letters are thus wholly unconvincing as love letters. Carrington calls them, with their mixture of 'dog-like devotion' and 'bland condescension', 'the common form of calf-love'. But this explanation is inadequate. Here was this young man, who had tried and failed to be so 'knowing' about love in his stories, writing letters that were clumsily unfelt. Calf-love is a not very well defined term for immature love: one might mean by it anything from the expression of the agonising and unforgettable unrequited love of adolescence to the sort of emotionless rhetoric so notoriously present in George Bernard Shaw's letters to Mrs Patrick Campbell. These letters of Kipling's are literary compositions in which all feeling is meticulously kept at a distance. Shaw's letters to Mrs Campbell are comic as a revelation of their author's ignorance of the real language of sexual love. Kipling's letters to Caroline Taylor are not comic; they are boring exercises. He may not have known how men make love to women, but he knew a very great deal more about tenderness between human beings (as is apparent in some of his stories) than he displays in this set of frigid and embarrassing declarations.

One of them, however, does not pretend to be about love. It is about religion: on 9 December 1889 he felt impelled to counter a strong (but erroneous) impression that Caroline had formed of him, namely, that he was considering becoming a Roman Catholic. She shared her father's Methodist faith, and seems to have been serious about it. It was something Professor Hill had casually said that worried her.

> Your slave was baptised in Bombay Cathedral into the Church of England . . . was brought up as you have read in that church, and confirmed . . . Does that satisfy that I am not a veiled adherent of the Church of Rome? You have got from me what no living soul has ever done before. I believe in the existence of a personal God to whom we are personally responsible for wrongdoing – that it is our duty to follow and our peril to disobey the ten ethical laws laid down for us by Him and His prophets. I disbelieve directly in eternal punishment, for reasons that would take too long to put down on paper. On the same grounds I disbelieve in an eternal reward. As regards the mystery of the Trinity and the Doctrine of Redemption, I regard them most reverently but I cannot give them implicit belief . . .
>
> I believe in God the father Almighty, maker of Heaven and Earth and in One filled with his spirit Who did voluntarily die in the belief that the human race would be spiritually bettered thereby.

For a doubting Thomas under pressure this is creditable. It is, after all, a conscientious denial of Jesus Christ as the Son of God. He could not and would not suppress his pessimism. This was plainly unorthodox. But the religiously minded Kipling who doubted the Christian faith was not going to take God's name in vain, and confess to a faith he did not possess. As for directly disbelieving in eternal punishment, even at the cost of also disbelieving in eternal reward: it was a pretty honest compromise in that age, even if homosexual feeling is not forbidden in the ten ethical laws.

In the McGoggin story, written some eighteen months earlier, he was, however light-heartedly, examining the consequences of atheism.

Attacking Comte and Herbert Spencer in the person of a narrator rather more knowing than he was in matters of religion, he plainly deplores McGoggin's 'rarefied religion' which 'only proved that men had no souls, and there was no God and no hereafter, and that you must worry along somehow for the good of humanity'. The critical tone, the wise denunciation of the insufficiency of this creed, are unmistakable. And Kipling needs must bring in an irrelevancy: that 'one of its minor tenets seemed to be that the one thing more sinful than giving an order was obeying it'. The necessity of obedience, thoroughly undermined by Kipling in *Soldiers Three* and elsewhere, is not relevant to the existence of a soul, of God or of a hereafter. But in Kipling's artificial system it must be so. There is the true system, too, buried in his creative work, and incomplete – by its very nature it is not as immediately accessible. In that, obedience to the orders of other human beings is not necessary, although it might be adopted for one reason or another.

But the two systems disconcertingly overlap. The false system is generated by painful need, the true by needful pain; the former is imperative, the latter humble. Once (in May 1918) his friend Rider Haggard, author of *She* and *King Solomon's Mines*, suggested to him, when he was feeling despondent, that he should be consoled by the 'fact that he had wide fame and was known as "the great Mr Kipling"'. He thrust this idea away with a 'gesture of disgust': 'What *is* it all worth? . . . We are only telephone wires . . . You didn't write *She* you know; something wrote it through you!' He meant this: no man resisted the terrors of being a 'celebrity' more than Kipling. Alas, his biographers have almost without exception assumed that Success must be a Very Good Thing, whatever else is not. They will concede that a Successful Man Needs His Privacy, but they will not grant Kipling's own hostility to Success.

What we see here is the process by which he built up the artificially rigid structure of his thoughtless conservatism, his false system. It is stiff with fear and tension. Kipling the conservative can't afford to see his own very real and sincere religious doubt in a sympathetic light. He relegates it to the altogether too absurd McGoggin. It worries him so much that he just won't regard it seriously. So while writing the story he sees only fitfully that McGoggin is in many ways a nervous caricature of himself: he can patronise him infinitely, diminish him, and make him of no account whatsoever. But when he came to write to Caroline, under pressure, his conscience would not allow him to lie, to make a conventional declaration of faith. Yet his religious feelings had not then more than started to develop; he had not begun to evolve a personal religion.

In the McGoggin tale (which is mixed in quality, but always revealing), Kipling goes on to delineate the atheistic faith. He will not 'say a word against this creed': it was 'built up' in fog-bound cities where 'a man grows to think that there is no one higher than himself'. In India, though, whence McGoggin has come, 'where you really see humanity . . . most folk come back to simpler theories'. Kipling's justification for this assertion could not honestly, as a sincere doubter without a personal religion, be based in faith. And it isn't. It is based, unconvincing and feeble though it is, on the only thing he knows: the imperial hierarchy of command. This is another example of the operation of his artistic conscience: he won't cheat in the matter of religion. If he had, then he would have avoided the matter of

God and Queen Victoria. Rhetorical cheating would have got him by with more aplomb.

What went wrong with McGoggin, Kipling continues, is that he couldn't keep his 'beliefs' to himself. The trouble was that both his grandfathers had been Wesleyan preachers (so of course had Kipling's own): 'the preaching strain came out in his mind'. So he needed everyone at the Club to know that they had no souls, too. Thus they would 'help him to eliminate his Creator'. It is clear that Kipling intended McGoggin to be, in this context, the fool that has said in his heart that there is no God – and he is a fool too, Kipling's daimon made sure of at least that. The wiser ones told McGoggin that certainly he had no soul: he was too young yet. But he must not assume that his seniors were as underdeveloped. (Here Kipling expresses hope for himself: he was twenty-one.) They tried to educate him by throwing cushions at him, calling him the Blastoderm, and 'strove to choke him' that way, as he was becoming an 'unmitigated nuisance'. 'Not a soul was interested in McGoggin's soul', the narrator light-heartedly puns.

McGoggin, 'all head, no physique and a hundred theories', continues to do his office work 'brilliantly'; but, like his creator, 'he could not accept any order without trying to better it'.

> That was the fault of his Creed. It made men too responsible and left too much to their honour. You can sometimes ride an old horse in a halter, but never a colt . . . he worked too much, and worried and fretted over the rebukes he received, and lectured away on his ridiculous creed out of office, till the Doctor had to warn him that he was overdoing it . . . But McGoggin was still intellectually 'beany' and proud of himself and his powers, and he would take no hint . . . One day the collapse came – as dramatically as if it had been meant to embellish a Tract.

One stiflingly hot day at the Club the Rains at last come, and usher in the cool. The heat of India was always a symbol, for Kipling, of evil and madness and chaos. It was something he had experienced, and he writes of it with a demonic intensity. A member says, 'Thank God!' McGoggin asks in his usual tiresome way: 'Why? I assure you it's only the result of purely natural causes . . .' and so forth. He is told to shut up, and, as he gets up to bring a paper to a member, appears to go mad. 'Perfectly conceivable – dictionary – red oak – amenable – cause – retaining – shuttle-cock – alone.' The doctor pronounces it not insanity but *aphasia*: 'complete loss of control over the speech and memory'. He is sent to the Hills to recover, but cannot understand how he could have lost control of his own speech and memory. We are given to understand that he spends the rest of his time in India as a sort of zombie: 'Something had wiped his lips of speech, as a mother wipes the milky lips of her child, and he was afraid – horribly afraid.' This is an interesting and dense simile: obsessive and unholy speech as the 'dirty' regurgitations or remnants of first food from the mother's breasts, wiped casually away. Yet does not the very impiety come from the mother, and is she not thus, although very obliquely, blamed, if only for giving birth? The story ends:

> So the Club had rest when he returned; and if ever you come across Aurelian McGoggin laying down the law on things Human – he doesn't

seem to know as much as he did about things Divine – put your forefinger
to your lip for a moment, and see what happens.
Don't blame me if he throws a glass at your head.

This, as well as being an incidental warning to himself, is about a
certain type of vanity. The vanity is that of the obsessed mind. And
Kipling did himself, and in spite of himself, become a McGoggin in his
insistent and obsessed imperialism. This obsessiveness made many of his
most grateful readers ashamed of owning up to a love for him; for years it
was not fashionable to consider him, although it was always more absurd
to dismiss him. Such sentences as 'This is not a story exactly. It is a Tract'
come perilously near to preaching, however facetious. He is preaching
against preaching.

Authoritarianism

When Kipling left India, then, the foundations of his imperialism were laid. But it was different in many ways from the other imperialism with which it inevitably became associated. His opposition to any kind of real self-rule for the Indians was based on his love for his own India: he did not want this to be changed by anyone, neither by interfering administrators who didn't understand the rules, nor obsessional atheists, nor, above all, by liberals who did not know anything about how tough the real world was.

What can only be called his authoritarianism brings us very near to the heart of the problem of why Kipling is, as C.S. Lewis put it, loved or hated, very seldom 'liked a little'. He is, Lewis brilliantly suggested, admired as a 'mistress or a country rather than a writer'. The common reader is as likely to be politically 'right' as 'left' in his views; he is even more likely, as the supreme arbiter of taste, to be both critical of a simplistic political divisiveness that prevents issues being taken on their merits, and self-critical in a manner that political dogmatists cannot afford to be. Since this common reader is devoted to seriousness he is likely to be interested in what Plato called The Good. He thinks he may be a political animal; but he values his reading more than much else in his life because he would like to divorce himself, but in a responsible manner, from politics as it is practised. He sets what he learns from his reading against what he knows to be his prejudices. This common reader, elusive though he (and she) is, may think of 'authoritarianism' either as a much discussed concept or, more vaguely, as an attitude common to such people as German Nazis, British reactionaries and Soviet communists. Thus the common reader has not been wrong to *worry* about Kipling.

C.S. Lewis thought that there were two things against him. One was that he compressed his stories too much, so that you could not always know what was going on, and 'it is all unrelieved vitamins from the first word to the last'. The other objection was that he was the 'slave of the Inner Ring' (the 'in-people'). 'The spirit of the Inner Ring is morally neutral – the obedient servant of valour and the public spirit, but equally of cruelty, extortion, oppression, and dishonesty.' The Inner Ring, a very elaborate thing for Kipling, and one that will be recognised by all his readers, is the secret society of those really 'in the know', those who fully understand by exactly what nods and winks 'things get done': callow fellows reprimanded, liberals given their comeuppance, ignorant lovers the boot, bullies their medicine, young-heroes-to-be the undeserved cane . . .

The Inner Ring is a more fictional sort of model than the so-called 'authoritarian personality', and it arises from a terrified insecurity. The sort of thing you would expect from a badly sighted, small, clumsy young chap who desperately wants to be one of the tough men, in on the great secret. Yet as Lewis also says, Kipling 'presented the magic of the Inner Ring in all its manifold workings for the first time'. But he can't stand outside it, Lewis continues, and criticise it. And surely, if he does show so clearly that we all need 'licking into shape', which may be true, then *justice* is very important? Kipling's schoolmasterly means of telling us that we all need lashing and curbing is unattractive, and may legitimately be criticised. But the medium is not all the message, and there is a nasty truth in the message. '*There ain't no justice*', felt the man who had been denied 'normal love'. His insistence on the absurdity and unmanliness of complaining at injustice is nonetheless, as Lewis says, reprehensible and insensitive. 'It is the ubiquitous presence of the Ring, this unwearied knowingness, that renders his work in the long run suffocating and unendurable,' Lewis concludes. But then, a sentence or two further on, he changes his mind. 'But he was a very great writer.'

Now how can someone whose work is *suffocating* and *unendurable* be 'very great'? Lewis was a careful and conscientious critic. Part of the confusion arises from the use of the wholly subjective word 'great': we all know what we mean by it when we use it, but we never understand it when anyone else uses it – unless we agree. Most of the confusion is sown, though, by Kipling himself, and by the dual nature of his achievement. Lewis means, 'and yet after saying that, I do like him very much.' We cannot even agree with ourselves about him.

It will soon be seen, then, that Kipling's personality is by no means irrelevant to the now accepted concept of 'the authoritarian personality' – accepted, I should say, by all those who would not wish to call themselves authoritarians. Undoubtedly this latter is a fictional model, based upon hostile generalisations about Nazis, anti-semites and American 'fascists' (all exceedingly unpleasant people, it may be claimed); but many of its findings have stood up well to eminently 'scientific' investigations carried out over the years: the model, if one is wise enough to remember that it is only that, may usefully be seen as relevant both to reality, and to Kipling. All in all, it is one of the better guides to the workings of the irrational world, and to the laws to which it prefers to conform. Let us, then, give a brief account of this celebrated model.

Authoritarians tend to look out for, in order to condemn, reject and punish, violations of in-values ('the Inner Ring'); they are opposed to the imaginative and the tender-minded. They tend not to have parents but rather, in the words of one commentator, 'Mother's Day' and 'Father's Day'. Their parents are paradigms, not real people at all. The parents of the authoritarian are frozen, by fear and anxiety, into faultless idealised stereotypes. Like Kipling, the authoritarian is explicitly (as distinct from thoughtfully or reticently) ethnocentric. He projects his own faults onto other people. Thus the authoritarian homosexual, who will tend to lump homosexuality together with dirt, Jewishness, striking workers, unions and Blacks, as generally bad (because his father and mother, the police and other authority figures taught him this), will repress his homosexuality and call for the castration of perverts. If he is or feels himself to be a weakling then he will extol strength, and so forth. He is dogmatic. Interestingly, in view of the Kiplings' difficulties over social position in India, one of the factors in the formation of an authoritarian personality is parental anxiety over status. All this is familiar enough, and is now often turned into jargon by self-avowed liberals who draw it out of books – and who frequently are themselves concealed authoritarians.

This apparent authoritarianism is important because it spoils a part of Kipling for us. Or it at least worries us until we can understand it. It cannot be ignored or swept under the carpet or modified (even Angus Wilson tries to modify the anti-semitism by referring to the evidence that he was in some ways 'in favour' of Jews – this implies some sort of concession on his part, and that is not good enough). He is worth rescuing from this morass, but it cannot be done by pretending it is not there. The fact is that Kipling's public views are, for the most part, unpleasantly familiar. As we shall see, Kipling really meant something else, and so the rant is frequently interrupted and modified by good sense. He distrusted all politicians, but made the error of aligning himself with ones so extreme as to be unfit for office. He must be said to have lacked a sense of responsibility in that respect: his art has a valid message which is in certain disconcerting ways analogous to his ugly political message; it is a deeply gloomy one, but quite different from the ill-tempered stream of polemic which issued from him. We know (or, at least, I am suggesting on the only sort of evidence that would, in the nature of things, be available) that he had reason to imagine himself as secretly on the side of evil and chaos, which in the perception of society at that time he indeed was.

Kipling, like his left-wing counterpart George Bernard Shaw, admired Mussolini uncritically. When an attempt was made on the Duce's life by an Irishwoman, Lavinia Gibson, he rejoiced in pointing out that she was not a British subject but a 'Free Stater', and therefore she came into the category of people who had 'foot and mouth' disease. People are entitled to their lapses in private – but Kipling's lapses of that kind are unrelieved by humanitarian considerations. He recommended Mussolini to many of his correspondents, extolling him for saving money by forbidding strikes: he was a 'strong man ruling alone'. He was worried lest the assassination attempt might have damaged his eyesight. The victory of the British government over the General Strike was a 'victory for civilisation'; he refused to consider what conditions might have led to its happening in the first place. In other words, on this matter, he was totally blind to justice. He could not understand that the terms on which the General Strike was settled would lead inevitably to the eventual return of an effective Labour government (which it did in 1945), that the pendulum would swing the other way for a time. He would not countenance, and his polemic never makes the least allowance for, those manifestions of history which he did not like. He is quite as blind in this respect as any dedicated Stalinist. He could not see that the wing of conservatism which profoundly and truly desired reforms was anything other than socialist. Had he lived to hear Macmillan quip that he had been the most socialist prime minister of the century, he would not have been amused. Conservatives claim with justice that they as much as Labour (and Liberals) fathered the welfare state. That would have meant to Kipling that they were socialists. It simply is not true.

His objections to such things as the welfare state are cogent; but they are robbed of all force because they do not concede that the

motives behind it were not all foolish. Kipling lacked the compassion
of that true Tory, Dr Johnson. He saw all the virtues of strong rule
by one man (such as Mussolini's), but none of the pitfalls. He was
insensitive to man's ill-treatment of man on the flimsy grounds that
life is nasty, brutish and short and that we all need licking into shape.
He irresponsibly incorporated his fascination with punishment into his
polemic. His objections to Nazism were based not at all on Hitler's massive
internal violations of decency, but on his dislike for 'the Hun'. His views
on the Indian question were characterised by a rudeness about Indians
unworthy of him. He was not a man who ought to have unmagnanimously
reproduced the nasty cheap chat of every white man's mess throughout
India. He had satirised that kind of society, and had pointed out the
shortcomings of British rule. 'His dislike for Indians who had received
a Western education was both irresponsible and indiscreet,' writes the
Indian admirer of *Kim*, Nirad C. Chaudhuri, 'and in the light of what has
followed almost foolish.' He thought that the word 'suffragette' 'stank'. He
told the closest of all friends, Rider Haggard, that 'we owe our Russian
troubles, and many others, to the machinations of the Jews' (December
1919). Even Haggard demurred, adding to himself that he was inclined to
believe that 'one can insist too much on the Jew motive'; the truth was,
he gallantly conceded, that 'there are Jews and Jews'. The late Maurice
Bowra, who encountered him in the summer of 1921, recalled that he
called Jews 'yids' (in company), railed against Zionism and Balfour, and
'gave the impression that his views were formed less on reason than on
rather hysterical emotions'. While Hitler and his gang were persecuting
Jews and actively planning their destruction – the announced policy of
their party, and no secret to anyone, especially of the Inner Ring who
knew everything – Kipling, writing in 1935 in *Something of Myself*, had
this to say:

> It is true that the Children of Israel are 'people of the Book', and
> in the second Surah of the Koran Allah is made to say: 'High above
> mankind I have raised you.' Yet, later, in the fifth Surah, it is written:
> 'Oft as they kindle a beacon-fire for war, shall God quench it. And their
> aim will be to abet disorder on earth: but God loveth not the abettors of
> disorder.' More important still, my bearer in Lahore never announced
> our good little Jew Tyler but he spat loudly and openly on the verandah.
> I swallowed my spittle at once. Israel is a race to leave alone. It abets
> disorder.

It would have been better to have said nothing than perpetrate this
uneasy tat. The sort of feelings Kipling had about Jews crop up unhappily
often in the literature about authoritarianism. Angus Wilson, who has no
explanation for the passage quoted above, claims that his abusiveness
about Jews was simply 'a sort of slang . . . that we have come to associate
with anti-semitism'. This fudges the issue: it was anti-semitic. We must
not, as so many do, assume that this slang implied support for the Final
Solution, which had not then been invented. But it was in the process
of being invented, and that inhumane, facetious and unfunny abuse, far
from being good-natured, was part of the process. Wilson draws our
attention to Kipling's appreciation of the 'Jewish contribution to Western
civilisation', expressed in such stories as 'The Army of a Dream'. But, as

he (not an anti-semite) knows perfectly well, this is merely being 'fair to the Jews', and is anti-semitic in spirit. The man who thinks communism a Jewish conspiracy is an anti-semite; the man who thinks that the Jews 'abet disorder' any more than any other group of people is anti-semitic (it is the envy of their efficiency, on the part of ungrateful host peoples, that abets disorder). Never mind what 'due' he may think from time to time he would patronisingly like to give Jews. Wilson does comment that the 'whole concept of racialist Anglo-Saxon superiority which these clever people' – including Kipling – 'truly believed seems now as absurd as it is repugnant'. That belief included distrust (or worse) of Jews. That said, it must also be acknowledged that Kipling expressed oblique guilt for his guttersnipe feelings, both in the stories to which Wilson draws our attention and in the title of one of his most cryptic and profound poems: 'The Prayer of Miriam Cohen' – which no one has been able to understand.

Any writer could compile a sizeable anthology of Kipling's writings legitimately entitled something like 'Kipling the Inhumane'. It would be easily done. But it would be unfair, because another anthology with the legitimate title of 'Kipling the Tender' could also be compiled.

For the whole of his life Kipling the mask, as I think it is fair to call the public-man-with-the-opinions as distinct from the just as famous but understandably more mysterious recluse-with-the-secrets, was obsessed with the notion of an 'in-group', the 'Inner Ring'. He met people of all creeds in Freemasonry, in order to satisfy his religious eclecticism, and he also tried to find in Freemasonry a secret society for the advancement and preservation of humanity (such as his idol Cecil Rhodes, another repressed homosexual, seriously suggested should be founded). But Freemasonry was probably too banal in practice: Kipling's pictures of its operations in some of his later stories are highly idealised, and do not reflect the activity of any actual Masonic lodges. He was still an active Mason in 1912, but not much is known about his involvements, certainly slight, after that.

Kipling was a critical authoritarian: he examines rigidly (as in McGoggin), he investigates the psychology of submission, and he was opposed to the subjective, the imaginative and the tender-minded, while being highly subjective, very imaginative and exceedingly tender-minded. His tender-mindedness would have involved him in more sensitive communication with his own sex than society thought nice or right. This can certainly be described as a feminine characteristic. His disappointment at not being able thus tenderly to express himself reinforced the sharpness of his ironic questioning of authoritarian set-ups when he did criticise them – as when he suggests the 'impossibility' of 'the entire system of our administration' being wrong. Just as he defended the Anglo-Indian status quo because he genuinely loved *his* India, so he felt that toughness was the only means of preserving real tender-mindedness, an essentially private thing. There is some truth in this view, although one can take the toughness much too far through motives of unacknowledged sadism and bitterness. Kipling could be sentimental, yet he also explored real tender-mindedness, despite and because of his fear of it.

Kipling did have in his nature a great longing for submission: he was, I should think, the 'woman' in any idealised homosexual fantasies he may have allowed himself, or in those dreams over which he had no control. The *frisson* which such events as executions and floggings had for him exists mostly in his contemplation of the awful absolute need for submission on the victim's part. In *Stalky* he tries to make this into jolly good fun. But jolly good fun of that kind leaves its scars. Kipling's love of the concept of obedience, which he always preached as sacred (but he could countenance its non-observation in those who, like his three soldiers, were strictly in the know), is based on his fatalism, and his fatalism is based on a sense of ineluctable doom arising from the fact that the exercise of freedom is impossible for him in the sense that he cannot express himself as his nature wishes. Everything flows from that: his rebelliousness, his worship of the past, his insistence upon what is, in Christian terms, original sin. When he wrote such lines as these from 'The Benefactors',

> Ah! What avails the classic bent
>   And what the cultured word,
> Against the undoctored incident
>   That actually occurred?

> And what is Art whereto we press
>   Through paint and prose and rhyme –
> When Nature in her nakedness
>   Defeats us every time?

he was probably unaware that he was expressing some of the more emotive tenets of naturalism. He was aware, though, of his need to submit to Nature, and his need therefore to express the philosophy of Social Darwinism:

> When in this world's unpleasing youth
>   Our godlike race began,
> The longest arm, the sharpest tooth,
>   Gave man control of man.

Ironically, this would have served well as an epigraph for any one of the Social Darwinist primers which were, in the time of Kipling's youth, being written for all levels of society. The term had been coined by none other than Herbert Spencer, one of the two villains of 'The Conversion of Aurelian McGoggin', in 1876. The poem ('The Benefactors', which stands on its own in the *Definitive Edition*) goes on to demonstrate how, in the unpleasing youth of man, someone thought of casting a stone to make the tooth insufficient, and so forth. At all points in the process it is 'pain and fear' that do the teaching:

> It is not learning, grace, nor gear,
>   Nor easy meat and drink,
> But bitter pinch of pain and fear
>   That makes creation think.

Spencer, who had previously in some respects anticipated the findings of *The Evolution of Species*, wished to apply the concept of natural selection to the interpretation of human social evolution. In doing so he and his too eager followers crudely *mis*applied a biological theory without taking into account historical, cultural or social factors. Kipling's hostility to culture in 'The Benefactors' is characteristic of the Social Darwinist. But his Social Darwinism was not itself typical of the popular product, since it lacked optimism and was not offered as a substitute for religion. He may well have been influenced, too, by *The Martyrdom of Man* (1872), written by William Winwood Reade, nephew of Charles Reade. Reade left Oxford without a degree, went to Africa to discover that the gorilla was the most timid of creatures, returned to England to learn science, tried to be a doctor, rushed off again to Africa to fight in the Ashanti War, exhausted himself, and died at the age of thirty-seven. But his facile and excited book, an account of the 'maleficence of religion', made a huge impact at the time, and influenced people strongly for or against.

Authoritarian thinking derives from a conviction that the course of life is determined by forces wholly indifferent to the hopes, wishes and fears of the individual. But such a conviction (not necessarily wholly wrong) on the part of an individual by no means presupposes that he is an authoritarian. There is plenty in the earlier Kipling to show that he felt that his and everyone else's life was determined by indifferent forces – strikingly in, for example, 'Without Benefit of Clergy'. But the view of life which eventually emerges from his creative work, to the extent that it is coherent, bravely tries to leave that conviction behind. As a homosexual by temperament, not able fully to resist the 'undoctored incident that actually occurred', the notion that individuals are without choice would have had even greater appeal for him. But he left it behind him inasmuch as it might have seemed, at least to his daimon, to be a lazy way out. Still, he was always tempted towards fatalism. He may have been predisposed to a general acceptance of Original Sin (the great enemy of the liberal, and the thorniest of the thorns in the sides of his splendid schemes) by some vein of Calvinism in him.

Erich Fromm in one of his books analysing the phenomenon of authoritarianism declares that 'the miracle of creation' is outside the range of the authoritarian's experience. That is true. The authoritarian envies creation and demeans women or institutionalises her, like an animal, as breeder (as the Nazis did). But this miracle was not outside Kipling's range. It could not have been, because he was all too clearly an inspired author, who pointed to a daimon as the source of his inspiration. He thought this daimon came from without, but really it came from within. This is interesting. For if we look at Kipling as one who struggled with and rejected, as an artist if not as a polemicist, all the impedimenta of authoritarianism, then here he is trying to account for a sort of creation which he knew well *as* miracle, but a miracle that for him, because he feels 'unworthy', comes entirely from without. He illustrates this masterfully in his story 'Wireless', an account of inspiration which may not be true, but which has an astonishing authenticity.

Kipling, then, was a victim of the sorts of disturbance that lead to authoritarianism, but the best of his art somehow escaped it. In doing so he conducted some fascinating and dangerous investigations of the particular psychological territory he inhabited. In philosophy there is a term called 'privileged access', which refers to an observer's relationship to the contents of his own consciousness. When a man makes art, he allows such access to his reader, even if he is fanatical in his determination to remain 'private'. Hence the notoriously 'enigmatic' nature of Kipling's writings, variously and irritatedly described, even by his admirers, as elliptical, lacunose or compressed. He knew, however, that such access can only be achieved by self-knowledge and then by intuition.

Moeller van der Bruck, a writer regarded as one of the fathers of the Third Reich (although he killed himself soon after it was established), wrote in his book *Der Dritte Reich*: 'The conservative believes ... in catastrophe, in the powerlessness of man to avoid it, and in the terrible disappointment of the seduced optimist.' We are here put right into the area explored by Kipling. In all his writings about India, and later about the Empire, he points towards some nameless catastrophe, that

> certain darkness into which the soul of the young man sometimes descends – a horror of desolation, abandonment, and realised worth-lessness, which is one of the most real of the hells in which we are compelled to walk.
> I know of what I speak ... But I can tell you for your comfort that the best cure for it is to interest yourself, to lose yourself, in some issue not personal to yourself – in another man's trouble ...

He said this in an address to students in Canada in October 1907. The idea of the abyss, a terrible pit of black depression akin to that suffered by those with 'religious mania', often occurs in Kipling. It is nothing less than a fear of eternal damnation, arising from a sense of a God who could malignantly trap beings in a life they did not ask for, and then fail to elect them. Calvinism is an especially horrible case, perhaps, of mankind's multitudinous attempts to escape from its sense of the inevitability of fate, that is to say from the notion that whatever it does, it is doomed to fulfil its destiny like clockwork. Calvin proposed the notion of election as a necessary assumption for the efficient fulfilment of fate: the profitable pursuit of power. That the victims of depression have not always been taught to believe, or intellectually do not conceive of, a formal Christian hell, is to miss the point altogether. Kipling's Calvinist heritage must have reinforced his experience in this abyss. This sense of life as a thing with power to propel men into sudden inexplicable blacknesses in which all their most private guilts and schemes glare at them, helps to explain Kipling's drift into a public authoritarianism. Once this involvement has been accepted as ugly, as unjustifiable, as an undoubted disappointment to his readers, and, above all, as something he tried (in his oblique way) to come to terms with, we may be able to lose our uneasiness and come to some terms with it.

To those neo-imperialists who have come so far with me, and remain, I can only appeal: is not your belief a fantastic dream, a dwelling in the past, a misreading of the present course of history? If it helps, then I unhappily concede that the present course of history is far worse than even your dream ... It is my dubious consolation, too, that we have not yet had any government of the people, for the people, or by the people – unless some politician may be identified who is the people.

Roger Brown, an American social psychologist, has given a witty and accurate appraisal of the literature on authoritarianism, and has compiled a valuable list of statements which are supposed to constitute the 'potentially fascist syndrome'. His book was written in 1965, and since then there has been the upsurge of both the so-called New Left (in particular the events in France in 1968) and the counter-upsurge of the New Right. In other words, a great deal has happened since then. In both America and Britain governments nominally of the right have triumphed. They are not governments of the extreme right, but they are not of the centre, and those who wholeheartedly support them are often of the extreme right. The American government has successfully reintroduced capital punishment, and the British government (or its head) has repeatedly tried to do so. Both governments have denounced communism as the ultimate in evil – only now to come to terms with the foreign policy of a master of publicity. Kipling would have enjoyed all this, and the enmity towards the welfare state (even though one of the doctrinaire inventors of the concept was the imperialist Joe Chamberlain); but he would have disapproved of a female prime minister, and he would have abhorred 'doing business with the devil'. Kingsley Amis, one of the better writers of our time, a public supporter of these governments, and a fine critic of Kipling, has said that 'Rudyard resurrected would have a plenitude of . . . urgent business on his hands.' I do not think that he means that this would properly include regaining India; but I do not think, either, that he is quite making a joke, although he is perhaps being provocative, as is his wont. In my distinction there is, in Kipling's work, a crude polemic on the one hand, and a creatively modified conservatism on the other. It is instructive in this connection to look at Roger Brown's compilation of statements that, allegedly, 'constitute the potentially fascist syndrome'. I have adapted the following list from his 1965 book:

1. *Conventionalism. a*: Obedience and respect for authority are the most important virtues children should learn; *b*: The businessman and the manufacturer are much more important to society than the artist and the professor.

2. *Authoritarian submission. a*: Young people sometimes get rebellious ideas, but as they grow up they ought to get over them and settle down; *b*: Science has its place, but there are many important things that can never possibly be understood by the human mind.

3. *Authoritarian aggression. a*: Sex crimes . . . deserve more than mere imprisonment; such criminals ought to be publicly whipped, or worse; *b*: If people would talk less and work more, everybody would be better off.

4. *Anti-intraception. a*: When a person has a problem or worry, it is best for him not to think about it, but to keep busy with more cheerful things; *b*: Nowadays more and more people are prying into matters that should remain personal and private.

5. *Superstition and stereotype. a*: Some day it will probably be shown that astrology can explain a lot of things; *b*: Some people are born with an urge to jump from high places.

6. *Power and 'toughness'. a*: People can be divided into two distinct classes: the weak and strong; *b*: Most people don't realise how much our lives are controlled by plots hatched in secret places.

7. *Destructiveness and cynicism*. *a*: Human nature being what it is, there will always be war and conflict; *b*: Familiarity breeds contempt.

8. *Projectivity*. *a*: Wars and social troubles may someday be ended by an earthquake or flood that will destroy the whole world; *b*: Nowadays, when so many different kinds of people move around and mix together so much, a person has to protect himself especially carefully against catching an infection or disease from them.

9. *Sex*. *a*: The wild sex-life of the old Greeks and Romans was tame compared to some of the goings-on in this country, even in places where people might least expect it; *b*: Homosexuals are hardly better than criminals and ought to be severely punished.

It is somewhat alarming to discover that this set of statements (familiar to us as 'taxi-drivers' talk, though we can all be occasional taxi-drivers), taken together, correlates positively to 'the authoritarian': 'Do you know him . . .?' asks Brown. 'It seems to me that I do . . .' He goes on to point out that Adorno and his fellow authors, who originally compiled this list, had found a 'superficially heterogeneous set of opinions that had, as a total set, some kind of psychological unity.'

Do you think you know your Kipling? Do you recognise him? Look through the list of statements, taking them in order, one by one. He preached obedience; he decried the artists; his stories are full of examples of bumptious young people being taught to 'settle down'; he gave science its 'special place' but went so far as to beg God ('The Prayer of Miriam Cohen') to hide his secrets from us; I do not know what his attitude to sex crimes was, but one can imagine; he preached the gospel of work, and was one of the first 'poets of work'; throughout his life he recommended the diversion of attention from one's own worries to other things; he preached privacy; clearly he thought there was 'something in' astrology; he was a fatalist; he believed in 'strong men'; he was obsessed with secret plots in high places; he believed that violence was necessary, because of the nature of human beings; he believed in hierarchies and 'respect'; the notion of great catastrophe haunts most of his work; his experience in India made him cautious about infections and diseases.

The category 'sex' is a separate issue, and particularly so here. Kipling said less about this subject in public than about most others, although he was perpetually insistent about 'swine' in educational institutions who practised 'filth'.

But when asked by Hugh Walpole – a lifelong paedophile who had offered himself to Henry James (who answered *'Si vieillesse pouvait'*) – what he thought about the row concerning the banning of Radclyffe Hall's monotonous, courageous lesbian novel *The Well of Loneliness*, he answered, in Walpole's words, that there was

> too much of the abnormal in all of us to play about with it. Hates opening up reserves. All the same he'd had friends once and again he'd done more for than for any woman. Luckily Ma Kipling doesn't hear this – but she's had her ear at *his* keyhole for so long that, without hearing anything, she nevertheless suspects and turns her dull eye on to me as much as to say: 'Now the moment you're tiresome you *go*, so if you want to stay with him you'd better behave'. Nor do I blame her. She's a good strong-minded woman, who has played watch-dog to him so long that she knows now just how to save him from any kind of disturbance,

mental, physical or spiritual. That's *her* job and she does it superbly . . .
so she takes him, wraps him up in her bosom and conveys him back to
their uncomfortable hard-chaired home. He is quite content.

It is significant that Carrington cuts the more critical parts of the
remarks about Carrie (Caroline Balestier, Kipling's wife) when he quotes
from this passage of the vain but good-hearted Walpole's diary. He
was probably aware that Elsie Bambridge would not have read Rupert
Hart-Davis's biography of Walpole, where it was first quoted. The above
quotation (especially the word *'suspects'*, which reinforces other evidence,
and of course the odd sentence beginning 'All the same he'd had friends
once . . .') seems to speak for itself: in those days of oppression homosexuals recognised and appreciated one another, even if they muted that
recognition in deference to custom. By that time Kipling was probably
'not homosexual', but if he was anything sexual at all, and it is hard not
to be, then he would dwell emotionally in homosexual memories.

As to the rest of the items in Brown's 1965 list. They are not surprising to
us because, among other things, they remind us of Kipling. They may be
surprising, though, because many of them seem innocuous when taken in
isolation. Any humane person, looking through them, might say of many
of them: 'well, I might, in these times, have come to believe in something
like that, if not quite all of it, but does my cluster of assumptions make
me a potential Nazi?' It is here that Kipling is relevant.

Kipling's ethos is concerned with current affairs. We are rewarded by
his creative work and so we reasonably ask such questions as: would he
have believed that human nature is so awful and essentially wicked that
nuclear terror and pollution is our only protection against it? We are living
on the edge of the kind of eschatological chaos, absolute death, darkness,
of which the imaginative Kipling, in particular, has helped to make us
sensible. This is so familiar that it has been trivialised, and all the television
channels in the 'free world' are permitted to trivialise it. Our leaders, or,
rather, those whom we tolerate as our leaders, have realised that such
trivialisation does not operate any more against their essential interests
than does 'satire' of the institutionalised kind. By trivialisation I mean
some such affair as the present (late 1987) unfashionableness of nuclear
weapons: everyone has denounced them, a treaty has been signed which
is going to lead to a new dawn for mankind, and everyone continues to
work on new prototypes. Kipling would have appreciated all this.

If we call certain writers 'great', then the nature of their message is
important. Walpole, again in his diary, said that Kipling was 'a zealous
propagandist who, having discovered that the things for which he must
propagand are now all out of fashion, guards them joyously and lovingly
in his heart, but won't any longer trail them in public'. That was true: by
then (1928) he tended only to trail them to captive audiences, or to those
who agreed with him. But in fact they were 'out of fashion' only amongst
the intellectual or 'enlightened' section of his readership. Such ideas are
not old-fashioned now. They never will be old-fashioned. They are not
old-fashioned in the Soviet Union, where they masquerade, the same as
ever, under names more acceptable in a communist society. They have
lined themselves up against proposed reforms; certainly these will lead to
more 'free comment' and 'satire' in any case. Would a Russian Rudyard

Kipling born and bred in one of the Soviet colonies, say Hungary, have in time returned there and come to deplore those changes as threats to the brotherhood of man?

I have argued against acceptance of what I call Kipling's polemic on the grounds that it is too one-sided, that it incorporates personal sadistic elements which have no business to be contained within it, that it is impracticable, obscurantist and unrealistic, and inhumane, that it refuses to take account of individual good will, that it ignores under the thoughtless rubric of wickedness all that it too mindlessly dislikes. That remains my position. If you can rid yourselves of any prejudices such as that Kipling is not a major writer, or that major writers somehow have to be defended from their lapses, or that they they are not really lapses (this is the burden of Noel Annan's extraordinarily disingenuous attempt at a defence, to which I shall refer later) – then it will very likely be yours, too.

We have seen the statement 'Human nature being what it is, there will always be war and conflict.' That is certainly 'vilification of the human', says Brown in his summary. Is it? Is your or my or Kipling's pessimism 'vilification' of the human? Yet we rightly say that there would be no change to bad conditions, no reform, if there were no liberals. That is my own position, so long as it is granted that liberal has a small 'l', and might therefore belong to almost any party or school of thought. So, as a reader of Kipling, I neither forgive nor want to forgive him for his extremism.

But perhaps the folk, a concept of which Kipling had a very keen awareness, need protection not only from fascists and potential fascists and perhaps even enlightened or 'democratic' dictators but also from good liberals. Perhaps liberals really are *sometimes,* or *too often,* as Kipling makes them appear in his tendentious stories, ridiculously *unwise*. Otherwise why all those *wise* ('something in that, undoubtedly') *conservative* proverbs.

If this is true, then the folk won't get any sort of protection from Kipling the polemicist. None at all. They need more of the sort of wisdom that is inherent in their huge store of conservative proverbs. They need a continual flow of humane feeling, experience and mellowness. We cannot keep beating Kipling over the head for not being a liberal. He was never that. But we may find in much of his art, in all his best art, a continual humanisation of the sorts of authoritarian statements we have been looking at and discussing. We won't find it in 'If'. That is empty, has no life in it, refers to a string of excellent platitudes but never illuminates them and is modelled upon a person (Dr Jameson of the Raid) who now seems absurd. What we need to discover is just what work Kipling did that fills in the clichés of 'If' with detail and real life and real example. Then he gains the value of at least the best proverbs, and becomes a part of the life of the folk: of our lives.

London

Kipling, in the company of Ted Hill, Caroline Taylor and their cousin Edgar Taylor, docked at Liverpool on 5 October 1889. In a day or two he was in London, still for the moment in their company. His arrival in London was in accordance with his Scheme. He was determined to stick to this.

He did not write much to his parents about how he was getting on, and his mother complained. He felt it was time that he got away from the 'Family Square', and clearly he did not know what to say for himself. For the first time in his life since the Southsea episode, he was fending for himself; but now he was on the verge of his twenty-fourth birthday. He did however write to Mrs Hill, when she left, and he continued his series of stiff conventional love letters to her younger sister. He stayed for a time with the Burne-Joneses, went to Paris for a few days, and finally settled in rooms in Villiers Street.

Villiers Street is still there, under the same name, and the house the third floor of which Kipling inhabited is marked with a plaque. It is now merely depressing; then it was a mixture of squalor and romance. The Strand runs by Charing Cross railway station; parallel to and south of it runs the Embankment. Villiers Street, comparatively narrow, connects the two. Kipling could look down it at the River Thames, with its constant traffic, and up it towards the Strand, then as busy as it is now, and crowded with horse-drawn vehicles of every description. Opposite was Gatti's Music-Hall. 'The Charing Cross trains rumbled through my dreams on one side, the boom of the Strand on the other.' As always, he had women to help him settle in, in this case Ted Hill and the supposed object of his love, her sister Caroline. The relative he saw most of at this time was 'the beloved aunt', Burne-Jones's wife, whose presence, along with that of other aunts, ensured that he would not starve. He set out to woo the literary world, but, characteristically, by getting them, for the most part, to come to him. On his door he pasted the facetious notice: 'PUBLISHERS: A CLASSIC WHILE YOU WAIT!' The room sounds, as Birkenhead describes it (this is the fullest description we have) as though it was Kipling's later large study at Bateman's *in parvo*. There were eastern rugs and mats and a Japanese screen; all was soon coloured by the smoke of Kipling's incessant pipe, cigarettes and cigars. He was afraid, but he kept his nerve. In this gaslit room, Birkenhead writes,

Kipling toiled with intense concentration . . . in his working clothes, a loose dark suit, buttoned high to the throat like a workman's blouse, and a tassel-less scarlet fez which he had the habit of thrusting backward. He suffered from bouts of depression. 'There are five million people in London this night, and saving those who starve, I don't think there is one more heartsick or thoroughly wretched than that "rising young author" known to you as: Ruddy.'

The letter Birkenhead quotes from was to Mrs Hill, not to his parents.

He now really was a rising young author. He must have broken his general rule about the literary world coming to him when he called on Andrew Lang, who took him to the Savile Club, where he would soon have met Hardy, Sir Walter Besant (founder of the Authors' Society), Haggard, Gosse, James, the literary historian George Saintsbury, and many others. He also seems to have approached W.E. Henley rather than vice versa, although the latter had been eagerly awaiting his arrival. Kipling at once took to the angry imperialist and promoter of outdoor sports, editor of the *Scots Observer* (later the *National Observer*), and to his ferocious politics:

> Henley's demerits were, of course, explained to the world by loving friends after his death. I had the fortune to know him only as kind, generous, and a jewel of an editor, with the gift of fetching the very best out of his cattle, with words that would astonish men. He had, further, an organic loathing of Mr Gladstone and all Liberalism.

Henley had 'no sense of public decency': he printed an intemperate attack in verse on the Liberals which *The Times* had refused (though it quoted it later), and thus endeared himself to Kipling, who really knew very little about politics, forever. This admiration did not prevent him writing, characteristically and angrily, to Trix, when he heard that Henley was speaking of him as one of his 'young men', 'Henley is a great man; he is also a cripple, but he is not going to come the bullying cripple over me, after I have been in harness all these years.'

He was by now beginning to harden into the anti-Liberal imperialist familiar to us. His articles written in India while he was working for the *Pioneer* show that he had been going that way; now all pretence to any other attitude was dropped. The front he presented was bohemian enough, in particular the fez; but it was a virile and highly aggressive bohemianism. He was in demand, and up to his ears in work. He was soon making money, too, as he tells us in the autobiography. He was beginning to enjoy the praise of his peers, all of whom he met at the Savile (to which he was elected in 1891). He selects for mention, in *Something of Myself*, Besant, Gosse, Hardy, Lang, Eustace Balfour, Herbert Stephen, Haggard, Saintsbury and Walter Pollock.

He felt he owed a great debt to Besant not only for *All in a Garden Fair* but also for the good advice he gave him. Besant told him to 'keep out of the dog fight': if you are 'in with one lot you will have to be out with the other', and things will 'get like a girls' school where they stick out their tongues at each other when they pass'. Besant introduced him to the literary agent A.P. Watt, whom he employed until his death, and with whom he never had a dispute.

He found Gosse sensitive, and thought him 'fearless' when it came to 'questions of good workmanship'. Gosse has come to succeeding generations to look something of a charlatan and even a crook. He was sexually furtive in an unattractive and apparently hypocritical manner, his scholarly work was not as good as his contemporaries believed it to be, and his criticism was until recently ignored or judged as feeble – some of it is certainly due for reassessment. Even so, Roger Lancelyn Green's judgement that he was a 'major' literary critic and biographer is plain wrong – especially as Green dismisses Oscar Wilde as a lightweight critic by comparison. Much worse, Gosse was up to his navel, if not his neck, in the notorious T.J. Wise forgeries. But he did leave one small masterpiece, *Father and Son* (1907), and he did enjoy the confidence of such men as Hardy (who had his reservations about him) and, to a lesser extent, Kipling.

Gosse wrote about Kipling in the *Century* magazine in October 1891. He observed that before his advent 'the fiction of the Anglo-Saxon world ... had become curiously feminized'. Novel writers had become, he went on, 'extremely refined in taste and discreet in judgement'; 'there was a great void'. He then hit the nail on the head by pronouncing that Kipling had filled his void with 'exotic realism' and 'vigorous rendering of unhackneyed experience'.

Rudyard remembered Hardy for his 'grave and bitter humour'. Hardy, for his part, first became acquainted with the work of the rising young star over the Easter of 1890. His friend Sir George Douglas came on a visit, and Mrs Hardy read the company a story by Kipling in a magazine. So much by Kipling was then appearing that it is not possible to say what story it was, but this company disliked it: '"What is he driving at?" was our unanimous verdict,' Douglas later recalled. But by May Hardy was reading him with serious attention, noting down summaries of some of the stories in *Plain Tales* and enthusing about the poem 'The Ballad of Fisher's Boarding-House', which begins

'Twas Fultah Fisher's boarding-house,
    Where sailor-men reside,
And there were men of all the ports
    From Mississip to Clyde,
And regally they spat and smoked,
    And fearsomely they lied.

They lied about the purple Sea
    That gave them scanty bread,
They lied about the Earth beneath,
    The Heavens overhead,
For they had looked too often on
    Black rum when that was red.

Hardy selected 'Lisbeth', 'Thrown Away', 'Yoked with an Unbeliever', 'The Other Man' and other stories for special mention, and called 'The Strength of a Likeness' 'an excellent story of the delicate sort'. He came to deplore Kipling's politics, remarking, when he got the Nobel Prize, that one could scarcely connect him with the idea of peace; but now in 1890 he selected the line, 'What part have Indian exiles in their mirth?' as being like 'the cry of a race in trouble'. He shrewdly saw that Kipling 'adroitly mixed two tones, the gay & the bitter'.

Kipling does not mention Henry James in his autobiography except briefly as having been at his wedding, although he would have met him early in his time in London, at the Savile Club. They were quite close for a year or two, and Kipling continued to visit him at Rye, from Bateman's, for several years into the new century; but they drifted apart a little after the Kiplings went to America.

James's comments on him were acute from start to finish, as were Robert Louis Stevenson's. The two men wrote about him to each other. Stevenson, until the advent of Kipling, was the most sheerly popular serious writer of the time. When he married his strange American wife Fannie, Henley (Stevenson's as well as Kipling's mentor), chose to quarrel with him. James contented himself with acid comments on the marriage. On 21 March 1890 James told Stevenson that his 'nascent rival' had already killed off 'one immortal', Rider Haggard, and that he was the 'star of the hour' with his 'extraordinarily observed' tales of barrack life and Tommy Atkins. Stevenson wrote in August of the same year, 'Kipling is too clever to live', and then followed this up in December with further comments. Kipling was, he told James, the most promising young writer to appear since (ahem) himself. But he alarmed Stevenson

> with his copiousness and haste. He should shield his fire with both hands . . . surely he was armed for better things than these succinct sketches and flying leaves of verse? . . . If I had this man's fertility and courage, it seems to me I could heave a pyramid . . . the fairy godmothers were all tipsy at his christening.

By 1892 Stevenson was developing reservations. To his friend Charles Baxter (18 July) he compared Kipling unfavourably to Henley, 'How poorly Kipling compares! He is all smart journalism and cleverness . . . there is no blot of heart's blood and the Old Night.' To James (5 December) a few months later he reiterated his doubts. By then he thought, as in fact George Meredith did, that Barrie was the coming man. A year later, to Richard Le Gallienne (28 December), he wrote that Kipling, 'with all his genius', was moving in the wrong direction: in that of 'the British pig', 'the style-less . . . the shapeless . . . the slapdash and the disorderly'.

James, writing to Stevenson in January 1891, called Kipling an 'infant monster', and enclosed his introduction to an American edition of Kipling's stories called *Mine Own People*. *The Light that Failed* had just appeared, and James thought it cut 'the ground somewhat from under my feet, inasmuch as I find it the most youthfully infirm of his productions (in spite of great "life"), much wanting in composition and in narrative and explicative, even implicative, art'.

Later (5 November 1896 in a letter to Jonathan Sturges) James praised the collection of poems called *The Seven Seas* (1896): 'I am laid low by the absolutely uncanny talent.' But he qualified this by describing it as all *'violent'*, 'without a dream of nuance or a "hint of distinction"', 'with never a touch of the fiddle-string or a note of the nightingale', 'full of the most insidious art'. He thought that Kipling's 'coarseness' was 'absolutely one of the most triumphant "values"' of the best poetry, and singled out the poem 'The *Mary Gloster*'. By the next year he was getting a little weary of it, and told Grace Norton (25 December) that while Kipling's 'ballad future may still be big', his prose future had 'much shrunken in the light of one's increasingly observing how little life he can make use of'. He found 'almost nothing of the complicated soul or of the female form or of any

other question of *shades*'. To Charles Eliot Norton, Kipling's friend as well
as his own, James again expressed his 'reserves' a couple of years later (28
November 1899): he could not swallow the

> loud, brazen patriotic verse – an exploitation of the patriotic idea, for that
> matter, which seems to me not really much other than the exploitation
> of the name of one's mother or one's wife. Two or three times a
> century – yes; but not every month. He is, however, such an embodied
> little talent, so economically constructed for all use and no waste, that
> he will get again on a good road – leading *not* into mere multitudinous
> noise. His talent I think quite diabolically great; and this in spite – here
> I am at it again! – of the misguided, the unfortunate Stalky. Stalky gives
> him away, aesthetically, as a man in his really now, as regards our roaring
> race, bardic condition, should not have allowed himself to be given. That
> is not a thing, however, that, in our paradise of criticism, appears to
> occur to so much as three persons, and meanwhile the sale, I believe, is
> tremendous.

These are among the wisest remarks ever made about Kipling, and one
can forgive James, whose own sales were disappointing to him, for his little
burst of envy about the popularity of *Stalky*, which was, after all, just what
James said it was, and even worse. The remarks about patriotism are true,
too: Kipling did overdo it. It is also true that Kipling, in James's brilliant
definition here, was an energetic little engine of a man, constructed for
'all use and no waste', and that he did, after all, get back 'upon a good
road'. That road led to *Kim*, as well as some of the later stories. Kipling
could not keep himself down.

In his introduction to *Mine Own People* James examined the question of
just why Kipling was such a rising star in the literary firmament with more
characteristic acuteness than any other critic. It is in certain respects
a cautious piece, since James begins by discussing the phenomena of
'freshness', novelty and enjoyment in literature, and he makes sure to
emphasise that these 'flit by' very fast. 'The tormenting part . . . is that, in
any particular key, it can happen but once – by a sad failure of the law that
inculcates the repetition of goodness.' He saw that Kipling, a 'strangely
clever youth', had 'stolen the formidable mask of maturity'. He saw that
much of the 'experience' in the stories was 'vicarious':

> I cannot overlook the general, the importunate fact that, confidently
> as he has caught the trick and habit of this sophisticated world, he has
> not been long of it. His extreme youth is indeed what I might call his
> window-bar – the support upon which he somewhat rowdily leans while
> he looks down at the human scene with his pipe in his teeth . . . Mr
> Kipling's actual performance is like a tremendous walk before breakfast,
> making one welcome the idea of the meal, but consider with some alarm
> the hours still to be traversed.

Upon *Mine Own People* hangs a tale from which we may learn a great deal
about Kipling's ferocity when he felt that he was being exploited. Besant
had introduced him to the admirable agent A.P. Watt (this family firm, before falling into other hands in the 1960s, represented not only Kipling, but
Galsworthy, Graves and a host of other grateful and well-served authors)
almost as soon as he arrived in England. Watt made a sale to Harper's of

'The Courting of Dinah Shadd' in January 1890, and then of other stories, for their *Weekly*. In the autumn of 1890, just after Kipling had set out on a course of world travel in order to improve his health, Harper's collected the stories, and, it seems, helped themselves to one more, in a paperback edition in September, with an introduction by Andrew Lang. When Kipling had been in America in 1889 he had offered to write for Harper's, and had been told, 'Young man, this house is devoted to the production of litera- ture.' Any young writer would want to revenge that, although it should be remembered that Kipling had not endeared himself to many Americans with his brash, ignorant and knowing remarks about their country. The American novelist, critic and friend of James, W.D. Howells, had just referred in another Harper's magazine, the *Monthly*, to Kipling's 'jaunty, hat-cocked-on-one-side, wink-tipping sketches'. Exhausted by overwork, with the strain of dealing with his sudden emergence as a master, and with all manner of personal difficulties, he was in no mood to be amused. He blew off steam to Henley:

> Today I receive a note from Harper's announcing that they have reprinted in book form . . . They will give it their own title. (They have given it their own title.) They have not had the decency to apprise me of their intention, and to complete the insult they fling a £10 note (the wages of one New York road scavenger for one month) at my head . . . Rather less than 12 months ago that firm in a letter one line and seven words long told me that they would not republish *Soldiers three, the Gadsbys*, and all the rest . . . This month's Harper's magazine brings in an elaborate patronization of me . . . When the man was writing that, his blasted owners were stealing my work. The critic himself was criticizing stolen work with adjectives stolen from England . . . When a burglar . . .

and so on. Someone in Harper's had been unforgivably rude the year before; apart from that, no one was playing the villain. It was simply that the copyright laws between Great Britain and the United States had not yet been cleared up, so that injustices could be legally perpetrated on both sides of the Atlantic. Harper's were no worse than anyone else, and better than most. They were not acting outside the law, although of course they were acting towards Kipling (and any other author to whom they chose to do this) with an unjust and patronising insolence. But they did not mean it that way. Not some but many less reputable American houses were plain villains.

Kipling decided to fight. The editor of the *Athenaeum* took up his case, and Harper's published a statement there by way of reply, conceding that they had rejected his earlier work, but pointing out that what they had published was superior; they had not meant to insult him by offering him £10: they were following custom. He replied to this with an angry letter, rather foolishly accusing Harper's of sharp practice. Tact would have been better.

At this point Sir Walter Besant had to step in. As founder of the Authors' Society, he knew that a Copyright Bill was before the House of Representatives and that it might well become law by the next summer (it took longer). He did not want to offend a big and gentlemanly American publisher at such a stage: all would be well soon. Thomas Hardy was awaiting the serialisation of *Tess of the d'Urbervilles*; he did not want to go on seeing his books pirated in America by unscrupulous firms. Besant and Hardy therefore, together with the then popular Scottish novelist William Black (author of *The Princess of Thule* (1874) and other pleasant romances) wrote a letter defending the reputation of Harper's. Most of the original draft text of the letter was almost certainly by Besant; probably the three men went over it when they met at the Savile. Hardy – put up to it by his own new English publisher, James Ripley Osgood of Osgood, McIlvaine & Co., a 'semi-autonomous subsidiary' of Harper's – had reason to be personally grateful to the New York firm, which had also published most of the novels of Besant and Black over the years.

The letter tried to spare Kipling's feelings but did not notably succeed, for he published in the *Athenaeum* a satire called 'The Rhyme of the Three Captains' – the three captains being, of course, Besant, Black and Hardy. The letter did not in fact much offend Kipling's feelings, and Carrington calls the satirical poem 'spirited' (right) and 'effective satire' (wrong). Carrington points out that the action made Kipling feel independent of 'literary grandees'. Carrington also mentions Besant and Lang (who had supplied the introduction to the offending volume); but Kipling wanted to be independent of all 'grandees' – and not to be equal, but the best by a long chalk. As for the poem: it is lively but it is not appropriate. Possibly Kipling did not know the full circumstances. If it were effective satire then it would be a famous example of an injured author fighting for his rights; but it is not. The episode did not do Kipling much harm, but it did not do him good, either.

Despite the success that had come to him, he was not happy in London. He was overworking, but it was not overwork that was making him un-happy: overwork can, at least for a short time, keep a person as happy as lack of employment. Apart from whatever was troubling him inside – his disturbed sexuality and his uneasiness about his literary status – he hated the city, even as it fascinated him and compelled him to wander in it as he had wandered in Lahore. James ('B.V.') Thomson's powerful poem *The City of Dreadful Night* had haunted him from his boyhood at USC; so much so that he used it for the title of an early prose sketch. Cities seemed to him full of corruption and of his own particular sense of original sin. London, the largest city he had yet seen, must have seemed infinitely the most teeming with wickedness. His only solace was the music hall, to whose unpretentious warmth and lack of respectfulness he could heartily respond. But although the music hall was the sole province of the working class, Kipling found nothing but 'lack of self-respect' in working-class aspirations. This, he told various of his correspondents, was not less than 'revolting'. It was not as if he could accept the phenomenon of people wishing to better their lot as inevitable; he condemned it lock, stock and barrel, and had very definite notions about how the poor must *not* better themselves. One is sure that the poor were wrong – but Kipling's attitude was impractical, inasmuch as he did not even allow them their aspirations. But to what purpose did he hold these insensitive views, which were after all contradicted by his wholehearted response to the music hall, as well as to the woman of the slums, as recorded in the story 'The Record of Badalia Herodsfoot' (an important source for Somerset Maugham's *Liza of Lambeth*)?

The answer is that, as he met with success, so his views began to harden. He decided to identify himself with the Anglo-Indian views to which he was used. He exaggerated them and stuck to them, and allowed in his mind – but his heart was less inflexible – for no other. He felt bound to line himself up with those who condemned 'arty' people, choosing to ignore (and he got away with it) that he was inevitably one himself. *He*, after all, was not a soldier, administrator or any kind of knowing tough guy. On a foggy day in November 1889, he had written the now famous 'In Partibus', which he described to Ted Hill as, 'the wail of a fog-bound exile howling for Sunlight'. The *Civil and Military* and the *Pioneer*, in both of which it was published, called it 'amusing doggerel'; the relevant stanzas are:

> But I consort with long-haired things
>   In velvet collar-rolls
> Who talk about the Aims of Art,
>   And 'theories' and 'goals',
> And moo and coo with womenfolk
>   About their blessed souls.
>
> But that they call 'psychology'
>   Is lack of liver-pill,
> And all that blights their tender souls
>   Is eating till they're ill,
> And their chief way of winning goals
>   Consists of sitting still.
>
> Its Oh to meet an Army man,
>   Set up, and trimmed and taut,
> Who does not spout hashed libraries
>   Or think the next man's thought,
> And walks as though he owns himself,
>   And hogs his bristles short.

Kipling did reprint these popular verses, but never in the various issues of the mammoth *Definitive Edition* of the poems. They were only for the eyes of his old Anglo-Indian audience, and are indeed only doggerel. Nonetheless, he meant them to a degree, and soon after the copyright row echoed them in a letter:

> London is a vile place. The long-haired literati of the Savile Club are swearing that I 'invented' my soldier talk in *Soldiers Three*. Seeing that not one of these critics has been within earshot of a barrack, I am naturally wroth. But this is only the beginning of the lark. You'll see some savage criticisms of my work before Spring. That's what I'm playing for.

During the whole of this trying time his health was poor, in part because of the recurrence of 'Indian fevers', whatever exactly these may have been. Probably they were psychosomatic. His parents came on leave to London, where they stayed in Kensington, in May 1890. They had been preceded by Trix in February. He told her then that he had been 'mistaken' in his 'love' for Caroline; that he had met Florence Garrard by chance in the street, and that his old feeling for her had thus revived. He was therefore still anxiously working out this old false vein: an artificial vessel into which he nonetheless poured out real passion and real resentment. Interestingly, Angus Wilson very rationally suggests that because Florence lived for the whole of her life with one friend – Mabel Price – possibly Kipling had 'by chance, embarked upon a romantic quest that was stillborn from the start'. This can only be conjecture, but it would be irony indeed if it were true. When Kipling told Trix of Flo's death (Birkenhead surmises that he heard a false rumour) he added, 'she never took the least care of herself'. Presumably this meant that she did not respond to Kipling as he thought she should have done.

Kipling became dependent upon his parents once more when they arrived in London. His father came, supportively, to work with him in Villiers Street in the daytime. By 15 August (according to Lockwood) he had finished his first draft of *The Light that Failed*, which was published in its 'conventional' version – we shall discuss this further on – in *Lippincott's Monthly Magazine* in January 1891. This novel, written on the edge of breakdown, was the most carefully self-revealing book he ever wrote, and he made sure not to repeat his mistake. He was always much more reticent in his poetry – or he meant to be. But what had he achieved by then in this form?

He told Caroline Taylor in a letter of 9 December 1889 that he was not a poet and never would be, 'but only a writer of fiction who varies fiction with verse'. Was this a serious attempt at self-evaluation, and is it true?

Apart from the verses collected in odd volumes such as those in the Sussex edition of his works, and eventually all together by Andrew Rutherford in *Early Verse by Rudyard Kipling 1879–1889* (1986), Kipling eschewed 'personal lyrics'. He was not a love poet, according to the *Definitive Edition* of his poems, which appeared in 1919, 1921, 1927, 1933, and (posthumously) 1940, each time being added to.

But what had he achieved as a poet by the time he published his second and his third collections (if we don't count privately issued gatherings), *Barrack-Room Ballads* (1892), and *The Seven Seas* (1896)? Apart from a handful of poems written in India, such as 'The Ballad of Boh Da Thone', the poems of *Barrack-Room Ballads* were written after he reached London in the autumn of 1889. There is an improvement on the poems of *Departmental Ditties*, as would be expected. Kipling had found his own voice, and Henley was right to endorse this new genius by publishing all he sent him in the *Scots Observer*. The first major poem Henley published (others appeared in *Macmillan's Magazine* and elsewhere) was 'Danny Deever'. This does not have merely Anglo-Indian appeal: it is universal, and is still one of the few poems about an execution to have a genuine *frisson*. The man who wrote this is a true poet: he has read the ballads and he exploits them with brilliant flair. That same naturalistic relish to which I have already drawn attention is seen here, although in a highly concentrated and dramatic form. This is as good, perhaps, as a (short) literary ballad could then be. One can only note what subjects have a *frisson* for this young man, and note – as I have already done – the mentalities of other poets similarly moved. His judgement of himself to Caroline Taylor as 'not a poet' is given the lie by 'Danny Deever', as well as by other poems. It may be unpleasant, as so many have found; but that does not rob it of its power.

T.S. Eliot, in his confused plea for Kipling's verse made at the beginning of the Second World War, suggested that it was 'great verse', rather than poetry. We do not, he suggested, possess the right tools to judge it. But he conceded that 'Danny Deever' was poetry.

Eliot's plea for Kipling is one of his more contorted and disingenuous critical efforts. But it deserves attention as a plea from a man of the extreme right for another of the extreme right. It is disingenuous because in it Eliot hopes for a time when the notorious *odium politicum* would cease to operate. What he means is that he is worried about Kipling's lapses from good literary taste but loves and yearns for the overtness of his politics. For all his delicacy and literary elegance, the anti-semitic Eliot's own politics were as coarse and as vulgar as Kipling's; they were also more ignorant, and less deliberately so, since Kipling was British, whereas Eliot was an American with aspirations to become a right-wing English gentleman, something he could never be, and something he did not really understand.

Eliot, whose emotions were isolated from his intellect in a very odd manner, privately thrilled to the jingo in a way that Kipling's educated English readers, Tory or not, seldom have. But he could not admit as much. Yet one can hardly call for the rehabilitation of a poet and then state that he is seldom a poet, only the author of 'great verse'. As so often when the emotive word 'great' is employed, there is something wrong with the critical argument. Usually this is simply because it ceases to be critical. But here what is wrong is Eliot's unacknowledged enjoyment of Kipling's vulgarity. One aspect of Eliot was that he was a secret vulgarian (there is abundant evidence for this judgement). Kipling was, notoriously, a public vulgarian.

Eliot's criticism of Kipling would have been that much more valuable had he felt himself able to admit his own prejudices. But he was not in a sense wrong to thrill to the jingo, if only because much of Kipling's verse does give pleasure as verse, however obtuse the jingoist sentiments he is expressing. As Orwell said in his pioneer essay, one would have to be a liar or a snob to deny that this merely sensuous pleasure frequently exists. It is the same with much of the verse of one of Kipling's models, Swinburne. No less a critic than the almost excessively refined Henry James admitted its presence. If the rhetoric of Kipling's imperialistic verse had been ineffective then it would long ago have ceased to infuriate liberals. It might have been better for Eliot and for literature had Eliot allowed himself to write crude verses straightforwardly denouncing Jews, liberals, democrats, would-be French regicides and enemies of Catholicism: this side of him would not have attracted more odium than did the frigid extremism he vainly tried to conceal – the sort of lack of sensibility that led him to say, just as Hitler was about to take power, 'The population should be homogeneous . . . reasons of race and religion combine to make any large number of free-thinking Jews undesirable . . . a spirit of excessive tolerance is to be deprecated'. I quote this because it resembles some of Kipling's utterances, but is far worse than anything Kipling wrote, and all the more so for coming from a man who was supposed to be so civilised. That it came about through ignorance is no excuse: such unrealistic aloofness is chillingly repulsive. In fact there is a deep *snobisme* in Eliot's plea for Kipling, whose borrowings from the music halls, if indeed they can be characterised as mere borrowings, are far less self-conscious than Eliot's, which came a quarter of a century later and which owed so much to Kipling.

When Kipling does escape from his nasty 'snarl of middle-class gentility' about the disgustingly unashamed aspirations of the poor, he escapes altogether. 'Mary, Pity Women!', which first appeared in *The Seven Seas*, is justly famous, but still underrated. Some still believe it actually to be an old music-hall song. As Angus Wilson points out, it is the father of all the 'proudly amoral "My Man"' songs, and remains better than any. The feeling in it is entirely vicarious, but all the purer for that. Here for once we do see Kipling as lyrical poet, decently indulging his femininity, and improving on the music-hall songs that so inspired him. It is also democratic in the sense that Whitman (a poet Kipling had admired since his schooldays) achieved, and which Eliot could never have achieved. One might say that Kipling, because he allowed his crudity full rein, could reach these heights; Eliot, whose snobbery inhibited him from such forthright expression of his just as crude views, was thus prevented. 'Mary, Pity Women' is worth quoting in full as a reminder of what Kipling could do, of how free he could become of the agonies and angers that possessed him, of the simplicity with which he could identify with women. No wonder Brecht enjoyed him!

You call yourself a man,
　For all you used to swear,
An' leave me, as you can,
　My certain shame to bear?
　I 'ear! You do not care –
You done the worst you know.
　I 'ate you, grinnin' there . . .
Ah, Gawd, I love you so!

Nice while it lasted, an' now it is over –
Tear out your 'eart an' good-bye to your lover!
What's the use o' grievin', when the mother that bore you
(Mary, pity women!) knew it all before you?

It aren't no false alarm,
　The finish to your fun;
You – you 'ave brung the 'arm,
　An' I'm the ruined one!
　An' now you'll off an' run
With some new fool in tow.
　Your 'eart? You 'aven't none . . .
Ah, Gawd, I love you so!

When a man is tired there is naught will blind 'im;
All 'e solemn promised 'e will shove be'ind 'im.
What's the good o' prayin' for the Wrath to strike 'im
(Mary, pity women!), when the rest are like 'im?

What 'ope for me or – it?
　What's left for us to do?
I've walked with men a bit,
　But this – but this is you.
　So 'elp me, Christ, it's true!
Where can I 'ide or go?
　You coward through and through! . . .
Ah, Gawd, I love you so!

All the more you give 'em the less are they for givin' –
Love lies dead, an' you cannot kiss 'im livin'.

Down the road 'e led you there is no returnin'
(Mary, pity women!), but you're late in learnin'!

You'd like to treat me fair?
    You can't, because we're pore?
We'd starve? What do I care!
    We might, but *this* is shore!
    I want the name – no more –
The name, an' lines to show,
    An' not to be an 'ore . . .
Ah, Gawd, I love you so!

What's the good o' pleadin', when the mother that bore you
(Mary, pity women!) knew it all before you?
Sleep on 'is promises an' wake to your sorrow
(Mary, pity women!), for we sail to-morrow!

The poor were for Kipling different from the 'pore', but he had a real feeling for the latter, even if he did only know them in an artificial manner. This poem is, yes, sentimental; it is pastiche; it is only a minor poem. But there is a genuine (and rare) poetry of sentimentality, and that is what Kipling perfectly captures here, for all – or is it because of? – the stereotyped nature of the situation. Nevertheless the situation is real, it did happen frequently, and did provide writers with much material. It is not without its pathos. If you are going to explore a cliché for its human possibilities, very considerable here, then it is best done thoroughly. Kipling here does more than justice to it. W.H. Davies was to achieve similar pathos in his lyric spoken in the person of a dying old woman, with its heartrending refrain: 'Don't touch that bird of paradise, perched on the bedpost there!'

There are other pleasant poems in Kipling's second and third volumes, although it cannot be said that they abound or that they are major. Kipling was a minor poet: neither his thinking nor his view of life developed in his poetry. In some poems he exploited the dramatic monologue method of Robert Browning, one of the most influential poets of the past two hundred years. This debt was shared by many, even most, of the poets of his time, and it was not a secret – Kipling made no claim, tacit or otherwise, to the effect that he was original. But he was original.

One of the most interesting of the poems is 'Tomlinson', which first appeared in the *National Observer* in January 1892. The monologue in it, however, is 'framed' by another narrative, in Kipling's familiar manner. It deals as thoroughly with Kipling's hatred of certain kinds of what Angus Wilson calls 'civilised urban nullity' as any of his poems. It is a vigorous and a striking poem, of superlative energy, but it is not quite successful. The sin of the rich Tomlinson of Berkeley Square is that he has not lived. Peter won't have him in heaven because he has 'read . . . heard . . . thought', but, 'By the worth of the body that once ye had, give answer – what ha' ye done?'. The devil won't have him either:

'Do ye think I would waste my good pit-coal on the hide of a brain-sick
                    fool?
'I see no worth in the hobnailed mirth or the jolthead jest ye did
'That I should wake my gentlemen that are sleeping three on a grid.'

Tomlinson, his 'houseless soul' filled 'with the Fear of Naked Space', becomes desperate:

> 'For I mind that I borrowed my neighbour's wife to sin the deadly sin.'
> The Devil he grinned behind the bars, and banked the fires high:
> 'Did ye read of that sin in a book?' said he; and Tomlinson said, 'Ay!'
> The Devil he blew upon his nails, and the little devils ran,
> And he said: 'Go husk this whimpering thief that comes in the guise
> of a man:
> 'Winnow him out 'twixt star and star, and sieve his proper worth:
> 'There's sore decline in Adam's line if this be the spawn of Earth.'

His putative soul is chased by 'Empusa's crew', who 'weep that they bin too small to sin to the height of their desire'; but they find he has none – he has never done anything except read and steal notions from others. The devil does not care to anger his gentlemen 'for the sake of a shiftless ghost'. The 'mangled soul' prays 'to feel the flame', and the devil almost relents on the grounds that 'the roots of sin are there'. Tomlinson has tried to bring witness to both his virtues and his sins, to Peter and the devil respectively, but Peter replies, 'For the race is run by one and one, and never by two and two'; and the devil replies, 'For the sin ye do by two and two ye must pay for one by one!' But at least the devil sends Tomlinson back to earth, so that he may discover 'worthier sin'. He tells him: 'And . . . the God that you took from a printed book be with you, Tomlinson!'

Although the poem has fine passages, and is something of a tour de force, it shares a weakness with all Kipling's poetry except the best: it is not self-contained. This is to say: it depends upon something outside itself – upon the existence of an attitude that does not really have anything to do with the story it tells or with the original impulses that generated it – to gain its effect. Browning's dramatic monologues at their best do not rely on such outside props, such received attitudes. For all the vigour of some of the language, this poem relies on the notion that ideas and thinking are offensive. Kipling cannot find a convincing narrative centre to generate such a point of view. Tomlinson has not been a 'man'. The moral, 'actions count for more than words', is not truly examined and has not been truly observed in such phenomenological details as we are given of Tomlinson's life. We should need to be given more of such a life. And the truth is, maybe, that everyone is frustrated by too much thinking and too little action, by their tendency to sickly o'er intentions with the pale cast of thought. The battlefield is not really of much use when it is left behind – and battles do not last very long.

The audience whose attitudes Kipling here has in mind is his familiar Anglo-Indian one. But it would not matter, from the point of view of the poetic integrity of the piece, what audience he had in mind. It might have been one composed of gentle liberals and anti-imperialists such as his old headmaster. If a poet depends upon any set of received ideas – unless he is using irony – he evades the nature of his own inspiration, whose precise task is to subvert all received ideas, even if they are eventually verified. The hyper-romantic assumption upon which 'Tomlinson' rests, that ideas are no good but that actions arising from the heart's – not books' – recognitions are, is not examined and demonstrated in the created psychological circumstances, which are too sketchy to be convincing.

As we shall see, 'Tomlinson' was written at a time of serious crisis for Kipling. He had just got married; his closest friend had not long since died; he was thinking about leaving London. It is thus self-critical. But such details of Tomlinson's life as might have provided an objective correlative are lacking. All that can be said is that Tomlinson might very well have been a writer. There is nothing to suggest that he might not have been, and much to suggest that this is the very offence of which he is guilty. The poor crew of Empusa tells the devil:

> '. . . The soul that he got from God he has bartered clean away.
> 'We have threshed a stook of print and book, and winnowed a chattering
> > wind,
> 'And many a soul wherefrom he stole, but his we cannot find.
> 'We have handled him, we have dandled him, we have seared him to the
> > bone,
> 'And, Sire, if tooth and nail show truth he has no soul of his own.'

Kipling dedicated *Barrack-Room Ballads* to the now dead Wolcott Balestier in embarrassingly effusive verses which had previously appeared in different form in Henley's paper on 27 December 1890, and, on the same day, in the *St James's Gazette*. The title in Balestier's lifetime was 'The Blind Bug', and in the *Barrack-Room Ballads* version the last three stanzas have been changed as a tribute to Balestier. The dedicatory poem, presumably incorporating the values that Kipling wanted to remember Wolcott by, is a tribute to 'doers', to men unlike Tomlinson. The imagery once more draws upon stars and the vastnesses of outer space, but does so less successfully:

> Beyond the path of the outmost sun through utter darkness hurled –
> Farther than ever comet flared or vagrant star-dust swirled –
> Live such as fought and sailed and ruled and loved and made our world.
>
> They are purged of pride because they died; they know the worth of
> > their bays;
> They sit at wine with the Maidens Nine and the Gods of the Elder Days –
> It is their will to serve or be still as fitteth Our Father's praise.

These doers, unlike Tomlinson, 'whistle the Devil to make them sport who know that Sin is vain'. They are 'cleansed of base Desire, Sorrow, Lust and Shame'. And in the last three stanzas, now written especially for Wolcott Balestier, he is seen as a paradigmatic doer who

> scarce had need to doff his pride or slough the dross of Earth –
>
> E'en as he trod that day to God so walked he from his birth,
> In simpleness and gentleness and honour and clean mirth.
>
> So cup to lip in fellowship they gave him welcome high
> And made him place at the banquet board – the Strong Men ranged
> > thereby,
> Who had done his work and held his peace and had no fear to die.
>
> Beyond the loom of the last lone star, through open darkness hurled,
> Further than rebel comet dared or hiving star-swarm swirled,

Sits he with those that praise our God for that they served His World.

So we have here, in a poem for the most part earlier in time than 'Tomlinson', a fairly exact clue (inasmuch as this sort of thing is capable of being exact, for none of it bears much intellectual scrutiny) as to the nature of Tomlinson's sin. It is very close to what Kipling felt about himself. But, just as he had to turn to an old poem to write about Balestier's death because he could not possibly say what he really felt about it, so Kipling found it hard to deal with his theme of being a writer who despised writers (that is, himself most of all); he stopped short when he came to the point at which he had to define in imaginative terms the kind of writer he despised most of all.

There are one or two lyrical poems in *Barrack-Room Ballads* that do manage, almost under the guise of convention – as if Kipling did not want them to be particularly noticed – to convey his more personal concerns. While in India he wrote a portentous piece of nonsense in a letter, from which I quoted apropos of Florence Garrard, about love and death. 'The Explanation', which first appeared in the *National Observer* on 1 February 1890, is less unconvincing than that passage, although it does not make much sense at it stands. It is written under the direct influence of the Jacobean lyrics which he had so assiduously studied and which he so admired. He was one of those Victorians who knew in exactly what sense Donne was the 'grandfather' of Browning.

> Love and Death once ceased their strife
> At the Tavern of Man's Life.
> Called for wine, and threw – alas! –
> Each his quiver on the grass.
> When the bout was o'er they found
> Mingled arrows strewed the ground.
> Hastily they gathered then
> Each the lives and loves of men.
> Ah, the fateful dawn deceived!
> Mingled arrows each one sheaved.
> Death's dread armoury was stored
> With the shafts he most abhorred;
> Love's light quiver groaned beneath
> Venom-headed darts of Death.
> Thus it was they wrought our woe
> At the Tavern long ago.
> Tell me, do our masters know,
> Loosing blindly as they fly,
> Old men love while young men die?

The diction here is too stilted to make for complete or even near success; but the poet is trying to say something out of the ordinary. Indeed, could any of the contemporary readers of the poem have paused to consider what exactly it meant? Certainly it is characteristically fatalistic, the mix-up to which it bitterly alludes being attributed to a drunken bout between two gods (or, strictly, personifications). But what about the nature of the mix-up? To be successful this mix-up would have to be a universal one, in order to justify the 'metaphysical' neatness of the poem, and so that readers would feel the pleasure of recognition of a truth. But this is not a familiar situation, and not one many readers would be able to recognise: Kipling perhaps hopes that the epigrammatic force will draw attention away from this. Instead, no one has taken much note of the poem. What is he actually saying?

First, the theme of young men dying in war did not become really familiar in English poetry until during the First World War. There is one main exception: A Shropshire Lad. Where of course we meet it is in ancient Greek poetry, upon his knowledge of which A.E. Housman more or less explicitly draws (doubtless he would have said as a classicist) in A Shropshire Lad. Housman's main themes are reminiscent of Kipling's, in fact: they are exile, war and youthful death. I have already quoted one poem by Housman, but let us consider another even shorter one:

> He, standing hushed, a pace or two apart.
>   Among the bluebells of the listless plain,
> Thinks, and remembers how he cleansed his heart
>   And washed his hands in innocence in vain.

We know that this, although necessarily enigmatic, and very poignant and tender in mood and rhythm, is about a man standing a pace or two away from another man, probably a young one, possibly even his student, for whom he suddenly feels an irresistible desire. (We don't need Psalm 73, 13, to help us with it: the poem is a variation on this, not a key to it.) Housman hints with extreme delicacy at the 'abnormality' of the situation – for it was abnormal then, and men were not expected to write lyrics to other men – by putting woodland flowers in a place where they do not grow 'naturally': into a *listless* plain, one 'destitute of purpose or inclination for some object or pursuit'. Kipling, too, has this strange theme of darkness and guilt, although he puts it in the form of a kind of myth (unfortunately too vague) which he partly derives from Buddhism – in that all is *maya*, illusion – and partly from his pessimistic and undoubtedly gnostic conclusion that the Forces of Darkness can only be opposed, never defeated.

In 'The Explanation' Kipling tells us that young men are killed in war. We are surely entitled to infer this: he can't mean that they are in the habit of just dying otherwise. Although he knows that they die to him because he must deny them to himself, as objects of desire and as people to love (and thus in that aspect not objects) he isn't saying enough to let on. Housman, on the other hand, was directly, if necessarily discreetly, inspired to make something of his poetry by the trial of Oscar Wilde in 1895. Eventually he went abroad and indulged his tastes as best he could. Kipling's way was different: he told himself as little about his own nature as he could, because he knew he could not endure it. He was not a sophisticated scholar, like Housman, but one who praised army men at first because he wanted to be one, and then later because, even more, he wanted to love and be loved by young army men. So he cannot as a poet be as poignant and clear (once you know the secret – but it is clear enough from the poetry) as Housman is, in the fragment quoted above.

Housman's message to himself could be clear, too. Kipling has got to achieve epigrammatical neatness in his little poem, but he can't say what he really means and he doesn't even know that he wants to say what he means: 'the men of action I love get killed, while the men like me who aren't fit for it, being mere writers with poor sight, love them'. For 'old' therefore read 'unfit', 'never-on-the-battlefield', 'not-in-on-the-action' or even 'not-allowed-to-say-what-we-feel'. We are permitted to speculate upon a Kipling who *was* allowed to say what he felt . . . But such speculation will lead us nowhere.

I quoted the lovely and unhappy Housman lines mainly in order to demonstrate the pathos of a homosexual's situation at that time, and in order to draw attention to the equal pathos lying behind some of Kipling's bluster. It puts him in quite a new light. Who could, now, not forgive his excesses? One can now so easily appreciate the sudden and uncharacteristic tolerance he showed to Hugh Walpole when the subject of Radclyffe Hall's novel came up.

'The Explanation', then, could read:

> Love and Death once ceased their strife
> At the Tavern of my life.
> Called for wine, and threw – alas! –
> Each his quiver on the grass.
> When the bout was o'er they found
> Mingled arrows strewed the ground.
> Too hastily they gathered then
> Each the loves and lives of men.
> Ah! The fateful dawn deceived!
> Mingled arrows each one sheathed,
> Love with Death got quite mixed up,
> To make for some a bitter cup:
> Death's dread armoury was stored
> With the shafts he most abhorred!
> So my love's quiver groans beneath
> The venom-headed dart of Death.
> All I love must die to me
> Or else I sink in perfidy.
> Then it was they wrought my woe
> At the Tavern long ago –
> Would I were not so rankly fixed,
> That my arrows were not thus mixed!
> But that is how they wrought my woe
> At the Tavern long ago.
> Tell me, masters, do you know,
> Loosing so blindly as you fly,
> That each I love must quickly die –
> All deaths in war I have to praise
> As though 'twere Death I would embrace?

The reason for making this change to the poem is that the original does not make sense except in the most strained way. Not all young men do die (the First World War had not then been fought). Most of them love. And in what sense do 'old' men love more than their young counterparts?

A monologue more successful than 'Tomlinson', written in Vermont in 1894 and published in *The Seven Seas*, is 'The *Mary Gloster*', one of Kipling's more successful, vigorous and original poems. This is the dying speech of a self-made, risk-taking tycoon ship-owner to his apparently worthless son.

It is an example of how a poet may legitimately make use of another poet without stealing from him. The method is Browning's, but the treatment is the author's own. The poem is genuinely dramatic, the speaker is endowed with increasing psychological life as his desperate tirade continues, and there are no really bad lapses, only one or two rhythmic failures such as are seldom found in Browning's best monologues. Here Kipling has found an objective correlative, and, if he is solving any personal problems, then that, as in some of the stories we have already looked at, is incidental, a matter for the literary biographer rather than for the literary critic.

> I've paid for your sickest fancies; I've humoured your crackedest whim –
> Dick, it's your daddy, dying: you've got to listen to him!
> Good for a fortnight, am I? The doctor told you? He lied.
> I shall go under by morning, and – Put the nurse outside.
> Never seen death yet, Dickie? Well, now is your time to learn,
> And you'll wish you held my record before it comes to your turn.
> Not counting the Line and the Foundry, the Yards and the village, too,
> I've made myself and a million; but I'm damned if I made you.
> Master at two-and-twenty, and married at twenty-three –
> Ten thousand men on the pay-roll, and forty freighters at sea!
> Fifty years between 'em, and every year of it fight,
> And now I'm Sir Anthony Gloster, dying, a baronite:
> For I lunched with his Royal 'Ighness – what was it the papers had?
> 'Not least of our merchant-princes.' Dickie, that's me, your dad!
> I didn't begin with askings. I took my job and I stuck;
> I took the chances they wouldn't, an' now they're calling it luck.

These opening lines establish that Sir Anthony is a magnate of importance, that he is vulgar, and that he is disappointed in his son, whom he despises (he doesn't think he could die bravely) and in whom he can see no apparent trace of himself. Perhaps the vulgarian is a narcissist? He wants to emphasise that he took the risks that others – some of whom now serve him – would not. He wants to emphasise, too, that he was married at the early age of twenty-three, as if to reinforce the massive nature of his youthful risk-taking, and as if women really were as bad as all that. To his wife, he says, he owes his money and what he thinks of as his manhood: 'And your mother saving the money and making a man of me'. It was his wife who encouraged him to seek his fortune, borrow money and take further risks. But then she died while they were on a voyage:

> And we dropped her in fourteen fathom: I pricked it off where she sank.
> Owners we were, full owners, and the boat was christened for her,
> And she died in the *Mary Gloster*. My heart, how young we were!
> So I went on a spree round Java and well-nigh ran her ashore,
> But your mother came and warned me and I wouldn't liquor no more:
> Strict I stuck to my business, afraid to stop or I'd think,
> Saving the money (she warned me), and letting the other men drink.

So, with the ghost of his wife as an advisor, he went on to prosper, and did it by going boldly for the best and yet the most economical – a partner called M'Cullough is reprimanded, if only by implication, for wanting to do things a little too finely: they must not be, to take up again the metaphor of C.S. Lewis, too full of vitamins. People asked Sir Anthony how he managed to do so well, and he 'gave 'em the Scripture text': 'You keep your light so shining a little in front o' the next!'

On his way to a fortune he had put his credit aside for Dick, whose character, as his father sees him, we now get to know better:

> I thought – it doesn't matter – you seemed to favour your ma,
> But you're nearer forty than thirty, and I know the kind you are.
> Harrer and Trinity College! I ought to ha' sent you to sea –
> But I stood you an education, an' what have you done for me?
> The things I knew was proper you wouldn't thank me to give,
> And the things I knew was rotten you said was the way to live.
> For you muddled with books and pictures, an' china an' etchin's and fans,
> And your rooms at college was beastly – more like a whore's than a man's;
> Till you married that thin-flanked woman, as white and as stale as a bone,
> And she gave you your social nonsense; but where's that kid o' your own?
> I've seen your carriages blocking the half o' the Cromwell Road,
> But never the doctor's brougham to help the missus unload.

We learn, further, that, according to his father, the only manly thing Dickie ever did was to survive where his brothers and sisters didn't ('Only you, an' you stood it'); he is a 'liar' (but no instance is given), 'idle' and as mean as 'a colliers whelp/Nosing for scraps in the galley'. He is therefore to have all the money in trust with interest paid: his father won't give it to him, as he 'made it in trade': the capital will go back into the business. Dickie's insincere wife will be furious, but Sir Anthony's own wife wouldn't have been able to stand her, and 'anyhow, women are queer . . .' 'She carried her freight each run' – he is always concerned to compare his wife to this complicated piece of machinery which he named after her, just as Kipling would compare his son to a machine on the occasion of his birth.

So Sir Anthony is dying choked with resentment, and is inflicting his vulgarity ('unload'), loneliness and rage on his son and on his daughter-in-law. Is this lusty and robust coarseness justified by any set of actual circumstances, is it just comic, or what? More of the dying man's attitudes are revealed, to allow us to judge. His daughter-in-law, he is sure, would affect grief – 'Grateful? Oh, yes, I'm grateful, but keep her away from here.' He then goes on to speak of his mistress. 'But give pore Aggie a hundred, and tell her your lawyers'll fight./She was the best o' the boiling . . .'

> I'm in for a row with the mother – I'll leave you settle my friends.
> For a man he must go with a woman, which women don't understand –
> Or the sort that say they can see it they aren't the marrying brand.
> But I wanted to speak o' your mother that's Lady Gloster still;
> I'm going to up and see her, without its hurting the will.
> Here! Take your hand off the bell-pull. Five thousand's waiting for you,
> If only you'll listen a minute, and do as I bid you do.

It is at this point that the attentive reader realises that the speaker has profound anxieties, and that all is not quite as straightforward as, initially, it seemed. Perhaps Kipling began writing this with the idea of denouncing arty ungrateful childless snobs from the mouth of a dying old buccaneer;

but it has got out of hand by now. Dickie performs only one action during
the entire monologue, and this is to put out his hand to the bell-pull to
be shown out when his father starts talking about his mother in a vulgar
manner. Sir Anthony admits that only in death is he able to 'up and see' his
wife 'without its hurting the will'. So did she in fact ever share his attitudes,
out of which spring his hostility to his son – or did she deprecate them?
'They'll try to prove me crazy, and, if you bungle, they can; /And I've
only you to trust to! (O God, why ain't it a man?)'

Having insulted and abused but also been honest with his son (as we
variously wish to look at it, with only the speaker's word to go on), he
has to ask a favour of him. It must be this necessity that has brought his
resentment of Dickie's disappointing lack of what he feels are the manly
qualities to the surface of his dying mind. The matters which are worrying
him are quite complicated:

> There's some waste money on marbles, the same as M'Cullough tried –
> Marbles and mausoleums – but I call that sinful pride.
> There's some ship bodies for burial – we've carried 'em, soldered and
> packed;
> Down in their wills they wrote it, and nobody called *them* cracked.
> But me – I've too much money, and people might . . . All my fault:
> It came o' hoping for grandsons and buying that Wokin' vault . . .
> I'm sick o' the 'ole dam' business. I'm going back where I came.
> Dick, you're the son o' my body, and you'll take charge o' the same!
> I want to lie by your mother, ten thousand mile away,
> And they'll want to send me to Woking; and that's where you'll earn
> your pay.

This is an absurd request on the part of a rich man, whose last wishes
would certainly be observed whether he had bought a posh vault at Woking
or not. Yet he asks Dickie, on the pretext that his father's death has 'upset'
him ('You write to the Board, and tell/Your father's death has upset you
an' you're goin' to cruise for a spell' – he'd like the Board not to know
what he thinks he knows about Dickie's attitude to him), to take a cruise
on the *Mary Gloster* and to drop the ship and his body, hugger mugger, by
his mother's. It is all arranged, and the necessary favours will be granted
by old friends who have reason to be grateful (Kipling can never resist
the Masonic touch, even when he does not have Masonry specifically
in mind). While he insults Dickie in making the request, he does add that
'you'd like the *Mary Gloster*' . . . His old friend McAndrew (who figures
in the 'Hymn' of his name), whom he has never invited to dinner but who
will 'see it out', will pay him his five thousand pound bribe and take him
back when he's scuppered the boat with his father inside it. Sir Anthony
'made himself and a million, but this world is a fleetin' show,/And he'll
go to the wife of 'is bosom the same as he ought to go . . .

He does want the *Mary* scuppered, even if the wife of 'is bosom whom by
then he'll have joined would have thought it a waste. He can't help adding,
'For my son 'e was never a credit: 'e muddled with books and art,/And
'e lived on Sir Anthony's money and 'e broke Sir Anthony's heart.'

Since a rich man can buy everything but love, this isn't a necessary
request. It is a plea for a gesture from the allegedly arty and snobbish son.
Will he do it for his father even while he is left in no doubt as to what his

father thinks of him? Sir Anthony is so lonely that he assumes Dickie will
feel no grief for him: he is offering to pay him to feign it. Still he cannot
learn that 'upset' at death or anything else cannot be bought. Our thoughts
ought – but perhaps not enough readers' do – to go to the son at about this
point: what does *he* think of all this?

Suddenly the monologue changes: it is now addressed not to the living
but to the dead, to his wife, Mary, whom he wants to join, lying in the
Macassar Strait. But Dickie hasn't left, and is still listening.

> The only one you left me – O mother, the only one!
> Harrer and Trinity College – me slavin' early an' late –
> An' he thinks I'm dying crazy, and you're in Macassar Strait!
> Flesh o' my flesh, my dearie, for ever an' ever amen,
> The first stroke come for a warning. I ought to ha' gone to you then.

What is troubling him, apparently, is that his purchase of other women,
to whom however he never 'talked . . . secrets', might prejudice in some
way his wish to lie beside her at the bottom of the sea. Whether he had
these women before or after Mary's death, or both, is not made clear, but
'a man must go with a woman, as you *could* not understand.'

It is therefore not clear, either, whether he feels that Mary objects to his
being unfaithful to her in life, or to her memory, or both. But a later line
shows that it does not matter since (he hopes): 'the wife of my youth shall
charm me – an' the rest can go to hell!' Yet, is the repeated and inarticulate
complaint (if it is a complaint) that she *would* not understand that a man
has to 'go' with a woman a memory of old conflicts or just a recognition
of how Mary, his only love (evidently), was? We are entitled to ask, since
he 'went' with her, how she is for him, in some sense, 'not a woman'. We
are further entitled to infer that he used her like a 'whore' (like, say, Aggie)
but in some way knew that she was not one.

As in many dramatic monologues which are addressed to second
parties, the latters' silence is pregnant. His dying mind is trying to make
the *Mary Gloster*, his property, the foundation of his Line, into Mary herself.
He repeats, with reference to the women he's bought, that he is thankful
to God that he 'can *pay*' for his 'fancies': previously this remark was made
apropos of his being able to 'patch' and 'lay aside' the *Mary* for this
last purpose. Even now he is worrying about *wasting* five thousand – but
what is that to him if he can be in the haven 'where I would be'? He is
trying his best to take his money with him although he knows he cannot.
He proclaims that he believes in the Resurrection from his plain man's
understanding of the Bible, but 'I wouldn't trust 'em at Wokin'; we're safer
at sea again'. 'I'm sick of the hired women. I'll kiss my girl on her lips!'
Dickie, he adds in a vicious parenthesis, will certainly go to hell in any
case . . . At the poem's close the speaker lurches into uneasy and inchoate
but ecstatic sexual metaphor:

>   I'll lie in our standin'-bed,
> An' Mac'll take her in ballast – an' she trims best by the head . . .
> Down by the head an' sinkin', her fires are drawn and cold,
> And the water's splashin' hollow on the skin of the empty hold –
> Churning an' choking and chuckling, quiet and scummy and dark –
> Full to her lower hatches and risin' steady. Hark!

That was the after-bulkhead . . . She's flooded from stem to stern . . .
'Never seen death yet, Dickie? . . . Well, now is your time to learn!

This monologue is always taken as an unequivocal expression of Kipling's own views. Even Angus Wilson, while of course perfectly aware of the elementary error of attributing to writers the views of their characters, claims both that 'The *Mary Gloster*' was an attack (so to say) on his youthful 'aesthetic' self, the boy who decorated his study in a Pre-Raphaelite style at USC, and that in the poem itself, as in 'McAndrew's Hymn', Kipling

celebrates not the machines, but the men who work them . . . Both are positive hymns to the life force. They work perfectly . . . The celebration of the ruthless life-force of a self-made man . . . is really the only work of those Vermont years that fully suggest any strong influence from his newly adopted country.

Now this is venturing into dangerous territory. Granted that it is irresistible at a merely superficial level to see it as an expression of Kipling's own attitudes, because those attitudes were so baldly stated and are so well known, it seeks, however unwittingly, to deprive him of his stature as an imaginative writer. Imaginative writers, and particularly poets, go against themselves. The more of a vengeance with which they do it – if they truly do it, and are not playing a literary game – the more powerful they are likely to be as writers. And once again, Kipling, certainly initially spurred on by superficial loathing (and fear) of his very brief and youthful Pre-Raphaelite past, has undermined himself. He did not do this to any great extent in poetry: he was a minor poet with a 'line' in patriotic stuff that has little relevance to his poetic achievement. He saved the larger part of his genius for fiction. But in this poem as much as in any the imagination has free rein.

Dickie, the son, doesn't speak a word (of course). Our patience has to be worn very thin indeed before we will make as if to abandon a dying parent. We only ever see Dickie as he is perceived by his father. We watch him go for the bell when he can't stand any more of what must be familiar rant. But the poem is written by a man who is himself preoccupied with 'books and art'. Any reader must know that – and to that extent the knowledge, although incidental, is part of the text. What any reader may not know, although most by now should, is that he has married an American wife, this creator of Sir Anthony Gloster, Baronite, who insists on her husband and herself dining every evening (usually alone) in full evening dress, Kipling in white tie and tails, his wife in a low cut gown with train – and on keeping a properly dressed English butler, and on touring the Vermont countryside in a carriage driven by a flunky wearing top-boots, doeskin breeches, blue coat and top hat. She has given him a child and will give him two more – but anyone could be forgiven, in wild Brattleboro, for thinking her a snob, and if not 'thin-flanked' then at least 'as stale and white as a bone'. This must have been the sort of thing, allowing for their lack of Kipling's linguistic gift, that her neighbours said about her. It was not lost on her husband. He has got 'social nonsense' from her, too – or so they say, and so says her brother. There is also (as we shall see) evidence that he did not much care for it. But that is biographical knowledge and it is not part of the text of the poem. That the author is a muddler with books and art has, though, got to do with the poem: because it is a poem, it is in a book, and it has art as well as verve and the rest. That his wife appears a snob to her neighbours has nothing to do with it, or is at least not in it. But let us consider the text itself again, to see if it really is a 'celebration of the ruthless life-force'. It is not. The vigour of the expression, the authorial pleasure in the coarseness, the vulgarity, the vitality, the rhythmic energy: these are all examples of the life-force trying to assert itself against the fact of death. But the monologue itself is nothing less than a relentless (possibly reluctant – although there is no real reason to suppose that) exposé of the emotional paucity of materialism. The application of common sense, not of any attitudes of mind, immediately reveals them.

The boy Dickie, we learn, had a feeling for his mother ('you seemed to favour your ma'). Perhaps this was because he reacted unfavourably to his father's coarseness, or to his tyrannical insistence that he become a 'man'. Sir Anthony's notion that his only surviving child should do what his father has done is, by any standards, intolerable and cruel. Such parental tyranny, like arranged marriages, is part of the stuff of folklore and even of popular novels. Maybe after all Dickie was like Kipling himself and favoured books and art – and thrilled to the appeal of the ruthless life-force, and thus loved his father unknown to the old man . . . Perhaps the ruthless life-force frightened him, too.

Robert Browning's overt views were much less clear-cut than Kipling's. We puzzle over some of his monologues from the time we attend school. Some of the less good ones seem designed for it. Kipling's views are so overt, indeed, that we fondly imagine that we need not puzzle over his. But a dramatic monologue is above all a revelation of character. We are entitled to apply common sense to it, and we then discover which monologues stand up and which don't. This stands up. And when we apply common sense to it, we find that Dickie has probably been badly done by. Here is a man who wants his son to follow in his footsteps and who is not going to be merely disappointed if he does not: he is going to be plain abusive. It is suggested that Dickie and his wife are snobs – but only in the crass perception of Sir Anthony. Yes, that perception is salty and energetic. It is also crass. It is nowhere charged – and this suggests strongly that it cannot be – that Dickie is a thief, or in any way 'immoral' (by his father's lights), or that he does not possess good taste, or that he did other than well in his namby pamby studies at Harrer (cousin Stan went to Harrer) and Trinity. It is true that he rejected what his father 'knew was proper' and asserted that what he 'knew was rotten' 'was the way to live'. But this points to no more than a clash of viewpoints, such as had happened between Kipling and his own father over *Mother Maturin* and perhaps over other things. It is true that we know that Kipling himself wrote not very good poems questioning the values of education when it came to fighting, and that the mention of Walter Pater made him 'sick'. Perhaps now he is questioning that view as expressed by Sir Anthony, who wouldn't have heard of Pater or Oscar Wilde except as 'rotten' (he is dying just one year before this is confirmed by the Wilde scandal. He would have told you so – nothing like as clean and decent as his feelings for old Mac). For Kipling does not choose to make Sir Anthony very credible, in the modern journalistic sense of that word. He does give him vigour, but then the life-force is, above all, vigorous. 'That is what is so difficult about it', one can hear some namby-pamby childless Harrer man drawling from his carriage. Vigour is not the same as 'credibility'. Sir Anthony believes his son to be a failure. But there are no clues to suggest that he actually is a failure.

All Sir Anthony can assert is that 'a man must go with a woman'. What does that mean? If the women he bought seemed to 'understand' this, being not of the marrying brand, then why not want Aggie (the best of the boiling) in death? Why this wish to return to his wife now he is close to death? Surely a woman who 'understands' is a jewel compared with one who does not? But Kipling is revealing Sir Anthony as the possessor of meaningless and familiar values. The wife is for childbirth ('unloading') *and* spiritual love (meaning Harrer for the boys and all that, perhaps?), and the Aggies of this world, the whores, are for what a 'man must do'. Who in all sincerity is to assert that the disgustingly educated Dickie does not have and do *both* with his thin-flanked, white, stale, childless but enlightened wife? After all, Sir Anthony has heard, he says, that even the faithful McAndrew, 'stiff-necked Glasgow beggar!' (euphemism for the affectionately intended 'bugger'), has prayed for his soul. That is evidence of another point of view. Perhaps Mac prayed for the soul of this tough, colourful man of his word who is also such a reprobate, a womanizer and such a bad, and therefore deeply unhappy father . . .

We know nothing whatsoever bad about Dickie (unless giving parties is bad). We know nothing bad, either, about Dickie's wife, whose grief, so sneered at by her father-in-law, may be sincere. Perhaps her tears have been the genuine tears of an enlightened woman who has always felt awkward: sorrow to see the light in this tough, spiteful, obstinate but vital old man going out at last . . . Such questions of attitude are left entirely open.

So these last wishes are the grotesque if touching and eloquent fantasy of a man who thinks he can buy everything with money ('Thank Gawd, I can pay for my fancies!'), who is so clumsy that he cannot separate a 'fancy' from a wish, even his own final one. But his last desire, less ignoble than the fancies of his life, is not quite a fancy. He cannot buy it and he believes that the world thinks him 'crazy' because of it. He could have arranged what he wanted with McAndrew, easily. But he needs Dickie, flesh of his flesh, to do it. Yet he knows that he cannot ask, 'Would you do this for me, son?' He hasn't earned that right: to ask in love. He cannot understand that the silent Dickie might well admire in him at least this wish. He can't say: 'Dickie, in a stupid sinful fit of pride I bought a posh vault at Woking, it was when I thought you might have kids. Now I'm dying I've changed my mind. I do believe in the Bible and I've always read it, so I believe in the Resurrection and eternal life. But I want to be with your ma. I don't hold it against you that you've no kids. All mine but you died, and then Mary did too. Now if *you* took me out to the Macassar Strait where I left her, *you'd* understand. *They'll* think I'm cracked. Will you do it for me, son? I'll see you're not out of pocket of course. Mac would do it alone, but . . .'

The real subject is why Sir Anthony can't ask that of his son – and why he is convinced that Dickie, too, like the rest, thinks he's cracked. (Perhaps he is the only one who knows he isn't. Perhaps not.) His tragedy is that he has not left himself enough room to learn, or start to learn, the simple language of love and affection. He knows that this language exists, but has all his life conveniently located it with his wife in the Macassar Strait, and so has allowed it to rest there. Now that he can't buy anything more, he wants to go there, and he wants to be transported there, with love, by flesh of his flesh. His last words amount to a kind of inarticulate orgasm that is as fear-ridden as his ever were – except with Aggie, who 'understood' and is going to be paid for it, but who could probably make no further comment than the question, 'feel better dearie?' We do not know and do not need to know whether Dickie does understand or not. But he is the sort of man who reads good books and so he might understand. It would add some pathos if Dickie were found to be, indeed, a rotten, idle, snobbish little rat who couldn't and didn't. But Sir Anthony at this final stage of life has not gained the emotional authority, despite his vigour, to any response at all. So, tragically, we aren't told: it is irrelevant. Even if Dickie were to do as he was asked, he couldn't have done it with a loving heart.

So he turns desperately to the dead Mary ('pity women'), and appeals to her. It is all very well, any listening Dickie might think, to say that you're sick of whores and want to kiss your own girl on the lips at last – but it depends on when you say it. This is a bit late in the day. Sir Anthony's crassness has clearly been an issue between him and his wife; and it is weighing now on his mind. A man has to go with a woman, which Mary just *would* not understand. So the poem ends in a welter of sexually charged chaos, 'quiet and scummy and dark', the dying man speaking to his dead wife with the listening son – supposed to be in some way reprimanded for not being the object his father desired rather than his own real self. Yet one of the joys of having children, is to be able to have the true vision of their becoming unpossessed and free and themselves. There is some poignancy in Sir Anthony's desire for burial at sea, in his own ship, and with his wife. But the real poignancy, and the final poignancy, is reserved for the fact that he has engineered himself into a position in which he cannot be loved by anyone at all. And it is interesting that in his last thoughts only one person, whom he never invited to dinner, and who prays for him, thinks enough of him to be loyal to him: McAndrew. The ending incidentally causes the reader of the 'metaphysicals' to wonder if Kipling knew what 'death' so often meant in their poems. It seems that he did.

So Kipling as a poet is able, at his best, whilst apparently indulging himself in 'celebration of the ruthless life-force', to question the ultimate value of any kind of ruthlessness. But it is not only his still imperialistically minded readers who woodenly insist on confusing the authorial voice with that of the speaker in 'The *Mary Gloster*'. It is an eminently understandable confusion. But to take that view is to be seduced by the power of rhetoric against Kipling's true artistic intentions, and to make him out to be a less subtle poet than he is.

It is preposterous to suggest that Kipling the man, the polemicist, would ever have subscribed to any such 'humane' reading of this poem as I have given above. But something in him gave his readers the clear chance to make such a reading. He understood the dangers of such bluster as Sir Anthony's only too well: from self-knowledge. As so often, he undermined what seemed to him, for most of the time, to be one of his life's most cherished projects. That is what poets, whatever they may be like as men and women, do.

Wolcott

Kipling first met Wolcott Balestier either at the very end of 1889 or the very beginning of 1890. We can date their intimacy from June 1890. Their friendship is one of literary history's most famous – and most mysterious. What was its real nature?

Joseph Nerée Balestier, the paternal grandfather of Wolcott Balestier and his brother and two sisters, was born on a plantation in Martinique. He was of a Huguenot family which emigrated from France to America during the eighteenth century. He went to Chicago during the land boom in the years before the Civil War to make his fortune in real estate, and made it. While in Chicago he met and married a woman of notable family, Caroline Starr Wolcott, and after living for a while in New York, where he practised law, he and his wife settled in Brattleboro (1868), a fashionable watering place on the Connecticut River, in Windham County, Vermont, only a few miles north of the state of Massachusetts. He believed that the waters might cure his gout, rheumatism, or whatever afflictions it was that he owned. Doubtless they did. He and Caroline lived on their farm, Beechwood, and it may have been memories of their grand style that gave their granddaughter, also named Caroline, ideas when she went to live in Brattleboro some twenty-five years later. Certainly they dressed for dinner, and certainly there was a choice of wines. But their servants were not English, and, though talked about, they were not ostentatious. Joseph Balestier died in 1888. His widow lived on until 1901, giving much of her time to the local Unitarian church. She was known and long remembered as 'Madame Balestier'. Insofar as the family had a ruler, it was her: those who did not want to be under her sway didn't challenge it, but kept a respectful distance. She seems not to have been particularly intelligent, but very practical and sensible – and that, intelligence being so expensive a luxury, was why she had what could be called a successful life.

Among their sons and daughters was Henry, who died young and did not outlive his own father. He married Anna Smith, an Episcopalian, who may not altogether have pleased the old lady by taking her son off into another church. Anna was the daughter of a famous international lawyer and judge, Erasmus Peshine Smith, who was advisor to the Emperor of Japan on matters of international law. They had four children: Charles Wolcott, always known by the second of his Christian names, Caroline, 'a little active clever woman', said to be like her paternal grandmother in character, rather plain in appearance, Josephine, charming and regarded as a beauty, and Beatty, the youngest.

Beatty, although as intelligent as his elder brother, lacked the application to make a fortune, and was always complaining that he had no cash. He was the beloved of his old grandmother at Beechwood, although he eventually quarrelled with her when someone in her household declared that he was a forger (he was not that, but might have signed a bill in someone else's name, just to do them a favour). He was, said his friend, the waspish theatre-critic Alexander Woollcott, 'violent, warm-hearted, disorderly . . . a charming, contentious rattlepate'. He was a lover of exploits with dogs and horses, and famous for them locally. He would do anything for you except give you money, which he never had; if you dunned him for a bill you were not popular – and for some time no one did. He had a tongue 'like a skinning-knife' when he was drunk, and he often was. Still, let's have a drink and forget it. Don't let's spoil life by being too serious about it. Everyone's a bit crazy and that's how it's meant to be. Of course we'll be as serious as we must be tomorrow. Everyone means to be honourable. Here's how. His neighbours at Brattleboro, where he lived for his whole life, would have been devastated had he fallen on really desperate times; he never quite did, although he drifted nearer and nearer to them as he grew older. He might have made an athletic popular film star had he been born a little later. He had all the stamina his elder brother lacked, had some of the same charisma although none of the acumen (or cunning?) and staying power, and was better looking but lacked the sorrowfully appealing ears. He died in time to avoid total desperation (he petitioned to be merely bankrupt within a short time of the Kiplings' arrival in America – but that was nothing to him), in 1936, a few months after Kipling, the worst enemy of his good-natured, turbulent and troublesome, but unpuzzled life. Or was his worst enemy the plainer of his two sisters, the woman without whom his brother-in-law might have been goddamned all right?

Wolcott was the white hope, though, and he grew up adored by his two sisters and his widowed mother. He had enormous and unquestioned confidence in himself. His one handicap in life seemed to be that he had what was then known as a 'weak chest', but the sense of fragility it brought with it, the delicacy, attracted people to him still more. He had charisma, was a live wire, carried everyone along with him in his enthusiasm for whatever he was doing. At Cornell, where he studied 'Early English' without achieving any particular academic distinction, he was the 'idol of his classmates', whom he joined in every conceivable prank – but never overstepping the bounds of propriety. He later studied at the University of Virginia. While still attending school in Rochester he had been a cub reporter on the *Rochester Post Express*. He worked as an assistant librarian in New York, then again as a journalist. At the age of twenty-two he published a novel, *The Potent Philtre* (1884). This was followed by other novels and some short stories; moralistic (*A Victorious Defeat*, 1886), but cast in the mould of Howells – the same Howells who patronised young Kipling in *Harper's* – whom he met and by whom he was encouraged. He was in Colorado in 1885, and out of this came his least insubstantial work of fiction: a novel of the mining camps, *Benefits Forgot* (1892), which was first serialised in *Century* magazine. When James supplied an introductory memoir of him in a posthumous book of three stories, *The Average Woman* (1892), he made the best of it. His other book is the collaboration with Kipling, *The Naulahka* (1892), a sort of 'Western' about a Californian speculator in India. It has not been underrated, as both Angus Wilson and Kingsley Amis claim. It has been judged alongside Kipling's works and,

rightly, found wanting. It is unsubtle and unenchanting. Had it been by
Wolcott alone it would have been pallid stuff indeed. But the American
bits, nominally by Wolcott, have been excitedly gingered up by Kipling.
It is a rollicking good yarn, but absolutely nothing more than that.
Wolcott found employment eventually with the New York publisher John
W. Lovell, who sent him to London as agent in 1888, a year before Kipling
arrived there.

There is a fading photograph of Charles Wolcott Balestier. As with
almost all of those who are supposed to have had charisma, it is at first
hard to discern what all the fuss was about. But he looks very determined.
He has a pencil to his lips; he is at a table covered by a thick carved or
embroidered cloth; his elbow is resting on it, and there is a pad of paper by
him. Obviously he is posing for the picture: he looks a little uneasy in spite
of himself. The table is mounted on a single pedestal with lion's claws on
castors, as were fashionable in those days. He has abundant hair, parted in
the middle, a high forehead, huge staring eyes. Only one of his enormous
innocent ears is visible in the print, but it is so desperately prominent that
perception inexorably supplies the other – and the two ears, one real and
the other a necessary illusion, stick out so much that he looks as though at
any minute he might take unwitting flight. He is very 'interesting' looking,
and we are told that he was 'pale'. The wing-like ears add to his delicacy,
and must have excited women and others who could love men. He has
been 'caught' in pensive mood, but knows that he has been thus caught.
A highly ambitious and capable man who means to be a coming one. He
is going to 'astonish the world' (says Carrington), and as a writer, too. Why
not? It is exceedingly important to his enterprises that he should be able to
take people aside and say, 'I'm a novelist myself.' Indeed, it is of paramount
importance to him, and right now, about the time Kipling arrives in London, it is a cause for some irritation; it is the one thing that is not going too
well in his life, this fiction business. For he must know that on his own he
has not yet been too good: clumsy, newspaperish, superficial. His works
are not getting him the attention he requires. But he has the friendship of
so many who are getting attention . . .

Edmund Gosse was excited by this young man, and when Balestier
suddenly died of typhoid in Dresden in December 1891 wrote a memoir of
him for the *Cosmopolitan*, which he subsequently reprinted. James wrote of
him, too, at length. Gosse claimed that he made more friends in London
than 'any living American'. Wolcott was aware that English writers were
unhappy about the pirating of their works in America, and he could sense
that the time for an international agreement of some kind was approaching.
He presented himself as the young man who would solve the problem. The
only way an English author could get round being pirated in America was
to come to an arrangement with an American citizen. This was difficult,
and very few were able to do it. Wolcott Balestier now set himself up as
an honest American citizen with whom a writer *could* come to a profitable
and just arrangement. He bought up the sheets of books before they had
appeared in Great Britain, and he paid advances for them, apparently
sometimes out of his own pocket. There were others doing the same thing
at the same time, but he was infinitely the best at it. When he went to see
the ageing Meredith on Box Hill he was there, his sister Josephine wrote in
a letter home, for seven hours, talking. He met Hardy and his wife, Besant,

Mrs Humphrey Ward, Mrs W.K. Clifford, William Black – everyone. However sensitive and understanding he really was, he had the gift of being interesting. He opened an office in Dean's Yard by Westminster Abbey, and, if he was not visiting a writer or at a writer's party, he was usually there, working until after midnight. He had an assistant, a young man from Brattleboro. He wanted the best authors, he told each author he was the best, and he would give all these best authors the best deal. He would, too. Wouldn't you have liked him if you had been an author with an American readership? Had he lived, he might have become a very big publishing man indeed. At the end of his short life, his novel with Kipling almost finished, he went into partnership with a young man who did become such a giant, William Heinemann. The firm of Heinemann and Balestier was all set to challenge Baron Tauschnitz's monopoly of continental editions of English-language writers. The enterprise, the 'English Library', was Balestier's reason for being in Dresden when he fell victim to typhoid, and hadn't the stamina to pull through. His sister Carrie, who nursed him throughout this last illness, said that she knew he was very seriously ill when he refused to allow her to ring for a second time for the maid. Angus Wilson notes how characteristic·it was of Carrie to say this.

The tone of the memoirs of this meteor that crossed the London literary world of the very late 1880s and early 1890s tends to the reverential. This is understandable. There is, however, more than a hint – in Gosse, for example – that Wolcott was pushy and far from perfectly educated in matters literary. He was a man who set out to seem indispensable to British authors, and they were not going to want be too critical of his manners. Publishers take care how they talk about the authors they like and publish, and authors are equally careful in what they say about their mentors' tastes. Even F. R. Leavis, not a man smelling of sweet violets, indeed the Mr Misery amongst literary critics of his day, was never heard to denounce the unappealing Bloomsburyean tastes of the House of Chatto, even though he could easily have done; and its gentlemanly bosses would always excuse themselves, as is well known, if asked about Leavis's latest ill-bred if in part perceptive attack. This is probably how it should be, as it tends to bring the best out of both parties, especially when the author and the publisher are ones of account – as Leavis and Chatto certainly were.

Wolcott, then, was 'no Adonis' – as Hilton Brown, author of an early life of Kipling beholden only to Trix, puts it. As Brown says, Wolcott was brash, his accent grated, he collected labels naming exotic places he had not visited and stuck them on his trunks and cases, he patronisingly addressed all women as 'Miss', and he was an American publisher 'bent on Getting Things Done'. When he died the good things got recorded and the rest did not.

But, as will shortly become apparent, he divided those who knew him. All 'indispensable' people do this to some extent. Wolcott was coming to be a bit indispensable. Naturally, he prompted gush: he set up good cash deals, and there is nothing like good money for producing good gush. Justin Macarthy, a critic, novelist and politician almost forgotten except for the comments he made on Kipling, called Wolcott 'a young man of singular and varied intellectual gifts with a sweet and lovable nature'. There is no evidence of intellectual gifts in his writings. Was he just a good business man? Miss Mary Gleed Tuttiet, who wrote melodramatic novels under the name of Maxwell Gray, waxed almost as lyrical about Wolcott, in one of her dedications, as Kipling did in his adapted verses in front of *Barrack-Room Ballads*. But the two men who said the nicest things about Wolcott – Kipling never said much – were Edmund Gosse, who did not quite keep his reservations to himself, and Henry James, who did – although his convoluted manner in itself carries the implication of all the reservations in the world. After his death James wrote to Mrs Balestier:

> Your letter . . . gives me now my only occasion to *name* dear Wolcott articulately and feel that I still hold on firmly, in the cold rush of time which makes a wind as from the passage of an ice-flow, to the reality of his brief presence here. His ghostly photograph is on the wall of my room and looks down at me as I write you late at night in this silent sleeping little town – as with a melancholy consciousness of what I am doing.

James's expression of his emotions is inevitably contrived inasmuch as he is trying to do justice for another's sake. But he was clearly much moved by Wolcott. That Gosse, too, who was clever at conveying his real meaning through words acceptable to society, should feel 'a thrill of attraction', should note the 'mixture of suave Colonial French, and strained nervous New England blood', and comment on 'the capricious contrast between this wonderful intelligence and the unhelpful frame that did it so much wrong', suggests that he may well have exploited his charms, and that men of a certain disposition, as well as women, may have overrated his mentality (just as the susceptible James did the young Hugh Walpole's). James, as someone has said, was used to his swans being geese. Whistler and his wife fell for Wolcott's charms. So did Austin Dobson, Alma Tadema, George Meredith, Jean Ingelow, Kate Greenaway and a host of other luminaries. Arthur Waugh, publisher and man of letters, father of Evelyn and Alec, who worked for Wolcott, spoke of his 'chameleon power with people'. Wolcott's whole family came to tend and admire him in his conquest of London. First Josephine. Then Caroline, who simply took him over lock, stock and barrel, looking after him at his Kensington house and in the holiday house he took at Freshwater in the Isle of Wight. Eventually Mrs Balestier, his mother, arrived – and Beatty and his wife Mai.

But Beatty had to be 'repatriated', which was a disappointment, as was Mrs Balestier's discovery that literary celebrity didn't get one into 'society' (as Carrington puts it). Beatty didn't add to Wolcott's reputation. He went to the docks one afternoon and remembered with grim pleasure for the rest of his life just how drunk and incapable he got. Alexander Woollcott alluded to 'uneasy recollections of his striding through the Savoy, stewed to the gills, dragged by several leashed wolf-hounds'. One can only surmise what Caroline would have thought of this slur on her brother's name. But this brother Wolcott, the saved one, was he shallow or did he have depths? The question can't be answered now. He was sensitive enough to have given help to Henry James in an hour of need. James had, one wet night, to attend a performance of *The American* in a dreary provincial town. James's need, so base to himself, for vulgar success in the theatre was his Achilles heel, and he was delighted to have a commiserating Wolcott by his side. Perhaps, though, he sometimes found Wolcott's refusal to recognise an obstacle, his 'Napoleonic propensities', a trifle wearing. But then he also speaks of Wolcott's talk being 'traversed by little wandering airs of the unsaid'. This is an exquisite observation, and would, from James, lead one to suppose that Wolcott was indeed a deep and sympathetic person. But could it not mean, merely, that he appreciated or shared James's own private predilections and made that apparent in a most graceful way? Again, in any case, doesn't everyone make little pregnant silences? Is James working up a special case, as he so often and so kindly did?

There is no mention of a girlfriend anywhere, and perhaps that is unusual in so live a wire; maybe Wolcott was just too busy. The odd bits of his writing that survive, a few letters, are, like the fiction, insipid and feeble. He was a man who relied on personal charm to get his way. Just as his early employee (at £1 a week) Arthur Waugh alluded to his 'chameleon power with people', so Henry James wrote of the 'subtlety' of the way in which he could put himself in the place of, empathise with (he might have said), the man – or, James was careful to note, the woman – of letters. He must have been used to getting his own way, and, adored by his family, possibly very chagrined when he did not obtain it. Gosse noted the *care* with which he dressed himself, 'a carefully dressed young-old man', an 'elderly youth' with 'sensitive ears' (did he exploit, for the susceptible Gosse, that sense he gave of being able to break into charming flight?). Other adjectives were used of Wolcott which do not come over either from his own fiction or from his (American) bits of *The Naulahka*: exotic, curious, peculiar, mobile, whimsical, boyish, exuberant, elastic, fatherly . . . All things to all men? An empty barrel?

Kipling was not, it seems, introduced to Wolcott Balestier by Edmund Gosse, as is so often stated. It is conceivable that Gosse was there when they first met, but he had nothing to do with it. The meeting took place in the house of Mrs Humphrey Ward (1851–1920), an interesting if somewhat sensational best-selling author whose *Robert Elsmere* (1888) has recently been reprinted. Mrs Ward, born in Tasmania, the granddaughter of Thomas Arnold of Rugby, was intelligent and articulate but a little too earnest; her best novel is *Helbeck of Bannisdale* (1898), but *Robert Elsmere* is worthy, too. She doesn't often get her due today. This may be because she was an anti-suffragette, although a quite interesting one. In any case Balestier had her on a string, just as he had James (the phrase is Carrington's). There was no result from this meeting between Rudyard and Wolcott, or from any others that may have taken place towards the end of 1889 and the beginning of 1890. Maybe they met again at the house of the widowed novelist Mrs W.K. Clifford, née Lucy Lane, of a Barbados family, a writer less heard of today than Mrs Ward, but one as deserving – and in certain respects more so, since she was less stridently propagandist.

Mrs Clifford was very useful to Kipling when he first arrived in London, but does not get a mention in Carrington's biography. Like many enterprising, gifted and courageous Victorian women – Mrs Oliphant is the paramount example – she managed to prevail against the general climate of opinion, and to become well known as a dramatist and novelist. She had two daughters to support, but was not as seriously in need as Mrs Oliphant had been when her husband died, since the latter had to keep sons at expensive public schools; but she was seriously enough in need. She had quite recently published the best of her novels, *Mrs Keith's Crime* (1885), and she was then working on the (for that time) bold *Love-Letters of a*

Worldly Woman (1891). She was helpful and generous to young writers, and introduced Kipling to many useful people. Birkenhead is assuredly right in his suggestion that she also taught the young man some manners, and helped him to round off some of the very awkward corners, in the most tactful way. She was a shrewd woman, and may well have had a deeper understanding of his complex temperament than he would then have thought possible. But that silly and sad 'genteelising of the past' to which Angus Wilson draws our attention has been at work here, since it cannot be said that Carrington's admirable biography is altogether free of it. This is a pity, for Mrs Clifford, besides being someone well worth studying for her own sake, did a great deal for Kipling, more perhaps than anyone has thought possible. She had received his work from India, and did much to spread about its worth amongst intelligent readers. Kipling was happy at her house, liked her daughter, and enjoyed her cat Scuttles, for whom, Birkenhead tells us, he wrote an inscription: 'My name is Scuttles. I live at 26 Colvin Road. Please take me home.'

But alas, she could not be admitted into the Kipling legend. The reason is unfortunate and understandable. It happened before Kipling knew Wolcott well, and when he had no inkling at all that he would one day marry Caroline. He and Mrs Clifford went to the theatre. In a box sat Wolcott and both his sisters. Mrs Clifford must have made a remark that many people had made, perhaps to the effect that Caroline looked pretty grim by the side of her beautiful sister and lively brother. When he became engaged to Caroline in about May 1891 he had to put an end to the friendship, which he did by sending her a telegram. Until her death in 1929, not so very long before his, she regretted her words – she told Mrs Belloc Lowndes, the novelist, that whenever she saw him on social occasions 'a sensation of such pain filled her heart that she had to leave the room'. He must have known what he owed her, and must, too, have wondered about her words.

Wolcott at this time was, as I have mentioned, suffering from an embarrassment. We may conclude that he felt it keenly. He was anxious not only to further his publishing career, but also his writing career. In a word, he was exceedingly ambitious. We don't know much about him, except that he was most people's darling; and even our knowledge of his association with Kipling has to be pieced together from scraps of information here and there. But it is reasonable to suppose that, an intelligent or at the least a shrewd man, he was deeply envious of successful writers, and wanted to be one. He may also have been aware that he was not a good writer himself, that he had not got it in him – had not got that raging curiosity that needs to know the truth about his fellow human beings and what they are doing here. Possibly he realised that he had not yet done very well, that the praise of Henry James and the like was the praise of gratitude and a salute to effort rather than the recognition of genius; perhaps he felt that he could make it yet. Like many Americans then and now, he wanted to succeed, and he wanted to succeed in a big way. To be a big publisher is to revolve around Great People and get vicarious satisfaction as the 'man behind them'. That would have been Wolcott's fate. But he was still very young, and was still making a bid to be one of the Great himself.

Wolcott would not have cared much for Henry James's brother William's definition of success. This did not come until 1906, in a letter to H.G. Wells. But it was always an assumption in the minds of both the James brothers.

'The moral flabbiness born of the bitch-goddess SUCCESS. That – with the squalid cash interpretation put on the word success – is the disease of our nation.' Had he lived, Wolcott would eventually have found his way to Hollywood – and would generously have taken all his friends' works with him to be scripted, filmed (in the more fortunate instances) and travestied. Kipling felt fairly glad, throughout his life, that he was able to avoid much of that sort of embroilment. He must have worried, in connection with such thoughts of success, about Wolcott's advice to him – and doubtless his mother's, too, but he was more used to that – with regard to the end of *The Light that Failed*. But this is somewhat to anticipate matters.

What Wolcott thought he could do successfully was in some way to convey the new spirit of America, the frontier spirit, the sort of thing he had tried and failed to do in *Benefits Forgot*. He had roughed it in Colorado, or said he had, and Kipling was rapturous about that kind of thing, as we see from a poem he did actually write for Wolcott (afterwards he changed the sex of the person addressed in it), 'The Long Trail'. Wolcott must have felt that his good friend James was quite unable to do anything like that. But before he knew, or rather before he started to chase Kipling, with this purpose in mind, he seems to have been willing to consider anything.

What he was after was a collaborator. He wanted help, and saw nothing discreditable in it. 'Say, would you write a novel with me?' 'Could I assist you in your next novel with American colour? There's a great demand for that sort of thing, you know.' Chameleon-like with men and with women, he would have varied his approach with great shrewdness. But it wasn't working. He must have felt that he was approaching his Waterloo. Hilton Brown points out that in the London of that time, considerably 'chillier' than America, such proposals were 'not very heartily received'. As Kipling arrived in London, Wolcott was 'smarting under a series of minor rebuffs'; writers did not want to collaborate with him. He was a great admirer of *Robert Elsmere*, and on the strength of his admiration he had asked Mrs Humphrey Ward to write a novel with him; or at least he had asked if he might collaborate with her.

She rejected the proposal outright. Mrs Ward was almost ten years Wolcott's senior, and although *Robert Elsmere* was only her third novel, and her first success, she might well have felt put out and upset. Certainly Wolcott did have her 'on a string': he was managing the publication of her much pirated novel, which some critics have felt 'played a part in the intellectual evolution of America' (this is only too likely: it is not that good). But the rebuff to him would then have been all the more severe, although he was evidently the sort of man to bounce back very quickly. Maybe she was so taken aback that she expressed herself with some unaccustomed nervous vehemence.

It is at this point that chronology becomes a little confused, because we have few personal details of the all-important Kipling–Balestier relationship. What we know is that, in Carrington's words, 'no man ever exercised so dominating an influence over Rudyard Kipling as did Wolcott Balestier during the eighteen months of their intimacy.'

The first meeting with Balestier must have been preceded by a conversation between Gosse and himself which the latter recorded. Or must it? If Gosse was not at Mrs Ward's when Kipling first called there, towards the end of 1889 – and it is not likely that he was – then Balestier could have been aware that he didn't know about the first encounter, which was presumably casual. It is easy to see why most readers have believed that Gosse brought the two men together. By 12 July 1890 Wolcott could write to William Dean Howells that 'lately I have been seeing even more of Kipling with whom I am writing a story in collaboration. The scene is to be partly far Western American (W.B.) and partly Indian (R.K.).' He also succeeded in reconciling Kipling to Howells. Both these achievements would have been a considerable feather in anyone's cap. The literary world might not have been surprised to hear that Kipling was collaborating on something with, say, Barrie, or Stevenson (had Stevenson been around to collaborate with), or even Gosse himself (whose output, however, apart from a few flaccid poems, was not very 'creative'). But Balestier! Wasn't he that bumptious man who was fixing up so many deals for English writers in America, and hadn't he helped straighten up things for Kipling? Not quite a gentleman, though, was he? Yes, there was some fiction of his, but had anyone much read it? He'd done very well for himself, then, hadn't he? And so he had. Everyone has wondered: how did Balestier do it? And the novel is certainly not as good as to explain this in the simple terms of Balestier's gifts. He had none. He was barely competent on his own.

As Edmund Gosse told the story, he had been reading *Soldiers Three* and told Balestier to watch out for Kipling. 'Rudyard Kipling?' asked Balestier with 'elaborate indifference', 'is it a man or a woman? What's its real name?' What a question to ask at the initial stage of such a relationship!

But according to the most reliable witness of all, Arthur Waugh, in his account of his life in publishing, *One Man's Road* (1931), Balestier, at some time before the acquaintance ripened into friendship, sent him round to the room in Villiers Street with an urgent note in which he begged to have a glimpse of a new story, *The Book of the Hundred Mornings*. Kipling said: 'Extraordinarily importunate person, this Mr Balestier. Tell him that *The Book of the Hundred Mornings* is all over my bed and may never get finished. Tell him to enquire again in six months.' The 'elaborate indifference' suggests that Wolcott really was after Kipling for his own purposes.

But Kipling may have sent something, and probably did: Gosse says that when, three days after first talking to Wolcott about Kipling, he went into the office just outside Westminster Abbey, the desk was covered with Kipling's Indian books. Everyone is agreed that there ensued a courtship or pursuit of Kipling by Balestier, for the purpose of gaining him as a collaborator, and that Kipling put up resistance, or a show of it, but eventually gave way. *Naulahka* is a Hindu word denoting 900,000 rupees, and it is also applied to a fabulous jewel: it should be *Naulakha*, and this was how Kipling spelt it when he gave the name to his Vermont house, but in reprints of the novel the mistake is preserved, and I assume that Kipling kept it that way because he wanted to remember his friend through it – no doubt it was Wolcott's original error in typewriting. Not only do we find Wolcott writing to Howells in July 1890 that the novel is now being written but we also find, in the same month, Josephine writing to her mother:

> After the authors' dinner the other night Wolcott and young Kipling talked until four in the morning. They are growing fast friends; they are very congenial, dove-tail finely. I think it rather picturesque that the two London literary infants should play so prettily together.

Philip Mason, discussing the misogyny of *The Light that Failed*, and the theme of 'physical tenderness between men' in it, writes:

> It has been a commonplace to think of the Victorians as hypocrites because they were silent about much of which they were well aware. But, largely because of that silence, they were often not so hypocritical as innocent. Of course, there cannot have been Victorian men unaware that homosexual acts sometimes took place – but they regarded this as a strange and on the whole rare vice. They were unaware of the many half-shades of emotion and behaviour that are commonplace today, and most of them would have indignantly repudiated the suggestion that there was any sexual element in the platonic male affection that played so large a part in their society. But schoolmasters, dons, army officers, who devoted their lives to looking after young men, were at the heart of Victorian greatness; their charges were the loves of their lives. For most of Kipling's life, this was not so with him. He liked being with men, but it was to women that he looked for fascination and attraction. Sore from Flo Garrard's rejection, he felt himself thrown back on men for an affection that was safe, warm and intelligible. And into this mood was projected a young man who carried with him an atmosphere of intellectual excitement and animal magnetism.

This is well said, but too delicate – and does not go far enough. It is too polite, and does not take account of what Kipling called in 'The Benefactors' 'the undoctored incident that actually occurred' – a realisation *is* an incident. You can put it out of your mind; but it is there, and if affects you. Readers will note the contradiction between the first and second sentences. You cannot be well aware and 'innocent' simultaneously. But Mason, a little reprehensibly, feels that he wants to 'excuse' Kipling's behaviour by demonstrating it was 'healthy' and basically heterosexual. After all, he likes Kipling a lot really – though critical of his excesses – and he simply would not like it if Kipling were homosexual.

But what does he mean by 'animal magnetism'? Isn't that a bit close to the bone? Besides, the Victorians weren't *unaware* of these various shades of emotion that 'are commonplace today': they repressed them, and kept quiet about them – and because they did so, and they were not 'commonplace', the whole atmosphere was redolent with them. Everyone knows the effect of Jane Austin's reticence! An intelligent man or woman who represses a strong emotion will every now and then be caught unaware of his or her repression, and will be shocked and put out. Just as a few Victorians were so obsessed with nakedness that they put little knickers on the legs of chairs (though this was not as common a practice as some suppose), thus endowing them with an eroticism they had not previously possessed, so the 'Platonic' love of some others for boys and young men was made to be a very guilty thing stinking of crude lust. This made teachers and others feel even more guilty than their culture already did, and so made them either defy it in secret – or repress it even more fiercely.

Angus Wilson, however, says, simply and suddenly, as though he has made up his mind that he has got to say it somewhere,

I think it likely that Kipling was much in love with Wolcott. Worry
about the nature of his own feelings may have played some part among
all the other anxieties crowded in on him in those brief London years. Yet
I believe it to be more probable that he did not allow himself to glimpse
anything that was unorthodox in his feelings for his friend. To suppose
that Kipling's life would have been different had Wolcott lived, as is
often said to me, is greatly to misunderstand both Wolcott and Kipling,
and more still such men in the age in which they lived. In any case,
excellent friend and useful literary collaborator though Wolcott was, his
attitude to the marketing of Kipling's work was much the same as his
sister inherited.

This is undoubtedly right, too, but again it does not go far enough.
Wilson's book on Kipling is the best all-round one because he is a sensitive
and truly distinguished practitioner of fiction, because it is critically and
psychologically knowing in a way that the authors of the other books,
for all their excellencies, simply aren't, and because in addition to all
this Wilson has a heart of gold – is, in a word, humane. But what he
reluctantly says here – reluctantly because it does open up a whole new
field of enquiry, or can of worms – is inadequate. Judges and others in
authority who were extra hard on 'perversion' because they were in
effect quite unconsciously condemning such 'unorthodox' tendencies in
themselves were, in the bad old days, two a penny. They spent lifetimes of
self-deceit, and to a certain (too limited) extent could genuinely sublimate
their feelings in 'innocent' activities. But Kipling, though not an intellectual, was a writer and one of the most famously subtle (as well as famously
brash) men of his time. Such a man can't be 'much in love' with another
man, and not allow himself to glimpse the 'unorthodox'! In any case, if he
did succeed in this, why should he 'worry' about 'the nature of his own
feelings'? Such different emotions and anxieties could all have co-existed,
but it would have been on a number of levels, conscious, semi-conscious,
unconscious, and so on, and it would have required a great deal more
discussing than it gets in Wilson's book.
    What about the question of physical desire? The mechanisms of
repressing this are complex indeed: such feelings were the 'terrible
temptations' of which so many of the Victorians, including Kipling,
spoke – and when they did they could achieve temporary compassion.
    The language of the passage I have quoted above demonstrates its
writer's uneasiness in understanding this aspect of Kipling. Indeed, there
is always a great deal of resistance to such investigations. Whatever the
public line about matters sexual may happen to be at the time – and it
is always silly, because, as I have already quoted Malinowski as saying, sex
really is dangerous, and danger evokes silly generalisations – it is wise
to adhere to it. It may be a Victorian view: it may be a tendency to conceal
it all; or it may be 'modern': to pretend to open it all up to public scrutiny.
So it is asked, what does it matter? Why must these 'Freudian' (a misuse
of the word in this context) critics keep going on about sex? Thus some
critics and readers will call me 'morbid'. I sympathise with them.
    It matters very much, however, because the nature of sexuality
pervades, and must pervade, the work of any writer of fiction. The
nature of sexuality pervades life. We are present on earth because of
sexuality, and acts of sexuality are not performed with quite the same

ends in mind as are acts of elimination. Jung and others were right to question Freud's undoubtedly morbid preoccupation with the explicitly and specifically sexual, with the genital; but if we take the word 'sexual' to embrace such emotions as those of love and parenthood ('We spurred our parents to the kiss/Though doubtfully they shrank from this'), then their preoccupations lay in almost the same area. They are, simply, less specifically genital than classical Freudianism seems to demand. Kipling loved children, and innocent children are brought into being by less than innocent sex; if it were innocent sex then it would not be our familiar world, of which Kipling's vision was so dark a one.

Wilson says that Kipling was much *in love* with Wolcott. Then he says that Kipling may have worried about that. Then he says that it is *more probable* that he did not allow himself to have any glimpse of the 'unorthodox'. At the least Kipling must have been confused! There is a type of man who gets involved with another man emotionally, but has no feelings at all about his body. He does not want to make love to him, or be made love to by him. This is called friendship. Wordsworth and Coleridge were at one time very close, and they had powerful emotions about each other; but we are surely right in thinking that they never wanted – consciously, subconsciously or unconsciously – to make love. Did Kipling and Wolcott, sitting up night after night, make love? I don't think so. But then, after all, why not? Perhaps Leon Edel is right, as far as he goes, when he says that between Rudyard and Wolcott it was a case of 'camaraderie and love, almost at first sight. Platonic, quite clearly. Both would have been terrified at any other suggestion.'

But *is* he right? For isn't he managing both to be patronisingly 'Freudian' and simple-minded at the same time? Really we cannot say whether Rudyard and Wolcott made love. Who is in the least interested in what they may have *done*? Just pressures of the hand, perhaps. If critics like Edel didn't come along to inform us that their relationship was, oh, so definitely Platonic, we should not think about that. We don't talk about the Wordsworth–Coleridge relationship as 'Platonic' because we don't feel the need to. One cannot tell, especially in Victorian times when such things were so taboo, whether they occurred or not. The participants probably felt deeply guilty (although there was a 'decadent' enclave whose members defiantly did not), but they most certainly did not let on to others. When Henry James, who never so far as we know indulged himself in any sexual activity, and invented an 'obscure hurt' to account for it lest the world should enquire why he was unmarried or why he did not frequent brothels, heard about Oscar Wilde's troubles he denounced him in the most hypocritical terms imaginable. The James- and Kipling-directed young Willa Cather, who was a homosexual but did not want it discussed at all, condemned Wilde for his 'evil' and 'baseness'. I am not sure if Cather felt she had to, or not. Both she and James were major novelists. And one can note that James felt that Oscar Wilde had let the side down badly, too. In one sense he did.

There was in the Victorian era, as well as a lot of Edel's camaraderie, choirboys with beautiful voices, stirring young guardsmen on parade, and terrified Platonism between men, some supra-Edelian sophistication, too. It penetrated into our own era and only very gradually began to fall away after homosexual acts were made 'legal'. It still exists among members of

the 'best circles', who are connoisseurs of the extra delights offered by
the furtive, the forbidden, the artificially corrupt. It does not figure in any
of the many formal and official or semi-official biographies of Winston
Churchill that he, not a homosexual, went to bed with Ivor Novello (when
Somerset Maugham asked him what it had been like, he replied, 'very mu-
sical'). Fancy if that had been known during the war, when Novello went
to prison for a petrol offence! But if one is asked to provide a comment,
the only appropriate one would be: 'Why the hell not? It's their business.
If only Mrs Thatcher had been to bed with Meryl Streep, or, failing that,
Arthur Scargill, or even better, both!'

This remark is in bad taste. So were much of Churchill's politics and
his early admiration for Mussolini and very early admiration for Hitler. But
the essence of his part in the Second World War was not in bad taste, any
more than Queen Elizabeth's was at the time of the Spanish Armada. Was
it soiled by his experiment with Novello? Churchill's experiment should
have been his own affair. But we do not possess that kind of purity. One
has to work at the notion that Kipling's love experience, whatever it was,
was pure, too – and has to drag it out in the open to do it, because everyone
is so busy apologising for his ever giving anyone doubts . . . He couldn't
have realised, he couldn't have been aware, it was Platonic . . . Let it be
whatever the whole complex of terrors and tendernesses of life made it to
be! One is reminded of the reaction of one nineteenth-century critic to the
suggestion that Shakespeare's love for the young man of his sonnets might
have had anything 'abnormal' about it: 'What! The great Bard! Shame!'

Now Wolcott was a charmer. It is just possible that he had some of the
sort of sophistication I have discussed, and that he tempted Kipling – because he badly wanted something out of him. He was after all a buyer and
a seller, a business man. Wilson puts his finger on something else when he
points out that Wolcott's attitude to the 'marketing of Kipling's work was
much the same as his sister inherited'. Wilson is touchingly just to Carrie,
except that he cannot quite bring himself fully to admit that she was a
ferocious old battleaxe and of little use to anyone but her husband, and
frequently not even to him. She was disliked, and with good reason. But his
defence of her is decent and cogent, and those who research Kipling's life
in depth do become fonder – not the contrary – of her. She was a genuine
hero (not heroine). She was the only wife Kipling could have had. Wilson's
final verdict is that she was the player of a difficult role: 'the celebrity's
helpmate'. Feminists won't thank him for that; but she was, after all, herself
a virulent anti-feminist. Wilson's view of her attitude to Kipling's art, in
connection with his remark about her elder brother's to it, is that she was
'touching', as when she said of one of Kipling's books, 'I do think some of it
will live', or when, weeping, she came out of a performance of J.M. Barrie's
Dear Brutus, complaining 'He had no right to do it!'. He has no doubt that
Kipling kept 'the deeper meaning of his work' to himself.

I am not quite so sure about that, although the sense in which I am
not so sure about it is a strictly non-literary one – and at least the story
about the Barrie 'what-might-have-been' play demonstrates that Carrie had
emotions, if anyone has doubted it. I reckon all writers hang on to their
deeper meanings if they think they have them – the less they think about
that the deeper they may be, unless they are literary butterflies. The reason
for literature is in any case non-literary: this is a paradox that few academic

critics have bothered to work out. There is no question of Carrie having had any intellectual or 'literary' appreciation of her husband's art. So did her brother Wolcott have any? Or did he feign it?

A tale really may well hang from this question of Wolcott Balestier's care about Kipling's art, and Wilson has done very well to draw our attention to it. As for their relationship, I think it is as likely as it is unlikely, or as unlikely as it is likely, that it was physical. One just cannot know. *That* is unimportant, so long as no one is going to think it a shame, a pity, dwelling on nasty and unnecessary and 'morbid' matters. Literature does dwell, among other things, on what society holds is nasty, unnecessary, even 'morbid' – on what society likes to hide and may need to hide. *Bon-ton* writers have to collaborate with society in this, while seeming to criticise it; most of them do. Perhaps society is becoming so open about 'horrors' because the place of literature is rapidly being taken, so far as the media are concerned, by various *ersatz* substitutes for it. Sexual relations would not be whatever they are if they were conducted in public, and it has not quite come to that yet. What is possible is not only that Kipling loved Wolcott, but also that he loved too well and too unwisely.

But in order to discover how it really may have been between these two men, it is necessary to examine Kipling's first novel, *The Light that Failed*, first published – by Wolcott's good graces – by J.W. Lowell in New York in November 1890; it appeared in *Lippincott's Magazine* in January 1891. Then it appeared in a new, longer version in March 1891, published by Macmillan. In that form it was, and has been called, 'practically an anti-feminist tract'. Balestier's publication of it did not prevent Rand McNally pirating it in America, either. They printed from the magazine version. Kipling began the novel in about February or March of 1890, and had finished it by August. He does not seem to have made a fuss about the Rand McNally theft. What was on his mind?

The Light that Failed

In February 1890 Kipling met Florence Garrard again on the street in London. Trix came back to England with her new husband on 11 February 1890 and soon went to where Kipling was living in Villiers Street. She was horrified at the state he was in. Yet February and March were the two months of Kipling's decided triumph in London. 'Danny Deever' appeared on 22 February in the *Scots Observer*, and was followed by a poem a week; everything that came from his pen, and much did, was gaining maximum attention. David Masson, the learned Scottish critic and professor who wrote the huge definitive life of Milton exclaimed, 'Here's literature! Here's literature at last!' On 25 March *The Times* started the Kipling boom in earnest by devoting a leader to his genius. This cannot have happened to so young a writer before or since. He could write to Caroline Taylor (7 February, a few days before Trix saw him and found him so ill and despairing) that he was being chased by 'several publishers' (they were, he told her, like 'Jew Hawkers' by the time he had done with them), and that he is nobody's fool and isn't going to fall for anyone's offers.

Kipling was in a state of high excitement which alternated with the deepest depression. He was exploring London and the music halls, exeriencing great (mental) fascination with the hordes of prostitutes he saw everywhere around him, and with the seamy side of the metropolis in general; but his new fame had not gone to his head to the degree it would have done with most men. His excitement was punctuated with despair. He saw his privacy destroyed, and himself destroyed by his privacy. He told Trix on that February day that his engagement to Caroline Taylor had been an error, that seeing Florence Garrard in the street by accident had awakened the old infatuation. Trix told him how kind Mrs Hill had been to her and her husband when they were in Allahabad: she said that his face then 'began to work', as he admitted that his feelings for Caroline Taylor had been a mistake – and that Flo still had a hold over him. He was ill at the time, but with more than influenza, his sister thought. All this time he was working, and over the next few months he produced 'The Courting of Dinah Shadd', 'The Man Who Was', 'Without Benefit of Clergy', 'At the End of the Passage', 'The Mark of the Beast' and 'On Greenhow Hill', as well as poems and, of course, *The Light that Failed*.

He was paying some attention to Flo throughout this spring and summer, although there are few details. Trix thought Flo was 'unnaturally cold'; but it is possible that Flo did not much like Kipling as a suitor, or men in general. Kipling in any case worked himself up into an apparent frenzy over her 'coldness', and made it his official romantic preoccupation – to the extent that a cold girl's refusal of a warm-blooded man is the main theme of his first novel, which he now started to write, and also of his second novel-in-collaboration, although that one ended 'happily' with a change of heart.

So far as his family was concerned, this was the unhappy and exhausted front he was putting up. He had left India and them only five or six months ago, had achieved success on his own terms – but was now wanting them back. And they all came back. First Trix in February, and then his father and mother on leave, in May. After that he spent less time in Villiers Street, since in the early summer he worked with his father, sometimes in his own rooms but also in Kensington where they were staying, first in Wynnstay Gardens and then in Earl's Court Road. He even went down to his old school, accompanied by his father; the boys were given a half-holiday in his honour.

So the official version, as given by Carrington, is that Kipling's 'prolonged ill-health and unhappiness in 1890 were the consequence' of a 'mental conflict' over Flo: according to his custom, says Carrington, he shut it up in his own heart, 'leaving no scrap of direct evidence to mark the progress of his love affairs'. Thus he plunged himself into work with a 'reckless energy', leaning on the old 'family square'. I think, however, that since he had boasted of his 'wenching' when a schoolboy, he would have been altogether more forthcoming about his heterosexuality – had he had it – than he was.

There were other conflicts. I think he had become aware of his own nature in India, years back; 'The Explanation', the first of all the poems he printed in the *Scots Observer* (1 February 1890, three weeks before 'Danny Deever') makes this perfectly clear. I do not assert that the attraction to Balestier had then manifested itself; but it may very well have done. It could have been a case of love at first sight. After all, Balestier was after Kipling, for his own purposes, from the start. So Kipling was aware that Wolcott wanted his attention. For how long did Kipling resist? Certainly Arthur Waugh's story about going to Villiers Street on Wolcott's behalf to ask for work-in-progress shows that the courtship was proceeding. 'The Explanation' is not the poem of a man about to be re-swept off his feet by a woman he had seen, or pretended to see, in a romantic light some years back. But we must remember, at the same time, the pressure on men to be 'normal'. And, as we already know, his original feelings for Flo have impressed every commentator as having been as essentially false as his feelings for Caroline Taylor. There is something wrong with his expression of these feelings – but no one has been anxious to put a finger on the reasons for this falseness. No one, of course, felt it as keenly as he did. His need to seem 'normal' in the eyes of his contemporaries was keen: the social pressure was extreme, and for Kipling more than almost any other man living the term 'contemporaries' embraced all who could read. No wonder he wanted firmly to disassociate himself from any relics of his early Pre-Raphaelitism. Any serious writer is vulnerable, for he is baring his soul, however hard he may try to make a virtue of not doing so; Kipling was doubly vulnerable because of his 'philosophy' of action, now rapidly being developed in his journalism, which was attracting much attention. Critics could and did write some wounding things.

Richard Le Gallienne, a quite discerning self-critical aesthete whose fiction and criticism do not deserve the oblivion into which they have fallen, wrote a fairly hostile but intelligent book on Kipling in 1900. (He modified his view in an essay of 1919, which is also an essential part of the history of Kipling criticism.) Le Gallienne's 1900 study embodies what might be called the responsible 'case against' Kipling at it stood at the turn of the century; Gosse and a number of other intelligent readers felt, by then, more or less the same way as Le Gallienne, with differences over details. Le Gallienne could not reconcile the overt 'religiosity' (as in the patriotic poems and utterances), as he called it, with the cynicism. He found him brutal and 'heartlessly vulgar'. He states the case as responsibly and as well as anyone else, and he requires answering; in certain respects he cannot be answered. But Kipling cannot have been other than disturbed when Le Gallienne wrote, apropos of *The Light that Failed*, that he was 'a war correspondent in love with soldiers'. That kind of thing would have been said ten years earlier in the clubs . . . It was towards such innocent-seeming remarks (I do not believe Le Gallienne intended to be offensive, for he was the kind of man who, had he guessed, wouldn't have raised the matter at all) that Kipling must have reacted most unhappily. But that after all does provide the explanation for Kipling's imperialistic politics. By this I do not mean that he did not believe in his political views; but he would not have expressed them so vehemently, ultimately robbing them of what power they possessed, had they not had the particular emotional charge behind them that they did.

It is hard to say exactly when Kipling started *The Light that Failed*. But all the time he was writing it, and for some time after that, he was exercising his polemical powers in favour of his political views. Thus in June or July 1890 he wrote, with some tactful help from his father, the satirical sketch 'The Enlightenments of Pagett, M.P.'. This appeared in both the *Contemporary Review* and the *Pioneer* for September. It was not included in the ordinary collected edition of his works, but did appear in a 'De Luxe Edition'. Pagett M.P. is not really the same invention as the one attacked in the poem 'Pagett, M.P.' ('Pagett, M.P. was a liar, and a fluent liar therewith'); he is a radical who is enthusiastic about the Indian National Congress. He is made to be ignorant of India and Indians; but this does not work, since his feeling for minorities and his views as to where political power should lie are nothing like as stupid or vicious as Kipling wants them to be. Liberalism is at its worst when it is pseudo-liberalism; it is thus not liberalism. But this Pagett is recognisably liberal, and his hopes for humanity need to be crushed on better grounds than Kipling provides. It was with this piece that Kipling began his imperialism in earnest, and it is significant that it should have developed at this time.

The poem 'Cleared' was one of the earliest printed by Henley (8 March 1890). This, 'In Memory of the Parnell Commission', demonstrates that Kipling's imperialistic thrust had its roots more in his hatred and fear than in his lovingness: always, in his polemic, the loathing of the liberal carries more weight and conviction than the love of the (partly fictitious) romantic federation of supervisors of those who carry out the administrative work. It is worth looking more closely at Kipling's perception of the situation depicted in this poem.

Kipling was interested in Zola, and he had not been more than two or three weeks in England when *The Times*, in one of its outbursts of moral indignation, took up the name of this notorious French sensualist: Parnell's personal conduct, thundered an editorial, was one of 'dull and ignoble infidelity untouched ... by a single ray of sentiment ... comparable only to the dreary monotony of French middle-class vice, over which the scalpel of M. Zola so lovingly lingers'. Parnell had just been (unfairly) criticised by the judge in the O'Shea divorce case, in which he had been named as co-respondent. Gladstone, amidst the convulsion of indignation that possessed the nation at this time, exclaimed on countless occasions, 'it'll ne'er do!' Letters from his Liberal supporters poured in upon him: he must sever all connections with Parnell. But, to his credit, he refused to act as moral judge in public. He contented himself with warning Parnell of the political consequences of his continuance as leader of his party. The affair was important to the Liberals because it threatened the cause, so hated by Kipling, of Irish Home Rule. Quite what he would have made of the advice the public man he was to revere above all others offered Parnell is problematical. Cecil Rhodes, all for Home Rule on the pragmatic grounds that the arrangements would eventually suit his own imperialistic ideals best (he had put money into it), wired from the Cape: 'RESIGN – MARRY – RETURN!' I do not suppose this matter was ever discussed between them.

O'Shea was a blackmailer and fraud who had condoned Parnell's relationship with his wife throughout; but Parnell, over-confident, refused to take Rhodes's and the Liberal Party's advice, and temporarily back down. His contempt for public opinion was vitiated, however, by his own political ambitions; but he refused to acknowledge this. He allowed himself to be re-elected as leader of the Irish Party without letting the views of the Liberals be known. Gladstone lost his head and allowed a letter to Parnell, originally confidential, to be published; Parnell then also lost his head. This led to the break-up of the Irish Party and, eventually, to an end to the Home Rule cause.

The verdict of the Parnell Commission was given on 13 February 1890. A panel of three judges had been appointed by Parliament to investigate claims that Parnell had in a letter justified the terrorist Phoenix Park Murders of 1882. It was obliged to clear Parnell, especially since it had already been shown – during F.H. O'Donnell's libel action against *The Times* – that certain letters he was supposed to have written were forgeries. The forger of them killed himself in Madrid on 1 March 1889. But Salisbury, the Tory Prime Minister at this time, had made it clear that he believed Parnell capable of writing them. He knew very well that Parnell wasn't – and, indeed, the latter's original denunciation of the murders was perfectly sincere, since they were a great inconvenience to his cause.

'Cleared', although vigorous, shows Kipling at his worst. He hated the Liberals (and, in truth, even Tory liberalism), and would use any excuse to discredit them. The vigour of his poem is quite spoiled by the purposes towards which he directs it. It is also spoiled, and reprehensibly spoiled, by the partisan emotion he is assuming in sympathetic readers. As always with Kipling at his worst – and I am offering a deliberate example of him at his worst – he is not a man speaking to men, as Wordsworth rightly demanded poetry must be, but a man ranting to an unenlightened section of humanity that he nastily assumes is, or ought to be, in some kind of strenuous and unpleasant majority. He thus wasted much energy.

Society may well earn a few of its individual monsters – he is a monster here – by its hypocrisy and cruelty; it may and probably was – in the last analysis – social pressure that made Kipling the polemicist determined to demonstrate that he was no namby-pamby, long-haired pansy democrat; but it is still a shame that he had to express himself in such inhumane terms. This has nothing to do with not liking Liberals or liberals. It should be emphasised that it is by no means the case that the compassion shown in a story like 'The Gardener' can only come into being as a result of performances of the nature of 'Cleared'. It happens to be so in Kipling's case, and makes him horribly peculiar, and, when he is horrible, peculiarly horrible.

Lord Salisbury was merely a politician, although in many ways an admirable one, and doubtless when in 1886 he made his famous and successful (in the sense that it certainly helped his party win the July election of that year) speech deriding the Irish as 'Hottentots', and scorning any idea of their capacity to govern themselves, he was not much bothered as to whether he meant it or not. Although politically a very skilful man, he was 'essentially negative' (Lord Blake in his invaluable *History of the Conservative Party*). The fact is that his subsequent 'explanation' of his harsh language about the Irish made no difference to majority British opinion that he was right; he knew it would not. But, as anyone would now agree (many of the seeds of the present troubles were sown at this time), it was not 'opinion' at all, but ignorance and prejudice to which he was deliberately appealing. It seems that *The Times* was not, after all, as used to be believed, behind or involved in the conspiracies to ruin Parnell; morally it was, though. Nor does one have to condone or admire Parnell to see that when Salisbury said in 1886 that 'politics is Ireland' he wanted to win an election, not pursue a just cause. More than any other politician of his century, Salisbury was interested in winning elections and then casually ruling – rather than in much else. Although he disliked democracy he was singularly democratic in the way he treated his cabinet. One would hardly think that he was in power in 1890 when 'Cleared' was published, but this is the case. Gladstone's Home Rule Bill of 1893 failed when the Lords rejected it, and the path was open for the formation of Sinn Fein, and then of the IRA.

But it is not a question of retrospective hatred of Gladstone. It is a question of pouring vehement emotion into a cause that Kipling knows is popular, and thus ingratiating himself with the 'severe' and 'strenuous' people who support it. One can't say that Home Rule for Ireland gets a just airing in anything he ever wrote about it. His cause is bad because it bases itself on inhumane impulses, because it tries to equate Irishmen with 'savages', and because it appeals to mindlessness and not to justice or reason. One may like or dislike the Irish Republic, or think nothing about it at all; but in it, after its civil war, the Irish rule themselves no worse than anyone else. The cause's, and Kipling's, ill-will still contribute something to that murder and violence which Englishmen like Kipling call 'Irish'. The tragedy of Ireland is perhaps ultimately 'tribal', as many Irishmen suggest; but it lies in history, too – and England cannot be absolved of responsibility.

Help for a patriot distressed, a spotless spirit hurt,
Help for an honourable clan sore trampled in the dirt!
From Queenstown Bay to Donegal, oh, listen to my song,
The honourable gentlemen have suffered grievous wrong.

Their noble names were mentioned – Oh, the burning black disgrace! –
By a brutal Saxon paper in an Irish shooting-case;
They sat upon it for a year, then steeled their heart to brave it,
And 'corruscating innocence' the learned Judges gave it.

This goes on until the famous conclusion, which led *The Times* itself to
refuse the poem – Frank Harris at the *Fortnightly* set it up but cried off at
the last moment:

If black is black or white is white, in black and white it's down,
You're only traitors to the Queen and rebels to the Crown.
If print is print or words are words, the learned Court perpends:-
We are not ruled by murderers, but only – by their friends.

It is not possible to conclude, from this poem, that one of Parnell's
supporters had won a libel action against *The Times* (the 'brutal Saxon
paper') very largely on the grounds that a journalist called Richard Piggott
had forged 'his' letters about the Phoenix Park Murders. Kipling doesn't
stand condemned because he didn't like Parnell, who was after all, like
Salisbury, merely a politician. He stands condemned because he is using
the brutality of the Phoenix Park and other terrorist murders to attack
Liberals on the grounds that they don't understand that the Irish are
'savages' who must learn to be ruled by the English. He doesn't have the
tenderness for the Irish that he has for the Indians. There is no Strickland
to go amongst the Irish in Kipling's works. He is therefore making himself
a part of the attitude that will always promote such ugly violence as was
seen in Phoenix Park in 1882.

Kipling was not capable of *thinking* about the issue at all. And, because
it is a poem of thoughtless ill will, 'Cleared' fits no situation, and can be
quoted in support of no cause at all. If this were a mere lapse, then it
would not be worth discussion. But such violence flaws most of his
political poetry, which appeals unsubtly if with high energy to the
violent in its reader – and then expects praise for it. This is not to say that
Kipling's voice in that last decade of British imperialism was in any way a
complacent one; but that is another story.

Yet it must be added that extreme and sudden popularity of the
sort Kipling so quickly obtained would have corrupted almost any writer
absolutely. After all, he alone has had to withstand such widespread fame.
He alone can tell us anything about it. Other writers have become popular,
but not quite as popular or quite as suddenly. Only Kipling has combined
the two functions of famous personality and writer. There was an angry
vein in him from the beginning, long before he became popular. Because
he didn't become corrupted by his fame, because he fought so hard
and so unusually – indeed extraordinarily and even heroically – against
becoming corrupted, one is bound to see the problem in a different light.
He did, yes, write partisan verse; he did misuse his vigour. His hate, when
it is just hate, doesn't have the sheer energy and wild humour possessed by
other famously enraged writers: Bloy, Céline – and of Englishmen, Swift,

in whom he was much interested. But at the time he was cultivating his hatred, in pieces like *Pagett*, he was simultaneously struggling to retain his artistic integrity in a unique way. I have shown how thoroughly he could go against himself in his poem 'The *Mary Gloster*': how the effect he creates, for any sensitive reader, is exactly the opposite of what it looks like and, very likely, of what he intends (or intends before his imagination takes over). This poem, like so many other things in Kipling, is a triumph of the imagination. It creates its own justice, and in doing so defines it – just as a society without 'leaders' might, if allowed to come into being, define order. In the more important later stories it happens again, especially when revenge, hatred, pain in the mind, and related themes, are dealt with. Yet in 'Cleared' Kipling inflames dangerous feelings.

But let us go forward twenty-five years and look at what he wrote when his cause was just, and when the times really did call for a savage satire. The poem is 'Gehazi'. Its occasion was the Marconi scandal. At first the rumour had it that three members of the government – a Liberal one, Asquith being Prime Minister – had enriched themselves by using information in their possession as ministers. The ministers were Lloyd George (Chancellor), Rufus Isaacs (Attorney-General) and Sir Herbert Samuel (Postmaster-General). Samuel had done nothing, and this was soon admitted. A select committee cleared the other two of corruption, but the conservative minority on it condemned them (1913), and with proper cause. The impact of the scandal was increased when Asquith, in a fit of sublime and incomprehensible irresponsibility, appointed Rufus Isaacs Lord Chief Justice – only six months after the scandal. The whole country knew that Isaacs was a crook, and therefore saw where corruption could lead. Gehazi was the name of Elisha's servant who got, by corruption, a reward from Naaman that his master had refused.

> Whence comest thou, Gehazi,
>   So reverent to behold,
> In scarlet and in ermines
>   And chain of England's gold?
> 'From following after Naaman
>   To tell him all is well,
> Whereby my zeal hath made me
>   A Judge in Israel.'
>
> Well done, well done, Gehazi!
>   Stretch forth thy ready hand.
> Thou barely 'scaped from judgment,
>   Take oath to judge the land
> Unswayed by gift of money
>   Or privy bribe, more base,
> Of knowledge which is profit
>   In any market-place.
>
> Search out and probe, Gehazi,
>   As thou of all canst try
> The truthful, well-weighed answer
>   That tells the blacker lie –
> The loud, uneasy virtue,
>   The anger feigned at will,
> To overbear a witness
>   And make the Court keep still.

Take order now, Gehazi,
   That no man talk aside
In secret with his judges
   The while his case is tried.
Lest he should show them – reason
   To keep a matter hid,
And subtly lead the questions
   Away from what he did.

Thou mirror of uprightness,
   What ails thee at thy vows?
What means the risen whiteness
   Of the skin between thy brows?
The boils that shine and burrow
   The sores that slough and bleed –
The leprosy of Naaman
   On thee and all thy seed?
     Stand up, stand up, Gehazi,
Draw close thy robe and go,
     Gehazi, Judge in Israel,
       A leper white as snow!

I cannot quite agree with Lord Blake, who calls this 'one of the greatest of hate poems': one has to think of some of Sassoon's and Owen's war poems, of Skelton, of Pope, even of William Carlos Williams on the Sacco and Vanzetti case ('But after all, what swayed heaviest/against you was that you were scared when/they copped you . . .'); but it is pretty good. It is one of the last poems written in Great Britain to speak for a scandalised common people.

One unfortunate result of the Marconi scandal and Isaacs' subsequent elevation was that it added to the impact of the anti-semitism then being touted, with some 'success', by Belloc, Chesterton and others. Kipling had no connection with this movement; and it cannot be said that he took any opportunity, in this poem, to ventilate the anti-semitic feelings that swept over him from time to time. He simply sums up in an apt way the feelings of the public. The poem does not nastily wish that Isaacs be afflicted with illness: it simply exploits the Bible story to the full in alluding to the punishment Naaman received for his deception and greed. One moved by straightforwardly anti-semitic motives, such as Belloc, would have implied that the whole Jewish people were thus tainted. There is no such absurd suggestion here. The historical context is wholly Jewish, and so therefore is the punishment.

So a worthy cause *could* inspire Kipling. In this poem there is no disingenuous calling upon values outside of the poem, no stereotyped accusations of treason and disloyalty that don't arise from the subject-matter. The indignation, not righteous but merely right, generates its own values. The crook appointed to give justice to all is exposed as the social leper his ambition (in accepting the post) makes him to be.

The imperialism that was hardening in Kipling during 1890 is rampant in the story he wrote in December 1889 or January 1890, before he met Flo in the street: 'The Head of the District' (it is included in *Life's Handicap* and first appeared in *Macmillan's Magazine* for January 1890). This has always seemed to play into the hands of such democratically outraged detractors of Kipling-as-evil-imperialist as McClure. McClure quotes the passage in which the much loved dying head of the district, Yardley-Orde, tells his escort of Indians that 'though ye be strong men, ye are children'. Kipling, McClure says, maintains that 'the Indian . . . is a peculiar kind of child, one who will "never stand alone"'. As he then goes on to say that 'such conversations undoubtedly occurred', he shows that he is falling into the old error of attributing to the author the statements of his characters; and as he then adds that the head of the district is guilty of an 'enslaving lie' one must assume that his instructions to authors include one to the effect that not even a character in a story may be permitted to deviate from a (not admirable because wooden) anti-racist line. Of course it is not as simple as that: Kipling was then at the height of his powers, and nothing he wrote is without some power. But the story is in fact wrecked by ideas from outside of it.

It is not properly about races at all. It is about a man, Yardley-Orde, doing a job of work as best he can and with the best will in the world. He does think of his loyal Indians as children. He is paternalistic. The story isn't about the shortcomings of paternalism. There are good paternalists and there are bad paternalists, sensible paternalists and silly paternalists. Paternalism may be a bad thing; but there are degrees of it. Of course Orde has 'ethnocentricity', such as everyone does – but his words aren't even centred in that, and he would have applied them to anyone whom his work called upon him to defend and protect and look after, whatever their race. People in the mass (such as the present House of Commons or any other legislative assembly anywhere in the world) are, whether black, pink, yellow, white or any other colour, or masked, very much more like children than individual adults. The race of Yardley-Orde's Indians is only important inasmuch as it is to India that fate sent him. He might have been a good prison-governor or a good headmaster or a good army officer. As Kipling said in another context, and not (alas) very effectively, 'When two strong men stand face to face . . .' Kipling knew this, too. All the more pity then, that having seen to it that Yardley-Orde's words are in character, and be damned to po-faced self-righteous pseudo-liberalism, he should resort to shameful manipulation. As Wilson says, the story contains so much offence even to the non-squeamish that its humane meaning becomes submerged. No one ever appointed or thought of appointing a Bengali Hindu to rule over a Moslem district, as happens in the tale, and no Bengali Hindu could have been quite as absurd as Chunder Dé.

The wonderful opening to the story, the halt by the swollen Indus, the wife, Polly, waiting on the other bank, the man who is going to die before she can reach him, his worries about how she is going to manage, 'Man that is born of woman is small potatoes and few in the hill' – all this is wasted and spoiled. One becomes tired of having to pick out from spoiled goods the tiny wonderful bits. The narrative begins to tail off within a page or so of the opening, when Orde talks to the Indians: his goodness is convincing, certainly, but the dialogue on both sides becomes contrived. The portrait of Mr Grish Chunder Dé that follows is poisonous, because its satire isn't – once again – based on a truth. The imitation of English ways by Indians had a funny aspect, but was not a fit subject for sharp satire because it was a good-hearted matter. The master or mistress of humour who could convey the sense of fun could have been Kipling, but, alas, wasn't. And the tale slowly degenerates until it depends on Tallentire's

Alice Kipling aged about forty-five
(National Trust/University of Sussex)

Lockwood Kipling aged about fifty
(National Trust/University of Sussex)

Rudyard aged about six   *(National Trust/
University of Sussex)*

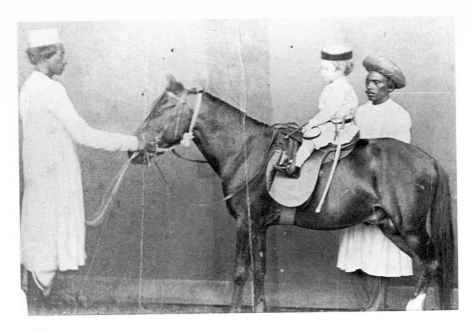

Emperor on horseback with servants: Rudyard aged two *(National Trust/University of Sussex)*

Rudyard, in the middle of the group wearing glasses, at school in Westward Ho!, *c.*1880 *(National Trust/University of Sussex)*

The wily Milner: imperialist *sans
maîtresse*, c.1901   *(National Portrait
Gallery)*

The gun outside the museum of Lahore,
as described in *Kim*   *(National Trust/
University of Sussex)*

Trix when she captivated Kitchener,
before her collapse   *(The Kipling Society/
Steve Richards)*

A selection of first edition covers
(National Trust/University of Sussex)

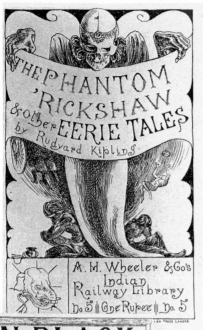

Wolcott Balestier, the man Kipling loved
(The Mansell Collection)

The enchanting Josephine, *c.*1895
(National Trust/University of Sussex)

The old story: Boers punish Kaffirs (here, for serving the British in the Boer War)

A Lockwood Kipling design for *The Second Jungle Book* (*National Trust/ University of Sussex*)

One of Max Beerbohm's caricatures of Kipling, drawn in 1898 (*British Library*)

Kipling in his study at Naulakha
(*Library of Congress*)

One of the earliest and best of the Mr
Tenpercents, A. P. Watt (*A. P. Watt/
Steve Richards*)

Will Rothenstein's portrait of Kipling
(*National Portrait Gallery*)

1925: the Kiplings
attend the first
court of the season
at Buckingham
Palace *(BBC
Hulton Picture
Library)*

Bateman's: the
'overground
dungeon'
*(National Trust/
John Bethell)*

Kipling in full
public spate: at
the Mansion
House during
World War
One *(BBC
Hulton Picture
Library)*

telling an Indian that, whoever is sent to rule over them, it'll be a *'man'*. By that time we've forgotten that Orde was, just initially, shown to be a man – not merely called one in a blustering and rhetorical appeal to base emotions.

The Light that Failed is not, by common and by Kipling's own consent, a successful novel. But it was important to him when he wrote it, important to him as an artist and a creative writer, important to his integrity in those capacities. He was trying to make sense of his life. When the version we now read was published, in March 1891, it bore the note that it still bears: 'This is the story of *The Light that Failed* as it was originally conceived by the Writer'. He never removed this, and he never reprinted the earlier, shorter version with the 'happy ending' (which appeared in November 1890). The note is edged with anger; there is a reprimand to someone concealed within it. To whom? His mother? His father? Wolcott Balestier? Himself, anyway, for having given way to someone. Balestier was then still alive and very much kicking. I have no doubt that the reproach was to Balestier for impudently printing, without permission, a short 'happy' version with which Kipling had been merely toying – under pressure from both his mother and Balestier himself. But that must remain conjectural: there is no direct evidence for it.

The novel was a critical failure, Kipling's first really wrong step from that point of view, though only a temporary one. There was no obvious successor to Dickens at the time he was writing it, and he must have hoped to fill that place in the estimation of critics and public alike. Thackeray and Trollope were dead. Hardy was much read – interestingly, he now outsells Kipling by a quite considerable ratio – but neither liked nor understood by many reviewers. The prolific Gissing, who had published eight novels in the 1880s, and who had started the new decade with *The Emancipated*, was too drab (though substantial) to be considered as major. Meredith was too unconventional, and even now his work presents great difficulties. *The Case of General Ople and Lady Camper* (1890) presented no challenge to any aspiring novelist, Grand Old Man though Meredith was. So Kipling's uncertainty about his first novel reflects much frustration and puzzlement; it also reflects a conflict between God and mammon, between imagination and commerce, between the expression of the truth and the fear of starvation and ignominy.

But *The Light that Failed* was not a popular failure, and has sold well from the time of its publication until today. Everybody who cares about good fiction has read it, and all those agree that it is not a success. But it is nonetheless important in the Kipling canon, which cannot be said for *Captains Courageous*, a better but lower-powered work about which no one is much bothered either way.

The secret of why it only didn't *quite* work out was aptly laid bare by the able poet and critic Lionel Johnson. Kipling, said Johnson, reviewing the novel in the *Academy* in April 1891, doesn't have a 'clever trick', doesn't have a 'happy knack', doesn't have a 'flashy style': no, what he has is 'real instrinsic power'. Yet Johnson warned of Kipling's tendency to 'brilliant vulgarity', and clearly he found the novel brilliantly vulgar. In *The Light that Failed* his power is frequently misused; but it is still sporadically there.

When anyone now talks about *The Light that Failed*, they refer to the version 'originally conceived by the Writer'. In the first edition the original text is truncated, and Dick and Maisie end up engaged to a chorus of singing journalists. This is a sentimental abuse of the author's concept of Maisie (in giving her that name he must have been aware of Sir Walter Scott's poem 'Proud Maisie'). Whatever may be wrong with the original, this first published version is a travesty and a disgrace to its author's intentions. Young writers should be allowed to make their own mistakes, and should not be interfered with. It is clear from Kipling's brief note to the first issue of his own version that he much regretted taking other advice, or, possibly, having it forced upon him.

In Kipling's own book, then, and not the shambles of it issued in November 1890, the narrative begins with two adolescents experimenting with a revolver; the girl, Maisie, almost wounds Dick Heldar, the boy, when she fires it. There is a goat present, and, firing the last shot, Dick's aim is spoiled. But he reckons that he has the love of Maisie, who has allowed him to kiss her. Few readers would seriously consider that she had pledged herself to him; but Dick Heldar does. All Maisie says in answer to Dick's 'You belong to me, for ever and ever', is 'Yes, we belong – for ever. It's very nice.' One trouble with the book is that Dick's flaming unrequited love for Maisie isn't convincing. But something about *him* is. Barrie, at one point considered a rival to Kipling, shrewdly said in his review of it: 'His boy and girl . . . are man and woman playing in vain at being children.' 'We see at once,' Barrie went on, with typical Scotch percipience and wit, 'that his pathos is potatoes. It is not legitimate, but it produces the desired effects.' 'Girlhood is what is wanted, and so far it has proved beyond him.' Maisie, Barrie rightly says, is a 'nonentity'. The trouble is – did Barrie recognise it? – that Kipling was not really much interested in girls. If Maisie's red-haired friend, the one who wanted Dick (*not* an autobiographical touch, the woman in question protested many years afterwards), 'came into the light of day she might prove as dull as Maisie'. 'His chief defect is ignorance of life.' But he was less ignorant of life by that time than he was desperately ignorant of women, for whom he had, like almost all those with misogynistic tendencies, an equally desperate tenderness.

It is this dullness of Maisie that gives the game away. Like Kipling with Florence Garrard, Dick is playing some passionate game in which he is projecting whatever it is he really feels, a burning confusion, on the *figure* of Maisie. As it is she exists only in Dick's embittered or excited perception. Had he succeeded in defining his own feelings exactly he would have written a classic first novel. But who would have published it? Who could have published it? Not Wolcott Balestier, assuredly. He wasn't after that sort of notoriety, or a novel that would consist of a triangle of him, his managerial sister and the great young author whose attention he had seduced. So the novel is a classic of a shambles of a classic.

The scene rapidly moves from childhood to Dick's young manhood. He is a war-artist (Kipling's fantasy of himself-as-artist in battle, which he was to try to fulfil in the Boer War): we see him, in an undoubtedly powerful but repulsive battle-scene, receiving the wound that causes him to be blind. Stephen Crane, that other writer who had never heard a shot fired in anger when he wrote his war book, was much influenced by this one – and also stole and improved on a metaphor twice employed by Kipling. In the opening chapter of Kipling's book a puddle catches the sun and turns it into 'a wrathful red disc'. Later on (Chapter IV) it shines over the Thames for a moment, after fog has lifted, 'a blood-red wafer'. Crane has the sun 'pasted in the sky like a blood-red wafer', which was praised by John Berryman as original – and 'pasted' was.

The opening scene is good action writing, but is more evidently written by someone who has not seen battle than *The Red Badge of Courage*. Crane understood the necessity of cowardice and fear more consistently than Kipling, who tended to attribute it only to the lower orders. Crane is more mature. Kipling is over-heroic, and the relish in violence is nasty. This battle scene has too much in common with the notorious one of the baiting of the cardiac publisher.

Early on, when Dick has returned from the Sudan and is becoming a famous artist (just as Kipling, already being pirated by American publishers, was becoming famous), the head of the Central Southern Syndicate tells him that he can't have back about one hundred and fifty of his sketches because 'in the absence of any specified agreement the sketches are our property, of course'. When the man first entered the room Dick had said to himself, 'Weak heart . . . Very weak heart'. Dick is therefore made by Kipling, Boys'-Own-Paper-like, to request a 'younger man' with whom to deal. The publisher refuses. Dick thereupon circles him and threatens him, thus humiliating him and making him afraid of having a stroke on the spot. It is a remarkable flaw in the book, it is one which runs through all Kipling's writing, and it spoils the effectiveness with which all the violence is depicted in *The Light that Failed*. We only have to read Stevenson's action scenes to see how much more maturely, how much better, how much more wholesomely, this kind of thing can be done. The justification for Dick's bullying is supposed to lie in his memories of being near starvation. Anyone can sympathise, and no one better than an author. But there is something gravely wrong: this is cheap fantasy. It might have been effective if that kind of behaviour were perceived by the narrator as a flaw in Dick – but it is supposed to be appealing. Kipling is a little boy again, wanting his own way, owning his righteousness rather than asserting his rights.

Yet there is a curious honesty and straightforwardness about the book, in the positively naive way that Kipling puts his own puerile aggressiveness, his sexuality and his artistic conscience at stake: his loyalty to what he would soon call his 'daimon'. The absurd lapse, though repulsive in detail, is almost appealing. A writer less passionate or less clearly aware of the opposing values of art and commerce would not have allowed himself to be so childish, either in the scene depicting the baiting of the publisher or, even, in the battle scenes. In the first of these, and the main one (there is only one page of action at the end), the level of writing initially achieved is very high.

> The camel-guns shelled them as they passed, and opened for an instant lanes through their midst, most like those quick-closing vistas in a Kentish hop-garden seen when the train races by at full speed; and the infantry fire, held till the opportune moment, dropped them in close-packed hundreds.

'Close-packed hundreds' is impossible, but is how it might have been remembered by a participant. All this is marred by two details: Torpenhow's blinding of an Arab, and Dick's 'calling aloud to the restless Nile for Maisie', simply a sudden intrusion into the texture of not just fantasy, but schoolboy fantasy. The eye-gouging is further spoiled by an allusion later in the book: Dick, when he has become blind, says to Torpenhow, 'D'you remember that nigger you gouged in the square? Pity you didn't keep the odd eye. It would have been useful.' This might have been good in the mouth of a more finely conceived character; but here is the writing of a gifted, brutal schoolboy who may grow up, not that of a mature novelist. Torpenhow, being himself an aspect of Kipling, is shown as the newspaperman who is nonetheless as tough (and tougher!) than even a soldier. In the battle passage it might almost seem that the entire war is being conducted between a horde of enraged but not ignoble savages and a journalist and his artist friends. It would have been brilliant if Kipling had been able to see Dick for the boastful and violent man he is, the fantasy artist-soldier, and had wanted to show him up; but he is wrapped up in him because he knows that he is himself. Had he himself been caught up in a situation like that, he guiltily tries not to reflect, he would bloody well run away. It is true that the narrator talks of Dick's arrogance; but he heroises it rather than analyses it. So far as Maisie is concerned, it is as if Kipling wants the reader to blame her for being so ungrateful after Dick has been so brave in battle and called out for her: the obstinate male insisting that male heroics oblige women to reciprocate passion without question. He is crying out for a woman's compassion, motherly love transferred to a girl, but he requires this matchless experience through Dick: his having not earned it shows.

An interesting detail is that Dick's 'aim' is once again spoiled. In the first chapter it was spoiled by – as the girl's hair is blown by the rising wind and she calls the goat Amomma 'a little beast' – a sudden darkness 'that stung'; here it is spoiled by the memory of that incident, a voice saying 'Ah, get away you brute!', the voice of someone scaring something away, a crack in the head, a darkness 'that stung' . . . Here is a vivid sense of the blindingness of sexual encounter, not experienced by Kipling with women. He does not know what he will find.

Victorian sexual symbolism, as in some of the very early Henry James, was obvious, 'innocent' and in a sense pure. Freud had not yet come to make everyone self-conscious, and the symbolism worked much better and less consciously. Blindness here is impotence, lack of creative virility, fear that homosexuality may cripple creativity – and the goat and the 'brute' are lust. They may also represent, although more remotely, the cultural obligations that a man feels to desire women. The book is full of crude insistences about the sexual encounters of the jolly males in it, with 'loose' women – to the point that one suspects them. The blindness metaphor crops up often in Victorian literature, and Carrington refines it when he supposes it to be a symbol of 'failure in love'; he cites *Jane Eyre, Westward Ho!, Martian* (Du Maurier) and *Aurora Leigh*, from which Kipling derived detail for *The Light that Failed*. The essential connection lies in the revelation (sight) believed inherent in romantic consummation. In mythology the process of sight is symbolic of understanding.

The 'spoiling of the aim' in this novel is an adumbration of the blindness theme: desire (goat, brute) destroys the will to work. At the same time, the firing of a revolver has an unmistakably phallic significance. It is silly and immature (just as men often are), over-obvious, and irritatingly and glibly over-used – but one that is responsible for much death and destruction. In *The Light that Failed* the case of the bullets whining away off target is poignant, a hint of something else the author wants. In the first chapter, the 'thoroughly fouled revolver' kicks 'wildly' in Dick's hands – a reminiscence of onanism (although Onan actually seems to have been guilty of *coitus interruptus* rather than masturbation – we will give the word Kipling would have used if he had dared) when he was not too tired at USC? The bullet of the spoiled aim goes 'singing out to the empty sea'. In the second chapter the bullet goes out over the desert. There is a sense of hopelessness in 'firing' at all.

Kipling was prompted to write the book in the way he did by two events: his accidental meeting with Flo in the street, and his meeting with Wolcott. He could express his passions outwardly by use, so to say, of running into the *femme fatale*. Perhaps he even lurked in alleyways until she emerged, so as to 'run into her'. He knew where she was to be found. All the time that he was actually writing the novel, he was attempting vainly to whip up not only Flo's interest in him, basing his hopes unfairly and with deliberate hopelessness on the past and merely adolescent encounter, but also his own interest in her. (What would have happened had he been confronted with reciprocated passion? He would have set off instantly on the world voyage he did not take until the end of 1891 . . .) The book was finished by August, but must have been interrupted by the writing of the substantial and superior stories of that spring and summer. He even went to France at the beginning of May to see Flo for a few days. Yet all that rage and desperate uneasiness was in part generated by a culture which could not accept feelings of the kind he experienced. He felt himself a part of that culture, too. Few men of those times had the courage to work it all out in a novel that was trying to be true to the situation. Kipling botched it; but he managed to drag out into the semi-open most of his problems. Later he became more cunning.

The Light that Failed is indeed in many ways an 'anti-feminist tract'. But Kipling tries harder to be fair than he is generally given credit for. Under the 'tarred throat of a forty-pounder cannon' Maisie exclaims to Dick, in the midst of his vain attempts to win her love – they are back on the beach – 'Now, if Amomma were only here!' She means, innocently but provocatively, 'if only we were children again!' (She also means, of course: 'I wish I could have lust for you!') Dick asks 'doesn't it make any difference?' and she answers, eventually, that she knows what he wants, but can't give it to him, and doesn't 'understand what that feeling means'. She despises herself for it, as such women usually do – even if they are asked not to do so. Other men have 'interrupted' her when she was in the middle of her own work (this is mentioned twice in the course of the novel). Dick is never convincing in his physical passion, and it is obvious why the whole thing has the air of something forbidden. But what is happening here is that Kipling forgets Dick altogether, and tries, through his presentation of Maisie, to project his own feelings of sexual disinclination and inadequacy towards women. That is why it is unconvincing. Maisie becomes both the vessel of Kipling's own feelings towards women, and also the young man whom Dick wants but towards whom he wishes to remain 'spiritual'. But at an even more primitive level she is something else, as will become apparent. I am sure that Kipling did exploit one characteristic of the real Maisie which he was easily able to intuit: her coldness and dislike of being touched. There are similar characters in Willa Cather's novels. (It should be noted that there is social pressure upon them, too, to 'conform'.)

The other conflict in the novel is between true and false (commercial) work. Kipling here, with great honesty, ignores the compromise most commonly available to writers or artists: that their serious work gains them a modicum, and that (later at least) they well understand the difference between real and false work, and so can earn from some hack work without trying, falsely, to ingratiate themselves with unauthentic and uncompelled work. He causes Dick to be a brilliant artist and Maisie to be a dedicated one who is, however (like Wolcott), no good. When at the beginning Dick has some hope of winning her he curses '"all varieties of Art"', because he will have to '"talk about Art, – Woman's Art! ... it did me a good turn once, and now it's in my way. I'll go home and do some Art"' He goes home, thinking on the way that his relationship with Maisie is 'ten times worse than owning a wife' because he won't be able to look after her when she and her red-haired companion become ill through eating improperly (a strange notion, and a somewhat maternal one). Probably Kipling's mother was on to him continually about eating properly.

Torpenhow comes into his studio one evening at dusk and looks 'at Dick with his eyes full of the austere love that springs up between men who have tugged at the same oar together and are yoked by custom and use and the intimacies of toil'. 'This is a good love,' the narrator adds, 'and, since it allows, and even encourages strife, recrimination, and the most brutal sincerity, does not die, but increases, and is proof against any absence and evil conduct.' But is it proof against 'any evil conduct'? Why is such conduct (whatever it is) 'evil'? The male camaraderie stuff in this novel has been properly criticised: even allowing for the Victorian context, it is still nauseating, and strikes an embarrassingly false, almost pornographic, note.

That evening Dick has a good chat, as he might have styled it, with Torpenhow, who asks him if his liver is out of order. 'I don't think we could misunderstand each other,' Dick tells him. It is the sort of thing that a young man says to a lover. Torpenhow asks him if the trouble with him isn't 'a woman' (disturbing and troublesome object, this). Dick denies it, but Torpenhow knows and is supposed to understand. What Kipling omits, and what he ought to have put in, was that Torpenhow was jealous. But in that case *The Light that Failed* would have been a different, and unpublishable, novel. He would never have settled for something as honest but necessarily watered down as *Tim* (1891), by Henry James's friend Howard Overing Sturgis (this tale of a younger boy's devotion to an older one passed as 'innocent' until recently; it is not as truly innocent as it might have been had Sturgis been able to express his actual feelings).

The Light that Failed, then, certainly is, in an elementary sense, an 'anti-feminist tract'. On the surface Kipling has many muddled and silly ideas about women, officers' mess talk, stuff about being 'manly' – it is all perfectly silly and perfectly obvious. But the book could not, generally, be read more deeply in its time; and, because it was thus read, so it has been ever after. It is a shambles, though, and no one has been able to see how it really tries to work. It doesn't succeed because it could not, and in any case Kipling couldn't work out his complex destiny in the form of the novel (except to a limited extent in the partially Pre-Raphaelite exercise that is *Kim*). He was, however, doing that in the stories he wrote contemporaneously.

I do not feel the least qualm in taking *The Light that Failed* to pieces, whereas, even as a critical biographer, I have felt some qualms at trying to do so to certain of Kipling's beautifully integrated stories. But *The Light that Failed* is already in tatters. It will be recalled that Gide took Proust to task for making some of his young men into women in his fiction – Gide, after all, though he turned down Proust's novel for the *Nouvelle Revue Française*, had himself been as bold as it was then possible to be about his own ambisexuality. A number of other sexually ambivalent writers were forced to do this, too. In the (critically) neglected *Of Human Bondage*, Somerset Maugham actually managed to create a character who, almost successfully, carries the attributes of both sexes. This is certainly what Kipling did in *The Light that Failed*, although I doubt if he knew it at the time. The procedure may well account for the chaotic power that is in it. But because it is chaotic and confused, and because the process was unconscious, no scheme underlying it could be consistent. Nonetheless, it is clear that Maisie-as-would-be-artist is Wolcott Balestier, and that the red-haired girl is his sister Caroline. Torpenhow, as well as Dick, is Kipling himself, although he doubles as ideal chaste (but wrestling) lover of Dick, and provides a contrast to Balestier, who is seen as both a physically suitable and an emotionally (or intellectually – so far as Kipling could conceive of this function) unsuitable lover. Few personal characteristics of any of these people are involved. But that, allowing for many local shifts and confusions, is who they really are. And the history of Kipling while he was writing the book is in important respects recorded in the book itself (the final version, the one conceived by him, that is). 'He lived it as he wrote it,' as Carrington says.

Did he write the longer version first, then do a 'happy ending' version? Or did he write the happy ending version first, and only after that write it as he felt he had originally 'conceived' it? We do not know. It does not much matter, in the sense that he might have shaped it from drafts already in part written. When Lovell published the shortened version in November 1890, as No. 25 of their Westminster series (they were very shortly afterwards to become known as the United States Book Company), the copy they deposited for copyright purposes in Washington is said to have been the one published by Macmillan in March 1891. Kipling made further revisions to the texts published in 1897 and 1899, but these don't alter the book substantially. He was always evasive about it – perhaps he later realised who really was who – and in his autobiography claimed that it had been prompted by his reading of *Manon Lescaut*. But, as Carrington has shown, it owes more to Elizabeth Barrett Browning's narrative poem *Aurora Leigh*, itself written at a time of extreme psychological crisis for its author.

Gosse stated that Balestier claimed that he had made 'a personal conquest' of Kipling, and that he obtained his agreement to collaborate in a novel 'within a week'. They could not have begun work until, at the earliest, late May or June. But they could have talked about it – Kipling reticent – for a month or two, or longer. It is quite possible that Kipling may have considered, or Wolcott may have suggested, a collaboration on *The Light that Failed*. Whether what Gosse says about the period of only a week elapsing between Wolcott's starting to court Kipling, and Kipling's giving way, it is clear that Wolcott had to wait for a time before actual work could begin. That Kipling must have felt artistically compromised goes without saying. No praise of Balestier's fiction by him is extant; he never used his considerable influence to keep it in print. No doubt he felt silence was best.

Kipling's surrender to the influence of Wolcott has amazed all his biographers. Hilton Brown, reflecting some of the gossip about it at the time, describes it as 'altogether incredible'. Wolcott had the man who 'during those seven long years in India had most unquestioningly walked by himself!' 'pinned down': there 'is really no accounting for this extraordinary occurrence which is made the more fantastic by the fact – which must have been obvious to Kipling – that Wolcott as a writer was at best third-rate . . . There is nothing for it than to accept Wolcott's own version of a "personal conquest" . . .' Such wondering gossip makes it abundantly clear why Kipling needed the cover of a heterosexual attachment – best that it be 'hopeless', too, so that he need not become embroiled.

There is a way to account for it all, though: the obvious one, which only Wilson has acknowledged. It is not so remarkable, although one accepts it with a sense of shock. It accounts for much of the 'enigma' of Kipling. But there arises the question of the resentment and rage which Kipling would have felt at being thus in harness. Romantic love does not end happily unless it changes. Its course is not altogether happy, either, although it is punctuated by ecstatic moments. Rationality is traded for ecstasy.

Kipling's complex set of feelings account for the strong theme of artistic integrity running through *The Light that Failed*. Near the opening, Dick cynically pretties up a picture of a soldier he has painted, in order to give it more value on the market. This episode emerges from a generally autobiographical context, during which Dick describes his contempt for the people who are now making him famous. Kipling himself was suspicious of his popularity, and even used to bait literary 'experts' by making up names of 'famous' writers to test their honesty (he tells us in *Something of Myself*). Like any true writer, he enjoyed genuine appreciation more than mindless adulation. He saw merely fashionable praise as insulting; he liked the 'fun', the 'fuss', but only 'almost' liked those who made the fuss and paid the money. This wasn't just arrogance; it was also an astonishing assertion of artistic conscience in Kipling, who, even in the midst of all the fuss that was being made about him, was determined to try to keep his head. He was vain, but deeply conscious of being so.

Dick's painting was of a 'dishevelled, bedevilled scallawag . . . He wasn't pretty, but he was all soldier and very much man' (one thinks of 'Loot'). The market wanted something more 'restful', so 'Result, military tailor's pattern-plate. Price, thank Heaven, twice as much . . .' Torpenhow–Kipling–conscience puts his boot through the canvas of this rubbish. 'What can you expect from creatures born in this light,' Dick protests, 'if they want furniture-polish, let them have furniture-polish, so long as they pay for it.' Torpenhow points out that these 'are the people you have to work for, whether you like it or not' (one thinks here not only of the 'critics' but also the 'common reader') and Dick gives in, although only temporarily. This passage reflects the conflict going on in Kipling, and interestingly relates it to his feeling for the 'long trail' (to which subject we shall come), to his desire to get away from home, to be a gipsy, a wanderer, accountable to nobody. *The Light that Failed* at a certain level (it has so many), and perhaps the least unsuccessful one, is a fable of artistic integrity, creative integrity, triumphant through suffering. That Dick's picture is of a *soldier* is, again, an example of courageous honesty. Again and again Dick is tempted to be brutal, to surrender. But that brutality also takes him on a camel, blind and denied the capacity to practice his art, 'punished' (he thinks of himself as 'learning a punishment hymn at Mrs Jennett's') to his death in the arms of Torpenhow, who has been conscience, ideal lover and now, at last, a Wolcott impossible in life.

One must remember that at about this time Kipling read a headline from New York all about himself: 'WILL SUCCESS TURN HIS HEAD?' But he had also written (March 1890), to Kay Robinson, his old mentor in India, that it was as 'selfish to work for the trinity . . . Money, fame and success' as it was to 'lay siege to a woman'. 'No man can be a power for all time or the tenth of it' (the parallel to this in *The Light that Failed* is when Dick tells Maisie that 'four-fifths of everybody's work must be bad'). What a person was going to be able to achieve was 'in God's hands absolutely', and he is best not to think too much about his soul, for this will breed 'self-consciousness and loss of power'. Then Kipling added: 'Pray for me that I do not take the sickness which for lack of understanding, I shall call love.' He knew that Robinson could not know what lay behind that remark, which has been taken as merely misogynistic. He went on to inform Robinson that, come what might, he had to do his work in his own way. By now he had perhaps grown used to the existence of Wolcott Balestier, and was trying not to be in love with him. Among Victorian homosexuals, Housman, we know, talked to very few. But he was able to 'come out' to someone. Likewise John Addington Symonds, whose recently published autobiography tells us so much. T.E. Brown, the Manx poet and master at Clifton, who was married, has an unequivocal (and nobly frank and intelligent) passage in one of his letters about his real feelings for some of his pupils. Kipling is unlikely ever to have talked to anyone at all, except Balestier himself. But there is a single exception, to whom we shall come.

Kipling had experienced a dual shock: full recognition of the fact that he was 'victim' of a 'forbidden' love, and simultaneous recognition that love did not bring with it understanding. I do not see how he and Balestier really could have understood each other over the question of literature. No one, in fact, has even supposed that they could. If he loved Balestier – and I see no other explanation of his behaviour – then this must have been a terrible disappointment to him. He may have hidden it for a time, and chosen to enjoy what he liked about his friend. But would this enjoyment not have been continually interrupted by Wolcott's crassness? It has always to be remembered that no writer in English has been more intensely serious about his vocation, and that Wolcott was, after all, wholly concerned with the bitch Goddess. Could there have been, in this friendship, some feeling in Rudyard akin to Shakespeare's towards the Friend, the young man, as expressed in the *Sonnets*? Kipling's concern with fame and its corrupting potential is in proportion to his popularity – and that was very considerable. When he became something of a political bore, and critical fashion turned against him, he was still widely read, even though his sales went down. His best work did not deteriorate.

He therefore chose, as an overt course, to exploit his largely feigned disappointment with Flo Garrard in his novel. The conflict over Wolcott is expressed as though it were a conflict over Flo. What was not feigned about the disappointment with Flo was, no doubt, her refusal to provide him with a 'permitted' haven for his emotions. His bias was towards his own sex, but he was by no means immune to women, even if all the 'wenching' he implies never took place. There is no doubt that he personally felt that her sketches were no good. That was the traditional Kipling family view of them. But then they resented her. So he thus, perhaps half-revengefully, represents them as being bad in the book.

But at a deeper level she is Balestier, with his wretched lightweight useless talent. After all, even if those who admire *The Naulahka* are right (but the enthusiasm scarcely stands up to critical analysis), not much of it was by Wolcott, even if Kipling let him pretend it was. What Wilson and Amis are admiring are the Kipling touches. They say nothing of the absurd and psychologically false ending. No doubt Kipling did make Balestier feel good, too: the author of good sentences that had been very tactfully re-structured by Kipling. They worked together, Wolcott at the typewriter, Kipling pacing about.

But there is an inevitable confusion as to who is who at certain points in *The Light that Failed*. When Dick suggests to Maisie, with what some might take to be insensitivity, that he paint a picture and she sign it, she is, of course, Balestier wooing him – and he being artistically reckless. That must be taken as a direct reference to the collaboration, a proposition that sent Kipling into an immediate psychological crisis. He must have resisted the suggestion to collaborate; perhaps, loving the eager Wolcott, he did desperately think of this as an alternative. She is Balestier whenever intercourse about art concerns them. But she is Flo whenever she *talks* about her own work (she has her counterpart in the eventually defeated Kate in the Kipling–Balestier collaboration itself), and the necessity not to have it interrupted. When Dick judges the work she is, of course, Wolcott. She may even also be Kipling himself in this respect! *The Light that Failed* does not possess integrity of character, there is scarcely any psychology in it, and, insofar as it consists of wodges of opinion or outlook, anyone may be anyone: the best one can do is to pick up on the more consistent elements. As Maisie, Flo, the girl devoted only to her work, she is also, as has been pointed out by more than one critic (first, I think, by Betty Miller), one of the earliest, if not even the earliest, example of the so-called 'new woman'. This 'new woman' is certainly adumbrated in novels such as those by Kipling's generous mentor Mrs Clifford, and, more familiarly, in *Hester* and other novels by Mrs Oliphant. This 'new woman' comes most profoundly into her own in *Jude the Obscure*, of course, as the maddening, cruel and yet fascinating Sue Bridehead. Kipling's own introduction to her, apart from what he learned from Mrs Clifford, must have been through Ibsen's *A Doll's House* – which he didn't like. Kipling was overtly horrified, and no doubt his mother was; but he was also fascinated.

Maisie as blinder of men, Maisie as Delilah, Maisie as destroyer of a man's work, is Wolcott, though, even more than she is a 'new woman'. She almost blinds him on the beach when she carelessly fires his own revolver at him. That opening displays her as male (armed with a revolver). Such a thing never happened with Flo, although she did once have a goat. Then in battle Dick gets the wound that will cause his blindness. But we are given to understand that 'mental anxiety' has greatly accelerated the process of blindness. The Melancolia which is (unconvincingly in artistic terms) Dick's masterpiece and which is destroyed by Bessie is *The Light that Failed* itself; this destruction is the representation of it in its truncated and sentimentalised version, a version that saw the light only through Wolcott's hideous insensitivity. The act of its defacement by a jealous whore oblivious to everything decent in life, is precisely what Kipling thought of himself for allowing it to go forward. That much, just the destruction, is contained in the truncated version itself. And Bessie, too, is thus Balestier as he really is: a dirty opportunistic destructive whore. The truncated version, whether written first or no, omits almost all of the discussion about art (one can hear the voice of the commercialist advising – if some of that material existed in draft – 'don't put that stuff in, Rud, readers are not interested in the values of art, but in romance and battles').

Dick knows perfectly well that Maisie will use him 'as he used Binat' (a spoiled and drunken artist in Port Said whose degradation Dick has used as copy just as writers use everyone they know as copy), but he is resigned. He knows that what Torpenhow has told him is true: that for his own tendency to cynicism alone he will get a 'tremendous thrashing'. Then follows (Chapter VI) a probably accurate if tactfully disguised account of what Kipling thinks of Wolcott's already published or finished works of fiction. Dick, identifying the 'thrashing' Torpenhow meant as his state of frustration over Maisie, crosses the park and thinks that although the Queen 'can do no wrong' (the 'thrashing' of being 'bound hand and foot' to 'the Queen' – an essential part of the art of being-in-love) 'certainly she has some notion of drawing'. He tells himself that Maisie's paintings are 'reproductions on which advice would not be wasted', a frigid and ambiguous realisation. He has wanted, Sunday after Sunday, to kiss Maisie rather than talk 'connectedly' about 'the mysteries of the craft that was all in all to her'. He has meanwhile learned to hate the red-haired girl 'on sight'. It is hard not to connect this devoted red-haired girl with Caroline, Wolcott's sister, 'always watching him'. Caroline was always there when he visited Wolcott; they first met at Wolcott's office in Dean's Yard, when she had come to consult her brother about housekeeping; she had not, though, been present when they first met, since she had not then arrived in England. Kipling then shows us Dick being inspired to preach his own gospel of art to Maisie, with its brutal realism about the public and the amount of work that is likely to be any good; he now tells her that, while he likes a certain 'grim Dutch touch' to her painting, he thinks she is weak in drawing. He tells her not to be 'immoral' by trying to 'carry a bad thing off' with 'flashy, tricky stuff in the corner of a pic'. Maisie–Wolcott protests: 'She did not care for the pure line.' Maisie does not react at all happily to Dick's exhortations about art and not minding what other people do, and he

paused, and the longing that had been so resolutely put away came back
into his eyes. He looked at Maisie, and the look asked as plainly as words,
Was it not time to leave all this barren wilderness of canvas and counsel
and join hands with Life and Love.

Clearly Dick here thinks of marriage as being without the nonsense of
Maisie's art. This has been looked on as misogynistic or at least anti-feminist
(anti-'new woman'), and it is; but to the extent that Maisie's own shallow
attitudes – and they are shallow, as may be seen even from what I have
quoted of them – are Balestier's, it is not. Kipling's attitude, then, towards
'Life and Love' was vague; but its outlines are clear enough. One of these
confused attitudes he expressed to Kay Robinson: he is going to go his
own way, and it is awful to him (he also told Robinson) that 'each Soul
has to work out its own salvation'. Another is expressed by the poem he
wrote (and later altered) some time during this unhappy period, called
'The Long Trail'. Whereas the received version of this, the one appearing
in *Barrack-Room Ballads*, exhorts a 'lass' to 'have done' with the 'Tents of
Shem' (by which Carrington suggests Kipling might have meant a contract
Balestier intended to sign with Heinemann), an earlier, and preserved, draft
has 'lad'. 'Have done with the Tents of Shem, dear lad',

> We've seen the seasons through,
> And it's time to turn on the old trail, our own trail, the out trail,
> Pull out, pull out, on the Long Trail – the trail that is always
> > new!

This ends:

> The Lord knows what we may find, dear lad,
> And the deuce knows what we may do –
> But we're back once more on the old trail, our own trail, the out trail,
> We're down, hull-down, on the Long Trail – the trail that is always
> > new.

Now I am far from suggesting that Kipling was here exhorting Wolcott
to share with him those undoubtedly mythical pleasures of naval life so
unfairly characterised by Winston Churchill as 'rum, sodomy and the lash',
and feel sure that he was disinterestedly interested only in the limited use
of the last-named. In suggesting that he was, however, exhorting Wolcott
to follow him to a free and wandering life (the place of literature in this is
unclear), I am simply following all his other biographers.

The exhortation to take the trail is what Dick tries to beg Maisie in
one of the sections (Chapter VII) he added to the novel. There is perhaps
more than a tittle of evidence, apart from the fact of what most critics
think, that he did write the expanded and 'unhappy' version, or at least
put it together, after he had published the first 'happy' one. The copy
deposited in Washington in November 1890 cannot possibly be identical
to the one published in March 1891 in England. In an undated letter to
Macmillan, clearly belonging to the time when they were putting the
revised and full version through the press, he wrote (from Villiers Street):

I am forwarding with this the typed [sic] of an extra chapter (No.8) for the Light that Failed, and should be glad to see proofs of the first pages of the work as soon as possible.

That letter must have been written a few days, at most a couple of weeks, before the following, of 16 February 1891:

Enclosed please find last proofs of The Light, also the Dedication. The l'Envoi must be printed after the blank page and not facing the conclusion of the story. I have not yet received the revise of Chapter IX. Kindly send as soon as possible.

Now 'The Long Trail' first appeared, under its eventual title, in the *Cape Illustrated Magazine* for November 1891; after that it became 'L'Envoi' to *Barrack-Room Ballads*. Did Kipling intend to print some earlier draft of his poem in *The Light that Failed*? It seems possible. But Carrington, who, as I have said, believes that 'the Tents of Shem' may refer to a specific contract with Heinemann from which Kipling was trying to dissuade Wolcott, states that Kipling's parting from Carrie in August 1891 – when he went off on his voyage to South Africa and beyond – was the occasion of the poem. If so, it must have been of a new version of it. But such an argument is confused and unconvincing.

Everyone asks to what 'the Tents of Shem' may refer. Mason wonders if it might refer to 'some specific Jewish association'. He is worried because he thinks that the specific context of the piece wants 'towns, not tents': 'places of luxury or at least comfort'. The reference belongs to *Genesis*, 9: 27, and is cryptic in itself. The Noah of this little tale doesn't really belong to the Noah of the Flood tradition; but Kipling could not have known that. The story is thus. This Noah, a nomad, and the first tiller of the soil (or first farmer) founded wine (so to say: he planted a vineyard). Naturally enough, in experimenting with it, he 'was drunken; and he was uncovered in his tent'. No scholar yet can make certain sense of the story from now on. Canaan (for those who have looked it up in their Bible: the reference to Ham is the result of an intertwining of two genealogical traditions and hence a textual confusion; it need not concern us here) 'saw the nakedness of his father, and told his two brethren without'. Shem and Japhet went in to their father and covered him up, taking care not to look on their father's nakedness. Noah awoke from his stupor and 'knew what his younger son had done unto him'. He cursed Canaan to be the slave of his two brothers, and said: 'God shall enlarge Japhet, and he shall dwell in the tents of Shem; and Canaan shall be his servant'. Professor John H. Marks of Princeton University writes of this passage:

Canaan's wrongdoing probably consists in ridiculing his father in what he reports to his brother . . . though more may be implied in vs.24. Japhet occupies the *tents of Shem* . . . the references may be to the Canaanites, Israelites, and Philistines; but historical precision is impossible.

We may now leave speculation on the subject of what the text actually means (or meant) for speculation on what Kipling, who was familiar with the Bible, understood by it. What would originally have appealed to him was the simple and humorous detail of what happened to the inventor of booze. He himself never had a problem with drink, although he liked it, and in the last twenty or thirty years of his life his wife saw to it that he didn't 'have too much', especially when he was talking to old friends. The phrase 'the tents of Shem' only became known at all when his poem 'The Long Trail', as a whole, entered the language. But no one has ever had the least idea of what he meant by it, and it is highly unlikely that he was aware of what he made of, if indeed he made anything of, 'the Tents of Shem' part of the passage. But he had an ear for phrases. The second edition of the Religious Tract Society's popular *Bible Cyclopaedia* of 1868 glosses Shem simply as the eldest son of Noah from whom the Jewish race, and through it the Messiah, are descended. I think that Kipling's sudden coinage of 'Tents of Shem' for 'London' (that is what it must have meant to him, as Mason rightly suggests) was unconsciously (not consciously!) drawing on a number of associations. The first of these was of course the passage in *Genesis*, 9, and in particular verse 24, where Canaan's father knows what his son has done: 'he knew what his son had done unto him'. That has possibilities even for Professor Marks, and these possibilities arise from the fact that Canaan saw his father's nakedness when (apparently) he ought not to have done: after all, the other two brothers cover him up and don't gaze on him, actually turning the other way as they cover him up. This would have struck Kipling when he first read it as puzzling. The only possible inference, apart from the simple one that Canaan saw his father's nakedness when he oughtn't to have done, is that he ridiculed him, by buggering him and then saying something to his two brothers like, 'I found him in a stupor so I buggered the old sod.' It is an insult to one's father to bugger him, and the more especially if he is drunk. But the specifics don't matter. Later it came to the surface of Kipling's mind as a 'forbidden thought'. A new word just then current, from the East End, and popularised in the *Referee* newspaper, was *shemozzle* (*shlemozzle, shimozzle* and other variants) from Yiddish *schlem*, 'bad luck', and thus meaning 'a difficulty'. This is actually an entry (but with an incomplete explanation) in *Slang and Its Analogues*, upon the first volume of which no other than W.E. Henley was working with his friend J.S. Farmer. However, the bell rung in Kipling's mind is less that word, although it did start to gain currency in 1889, than the word *shame*: the 'tents of *shame*'. Not being in the least consciously aware, then or later, of this set of associations, it remains unorganised and merely suggestive. One other cementing association, though, must, alas, be mentioned. Kipling was obsessed, as were so many men of his generation, with a nasty Jew-commerce equation. He was always speaking of 'Jew hawkers' and suchlike: clearly the Jewish mentality, in his estimation, and especially when he was not giving the matter thought, was identical with the buying and selling (in modern terms the 'marketing') mentality. So, however, was Wolcott Balestier, who really was a buyer and seller. In a sense, therefore, Carrington is right: Kipling's attitude towards Wolcott is: 'Stop this Jew-like buying and selling and talking of partnerships with Heinemann and come away with me to lead the roving life! Leave the tents of Shame where we saw (or wanted to see) each other's nakedness!'

The full set of associations, then, is this: seeing another man's nakedness (wanting to see this) – doing something *shameful* and sexually forbidden – *shem*mozzle, trouble – *Shem* – tribes of Israelites selling and buying: 'leave all that and come to sea, the lash, the drunken sailor (of whom he speaks in the poem) and the open prairie'.

Now let us look at the red-haired girl in more detail. What is her function in the novel? Why does Kipling bring her into it at all? Could it simply be that he wants his revenge – as so often he did – on the woman he thinks is preferred to him by Maisie? That he is going to settle *that* score once and for all? If we know our Kipling, then we certainly can't put that past him. But, if it is the case, he doesn't give her, or, to be more precise, give to her discomforture, much of a dominant role in that respect. She is not ridiculed or diminished or made unattractive. The emphases are elsewhere; but these are by no means withheld or restrained or merely incidental. The girl does a sketch of Dick's head for which he sits, as 'he could not well refuse'; he thinks of those he has used for his own art, especially the drunken Binat (again): 'Binat who had once been an artist and talked about degradation'. Although a mere rough sketch, the drawing – which is spoiled when it is dropped into the stove – 'presented the dumb waiting, the longing, and, above all, the hopeless enslavement of the man, in a spirit of bitter mockery'. The girl tells Maisie that Dick hates her, but the narration differs: 'she was not altogether correct'. Dick does regard her as 'unwholesome', though, for reasons that are not altogether clear. Is it because she sees into the nature of his love for Maisie? Isn't this Carrie standing around, plain-faced, no *jolie laide* even, knowing, if not fully understanding, what is going on?

Torpenhow and the awful 'Nilghai', one of Kipling's most tiresome 'masculine' creations, have no doubt of the nature of his love: it is 'punishment'. Torpenhow would gladly take this 'punishment' for him, but no man can save his own brother, and Dick must learn his own lesson in this 'war'. Kipling ought not to be criticised too harshly for depicting the course of doomed love as a 'war': the course of true love does not always run smoothly, and Dick is after all continually shown to be biting on granite in his pursuit of Maisie. Even if there is some misogyny here, the actual disturbance arises from other feelings.

When Maisie agrees to go out with Dick, in a passage not appearing in Chapter VI of the first published version, there is more business with the red-haired girl, showing that Kipling had her function very much on his mind. After a remark from Dick that ought to be framed and hung on the wall above every writer's desk – 'overwork's only murderous idleness' – Maisie tells her companion that she is going out with Dick on the next day. The girl answers that he deserves it, and that she will scrub the floor of their studio. The next morning

> The red-haired girl drew her into her studio for a moment and kissed her hurriedly. Maisie's eyebrows climbed to the top of her forehead. She was altogether unused to these demonstrations. 'Mind my hat,' she said, hurrying away, and ran down the steps to Dick waiting by the hansom.

This is perceptive, if only incidental. How much, one so often wonders, did Kipling, or at least the intuition of Kipling, really miss? The detail about the hat perfectly captures the temperament of a naturally cold person who is irritated by physical demonstrations of spontaneous (not sexual) affection – just as the girl's gesture perfectly captures her generous desire to transcend her jealousy of her friend, who will never, because she is incapable of it, make anything of Dick's passion for her. Such writing offers a lesson to any class in creative writing of the precept, 'never explain, demonstrate!' But there is not enough of it in *The Light that Failed*. This chapter ends with the girl lying alone in her own room, dreaming of being kissed by Dick. She bursts out in rage at a cleaner who comes in, and feels that she has betrayed a *'shameful'* secret.

Chapter VII is probably the worst part of the expanded version. It acts as a smoke-screen for Dick's real feelings by exhibiting the ruthless heterosexual artist enjoying what is clearly regarded as one of the most disgraceful of possible mixtures: a 'Negroid–Jewess–Cuban' (*'with morals to match'* – my italics). What's more, she belongs to the skipper of the ship in which Dick is travelling, so that in enjoying her he is taking a calculated risk of being killed (such is the implication). Being 'immoral', this woman resembles the Aggie of 'The *Mary Gloster*': she 'understands', and the implication is that she is as 'good' at lust-making as she is morally bad. Kipling really does at times give the impression that he shares the male myth that 'forbidden' and 'immoral' women are the hottest stuff between the sheets, and even that the whole thing goes down best with liberal shots of alcohol – and the creation of great art to boot! But whereas Sir Anthony Gloster, baronite, is a mere shipowner, Dick is an artist (the details of his artistic success don't, incidentally, make sense: they are based on ideas learned from Pre-Raphaelites, and aren't up to the mark in the sort of painting that was being successful just then – Balestier should have sent his young victim to Whistler, who knew), and is furthermore shown as achieving true artistic success (only stevedores see the masterpiece).

> 'Why don't you try something of the same kind now?' said the Nilghai.
> 'Because those things come not by fasting and prayer. When I find a cargo-boat and a Jewess-Cuban and another notion and the same old life, I may.'

This is repulsive and contrived. Yet one feels a certain sympathy with Kipling because what he is really wanting to do is express his feelings about going off with Wolcott and producing (perhaps) a real but private art: of achieving self-realisation through a love forbidden by society, in wide open spaces free of society. But he cannot (and one cannot blame him) here represent that love as forbidden enough. Great art does, it is true, go with the subversive – as that not very subversive man Thomas Hardy said – but it does not go with the commonplace mythology of the subversive: with the stockbroker's dirty weekend at Brighton with a bit of hot stuff. Later Torpenhow answers Dick's assertion that a woman *can* be 'a piece of one's life':

> 'No, she can't.' His face darkened for a moment. 'She says she wants to sympathise with you and help you in your work, and everything else that clearly a man must do for himself. Then she sends round five notes a day to ask why the dickens you haven't been wasting your time with her.'

In Chapter IX the red-haired girl once more takes up her cryptic role. Maisie has an idea for a picture. She has picked this up from the girl, who has been reading James ('B.V.') Thomson's truly impressive *The City of Dreadful Night* to her. Now this was one of Kipling's own favourite poems, to the extent that he borrowed its title for his book of sketches first published in India in 1890. The girl reads out some of the passage about what Thomson spells as the 'MELENCOLIA', which Kipling corrects to 'Melancolia'. This is the 'bronze colossus of a wingéd Woman', who gives (in a stanza unquoted by the girl)

The sense that every struggle brings defeat
  Because Fate holds no prize to crown success;
That all the oracles are dumb or cheat
  Because they have no secret to express;
That none can pierce the vast black veil uncertain
Because there is no light beyond the curtain;
  That all is vanity and nothingness.

The last stanza of this undoubtedly powerful although excessively depressed poem (published in 1880, written during 1870–4; Thomson died, a hopeless drunk, in 1882) is also centred on this statue; the last three lines have always reverberated in the minds of readers of the poem:

The moving moon and stars from east to west
  Circle before her in the sea of air;
Shadows and gleams glide round her solemn rest.
  Her subjects often gaze up to her there:
The strong to drink new strength of iron endurance,
The weak new terrors; all, renewed assurance
  And confirmation of the old despair.

It is astonishing to recall that Thomson was also the author of the lines,

Give a man a pipe he can smoke,
  Give a man a book he can read;
And his home is bright with a calm delight,
  Though the room be poor indeed.

But that was written when his mentor Bradlaugh (a philanthropist favoured by Kipling) was exhorting him to lay off the bottle and write to please the public.

The red-haired girl understands, but Maisie doesn't, and Dick tells her,

'You haven't the power. You have only the ideas – the ideas and the little cheap impulses. How you could have kept at your work for ten years steadily is a mystery to me . . .'

Balestier had then been trying to write fiction for ten years. When Maisie tells the girl that Dick is selfish to have gone off (she appears not to register his forthright condemnation of her work as consisting of 'cheap impulses'), the girl 'opened her lips as if to speak, shut them again, and went on reading *The City of Dreadful Night*'. Dick decides to do another masterpiece: a Melancolia of his own which will 'humble her vanity'. He is very troubled and mentions to the dog, Binkie (not on the whole one of Kipling's most successful dogs), 'something' about 'hermaphroditic futilities'. Kipling can't have thought very deeply about what he was saying here. The word itself, which he got either from his beloved Ben Jonson's *A Staple of News* (there used in a sexual sense) or from Swinburne's *Miscellanies* of 1881 (there used in a non-sexual sense), must have welled up from his unconscious. What he thought he meant, alas, was that women aren't fitted to be artists.

When the time comes for poor Maisie to go to France again, in order to pick up the necessary knowledge to create her masterpiece, the red-haired girl does not look 'lovely'; the implication is that she doesn't want to leave Dick behind. Maisie allows Dick to give her a kiss, from which she tears herself away angrily, and then the girl comes up to her with eyes 'alight with cold flame':

> 'He kissed you!' she said. 'How could you let him, when he wasn't anything to you? Oh, Maisie, let's go to the ladies' cabin. I'm sick, – deadly sick.'

This must reflect Kipling's reaction to Caroline's silent yearning after him, and, doubtless, his own lack of interest in her at that time. The actual engagement, or 'understanding', between him and Caroline came about May 1891, but the affair, says Carrington from 'private information', never went 'smoothly'. Its secrets, he says, went with the two of them to the grave. His reticence over this, and his plain and scrupulous insistence that it was an odd and not exactly a happy marriage, puts a proper emphasis on all this. It was a dark marriage.

The difficulties Kipling was passing through at this time in his life are highlighted by a particularly gruesome (and highly effective) metaphor in the chapter (X) dealing with Dick's receipt of the news of his blindness. Whereas Chapter VIII is generally weak, this is, for the most part, powerful and written at a high pitch of excitement and despair. Dick is wondering 'what the darkness of the night would be like', when he remembers a 'quaint' scene in the Sudan:

> A soldier had been nearly hacked in two by a broad-bladed Arab spear. For one instant the man felt no pain. Looking down, he saw that his life-blood was going from him. The stupid bewilderment on his face was so comic that both Dick and Torpenhow, still panting and unstrung from a fight for life, had roared with laughter, in which the man seemed as if he would join, but, as his lips parted in a sheepish grin, the agony of death came upon him, and he pitched grunting at their feet. Dick laughed again, remembering the horror. It seemed so exactly like his own case.

This is wrenched, extreme, and, strictly, impossible; it could not have been written by a man who had seen even the very least action. But it has power as a true metaphor of how Kipling felt. Dick then asks the dog where Moses was when the light went out (referring presumably to *Exodus*, 1: 21–9), and immediately makes a reference to Marvell's 'To His Coy Mistress'. Drunk, he sets about the making of his masterpiece, which is to be a 'Melancolia' mixing the characteristics of Maisie and the angry Bessie – he requires a specifically angered Bessie around him as he drunkenly paints. Bessie is angry, in any case, because Dick has 'rescued'

Torpenhow from her embraces, and has actually told her, after she has 'shrieked with rage', that in so doing he has saved her from 'making love to some drunken beast in the street'. When Torpenhow returns Dick

> began to whimper faintly, for joy, at seeing Torpenhow again, for grief at misdeeds – if indeed they were misdeeds – that made Torpenhow remote and unsympathetic, and for childish vanity hurt, since Torpenhow had not given a word of praise to his wonder picture

and they walk up and down with arms around each other's shoulders: Bessie, seeing it all through the keyhole, 'said something so improper that it shocked even Binkie, who was dribbling patiently . . .' One can imagine what it was she said – but did Kipling?

Kipling's youthful notion that drunkenness goes with the great art conjured out of romantic despair was a decadent element in his first novel. It seems to have been a despairing equation of wanderlust-with-Wolcott and forbidden love and art-achieved-somehow. Certainly he came near to giving himself away when he had Dick, out on a walk and seeing the Guards on parade, tell Torpenhow, 'Oh my men! – My beautiful men!' This could be explained as the exclamation of a blind artist as he senses the presence of his best subjects; but that will hardly wash in view of what we already know. It has been much remarked upon.

The words to the tune to which the men are marching are supplied by Dick:

> He must be a man of decent height,
>   He must be a man of weight,
> He must come home on a Saturday night
>   In a thoroughly sober state;
> He must know how to love me,
>   And he must know how to kiss;
> And if he's enough to keep us both
>   I can't refuse him bliss.

The red-haired girl returns to haunt the scene, but not before more of the intimate masculine business that has so signally failed to impress readers of this novel. Torpenhow says that he cannot go to the new war. The Nilghai, 'fat, burly and aggressive',

> says something uncomplimentary about soft-headed fools who throw away their careers for other fools. Torpenhow flushed angrily. The constant strain of attendance on Dick had worn his nerves thin.

There then follows a coy reference, a kind of awkward red herring, to Dick's having cut the Nilghai out in an 'affair' at Cairo. Men will be men. Then Dick's state of mind is discussed, and it is decided to appeal – but unknown to Dick – to Maisie to come to him out of pity. Torpenhow is sent off to France to make this appeal, and he arrives – being endowed with USC enterprise – on a horse borrowed from a French Army cavalry squadron, all of whose officers he has 'drunk under the table'. Maisie has just disgustedly watched a couple kissing. As her selfish and petty thoughts are recorded – there is not much misogyny here, really: Maisie is just a cold person who happens to be a girl, but might just as well be a man – the red-haired girl, tossing and turning in bed, provides a silent contrast. When Torpenhow brings the news of Dick's blindness the girl is silent no longer, telling Maisie that if it were her she would go to him and kiss his eyes until they got better.

The confrontation between Dick and Maisie in London is one of those that makes the book appealing; only its strained and wrenched context renders it incredible. The revelation to Dick, and to herself, of her essential shallowness, and her consequent self-hatred, rings true. The 'Melancolia' (into which in fact the painter has incorporated a 'flagrant' 'trick' to which he felt 'entitled' – see how Kipling keeps on at this *motif*) is, in its destroyed state, perhaps a representation of what Kipling really thought about the creation of valid work in the company of Balestier. The detail of Dick's having incorporated trickery into it is an exceedingly subtle one. Real writers feel their salvation depends on understanding these things – and few real writers, especially those embarrassed by their fame, do not lapse. Kipling understood it perfectly. But he loved to leave in a few knowing tricks.

The famous sentence 'And that was the end of Maisie' is preceded by detail of her thoughts about the red-haired girl, clearly essential in Kipling's by now utterly confused scheme. She had 'never feared her companion before'. And the degree of 'her scorn of herself' has never been so great. But still the red-haired girl has a part to play. Dick, realising that only a 'lingering sense of humour' has allowed him to survive, receives a letter from her:

> I could have given you love, I could have given you loyalty, such as you never dreamed of. Do you suppose I cared what you were? But you chose to whistle down the wind for nothing. My only excuse for you is that you are so young.

In September 1891, when he was in Cape Town, Kipling made friends with the novelist Olive Schreiner, author of *The Story of an African Farm*. She asked him, Carrington tells us, 'about the background to *The Light that Failed*'. He wrote to her:

> If all the girls of the world sat quiet and still, at the right moment, by all the men of the world, when those were in trouble, we should all be perfectly happy instead of being hurt and worried. I'll show you about this time next year why Maisie was made as she was.

This is cryptic. 'The reader may interpret this letter as he will,' writes Carrington. It may refer to a book or poem that Kipling plans, or it may refer to some more personal plan such as marriage. It may be about nothing, or a device to put the shrewd Olive Schreiner off the scent. But certainly it puts one in mind of the red-haired girl and her strange function in the novel.

Confusions

It has been suggested that a strong influence on Kipling over the matter of the first version of the *The Light that Failed* was Alice Kipling. This seems likely. But it does not preclude Wolcott's influence, too. When Kipling published the 'sad' version, he added at the beginning the 'Dedication':

> If I were hanged on the highest hill,
> *Mother o' mine, O mother o' mine!*
> I know whose love would follow me still,
> *Mother o' mine, O mother o' mine!*

and so on. This was supposedly to appease her. Probably that is the case: he didn't like defying her, or making her unhappy, but he had to make his own way. It served, too, to express his feelings of dependence upon her in those difficult years.

But Wolcott published the first edition, and so must have been 'on Alice's side' in the matter. It is likely that he infuriated Kipling by more or less forcing him (taking advantage of the parental view) to the publication. Possibly, an opportunist realising that he had Kipling's adoration, he got hold of a copy and just sent it to press – then informed the author. What would Kipling, feeling as he did about interference, let alone the watering down of 'offensive' material, have been able to do in face of the *fait accompli*? We may picture him feeling the same rage against Wolcott as he felt against Harper's and the other pirates; but unable to express it, both because he loved him and because his mother 'liked' that version. This would explain the venom of the noisy and ineffective poem against the pirates, overtly directed at Hardy, Besant and Black and their letter defending Harper's. It all occurred at about this time.

All this would have put Kipling, who was already overworked, into a worse and even more confused frame of mind. Clearly there was some quarrel, because he must have made up his mind to issue his own version with Macmillan within a week or two of the publication of the first. He would have put in the dedication as a second thought. Whenever he was most angry with his mother, he instantly protected her – just as with this sickly quatrain. What could she say when she read that, however much she deplored the gloom or nastiness of the novel? Her views of the book, doubtless bound up with her fears – some of them intuitive – for her son, will have had much weight with him, whether he resented them or not. Perhaps she saw something in the longer version that worried her. One can sympathise with her as a mother, as with Kipling and his need to print the version of his book he wanted to print. There was even some trouble with Kipling's agent, Watt, about the extent of Wolcott's influence on him.

Watt, not Wolcott, handled the Macmillan negotiations. But the details of this row have been suppressed.

Kipling was prolific and worked fast. Yet at Wolcott's death, at the end of 1891, *The Naulahka* was unfinished, and he had to put the final touches to it while on his honeymoon trip. Possibly he rewrote Wolcott's bits. Work on it went slowly: from July 1890 at the latest, until August 1891, when Kipling went off to Cape Town after staying at Freshwater in the Isle of Wight with Wolcott and Carrie in the house they rented there. Kipling never saw Wolcott again after that. He not only had the stories and the novel and poems on his hands, but he was also considering the publication of a form of the novel he had partly written in India, *Mother Maturin*, or *Hundred Mornings*. This was never finished, but various references to it tell us that he did not abandon the idea of it until *Kim* took its place.

He would have told the importuning Wolcott that he was busy struggling with this work, and that there was no question of collaboration on it, in view of the subject matter. A compromise was reached when they agreed to an adventure novel, in which Wolcott would be responsible for the American bits and Kipling for the Indian. Undoubtedly Kipling did throw caution to the winds, and allow his enthusiasm for Wolcott himself to become enthusiasm for his fiction-writing. He did enjoy working with him. But he was indulging himself in a falsehood, and it made him unhappy. He must already have known that anything good in *The Naulahka* (the description of the Rajput King's court, in fact, is the sole outstanding part) would be by him. The fate of *The Light that Failed* must have brought this home painfully. It is a novel all about flawed art and destroyed masterpieces. And the collaboration is itself a replica of the early version of *The Light that Failed* in that it is a tale of a man who loves a woman who feels that, since women must give the whole of themselves in marriage, she ought not to marry, since she can't give the whole of herself. Kate's 'submission' at the end is manipulated; there is no attempt to resolve this problem, psychologically or otherwise. On 18 February 1891 Wolcott wrote to Howells to tell him that he and Kipling had done 'rather more than two-thirds' of it – yet at the end of the year the last serial instalment was not ready. There may have been a row when the new version of *The Light that Failed* came out in March. Whether there was or not, little work was done on the new book over the next months. After Kipling left England in August Wolcott was doing work on it by himself, and reported progress on it by cable. Had Kipling given up interest in it, and did he leave mainly to escape not only from Wolcott but also from the pursuing Carrie, whom he seems to have promised to marry? Did he regret all the Balestiers and go off alone on the, in his own mind, long trail?

There were other tensions. The Kipling parents' reaction to Carrie was not favourable from the very start. Alice noted: 'That woman means to marry our Ruddy', and did not like it. Lockwood said that she was 'a good man spoiled', which cannot be interpreted as other than a hostile remark, especially coming from a notably unmalicious man. It is true, too, that in the early photographs we have of her, she manages to look mannish. Apparently Alice never came to like Carrie, and even frequently denied herself the undoubted pleasure of her son's company in order to avoid his wife's. It was Lockwood who usually visited the Kiplings, and who stayed with them. Alice did not believe her son happily or satisfactorily married.

This in turn of course put Carrie's back up. Perhaps she felt Lockwood's acceptance, too, to be no more than diplomatic. After all, if he thought her a good man spoiled, then she would have registered this. When Kipling wrote to his Aunt Louie on the day before his wedding, he told her that he and Carrie had been 'through some deep waters together'. He said that the affair had been going on for 'rather more months than I care to think about in that they were sheer waste of God's good life'. No doubt, so far as Aunt Louie was concerned, Wolcott and his sister were the same outfit.

In May 1891 Gosse wrote a friendly review in the *Century*, in which he said:

> The private life of Mr Rudyard Kipling is not a matter of public interest, and I should be very unwilling to exploit it, even if I had the means of doing so.

Clearly the private life of Kipling was a matter arousing great curiosity, as Gosse makes clear by denying it; it is worth recalling that the pressure upon him in this respect was near to intolerable. He was perhaps the first famous man (outside politics) to gain the full attentions of the modern press. Even the most voracious reader of newspapers will admit pity for the victims of the reporters. Kipling's hatred for them is understandable. He was one of the earliest victims of the popular press; he failed to handle it well, although he got better at it. American reporters were soon able to revenge themselves on him for his early indiscretions.

Gosse's criticism in his *Century* article is perceptive. He draws attention to the figure of Strickland in the early short stories (Strickland reappears as a minor character in *Kim*), saying that Kipling sets his 'regime' over that of the prig (such as McGoggin and Golightly). Kipling introduces Strickland, Gosse continues, 'always with extreme approval'. Strickland can't simply be dismissed as a 'racist' figure, as he is by McClure. He is melodramatically conceived, but also genuinely mysterious. He is someone who needs to be investigated not for what his creator does say about him, but for what he does not say. Like Conan Doyle's Sherlock Holmes, he is essentially a decadent figure, but is presented as something other than that. Conan Doyle made Holmes into a detective, on the side of the 'good', but also implied or stated that he was into drugs, 'fiendish' violin playing, and other unstated decadent matters. Holmes and Moriarty are very obviously two sides of one coin; but Conan Doyle did not wish to press this.

Strickland, significantly a policeman, is conceived along very similar lines and at exactly the same time (1888); the excessive respectability of the time generated such ambiguous fictional figures. Strickland transcends his doubtless – as McClure claims – dogmatic origins. What we feel about Strickland is that we'd like his 'secret life'. And that is just what we are not going to get from the author, who could not give it. Our own imaginations therefore provide us with it. The problem with such righteous approaches as McClure's is that they start but then stay at overt authorial intentions. Conan Doyle had no idea whatsoever that his Holmes adventures (he was always trying to rid himself of them) were highly advanced literary criticism as well as exquisite mini-classics, holding within them not some, but all of the ambitious critical ideas to be put forward during the

twentieth century. Kipling did not know either, that with Strickland and
other creations, he too was an advanced literary critic. He remained a
naive writer. But he had some odd speculations: far more so than his
friend Conan Doyle. You can never be sure what he did or did not know.
We find from 'The Man Who Would Be King' that he knew that an empire
might fail if one of its founders has a defect of character. He had been
through 'deep waters', and (he might have added), through the fire. He
had been through these agonies with Caroline, much more naive as a
reader and literary critic than her husband was naive as an author. 'I do
think some of it will live.' She meant what she said, and, naturally envious
of her husband (who would not be?), she said it reluctantly. Every wife is
a critic of her writer-husband if she reads at all! She was always at Rud's
side when he was deconstructing, the authoritarian himself destroying
'authoritarian unity' (a sin of the old stuff).

Gosse ended his long piece on Kipling by quoting from 'Mandalay',
from the line beginning 'Ship me somewhere east of Suez'. He then added:

> Ah, yes Mr Kipling, go back to the far East! Yours is not the talent to bear
> with the dry-rot of London or of New York. Disappear, another Waring,
> and come back in ten years' time with a fresh and still more admirable
> budget out of Wonderland!

In other words, go off and become another, British, better, Pierre Loti
(a lush French novelist with whom Kipling was oft compared). Gosse's
judgement was influenced by his feeling that *The Light that Failed* showed
the 'limits' of Kipling's genius. But this, while perceptive, wasn't a bit
offensive – it might even have been advice given in collusion with the
Kipling parents, who were not only worried about their son's health but
didn't want to see Rudyard in the keeping of Carrie; it was also very likely
prompted by Kipling's own talk of wanting to shake the dust of England
from his feet. He soon did so, for a time. Previously, in September 1890,
he had gone off to Italy, to stay with Lord Dufferin; but he had not been
much restored, although he enjoyed himself while he was away. In fact
he came back to what was soon to develop into a row about pirating, and
the row (as I think) about the issuing of the short version of *The Light that
Failed*. Carrie was in pursuit of him, Wolcott was putting certain sorts of
pressure on him, and he must have felt that his parents were too.

In May 1891 Kipling did go off; at least, he tried to. Trix's version of
this, given to Hilton Brown, is that Rudyard was running away from Carrie
and his engagement to her ('Shot like a rabbit in a ride, indeed!' comments
Brown). She said that he broke off the engagement on the grounds that his
health was undermined by overwork, but undertook to take a sea-voyage
and American holiday in order to discover if it could ever be restored.
His uncle Henry (Harry) Macdonald, who lived in New York, he had
met and (he said) liked when he was last in America. Harry was a failure:
after he abandoned the Indian Civil Service because his fiancée would
not go to India (she then jilted him) he took the long trail, but did not
make much of a success of it. Kipling now set off with his other uncle,
the Methodist minister Fred Macdonald, to see him again. He travelled
supposedly incognito, under the name of Macdonald, but either gave
himself away or was found out, owing to his 'brilliant conversation' on

board ship. The reporters were waiting for him in New York, as the man who 'had insulted America'. One newspaper reported him as 'speechless with a diseased throat'. But he soon returned to England, leaving Fred behind in New York: Harry had died while they were on their way.

It seems likely that when Kipling was angry with Wolcott for publishing the false version of his novel (however exactly that came about), Carrie, desperate to become his wife, probably took his and not her brother's side: she sympathised with him. If Alice was right, and she had decided to marry Kipling, then here she would have had a heaven-sent opportunity. Alice must have been all for the 'happy version', and Wolcott, who published it, likewise. No one, then, of his own close circle, supported him. Lockwood was probably as non-committal as he dared. If Carrie stood by him then, she could capitalise on it afterwards. If she capitalised on it too much, then she might have entrapped him – or, what is the same thing, he might have felt entrapped. So he fled. Then he got back, and presumably – turned away by Henry's death – he still pleaded exhaustion. Soon (21 August) he was off again. But what happened on that July holiday at Freshwater, when the three of them, Kipling, Carrie and Wolcott (ill), were all together for the last time?

It is not a discredit to Carrie if she felt desperate. She felt herself to be plain to ugly, and the object of derisive comment – most of which has doubtless, and decently, been suppressed. This is to say no more than that photographs of her when young show a woman in whom good nature, sweetness and light have not prevailed. She looks sullen and imperious, a woman determined to compensate for her lack of the (popularly conceived) feminine virtues by fulfilling the role of a masterful man. But that does not mean that she lacked the feminine virtues, only that she lacked what she thought they were – that is, what people said they were, and that may have been why she didn't much like people.

What was it that Mrs Clifford said in that theatre? The polite equivalent of, 'What a bossy looking bitch! God help the man who's unwise enough to get hitched to her!'? We know what Lockwood said, and that amounts to much more than a 'mere remark' on 'her universal competence', as Carrington would like the ardent Kiplingite to understand it. *A good man spoiled!* It is worth contemplating.

In order to be just about the life within an apparently unpleasant person – and Carrie was regarded as that – you have to tell the truth about how others perceived her. For I have only spoken about Carrie in the perception of others. Those who cannot stomach the fact of Kipling's love for Wolcott – and that is everyone except Angus Wilson, who knows it perfectly well and does not seek to deny it – the marriage is explained on the grounds that 'Wolcott fostered the match, that Wolcott on his death-bed commended the care of his family to his friend Rudyard, that Wolcott's wishes were accepted by Rudyard as obligations'.

Carrington, who says this, adds: 'this does not imply that Wolcott's sister was hurried into a match'; and he comments that the marriage was more satisfactory to Kipling that it was to the person described by Henry James as 'poor concentrated Carrie'! What he must mean is that Carrie was so pathologically depressed and overbearing that no marriage could have been any more satisfactory to her than life itself. When Beatty Balestier in Brattleboro first heard the news he thought that it involved

Josephine – so did several people in London. Clearly they could hardly believe it; just as, eighteen months or so earlier, they could hardly believe that Wolcott Balestier had seduced Kipling into an agreement to collaborate on a novel with him. Other biographers say the same as Carrington. Birkenhead writes: 'They had been through so much together, were united by a common love of the dead man, and drawn yet closer by the pangs of bereavement.' Mason writes that the marriage was a 'death-bed bequest from Wolcott to both partners':

> Wolcott stirred and excited him; he fell under his spell. Then he met his sister and she was included in the glow of romantic affection he felt for this young man who so warmly admired his work and entered so eagerly into his plans. Then he fled – but from what exactly we do not know. When he came back Wolcott was dead, and, whatever the circumstances of his flight, it is surely safe to suppose that Kipling reproached himself for things left undone and unsaid, for time lost that might have been spent with his friend. If there had been some difference between them, then the feeling of reproach would have been stronger. It would surely be enough to push him over the brink on which he had hesitated; it had been Wolcott who had brought Rudyard and Carrie together, and shared love for Wolcott had drawn them closer. To marry Wolcott's sister would give some degree of immortality to the relationship that had meant so much to him.

This is a good example of the sort of difficulties into which sensible writers are drawn when they want to ignore the obvious. Something more is needed to explain this marriage. It could not have been love at first sight. Had it been that, then Kipling would have been relieved from the time he saw Carrie, and would hardly have run away at least twice – or written a poem ('The Long Trail') to Wolcott begging *him* to come away with him.

Wolcott went to Dresden in late November 1891, on business to do with his and Heinemann's plans for cheap imprints, to rival Tauschnitz. When he left London he is said to have been already infected with typhoid. A stronger man might have survived the onslaught, but, apparently, he never looked as though he was going to. He first fell ill at his hotel, but was soon sent to a hospital. By a coincidence William Heinemann's wife was visiting Dresden for pleasure. Hearing of the trouble, she at once sent for Mrs Balestier and both daughters. They came from Paris (Henry James said). Mrs Balestier and Josephine were distraught and unable to cope. But Carrie could and did. She at once sent for Henry James, and he instantly left for Dresden. Carrie may have cabled to Kipling before Wolcott died (on 5 December): a cable he could not have received until he arrived at Colombo on 10 December. Anyhow, she certainly wired him, with a summons to come at once, when Wolcott died. He received this at Lahore, where he was visiting his parents. According to Carrington, he skipped Christmas Day with his mother and father and was back in London in fourteen days. Birkenhead, using Carrie's diaries (now destroyed) as his source, says that Kipling did spend Christmas Day with his parents.

Henry James, in a letter of 10 December 1891, described the funeral service, conducted by an English chaplain. 'The three ladies came insistently to the grave ... By far the most interesting is poor little concentrated Carrie . . .' He drove back with her, alone, from the cemetery: 'She wanted to talk to me.' What did she tell him? He never told anyone. He spoke of her 'emotion' as 'almost manly', as Lockwood might have done, had he been present. She seemed to James 'remarkable' in her 'force, acuteness, capacity and courage . . . a worthy sister of poor dear big-spirited, only-by-death-quenched Wolcott'. A couple of days later he described her as 'a little person of extraordinary capacity'. The day after that he wrote to his brother William and spoke of Wolcott himself, saying that, although Wolcott's 'writing . . . was his real ambition', this writing would 'give those who didn't know him but little idea of what those who *did* know him (and I think I did so better than anyone) found in him'. James could not have expressed his lack of faith in Wolcott's literary merit more clearly – and this in spite of what must have been a markedly sentimental interest. In the letters he wrote from Dresden James emphasised that his own debts to Wolcott were to the tradesman, and not to the literary man; but he was emphatic, without being too specific, about his personal qualities. One wonders, though, just how appealing Wolcott Balestier was to men who didn't have a special interest in young men. How much did James agree with Gosse about Wolcott's 'pushiness'? It would be fascinating to know what he would have said (indeed, did say to someone, no doubt) informally, about Wolcott.

There is one queer detail, at least in Carrington's account, of the events leading up to the marriage. Kipling returned on 10 January. But Carrington tells us that, in Brattleboro, 'it was not known . . . until *28 December* that the man who had been collaborating with Wolcott was to marry Wolcott's sister' (my italics), though for several days Beatty 'did not know which sister'. This suggests one of two things. Either that Kipling and Carrie had already agreed to marry on his return; or that she jumped the gun and told everyone that this was the agreement, when in fact it wasn't, or wasn't quite. We can rule out entirely any idea that Kipling sent a wire to Brattleboro reading 'AM GOING TO MARRY CARRIE NOT JOSEPHINE'. It must surely have been the first of the two alternatives, since even Carrie could not have felt that she had quite so strong an ascendency over this hardly acquiescent man. It may be that he sent her a wire telling her that he would marry her; but one would imagine that he would have left the matter for discussion. Telegrams are not a good medium through which to conduct marriage negotiations.

If Kipling had agreed to marry on his return, or had agreed that he would do so on the condition that he felt restored – 'was fit for you' was how he would have put it to Carrie – and his 'nerves' in better order, then he certainly hung about, and thought of hanging around for even longer. He spent three weeks in Cape Town in September, may have met Rhodes for the first time, and made friends with the naval men at Simonstown (Carrington says that 'sailors were new types of men whom he now began to study with his penetrating eye'). Then he went to New Zealand. At that point he fully intended to go for three months to Samoa to see Stevenson. Carrington seems to give three reasons why he did not:

When he arrived in New Zealand it was his intention to extend his tour for another three months in order to see Stevenson in Samoa, but something in London called him home, and he was unwilling to stay too long in the Antipodes. In Wellington he had been ill and frustrated, and the Shipping Office persuaded him that Samoa, with no regular sailings, could not be fitted into his itinerary. Perhaps with relief, he abandoned the side trip.

Birkenhead, presumably working from the same material, says:

> Kipling had hoped to sail from Auckland to visit Robert Louis Stevenson in Samoa, and the enchanted islands of the south, but the master of the little Samoa-bound fruit boat was too drunk to offer any reasonable hope of safe arrival. He decided instead to revisit India.

Clearly Kipling was confused and in no hurry to get home. Pressure was being exerted upon him by his mother and probably his father *not* to marry Carrie. It hardly matters how they conducted themselves (since Southsea they had become Rudyard experts, so might even have begged him, strategically, to go ahead with the marriage): he knew how they felt. Pressure was being exerted from the other side by Carrie herself. We have no means of knowing what Wolcott ever felt about it, if anything, or what he said about it. But since the strongest of his ambitions was to be a successful writer – Henry James wouldn't have got that point wrong – it is not hard to assume that he would have urged Kipling to marry his sister. His conquest of him would then have been complete. So Wolcott, with whom he must recently have quarrelled – but forgiven – for other reasons, may also have been putting pressure on him. The discussions must have been pursued at great length while he was staying with the Balestiers at Freshwater, and must have been exhausting for him. It was during this visit that he wrote one of the most poetic of his short stories, the magnificent 'A Disturber of Traffic', published in September and then collected in *Many Inventions* as 'The Disturber of Traffic'.

Thus he was in very severe emotional trouble in the years 1890 and 1891. I have made it clear enough where I think the roots of that trouble lay. It may be that Leon Edel is right, and that he was only 'in love' with Wolcott Balestier 'unconsciously'. But that makes him out to have been a bit of a simpleton – not just a non-intellectual. I have made it equally clear why I think such an interpretation, in the case of a man like Kipling, who was so concerned with truth and with the nature of inner feelings, is unsatisfactory. What puzzles me still, though, is how the marriage to Carrie finally came about. What was the nature of the understanding between them? It must have been such that when he landed in England on 10 December they could decide very quickly indeed to be married: they applied for a special licence on that day, for the marriage took place on 18 January at All Souls, Langham Place. Henry James gave the bride away. The best man was Ambrose ('Ambo') Poynter, son of Kipling's Aunt Agnes and Sir Edward Poynter. The four other members of the congregation were Gosse, his wife, their son Philip, and William Heinemann. James wrote:

> I saw the Rudyard Kiplings off . . . she was poor Wolcott Balestier's sister and is a hard devoted capable little person whom I don't in the

least understand his marrying. It's a union of which I don't forecast the
future though I gave her away at the altar in a dreary little wedding . . .

Biographers have been puzzled by the 'mystery' of why Kipling should
have changed the addressee of 'The Long Trail' from 'he' to 'she'! But there
is no mystery. A large element in resistance to my interpretation must be
based on irrational distaste. Some commentators will say, at this point,
that the sexualities of writers don't matter, and ought not to be discussed.
There is a brief answer to that: they matter to the writers, and therefore
they matter to the work they put out. So we are free to blind ourselves
to it, or we are free to enquire into it. The matters that concern writers
get into their work.

My interpretation of these few and scattered facts, then, is that Carrie
was able to seize Kipling for life because of his vulnerability in the matter
of her brother. Three years older than Kipling, she was not a happy young
woman, and she did not impress anyone at all favourably. No one ever
liked her. She would have been written off, in contrast to her younger
and much better-looking and more socially responsive and cheerful sister,
as well nigh unmarriable. No wonder they believed in Vermont for a few
days that it was to Josephine that the famous author was to be married.

But the ugly, charmless and awkward victims of such talk sometimes
have wills of iron. Carrie had wanted Kipling from the time she first
saw him. Her disposition was a jealous and proprietory one. It is hard
to say to what kind of woman, and indeed to what kind of physique in
women (if any), Kipling was susceptible. But it is not likely that, out of
kilter with his fellow men, his attentions were much directed towards
poor Caroline Starr Balestier, whose reserves of charm and sex-appeal,
if she had them, have been wholly concealed by history. What I am
saying is cruel; but Carrie, not even endowed with much intelligence,
wit or emotional resource, did not feel it as cruel. She registered it with
shrewdness, though, and she determined to hitch herself to a new star
of the firmament whose courses through space she could and would
supervise. She was one of those who pay back life, in the form of the
people they encounter on their journey through it, for what life, in the
form of fate, inflicted on her. But she did have feelings, and although
these feelings were not generous towards others, and are not open to
much misinterpretation, they should not, as feelings in themselves,
and unexpressed, be misunderstood. There was great uneasiness in her
daughter Elsie's mind about how her mother would be portrayed by the
prospective biographer of her father. Birkenhead clearly messed that up,
as well as making a point of certain aspects of Kipling's character that
she didn't want mentioned; Carrington understood this, and dealt with
it tactfully – so in a fit of scrupulous generosity she added what she did
to his biography, and it is pretty damning:

My mother introduced into everything she did, and even permeated the
life of the family with, a sense of strain and worry amounting sometimes
to hysteria. Her possessive and rather jealous nature, both with regard
to my father and to us children, made our lives very difficult, while her
uncertain moods kept us apprehensively on the alert for possible storms.
There is no doubt that her difficult temperament sometimes reacted ad-
versely on my father and exhausted him, but his kindly nature, patience,

and utter loyalty to her prevented his ever questioning this bondage, and
they were seldom apart. She had great qualities: a keen, quick mind and
ready wit, a business ability above the average and loyalty and kindness
to old friends; but above all, an immense and never-failing courage in
pain and sorrow, both of which she bore unflinchingly. My father's much
exaggerated reputation as recluse sprang, to a certain extent, from her
domination of his life and the way in which she tried to shelter him from
the world. To a certain degree this was a good thing and enabled him to
work without too much interruption, but he needed also the stimulus of
good talk and mixing with people, and as the years went on and his life
became more restricted, he missed these keenly.

This is admirably honest, and goes further than most loyal daughters
would like to go. Elsie had put up with Carrie's interference in her married
life that was intolerable, and, finally, pitiful. One would wish to add only
a little to it, and that but a mere corollary. For 'rather jealous' one must,
in the light of other evidence (including that of Kipling's rare but known
complaints at his domestic circumstance, recorded by Birkenhead but
not by Carrington), substitute 'pathologically jealous'. Of course, although
what is said of Kipling's 'utter loyalty' is true, it is not and could not be
true that he 'never questioned' his 'bondage' (a harsh word). He remained
true and loyal to the extent of his capacity; but his work speaks often
and eloquently of his bondage, of the double life – domestic existence
and the world of the imagination into which, as Carrington himself is
certain, Carrie could not follow him. But he went through that work so
carefully that there is little *ostensible* trace in it of what he thought he
had to say (different, as in all writers, from what he really had to say:
when the writer of an imaginative work knows for certain what he has
to say, then the work will be dead, without excitement, and not written
in excitement). Hence his famous 'obscurity'.

From the very beginning there was something to conceal. Carrington
happily describes Rudyard and Carrie as 'lovers', yet also refers to the
'Wolcott–Carrie–Rudyard triangle'. Can he or anyone else seriously think
that Kipling suddenly, naturally, fell in love with Wolcott's sister because
Wolcott so decreed on his death-bed – and decreed, at that, only to
Carrie? She may well have told everyone that Wolcott had 'decreed' it.
But had he?

Suppose that, knowing he was dying, and having nothing more to lose,
he told Carrie, instead, of the nature of Kipling's friendship for him? Of the
nature of their relationship? Of how he, too, felt about Kipling? Perhaps,
a decent man at heart, but too ambitious, he confessed to Carrie that he
had used Kipling's 'unnatural' love for him, that he had put him into a
very bad way, that he had set his life up so that he would never dare to
be married for fear of how he would acquit himself, of how he, a man
of 'unnatural' appetites, could ever care for and protect a wife, in the
way in which proper men should? 'I ruined him, Carrie, but you love
him, tell him that you know, that I told you – and that you'll accept him
even so. Would you do that for me, Carrie? Give him children, make
him feel normal in the eyes of the World, he'll change, he'll put all that
behind him.'

Carrington says that *The Naulahka* had been planned as a romance with
a happy ending:

Again, his personal romance had been clouded by a disaster, the death of Wolcott, 'the brother of his beloved', a tell-tale phrase that is applied irrelevantly to the hero ... Kipling's heart, however, was not in the book, as is shown by the verse chapter-headings which he added after Wolcott's death.

These epigraphs may, superficially, tell the tale of *The Naulahka* as Kipling and Wolcott Balestier planned it. But Kipling's choices – presumably made on board the *Teutonic* as it steamed away with him and his new wife, but perhaps afterwards when the time came for publication in volume form (they aren't in the version printed in the *Century*) – are interesting, and Carrington is right, if exceedingly ill-advised, to direct the attention of the curious towards them. That a definition of the nature of Kipling's intentions towards Carrie at this time would strain the notion of honour, as of love (but not erotic love), goes without saying. Kipling must have known from the outset that Carrie could not follow him into the subtler levels of his art – and he was a subtle writer. Many marriages break down when erotic and romantic love break down. Kipling knew from the beginning that there was no romance. Romantically, Carrie was simply the ghost of Wolcott. He would have intended to change that. But can anyone make that sort of change? Doing his marital duty, was he not sodomising (O shameful thought!) Wolcott? No wonder he was confused, and no wonder he became fanatical about his privacy.

The first interesting chapter-heading to *The Naulahka* is that to Chapter IV, which is about the 'trade' Nicholas Tarvin does with Kate. He says that he will get her the necklace, and actually describes this as a 'trade'. The heading is, as so often with Kipling, very obscurely connected with the subject-matter. It is 'quoted' from 'The Grand-Master's Defence', and it is hard not to see the 'grand-master' here as anything but the secret and detached strategist, the moralist defending his position to his peers. Part of the Shakespearean-Browningesque pastiche reads: 'My love was safe from all the powers of Hell – /For you – e'en you – acquit her of my guilt.'

The marriage to Carrie had indeed been a 'trade', on Kipling's side, but the guilt is his, not hers. It was (the speaker in the dramatic verses continues) for the sake of Sula, 'My city, child of mine, my heart, my home, /Mine and my pride – evil might visit there!', that he committed himself to his 'Heaven', his 'love'. Or that is what it seems to mean. 'It was for Sula and her naked ports/ ... Our city Sula, that I drove my price – /For love of Sula and for love of her.' This can be made to apply to the story, although there is a very severe sense of strain. But Carrington's insight as to its real application is absolutely right. Inasmuch as we believe, with good reason, that Kipling had charge of the conception of *The Naulahka*, that conception would have had relevance in his mind to the 'Carrie situation': he would have discussed this with Wolcott, have heard what a martinet Carrie was, how much she was at a disadvantage in her feelings about Josephine (they were never in the least close), and, certainly, other unpleasant things. The novel describes itself as 'a story of East and West'. Sula, in the verse heading Chapter IV, is very much the East, is even, simply, in its context, Kipling's India – but possibly it is 'the long trail', too: the life away from fame, the 'world', newspaper reporters,

but not really away from private artistic endeavour. Java, though, comes
into the web of personal notions once again: as the setting of that crucial
story written at Freshwater, 'The Disturber of Traffic'. Tarvin promises
not to follow Kate when she goes off to India to become a medical
missionary (he believes that his own mission is to persuade her that the
crown of womanhood is motherhood, a notion she resists, although she
doesn't actually accuse him of wanting to get directly at her on a glorious
pretence), but by travelling in the opposite direction meets her. This was
prophetic.

But had Kipling had an idea, while he was collaborating on the book,
that he wanted to go back to India, eventually – after a long sojourn on
the trail – and did he fantasise that he could cause the ambitious young
publisher to come with him, perhaps to become a successful publisher
there? There was scope for it. His own initial success had been in India.
He then saw himself as an Anglo-Indian by nature; his parents were soon
to return there, so that he would no longer have their support in London.
But when it came to it, he could not take his bride to Lahore, or he
would have gone straight there. They, his mother in particular, did not
like her – and they were probably furious.

The heading to the short Chapter VII of *The Naulahka* is 'from' a 'work'
called 'op. 3', and it tells of the two sorts of pleasure: the pleasure got
from art, and the pleasure got from 'a water-tight, fireproof, angle-iron,
sunk-hinge, time-lock, steel-faced Lie!' The lie immediately referred to
here is Tarvin's, who wants to ingratiate himself with the Estes family at
Rhatore to further his own ends. But in Kipling's mind it referred to his
'love' and to his determination to change it into real, full love. Whatever
gestures of independence Carrie may have felt prevailed upon by her
pride to make, they are unlikely to have been substantial. The situation
during the fake courtship into which Kipling found himself thrust, in the
interests of his relationship with Wolcott, was essentially one in which he
was the pursued, and Carrie was the pursuer. So if Kate's reluctance does
have an objective correlative, then that would be Wolcott's reluctance to
accompany Kipling on the long trail (ending, as I suggest, in India). We
then have the odd situation of Kipling's master-minding the collaboration
into which he had been forced, and expressing in it – without Wolcott's
knowing – the urge to travel with Wolcott, an urge which was really
the sublimation of his love for him. The chapter (IX) in which Nick
'accidentally' catches up with Kate, who is furious, at Rhatore, is headed
(it is 'from' 'In Shadowland'):

> We meet in an evil land,
>   That is near to the gates of Hell –
> I wait for thy command,
> To serve, to speed, or withstand;
>   And thou sayest I do not well.
>
> Oh, love, the flowers so red
>   Be only blossoms of flame,
> The earth is full of the dead,
> The new-killed, restless dead,
> There is danger beneath and o'erhead;
>   And I guard at thy gates in fear
> Of peril and jeopardy,

Of words thou cans't not hear,
   Of signs thou cans't not see –
And thou sayest 't is ill that I came!

Kate in the novel does indeed say that it is ill that Nick came – women frequently do when their minds are divided. In the book she is simply a Maisie who is better advised. But beneath the surface Kipling seems to be saying to Carrie, 'There are evil impulses in our union in marriage; I wait for you to give me guidance, but you, hearing what you heard from your brother, continue to say that I am bad throughout. But Carrie, Wolcott is newly dead, his spirit still disturbs us with love – yes, I'm worried about myself and the future of my impulses, but you don't understand, and continue to be full of foreboding.'

The fact is, as we shall soon see, Carrie was a depressed person, temperamentally inclined to look at everything in a gloomy light: she was depressing her husband even now. I think that she had always felt humiliated at being in love with him – that is a feeling few who are deeply in love miss: hate for the disturber of their inner peace – and that when she heard from Wolcott about her future husband's nature, found that she was able to get her way over him by, so to say, taking him on sufferance. Any hint of the 'abnormal' would have been not less than terrifying to her dull mind. It was to Kipling himself, but he could have his quiet and private conjectures about the true rightness of social attitudes, and even the reasons for them. His reaction when Walpole brought up the homosexual novel of Radclyffe Hall was, as we have seen, surprisingly tolerant for a man who had cast himself as the reactionary amongst reactionaries. So he felt grateful to her for taking on a man who was secretly wicked, 'evil', for (soon) making him into a father – allowing him to be so, when he 'wasn't entitled to it'. Thus her grudging and 'jealous' attitude, 'I do think some of it will live', isn't so much stupid and naïve, or isn't only stupid and naive: it means, 'in spite of his terrible evil nature, a little of what he has written may live – how amazing!'

That was just how she saw it. And she did love him, and she proved her love to herself and him by taking him on. He would have 'proved' himself to her by 'eradicating' his 'evil' streak. She would have been consoled, but, his manager, would not have let him forget the nature of what she had done for him.

She, Carrie, carried the great burden of his 'sin'. So he went along with it throughout his ever more constricted life, increasingly cut off from the company of others, increasingly identified in the public mind – and unpopular amongst liberals for it, to the point when he was famous but written off – with the only sort of political and social position that she could be expected to take, sharing the great evil secret with – oh, loyal Carrie, yes indeed, but *understanding* Carrie, oh no, not really. Kipling most astonished everyone who knew anything about him in two ways: consenting to collaborate with a literary trifler, and marrying a gloomy dragon. He amazed them because he had manifested his independence in as forceful a manner as any writer ever has. His love for Wolcott was his undoing, and thereafter his only outlet for protest was to be in violence – not in physical violence, but in the savagery of his ostensible position – and that was her position, so he dared not modify it!

Kipling's world was an evil land, near to the gates of hell. Carrie would never have allowed him even to question the 'evil' of it. But secretly question it as some fundamental injustice of cruel fate of course *he* did. Her eye was only as watchful as it could be: it was a gaze of woman's intuition (than which there is nothing more formidable in the world), but not one of intelligence. She was jealous of his fame and jealous of his genius (that genius which Henry James so shrewdly described as being 'complete' in him, but divorced from *'fine intelligence'*), and she won't have spared him.

Carrie certainly wasn't a *rotten* or an *unwholesome* human being; but she was equally certainly what we should call not a very nice piece of work. The right epithets are: unsweetened or sugarless, a bit off (but not rank). But she wasn't quite unlovable, and her throughout-life-deepening gloom is poignant. Kipling learned to love her at very great cost to himself, and this must have transformed her a little in his eyes. The way he learned to love her was by discovering the radiance of her motherhood. Indeed, the most poignant of all aspects of her unhappy and mean life was her softness at the fun affectionately offered to her by her son John, and the terrible and meaningless manner of his death. She wouldn't have felt that girls were as important as boys.

The character of Carrie provided much of the raw material upon which Kipling the writer worked. It is not unlikely that when she told him she would marry him (concealing her aching need and humiliating love), she did so on some such grounds as that 'becoming a father' might 'cure' him: she would give him this. I repeat, she was a bossy woman, and she would have made sure from the outset that she was his master as well as the sacrificial mother-to-be. He got no respite for being a genius from *her*. No respect. She ran her world. It is hard to believe this, but it is the case. It was a great concession from her that the work of this evil man might, some of it, last. These were the undoctored incidents that actually occurred. Thus his heading for Chapter X of *The Naulahka*, 'from' 'A Song of Women':

> Ye know the Hundred Danger Time when, gay with paint and flowers,
> Your household gods are bribed to help the bitter, helpless hours;
> Ye know the worn and rotten mat whereon your daughter lies,
> Ye know the *Sootak*-room unclean, the cell wherein she dies;
>
> Dies with the babble in her ear of midwife's muttered charm
> Dies, spite young life that strains to stay, the suckling on her arm –
> Dies in the four-fold heated room, parched by the Birth-Fire's breath –
> Foredoomed, ye say, lest anguish lack, to haunt her home in death.

But why do the verses at the chapter-heads in *The Naulahka* highlight the 'evil' of the East, and of India in particular? Since they are essentially personal and private, related only nominally to the content of the novel (and occasionally not even that), this can be explained only by a conviction in Kipling – at an exclusively private level – that for him India, or living in India, was 'evil'. It is often remarked upon that Kipling, an inveterate traveller, never chose to return there. Why not, unless he had some superstitious dread of it? It was where he had learned of his own nature, that threat to his hopes; it was where Wolcott (but this is my conjecture) had refused to go; it was where there dwelled people he knew only too well were as supremely human as anyone else anywhere else. (Strickland is hated by the 'natives' because he understands them too well.) '. . . I fled from a Fear I could not see,/and the Gods of the east made mouths at me.' This is quoted from 'In Seconee' at the head of Chapter XII. At the head of Chapter XVIII the last stanza of 'King Anthony' reads:

> Now we are come to our Kingdom,
>   But my love's eyelids fall,
> All that I wrought for, all that I fought for,
>   Delight her nothing at all.
>   My crown is withered leaves,
>   Now she sits in the dust and grieves.

The epigraph to the penultimate chapter, XX, is recondite indeed. How does Carrington think these verses apply to the 'Carrie–Wolcott –Rudyard triangle'?

> Our sister sayeth such and such,
>   And we must bow to her behests;
> Our sister toileth overmuch,
>   Our little maid that hath no breasts.
>
> A field untilled, a web unwove,
>   A bud withheld from sun or bee,
> An alien in the courts of Love,
>   And priestess of his shrine is she.
>
> We love her, but we laugh the while;
>   We laugh, but sobs are mixed with laughter;
> Our sister has no time to smile,
>   She knows not what must follow after.
>
> Wind of the South, arise and blow,
>   From beds of spice thy locks shake free;
> Breathe on her heart that she may know,
>   Breathe on her eyes that she may see.
>
> Alas! we vex her with our mirth,
>   And maze her with most tender scorn,
> Who stands beside the gates of Birth,
>   Herself a child – a child unborn!
>
> *Our sister sayeth such and such,*
>   *And we must bow to her behests;*
> *Our sister toileth overmuch,*
>   *Our little maid that hath no breasts.*

This is extraordinary. It can be made to refer to the story, but only enough to justify it as such to Carrie or any other unwary reader; but clearly that is not its meaning to Kipling, who has thought of what he wants to say, and then fitted it to the story.

It is, once again, a variation on an Old Testament obscurity. It is thought that the 'little sister that hath no breasts' in *Song of Solomon*, 8, refers to male suitors. But it is enough that it is highly erotic (Kipling's age was worried about this, because they had to admit that the Book was canonical – of course he knew very well that it was erotic) and that the chapter begins:

O that thou wert as my brother, that sucked the breasts of my mother!
when I should find thee without, I would kiss thee; yea, I should not be
despised . . . We have a little sister and she hath no breasts: what shall
we do for our sister in the day when she shall be spoken for?

Comment here is superfluous.

The epigraph to the last chapter relates to Kipling's 'Law', the chief
leitmotif in his works, but one tantalisingly never fully defined by him. Had
he ever felt able to define it, though, he would have lost his imaginative
powers. As it is, if we think of it as a representation of his 'soul', then,
as he told Kay Robinson in his letter of March 1890, he wisely chose
not to think of it too much: 'for that breeds self-consciousness and loss
of power'. However, he provides parts of a definition of it, and the most
important of all these is that the Law is opposed to the evil Powers of
Darkness, Disorder and Chaos. He never really got clear, even though
he did much question himself on the subject, of the concept that his
own sexual nature was a part, not of the Law, but of what it opposed.
But that stands well enough, in his most imaginative work, as a metaphor
for all 'evil' sexuality, or rather for the element of lust in it, insofar as this
is isolated from feeling. Kipling's homosexuality, or rather, the streak of
homosexuality in him, was not neurotically contrived, but pure: it existed
in him, naturally, from the start – this is why the social threat to it is so
poignant in his case.

The Law is not a satisfactory concept in Kipling. This is not because of
its ambiguity – such a concept is bound to be ambiguous – but because
of the nature of the ambiguity he gives to it. Too often he means whatever
he wants to mean by it when he is angry or unbalanced, when his
imagination is stifled by this or that rage or fear. This chapter-heading is
one of earliest references to it in his work.

The Law whereby my lady moves
    Was never Law to me,
But 'tis enough that she approves
    Whatever Law it be.

For in that Law, and by that Law,
    My constant course I'll steer;
Not that I need or deem it dread,
    But that she holds it dear.

Tho' Asia sent for my content
    Her richest argosies,
Those would I spurn, and bid return,
    If that should give her ease.

With equal heart I'd watch depart
    Each spicéd sail from sight,
Sans bitterness, desiring less
    Great gear than her delight.

Yet such am I, yea such am I –
    Sore bond and freest free –
The Law that sways my lady's ways
    Is mystery to me

This is as near as Kipling could come to a love poem to his wife. It
is not an erotic poem, because it is an honest one. He is stating here,

plainly, that his way of loving is not yet his wife's, but that he will follow her 'Law'. It is not a good poem because it is furtive (it had to be), and, chiefly, because it has no density of poetic language. But it is moving and poignant in the context of his life, and, once more, it modifies our antipathy to Kipling's inhumane statements and to his cruelty. Nothing better or more straightforwardly explains Kipling's devotion and loyalty to Carrie: these were 'deep waters' indeed.

God's Darkness

By the early Nineties, Kipling was fast gaining mastery over the short-story form. It took, however, more than forty years from the time of his death, in 1936, for him to achieve recognition as one of the masters of it in the English language. It was until quite recently unfashionable to give him more than a sentence or two in so-called 'surveys' of the short story. Critics, creatures of fashion, felt that they ought to be ashamed to own up to a liking to him. (The same now applies to the works of George Moore, who waits in the wings to be 'rediscovered'.) Yet Kipling's imperialism never much hindered his popularity, except with the intelligentsia. Alas, now that he is fashionable again (but sells less and less), the criticism is not always much better than it ever was.

'The Man Who Was' (April 1890) is less a story than a substantial sketch. An officer of the regiment long listed as 'missing' turns up in terror and rags on a night when the mess is entertaining an arrogant Cossack officer. He is at first mistaken for an Afghan thief. A prisoner at Sebastopol, he refused to apologise to a Russian colonel, and so spent thirty years in Siberia. He dies three days later. Here Kipling shows perspicacity about the political nature of the Russians, but little understanding of or even interest in what they are like as individuals. The story has a nasty anti-Jewish paragraph, and, although professionally executed, is not one of his best. It was much admired at the time.

'The Courting of Diana Shadd', which appeared in the previous month, is authoritative, and compelling; it was regarded by both Lionel Johnson and Henry James as an example of Kipling at his best. Here he adds a tragic dimension to his soldiers-three achievement. He was already trying to work India slowly but surely out of his system. Were this story to be read by a good Irish actor, he would have to override the 'markings', and take his own course; apart from that, Kipling's colloquial achievement here is as good as it ever was, and is occasionally Shakespearean – or, more appropriately, Hardyean. It is immediately apparent that the author of this story about Mulvaney has had much more experience of life than the author of the earlier *Soldiers Three*, in which he also figured.

It has a dark ending. Mulvaney fools about with another girl, Judy, but nevertheless wins Dinah, who forgives him. Judy's mother drunkenly curses them both, but then forgets what she has been saying. But Mulvaney insists that the curse is beginning to come true: his first child dies. We take leave of him stark against the sky, with vultures tearing at his liver. This is a powerful story of a simple man feeling oppressed by fate and by the complexities of his own sexuality. The dark side of Kipling's genius all too often come out in brutality; here it emerges in perfectly judged form.

GOD'S DARKNESS

'On Greenhow Hill' (published in August 1890) again shows Kipling at his best, and contains such passages as this, describing Ortheris on a 'soft pine-needled slope' in the Himalayas:

> He buried his nose in a clump of scentless white violets. No one had come to tell the flowers that the season of their strength was long past, and they had bloomed merrily in the twilight of the pines.

The frame story is of the three soldiers lying in wait for a native deserter who is bothering the men by crying out at night. He calls to his old comrades, Indians enlisted in the British cause, to come out and 'fight against the English. Don't kill your own kin!' Mulvaney, Ortheris and Learoyd go out, in a merely sanitary operation, to kill him. While they wait, Learoyd, reminded of his native Yorkshire by 'the bare Himalayan spur', and conjecturing that the man they await might originally have deserted for the sake of a girl, tells the tale of his own early romance, the consequences of which led him to volunteer.

When young, he became separated from a drinking party, fell down, and broke his arm. 'Liza Roantree rescued him, and they became sweethearts. Because of her he joined the Primitive Methodists. The Preacher came to Greenhow, and

> It seemed I wor a soul to be saved, and he meaned to do it. At th' same time I jealoused 'at he were keen o' savin' 'Liza Roantree's soul as well, and I could ha' killed him many a time.

The preacher turns out to be, in Learoyd's crude terms (something like those of which Kipling himself, as polemicist, was capable), to be a man and a half. Some of the Primitive Methodists, but not the preacher, who speaks up for Learoyd's dog, Blast, feel that the dog is 'worldly and low', but Learoyd won't give him up. Then 'Liza Roantree falls ill and dies, but before she does so tells Learoyd that it is he whom she has loved. He joins the army and has been 'forgettin' her ever since'. The story ends as Ortheris shoots the deserter:

> Seven hundred yards away, and a full two hundred down the hillside, the deserter of the Aurangabadis pitched forward, rolled down a red rock, and lay very still, with his face in a clump of blue gentians, while a big raven flapped out of the pine wood to make investigation.
> 'That's a clean shot, little man,' said Mulvaney.
> Learoyd thoughtfully watched the smoke clear away. 'Happen there was a lass tewed up wi' him, too,' said he.
> Ortheris did not reply. He was staring across the valley, with the smile of the artist who looks on the completed work.

In this tale, with the detail about the dog, Blast, Kipling begins to demonstrate an awareness that the world of human beings depends on its attitude towards the natural world, in particular the unsullied and less complicated world of animals. He recognised that although animals have no intellect, they have emotions. This awareness – even when it becomes sentimental – greatly compensates for his insensitivities in other areas.

Trix claimed that Kipling was greatly helped by his father in the composition of 'On Greenhow Hill'. It bears a resemblance to Lockwood's own youthful romance 'Inizella', and it may be that Kipling found it pleasant to put his father right creatively by means of, so to say, using his material and so seeming indebted to him.

The two other of the earlier stories, 'The Mark of the Beast' and 'The End of the Passage', both first published in July, are 'horror stories', although in no wise to be linked in any way with the contemporary genre thus labelled. The serious tale of terror seeks to examine and sometimes even to explain what is terrifying and why it is terrifying: it is not generated by any juvenile desire to 'be horrible'; the sense of terror is involuntary, as in *The Turn of the Screw*.

These stories aren't, though, on a level with the two just discussed. There is some reversion to old bad habits; for example, the uneasy and obsessed male privity of 'some were married, which was bad, and some did other things which were worse'. But such obsessions serve to demonstrate what was on Kipling's mind at this time: marriage seemed to represent a prison, although one which protected a man from 'sin' or 'worse things' – whatever Kipling thought those to be. (It was a common Victorian notion.)

'The Mark of the Beast' is a Strickland story, and Strickland represents, for Kipling, the Englishman just 'saved' from the rich disaster of the chaos represented by 'natives': he 'knows as much of natives of India as is good for any man'. This confers upon the natives of India a power not generally acknowledged by Anglo-Indians. The story was first written some years before, in India, but we do not know to what extent Kipling altered it. That he chose to publish it in 1891 suggests that he may have rewritten it.

The narrator and Strickland have to see a drunken man home. The man, Fleete, pulls away from them and grinds his cigar-butt into the 'forehead of the red stone image of Hanuman', the monkey-god towards whose power Kipling is here pointing. It may be that he is also faintly hinting at the consequences of human disrespect for animals, a clear theme of later work. A naked leper, a 'silver man', emerges, and touches Fleete's breast with his head. A priest then tells Strickland that Fleete has done with Hanuman, but that Hanuman has not done with him.

The next morning the marks on Fleete's breast have turned black. He becomes hungry for raw, bloody and eventually 'gristly' chops, which he bolts down. His horses turn against him, and are afraid of him. From this point 'The Mark of the Beast' turns into an ordinary werewolf tale, with the twist that Strickland, with his 'special knowledge', is able to 'cure' Fleete by capturing the silver man and making him take the evil spirit out of him. The paraphernalia of the cure itself is boring, even if it puts the contemporary non-literary practitioners of this 'genre' to shame. There are a couple of weak sequences in which Kipling implies that things too terrible to be printed occur. When Fleete is 'cured' he is given a sheet to 'cover his nakedness', and nakedness here, as in the Noah story, is insistently connected to the themes of terror and uncleanliness.

'At the End of the Passage' is a more elaborate tale. It begins very well. Four men are playing whist in intolerable heat. They have come very far to be together, but are 'not conscious of any special regard for each other'. They are heat-mad, but most of all the engineer Hummil, who is rude and at the end of his tether. One of the men, a doctor, spends the night with him. He has to give him two shots of morphia to get him off to sleep, to calm his fears. The exact nature of these fears is never made apparent (and herein lies the tale's main weakness), but we do learn two things: of a blind face 'that can't cry and wipes its eyes, a blind face that chases him down corridors' – and, later, of a double. When Hummil dies the doctor photographs his eyes, develops the film, but then destroys it. The double *motif* may well have been suggested by some such picture as Rossetti's 'How They Met Themselves'. Jeffrey Meyers has suggested that by hinting at the supernatural Kipling has, in this case, almost destroyed his story. This is a correct judgement: the sense of horror that Kipling was probably aiming at was a heat-crazed and overworked (as he was then) man driven into a sight of his true nature, or, rather, of his own 'id'. The supernatural is what is not needed here.

Kipling doesn't bring the supernatural into a comparable story, 'The Return of Imray' (originally 'The Recrudesence of Imray', from *Mine Own People*, and reprinted in *Life's Handicap*). In this tale Strickland takes over Imray's bungalow, and is puzzled by the behaviour of Imray's dog, Tietjens. Imray is in fact dead, above the ceiling cloth, which Strickland has to investigate because of some poisonous snakes. The remains of Imray descend (once again Kipling gives us a weak phrase: 'something that I dared not look at' – he would soon learn not to write in this jejune manner); his throat has been cut. Strickland discovers that one of the servants is guilty of the crime: he believed that Imray had put a curse on his small son, who had died. The guilty man allows himself to be bitten by one of the poisonous snakes rather than be hanged. The point of the story is that Imray did not know enough about the nature of the Indians. We have to be aware of the dangerous nature of what is strange and 'animal' (as Kipling might have put it) in us.

The 'animal' element in human beings really comes to the fore in the story he wrote at Freshwater in the Isle of Wight: 'The Disturber of Traffic'. This, his first completely successful story in his mature manner, is frequently called an obscure one. It is certainly true that Kipling gains some of his most telling effects from being deliberately enigmatic, obscure, condensed or recondite. But this story is not so cryptic for those in search of immediate, realistic, meaning, since it can be understood on those terms because it tells of a madman. Although it seems highly improbable, it is in fact, with cunning slavishness, imitating life. The reader is free to interpret Dowse's ideas as meaningless ravings, just as the people who eventually catch up with him do.

The epigraph to 'The Disturber of Traffic' is the extraordinary poem called 'The Prayer of Miriam Cohen':

From the wheel and the drift of Things
Deliver us, Good Lord;
And we will face the wrath of Kings,
The faggot and the sword!

Lay not Thy Works before our eyes
Nor vex us with Thy Wars,
Lest we should feel the straining skies

O'ertrod by trampling stars.

Hold us secure behind the gates
Of saving flesh and bone,
Lest we should dream what Dream awaits
The Soul escaped alone.

Thy Path, Thy Purposes conceal
From our beleaguered realm,
Lest any shattering whisper steal
Upon us and o'erwhelm.

A veil 'twixt us and Thee, Good Lord,
A veil 'twixt us and Thee –
Lest we should hear too clear, too clear,
And unto madness see!

I have quoted the complete poem as it stands in the *Definitive Edition*. As the original epigraph to 'The Disturber of Traffic' it lacked the third and fourth stanzas, and the words 'good' (line 2), 'kings' (line 3), and 'wars' (line 6) lacked initial capitals. 'Thy Works' (line 5) was, in the original draft, 'Thy toil'.

This is not good as a poem because, again, it lacks linguistic power. But it is effective, if immediately very obscure, as part of a story: the story is not complete without it, and it, conversely, is not complete without the story. An expanded paraphrase of it might, gloomily, read:

From the way things truly are, Lord, deliver us. Then we shall be able to meet mere physical misfortune. Don't lay bare to us anything that might demonstrate to us the nature of your labours (the real nature of things?). Just allow us the misery of our physical existence with its inevitable end: otherwise we should be haunted by dreams of what really does happen after death. Preserve us from any knowledge at all of your actual purposes, or you will spoil even the terrible illusion of peace that we occasionally can have. Keep a veil between us and you, God – otherwise the divine order, as we apprehend it, would cease to be order: the stars would seem to crowd in and obliterate the very skies. Put a veil between us and the true reality, unless we should understand your reality too well, and go mad.

Fundamental to the poem is the expression of our need to be protected from an understanding of God's purpose (i.e. from the nature of reality). This wish is cast into the form of the prayer of one who is both Jewish, and a woman. We begin to understand just how unimportant empires – even the British – really are to Kipling. All they are good for, despite all the fuss and the emphasis on discipline and order, is work: work to distract us from the real face of God. What is the 'personal unworthiness' Kipling spoke of? There was much Calvinism in his blood, and in any case fear of damnation is a common affliction of tender sensibilities. Such fears could be fought off by creativity. But Kipling does not state that damnation is what he fears. It is more likely, then, that pointing to the dreadful nature of reality itself is, to him, a form of damnation. In that case he was expressing a gnostic view of existence. At all events, gnosticism is immediately relevant to his strange mind, and his 'philosophy of life', in so far as he could express it, is gnostic in spirit.

One of the leading historians of gnosticism, Hans Jonas, points out that the gnostics were the first speculative theologians after the age of classical antiquity. There is certainly a sense in which Kipling may be regarded as a speculative theologian, with his notions of the 'Law' and his crypto-theological pronouncements. Anyone who has read *Kipling's 'Law'*, Shamsul Islam's useful exposition of 'Kipling's thought', will instantly recognise the similarity between the climate of thought (and feeling) revealed here, and that of gnosticism.

In Kipling the world is revealed as a terrible place. So it was with the gnostics. For the early gnostics the material universe was itself anti-divine, and man was alien in it. Something (they said) had happened in the godhead that had put it into a wrong condition. It was the task of gnostic theology to account for what had gone wrong, and to discover ways and means of putting it right. The gnostic explanations are frequently fantastical (and, in certain Iranian cases, exceedingly scatological, reflecting a hatred of the body and its functions that makes Swift look like a propagandist for sensuality).

This illuminates much that is puzzling about Kipling's thinking: his sense of deep personal unworthiness, his granting of all his genius to a daimon outside himself (in gnosticism the personality is false and material: the *gnosis* that is necessary to overcome it comes from outside the personality, or needs guidance or teaching, whose best function is to try to organise itself for a reception of the *gnosis*), his conviction (as demonstrated in the confusing and over-recondite tale 'The Children of the Zodiac') that something has gone profoundly wrong – and that individual men and women desperately need help.

Certainly Kipling did not understand gnosticism in an intellectual sense. Not enough historical knowledge of it was then available. It would be tempting, but a mistake, to try to parallel the detail of his stories with details from bizarre gnostic literatures – such as, for example, the Valentinian speculation. He may well have read a little on the subject, since he was a voracious reader of whatever he could get his hands on. But there seems to be little direct awareness in him of the gnostic's hatred of matter (as the antithesis of the spirit, which is invariably regarded as imprisoned in the flesh). His general anxiety and confusion about women does, however, reflect the gnostic attitude, which at certain points goes as far as to represent Jesus as saying that 'every woman that will make herself male will enter the kingdom of heaven' (*Gospel of Thomas*), but at other points elevates women to a status not then known. Some gnosticisms, indeed, are more 'feminist' in spirit than Christianity, and the great Christian enemies of gnosticism invariably noted with disgust how it attracted women.

But the most dramatic parallel between the thinking of the gnostics and of Kipling lies, as 'The Prayer of Miriam Cohen' makes clear, in the role given in both to the 'necessity of ignorance'. In the theological speculation of the second-century heretic Valentinus, one of the most influential of the gnostics, perfect repose is attained through the cultivation of ignorance: aspirations (which belong to the personality, a false and material thing) no longer arise. In the *Gospel of Truth*, a gnostic scripture discovered less than fifty years ago, materiality, existence itself, is formed from three experiences: terror, pain and confusion (*aporia*, 'waylessness': not knowing where to go). In Valentinus the *Sophia*, the evil wisdom, falls because she wishes to comprehend the greatness of God, whereas what she had to learn was that the father is incomprehensible. There is said, in Valentinus, to be an actual power which keeps people off from the greatness of the father, and 'consolidates' them. The power is called 'limit': *'horos'*. Mankind is to be saved by the raising of Wisdom from her fallen condition. All this is shockingly unfamiliar in the light of the 'orthodox' Christian thinking to which we have become used; but we cannot fully comprehend Kipling without making an effort to understand it. 'The Prayer of Miriam Cohen' is clear in the light of it; without it, it makes no sense.

Kipling's knowledge of gnosticism, which he may not even have registered under that name – it was and is an obscure, if not actually concealed, subject – was probably confined to Mithraism, a syncretic religion practised in the Roman Empire from the second to the fifth century. Certainly he assimilated some features of this. That he was interested in it is shown in his stories 'The Church that was in Antioch' and 'The Bull that Thought'. Some Christians such as Tertullian thought that Mithraism was a devilish parody of Christianity. But the God Mithras figures in both Zoroastrianism and Hinduism. The central act in the Mithraism practised in the Empire was Mithras's slaying of the bull. Mithraism was not gnostic, and was in fact a degenerate form of it; but there were many affinities, and the religion was deeply influenced, perhaps without knowing it, by gnostic texts and practices. The bull episode was interpreted as an act of creation, and salvation; it also had profound astrological significance; Kipling liked it because it took forms, under the Romans, which reminded him of Masonry.

One of the strong affinities with gnosticism in this popular and socially respectable religion was the account of salvation: the soul ascended through seven grades of initiation, and each of these was ruled over by a planet. In some, even most, gnosticisms, the (visible) planets (including the sun and moon) are the seven archons, and are seen as obstacles to be conquered by the soul in its ascent. Kipling's interest in Mithraism, well in evidence in *Puck of Pook's Hill*, too, must have arisen from his temperamental affinity to its gnostic elements as well as from his liking for its emphasis on purity, its imperial nature and its popularity. But we have to see Kipling's imperialism as a defence against terror rather than as a serious gesture to be carefully collated with the imperialist movement.

There is a clue to Kipling's intentions in 'The Disturber of Traffic', and, since Cohen is a common Jewish name, the clue seems to be a good one. Its source is familiar and unsurprising to anyone steeped, as Kipling was, in the Bible. Miriam ('High') was the elder sister of Moses who watched over the bullrushes in which the infant had been placed, and was instrumental in his mother becoming his nurse (*Exodus*, 2: 4–9, in which she is not named). In *Numbers*, 12: 1–15, she speaks with Aaron against Moses for marrying an Ethiopian, and against his divine authority; she is punished by being made leprous. But Aaron appeals to Moses, who appeals to the Lord, who (presumably) heals her after seven days. In the first verse of *Numbers*, 20, she is buried. But the most vital part of this Biblical clue lies in *Exodus*, 15. In verses 20–21 Miriam is seen in her role as prophetess: she leads the other women in song and dance.

So this 'Prayer of Miriam Cohen', pointing to the terrible conditions of the universe (the point is that the Miriam of *Exodus* knows the nature of God), is the prayer or song of a woman gifted with prophecy – and who through questioning divine authority has been struck down with leprosy. Here one of the people Kipling and his contemporaries frequently referred to in 'jocular' terms as the 'chosen people' is chosen by him: in the context of his profoundest beliefs. He was frightened of Jews, as so many had been in ages before him. That, too, comes out in 'The Church that was in Antioch'.

The story in 'The Disturber of Traffic' is told to the narrator throughout one night in a south-coast lighthouse. We discover from the first paragraph that the tale is about, among other things, the relationship between the divine order of things and the nature of art – or of a certain sort of art:

> The Brothers of the Trinity order that none unconnected with their service shall be found in or on one of their Lights during the hours of darkness; but their servants can be made to think otherwise. If you are fair-spoken and take an interest in their duties, they will allow you to sit with them through the long night and help to scare the ships into mid-channel.

Those who run the lighthouse service for the benefit of shipping are equated with the Divine (of the epigraph) at least by virtue of their associate name: Brothers of the *Trinity*. And there is further parallel to the epigraph: just as those verses beg God himself to deliver prophets (writers: those who seek to know how things work? – Kipling certainly showed a lifelong keenness to discover how things worked), so the Brothers of the Trinity do not allow the uninitiated into their lighthouses. Yet the uninitiated manage it – by being nicely spoken and taking an interest! This is evidently *against* a very strict law. These Brothers of the Trinity must after all know exactly what they are doing and why they do it. Having read thus far (and beware the reader who ignores Kipling's epigraphs) we are given to understand that although a wise woman, a prophet, prays not to discover how things work, yet others remain in the casual habit of trying to find out. The Lights, being the Lights of reality, given to us – strangers and afraid – to illuminate our journey, *scare* us away from the jagged rocks.

It is well to remember at what time Kipling wrote this tale: during his stay on the Isle of Wight, when he was pressed from two sides, by his forbidden beloved, and by his beloved's sister . . .

The frame story is simple. A spare engine is being used for the light, as the main one has had to be sent to London. It is going to be a very foggy night. A dead sea-mist has arisen 'out of the lifeless sea', a little ship is bleating out "fore he's hurt', as the keeper puts it to the narrator. The narrator has some doubts about where he is, almost as though he knew or wrote 'The Prayer of Miriam Cohen': 'It is no pleasant thing to thrust your company on a man for the night.' He is afraid of Fenwick, the keeper, boring him; he is afraid of boring Fenwick. Fenwick hardly knows the land 'except the lighthouse': is he, too, a sort of unconscious prophet, who knows about the workings of the lights without understanding them?

But they manage to get on all right, and Fenwick, discovering that the narrator knows a bit about the sea, becomes 'amazingly technical' – a characteristic touch for those who know their Kipling. 'I was forced to beg him to explain every other sentence.' 'This set him fully at his ease.' Thus one of Kipling's main themes is boldly iterated: the man who *knows the technicalities* can be *set fully at his ease*. (Kipling's own grasp of technicalities, as has often been observed, proves, on close examination by real experts, to have been well short of amazing.)

Then comes the tale itself, delivered by Fenwick 'in pieces between the roller-skate rattle of the revolving lenses, the bellowing of the fog-horn below, the answering calls from the sea, and the sharp tap of reckless night-birds that flung themselves at the glasses'. It concerns Dowse – Kipling's choice of names was seldom less than unerringly poetic – now a waterman at Portsmouth (where Kipling had spent such a long, unhappy time), 'once an intimate friend of Fenwick . . . believing that the guilt of blood is on his head, and finding no rest either at Portsmouth or Gosport Hard'. As Tompkins claims, this is Kipling's 'first full-sized experiment with the imperfect narrator'. He was interested in imperfection beyond all things.

Dowse was stationed in the Flores Straits, 'in charge of a screw-pile light'; it is a similar type of light now being operated by Fenwick. Fenwick does not know why Dowse accepted the position, but he did, 'and used to watch the tigers come out of the forests to hunt for crabs and such-like round about the lighthouse at low tide'. There was a man with Dowse in the lighthouse,

> but he wasn't rightly a man. He was a Kling . . . his skin was in little flakes and cracks all over, from living so much in the salt water as was his usual custom. His hands was all webby-foot, too. He was called, I remember Dowse saying now, an Orange-Lord, on account of his habits . . . An Orang-Laut, of course, and his name was Challong; what they call a sea-gypsy. Dowse told me that that man, long hair and all, would go swimming up and down the Straits just for something to do; running down on one tide and back again with the other . . . Elseways he'd be skipping about the beach with the tigers at low tide, for he was most part a beast . . . Dowse told me he wasn't a companionable man, like you and me might have been to Dowse.

There is much out-of-the-way information here, picked up by Kipling on his travels. We are told that a skipper said he'd never go through the Bali Straits again, 'not for all Jamrach's', and Fenwick asks the narrator if he has heard of Jamrach's; the narrator says he has – but we nowadays may not have done. (Kipling is alluding to Johann Christian Carl Jamrach, 1815–91, son of a Hamburg dealer in curiosities who turned to trade in exotic wild animals in 1840, and acquired a monopoly in it: he would have paid extra well for carriage. He died in London, so Kipling would have heard of this, and assimilated its significance for places such as the East Indies.) Do Java tigers really go down to the shore at low tide and catch crabs? Has anyone checked this? It is a marvellous detail, and hardly matters if it is true or not. Some old salt doubtless told Kipling that he had seen such a sight. Now, through wholesale slaughter earlier in the century, these tigers are probably extinct. So who will ever see such a sight again (if indeed anyone ever really did)? And what about the sea-ape-man, the 'Orang-Laut'? These men certainly existed, and 'Orang-laut' ('Man' - 'Sea') was common usage in Malay. As Angus Wilson asserts, Challong is reminiscent of Caliban, although Dowse is a curious Prospero. Yet he does hold the secret, in his way, of the workings of the Lights – and his name suggests nothing so much as his fear that he will, himself and by his own nature, put them out – *dowse that glim!* Challong's God is the volcano Loby Toby, to which he prays when it is 'spitting red'.

After a year or so saving his pay and occasionally fighting and tipping Challong off the Light into the sea, Dowse's 'head began to feel streaky from looking at the tides so long': 'the only comfort he got was at slack water. The streaks in his head went round and round like a sampan in a tide-rip; but that was heaven, he said, to the other kind of streaks, – the straight ones . . .' He becomes obsessed with 'the nesty streaky water', and cannot help watching it. He tells Fenwick about it as if he were telling it of someone else: 'all as if he was in the next room lying dead'. The streaks 'preyed upon his intellecks'. This obsession, as it develops into psychotic behaviour, is a masterly description of an obsessional neurosis turning into a sort of schizophrenia which then (when he is at Portsmouth) becomes 'burnt out'. Anyone who reads through a textbook of psychiatry well supplied with case-histories will discover that Kipling has outdone even the most conscientiously recorded case-histories themselves: here again is the fiction that is 'of the nature of universals', rather than the 'singulars' given in the mere historical accounts.

Challong used to swim round and round the Light laughing at Dowse when he became sick, until the latter began to believe that it was the ships, and not the tides, that made the streaks. So he and Challong – who can only say the word 'Dam' – make wreck-buoys and eventually 'naked lights of coir', to scare off the traffic. When these and other obstacles are removed by naval officers Dowse believes, according to Fenwick, that 'all the navies of the earth' are 'standing round in a ring'. The passage describing Dowse's descent into madness as, naked but not having noticed it for a long time, he is taken on board a Survey ship, realising that 'dam' is 'mad' backwards, and singing, 'And when the ship began to move/The captain says, "Quack-quack!"', is inspired writing of the very highest order. He must have gazed out to sea from Freshwater and himself become aware of the 'streaks' in the water, and of how a man might be driven into madness by them. All the time Dowse knows that he is mad, but he cannot stop himself being mad except by looking up towards where his eye can 'become lost and comfortable among the rigging, which ran criss-cross, and slopeways, and up and down, and any ways but straight along under his feet north and south'. He is, Fenwick tells the narrator, 'cured of his streaks by working hard and not looking over the side more than he could help' (one is reminded of what Kipling said to Kay Robinson about the results of thinking too much about one's soul). But the obsession's place is taken:

He was much ashamed of himself; but the trouble on his mind was to know whether he hadn't sent something or other to the bottom with his buoyings and lightings and such like. He put it to me many times, and each time more and more sure he was that something had happened in the Straits because of him. I think that distracted him, because I found him up at Fratton one day, in a red jersey, a-praying before the Salvation Army, which had produced him in their papers as a Reformed Pirate. They knew from his mouth that he had committed evil on the deep waters, – that was what he told them, – and piracy, which no one does now except Chineses, was all they knew of. I says to him: 'Dowse, don't be a fool. Take off that jersey and come along with me.' He says: 'Fenwick, I'm a-saving of my soul; for I do believe that I have killed more men in Flores Straits than Trafalgar.' I says: 'A man that thought he'd seen all the navies of the earth standing round in a ring to watch his foolish wreck-buoys . . . ain't fit to have a soul, and if he did he couldn't kill a louse with it. John Dowse, you was mad then, but you are a damn' sight madder now. Take off that there jersey!'

'He took it off and come along with me, but he never got rid o' that suspicion that he'd sunk some ships a-cause of his foolishness at Flores Straits, and now he's a wherryman from Portsmouth to Gosport, where the tides run crossways and you can't row straight for ten strokes together . . . So late as all this! Look!'

Fenwick left his chair, passed to the Light, touched something that clicked, and the glare ceased with a suddenness that was pain . . .

A lark went up from the cliffs . . . and we smelled a smell of cows in the lighthouse pastures below.

Then we were both at liberty to thank the Lord for another day of clean and wholesome life.

Angus Wilson doesn't hesitate to see this story as a parable of the artist – Prospero fearing the 'animal side' (Challong) playing 'too large a part'. Tompkins is, for once, at something of a loss, even calling the tale at one point 'comic', then 'tragic', 'if we like'. Yet that is witness to its power, and she does note that Fenwick can 'never rightly come at what it was' that disturbed Dowse, thus justifying her view that Fenwick as narrator is 'imperfect'. Tompkins knows, too, that – for the first time – the epigraph is an integral part of the story, the beginning of the art-form Kipling invented and perfected. The epigraphs are important in earlier stories, but none of those are at such a high level. 'There is nothing,' Tompkins believes, of the extended meanings of the verses ('a plea to be spared the sight of God's toil in the universe, and the madness that follows the vision'), 'in the tale as it stands, and there could not be; but it is a latent potentiality of the subject.'

It is too easy to speak of figures in fiction (or poetry) as 'standing for the artist'. But nevertheless it is often the case, inasmuch as, even if there is no conscious artistry in people, or creativity of a deliberate sort, there is still a directed imagination in them, simply as a badge of humanity itself. It is this kind of imagination, indeed, that characterises the common reader, without whom the writer is nothing. Thus even the illiterate or very 'simple' person dreams – Fenwick and Dowse of course do. They are men whose lives are dedicated to giving guidance to others, to making safe paths for others. So do the authors of stories dream, and so do the narrators of them (and so do the readers). The dream is also there, for people who lead more dubious sorts of lives: the writer who battens on others for copy, the narrator of stories who sits listening to yarns in lighthouses while the keepers of the Lights do their essential work, as well as telling tales.

The reader often wonders, in a Kipling story, if such-and-such has actually happened, and, if it has, how it has happened. Is, to take a notorious example, 'Mrs Postgate' a fantasy, as so many critics claim? If it is not, then did the pilot – German or British? – really kill a little girl, or did the girl die in the way the village doctor believed she did? Is there a mixture of reality and fantasy here, of dream and reality, of appearance and reality? The emphasis is in any case not on appearance, nor on reality, but on the never-ceasing shift between appearance and reality. In 'Mrs Postgate' there is no solution, but the probing towards one enlightens us, and perhaps even informs us of how what we believe are events really do come into being. No one can really say, since these are stories, that anything at all ever happened.

Here the outlines are bolder than in 'Mrs Postgate'. The story is twice filtered: by Fenwick's account, and by the narrator's account of Fenwick. To add to that, there is Kipling's account of the narrator's narration. There is more overt symbolism in 'The Disturber of Traffic' than in 'Mary Postgate'. We are entitled to interpret it as an artist-art fable because of the prevalence of this theme in the rest of Kipling. Just as the keeper of the Lights goes mad in his worse-than-isolation, with only a 'beast' for company, so the writer could go mad in his, with only his violent and inarticulate, yet seemingly irrepressible and autonomous Id (or, perhaps to be more precise, the robot he is, with his desire for fame, admiration – his fantasy that his soul could have an audience) for company. Kipling does not make Challong a real beast. He had too much respect for real beasts for that. He makes him a human being without intellect and (almost) without speech. He can only say 'dam': damn (an expletive not a word), dam: mother (Caliban), and dam: thing-that-blocks, here, blocks from the explicitly human, i.e. speech. The Id is the term used by Freud to describe a neither good, nor bad, but simply morally neutral, morally immune, component of personality. We do not need to be literal Freudians to accept the term as a viable formulation of the psychopath within ourselves. The tendency of Freud's critics was to understand his concept of the Id, not as morally neutral, but as immoral and terrifying (Jung turned Freud's Id into 'the shadow'). Yet Freud's was a Victorian conception, and fits in well with the conventional Victorian notion of human sexuality, according to which women were 'fortunately' 'not much troubled' by sexual desire, whereas men were like 'beasts' who needed to keep their irresistible needs under the strictest control, and were prescribed, by the best authorities, weekly 'double-emptyings' within marriage. But for those who cannot stomach Freud in any form, the phrase *struggle against our own natures* sums the matter up exactly – Freud's formulation is useful simply because it illuminates what is meant, there, by 'nature'.

Dowse is ignorant of the higher organisation of his employers, the Brothers of the Trinity. He is but a tiny cog in this huge machine for the guidance of shipping. His moral awareness contrasts with Challong's lack of it. The business of the Brothers is not to control but to understand and navigate the treacherous tides and deep waters. They are to Dowse what Kipling's daimon was to him. Dowse does not do anything to the tides and

deep waters, but he heeds them. Just as Kipling did not do anything to his
daimon – the inspirer he obeyed – but heeded it and tried to do justice to
it. What hinders Dowse in his humble and vital work are Challong and the
persistence of the 'streaks' in the very tides against whose intricacies he
must defend others. It is from any obsession with those streaks, 'the wheel
and *drift* of things', that Miriam Cohen prays to be delivered. Fenwick
cannot ever 'come rightly at what it was' that drove Dowse mad – but
nor could anyone else. 'Overwork is murderous idleness.' Knowledge of
that nature of which we are a part would drive us mad; we must work
but never contemplate our work itself. The anguish behind the piece is
gnostic in its nature: haunted by the terrors of madness and, considering
where Dowse ends up seeking comfort, of the difficulties of salvation. It
is profoundly religious in nature.

Two more important stories of this period remain for consideration: 'The
Children of the Zodiac' (*Harper's Weekly*, December 1891, and then in
Many Inventions) and 'The Finest Story in the World' (*Contemporary Review*,
July 1891, and then in *Many Inventions*). 'The Children of the Zodiac' is
a highly complex and over-cerebral allegory which does not work. The
interpretations of it that have been offered by consistently baffled critics
hardly justify its obscurity. Carrington believes that its true meaning lies
in 'something between himself and the woman he was about to marry':

> All that can be said about it with conviction is that it deals with the
> marriage of a young poet, who dreads death by cancer of the throat,
> and that in 1891 Kipling was a young poet contemplating marriage, and
> ill with an affliction of the throat.

Tompkins sees it as confused, but puts emphasis on the astrological
symbolism. Wilson sees it as a parable of the artist and art. Mason,
admitting that, like others, he cannot fully understand it, speaks for
others too, when he says that he finds it 'moving' and with 'something to
say . . . on every page'. In the light of Kipling's persistently gnostic habit
of thought, it might now be possible, without falsely claiming that the
story is coherent, to add something to the comment that has already been
made on it. However, it should be made clear that it has no recoverable
meaning, and that only respect for Kipling has endowed it with any.
The story had personal importance for Kipling, since he chose to
place it last in the collection *Many Inventions*. No summary of it can make
the outlines quite clear: they aren't clear. It is a fable with many asides,
such as, in the first sentence, 'men were greater than they are today'.
This contradicts the spirit of the tale, which is about the beginnings
of mankind, at which time, we are told by Kipling himself, men were
particularly insecure. Kipling balances five signs of the zodiac against
six others. I can find no precedent for his scheme in what passed at that
time for astrological thought, and must conclude that he was not fully
literate astrologically: after all, astrology has very strict rules. The story
begins thus:

> Thousands of years ago, when men were greater than they are today, the
> Children of the Zodiac lived in the world. There were six children of the
> Zodiac – the Ram, the Bull, Leo, the Twins and the Girl; and they were

afraid of the Six Houses which belonged to the Scorpion, the Balance, the Crab, the Fishes, the Archer, and the Waterman. Even when they first stepped down upon the earth and knew that they were immortal Gods, they carried this fear with them; and the fear grew as they became better acquainted with mankind and heard stories of the Six Houses. Men treated the Children as Gods and came to them with prayers and long stories of wrong, while the Children of the Zodiac listened and could not understand.

This is a strange scheme, drawn entirely from Kipling's own imagination. What is most interesting about it is that he has arbitrarily omitted his own sun sign, Capricorn the Goat. In other words, at a personal level, he has, characteristically, cut himself out – at the cost of misrepresenting the zodiac. Was this the technical error to which he alluded in his autobiography, and which he claimed no one had ever spotted? I doubt it. There was some meaning intended; but this meaning is not accessible. But he also cut out Carrie, since her birthday was on the day after his, and she too was born when the sun was in Capricorn. At this personal level the story must, as Carrington believes, be a sort of message to Carrie, or, more likely, a message to himself about Carrie. Otherwise he takes five signs of the zodiac, turns them into six by unprecedentedly counting Gemini as two, and then opposes to them six other signs, which he distinguishes as 'Houses': Scorpio, Libra, Cancer, Pisces, Sagittarius and Aquarius. There is no precedent in any astrological scheme for this: in any astrological system the signs are signs, and the houses (eight or twelve, most usually the latter) are something different. (There is a connection, but this is tenuous and much disputed.) Some astrologers of Kipling's time would interpret the houses according to the signs they believed they represented; others would not. The houses almost invariably start from the Ascendant, which is the place (in degrees and minutes of arc) of the sign rising on the eastern horizon at birth. This was and is taken by most astrologers as being as important as the sun sign. If the generally received time of Kipling's birth is right, then his rising sign was Cancer, which plays an important part in this story, being the Crab that lies in wait, the killer. If Kipling was born some two hours later, then he would have had Leo rising. (He would probably have had a chart drawn up for him, if only for fun or amusement, since in India astrology was then almost a way of life.) Indian astrology is markedly different from Western astrology; but not in respect of the sun sign or the rising sign. If Kipling believed that he had Leo rising then that would explain why he represents himself (as the lover and poet and sufferer from cancer of the throat) as Leo. But this seems unlikely. Throughout his life he had a terror of cancer, which he thought was a disease to which his family was particularly prone. (The astrological sign of Cancer has no more connection, traditionally, with the disease than any other sign.)

The story itself does not work, perhaps because it was written before he was actually married, and thus – as a complex and ambitious fable – reflects a confusion not yet resolved by firm intention or by Wolcott Balestier's death. The boy Leo and the girl Virgo ('the Maid') devote their lives, as half-gods, to making men happy. The Houses, except for Cancer, tell them that they have nothing to fear from them: 'They knew nothing of Leo, and cared less. They were the Houses, and they were busied in killing men.' But Cancer tells Leo that, since he was born into Cancer, 'at the appointed time I shall come for you'. The Crab will also come for the girl. Leo comments that the oppressed Bull 'had a better fate, he is alone'. Whether Kipling had by then read of the central mystery of Mithraism, *taurocteny*, the slaying of the bull, is open to question.

Here Kipling seems to be expressing a fear of Cancer (the zodiacal sign, which he must have known was ruled by the moon – and which he may have known was 'exalted' in the sign of the Bull), which he has associated with the Crab; and to imply that half-gods will become mere men, and suffer the fate of men, if they love. But the tale lapses into confusion, and never begins to carry the weight of its complex symbolism.

One can only remark, yet again, that it resembles a gnostic type of fable: the various signs and houses and half-gods and men are distinguished from one another in a peculiarly gnostic manner. When the Bull, stung by the Scorpion, is dying, he says that he knows everything, but that he 'had forgotten'. This theme of the forgetting, or ignorance of cosmic or divine knowledge is wholly gnostic in spirit. The careful reader will find many other clues in this cryptic tale. It tries to deal with the arrogance of wishing for all the applause – something Leo becomes guilty of – and with the need for work and absence of fear. But it is not coherent. Perhaps at that stage of his life Kipling was incapable of making so ambitious a fable, or allegory, work. Elaborate allegory to which too much thought has been applied in the absence of sufficient imagination was not a form he could manage. There is no unifying factor.

'The Finest Story in the World' first appeared in the *Contemporary Review* in July 1891. Carrington's account of this could be understood to imply that Kipling wrote it during his first Christmas in London, but, whether Carrington was making use of special information or not, the fact that Kipling did not publish the story until July of the following year suggests that he was not satisfied with it until the late spring or early summer of that year. He may merely have sketched it out, or started it, over the Christmas of 1890. It has several sources. One of them was his cousin Ambo Poynter; he was an architect with unrealisable literary ambitions. As Kipling shrewdly put it to Mrs Hill:

> He estimates his poems not by the thing actually put down in black and white but by all the glorious inchoate fancies that flashed through his brain while his pen was in his hand.

There speaks the artistically successful writer as distinct from the failure. The precept – for such it may be called – is best summed up in what Mallarmé said to Degas when the painter protested to him that he had such 'good ideas for poems': poems are made not with ideas, Mallarmé told him, but with words. But Ambo was interesting to Kipling – for, any other considerations apart, failed writers are often successful readers – and had the sort of ideas that fascinated him. Probably the five-act tragedy in verse which he offered to Kipling was a grotesque failure, perhaps resembling Max Beerbohm's hilarious and deadly *Savonarola*; but then it would, also, have been full of the sort of material (however absurdly presented) with which Kipling was just then preoccupied. After all, Kipling was bound, as a young man just back from India with its mixture of religions, to take a syncretic approach to the whole question of belief. To one brought up in a strict Christian atmosphere (I am referring to Southsea), and moreover the scion of generations of Calvinists, the matter must have seemed to him as of paramount importance. Carrington says that Ambo, in the manner of the Victorians, 'throughout life was haunted by the notion that buried and even inherited memories reveal themselves in dreams'.

Other sources for the story are a now completely forgotten and unsuccessful novel, *Transmigration* (mentioned in the text), by Mortimer Collins, and Edwin Arnold's *The Wonderful Adventures of Phra the Phoenician*, which was just then being serialised in the *Illustrated London News*. Both these have reincarnation as their theme, and this, rather than the books themselves in any way, was what interested Kipling (and his friend Ambo Poynter). Reincarnation was almost irresistible to a man of Kipling's curious mind, especially as he had spent so long in India, where amongst Hindus it, or variations on it, are assumed to be fact. Reincarnation has indeed played its part in most of the major religions, Christianity being a notable exception – although amongst the early Christians the thinking of Origen approached it, and Giordano Bruno (certainly a gnostic) was burned for that and other 'heresies'. Various notions of reincarnation – particularly recurrence – lie at the heart of much kabbalistic thinking. Vulgarity is not inherent in the idea of reincarnation; but it inevitably lends itself to speculation of a coarse, ignorant and vulgar sort: that Kipling was aware of this is evident from 'The Finest Story in the World'. But it was more to him than a brilliant device. Being of a generally religious nature, though no Christian, he speculated endlessly upon the possibility.

'The Finest Story in the World' is concerned with Charlie Mears, a bank clerk on twenty-five shillings a week and a friend of the narrator, who is a writer. Charlie, however, is a would-be writer who can't write. He is defined as one who remembers his past lives only because *he can't make use of his knowledge*. The story is also about special sorts of 'valueless' knowledge. The narrator once travelled 'ten thousand weary miles' to discover from a man who had 'gone down with a leaking ship in a still sea', but had survived what the sea looked like 'when it topped the bulwarks'; he had to take this knowledge 'at second hand', but the absurd Charlie

> who had never been out of sight of a made road, knew it all. It was no consolation to me that once in his lives he had been forced to die for his gains. I also must have died scores of times, but behind me, because I could have used my knowledge, the doors were shut.

This points at a wish to write in a more positive way than Kipling at this time usually found himself able to do: the writer is a kind of seer, a human being who 'knows' – the adjective, 'valueless', employed to describe the knowledge of what it is like to go down at sea has a special ironic ring, as if to say, 'valueless to all those of you who don't know about the burdens of writers who *can* make use of their knowledge'. At the core of the story lies a paradox: the sort of people who have the material at hand to make a literary masterpiece can't do it; the sort who don't have the material at hand can. The narrator's ambition is not only to write a masterpiece (by using Charlie) but also to abolish the fear of death by 'proving' that reincarnation is a fact. The narrator is using Charlie with a certain degree of ruthlessness; he feels himself on the edge of an important experience:

> Obviously if I used my knowledge I should stand alone and unapproachable until all men were as wise as myself. That would be something, but, manlike, I was ungrateful. It seemed bitterly unfair that Charlie's memory should fail me when I needed it most. Great Powers Above – I looked up at them through the fog-smoke – did the Lords of Life and Death know what this meant to me? Nothing less than eternal fame of the best kind, that comes from One, and is shared by one alone. I would be content – remembering Clive, I stood astounded at my own moderation – with the mere right to tell one story, to work out one little contribution to the light literature of the day. If Charlie were permitted full recollection for one hour – for sixty short minutes – of existencies that had extended over a thousand years – I would forego all profit and honour from all that I should make of his speech . . . The thing should be put forth anonymously . . . I saw with sorrow that men would mutilate and garble the story; that rival creeds would turn it upside down till, at last, the western world which clings to the dread of death more closely than the hope of life, would set it aside as an interesting superstition and stampede after some faith so long forgotten that it seemed altogether new . . . Only let me know, let me write, the story with sure knowledge that I wrote the truth, and I would burn the manuscript as a solemn sacrifice . . . But I must be allowed to write it with absolute certainty.

The narrator comes to the conclusion that Charlie, for whom he has not a little contempt, would be 'safest' in his 'own hands'. Then he meets the son of the (impossible) official whom he made look so absurd in 'The Head of the District', Grish Chunder. Grish Chunder tells him that Charlie could be made to 'tell', but that '*if* he spoke it would mean that this world would end now – *instanto* – fall down on your head. These things are not allowed, you know. As I said, the door is shut.' The emphasis then falls upon the fact that (according to Grish Chunder, and perhaps to Kipling, too) while a Hindu is afraid to be kicked, he is not afraid to die, 'because he knows what he knows', an Englishman is not afraid to be kicked, but is afraid to die:

> If you were not, by God! you English would be all over the shop in an hour, upsetting the balances of power, and making commotions. It would not be good. But no fear. He will remember a little and a little less, and he will call it dreams . . . If that friend of yours said so-and-so and so-and-so, indicating that he remembered all his lost lives, or one piece of a lost life, he would not be in the bank another hour. He would be what you call sacked because he was mad, and they would send him to an asylum for lunatics.

Grish Chunder also tells the narrator that he will never write the book he wishes to write, even if it were to be done only for its own sake: 'Even then there is no chance. You cannot play with the Gods.' He prophesies, rightly, that whatever power Charlie does have, of remembering, will leave him when he becomes interested in a woman: 'One kiss that he gives back again and remembers will cure all this nonsense . . .' Failing that, Charlie would still forget: he would 'become immersed in the trade and the financial speculation like the rest'. All Grish Chunder, the wise man of this tale, will concede is that Charlie 'would be most good to make to see things'.

Here is the gnostic theme presented all over again. The narrator in quest of secret knowledge, but confused as to whether he wishes to make real use of it or 'human' use of it (for personal glory), and all the time knowing very well that, were it discovered, were it published, it would be ignored by a mankind in love with death. It is a pity that Kipling here did not deal with *recurrence*, and possible small changes in the recurred 'lives', rather than with *reincarnation*. A 'modern gnostic' would probably speculate that recurrence (living the same life over and over again, but with some changes) is all that is, so to say, open to men. But Kipling's intellect was deficient; at that level he was content with the pathetic mumbo-jumbo of Masonry. That kind of thing was of course 'in the air': not only was there the interest in Nietzsche, now mad but much publicised, but there was, too, the success of Wells coming up (1896), with his speculative *Time Machine*, in which he points out to the ordinary reader that there cannot be an 'instantaneous cube' – something not quite generally understood before that date, and to be dealt with at a mathematical level by Einstein within a few years. Einstein would demonstrate that time and space are one thing, but seen as separate things . . .

Kipling anticipates his later manner when he introduces a fragment of Charlie's actual writings. (He is one of the few writers not to shirk the exhibition of any wonders he wants to describe: he got out of the bad habit of exclaiming, 'what I am telling you is too horrible for words.') It is a piece of prose poetry describing Charlie's incarnation as a galley-slave, and is at the least greatly superior to the amateur nonsense that Charlie is understood to churn out. But Charlie is interested only in any 'profits' which might be forthcoming from 'that story'. Kipling goes to great pains to underline how Charlie doesn't understand the first thing about real writing. He thus even proposes to send an essay to *Tit-Bits* on 'The Ways of Bank Clerks'. He can only talk of his pasts when hypnotized by a gas-flame in a fire. When he falls in love with a tobacconist's daughter he loses his power altogether, and, the narrator concludes, 'had tasted the love of woman that kills remembrance'.

This is not a misogynistic ending, as it has been taken to be: it looks forward to Kipling's mood at the time of his marriage, and to what he wrote then. For him, the love of a woman would act as a veil, that veil referred to in 'The Prayer of Miriam Cohen'. Charlie in this story was probably suggested by Ambo Poynter – but he must also be the bad writer, the commercialist (Charlie is pointedly described as grasping), the man lacking in vision who, with such a terrible irony, *can* remember his past lives: *Charles* Wolcott Balestier.

Marriage

After the wedding Rudyard and Carrie parted at the door of the church: she had to go to nurse her sick mother and sister. The marriage was not generally popular, but Kipling was very happy, or, if he was not, he told himself that he was – which for the time being was the same thing. It is likely that he felt that he had been granted the chance to make a new start, and so he was as genuinely happy as he had been for many years. He must have felt that the opportunity to love Wolcott-in-Carrie, and thus 'naturally', was a literally heaven-sent opportunity to 'normalise' himself – and therefore a task, too. He went to Brown's Hotel for a wedding breakfast with Ambo Poynter, and there signed his will. On the following day Carrie, with her characteristic grim humour, noted in her diary: 'We continue to be married.' When they left Brown's the manager gave them their accomodation as a wedding present. But Kipling was in a hurry to leave London, in order to make a voyage round the world. He was going to have his long trail. Yet once again – this time in Japan – it would be curtailed by circumstance. Thereafter he gave up the idea.

On 2 February 1892 he and Carrie left for Liverpool. They were seen off by the ever-affectionate Henry James, accompanied by Heinemann and, of all people, Bram (*Dracula*) Stoker. The next day the Kiplings set off on the S.S. *Teutonic* for New York. On board they had Henry James's friend, the historian and novelist Henry Adams, as a sympathetic fellow-passenger.

Kipling's overt personality quite soon became to a large extent that of his wife, who took immediate charge of him and his affairs, evidently by his own wish. He had had a mother, The Mother, and a father, The Father; it is hardly to be wondered at that Carrie became The Wife. Alas, he did not know much about marriage – or even he might have arranged matters a little differently.

The couple spent a short time as a guest of Beatty Balestier in his house, Maplewood, which was situated in the grounds of his fierce grandmother's estate, Beechwood. Kipling got on well at first with Beatty, his wife Mai Mendon and their daughter Marjorie. He took particular pleasure in the company of Marjorie: he had written to, and made part of his life, certain children (chiefly Mrs W.K. Clifford's daughter, Amelia, or 'Turkey') ever since he arrived in England, and had expressed his wish to have some of his own. What Carrie felt about Beatty is not known, but in view of the later events which she (at least in part, and probably in large part) precipitated, it is unlikely that she ever had much time for this rash brother, who might well have brought out all that was worst in her. Beatty's unforgivable sin was that he enjoyed his life without noticeably demonstrating any of the main virtues. Now he tried to give the Kiplings some ten of the seventy acres of his land as a wedding present. Kipling had already spoken of his rapture with the mountainous surroundings. But Carrie, who did not wish to be beholden to anyone, and least of all to this brother of hers, was not having any of it and took her husband and her brother off to New York lawyers. Finally Beatty conveyed eleven-and-a-half acres to the Kiplings for a nominal sum, and retained certain rights over it, including the use of it for pasture. This was to be the cause of trouble, and the Kiplings' eventual departure.

Kipling was himself happy, even if he was allowing Carrie to assume the ascendency over him which, when older, he would (though in acute privacy) occasionally regret. The landscape in which he was to live – although the original idea that they should settle there, amongst her folk, must have been Carrie's – enchanted him. He seemed perfectly happy to play second fiddle to Madame Balestier, called by Carrington 'the matriarch' who 'lived with her termagant Irish housekeeper', at Beechwood. Kipling was still brash and aggressive towards his enemies, the press; but privately of extreme modesty, and determined to be aware of personal 'unworthiness'.

After three days (they must have rushed to the New York lawyers) the happy couple left what was to be their new home to continue their honeymoon. First they went to Chicago, then to Canada, where Kipling admired the Canadian Pacific Railway and found the English smartness (as distinct from American sloppiness) to his taste. Waiting to sail for Japan in the *Empress of India* at Vancouver he learned that twenty acres of land he had bought from a crook there in 1889, on which he had paid taxes for three years, did not belong to him. Birkenhead adds a detail that Kipling himself must have enjoyed (or partly enjoyed): they now told him, 'You bought that from Steve, did you? Ah-ah, *Steve!* You hadn't ought to ha' bought from Steve. No! Not from *Steve!*'

They arrived in Japan on 20 April. Here Carrie was to a small degree somebody, since her grandfather was well remembered as legal advisor to the Emperor. They both enjoyed themselves, and contemplated (yet again) a visit to Samoa to see Stevenson. What now happened is best given in Kipling's own words:

> I went to the Yokohama branch of my bank on a wet forenoon to draw some of my solid wealth. Said the Manager to me: 'Why not take more? It will be just as easy.' I answered that I did not care to have too much cash at one time in my careless keeping, but that when I had looked over my accounts I might come back in the afternoon. I did so, but in that little space, my Bank, the notice on its shut door explained, had suspended payment . . . I returned with the news to my bride of three months and a child to be born.

He lost £2000 through this failure of the Oriental Banking Company, though he had a return ticket on the *Empress of China* to Vancouver, and the firm of Thomas Cook refunded them such passages as they had booked but not taken. They were not unnerved, and went about Japan 'as though nothing had happened'. They left for Canada on 27 June 1892. As Carrington pointedly observes, Kipling never went further east than Egypt again. Perhaps the main reason for this was that he wanted to live in his heart and mind with the India he had known, rather than ever come to terms with how it had changed. Certainly that part of him that was 'imperialist' now became confirmed. Everywhere, as Angus Wilson says, he looked for cornerstones of Empire; Canada was always his ideal in that respect. Wilson feels that Kipling's imperialism cannot be ignored. I agree, but whereas he (as a non-sympathiser) looks for intellectual respectability in it, I have looked at it as a channel for other emotions.

Wilson states that the practical programme of the imperialists was not 'silly' or 'immature'. 'Some critics,' he writes,

> have preferred to ignore this aspect of Kipling's thinking, dismissing his political ideas as silly and immature. All revolutionary ideas, whether of the left or of the right, are silly and immature unless and until they succeed. Kipling's, of course, where they are successful, filtered through the imagination . . . in the ideas of the Right Radicals, of the Imperialists, he was to find a programme of activity which accorded with those deep personal inner fears and desperate hopes that were the source of his art.

This does not go far enough. Much that is silly and immature succeeds – but is still silly and immature. After all, as Wilson says, Kipling 'was an artist not a thinker'. But when Wilson goes on to claim that the ideas of the imperialists have some intellectual respectability, he puts the emphasis in the wrong place. However that may be, I doubt if Kipling ever really reacted to any of these ideas other than on a purely emotional level. Wilson thinks that to equate the ideas of the imperialists – St Loe Strachey, Maxse, Alfred Milner, Joseph Chamberlain – with silliness is 'to equate maturity with the policy of the centre, of compromise': 'these political hopes must be considered seriously if we are to understand their pressure upon Kipling's imagination for the rest of his life . . .' But there is no need to take the ideas seriously, if they never impinged on Kipling intellectually – and there is no evidence that anything ever impinged upon him intellectually. He had the right 'instincts' – as they used to be called – about intellectuals and how awful they are; but intellectuals are by no means the only awful people (Hitler was not, for example, an intellectual). Kipling used imperialist emotion to support the non-imaginative flank of his world-view. It was largely an accident coincident on his parents' attitudes and his own experiences in India. He might as easily have become a wild and untamed Liberal, for all the true resemblance that imperialism has to the shape of his imagination. In other words, whenever that imagination is not working at full throttle – is not directed by objective effort – his bias distorts it, as we see in much of his verse. Wilson himself points out that Kipling, laureate of the imperialist group, was often 'gnomic' towards those he supported. Of course he was: at his best he went well beyond their imaginative range.

My point is that, insofar as imperialism was an influence at all on Kipling – and it was a considerable influence, even if it never quite penetrated to the core of his being – then it was a *bad*, and never a good, influence. Noel Annan, anxious to free Kipling from his reputation, has even tried to demonstrate that his 'thinking' was really in accord with such famous continental theorists as Durkheim; but, as I shall show at a later stage, that is not the case, and Annan's ambitious contention becomes grotesque.

The minute the Kiplings arrived back in Canada they heard by telegram that Madame Balestier had rented for them – perhaps decreed for them – Bliss Cottage, the hired man's accommodation on Bliss Farm, at ten dollars a month. Since they had, for the time being, no money, they could hardly complain. But Carrie may not have been pleased with the implied status, and the Swedish maid, Anna Anderson, whom she engaged – as if in silent protest against the necessity of living upon some kind of charity, or as the object of pity – cost eighteen dollars a month. Carrie thought this was too much. There was what Carrington called a 'family council' about whether to take up the offer of the 'storey-and-a-half high', 'seventeen feet to the roof-tree' Bliss Cottage; but one may guess that this consultation involved little more than Carrie's saving face. She had married one of the world's most famous young authors, and she was going to show everyone, not the least her own family, that she could influence him and, through him, events. Needless to say, the Kiplings were not without money for very long: there were royalties already due. In November Kipling received a cheque for almost $4000 from Watt. He never in fact had a day's worry about money after that sudden failure of the Oriental Bank. They never kept a servant for long, Kipling says in *Something of Myself*, for they all found the place too lonely, and one even left without taking along her trunk. Could Carrie's manner towards them have had something to do with this? It does not seem to have deterred Kipling much, although he tells us that he concentrated more on making comforts than on writing. The place was in fact very uncomfortable, and they risked either death from freezing or from fire when they installed an old hot-air stove. Perhaps because of this discomfort, or more likely because of the child born just after Christmas 1892, the only notable writing he produced in this period, apart from a few poems, was the finished version of one of his finest stories, 'Love-o' -Women' (about syphilis). Birkenhead differs somewhat from Carrington in stating that Kipling found he could work 'with zest in the crisp invigorating climate' and even that he wanted to buy this property, 'but the Blisses were not prepared to sell'. Probably the primitive discomfort suited his intentions – but by no means Carrie's, who had social ambitions of her own which she did not hesitate to put into effect. She was also turning out to be an expert business manager – much better, and more controlled and tactful in her dealings with publishers, than Kipling himself could have been. It seems, however, that his agent Watt usually had the last word – he was a smooth operator.

Their first child, a daughter, Josephine (yet another Capricorn, Kipling must have felt), was born on 29 December 1892. Birkenhead does not make clear on exactly what evidence he relies in stating that, while from the very beginning this attractive child was the very special apple of her father's eye (which we know), he at the same time 'felt a strange distrust in her destiny'. But it seems likely; for Kipling's life was characterised by strangely prophetic apprehensions and anticipations. He never took anything for granted for long. He could deny Josephine nothing. Yet Anna Anderson remembered that, when Josephine was born, he was disappointed because she was not a boy. He must soon have forgotten his disappointment. He said of a local bereavement that, had it been Josephine, he would never be able to 'think or speak of her again' – and that, after 1899, became a fact:

People say that kind of wound heals. It doesn't. It only skins over; but at least there is some black consolation to be got from the old bitter thoughts that the boy is safe from the chances of the after years. But it is the mother that bore him who suffers most when the young life goes out.

This, revealing the profound bitterness that was never far from the surface, was written later, after the death of Josephine, to another who had lost a young son. Always when he was brought any delight by life, Kipling instantly anticipated its being taken away. Yet he preferred to suffer such blows, rather than know the truth of God's purposes – to see through the veil of which he speaks in 'The Prayer of Miriam Cohen'. Meanwhile, in this flush of joy at being a father at last, the name of Wolcott Balestier could not be mentioned, and no photograph of him was allowed into the house. All of us have shocking moments when we resent the dead – and there is no doubt at all that Kipling suffered those, too.

Carrington valiantly endorses Kipling's own enthusiasm in *Something of Myself* for his do-it-yourself efforts around the house; but Birkenhead, who talked more extensively to the people of Brattleboro in the Forties, is certainly right when he says that 'in truth he was without resource in the simplest practical matters'. There is not a tittle of evidence to the contrary – just a polite legend. Birkenhead preceded Carrington in his visit there, and rather queered his pitch: they used to tell him that Birkenhead had been there asking the same questions. It seems that they had told Birkenhead all they had to say, and were tired of saying it again – nor would Carrington have much liked what he heard. The Kiplings were no more liked in Vermont than they were anywhere else, and there is no point in glossing that over.

Kipling's lack of resource in practical matters accounts for much of his delight in knowledge of them . . . He could not turn around a buggy properly, and had to be helped by a neighbour. He struck another as 'an uncommonly timid man'. So he was, in the sense that a part of him felt that his reputation as a writer was not quite the sort of reputation that he wanted: for the whole of his life the putative man of action – utterly helpless, dependent on others for the simplest tasks – would be inclined to obtrude himself. But he impressed many of the local people by keeping to himself except for those occasions when his curiosity overtook him.

However much pleasure he took in the hired man's cottage, Kipling was determined to build his own house – on the plot Beatty had tried to give him – and to name it Naulakha in silent and properly spelled memory of Wolcott, whose name was otherwise unmentionable. They began building in early 1893, and everything was handled by Beatty, probably because it was necessary to have Madame Balestier's approval – Madame Balestier still loved Beatty, and wanted him to make good.

'This was not to be a summer cottage, not a New England house but a mansion, replete with stable, barn, outbuildings that future generations of Kiplings might claim with pride,' said the writer Frederick Van de Water, who had Beatty's confidence, and who wrote an sharp, amusing account of the American years in *Rudyard Kipling's Vermont Feud* (1937). Van de Water thought that the seeds of the feud, although 'there was no surface sign of its presence', may have developed then. Surely, however, they lay in Carrie's attitude to her raffish brother: in his casualness, and in her gloomy dogmatism and almost pathological need to have her own way.

The house was on the slopes of Mount Wantastiquet, a 'gracious knoll' uphill and diagonally across the road from Beatty's own home, Maplewood. Van de Water says that Kipling 'gloated' over this landscape, and also describes how Kipling appeared at his small table (in Bliss Cottage) 'arrayed in full evening dress – Kipling in white tie and tails; his wife in a low cut gown with train'. But it was Carrie who gave herself, and therefore him, airs: he once confided to a neighbouring farmer, a Mr Waite, 'I envy you. Your day's work is finished. You can go in and wash up and sit right down at the table for supper. I've got to go home and put on evening clothes before I can dine.'

He may also have said something of this sort to Bliss, his landlord at the cottage. But such confidences were, throughout his life, very rare: only enough to tell us that a part of him rebelled against what I have suggested was the task he set himself, of gratefully adapting himself to his wife's wishes in every smallest detail, as a kind of religious duty to the one who had forgiven him. The impressions gained by Birkenhead chime in with what everyone else has to say: he stated that Carrie 'had a passion for the domination of others which she did not attempt to control' and that she 'greatly disliked being crossed'. That was the impression she gave to her neighbours, and Birkenhead picked that up from many of them, and reported on it. Certainly her insistence on their both dining in full evening dress was provocative and highly eccentric. It is as if she were determined to revenge herself on the world for her unhappy temperament – perhaps, too, for her husband's secret wickedness. Her good qualities came to the fore only when she was in charge. And there was one advantage for Kipling, which at least any writer will appreciate: all he needed to do was to write.

Nonetheless, while Kipling could be genial to those he liked – the doctor, James Conland, who helped him with the fishing background for *Captains Courageous*, Mary Cabot and her brother William, Charles O. Day, pastor of the Congregational Church in Brattleboro, Charles Eliot Norton (who was, however, at Harvard), Conan Doyle, who visited – he began to reflect upon Carrie's snobbish and gloomy stand-offishness, and developed a habit of occasionally atrocious rudeness towards those strangers to whom he happened to feel momentary and unexamined dislike. The Vermont people otherwise left the Kiplings alone, and they were well content. The impression Carrie gave to those amongst whom she had grown up was that of a woman who hadn't spent long in England, but had nevertheless 'returned to her native land with heavy Mayfair graces and accent that Vermont's climate seemed to nurture'. Her progress through Brattleboro's streets in her basket phaeton, driven by her coachman Matthew Howard dressed in 'top-boots, doeskin breeches, blue coat and top hat' seemed ridiculous and unfortunate. Thus the people of Dummerston – the name of the district in which Maplewood and Naulakha were situated – remembered Kipling as a 'friendlier spirit than his wife'. Kipling, they felt, 'might in time have become actually one of us, for he could unbend and warm men when he pleased'. Yet Van de Water thought that it might have been only his 'unfailing thirst for material' that unbent him. He was, said Dave Carey, the baggage master at the railway station, always 'listening for queer turns of speech that he could use. I never saw a man so hungry for information.'

So far as his own stand-offishness is concerned, it is most likely that he simply adapted himself to his wife's unhappy personality. He had not been much like that before marriage. Being a pessimist at heart, though capable of great temporary joy, this suited him. He thus remained 'an Englishman who looked down his nose and was monosyllabically frigid to those who from curiosity or simple friendliness sought his acquaintance'. When Beatty took him to a boarding house on Lake Raponda, nearby, he and Carrie (and his sister-in-law Josephine) 'spent several weeks . . . apart from all other boarders'. Josephine, having been in England too, was associated in the local mind with Carrie's high-falutin' ways. We hear nothing of their mother, much more of their grandmother.

When the house was built and they moved in all was well between Kipling and Beatty. The families had spent a merry Christmas at Maplewood, Kipling had written verses for Marjorie ('Winter in America; all the flowers go – /All except sweet Marjorie, blooming in the snow – ') and Beatty was given an early manuscript of The Jungle Book (1894, followed by The Second Jungle Book, 1895), which was the next big writing job. Carrington does not mention the vulgarity and lack of taste apparent in Naulakha, but, as Van de Water says, it

> was a large, expensive dwelling for that day and, by any standards, an ugly [sic]. Ark-like in outline, with long, low mass and ungainly angles, shingled walls and gray-green trim, it lay upon the knoll as though flood had cast it there.

This was, alas, mainly the result of the taste of Carrie – or, rather, of her need to appear superior to everyone else around her. This taste was thoroughly indulged and shared by Kipling. He called the house his ship, and it had 'chilling interior decoration'. Its architect, Henry Rutgers Marshall, was an over-confident man of no ability, and his desire to humour Kipling's whim to have it looking like a great ship on the swelling ocean of the knoll had only unfortunate results. It was built long and narrow, like a ship: and there was not much room. There was a porch attached to the side to the house, which led into an entrance hall, which in turn led into a sitting-room. Kipling had a library and work-room, which was, literally, guarded by Carrie from her 'boudoir' or 'office'. She used her authority as the necessary guardian of the writer's solitude as a means of exercising the absolute domination she craved. 'To this room,' Carrington says of Kipling's work-room, 'there was no admission past her chair.' Very few did get past the 'vigilant and unrelenting Cerberus', and then only those who had her approval. One guesses that Kipling had small say in this. Carrie called Naulakha 'Liberty Hall', but she 'provided', a neighbour said, 'only bare necessities and slender allowances', and gloomily 'made much of the difficulty of conducting a household so far from the source of supplies, and kept the machinery of life always in evidence'. In other words, whatever her fortunes, she whined; it was really only harsh adversity, such as death or critical illness, that brought out the unsour in her: her gloom could understand such things. No chance guest could have been offered lunch: thus did Carrie express her distaste and disapproval of the informality reigning in her brother Beatty's house, where people came and went as they pleased.

There is little doubt that Kipling was really a willing martyr, and knew that it was a part of his task never to cross Carrie. The whole affair is more easily explicable if we grant that she had agreed to give him 'a new start': that she 'had a hold over him', though not one that he (or she) so regarded. To whatever extent Kipling felt himself to be in a prison, he had built it as if with his own hands. But Carrie was his life's work. When he told Dave Carey that 'the men of any race were much less dangerous and savage than their women-folks', he knew what he was talking about. Whether or not he argued about the nature of women with Carrie there is no way of knowing; but when Dave Carey read 'The Female of the Species' years later, it 'was like hearing Kip say it all over again'. 'The Female of the Species' has been much decried as 'sexist'; it seems to me to be a powerful expression of feelings that many men, whether 'rightly' or not, possess. It is a poem of the second rank, exhibiting Kipling's too frequent fault in his poetry, of taking a set of more or less crude feelings as an assumption; but a compelling one, nevertheless. It does not examine the rank emotions it expresses, but it does express them memorably.

He had started *The Jungle Book* while in Bliss Cottage, but got down to it in earnest after he was settled into Naulakha, where he worked regularly, and in a total silence broken only (we are told) by his occasional cry to Carrie 'for a rhyme', from nine until one each morning. The products of the American period were the two Jungle Books, the poems of the collection *The Seven Seas* (1896), the novel *Captains Courageous* and the stories collected in *The Day's Work* (1898). Lockwood Kipling – whose presence was conducive to the composition of the Jungle Books in particular – came to stay shortly before they moved into Naulakha; significantly, he was not accompanied by his wife.

When Kipling at the end of his life spoke of his only having had to play the cards dealt him, he was perhaps thinking chiefly of Carrie, and of the strange part she had played in his life. Now she became not only his (invaluable) literary helpmeet, but 'banker . . . and farm superintendent'. 'If a hireling came to him for instructions, Kipling always answered: "You'd better ask my wife."'

Beatty resented being treated as a boy by this disagreeable sister, who doubtless would keep on reminding him, almost as if his good nature did not exist – no wonder, considering her own nature! – of what he hated most: reality. Carrie now appeared to wish to take it upon herself, since no one else would, to make a prudent man of him. She had him up to her house two to three times a week to do odd jobs, when she would give him the very least amounts of dollars consonant with his services. Never a bit on account from her! Until Naulakha was wholly finished, though, his services were considerable, and she sometimes had to pay out large amounts. Nor were there (perhaps surprisingly) any serious complaints about how he carried out his various commissions. All these amounts she recorded meticulously in her diary. Carrington says that in all Beatty had over four thousand dollars, equal to much more than forty thousand dollars today. But this useful source of ready cash began to dry up after the summer of 1893.

Van de Water has been accused of taking Beatty's side in the quarrel that was quite soon to follow; yet he wrote that Kipling's morbid lust for privacy made him shirk responsibility. He was galled by all save those elemental ties that bind a man to life. He craved, even then, that independence which he said, long after, 'signifies the blessed state of hanging on to as few persons and things as possible and leads to the singular privilege of a man owning himself'.

That craving may have brought him to Vermont. Beatty Balestier used it later with satanic skill to drive him away.

Van de Water wasn't, in fact, biased. He was, being a native of Vermont, simply somewhat more sympathetic to Beatty, and suspicious of Kipling's motives. But he is always fair. He questions whether Kipling wasn't being in part crafty in his hatred of reporters: 'his ostensible hostility to the press won him far more publicity . . . His very remoteness was a challenge.' Actually Kipling's hostility to the press was very real, especially as he had all – and had used all – the resources of a good reporter himself. Once a female journalist came from Brattleboro to Naulakha 'by sleigh in the dead of winter'. She collapsed from the cold and was taken in by the Kiplings and revived. But they threw her out in horror as soon as they discovered that she was a journalist. Kipling was, Van de Water shrewdly wrote, 'too peculiar a critter for anyone to want as friend'. It was the men of Vermont who had known Kipling while they were still children who spoke well of him: he always unbent to the young. In that area of life he was already building up a pleasant reputation. He lent toboggans to the pupils of the school, and would gather up children – even in his own working hours – to tell them enthralling stories. One lad, Merton Robbins, who was working his way through university by means of selling life insurance, made a sale of ten thousand dollars to Kipling (after he had asked Carrie for permission, something he made no bones about having to do); in return he was made to answer every conceivable question about his life at the university. Yet, Van de Water ominously wrote, Kipling 'had not yet become so firmly fixed that a single blast of scandal could not overthrow him and put him to flight'.

The Jungle

The two Jungle Books remain children's classics. They are, however, not so popular amongst today's children as they were amongst those of earlier generations. Writing in 1972, Gillian Avery, who had investigated the matter, said that Kipling's 'popularity appears to have declined . . . Only the *Just So Stories* survive as a universal favourite. The first *Jungle Book* is borrowed by Wolf Cubs, or by those who have seen the Disney film, but is usually returned without enthusiasm.' My own investigations confirm this, and the trend continues. Kipling's reputation as a children's writer was, thought Avery, 'artificially kept alive' because he is on reading lists. Yet, as she concedes, they are still classics. Like all such classics, they are for grown-ups, too. One says 'grown-ups' rather than 'adults' because this more appropriately describes the status of those of mature age who truly enjoy them: grown-ups willingly suspend their adulthood – in this particular case because they wish to dwell sentimentally or nostalgically upon their own childhoods.

Not all of us suffer, now, from the difficulty confessed by Tompkins when she discussed them: that it was hard for her to be dispassionate about them when they had so strongly influenced her in childhood. We have all read them, even if we are the children of self-consciously liberal anti-imperialists; we all remember them; but they have a less strong hold over our affections.

The books tell us much about Kipling, because in them he worked out, as far as he was capable, his notion of what he called the Law. But that is not to say much. Not being capable of serious thinking, he needed to express what he thought were his ideas through the comparatively simple channel offered by the form of children's fiction. As we have seen, he was now blessed with the achievement of fatherhood. Soon he found himself able to open up completely only to children. This ability to be so uninhibited with children – his successful entertainment of them, on board ship and elsewhere, began before the birth of Josephine – became fully developed as a result of his having to adapt himself to Carrie's zealous cautiousness. He discovered that she did not remonstrate with him when he opened himself up to children. If he opened up to adults, she would be on to him at once about allowing himself to be exploited. That was admirable and realistic, but must have created a negative atmosphere, and must have led to the cruel snubbing of decent and good-willed people as well as reporters out for some trivial story. She was more jealous, alas, than discriminate. This way of conducting himself became a habit. The practice of unbending to children, in life and on the written page, become a necessary release for him. It suited him because although children have wisdom, it is not the sullied or guilty wisdom of experience. He usually wanted to keep away

from that, and from what he called (much later) 'abnormalities' to Hugh
Walpole. Only children are not unutterably swinish (to employ his term,
if not his specific application of it). It has often been observed how
astonishingly childish, boyish, Kipling was – especially for so famous an
adult. This is true, and is to be seen in what James, with justice, called the
deplorable Stalky tales. The compensation comes from his feeling that he
could talk the language of children, almost as if he himself was no more
than a slightly older and more experienced child. The tone is grateful,
something from a much put-upon man with a sharp sense of sin who is
relieved by being among innocents. But the wisdom of what is actually
being said, of what is, so to say, being passed on from senior figure to
child for later use in life, is often in question. The detail has not been
much looked at, especially on the part of the ardent Kiplingite – and with
good reason.

Kipling when he was with children, over whom he cast a loving
spell, could suspend his experience of evil – his sense of unworthiness,
as he put it – and become an *aphorist*, safe in the assumption that, since
he was a grown-up dispensing real pleasure and giving genuinely felt
love, it would be understood by them as wisdom. Sometimes, however, it
was not wisdom, but ugly and over-emotional authoritarian propaganda.
Kipling became, through his cultivation of the form of children's fiction,
a self-conscious aphorist.

Even an unsuccessful aphorist has a certain advantage over his
non-aphoristic audience: only a very small proportion of that audience
likes to question the effectiveness of the aphorisms, because it might thus
be made to look simple-minded – might be exposed as incapable of 'seeing
the point'. Good aphorists (La Rochefoucauld, Cioran) are usually over-
cerebral people seeking relief in simplicity. They are seldom intellectually
wanting, as Kipling was. But the form can be a refuge for those who are
dissatisfied with their own intellectual performance. There is much more
than a touch of this in Kipling, who is by no means as good an aphorist as
he is sometimes taken to be. A wise aphorist needs to be witty, and wits
need intellect. Kipling was not witty.

Certainly he does not patronize or write down to children; and when he
writes in the way that children speak, it is more child-like than childish.
All in all, he pitches his actual language just right. There are lapses, but it
is not possible for any author to avoid these. Kipling, trying to escape from
his extreme individualism and his sense of disappointment, was trying to
be like a little child again – in the Gospel sense – and whenever he remains
in that mood what he does is right. But the mood does not prevail.

Tompkins' assertion that the Jungle Books fuse 'three worlds' takes their
near-perfection for granted; but otherwise it is accurate and thoughtful,
and lays down an excellent means of approach. Adapted from the scheme
suggested by a French critic of Kipling, Robert Escarpit, in his *Rudyard
Kipling: Servitudes et grandes impériales*, it agrees with him as to the first two
'worlds', but diverges from him as to the third.

First, as she says, there is 'the child's play-world': homely, simple,
'entirely congenial to a child's imagination'. This is a very 'Victorian' and
comfortable, secure world, for all its dangers. It has added nostalgic attractions nowadays for many older readers, who have become fed up with
false nihilism, pseudo-complexity and ignorant lack of moral purpose. Yet

there is much real nihilism at the heart of these books. But then that, if we revel in our own little bit of solipsist nihilism, is how we like to take it: in a very strictly moral framework. The atmosphere in these stories of the jungle and Mowgli is very often of a world of willed order menaced by the forces of chaos and darkness.

Then there is 'the world of fable proper'. In this world the beasts are less beast-like that allegorically human. Tompkins feels that the allegory is never pressed too hard for children; this hardly applies today, but it did in the days of her childhood. She is right when she says that these first two worlds are frequently 'inextricably fused'. As frankly moral literature the Jungle Books are in a category by themselves.

The last and most important of the three worlds is that of 'the wild and strange' – what Tompkins might well have called the poetic. This is what can't be fully explained or analysed, and must always be a component of an enduring literary work. It is present in the Jungle Books, but is not as all-pervasive as it could have been. For while Kipling was re-entering the world of childhood he was simultaneously indulging his obstinate solipsism. Had the personality of Carrie been different, he might have seen things differently. But his idea of unity with her was dutifully and, ultimately, false – false to his true needs.

The external sources of the Jungle Book stories are: Sterndale's *Mammalia of India*; whatever lore his knowledgeable father passed on to him (Lockwood was the author of the still charming book, *Beast and Man in India: A Popular Sketch of Indian Animals in Their Relations with People*, 1893); and, above all, the *Jataka* tales of India. Some of these fables go back as early as the fourth century BC and incorporate material of even earlier eras. One version, *Jatakamala*, was composed in about 200 AD by the poet Aryasura. They are Buddhist birth-stories – *Jatakamala* means 'Garland of Birth Stories' – which the nineteenth-century scholar Rhys Davids described as 'the most important collection of ancient folk-lore extant'. Each of the 550 stories tells of the Buddha in some previous incarnation, and each is a story of the past occasioned by some incident in the present. In practice, any ancient story served, provided the Buddha could be brought into it in an exemplary way. There are verses in each story, too – was that the basis of the form Kipling 'invented'?

Buddha appears in these tales in every human and animal guise – except as a female. Some of the beast fables resemble Aesop's, but the Jataka tales are more deliberately brutal. They teach not merely that men should be tender towards animals, but the equivalence of all life. 'The Ass in the Lion's Skin' is typical in its brutality. An Ass carries the goods of a peddler. When this peddler puts him into rice or barley fields, so that he can forage them, he throws a lion's skin over him so that he should not be chased off. Villagers gather with sticks and stones, he brays in fear – and is beaten to death.

In another tale which may have influenced Kipling a jackal eats into a dead elephant, and, finding shelter, goes to sleep. The carcass dries up and he cannot get out: he bobs up and down 'like a ball of rice in a saucepan'. Then it rains, the corpse softens and swells, light can be seen, and the jackal gets into the head and hurls himself at the exit. He emerges, but is stripped 'smooth as a palm-stem'. The panic and terror are inherent in the tale, but are missing in similar tales from outside India: the animals (each human being represents some animal in type) here have an 'inside life' and are not mere agents in the action. The influence on Kipling, clearly, was profound – as was the Buddhism he came at through this source, as distinct from his conscious thinking about the religion, which is often reflected in *Kim*.

The trigger for the Jungle stories must have been the birth of Josephine, or its anticipation; the author's most immediate intention was certainly to delight. But he wanted to instruct, too, even to warn (one recalls that revealing and extraordinary remark, written in a letter after Josephine's death, to the effect that one consolation for the death of one's child is that he or she will no longer be vulnerable to 'life's chances'). In the two Jungle Books Kipling did, as well as deliberately relax and successfully re-enter the world of childhood, consciously intend to be didactic; first and foremost in his mind, in this respect, was his wish to express the nature of what he called the Law. He never succeeded in defining this Law, primarily because it was an ambiguous, confused and, ultimately, defensive concept. On the one hand it represented his true, pessimistic, frightened attitude to existence. It was undoubtedly fuelled above all by his profound individualism – by his solipsism, his feeling that everything in the world was an obstacle to his self-expression. This was neither conventional – it could be seen as having been as subversive as gnosticism – nor easy.

Kipling's Law is seen as the most ancient of all Laws. It is inescapable, but it is also somehow arranged so as to look after 'every kind of accident that may befall' creatures. (We see there, incidentally, that it is in fact a scheme for the protection of the individual: it is uninterested in social mechanisms, save as a means of self-protection.) It is brutal, imperfect and pragmatic, and in the creation of it Kipling manages to express his dislike for Utopian schemes. In the poem (in *The Second Jungle Book*), 'The Law of the Jungle', the essentials are presented in an unsubtle and unambiguous manner: '*For the strength of the Pack is the Wolf, and the Strength of the Wolf is the pack*', and the famous final line: '*But the head and the hoof of the Law and the haunch and the hump is – Obey!*'

One has to remember that Kipling's own 'pack' was a pretty small one: he fiercely kept others out, and his only true solace was children, as yet unspoiled by life – a hideous thing full of 'chances' and 'accidents'. This 'Law' is wrong from Kipling's true emotional viewpoint: it is the *weakness* of the wolf (individual person) that is in the pack (masses). One can see that time and again reiterated in the 'morals' to his parables. Those 'in the know', in Kipling's writings, are those who 'know' that laws are made only to be broken . . .

Shashul Islam, in *Kipling's Law*, carefully and diligently tries to work out the nature of the Law – which he concedes Kipling himself could never define – as having for its basis reason, the common good, ethical values, law-making authority and promulgation, and custom and tradition. But in performing this service for us he gives the scheme a coherence that it does not, and could not, have. It is not that his analysis is not useful. Indeed, it is invaluable. But presented in this way, the essential simple-mindedness, even naivety, of it all, from an intellectual point of view, is seen: it reduces to a few conventional precepts. It would hardly satisfy any half-competent student of political theory, since it begs all the famous questions – or seems, even, to be unaware of them. It is no more than crude advice to people who are strangers and afraid in a world they never made: 'Go with the pack for your own good', it says. It never even says (as Durkheim always implies): 'You're *naturally* a part of the pack: you belong to it'. The only world in which one can be deliberately unaware of the elementary philosophical questions about individuals against society is, precisely, in a child's instinctive world. The value, or at least the interest, of the Law (and it is not one of the most interesting aspects of his work) in Kipling lies in what he does not say explicitly, in what he does not want to say (but feels) and in what he does not know he is saying. In other words, the concept is in itself a failure; but what he meant by it, or would have liked to have meant by it, is interesting.

In the story in *The Second Jungle Book* in which Hathi the old elephant tells of 'How Fear Came', Kipling consciously and ambitiously tries to reformulate the Fall. This particular story cannot be said to be a success, and, inasmuch as it has lived at all, this must be because it is part of the collection as a whole, and because its tone is right. Yet it is necessarily a key story, by which the overall conception of the Jungle Books must stand or fall. In the story told by Hathi, the aged elephant Tha is taken to be the all-wise one. He appoints the First of the Tigers to be Master. Disputes at this stage appear to have been the result of laziness. But the first of the Tigers kills a buck, and thus brings Death. The smell of blood makes him foolish. The Ape is then appointed Master; but he soon brings Shame. So Tha has to institute the Law. But in order to do that everyone has to know Fear. The creatures do not understand, and go about literally seeking Fear, in order to know it. The buffaloes said that Fear was a hairless creature sitting in a cave: Man. As soon as the inhabitants of the jungle saw Man, they withdrew and 'like kept to like'. Tha enables the Tiger to have one night of the year in which Man will be subject to him. On that occasion he is instructed to show Mercy. But he does not; thus he teaches Man to kill.

Whatever charm this still possesses for children is due to what Tompkins calls 'the pass-words and taboos' of the Jungle, which are 'entirely congenial to a child's imagination'. We have already seen how marvellously simple Kipling can be when he is dealing with almost impossibly complex material – as when, in 'The Disturber of Traffic', he is dealing with the fearfully complex delusions of madness. In 'How Fear Came' we have all the charm of the passwords and the taboos, and the power of the description of (for example) the jungle in drought. But of that simplicity we have none. It is, indeed, in its didacticism that the story fails. At that level, like 'The Children of the Zodiac', it is incoherent.

Since it was in the Jungle Books that Kipling first set out consciously to expound a philosophy of life, now is the appropriate time to consider Noel Annan's essay, 'Kipling's Place in the History of Ideas'.

The job of demolishing the notion of Kipling as no more than an apostle of extreme imperialism has already been well done. But, with few exceptions, such as the essay by Alan Sandison, 'Kipling: The Artist and the Empire', it was almost too well done. One might be forgiven for gaining the impression that the Kipling rehabilitated by W.W. Robson, John Bailey, Angus Wilson and other shrewd, interesting and valuable commentators, was either a liberal at heart, or that his politics did not matter. It has been disingenuous of a few recent critics to make such claims as that Kipling saw the menace of Nazi Germany before most of his countrymen, or that he was almost alone in discerning the cruelty of the Boers. Alas, he was not against either Nazis or Boers because of their cruelty. When he protested at and helped to exaggerate the extent of German atrocities after 1914 this was because he hated the Germans, not because he hated the atrocities. The humanity in him did not operate at a polemic level. His imaginative attitude to these peoples is another matter, as his stories about Germans demonstrate.

Kipling's politics were grotesque. He was provocative and brash and always too full of hatred, alienating himself from many readers. Fortunately Kipling never projected an epic of empire (*Puck* is no epic). I have sought to separate what I can of him from his politics, and to explain, with sympathy, why he developed such a set of opinions. Bailey, Robson and others can quite properly ignore Kipling's political opinions when they are examining his achievement in individual tales. But these cannot be ignored in the larger context of his life.

Imperialism was not a conspiracy to make money, or to benefit the wealthy, as has been charged. It was an accident. The Empire might just have 'paid' for itself – but if it did, then it certainly paid those who did not need further pay. But it did provide a far more capacious refuge for scoundrels than ever mere patriotism did. One must not, in loving Kipling for what he did give us, pretend that he was not in many ways monstrous. This is not a question of politics. Kipling was not politically educated, and ought to be described as an extremist rather than as a man with political opinions. In that connection, it is salutary to remember that it was the moderate right which he alienated – much more than the centre-left and the left, to whom he was a gift. Conservative thinkers did not like to see their ideas caricatured and rendered cruel and inhumane. Kipling, even in the Jungle Books, took advantage of the fact that cruelty was one means through which boys gained education; obsessed by this to the exclusion of so much else, he illogically concluded that cruelty was *the* means of education, and that it must therefore be promulgated. His law is in one aspect a Law of cruelty. Hence his excited admiration for Mussolini – the sole means of his interest in modern Italy. He did not see that Il Duce was a sawdust Caesar: he rejoiced, with unconscious sadism, in the cruelties Mussolini inflected on his fellow countrymen. That was educating them in the realities! So Kipling fails, except when he overcomes himself, at an important point: seeing that life is cruel, he seeks to exalt cruelty into a method of education to be forced on everyone. He was thus able to send his own son – despite his very real love for him – to a (then) militarily inclined school, to wish upon him his own ambitions, and to fiddle his admission into the Guards despite his poor eyesight, and thus to hasten his death. John Kipling, though loved, was for him little more than a vicarious hero. Kipling never said to him: 'What do *you* want, son?' One does not say this to accuse Kipling, but to draw attention to the self-critical feelings he had, and endured in silence. He never spoke of his feelings of guilt about having wanted to make his son into the hero he himself could not be. But he had them.

Annan seeks to elevate Kipling to the status of serious thinker, only then to deflate him as an apostle of a vague creed that he, Annan, thinks he dislikes. It is a pointless exercise, and it bears little relationship to the facts. But it is persuasively presented and sounds as though it has been considered. It is worth pausing over: it has been influential, and serves well to demonstrate the essential tawdriness of Kipling's thought, judged simply as 'thought', rather than as the outcome of a particular set of difficult circumstances.

Annan asserts that Kipling's conception of 'history and politics' is 'far more disturbing' than his supposed imperialism. He then states that he is the 'sole analogue' in late Victorian England to the three turn-of-the-century Continental sociologists, Pareto, Durkheim and Weber, whom he unwisely lumps together (it is Annan's business to have heard of the anthropologist Radcliff-Brown, another 'sole analogue'). His view of these three thinkers as sinister, disturbing and fascistic is, incidentally, an over-simplification: they were all quite beyond such considerations, and their ideas were much more delicate and well argued than were any of the ideas underlying imperialism.

Briefly, Durkheim, the French sociologist, son of a rabbi, insisted that what he called 'social facts' existed in their own right, and apart from individualistic considerations. He analysed suicide by means of official statistics and thought that he had demonstrated that suicide is related to degree of social cohesiveness rather than to individual decisions. (It was later convincingly shown, although Annan does not mention this, that the official statistics were inaccurate, and were biased in favour of the thesis.) Durkheim, who was a profound – and therefore often contradictory – thinker, believed that social facts existed independently of individuals and made sense in terms of their relationship with other social facts, and of what they actually did. Thus a ritual dance invoking a good harvest which might seem silly and superstitious really had a useful function: it was a metaphor by which all the people could affirm the importance of collectivity in their struggle for survival in a hostile environment. There might not be a good harvest; but, even if not, social solidarity is nevertheless promoted. Durkheim, himself an unbeliever – he was, although again Annan fails to mention this, an almost convinced guild socialist, utter anathema to Kipling – saw all religious practices as means of promoting social solidarity, and in his least inspired moments even had visions of a grand secular religion.

The work of Durkheim, Weber and Pareto had vital consequences, and led to crucial developments in anthropology and sociology. But Annan's sleight of hand in attempting to connect all this with Kipling is not short of breathtaking. He claims that Kipling resembled Weber in that he was not concerned with the truth or otherwise of religion, but with its social function. This is nonsense. Kipling was so desperately concerned with the truth of religion, that he actually wanted to be protected from it, to have a taboo on it. He thus, so far as he was himself concerned, sacralised it. True, such a story as 'The Disturber of Traffic' is concerned with society and with the way it works, but it is also concerned with the individual, Dowse, and with the place of his sanity in it. Such concern is in any case quite unrelated to social theory. Annan tries to draw parallels between what he sees as 'Kipling's social theory' (it could be inferred from what he writes that Kipling actually had read Durkheim, and discussed him, or that he evolved a conscious social theory *per se*) and a very vague and

selective set of ideas which he wrongly attributes to Weber, Durkheim and
Pareto – almost as if these very different thinkers were one man. He has in
mind Homans' 'Methodological Individualism', a theory which is opposed
to functionalism, and which asserts that all sociological explanation is
reducible to individual characteristics. But Annan does not tell us this.
In fact Annan is just dragging Kipling into this argument, and using him
for extra-literary purposes. Homans and other theorists argued that 'social
facts' were an abstraction, and that all functionalist arguments depend
ultimately on interpretations of individual behaviour. It is not necessary
to go into the merits or demerits of these theories here; but it should be
observed that Annan does not make the issues lucid, but over-simplifies
them for his own muddy purposes. Thus it suits him to present Kipling
as a unbeliever, as Durkheim was. He draws false parallels between the
anthropologist Malinowski's observations about ritual and utterances of
Kipling's. Malinowski, because he was a functionalist, is nonsensically
represented by implication as a sort of substitute for Durkheim, almost
as though Durkheim and Malinowski meant exactly the same thing by
functionalist, or as if both were sociologists. Thus, Malinowski is quoted as
saying (rightly) that 'precisely because savages understood that no magic
or ritual could bring the dead back to life, the need for regulating emotion
by ritual was all the stronger', and then suggests that Kipling's lines

> Unless you come of the gipsy stock
>   That steals by night and day,
> Lock your heart with a double lock
>   And throw the key away . . .

echo this thought. But there is no connection. Such parallels are fiercely
strained. For this poem, 'Gipsy Vans', which is an integral part of the
story 'A Madonna of the Trenches', is not an attack on gipsies, as Annan
represents it to be.

Kipling's famous 'harsh truth' about social relationships, set against
cant and even against official public school and army ideology (the most
famous example is the Jelly Bellied Flag-Flapper in *Stalky & Co.*), has no
affinity with Durkheim's thinking, which was in the first place prompted
by an earnest desire to reconcile individual with social pressures (an
aspect of it Annan chooses to ignore). Reading of Durkheim in this essay
one might imagine that he resembled a Frenchman like Péguy, who went
over from socialism to mystical right-wing nationalism. Durkheim was
never like that, and the subtleties and rich confusions of his writing never
reflect anything as heroically clear-cut. Annan presents Kipling's Law as
a social theory, but, as we have seen, it begs questions in a way that no
social theory could possibly afford to do, and is not even coherent. But a
single example ought to be given. Let us take the concept of obedience, so
important (or apparently so important) in Kipling. It is certainly important
in social theory, where it has to be justified. Obedience is something
Kipling always preached, and he refers to it decisively at the end of
the poem quoted above: 'The Law of the Jungle'. In terms of his own life
and the source of the vigour in some of his best stories – in *Soldiers Three*,
for instance – this makes no sense. The disobedience of his robust and
Falstaff-like rankers is, as we all know, the primary source of their life for

us. Kipling's account of his childhood at Portsmouth isn't by any means an exhortation to children in similar positions to obey. He tells us how he learned not to. We all know that subscription to obedience, in Kipling, is a means to disobey! Kipling is thus profoundly subversive, as well as conventional and conformist, and at no point in his work (especially at the point when he brings in his clumsy, pseudo-gnomic conception of the Law) is this sense of individual subversiveness intellectually justified. We are now confronted, though, with Annan's claim that Kipling, far from being an imaginative writer of fiction and poetry, and bounded as are all such writers by ambiguities and contradictions, is really no more than a political philosopher of unusual rigour! We should therefore expect the role of obedience in this remarkable and hitherto unacknowledged social theory to be particularly clearly justified. In such an early positivist and atheist theory as that of Thomas Hobbes the greatest attention is paid to the reasons why subjects must obey the admittedly unpleasant Leviathan of the state. But Kipling does not give any *reason* at all for his insistence on obedience, a principle which is consistently undermined throughout his work. There is simply not the kind of coherence in 'How Fear Came', or in any other part of the Jungle Books in that respect, that can even begin to express good philosophical reasons, aside from primitive fear, *why* people should obey. The Law, then, is a set of conventional precepts, such as,

> When Pack meets with Pack in the Jungle, and neither will go from the
> trail,
> Lie down till the leaders have spoken – it may be fair words will prevail.
>
> When ye fight with a Wolf of the Pack, ye must fight him alone and afar,
> Lest others take part in the quarrel, and the Pack be diminished by
> war.

which has the rhetorical power of 'I'm telling you, kids, as your entertainer and wise old friend who has had to grow up, that is how it ought to be', but no intellectual weight whatsoever, and not even the pretence of one. This is about as effective as political philosophy as scouting turned out to be in the prevention of war, pornography and all the other Victorian evils.

Annan, having thus set up the Law as though it were valid social theory, pronounces that it 'follows that those who broke the Law were outside the pale of civilisation'. But Kipling's best work is, sometimes compassionately, about that individual sense of aloneness which in itself 'breaks' the Law, which is in his own hands no more than a dummy to frighten away the ghosts. One has only to think of Dowse, who went mad in serving the Law. Annan is perfectly right when he draws attention to Kipling's purely instinctive (and religious-minded) anti-positivism, and his preference for schemes that cannot be rationally explained. But he forgets that Durkheim, of whom Kipling is a supposed 'analogue', wished to codify, in a rational manner, all the mysterious social facts that he alleged existed in their own collective right: his *conscience collective*. Kipling saw the positivism of Comte, which he rejected, as an attempt to give a scientific explanation of the facts of human social existence. Annan also forgets or ignores that one of the most powerful influences upon Durkheim was Comte. Annan actually states that Kipling worked out his theory of society 'thoroughly'! But one must at this point ask him to point to the coherence in the Law as expounded in 'How Fear Came'. After a circular discussion of *Kim* Annan suddenly reasserts that 'Kipling's scheme of things . . . rests on a highly articulated analysis of society in which none but socialized individuals exist'. The *chutzpah* of this would take one's breath away if it were not so patently absurd in the light of Dowse, of Dick Heldar, of Mrs Bathurst, of 'Click' Vicary (that so-socialised individual!) and all the others. Then, evidently anxious to escape before he can be discovered in the nonsense he is propounding, he adds, after claiming for Kipling a formidable 'mind', and a special *'cleverness'* (which he italicises), that 'he was not Social Darwinist, as Wells argued'.

Now this is, strictly, true. But it is true only because Kipling cannot be categorised as having held any position that is reached by rational thought. He was an emotional imperialist; but imperialism was never a position reached by thinking – and imperialism fed Kipling's work only in a negative way. In fact Wells was right inasmuch as all Kipling's emotional assumptions happened to be of a Social Darwinist type. That Kipling thought he hated Herbert Spencer is quite irrelevant: what he hated in him was the idea that everything could be explained scientifically – in the light of reason. If he had understood Durkheim he would have hated him for the same reason, as well as for playing with Utopian-socialist ideas. Social Darwinism, which reached its most offensive peak in the writings of the American William Graham Sumner (whom Kipling might well have read, and with sympathy), had both an emotional and an intellectual compo-nent. The intellectual one, that natural selection operated on society (or amongst races) was soon shown to be fallacious; but this was well beyond the scope of Social Darwinism's more emotional adherents, who merely pointed to it as an intellectual justification. This was still a popular view in the Thirties and Forties, and the sayings of the now happily forgotten Sir Arthur Keith were often quoted: that war was nature's pruning fork and that 'social evolution' demanded racial prejudice as a necessary mechanism in 'natural selection'. All that Kipling explicitly stated about society was Social Darwinist in spirit, whether he was aware of it or not. One of the bases of imperialism was the Social Darwinist assumption that the 'fittest' races would continue to dominate. Annan can hardly turn round and say that Kipling, as well as being a profound social thinker, as well as England's sole analogue to Durkheim/Pareto/Weber (take your pick) was not an imperialist.

Such anthropology (there is confusion between this and sociology in Annan's essay) as Kipling did absorb most probably went willy-nilly into his imagination, rather than fuelled his imperialistic assumptions. That is to say, he took from it exactly what his relaxed imagination wanted, provided there was nothing in it – no liberal assumptions – to offend him. I doubt if he was even open to any theories his reading-matter offered him. As he said to Rider Haggard in the passage quoted below, he wasn't a 'philosopher'. He was just a man who had passing thoughts. He did read the work of Sir Edward Tylor, deservedly regarded as one of the founding fathers of anthropology. In *Primitive Culture* (1871) Tylor put forward his theory of animism, the belief that 'primitive man' saw all natural phenomena as endowed with 'spirit'. By this he sought to account for religion: primitive men needed explanations of experiences such as dreams and loss of loved ones through death, and so arose the conception of soul. Durkheim opposed this notion, preferring to think of religion in terms of what it actually does. From what we know, Kipling simply delved into the two volumes of Tylor's book to get what he wanted from it. Thus, writing to Rider Haggard on 28 February 1925, he said, misspelling Tylor as Tyler (the Taungs skull, discovered in 1924, is about a million years old):

> By the way I don't believe anything ever was 'primitive' in the world after the time of the Taung's skull. I bet your early Gippos were as stale and world-used as any one on the planet now. And I bet, too, they knew it. You've gone back pretty far into history of the ages, and behind 'em, but I notice your people are much like our folk. It stands to reason old man that the world's *very* limited modicum of thinking was done millions of years ago; and that what we mistake for thought nowadays is the reaction of our own damned machinery on our own alleged minds. Get an odd volume of Tyler's *Primitive Culture* and see how far this squares with fact. Not being a philosopher, I haven't time to develop the thesis.

Now what is interesting about this, *pace* Annan and his belief that Kipling was a great social theorist, is that it demonstrates beyond any doubt that Kipling treated *Primitive Culture* just as a source-book, and no more. For Tylor's view, which had been taken up and developed by Spencer, and rejected as over-intellectual by Durkheim, was an optimistic and quasi-Social Darwinist one: he saw society as evolving: proceeding from animism, to ancestor worship, to polytheism, and then to monotheism. Kipling, in the letter to Haggard, is (unwittingly) denying Tylor's main thesis. But he was not concerned with it and almost certainly didn't know what it was, or how it had been developed in successive books. Curiously, what he is saying there is, in its entirely unsophisticated way, much nearer to the emotional position of Lévi-Strauss, who doesn't think that 'primitive' people are primitive at all, and would agree with Kipling that most of the real thinking was done at the year dot.

A much subtler essay than Annan's is 'Kipling: The Artist and the Empire', by Alan Sandison, who has read the stories with attention. He immediately concedes that 'Kipling vigorously beat the imperial drum'. Sandison sees at once that, in talking about society at all, Kipling was concerned, not with it, but with 'self and individual consciousness'. He praises him for what others have called his subaltern-worship, whose components, he thinks, are very like the 'few simple notions' recommended in Conrad's *Lord Jim*. That is a tenable position, but Kipling nervously overdoes it, and fails; Conrad, by underplaying it, succeeds. The trouble with Sandison's essay, for all its deep insight and careful attentiveness to Kipling's words, is that it tries to make him out to have been a consistent man. Sandison just can't accept that one part of Kipling thought it knew all about everything, while another knew that it did not, and therefore fruitfully speculated: was without any irritable reaching after fact or reason (as Keats so beautifully put it). Sandison falls into the error of asserting that Kipling believed in the 'artist's vocation', and chides Edmund Wilson for denying it – as though there were a straight choice between whether he did believe in it or whether he did not. It depends on what Kipling you want to refer to. Kipling the thoughtless and angry imperialist who wished he had been an efficient man of action did not believe in the artist's vocation because he wanted to be seen as a tough man despising it. Kipling the writer, on the other hand, could defend it – or, best, just get on with a job he could sometimes do. There are these different Kiplings and they have less relationship to one another than puzzled commentators like to think. It does not seem to make sense that there was a Kipling who delighted in his son John, and desired him to become whatever he would be happiest in being, and also a Kipling who could not resist living vicariously through an object called John who would fulfil his own crude military fantasies. But that is the case. Men consist of many such wholly disparate selves, and it is not often that these selves even know anything about one another (though some of them exist in clusters). In Kipling the awareness of this human peculiarity functions at only a low level; in Proust (say), a deeper writer, it functions at a higher level.

But Sandison is right when he says that 'community', for Kipling, 'is valued not for the particular morality on which it is based but for the effect it secures – the reassurance of the individual's integrity'. Unlike Annan, he has not mistaken the absence of much human psychology in Kipling's work for a lack of interest in the individual. He could, of course, have been less polite about the matter and substituted some more pejorative term for 'individual integrity'. Later he is less polite. He suggests that we read the stanza about the 'veil' in 'The Prayer of Miriam Cohen' as an indication of Kipling's recognition that 'the self seeks reassurance of integrity in society and commitment . . . But this involves sacrifice, for the creation of society means, for the individual, a partial surrender of integrity . . . every contribution to the society is an erosion of the self which it is designed to identify and protect.' I cannot myself see that these verses, prefatory to 'The Disturber of Traffic', can be thus interpreted, although they may carry that implication at one level. Would that Kipling's language had at that point proved richer and more poetic! But Sandison, in incidentally dealing the death-blow to Annan's thesis (as he says, 'in "The Mother Hive" the doctrine "we and the hive are one" is completely rejected'), is right that an intuitive awareness of the loss to the individual that communality entails is paramount in Kipling's work, where it functions with the same tragic intensity that loss of personal identity (in death) does in the work of Unamuno.

> For the eternal question still is whether the profit of any concession that a man makes to his Tribe, against the light that is in him, outweighs or justifies his disregard for that light.

Sandison quotes Kipling as saying this in a speech. It is a quotation Annan would have done well to ponder. The 'light' to which Kipling is alluding is the essentially lonely one of the sense of self-assertion that all men possess. He possessed it to a remarkable degree, and first became aware of it when he found himself at Southsea. Such phenomenological recognitions as this are not the result of thought, but of a finely developed sensibility. He did see the costs of what he called Man's 'personal independence of action' (doing what you want to do regardless – with him, it was not subtler than that!). If he seemed to have special reservations about the 'unworthiness' of the self in its loneliness, then these must be put down to his notions about 'abnormality', as he put it to Hugh Walpole. As

Sandison says, 'he was too jealous and uncertain of his own soul ever to be magnanimous, and a real, unhampered, outgoing warmth for humanity is present only sporadically in his work . . .' And this warmth, Sandison thinks, is too often 'reined and snaffled by his own selfishness'. This has to be conceded. There is the acute sense of the existence of tenderness in the work, implying that he, too, had felt it. But the work in itself is not tender. It is too afraid. Sandison quotes the end of 'The Children of the Zodiac', when Kipling suddenly loses control and turns on those who will dare to be tender, whom he calls 'little mean men, whimpering and flinching and howling because the Houses kill them and theirs, who wished to live forever without pain'. He thus withholds his sympathy for himself, for it is he who whimpers and complains and cannot be strong. That attitude is, as Sandison says, 'flawed': he is a 'mean-white', and not a 'true-blue', Conservative. Sandison sees that he never really cared about the Empire at all: 'His guilt was obvious to all – so obvious that it concealed the fact that he was not writing to express the Idea of Empire.' Sometimes the Kipling who whined irritably about the loss of a son (when most others did not, and behaved in the seemly manner Kipling himself recommended), is apparent in the work in an ugly way. For his attitude was egoistic and self-regarding. He told Haggard that he had been 'lucky' to lose his own son early: 'If he had lived to see this war he would have been dead or mutilated.' He tended to use the loss of John to express his sense of grievance against the liberals in the government, and he less frequently expressed the loss of *John*.

Trilling spoke of Kipling's 'snarl of defeated gentility'. Sandison calls it a snarl, rather, of 'dog in the manger'. No one, certainly, has missed the snarl. I think of it as the yelp of a man who had been doubly defeated in love: by the custom which he pretends to revere but knows it is a sacrifice to observe, and by death. This is the perpetual 'solipsist', as Sandison rightly charges, who has been forced to manufacture a false love and then to surround it with taboos. There is a sense in which Kipling was never happy, because the love of his life (his awful wife) was not spontaneous. But as a historian of the solipsist in his sad and necessarily lonely journey through life, the little savage deprived of his absolute authority, the historian who wants to live for others and once did, desperately, for one (who was not ideal), he has his high value. The two Jungle Books deserve to live for their ease of language, for their reflection of the soul of a man who wishes to become a child again; but they are redolent, too, of authoritarianism and ersatz cosy wisdom. They by no means represent Kipling at the peak of his achievement. They are the work of a man who is having it both ways: relaxing in an innocent world, but also one who is entrenching himself in a thoughtless, self-defensive creed. Those who read it as children are not made wiser by it.

Quarrel

'A dozen gaudy legends explain everything and nothing,' says Van de Water of the quarrel that ended the Kiplings' sojourn in America, where evidently they had purposed to stay permanently. Some say, and Kipling later claimed – but in dramatic circumstances – that this decision was reached for the sake of Beatty, because Wolcott had concernedly raved about him on his deathbed. Others may feel that Carrie wanted to make a point to her family.

In 1894 things had gone well. It had been Kipling's first year of peace and prosperity, and in the dwelling of his own choice. He told Carrie that he felt the 'return of a great strength', and the writing of the Jungle Books gave him concomitant pleasure. The part of himself that most frightened him he now felt he had under control: Mowgli, though uncertain whether he is man or beast, is nonetheless, as he is portrayed, still a child. The Victorians had in common that they regarded the 'beast in man' as terrifying but nevertheless in need of release. What better way to tame this beast than turn him into a child? Kipling managed, too, to achieve some slight proficiency in athletic pursuits: in snow-golf and in skiing, this latter being undoubtedly the height of his attainment. He and his companion the Rev. Day painted their golf balls red, and could make a drive of two miles – on the snow-crust. Socially, and among his few cronies, he gained a reputation for being friendly but 'anything but refined' (Mary Cabot). He liked to impress everyone with his knowledge of how things really were in the harsh world outside. He dressed roughly – the local people thought it was unsuitable for a genius – and did not mind being regarded as an eccentric. From America he continued to criticise namby-pamby liberals who did not understand that Britain needed her army and navy at full strength. He became equally angry, however, whenever any American made a criticism of England. He thoroughly enjoyed being a great big boy, playing his snow golf and writing simplistic but powerful patriotic verses such as 'Shillin'-a Day', and giving parties in his barn, complete with local fiddler, and with facetious notices such as 'Here are the marble pillars, Here is the gilded divan!' written out by himself. Every so often, though, self-criticism would come out, as in the long poem 'The *Mary Gloster*'. He armed himself with what Chalmers Roberts, an American who had known him and who was contacted by Birkenhead, called 'vicious precision' wherewith to attack American history, and was often incapable of separating the holder of an opinion he disliked from his personality.

How much he enjoyed the strict formality employed by Carrie is open to question. But a man can make himself enjoy all sorts of things if he sees no way out of them. The reason Carrie gave for this formality – although it was not her real reason, which may be put down to what Birkenhead calls her *folie de grandeur* and her lust for domination – was that it was necessary to keep the respect of the servants! One of these servants was the coachman Matthew Howard, who was said by the locals to keep his upright stance even when the horses tipped the carriage over. This may have compensated the Kiplings for the fact that, when applying for the job from England, he confessed to a wife and two children. He was told to come to Brattleboro with them. But it was then discovered that he had six more children, whom he 'filtered over', says Birkenhead, in 'discreet driblets'. He would engage a maid for Naulakha; then he would admit to being her father, and so on. Forgiveness was doubtless easier for Carrie because he had worked for an English peer. She was evidently a simple-minded sort of snob. But Kipling was then at the very height of his new fame, so that the style they lived in, while a little ridiculous, was made somewhat less so by his station. Nor was he yet thirty years old.

Kipling was probably the more inclined to accept all this formality, together with a perpetual air of embattlement with the outside world, because things had gone so badly in America between him and the press from the start. Even the Canadian press disliked him, and called him 'eccentric and conceited', 'haughty' and 'ungentlemanly'. The *Springfield Republican*, even nearer to his home, wrote that it was 'to be hoped that Mr Kipling will become acquainted with the B'boro people. It would broaded and deepen his mind and greatly improve his manners.' For all the sympathy we are inclined to grant him in face of the press, he was certainly ungracious, and he had certainly provoked opposition in his writings. Yet he had some healthy fear of the press, and, when hiding in barns from their attentions, would disregard advice to tell them to go to hell: 'they would write it all up in their papers'. He knew, since he had himself written people up in papers. The effect his inability to be pleasant to these vultures, which he must sometimes have regretted, had upon his image of himself, together with Carrie's entirely intransigent attitude, should not be underestimated.

It used to be said that Kipling must have had some disreputable secret, for only that could explain the degree of his desire for privacy and his unbending attitude towards strangers. Eventually this notion, which persisted throughout his lifetime, was forgotten. But when Elsie Bambridge died in 1976 it enjoyed a temporary revival. 'WHAT DID KIPLING'S DAUGHTER WANT TO HIDE?' asked the *Sunday Times*. Elliot L. Gilbert, the American critic who has written a good critical book about Kipling, *The Good Kipling*, and has edited a selection of his letters to his children, admits that Elsie Bambridge had done much to provoke such vulgar curiosity: she 'made herself notorious by severely limiting access to her father's papers' and by this reticence 'aroused suspicions that there was something in the history of the Kiplings requiring concealment'. Then, of course, she forbade Birkenhead to publish his biography without giving clear reasons. But Gilbert concludes this discussion by quoting Carrington: 'the secret in the Kipling archives is that there no secret.'

That is rather over-simplifying things. There was perhaps nothing 'incriminating' in the papers, but there was a secret. There must have been a secret if only because almost everyone who has ever lived has a secret, or a least something they regard as one. Could Kipling really be an exception?

Scepticism is salutary in the face of vulgar newspaper curiosity, to which we are all prone. But once again, as in the case of establishing that there was something more to Kipling than the famous brash imperialism, the job of 'establishing' that there is 'no secret' has been almost too well done. For, as Gilbert concedes, and as Carrington agrees, the fact that nothing sensational turned up when the Kipling papers found their way to the University of Sussex does *not* prove that there had not been something sensational in them before Carrington saw them, or before Carrie died.

But 'sensational' is not the right word. From the very start of her marriage Carrie made a habit of destroying all but a few incoming letters (such as Haggard's), and suppressing, too, almost all Kipling's drafts. She was altogether too narrow a person to have any sense that letters from famous or important people had any value of their own. The result of her jealous philistinism is that we do not know, for the most part, who wrote to Kipling, or what they said. It is quite likely that she suppressed much of interest pertaining to Kipling and to others. Kipling's own attitude to his public was resentful enough; she, while taking advantage of the privileges it brought her, took resentfulness to an absurd degree. Her hostility to any even sincere interest in her husband's work was legendary, and was noted by everyone. The reason she always gave for adopting these draconian measures was that she wanted to frustrate commercialism. Undoubtedly that was one of her reasons. But it was quite unnecessary. Kipling's papers, including his priceless drafts, showing how he cut his stories down to their final form, could have been put into the care of a university or a museum without any difficulty whatsoever. Indeed, what there is left of the papers has ended up in universities, notably Sussex and Durham. Watt could have looked after the matter without difficulty, and could have made whatever arrangements about access the Kiplings wanted. The archive could have been shut up for fifty years after the death of whoever the Kiplings had wished to stipulate. But can Carrie's jealous nature alone, of which no one has made any secret, be said to account for the mean procedure she did adopt?

I do not believe that jealousy or hatred of commercialism alone can account for the Kiplings' morbid obsession with privacy. Those who thought there was something peculiarly secretive about the Kiplings, but chose to speak of the 'riddle' or the 'enigma' rather than of the 'secret', were, in their way, right. Kipling had by 1893, and with the birth of Josephine and the Jungle Books, given up all disreputable hopes of taking the long trail. He had only Beatty, who took the long trail locally, to admire. He had given it a last try with Carrie, and it had not worked out. Doubtless he thought of the collapse of the Oriental Bank as a card dealt out to him by fate, and therefore one which he had to play. The long trail to him meant, among other things, the indulgence of his 'individual integrity'. He meant by that, mostly, the freedom to love as he wished. If, as I have suggested, Carrie was aware of the nature of his love for her brother Wolcott, and if she had gained her ascendancy by deciding to accept him despite that, then their joint sense that there *was* something to hide becomes instantly and completely explicable. Kipling would continue to write – perhaps now mainly to delight children – and would do his job to the best of his ability. They would exercise their right to privacy, and keep absolutely everyone from nosing in where they were not wanted or entitled. Carrie's guardianship of her husband, which became notorious within months of their settling at Brattleboro, then takes on an entirely different complexion.

It can now easily be understood why everything was taken to be so private. The morbidity of it all, noted by everyone, was generated by a very real fear, a fear that was not just a sense of shame, but one of disclosure. There was also a very real sense in which Carrie, especially given the nature of the era, did have the black on her husband, although whether she actually put it there is another matter altogether. The relationship has frequently been thought of as an abnormal one. So it was: strange and always, in one way, strained.

In 1894, though, all was as well with them as it ever would be. The Beatty situation must have been still good, since they left Josephine and their house and the staff in his charge when they went away. There is no doubt that Kipling liked Beatty very much, and that he gave him money (he still had some control over this) when he was in debt: Beatty would whistle outside the house, and Kipling would slip out with the necessary. He admired him as he admired dashing lieutenants: he got away with it, didn't he? Alas, Carrie was jealous of that, too.

They took a holiday in Bermuda early in the year, before visiting England and Lockwood and Alice. In Bermuda Kipling, with Carrie in close attendance, made friends with a sergeant, took tea with him in his married quarters, and wrote 'That Day' as a celebration of this meeting. He was never stand-offish with men in uniform. When they got back to Brattleboro before going off to England, they found that Beatty had got into debt; but this was amicably settled. Lockwood and Alice had settled at a little town in Wiltshire called Tisbury, but Rudyard and Carrie did not stay with them: Alice rented another house for them. While there Kipling continued with four of the Jungle Book stories. He also wrote some farcical stories such as 'My Sunday at Home', not his best. He enjoyed his fame in London to the full. Being with his parents always lent him confidence.

A conflict seems to have arisen at this point, although Carrington does not call it that. Kipling was so taken with England – and clearly he enjoyed the company of his parents, even if Carrie could hardly have been expected to, since they, and especially Alice, did not like her – that he thought of asking Ambo Poynter to design and build for them a cottage somewhere on the coast. But Carrie would not have it: there 'were several family reasons, she thought, why they must live in America'. She got her way, as she always did. But what were these 'family reasons' unless simply that the Kipling parents disliked her, and were sad to see their famous and successful son married to her? In his letters home to England, to such as Henley, Kipling made a virtue of his solitude. But how much did he enjoy it really, and how much did he care when they were forced to leave? He deeply resented the American policy of encouraging wholesale immigration – although he showed much sympathy to immigrant workers, and so once again contradicted himself – and he can hardly have been pleased when an outfit calling itself the Cornhill Press issued his *Times* essay 'In Sight of Mount Monadnock' as a 'privately printed' pamphlet in 1894. It was the Americans who did these things – not the English. He was so plagued by autograph-hunters that Carrie arranged with the *New York Herald* for his autograph to be sold at $2.50 a time – proceeds to the Fresh Air Fund. She did enjoy thwarting people: it was part of her passion for domination. But she was also very practical.

When they returned to Naulakha they had the services of the cockney coachman, Matt Howard, who was himself generally liked. There was, however, an exception: Beatty. The Kiplings used Howard to do odd jobs that had once been his province; they, or at least Carrie – but Carrie's will was by now Rudyard's will – were trying to ease him out. Acrimoniousness began to creep into the atmosphere. Carrington blandly states how much better 'brought up' Josephine was than her cousin Marjorie (Beatty's daughter), and how she became as bright as Marjorie although only half her age. The Balestiers, Carrington comments, 'lived a harum-scarum life'. This reflects Carrie's view of the matter, and it is unlikely that she bothered to hide it from anyone. She would tell Beatty that Marjorie was a bad influence on Josephine. Kipling cannot much have liked this. But he went along with it. Since she was a snob – there is no point in calling her anything else – one can imagine how all this was received by Beatty and his cronies: Beatty, who was always in the wrong because he always owed money, and was always being reminded of it by his superior sister, whose daughter had so many more of the benefits of virtue than his own did, and who was already making this evident by her greater cleverness . . . Furthermore, hadn't she shown him forbearance? Undoubtedly she had, too. We need to allow for Beatty's provocation of his sister to explain what followed. There can be no doubt that, as he found his work cut down and his presence unwelcome, he increasingly indulged himself in this pastime.

But early in 1895 Kipling, in his letters to Norton and others, still spoke kindly of Beatty. Carrie may have become increasingly neurotic and difficult in her search for domination of her family; in February she received a severe scorch when she opened an oven, which 'naturally upset her very much', Kipling told Norton. She made the best of it, and protracted the consequences by getting a painful inflammation of the eyelids. In this same letter he wrote:

> I have a yearning upon me to tell tales of extended impropriety – not sexual or within hailing distance of it but hard-bottomed unseemly yarns, and am now at work on the lamentable history of a big fat Indian administrator who was, in the course of duty, shot in his ample backside by a poisoned arrow, and his devoted subordinate sucked the wound to the destruction of his credit as an independent man for the rest of his days. One can't be serious always.

This is quoted by Birkenhead and Carrington. Carrington, though, unaware of course that Birkenhead had done so, omits the passage from 'and am now at work' to 'days', without ellipses: did he, or Elsie, think this distasteful, and feel that the great man's reputation ought to be preserved from such childish vulgarity? This, it must be added, leads one to suspect that if so innocent a matter can be excised, then any other evidence could have been, too. Silent bowdlerisation is no light matter. Minor errors, of course, are; but this cannot be an error: it is a suppression of a fact, no matter how comic or how minor. Carrie no doubt had as much say in the literary affairs of her husband as her compatriot Fannie did in the affairs of Robert Louis Stevenson – and to her we owe the loss of the first *Jekyll and Hyde* in the fire. Carrie did a great deal of moaning, and may well have tried to interfere in what Kipling was writing. If she suppressed much of this 'comic' kind then we owe her more than we owe Fannie Stevenson; but that is incidental and accidental. Dr Conland sent her off, or she got Conland to send her off, on a holiday to Washington, where they stayed in rooms for six weeks. She whined at the expense and, Carrington says, her hair turned grey. It is likely that at the time she was both troubled by Beatty and jealous of Kipling's fame. She could never be happy for long. Perhaps this is why it was felt by the Kiplingites that her diary must, after having been consulted for the details of Kipling's activities, be destroyed. People do not destroy such documents just for the sake of it: they destroy them because they feel they contain something discreditable – either to the writer, or, sometimes, to others mentioned. Birkenhead gives enough examples from it for us to judge how it must have read.

It was during these weeks in Washington that Kipling was taken to meet President Cleveland in the White House. He was disgusted by him and his associates, and called them 'a colossal agglomeration of reeking bounders'. Cleveland was anti-imperialist, and took the side of Venezuela (though for entirely political reasons) in a border dispute she was having with Great Britain; this perhaps accounted for Kipling's hatred of him, although Cleveland did not empower his Secretary of State, Olney, to send the famous 'strong note' on the question until July 1895. Theodore Roosevelt, whom he also met at this time, he liked, and remained in correspondence with for the rest of his life. Roosevelt's advocacy of the 'strenuous life' and his notion that to do good one 'had to speak softly and carry a big stick' were nectar to him; so far as Kipling was concerned he never put a foot wrong politically – especially towards the end of his life, when he tried to get America into the war against Germany. Both men thoroughly enjoyed arguing about the relative merits of Great Britain and America.

In 'William the Conqueror', a story in two parts which he began in March 1895 and published in the *Gentlewoman* at the end of that year (and then in *The Day's Work*), Kipling resumed his exploration of the theme of the emancipated woman, which he had begun with Maisie in *The Light that Failed*. Overrated at the time it appeared, it has been variously suggested to owe its central character to Carrie, to Ted Hill, and to the 'boyish young American girls whom Kipling so admired'. More likely it was Kipling's way of getting as close as he could to the memory of Wolcott, whom he must continually have seen in both Beatty and in the mannish Carrie.

Beatty was now giving serious trouble. As early as October 1894 Carrie was confiding her complaints of him to her diary: he had spoiled a 'glory of a day' with a 'complication'. In June 1895, after they returned from Washington, William James and his wife came to stay. William James had long before written diffidently ('I have been ashamed to write of that infant phenomenon, not knowing, with your exquisitely refined taste, how you might be affected by him and fearing to *jar*') to his brother to express his appreciation of this 'biggest literary phenomenon of our time', 'more of a Shakespeare than anyone yet in this generation of ours', who fed 'the public on his own bleeding insides'. At the time of this visit, there was trouble with Beatty over a tennis court, disagreements about the hay crop, and a row about draining the pasture. The Kiplings were about to go to England again for a few weeks, and this time they left Matthew Howard in charge.

Howard's efficiency was certainly held up as an example. These difficulties with Beatty – in his way as jealous a character as his sister – were annoying to Carrie, but, as Carrington suggests, 'ruin' to him. He began to drink more, and clearly began, too, to harbour feelings of revenge against his sister and her upstart husband. For quite some time – although not as much as a year, as was suggested in evidence – the two households were hardly on speaking terms. But Kipling tried to call on Beatty and failed to gain admittance, and vice versa – or so they both eventually claimed. The respectable Carrie cannot have liked Beatty's habit of ringing a great loud bronze bell hanging in his porch and shouting across the valley:. 'God damn it, come and have a drink!' But such behaviour tormented Kipling: he admired it, but had to pretend he did not when Carrie protested with all the vehemence of a woman used from childhood to the trail of havoc Beatty left behind him. Others, she could justly complain, always had to pay for his fun and generosity.

As Van de Water says, there must have been 'many seepages of incompatibility, jealousy, pride and anger into a volatile mixture'. The details were fiercely suppressed by Rudyard and Carrie; and even Beatty claimed, when he told Van de Water his side of the story in 1935, that it was the 'first time . . . he had told it to anyone'. 'And I'll be goddamned,' he added, with what Van de Water called a 'puzzled half indignant glare', 'if I know why I've told it to you.' Perhaps he was prompted by news of Kipling's death. Van de Water says he much wanted to hear the tale, but did not ask. Whereas Kipling, in writing his last book, omitted all mention of the affair, Beatty 'was proud of the enduring scandal he had fathered'. 'Scandal never shamed him. He was the word made flesh.' After his death a few months after Kipling's he quickly became a legend: drinker, horseman, spendthrift – and justice of the peace. He died bankrupt, wizened, almost a cripple, half-blind, wearing a cock's feather in 'the band of his hat that hid the wen on his head'. It seems more than likely that a character of this kind, and the brother of Wolcott to boot, would have attracted Kipling. He was, after all, even though he could hardly ever afford to leave his own district, very much of what might be called, in the Kipling context, a 'long trail' man. And it must be said that although he had a habit of getting things wrong, and delaying them, he seems eventually to have got them right – at least at this time of his life. Kipling had to admit in the Brattleboro courthouse that he had paid back every penny of any loan. How much the trouble cost Kipling in terms of personal friendship cannot be estimated. But, for Beatty, the world was either for or against him, and when he turned against Kipling he turned against him with a ferocity that could match anything the aggressive writer could bring forth. What must always have galled Carrie was that Beatty, for all his misdeeds, was more respected in his own country than ever she was. For all that he was a heavy drinker, people would go to him for advice – on how to get their taxes reduced, and even on 'the folkways of Vermont, precious if unnegotiable information'. Where he erred, as he so often did, they said, 'That's just Beatty.'

The Kiplings went off on 1 July 1895 for their holiday in London and Tisbury. When they returned they found things in good order, owing to Matthew Howard. And while Kipling was writing perhaps the worst of all his stories, 'The Brushwood Boy', and poems, Carrie was lending Beatty money and even guaranteeing his bills. There must still have been some sympathy between them, and doubtless Kipling kept up whatever pressure he could to keep things peaceful. When Carrie's mother came to stay at Naulakha over the Christmas of 1895 she tried to reconcile her two quarrelling children; but it came to nothing. Doubtless Carrie reminded her mother bitterly of what Wolcott had said when Beatty became engaged to marry the attractive Mai Mendon:

> But Beatty would choose nothing but the best, the best and the most expensive, so she is probably charming. In fact I have his word for it. But they both need a guardian appointed . . . If Miss Mendon would swear a solemn oath before her marriage never to buy anything for which they cannot pay at the moment, or let Beatty have a bill anywhere, she may be sure that will have a solider foundation for happiness than in any single resolution she can take.

But when they did marry it was Wolcott who looked after them, bringing them to England. Carrie was so cold to Mai that she disliked and distrusted her from that time onwards. Carrie undoubtedly had a sense of duty towards this brother, and she had probably used this in order to persuade her husband to settle in Vermont. But she was now finding his disobedience too hard to bear.

But Beatty and Carrie did have their vagrant childhood in common. 'We are all a little crazy,' said Beatty; whether she (or Josephine) cared for that way of putting it is not known. More significantly, perhaps, Beatty had, or had until very recently had, the love of the old Madame – which Carrie had never really had. The whole lot of them were, Carrington perhaps unwisely lets slip, 'as strong-minded' as the old woman, 'united by a strong family feeling and yet rather disposed to disagreement over their social responsibilities'.

In the meantime Kipling was in despair over international events, and decided, along with many others, that there would be a war over the Venezuelan matter. He was even asked to write an article for a New York newspaper on why he thought America could never conquer England. The Kaiser was taking advantage of the situation in South Africa. Kipling's daughter and second child Elsie, who became Mrs Bambridge, was born on 2 February 1896. A month before this, while he was worrying about it, he wrote (8 January) to Norton explaining how he felt. He was almost in a panic:

> I have arranged things so that C ought not to starve; and she has the house and all my copyrights to boot. You see it is obviously absurd for me to sit still and go on singing from a safe place while the men I know are on the crown of it; and it may be that when I am closer to the scene of action I may be able to help with a little song or two in the intervals of special correspondence . . . whether it be peace or war this folly puts an end to my good wholesome life here; and to me that is the saddest part of it.

One side of Kipling was restless and wanted a war – he was not satisfied until there was one, indeed, and one in which he could serve as a special correspondent. But Beatty alone quite soon became the main cause of his inability to remain in America. Cleveland's Venezuelan policy had been mostly an election ploy, and although it was his measures against inflation and his intervention in an Illinois strike that lost him the Democratic nomination (to William Jennings Bryan) in 1896, rather than his foreign policy, the threat of war between Great Britain and America was over almost before it had begun.

Kipling became restless, but, after the birth of Elsie, began to try to bring his old *Mother Maturin* novel to a successful conclusion. The germ of *Kim*, his one successful novel, began to form in his mind; but he yearned for his father's help with this, and was glad to turn to *Captains Courageous*, which was almost a collaboration with Dr Conland – Kipling made no secret of it – who provided all of the material for this story of a spoiled millionaire's son who learns his lesson the hard way, on a fishing trawler. It provided distraction from the quarrel between Beatty and Carrie, now threatening to come to a climax. It is a good boy's romance, and its chief virtue is the convincing manner in which Kipling was able to transfer Conland's memories of the fishing fleets of the 1860s into words. The didactic element in the book adds nothing to it. He wrote of the novel: 'It's in the nature of a sketch for better work: and I've crept out of the possible holes by labelling it a boy's story.' He finished it in October 1896 – by which time he was back in England.

Carrie was still backing Beatty's bills; but at the same time she was easing him out of the regular work he had been doing at Naulakha. Early one morning he was 'caught' – probably by Matt Howard, who must have seemed the epitome of foreign complacency to him – helping himself to Elsie's malted milk. One can imagine Carrie's comments. He took to drinking heavily and then coming up to the house to remonstrate with Kipling, who became too upset to write. At other times, when Howard was driving along in the coach, alone, Beatty would weave drunkenly about in front of him.

Now Carrie tried to get her mother to agree to cease to support his bills. Significantly, Anna Balestier would not do this, for it would have reduced him to bankruptcy. The family, ready always to admit that Beatty was a trial, believed that Carrie was pushing him too hard. They may well have blamed Carrie when Beatty did in fact, on 6 March, file a petition for bankruptcy. She never called on Madame Balestier with her new baby. It had now become a sordid row between a brother and sister, and both were determined to win. Kipling was caught up in it, whatever he thought. As most of us would, he took his wife's side. The family, knowing Carrie, took Beatty's. It is probable that, had Kipling crossed her in the matter, she would have had a nervous breakdown, or experienced another 'accident'.

Matters seem to have come to head over the pasture which Beatty had given to Rudyard and Carrie, but over which he retained some rights. Beatty's temper, though, had not been improved when he was approached by Kipling with an offer – a tactless offer that clearly came from Carrie. If he would go off for a year and find 'regular work' (and be out of sight and sound of Carrie), then the Kiplings would support Mai and Marjorie. What was more, Carrie herself would bring Marjorie up . . . Carrington, who does not try to defend Carrie too strongly over this, nonetheless states that Mai might have been the 'most vindictive' of all concerned. But is that the word to describe the feelings of a mother who has just received an offer from her sister-in-law to bring up her own child? Thus 'they schemed to save him from himself', but without consulting him – as Van de Water puts it. They should have know better than to put such an offer. Didn't he, Beatty, belong there, and weren't they the foreigners? Beatty of course showed neither contrition nor gratitude, but went for Kipling with as yet unexampled ferocity. Both men, egged on by their angry wives, retreated into righteousness.

The two families saw less of each other. The climax of the trouble, as Beatty remembered it, not necessarily entirely accurately, he described to Van de Water:

> We had a fight over property. And by God, I still think I was right. You know that mowing right across from Naulakha? I owned it then. Rud and Caroline wanted it. They were afraid that sometime it would get into other hands and someone would build a house there that would block their view. I told Rud I'd sell it to him for a dollar. I said to him: 'Hell, I don't care about the property as a building site. All I want off it is the hay for my stock. You agree to let me keep mowing it, and you can have it.' And then, by god, I heard that Caroline had had a landscape architect up and was going to turn that mowing into a formal garden. I didn't believe it but when they came one night to dinner at my house, I asked about it and Caroline said it was true. I told her: 'You're in my house; you're my guest but by Christ, once you've left it, I'll never speak to you again as long as I live.' We had a quarrel then, Caroline and I. Rud didn't say anything. He just sat there.

Beatty did not in fact own all of it by then; but he did have rights over it. Obviously Carrie had decided that, in order to spite her, he intended to sell it to someone who would build a house on it. Kipling didn't have the will to check her. He took her part and carelessly told a neighbour, a Colonel Goodhue, that for some time now he had been supporting Beatty: 'I've been obliged to carry him for the last year; to hold him up by the seat of his breeches.' 'By God, that's what he said. "By the seat of his breeches."' So repeated Beatty to Van de Water forty years afterwards, still indignant.

He was certainly indignant, and probably drunk, on the afternoon of Wednesday, 6 May 1896. Kipling loved riding his bicycle, especially when, like a boy, he could coast down hills with his feet on the handlebars. He may have been doing that as he returned home that day after posting a manuscript to London. He was on a small road between Maplewood and Naulakha when he ran into Beatty, who was driving his team of horses with accustomed savagery.

Kipling's behaviour after his experience with Beatty that afternoon will be understood by almost everyone. He was caught in a quarrel, not at all of his making, between two people he loved. But one of them was his wife. The trouble is that his behaviour was, apart perhaps from his initial action, too reasonable. Not too reasonable for us. Too reasonable for him. He can't have looked very good in his own subaltern-worshipping eyes, however good he looked in other people's. He hated scenes, but worshipped them from afar. Beatty reined in his horses sharply and skilfully and roared: 'See here, I want to talk to you!' He was very angry. Kipling had doubtless felt apprehensive about his brother-in-law's mood ever since the decision about turning the pasture into a garden had been taken by Carrie. The co-apostle of strenuous action fell off his bicycle and cut his wrist, picked himself up, and started rubbing it. He looked up at the tall brother of the man he had loved, the uncle of his children, the father of little Marjorie, from his height of five feet six inches, and was alarmed. He was to say later that Beatty was blue with rage. No, decidedly not white, or red, or green. Blue. Kipling may have felt that he was carrying a big stick, but he spoke softly and nervously: 'If you have anything to say you can say it to my lawyers.'

After this Beatty 'seemed crazy, his cheekbones blue with passion': 'By Jesus, this is no case for lawyers, I want you to understand that you have got to retract those Goddamned lies you've been telling about me. You've got to do it within a week or I'll kick the Goddamned soul out of you!'

'Let's get this straight. Do you mean personal violence?'

'Yes, I'll give you a week, and if you don't do it I'll blow out your Goddamned brains.'

'You will have only yourself to blame for the consequences.'

'Don't you dare to threaten me, you little bastard! Liar, cheat, coward!'

Most people have doubted that Beatty said anything about shooting. What happened, they think, is that Kipling went back, in a state of considerable upset – Matt Howard, who seems to have been following him, picked him up a minute or so after Beatty had vanished in a flurry of horses' hooves – and told Carrie what had happened. Now, as Van de Water observes, Mulvaney or Crook O'Neill of the Black Tyrone 'or any other of the valiant men whom Kipling sired would have dragged his traducer from the buckboard and done his earnest best . . .'

It would have been not short of damned silly for Kipling to have tried anything on with this tough farmer. But the fact remains that it would have looked better if he had. And one thousand times better from the famous describer of courage and enthusiastic friend of Theodore Roosevelt. 'It may be,' observes Van de Water unfairly, 'that authors of the most virile prose and verse are at heart the meekest of men.'

Kipling was deeply upset, and no match for Carrie. On the following morning she made him file a complaint against Beatty with Sheriff Starkey in Brattleboro. There is no direct evidence that it was her doing, but it is highly unlikely that Kipling would have done anything so rash without her pressing him to it. 'Those who knew the two men best supposed that they would have laughed off the quarrel if their wives had allowed them,' Carrington writes. As soon as the incident had occurred Beatty rushed off to a neighbour's house and recriminated with himself for having lost his temper. It was the complaint that finally hardened him. And if Mai disliked Carrie then Carrie had her own rudeness, patronage, tactlessness and sour nature to thank. She had tried and failed to make Beatty bankrupt and destitute (doubtless intending to reform him when he was thus down and helpless); now, since he would not listen to her proposals for his soul, he would have to rot in jail. What sweet revenge on a brother whose admirers could never discern his moral worthlessness, nor, perhaps, her own moral worth and good taste in people. Birkenhead tried to make out that Kipling was thinking of a country magistrate lecturing Beatty on the errors of his ways; his account suggests that the two Kiplings were as of one mind. But that is hardly likely. He must have been quite clear in his mind that he was setting the wheels of the criminal law in motion: a threat to kill is a serious matter. It is foolish of Birkenhead to paint him as a bewildered man in terror of his life. He was deeply upset and under the thumb of a wife bent on revenge. He was prevailed upon, in order to keep the act up, to obtain a pistol – and further humiliated when he offered it to the cockney Matt Howard, who said that he would use his fists, thank you. In fact no one ever believed that anyone was going to use a gun.

To call Carrie the sole villain of this sorry piece would hardly be fair. Beatty was a trial – although it is interesting that when the opportunity came, as it did in the courthouse, for Kipling to give details of his financial profligacy he could not deny that every penny he had lent Beatty had been paid back. Was he, one wonders, quite so awful about money as the partisans of Kipling make out? Probably. But Carrie made sure that the dice was loaded against him in that matter. One can sympathise with his sense of indignation that his own sister was out to destroy him on the grounds that she wished to improve his character. I doubt if he said that he would shoot Kipling. But the latter, as the known Laureate of the Deed, would quickly and eagerly have acceded to Carrie's promptings, and before long believed it himself. What Beatty probably said was that he would give him a good hiding. It had been an unpleasant incident, but it got blown up out of all proportion when Carrie forced her husband to draw up a complaint. He must already have felt a fool by the time he heard that Sheriff Starkey had arrested Beatty for 'assault with indecent and approbrious names and epithets and threatening to kill'. Not everyone believed that Beatty had threatened to kill. Most of the gentry backed Kipling and the ornery folk backed Beatty. But not all the gentry backed Kipling: they knew Beatty, and they knew Carrie, and the nature of the conflict between them. Decent people would have felt sorry for Kipling. But they knew very well that Beatty, while a rapscallion and a gambler and an occasional drunk, had never threatened anyone's life, did not carry a gun, and was much more of a good fellow than he was a bad one. Who didn't owe some favour to Beatty? Whereas Rudyard Kipling and his stuck-up wife . . . Beatty was a good-hearted person who would do things for you. Whenever did Caroline Kipling do anyone a favour? Reporters poured in for the kill: they were aching for revenge on the upstart little Englishman and his sour wife who had turned them away so often. Wasn't Mai Balestier claiming that when her husband had demanded some explanation from Kipling for the lies he had been spreading, he had started talking about lawyers? So he was frightened of his own brother-in-law, that good chap. There was a story here all right.

Kipling had suffered before. But this was the most humiliating position that he had ever been in; and the affair was public. He must also have thought about the wife who had got him into this muddle. Was this how people should behave on battlefields? As anyone but Beatty would have done, he dreaded exposure.

Beatty, predictably, was thoroughly enjoying himself. They all went in front of Judge William S. Newton ('Uncle Billy', Beatty's good friend of course – who was not?) on the Saturday morning. Newton, too, while taking the matter seriously, was thoroughly enjoying himself, and was doubtless delighted to get into the papers. Beatty admitted everything except the threat to murder. No, he said, he had merely told Mr Kipling that he would give him a good thrashing. 'Uncle Billy' then said that there was a case to answer, and that he must hold Beatty Balestier. But of course, he added, Mr Balestier would be able and prepared to furnish bond?

Beatty grinned hugely. No, he said, no: he was all ready to go to jail. Thus he was preparing the trap for Kipling. But did he not hate Carrie the most? Certainly later in life (his second wife Nellie said) he spoke well of Kipling, and even said at one point that if only he returned he would 'get all the bands in Brattleboro to play for him'; he never had a good word to say about Carrie, though. Now Kipling saw the trap his wife had dug for him: he would be talked of as the rich foreign author with the stuck-up wife who had cast his 'poor, obscure brother-in-law' into prison on a false accusation. He had been a journalist. He knew that the sympathy of respectable people like Conland or Goodhue did not matter a damn. He was going to be crucified by the press. And so he was.

But the decency and the generosity of the man now came to the fore. He was sorry. In a spontaneous gesture, forgetting Carrie, he took out a chequebook (he was allowed to have one in those days), flourished it, and said, 'I shall be glad to supply the defendant's bail myself.' An odd thing to do if he really believed that Beatty was out to kill him. But it was a telling and, for once, a warm gesture. One wonders what Carrie had to say about it. She described it in her diary as the worst day of her life. Beatty, delighted at the opportunity to remain on his high horse, refused Kipling's offer. But he was released on his own recognisance anyway, to appear on the next Tuesday to answer the charge. His triumph was to come.

Kipling was prostrate, and saw that the reassurances of his respectable friends such as Conland and the Rev. Day were hollow. He even thought that they were laughing at him while they gave him their sympathy – and perhaps a few were. It was the kind of thing that everyone enjoys, and Kipling, who had a coarse sense of humour himself, knew it very well. Had anyone taken Beatty's alleged threat seriously, or believed in it, then they would not have been so amused. He knew that he would lose face, and almost certainly he knew, too, that Beatty had never threatened him with death, merely with a hiding. He was suffering from a sense of 'unworthiness': he had not faced up to Beatty (as he saw it) with dignity, and he had then lied about it. Even if Beatty had said he would kill him, Kipling knew very well that he had not meant it. He had made a fool of himself. The most celebrated writer in the world had lost his dignity, and was being branded as a coward. Soon the papers were printing parodies of his verses, with stanzas such as this:

'What makes the Kipling breathe so hard? said the copper-ready-made.
'He's mighty scart, he's mighty scart,' the First Selectman said.
'What makes his wife look down so glum?' said the copper-ready-made.
'It's family pride, It's family pride,' the First Selectman said.

and

'What's that a-loping down the lane?' said the copper-ready-made.
'It's Rudyard, running for his life,' the First Selectman said.
'Who's pawing up the dust behind?' said the copper-ready-made.
'It's Beatty, seeking brother-in-law,' the First Selectman said.

Wretched stuff, but from Kipling's point of view there was a mite of truth in it. Hopelessly he watched the press pour in, all forty of them welcomed by Beatty – who had sold them his story – in stages and carried off to Maplewood, where they had whisky and talk with that good fellow and his pretty wife. He took them fishing. Here was his chance to score off that sister of his at last! Joseph Balestier, Beatty's favourite uncle, was brought in: he begged him to apologise to Kipling before it was too late. He would not. He saw his chance and was not going to let it go.

State Attorney C.C. Fitts prosecuted Beatty, who was represented by George B. Hitt. Colonel Kittredge Haskins appeared for Kipling, who acquitted himself well, but never stood a chance. He had to admit that he had said to Colonel Goodhue that he had been keeping Beatty 'by the seat of his breeches', or 'by the slack of his pants'. He had to admit that he had *not* been supporting Beatty for the past year – so he was in effect forced to retract what Beatty had in the first place asked him to retract. He was asked: 'Does Beatty owe you money?' and had to answer no, he did not. He had to answer all kinds of personal questions, sarcastically put by Hitt. He had, he claimed, settled in America in order to help 'this poor boy' at the dying behest of his concerned brother. Beatty burst out laughing. 'Ordinary business matters your wife takes care of?' He had to answer, 'yes', probably to a titter. When examined about his fear of being shot he had to admit that he had never seen Beatty with a gun, or known him to go about armed. But he said that he would not retract 'a word under threat of death from any living man'. Beatty was bound over to appear for trial in the following September, for disturbing the peace. But the case never came to court: the only witness fled. It was a situation, with the yellow press out for his blood, in which Kipling could not win; but he impressed a few reporters with 'glimpses of the depth and tenderness of feeling that contribute to his power'. Another paper praised his genius but chided him for his brusqueness, his failure to undertake local social responsibilities, to make more friends. Carrie was equally to blame for that.

He picked up a little, saw the poetry collection *The Seven Seas* into proof, carried on with *Captains Courageous*. But he knew he had to go, and on 28 August, his last day there, said that he only wanted to live in Bombay or Brattleboro, but could not live in either. But he would not admit that they would never return for some years. Much later, when Mary Cabot bought Naulakha from them, Carrie instructed that the words Kipling himself had carved on his desk, *Oft was I weary as I toiled at thee*, be erased. Lockwood's carving over the mantle, *For the night cometh when no man can work*, was allowed to stay.

Stalky

The Kiplings went straight to a large damp house, Rock House, at Maidencombe, near the south coast resort of Torquay in Devon. Although Rudyard's letters to American friends, such as Dr Conland and Mary Cabot, show that he was nostalgic for his New England home – and Carrie still spoke of their return 'under certain conditions' (the death or permanent incarceration of her surviving brother?) – he was for the moment happy to have escaped the recent nightmare. They did not like the new house, and later Kipling wrote a story, 'The House Surgeon', which is said to have been based on his dislike of it, though others dispute this.

From his window he had an idyllic view of the bay and the beach, which was used for lobster fishing. He took to going on fishing trips, and made friends with many local people; he was noticeably more forthcoming in his own country than he had been in America. He was given more freedom of movement by Carrie than he got later, after they had settled at Bateman's. The two of them would go out on a tandem, each imagining that the other was enjoying it.

Josephine kept on asking when they were going home. This upset her father, but, Carrie told Mary Cabot in a letter, 'Mr Kipling never talks of Brattleboro or reads a letter from America or does anything which remotely reminds him of that last year of calamity and sorrow.' That was his lifelong habit – not to refer to anything that had upset him – and from it one may even deduce those events which cut at him most deeply. It may be that the loss of his friendship with Beatty cut him, in this case, even more deeply than the humiliation he had undergone. Certainly the episode confirmed him even more strongly in his political views – ironically, since he had not acquitted himself at all as the philosophy of imperialism dictated. But he was obstinate, and was now looking for a chance to 'prove' himself as some kind of a man of action. Since he could not yet find a war to visit, he at first did this vicariously, in patriotic poems, and in the Stalky fantasy.

Carrie, like many writers' wives, was anxious that Kipling should please the nation, and there are hints that she was having some small success in preventing him from writing such stories as the one about the poisoned arrow. He told Norton that the people of Torquay made him feel he wanted to go out amongst them wearing nothing but his spectacles, so there was some threat of this mood becoming rampant in him; but the air was enervating and made him feel restless and watchful of international events in case he should be called to serve as singer of songs and correspondent. Later the mood did break out, and the result was *Stalky & Co.*

His genius, in these years, and until he took up *Kim* again, was at a low ebb. These are the years of the famous patriotic poems, of 'Recessional' and of 'The White Man's Burden'. But he was depressed at Torquay, and

Carrie told Norton that 'it's not easy to make Rud take what you are pleased to call his genius seriously. He does not believe in it, in the very least.' Norton had written an article on his poetry for the *Atlantic Monthly* (it appeared in January 1897, but evidently Norton sent a proof of it, or an advance copy, in December, for a letter Kipling wrote to Norton about it is dated 31 December 1896). Norton took friendly exception to the 'bad taste' of a few poems, but praised Kipling as a great imperialistic and moral poet; his article seems to have been calculated, among other things, to inspire the British literary establishment – with whom his word had some influence – to appoint Kipling Poet Laureate.

Kipling, with the reproof about tastelessness in mind, wrote back:

> We are both of us awed, and if the truth be told a little scared at your article . . . True it is, most sadly true that I have not been true to my duties but I did not know that I had been so untrue. As you know I love the fun and riot of writing (I am daily and nightly perplexed with my own private responsibilities before God) and there are times when it is just a comfort to let out with the pen and ink – as long as it doesn't do one any moral harm. I don't believe very much in my genius . . . there is the danger, it seems, of a man running off into William Watson's kind of wordy rot, if he, at a comparatively tender age, considers himself a poet . . . I will say just as one says to one's father, when one is little, 'I'll try to think and be better next time . . .'

Now that imperialism is past even its twilight, and the imperialist verse of those concluding years of the nineteenth century cannot really appeal in a retrospectively topical way to anyone younger than about ninety, it is easy to see that Norton was being over-respectable, and was in part wrong in reproaching Kipling for his bad taste. He was right enough when he reproached him (by implication) for being merely childish. But it is always a mistake to try to rein a poet in, and especially on grounds of respectability. Kipling's bursts of undutiful childishness, written when he was not worried about doing himself 'moral harm', usually yielded nothing of interest. Just occasionally, however, they did, even if it is of small account.

An example from these years is the little set of verses that got him, not praise, but much reproof, from the establishment which Carrie most wanted him to satisfy. This poem, 'The Vampire', is frequently quoted as an example of how unpleasant he could be.

His cousin Phil Burne-Jones, who had made a reputation for himself as a rather lurid and sensationalist artist, painted a picture called 'The Vampire', showing a young man lying prostrate on a bed while above him a standing woman, dressed in white, sneers in triumph. Kipling wrote a set of verses to be printed in the catalogue; later he included them in his *The Dipsy Chanty*, an illuminated selection of his poems done in eighty copies by an American, Elbert Hubberd, in 1899, and eventually (1919) in the *Definitive Edition*. The poem is by no means a major one, but is lively and evocative light verse, and much to be preferred to such pieces as 'Recessional':

> A fool there was and he made his prayer
> (Even as you and I!)

To a rag and a bone and a hank of hair
(We called her the woman who did not care)
But the fool he called her his lady fair –
(Even as you and I!)

Oh, the years we waste and the tears we waste
And the work of our head and hand
Belong to the woman who did not know
(And now we know that she never could know)
And did not understand!

A fool there was and his goods he spent
(Even as you and I!)
Honour and faith and a sure intent
(And it wasn't the least what the lady meant)
But a fool must follow his natural bent
(Even as you and I!)

Oh, the toil we lost and the spoil we lost
And the excellent things we planned
Belong to a woman who didn't know why
(And now we know that she never knew why)
And did not understand!

The fool was stripped to his foolish hide
(Even as you and I!)
Which she might have seen when she threw him aside
(But it isn't on record the lady tried)
So some of him lived but the most of him died –
(Even as you and I!)

And it isn't the shame and it isn't the blame
That stings like a white-hot brand –
It's coming to know that she never knew why
(Seeing, at last, she could never know why)
And never could understand!

Apparently Kipling was alluding to Phil's passion for the actress Mrs Patrick Campbell. The lines are not misogynistic – which they are always taken to be – unless one is prepared to grant that there are no worthless women; but the bitterness in them was no doubt a release of negative emotions about Carrie, about whom he was almost always suspiciously (and loyally) positive. That was about the only attitude he could take, short of leaving her, and it would not have occurred to him even to think of that. Indeed, in these years, in Torquay and then in Rottingdean, before chronic depression entirely overtook her, and away from her immediate family, Carrie kept him on a longer leash. But there is little doubt that she continually reminded him of his duties to his public, and of Norton's reproof. His answer was *Stalky & Co.* Carrington's bowdlerisation has drawn ineluctable attention to what must have been a chief feature of the intercourse in the Kipling household (we may assume that mother and daughter were of one mind in at least this): Rud's vulgarity must be controlled. Rud will have felt it his one safety valve. Dreadfully for Carrie, the public enjoyed it.

They gave up the Torquay house in the spring of 1897 and went to London, to a hotel, for a time. Carrie was expecting their third and last child, who was born at North End House, the Burne-Jones's holiday home in Rottingdean, on 17 August. Things had been deteriorating in Devon. The pleasure of the immediate relief from the American episode was spent. He wrote, of the depression that was threatening to engulf him, to Dr Theo Dunham, soon to become his brother-in-law as the husband of Josephine Balestier, in very early 1897:

> ... I've been rather out of sorts. Hipped and depressed from day to day, and this climate does not help ... So I went up to see a doctor. He reduced me to a state of highly improper nudity, and whacked and thumped and tested and did all the old tricks we know so well.
> 'Liver,' says I. 'Liver and ghastly depression.'
> 'Liver be sugared,' says he. 'You haven't a trace of a liver but you've got a colon rather distended with wind. Also you smoke too much.'
> Somehow it seemed to me I had heard that last remark before. Well the net result was that with a tonic, and knocking off tobacco, he pulled me out of the gloom and darkness that had been enveloping me. Being pretty much of the same dark temperament as I am you will understand what I suffered. Well, now I have felt serene – really at ease – for some weeks.

He met most of the famous people who were in London; he was elected to the Athenaeum Club in April (Henry James had seconded him, he told Norton in October 1896), and this gave him a convenient social base. He had had many visitors at Rock House, and even his mother had stayed with them for a time. There are, naturally, no details of the friction between her and Carrie. We should like to know more about what Alice really thought, and what her comments were, for she was a more intelligent woman than her daughter-in-law – and, for better or for worse, men tend to judge women, until quite late on in life, in the light of their mothers. All that material has been destroyed.

Kipling's chief joy at this time was the company of naval men of all ranks, and the chance, frequently taken, to go out in British vessels. Carrington goes so far as to state that he 'changed his allegiance', meaning from the army, 'to the Royal Navy'. First, in October 1896, he took to going down the railway to Dartmouth, where there was a training vessel, the *Britannia*. Here there were officers and cadets, and he was in his element: he always loved to hear details of how cubs were licked into shape without the 'decencies' being violated. In the story about a British whaling vessel, 'The Devil and the Deep Sea', he writes of a 'bright-eyed crew', 'desolate, unkempt, unshorn, shamelessly clothed – beyond the decencies'. He was very interested in the world beyond the decencies.

A little later he was invited to take a cruise with the Channel Fleet. As he told Conland, he was 'in oilskins chasing up and down the English Channel, playing at being a sailor'. That was just it. He did love to play at serious grand things. But how often did he think, when 'playing at being a sailor', of how he had conducted himself when Beatty had accosted him – when he had talked of lawyers and fear of being shot at? His jocular verses to a US Naval officer,

Zogbaum draws with a pencil
And I do things with a pen
But you sit up in a conning-tower
Bossing eight hundred men ...

To him that hath shall be given
And that's why these books are sent
To the man who's lived more stories
Than Zogbaum or I could invent.

hardly conceal his desperate hero-worship or his profound desire to be
a 'boss of men'. It is well to remember this, because when we realise the
vicariousness of his advocacy of the strenuous life – Theodore Roosevelt,
until the end, really did do strenuous things – we can the more easily put
a value on it in terms of his achievement. It meant an enormous amount
to him, but at the deepest level it hardly counted. It hardly counted when
he was, as he told Norton, perplexed with his own private responsibilities
before God. It might even be said that it was so superficial as to have gone
unnoticed by his daimon. But in his day-to-day life chagrin and envy could
be dissolved only by getting into vicarious action: watching others being
competent with various kinds of machinery, or waging war. He never did
have the least idea what it was actually like to be in charge of men, or to
work machines.

He and Carrie finally moved to Rottingdean, to the Burne-Jones's holiday
home, where John was to be born, in early June. Later they rented a house
called The Elms, on the same green. Cousin Stanley Baldwin, who had just
married into the Ridsdale family, was a neighbour. He was still a member of
his rich father's steel firm, and was not to become an MP for another eleven
years. The landscape around Rottingdean was not then, as Birkenhead
observes, 'pock-marked by the obscene debris of the speculative builder'.
Kipling found it pleasanter than Devon, the air better, and the immediate
neighbours more congenial. But he was not doing his best work. *Stalky* is
the prose counterpart of the imperialistic verses, and it is appropriate to
take these first; and to treat the celebrated 'Recessional' as paradigmatic.

He threw away his first draft of the poem. Sallie (Sarah) Norton,
daughter of Charles Eliot Norton, was staying with them at Rottingdean
and asked Kipling if she could look over the contents of his waste paper
basket. She discovered a poem about the Queen's Diamond Jubilee,
called 'After', and was struck by it. She tried to persuade him to take
it up again, but he refused, only agreeing to leave the decision to Aunt
Georgie. Aunt Georgie urged him to publish it. So he sat down, reduced
it to five stanzas, and sent it to *The Times* via Aunt Georgie, who was
just then returning to London. It appeared on 17 July 1897, and at once
established its author as the unofficial Poet Laureate. He experienced a
rebirth of his fame of seven years earlier; but this time the cause was
unworthy. 'Recessional' is a stirring piece, no doubt, and not one as
reprehensible as it has been made out to be; but it is not so much a bad
poem, as not a poem at all. It is not, as Walter Allen will have it, a 'great
hymn'. It is specious.

The best analysis has been made by Elliot Gilbert, who points out that the
actual words of the poem, in expressing imperial arrogance, contradict its
nominal notion of humility and impermanence. 'Recessional' has always
been taken by its admirers, such as Carrington, who waxes eloquent
about it, as a warning: 'Humility not pride, awe not arrogance, a sense
of transience not a sense of permanence were to be the keynotes of the
imperial festival.'

God of our fathers, known of old,
  Lord of our far-flung battle-line,
Beneath whose awful Hand we hold
  Dominion over palm and pine –
Lord God of Hosts, be with us yet,
Lest we forget, lest we forget!

The tumult and the shouting dies;
  The Captains and the Kings depart:
Still stands Thine ancient sacrifice,
  An humble and a contrite heart.
Lord God of Hosts, be with us yet,
Lest we forget, lest we forget!

Far-called, our navies melt away;
  On dune and headland sinks the fire:
Lo, all our pomp of yesterday
  Is one with Nineveh and Tyre!
Judge of the Nations, spare us yet,
Lest we forget, lest we forget!

If, drunk with the sight of power, we loose
  Wild tongues that have not Thee in awe,
Such boastings as the Gentiles use,
  Or lesser breeds without the law –
Lord God of Hosts, be with us yet,
Lest we forget, lest we forget!

For heathen heart that puts her trust
  In reeking tube and iron shard,
All valiant dust that builds on dust,
  And guarding, calls not Thee to guard,
For frantic boast and foolish word –
Have mercy on Thy people, Lord!

What Gilbert says sums the matter up. He could have added that it is an ingratiating set of verses, written up in a hurry, and appealing to shallow emotions. Posing as a warning against complacency, it was exactly what complacent people wanted to hear: that their sense of supremacy would be justified only if they were vigilant of it. It really does not matter who the much discussed 'lesser breeds' are. Are there, humanly, *any* 'lesser breeds'? That is what really matters.

The meaning is that there are people who are not British who can make trouble: they can't help not being British, but anyone not British, whether they can help it or not, can make trouble more easily. The God of the poem has chosen the British. Carrington talks of a 'sober and temperate sense of duty that justifies the will to power'. But what about power itself, and why should there be a will to it?

There is not a sentence in Kipling's poem – doubtless the product of a passing mood, and very properly thrown away by him – about justice, or moral worth, or what those qualities really mean. It is assumed without question that the British must be worthy of their God, who chose them. As for the 'warning that the proudest empire is ephemeral as a day's pageant' (Carrington): that is a perennial theme. There is no warning that this empire should respect its citizens for what they *are*; rather, it must expect the worst from them and keep them in order. Those are wild tongues that don't have *our* God in awe. A.P. Watt tried to read it aloud 'but broke down', he told the author. Well he might on his ten per cent (Kipling took no payment from *The Times*, but did not turn down any cash after that). People like to be reminded to look after their own interests in a suitably rhetorical manner, to be made to feel noble about their lust for power and their greed; what they do not like is to be reminded to examine their emotions to see if they are worthy, or to test the level of their being in the light of their living conscience. There is no sign here that Kipling understood what kind of trouble was brewing, or that he was prepared to look at both sides of any question. The poem is an exhortation to violence – not understanding, or sympathy – in the interests of power. It is also notably *anti*-patriotic: the assumption of a God who chooses the British (rather than any others) is irresponsible and false – Kipling could in fact have kept his point without being offensive had he dropped God.

But everyone was suddenly staggered by this unholy set of verses. The pacifist intellectual J.W. Mackail, Kipling's cousin Margaret's husband, and disliked by him for his academic remoteness, felt that there were 'all the signs of England saving up for the most tremendous smash ever recorded in history if she does not look to her goings'. In his cross reply to Mackail's congratulations Kipling expressed exactly the spirit in which he wrote 'Recessional':

> ... but all the same, seeing what manner of armed barbarians we are surrounded with, we're about the only power with a glimmer of civilisation in us. I've been round with the Channel Fleet for a fortnight and any other breed of white man, with such a weapon to their hand, would have been exploiting the round earth in their own interests long ago. This is no ideal world but a nest of burglars, alas; and we must prevent ourselves against being burgled. All the same, we have no need to shout and yell and ramp about our strength because that is waste of power, and because other nations can do the advertising better than we can.

The trouble with 'Recessional', as Gilbert rightly insists, is that it *does* really, 'shout and yell and ramp', even if under the pious guise of warning people that they should not do so. Complacency is in itself a sort of shouting and a sort of boasting. The poem is shallow and shabby, a product of Kipling's ability, not at all of his imagination. It warns against judgement and conceit and arrogance, but assumes those very vices without question throughout. The politics seem less distasteful, at this point of time, than silly, unrealistic and impractical. But the thinking, especially on the part of one who could be a true poet, *is* distasteful. No doubt the rhetoric appealed to many from a bygone age. No doubt because it is in the anthologies it is taught to the young as being a good patriotic poem. No doubt its metrical basis in a well-known hymn ('Eternal Father, Strong to Save') carries its crude message quite effectively. But it does not belong to a world in which anything is questioned. The message is: we're a splendid lot, the best there is, let's make sure we remain so! It is, in fact, a careless and derivative poem, being based (unconsciously) on Cardinal Newman's 'England' (which contains the lines 'We have no offering to impart/But praises and a wounded heart') and on poems by

Quarles and Emerson (who had written: 'And grant to dwellers with the pine/Dominion o'er the palm and vine'). Later the original manuscript was presented to the nation on the occasion of the crowning of George VI, and before that Sir Arthur Sullivan had wanted to set it to music.

Kipling meant it when he said that he did not believe in his genius. The artist in him knew very well that its fires were low. So, as a man with a huge reputation to maintain, he did what most people in his position do: knowing that his imagination was temporarily deficient, he relied on his ability. This was considerable. He was writing fewer short stories now, and *The Day's Work* (1898) is perhaps the weakest of his major collections. He still felt defeated by the Beatty episode, and was restless in his desire to seem worthy to himself once again. His chance would soon come, with war ('vigilance'). As Sandison says, he was selfish: in this case in requiring international conflicts in order to salve his own wounded ego. He was besotted by the navy to the exclusion of almost everything else. His words greeting the arrival of his son John, in a letter to a friend, are jocular enough; but they indicate the nature of his obsessions, his tendency to reduce everything to mechanical terms, and his unwillingness to consider his male progeny as a person in his own right:

> Ref: t.b.d. trials. My attention is at present taken up by one small craft recently launched from my own works – weight (approx) 8.957 lbs: h.p. (indicated) 2.0464, consumption of fuel unrecorded but fresh supplies needed . . . The vessel at present needs at least 15 yrs for full completion but at the end of that time may be an efficient addition to the Navy, for which service it is intended. Date of launch Aug. 17th, 1.50 a.m. No casualties. Christened John. You will understand that the new craft requires a certain amount of attention – but I trust ere long to attend a t.b.d. trial.

Kipling had started *Stalky & Co.*, which was eventually published in 1899, at Torquay, with 'Slaves of the Lamp'. The mild and gentle Crom Price was again a visitor, at The Elms, in October just before Rudyard and Carrie set out on the first of what was to be many winters in South Africa (8 January 1898). He was by then working steadily at the Stalky stories, and making an exhibition of himself by involving everyone in something he thought was irresistibly funny. He would read parts of them aloud to Ned Burne-Jones and to Price, and would keep asking Price, 'Do you remember that, sir?' Naturally, Price would politely reply, 'Yes, I remember that' to his now world-famous old pupil; but he did add, for his young friend Sydney Cockerell's ears alone, 'Yes, I remember many other things, too, that he might not wish me to remember.' Carrington adds, gratuitously, that there 'was no ill-will' in the remark. But he was not there.

Stalky, I should think, upset everyone except Kipling himself, and he must have been a trifle mad – his depression was balanced by little spurts of mania – to imagine that Price could fail to be irritated or at least dismayed by the fantastic portrait of him that Kipling was now drawing. It bears no relation to reality, since the Head in *Stalky* is a fierce flagellator who is not only all-wise but cheered by the assembled boys (especially when they are about to be flogged) throughout the book.

He was jerked into *Stalky* not only by feelings of inferiority, but by Crom Price's visit, and, most probably – initially – by the need to shake off his fit of depression. He shook it off, first, by defying his daimon and then by going off to South Africa, where trouble was brewing most promisingly and where indignation could be expressed and applauded.

Those many Victorians who suffered from what we today call clinical depression had no panacea: there was no electro-convulsive therapy and there were no drugs. So they either waited for it to pass, or, like Charles Kingsley and countless others, worked – or they drank alcohol until it passed (it usually did, but not, in many cases, for a long time), or, at worst, they killed themselves. Such depression most frequently first attacks adults in their early thirties. Sometimes it is accompanied by periods of equally undue elation; sometimes not. In Kipling's case his depression often manifested itself as increasingly agonising psychosomatic stomach pains – the distended colon the Torquay doctor noted. These developed, at some unknown point, into a duodenal ulcer which went undiagnosed for many years, and eventually killed him. The increasingly savage gloom and jealousy of Carrie, particularly after the loss of John, must also have exercised its effect. The dark atmosphere of Bateman's, still present, tells its own story. But all that, and more sorrow and silent suffering, was yet to come.

Price had undoubtedly been a good Head, with a wise and humorous way with his charges. He did not, however, impress them much. Only Rudyard. It must have been embarrassing for Price to listen to these fantastical tall tales spun out to him by the author of 'Recessional', who apparently assumed that his fierce flattery, amounting to hero-worship, was a fair exchange for his silence as to their authenticity. Here was an adult, just now the most famous patriot in the entire world, supposedly mature, inventing schooldays he had not had, and then rapturously re-living them in public. Perhaps it should be put down in large part to the humiliation he had received from his brother-in-law: reminded of his early humiliation and rage at Lorne Lodge, remembering that this had ended by his being put into the charge of a headmaster, a personal friend who had been told to keep a special eye on him because he was unduly sensitive and liable to exaggerate his sufferings, he now had to repeat the performance – to go back to school yet again, be put through his paces. Why not improve it all, then, and, by changing the character of Price to taste, make it a perfect retrospective experience?

Tompkins, in her discussion of the book, clearly felt uncomfortable with the 'fantasy' element, and she refers to it as such. But her case is that Kipling was consistently faithful to his daimon. Now at times, in certain works (the Mowgli stories are an apt example), the daimon both is and is not, so to say, there. In 'The Disturber of Traffic' or 'Dayspring Mishandled' the daimon is omnipresent. In *Stalky* it simply is not there at all. But Kipling deceived himself, at least for most of the time, into thinking that it was. It is difficult to recognise this, however, because of the enormous accomplishment with which he did the job. Despite that accomplishment, though, H.G. Wells was justified in writing, as early as 1911 in *The New Machiavelli*, that 'never was a man so violently exalted and then, himself assisting, so relentlessly called down'.

Because what Elliot Gilbert cleverly calls 'the good Kipling' has been gradually but thoroughly rehabilitated, the case pretty well made out, the naked hostility of the Leavis view (as trotted out by Boris Ford) discredited, we tend too easily to forget that Kipling did get relentlessly 'called down', and for very good and still valid reasons, of which *Stalky* was one. He felt it deeply, except in his purse, and reacted accordingly. There is not much point, however, in rubbing in the poorness, as poetry, of his imperialistic verses. The disingenuousness of these lies at a deep level: as Gilbert says, they are not politically but aesthetically objectionable. The rot, which was not protracted, started with *Stalky* (or perhaps with 'The Brushwood Boy'). This book has been a very proper embarrassment to his discriminating admirers since he published it.

Wells in 1911, with characteristic generosity, quoted 'The 'Eathen' ('The 'eathen in 'is blindness bows down to wood an' stone'), called it 'quintessential wisdom', and did not believe it more than a 'secondary matter' that Kipling 'could quite honestly entertain the now remarkable delusion that England had her side-arms at that time kept anything but "awful"'. Writing in 1927, however, he did attack the 'appreciative description of the torture of two boys by three others . . . excited to this orgy by a clergyman . . . In this we have the key to the ugliest, most retrogressive, and finally fatal idea of modern imperialism; the idea of a *tacit conspiracy between the law and illegal violence*.' Ultimately, towards the end of his own long life, Wells was puzzled, and found Kipling 'incomprehensible'.

Noel Annan approves of *Stalky*: 'to assert that boys in every age educate each other by cruelty is unexceptionable.' Such an argument amounts to 'asserting' that since murder is committed, it is 'unexceptionable' to pronounce it an excellent thing, and advertise its virtues. Kipling called *Stalky & Co.* a 'parable'. It is unexceptional to assert vigorously whatever is fact (Kipling learnt that lesson from, among others, Zola); but it is not unexceptionable to generalise moral precepts from those facts. In any case, is it a fact? I think that first of all it is parents and schoolmasters and 'world leaders' (and writers) who educate their charges by cruelty . . . What Kipling is doing in *Stalky* is in any case not *asserting* but *advocating* – perhaps these words are synonymous for Annan.

Throughout *Stalky* Kipling is famously and jollily against all precepts, all preaching: these are hypocritical and unctuous. In the meanwhile he is himself assiduously preaching. Just as in 'Recessional', where the words of the poem go against its avowed intention, so here do the didactic and parabolic tales go against the statements they make: they are themselves unctuous, and they gloat boastingly over the injustice and cruelty of which they tell. *Stalky* is not consistent: it preaches both obedience and disobedience; but the latter must be performed – indeed, we are left in no doubt, *should* be performed – under a certain set of rules. Then you are supposed to be able to be what is called today a regular guy (someone with enterprise), who can have his disobedience, or obedience as the case may be – who cares? – and eat it. Both the obedience and the disobedience are self-indulgent. *Stalky* is itself a self-indulgent, egocentric, egotistic fantasy. We should not need to make any fuss about it, were it not nervously incorporated into the Kipling canon; but it is. It ought not to be, because here there is no mercy, no humility, no sympathy. It is the fabricated revenge of a spoiled child, on circumstances. Tompkins, realising this and feeling uneasy about it, says that the hyperbole is not 'more so than those of many school tales of the period'. That has nothing to do with it. Kipling was a serious writer who should have known better;

the authors of the contemporary school tales were for the most part hacks who did not. Because she cannot bring herself to pronounce it unworthy of the daimon, she is obliged to justify it in Kipling's own terms, as a 'moral tract' and a 'parable':

> A wise negligence, particularly of the emotional side of a boy's life but also of his minor outbreaks and adventures, combined, when these get out of measure, with a sufficiently heavy discipline that makes no pretence to be perfect justice, is the best preparation for a resourceful, well-adjusted maturity, since it is not false to the general conditions of life.

But Kipling adored Price for having seen to it that his boys were so exhausted that they could not enjoy themselves in any swinish manner (as Kipling used to put it). That is integral to, although hardly mentioned in, *Stalky*. It by no means amounts to 'wise negligence', which is certainly the best philosophy to apply to adolescent sexual matters.

When in July 1894, Kipling went back to his school, on the occasion of Price's retirement, he was escorted by the head prefect, who many years later wrote to Birkenhead:

> ... oddly enough we were not impressed with some of his conversation as it partook of the immature schoolboy slang, and we were rather of the blasé age ... and didn't feel schoolboyish ... he would burst into quite boyish behaviour. In the tuck-shop he would always attach himself to the younger boys. I am afraid we, as high and mighties, rather stood aloof ... I recollect his rather boyish outlook on things ... I really only knew him as a grown-up schoolboy renewing the exploits of his youth, and I am bound to say that as a swollen-headed prefect he at times bored me – what a confession!

Although Kipling did know some of the *details* of how things worked, particularly the details of how the parts of a machine harmonised, and although he was able because of his fame to attend wars, there was a part of him that never grew up; he, who knew so much, was never able to discover 'what it was about' – as we have just seen, he failed to understand what ordinary senior boys at a public school were really like, probably because he had never been one. He could never accept his own passive role, of mere correspondent: he was always yearning to be the resourceful man of action himself. And because he could not accept this role, he was always just a kid in awe. That head prefect, who became General A.S. Little of the Royal Marines, did know what such things were about, and his apologetic confession to Birkenhead is just the kind of thing, of course, to which Elsie Bambridge objected – and all the more because she must have known it was true!

Roger Lancelyn Green, editor of the valuable compilation *Kipling: The Critical Heritage*, prints only two reviews of *Stalky & Co.* (he is as protectively selective as he can possibly be). One, anonymous, welcomes the book: it is 'spiffing', Mr Kipling knows his English boy through and through, his exposure of the practice of making boys refer to their 'sacred feelings publicly' is exemplary; yet even here he is told off for having, in 'his least satisfactory work', piled 'on youthful brutality beyond all need'. Even admirers, then, demurred. Green also gives Buchanan's famous piece, 'The Voice of the Hooligan', but not before he has denounced Buchanan as 'soured', and said that the lines of his attack on Kipling were to be followed by 'many so-called critics for reasons almost entirely divorced from literature'. But delight in cruelty is not an extra-literary matter.

Protectiveness, however, of the sort given by Green, will no longer do. Buchanan was indeed 'soured', as Green states, and he was an 'unsuccessful minor poet' whose destructive attack on Rossetti in 1871 had been by no means fair. But what he says of *Stalky*, and his general attack on the 'Hooligan' element in Kipling, is ably done, and requires a refutation which it has not had: critics, rightly convinced that Kipling is sometimes good, have decided that he must therefore *always* be good. Kipling, as I have remarked, got away with a great deal that he would not have got away with had he not had a grand reputation. We owe some magnificent stories to this fact (who would have published 'Mrs Bathurst' had it been sent in by an unknown writer?), but we also owe to it some bad books.

Stalky is one of the bad books. When Buchanan wrote that 'only the spoiled child of an utterly brutalised public could possibly have written *Stalky & Co.*, or, having written it, have dared to publish it', he was expressing himself too strongly, because, as I have said, the book is accomplished in an important sense: it is very readable. That, however, makes it all the more offensive. And was Buchanan really wrong to point out that in demonstrating that boys were not little sentimentalists, as poor Dean Farrar would have it in the unintentionally comic *Eric*, an easy target, he made them into 'little beasts . . . hideous little men'? True, the whole essay is cast in too strong terms; but most critics have been so anxious to defend, not Kipling's artistry, but his politics, that they have turned on Buchanan for being anti-imperialist, and for linking the book to 'recent political developments' (the Boer War had just then broken out). What Buchanan said was: 'the souls of Stalky and his companions *have* been looming large in our empire . . . But whether they really represent the true spirit of our civilisation, and make for its salvation, is a question I will leave my readers to decide.' This was reasonable. There was much in the conduct of the Boer War that was questionable. Dunsterville, the model for Stalky, was much put out by the appearance of the book, as he later told Birkenhead.

Buchanan was an over-embittered man; but how are we to explain the antipathy of Max Beerbohm? In extreme old age Beerbohm was found in his garden in Rapallo muttering with rage over something by Kipling, and remarking that it just ought not to be, just ought not to be. He had felt like that ever since the works of Kipling appeared, and his dislike survived Kipling's death. Unlike Buchanan, he was well aware that Kipling had genius, and often said so; but his many darts at him are among the most deadly and telling that were ever flung. That they did not come from an enraptured liberal humanist should give us pause for thought.

Carrington, extraordinarily, supposes himself to have been 'almost the first to utter an unkind word about this incomparable master of the smirk and titter'; but such language and such an angry tone give him away. Carrington had doubtless been made to feel small by Max; and was, like most of markedly unaesthetic bent, annoyed because he wondered whether he really saw the point of his jokes. 'Smirk and titter' is not at all descriptive of Max's genius, and, while he did allow Kipling to anger him personally, it was his humanity as well as his aesthetic sense that were offended. His nine caricatures, his two essays, and his famous parody (in *A Christmas Garland*) dispose of the 'bad Kipling' as he has not elsewhere been disposed of. His hatred did not distort his sense of what was acceptable and what was not acceptable. Roger Lancelyn Green in his collection shamefully refuses to print either the parody or the essays, and quotes Carrington with approval. He thinks that the parody fails to convey any real criticism! This mere irritation, wholly uncritical, at any dislike of his idol does no good to the ardent Kiplingite, and leads one to suspect (although it is only half-true) that he prefers Kipling the subtle political philosopher (à la Annan) to Kipling the imaginative writer. Beerbohm's parody contains too much telling criticism for the likes of Green and Carrington to stomach, and makes them merely resentful that 'their' Kipling should be vulnerable. Such people fail where Kipling did not fail: they do not understand that everyone is vulnerable; when they defend their idols, they defend themselves.

Elliot Gilbert, a more enlightened and useful critic of Kipling, in his collection *Kipling and the Critics* (1965), does print the Beerbohm parody. Its epigraph is from 'Police Station Ditties':

> Then it's collar 'im tight,
> In the name o' the Lawd!
> 'Ustle 'im, shake 'im till 'e's sick!
> Wot, 'e *would*, would 'e? Well,
> Then yer've got ter give 'im 'Ell,
> An' it's trunch, trunch, truncheon does the trick.

The sketch that follows this parody is not, as it happens, particularly malicious (the malice was saved up for the caricatures), and one might even think that a few of the tricks of the style – 'Now, when Judlip sighs the sound is like unto that which issues from the vent of a Crosby boiler when the cog-gauges are at 250' – that Beerbohm catches are affectionate.

A responsible American critic, Steven Marcus, has also contortedly tried to salvage *Stalky*. He concedes that it is a fantasy and a celebration of a way of life that never existed. But he believes it has a 'use': it shows us 'what, in part, we no longer are'. He does not add that it also shows us what no one ever was . . . He agrees that the accusations of cruelty that have been directed against the book are substantially true, and that it is pointless to deny them. However, this does not prevent him from putting it in a group of books explorative of youth that includes *Émile*: '*Stalky & Co.* is a classic of this sub-genre.'

Marcus then conducts an ingenious but hardly ingenuous argument by which he represents Kipling as being salutarily concerned to mount an 'anti-*Tom-Brown*ism': 'We are faced with a moral situation of some complexity and probably of deep-seated contradiction.' Marcus fashionably attributes to Kipling a kind of Freudian and modernist 'complexity', a confusion for which, as a Freudian *par excellence*, he can find praise: Kipling, thinks Marcus, has impulses which challenge his authoritarianism. Now of course he has. But they are not to be found in *Stalky*. Nor is the headmaster there 'a source of justice'. Indeed, he actually advocates injustice, on the savagely Annanesque grounds that life is going to be unjust and so his charges must be prepared for it.

Nothing could be so unsafe: proponents of such 'practical' theories of education do not allow for *who* thinks *what* unjust, or *when* . . . The flaws are perhaps too obvious. Kipling's confusions here about authoritarianism are not rich, but, regarded as thought, pathetic. When Marcus states that whether Price, or the Head in *Stalky*, or anyone at all 'could ever actually embody such qualities is not immediately to the point' ('what matters is that the boys believe he does') he himself is deliberately missing the point.

Marcus thinks that Kipling came across a great secret in the course of *Stalky*, which is that boys live a life which is 'passionately moral': they want desperately, Marcus thinks, to believe in all the traditionalist stuff that is handed down to them, hence their rebelliousness, which is nothing other than a revulsion from phoniness. He thinks, as Kipling did, that the Head's famous remark, 'I can connive at immorality, but I cannot stand impudence', is wonderfully wise and clever, a 'standing of these terms on their heads'.

Marcus concludes by telling the story of how Isaac Babel praised Kipling's economy of style – but does not trouble to remind us that this 'Russian-Jewish revolutionary writer' (revolutionary enough to be destroyed by Stalin) was not alluding to *Stalky*, which he would assuredly have entirely failed to grasp except as surreal fantasy. All this is a fine example of making the best of what you know very well is a bad job. It is as much nonsense to say that boys are passionate moralists as it is to say that they are violent psychopaths. They differ individually, and one cannot generalise. Marcus gets into the dubious position of praising the scene in which the heroic Head sucks the poison from the throat of a boy suffering from diptheria, and thus saves his life. After being cheered incessantly he naturally flogs a large number of boys before they go home. That episode is sheer sentimental (and sado-masochistic) fantasy, and is to be found in literally thousands of school stories from around Kipling's time until just before the Second World War. Usually it is a senior boy rather than a master who 'makes the sacrifice'; but the principle is the same, and the principle is fantasy – in part sexual fantasy. One definition of fantasy is that it is what is impossible in reality.

Kipling had already developed this vein of fantasy in the story he wrote not long before the Beatty crisis burst upon him, 'The Brushwood Boy'. Its hero, the dreamer George Cottar, has understandably been mocked by critics for his impossible perfection, and the sentence 'And she sat down on the bed, and they talked for a long hour, as mother and son should, if there is to be any future for our Empire' is very properly notorious; '. . . she kissed him on the mouth, which is not always a mother's property', which closely follows it, ought to be notorious, too. During this passage the mater is ascertaining that her son is still a virgin, and when she passes on this information to her husband, he laughs 'profane and incredulous laughs'. Here Kipling is smugly transforming a past of which he was ashamed into a spotless chastity. Worse is to come.

It is a queer tale, as well as an inept one. It does not work in the least. But it demonstrates, since it is almost destitute of imaginative qualities, what Kipling thought he wanted to do. It was written at the beginning of a period in his life during which he would not be in close touch with his daimon.

George Cottar has an involuntary dream-life. Each dream has the same starting-off place, a pile of brushwood. Plainly autobiographical elements are introduced, such as the seven-year-old boy's experience of 'Oxford-on-a-visit'; but the author is not on the whole keen to disclose that it is himself around whom he is weaving this curious fantasy. After all, he was never an impossibly successful sportsman and soldier, and he did not have an aristocratic upbringing in a grand country house. He had been the son of parents who always had some difficulty with their social standing, and who had to get on by means of their talents. There is one flash of the real Kipling in the (surely personal) recollections of seeing a performance of Pepper's ghost, of the 'provostoforiel' and of the little girl whose lisp mixes in with the voice of Pepper. But that is soon left behind. What is most interesting up to this point in the tale – the point at which George goes to school for ten years – is the terrifying figure of a *policeman*, who turns out to be 'Policeman Day', a 'Thing' that has the power to 'lead him back to miserable wakefulness'. The story is not properly worked out, because while George's 'real' life is paradigmatic of happiness and clean-cut military achievement and modesty, his dream life is perturbed. No reason can be adduced for this. One would not expect the day to be horrible to this happiest of men, of a character not unlike that of Tarzan, although not perhaps as physically strong.

George 'blossomed into full glory' as 'head of the school, ex-officio captain of games; head of his house, where he and his lieutenants pre-served discipline and decency'. The 'small fry' worship him, and he is, like the Head in *Stalky*, cheered wherever he goes (the source of Kipling's notion that public schoolboys cheer their masters and each other for most of their time is obscure); the women look at him and say 'That's Cottar'. 'Behind him, but not too near, was the wise and temperate Head, now suggesting the wisdom of the serpent, now counselling the mildness of the dove; leading him on to see, more by half-hints than by any direct word, how boys and men are all of a piece . . .' He does not (apparently) tell anyone about his dreams – but in any case 'ten years at an English public school do not encourage dreaming'. George progresses through Sandhurst with flying colours, but 'he did not know' that he bore 'from school and college a character worth much fine gold'. This is, simply, Kipling's own daydream. Paradoxically, he could indulge himself in this imaginary applause while the public did applaud him – but not as a man of action. There was someone in his life to discipline him, but not, alas, in this respect.

By virtue of his public-school training George 'kept his pores open and his mouth shut'. But he does have an inner life, although he does not want it: his dreams continue. He licks a few men from the lower orders into shape, and they come to worship him, and actually do sing his praises; he goes into action and (naturally) wins the DSO. Before he is made adjutant he wonders what man could possibly fill that place, and so forth. He is notable for not running after women. With a touch of what he takes to be realism, Kipling sees to it that his fellow-officers refer to him as Galahad – but they all look up to him nevertheless. Unpopularity with the in-group was not among the situations investigated by Kipling when he was in this mood. This is an example of Kipling's 'making much to-do about manliness', a tendency that, as the young Lionel Trilling wrote, does not go with actually being manly. When we want to praise Kipling for being sensible, as we might well do when we read of how he dealt with his enraged brother-in-law, we cannot do that in his own terms, for his own terms, as he prescribes them, are boastful and bullying. George Cottar would have known how to deal with Beatty, and would not have talked of lawyers. Nor would he have been afraid of a threat of shooting. Kipling, with Cottar, does make some small and pathetic effort to suggest, however vaguely, that a man ought to resist evil without self-glorification. This is to say: he makes him modest. But it is to no avail, and is unconvincing, because no man could achieve so much as Cottar and not have some struggle with self-conceit. But then the sort of men Kipling, in this incarnation of himself, worshipped, were not as he imagined them to be. Very few genuine men of action are boastful, swanking, swaggering, as he was; nor do they by any means all have the hatred of intellect that he demands.

To love the best of Kipling, we must see this unpleasant side of him, and recognise that even many of his friends must have been embarrassed and distressed by his swagger. As Trilling said (he was writing during a war) Kipling 'tempted liberals to be content with easy victories'. He did not help those who had the difficult job of making the laws to discover what governing was really like: he simply adored the administrators and ignored the rest. That was less reprehensible than childish. But it wasn't child-like, wasn't 'being as a little child'.

In India George's dreams become troublesome to him, for he is sometimes in terror: the policeman succeeds in giving him bad nights. But while we know that Kipling himself was a lifelong insomniac, who suffered terrors by night, we have to ask what the perfect and clear-conscienced George had to fear. In the story Kipling expresses his own fears as George's: but he had not the courage at that time to draw a portrait of himself, and so falsifies himself as the impossible, unconvincing and even ineptly created George. In 'The Disturber of Traffic' he was Dowse – whether he knew it or not.

There are curious details in the accounts of George's dream life. It is a mixture of terror and indescribable happiness. The companion is at first vaguely described: 'some one' in 'the reeds . . . whom Georgie knew he had travelled to this world's end to reach'. The sex of the companion is deliberately not revealed: 'He was unspeakably happy, and vaulted over the ship's side to find *this person*' (my italics). 'That person' guides Georgie, 'shows him a way'.

At this point 'They' are introduced, nameless creatures who are more dangerous to Georgie than the sinister seas. Also at this point, the so-far sexless companion acts as a guide. Later, after a spot of big-game hunting (the Kiplings possessed a tiger-skin in Vermont, but Rudyard did not shoot it, or anything bigger than a rabbit in his life) and promotion, George gets more deeply involved in his dreams. He is still helped by the 'person', and is 'filled with enormous despair' till he can meet this *person* again. They do meet again, in a garden 'surrounded by gilt and green railings, where a mob of stony white people, all unfriendly, sat at breakfast-tables covered with roses'. In some manner unspecified these unfriendly people (are they 'They'? – in the absence of any clue we must assume that 'They' are distinct entities) separate the companions, 'while underground voices sang deep songs'. Now the two meet again, and approach a 'huge house', in which a 'Sick Thing' lies.

> Now the least noise, Georgie knew, would unchain some waiting horror, and his companion knew it too; but when their eyes met across the bed, Georgie was disgusted to see she was a child – a little girl in strapped shoes, with her black hair combed back from her forehead.
>   'What disgraceful folly!' he thought. 'Now she could do nothing whatever if Its head came off.'
>   Then the thing coughed, and the ceiling shattered down in plaster on the mosquito-netting, and 'They' rushed in from all quarters. He dragged the child through the stifling garden, voices chanting behind them . . .

This is an odd passage. There is a hateful 'Thing', sick; there is Georgie's 'disgust' when he sees for the first time that the wonderful companion is a *little girl*, and his remark to himself to the effect, presumably, that since the companion is female and juvenile nothing could be done if the most horrible of all things happened, namely, that the Thing's head were to fall off; then on the Thing's cough 'They' rush in, presumably (again) in pursuit. It is totally confused, and would not have rated more than a rejection slip had it not come from the world's most famous living writer. Kipling was making an attempt to do justice to the emotional facts: that he had loved a man, who died, and then married his sister.

There is a clear hint that these dreams are 'unhealthy', since George also has 'ordinary' dreams, which are described as 'healthy'. The ones involving the discovery that his companion is a little girl, and the horrible sick (swinish?) 'Thing', recur until George is sent into action, upon the contemplation of which he 'nearly wept for joy'. How many of those with experience of danger and killing actually do 'weep for joy' when confronted with the reality? It is extraordinary that not one of Kipling's military or naval friends took him aside and told him, if not that he was making a fool of himself by taking such an approach, at least that he had got it wrong . . . After his heroic actions, and DSO, Georgie is given a year's leave. While on board ship, after passing Gibraltar, he has a further dream. Now the little girl has grown into a young woman, and the various horrible or threatening features of the dreams, although still evident, are at a greater distance.

Then he goes home and meets the girl of his dreams, who has shared all these adventures with him in sleep. An interesting detail is that the girl's name is Miriam. George exclaims to 'the pater': 'Sounds Jewish – Miriam', to which the pater replies, 'Jew! You'll be calling yourself a Jew next. She's one of the Herefordshire Lacys. When her aunt dies – '. The pater is then told to shut up, since the all-wise mater knows that to tell Georgie that she was heir to a fortune would cause him to have scruples.

Assuredly Kipling had a most curious mind. In the famously enigmatic 'Prayer of Miriam Cohen' the Jewish (and Old Testament) identity of the speaker is confirmed by the surname. This, like so many other details, must have some now inaccessible private significance. It cannot be a coincidence that Kipling chose this name for the dream girl, whose

Jewishness he now goes out of his way to deny. Probably many of his ideas about Jews were half-crazy and confused compounds of fear and respect. Miriam is also the traditional Jewish name for the mother of Jesus (Joshua). Whether he had this in mind or not, at any time, it is impossible to say.

In 'The Brushwood Boy' Kipling was trying to work out some ill-formulated private scheme. What can it all mean? Who are 'They', who are the people at the railway tables with roses who separate the two companions, and how do they do it, what is the 'sick Thing', what does this metaphor of meeting in a dream and discovering true love really mean? It is scarcely any wonder that Kipling's critics have not chosen to try to interpret this story. It is an example of irresponsible obscurity. Some feel that 'Mrs Bathurst' is, too; but there is a power in that tale which somehow suggests cohesion – and certainly there is no hint of the silliness of characterisation that there is in 'The Brushwood Boy'.

This private meaning is all there is, for the biographer (rather than the critic, who ought to have given up), to rescue, or try to rescue, from 'The Brushwood Boy'. It is well nigh inaccessible. Why, for example, is the sex of the dream-companion not made clear until a certain point? Why is the sex of the companion Mark 1 suppressed? Why is this companion a guide, whereas the Mark 2 companion is a (temporarily) disgusting little girl, so helpless that she has to be gathered up and led out of the presence of the coughing sick Thing?

This is Kipling's secretly scrupulous way of trying, at a time when his imagination is not working, to account for himself. The Mark 1 companion is male, but his creator cannot quite bring himself to say so. The sick Thing can only be what Kipling thought of as his own swinish indecency. And the at-first disgusting little girl, who turns into a woman (not, be it noted, a beautiful one), must be Carrie. Perhaps she is called, in the real life of the story, Miriam, because (although non-Jewishly) she represents the *veil* between Kipling and his real nature? Perhaps it is an obscure reference to the bargain Carrie and Rudyard made. This can only be speculation, but, however unsuccessful 'The Brushwood Boy' may be in artistic terms, it must have meant something to Kipling, and he must have meant something by it.

A Second Death

The Kiplings had not really liked The Elms, or at least Carrie had not, and no sooner had they got into it than Rudyard was sent out to house hunt. Some readers may object to my phrasing here. But it must be understood that Rudyard by now had become, as husband, the instrument of Carrie's will, which he could read like a book (and which she meant him to read like a book) and which he therefore learned to, so to say, anticipate. He took her grim nature as paradigm, and adapted himself to its iron will: almost became it. It is often not possible to say what he, Rudyard, would have liked or done in any set of circumstances: he did not live like that. Occasionally, however, one can read signs of inner and conscious rebellion. This did not become very apparent until some twenty years later – until after John had died. In return for all that, Carrie mothered and comforted him. There cannot in the nature of things be any 'evidence' for that. But I am sure that she took him to her bosom like a little child. It must have become less difficult for him when his own mother died.

Carrington tells the amusing tale of Kipling's visit to Dorchester, where Thomas Hardy took him to see a house owned by an old lady. Both men separately boasted of each other; the lady had heard of neither and was unimpressed. The two men made this an occasion, on their return to Max Gate, Hardy's house in Dorchester, to congratulate each other on their essential modesty and 'insignificance'. Later Hardy told H.W. Nevinson that he liked Kipling very much as a companion, and that he thought he would have been a 'very great writer' if the 'imperialists had not got hold of him'. At this time, before Rudyard and Carrie set out for South Africa in January 1898, and before there was any bad political tension between him and Aunt Georgie over the affair of that country, he enjoyed being amongst his relatives. Carrie may have felt that if they could not live satisfactorily amongst her family, then they should not amongst his. She not only had her diary – conveniently no longer available for critics to pick items from, and thus existent only in the form of Carrington's tactful and Birkenhead's not quite so tactful quotations – to which to confide her complaints; she had Rudyard, but of those complaints there is nothing but a silence pregnant with (probably guilty) outrage. Whether a difference between them on the matter of The Elms existed or not, after a few months and then a Christmas which Kipling enjoyed – this was the period of Crom Price's visit, as well of Henley's and others – he took Carrie off (8 January 1898) to the warmer climate of South Africa. It was seven years since Kipling had visited the Cape, and he had then been unmarried and in a very different and less certain state of mind. Carrie might have been feeling some jealousy, for in that summer Kipling was being extremely successful – mobbed by undergraduates when he visited Balliol, going to the beach and making jokes with Stanley Baldwin and with his beloved uncle Ned (though more dubious than ever about his misguided politics).

Perhaps in part owing to the troubles now nicely ripening in the area, Kipling eventually wrote a poem (quoted by Carrington, who believes it to have been written about 1899, but which is dated 1902 in the *Definitive Edition*) retrospective of this moment of his entry to South Africa, this coming 'to look at things'. This, 'Song of the Wise Children', is touching at certain points:

> We shall go back by the boltless doors,
>   To the life unaltered our childhood knew –
> To the naked feet on the cool, dark floors,
>   And the high-ceiled rooms that the Trade blows through:
>
> To the trumpet-flowers and the moon beyond,
>   And the tree-toad's chorus drowning all . . .

but in a sense, once again, specious. Characteristically, Kipling was trying to identify himself with the noble men at the outposts of Empire, when he well knew that his own nobility was of a different and more furtive nature – and that (in his own estimation) he was no Brushwood Boy to collect medals, over-modestly, for courage. The genuine emotions he used to convey this self-consciously Laureate-of-Empire piece had nothing to do with a South African childhood, since he had not had that; he had had India, Lorne Lodge and Westward Ho!. Lines such as:

> We have forfeited our birthright,
>   We have forsaken all things meet;
> We have forgotten the look of light,
>   We have forgotten the scent of heat.

take on a very different meaning when this confusion in their author is recognised. Yet the few phrases in the poem that are authentic and felt (for example, 'We shall go back . . . childhood knew') are based on his own experience.

Kipling on this visit established one of the apparently most important relationships of his life: that with Cecil Rhodes. But what might have been really important in it, to Kipling, was wasted. Had Kipling considered the complicated Rhodes, a repressed homosexual ('unmoved by women', Carrington says; but he does not say why), as a man in certain respects like himself (although Rhodes's homosexuality was fundamental to him in a way that Kipling's was, by now, not), the relationship would have had artistic and imaginative importance.

But Kipling registered only Rhodes's history as imperialistic hero, a part of a too consciously arranged scheme for dealing with personal problems – a 'guilty' past, the 'difficult' wife that had developed out of that – and did not register the man at all.

No one, of course, ever did. That was the idea. But of all Rhodes's friends Kipling alone might have fathomed him. Yet he could hardly afford to. He adored the cardboard figure, driven by its demons; but he was also attracted, and fascinated, by the real man. He dared not scratch it, though, for fear he should find something like, and yet horribly unlike, himself: a man driven into an attitude by inner horrors . . . Ah, but Rhodes was driven into *heroic action*, whereas he . . . The ghost of the little cyclist and his big rough brother-in-law must have at this point forbidden further speculation along such painful lines. Cecil Rhodes was quickly transformed, at such moments, into the Cecil Rhodes of history, striding aloft an imperial scene.

Rhodes, Kipling wrote in *Something of Myself*, had a habit of 'jerking out sudden questions as disconcerting as those of a child'. He once asked Kipling: 'What's your dream?' Kipling says he told Rhodes, 'You are part of it' – and, he tells us, he added that he 'had come down to look at things'. In fact he had come to evade the terrible challenge of his inner destiny, and to try vainly, yet again, to prove himself the man of action he could never be. He wanted then and was eagerly wishing to make, in the memorable words of the poet Sydney Keyes (of the Soviet General Timoshenko), 'the pencilled map alive with war'. The nature of his fantasies, throughout his life perhaps, but certainly in its earlier part, must have consisted of past incarnations of himself as various men of action, or sufferers made to labour (for example, a continuously lashed galley slave, in whose persona he could with masochistic delight imagine punishment of his sexual crimes). In that respect he is the bank clerk Charlie Mears of the 'The Finest Story in the World'. Quite soon he would begin to translate and transform these fantasies into more tales for children, at whose mental level such notions were conceived; in that one way at least could he purify himself of crassness, expel the merely juvenile aspect of such vain falsities.

He had always, instinctively, the aesthetic taste, and, as an artist and a creator, the power to distance himself from what was disgusting or hateful in him. He is said on the good authority of those who heard him to have been most wonderful as a storyteller to children. That true voice took him comfortingly and decently away from the inner demons from which more sensational, and more inept, authors cannot distance themselves – and with which they thus become identified. They do not master their material; it masters them. But Kipling, although without a confidant in the world, knew how to take care of himself in that respect.

Kipling, through Rhodes and Sir Alfred Milner, soon gained the position he sought in South Africa, which was one at the hub of public affairs. It was nectar to him. But the situation that was working up in Africa was different from his (or his father's or many other people's) view of it, or from the view he wanted to take of it.

Kipling started work on his poem 'The White Man's Burden' in June 1897. He finished it after he had visited South Africa, at the beginning of 1899, or possibly at the very end of 1898. It first appeared in *The Times* on 4 February 1899. He did not go to South Africa in order to make up his mind, but in order to confirm what he thought he thought; therefore he did not look too closely at what was really going on.

What can we make of 'The White Man's Burden'? It cannot really be described as a 'mixed' work. It is either superb or awful. Those who, like Angus Wilson, try to justify it, make a severe error. But then Wilson, for all his excellence, believes 'Recessional' to be redolent of 'humility', and does not see, as Gilbert sees, that the language of both poems is specious.

In February of that year, in Cuba, the U.S. battleship *Maine* was destroyed by an explosion for which the Spanish were blamed. As Carrington tells us, the Kiplings landed from their voyage from the Cape to learn of the news of the Spanish-American War. They stayed at Browns, and the American ambassador John Hay was their guest at dinner. Three days later there was another dinner; this time Hay entertained Kipling and Rhodes. Kipling therefore had a strong sense of being at the centre of things, which was exactly as he wished.

But 'The White Man's Burden' is ostensibly on the theme of *'The United States and the Philippine Islands'*. And the poem, regardless of its literary value (this is nil, although it employs skilled conventional procedures to gain its rhetorical effect) still divides people. Kipling had started it before the Spanish-American crisis developed; but he now employed it as the most fitting occasion for what he certainly thought of as one of his great set pieces. He had seen the reception of 'Recessional'. Another of his important heroes, and another real man of action, Theodore Roosevelt, gained fame as a Colonel of the 'Rough Riders' in Cuba, during the Spanish-American War.

It was all deeply disingenuous. Even Carrington, who candidly lives in a grand imperialist past, and loves Kipling for adorning it for him, grants that the feeling over the Spanish-American War was 'hysteric'. It was also deeply hypocritical: a colonial war conducted in a spirit of anti-colonialism. 'The White Man's Burden' was Kipling's message to his American friends to become imperialists. Wilson, recognising that it is unworthy trash, nonetheless tries to relate the poem to Kipling's 'daimon', which he rightly describes as 'his deepest creative impulse'. He tries to justify 'Recessional' as a guard against bragging, while 'The White Man's Burden' he justifies as 'the other great trust of preserving the voice that gave us Mowgli and Kim . . . and of ordering into a voice of art'. This is fanciful. 'The White Man's Burden' is uninspired, wrong, unrealistic, and humanly offensive in the deepest uncreative sense. Even the Americans to whom he ostensibly addressed it are not Irish or Italian, but only British. The words have no more than a fluent rhetoric to recommend them, and what they say is 'You people of *my* race (only), send forth your best to do our true duty, which is to serve (dusky) half-devils.' Politically adverse reaction to this has by now itself become conventionalised, often by those who misunderstand the very nature of nineteenth-century imperialism, or even believe it to have been 'right wing'. But, in a man of Kipling's capacities, its sheer folly as well as its unrealism cannot be allowed to pass without note.

Wilson writes:

> Of course, Kipling meant every word of his Imperial beliefs and gave most of his surface active life to them, but I am sure that the excess of the tensions they produced, his political frenzy . . . can only be fully understood if one grasps that his fears of anarchy . . . were also a reflection of the deep inner struggle between the anarchic, romantic childlike force of his creative impulse and the ordered . . . at times almost self-defeating pressure of the craft he imposed upon it.

This is well said, but omits two important facts. The first is that Kipling's 'anarchy' (as he saw it) coincided with his sexuality, and therefore with all his experiences, inner and outer, of his sexuality.

Secondly, his 'Imperial' vision was not only a response to his own cruel circumstances, but also a veil for his ferocity and contempt for others. We are reminded that from the word *daimon*, occurring in Homer and there meaning both *intermediate between man and god*, and something very close to *fate* (personal destiny), eventually came the word *demon*. In many people imperialism was doubtless misplaced patriotism, or stupidity; in Kipling – with his reserves of sensitivity and the responsibilities it entailed – it was sadistic, resentful, foolish, and, in one word, *demonic*, against his daimon.

In 1898 Sir Edward Burne-Jones died, and Trix became insane. The first event removed a humane influence from Kipling's life, and at the same time revived many happy memories. He had latterly found his attitude to Uncle Ned hard to maintain: a mixture of 'intellectual' contempt, or what he thought was intellectual contempt, and of warm affection. What he thought of Burne-Jones's infidelities is not on record. His exclamations against him have largely been suppressed; but probably when he wrote to Norton that Uncle Ned had been 'more to me than any other man', he (with one exception) meant it. His visits to Rottingdean, he told Norton, had 'changed my life'. I think that what he meant by that was that the visits relieved him from what he was beginning to find was the secret misery, the pressures, of his married life. Carrie's attitude to Uncle Ned's 'larking' must frequently have been grim. Ned, and childhood memories of Morris, himself a great larker, must have been responsible for Kipling's liking for the practical joke.

As for Trix's mental breakdown, not many details have been given about this, although Carrington records the event as a shattering of the 'happiness' of the 'Family Square'. She had been 'at the hub' of society in Simla, where her husband was stationed, 'far more beautiful' than her mother. But, Carrington adds, she seemed 'psychic' (we shall go into what is meant by that at a later stage) and 'unworldly', and to be moving 'in a land of phantoms'. When she had to be put in her mother's care at Tisbury in December 1898, she was either hysterical, or depressed, or both. It is clear enough, since she wrote fiction, that she was jealous of her brother's success – that was inevitable. All this time he was composing the *Just So Stories* for his daughter Josephine. They are, wrote Angela Thirkell, née Mackail – Aunt Georgie's granddaughter – 'a poor thing in print compared with the fun of hearing them told in Cousin Ruddy's deep unhesitating voice'. Without this, she felt, the stories are 'dried husks'. And so indeed they must seem to one who heard them first told.

The Kiplings might have gone to South Africa again that year, but Carrie wanted to see her mother; there were copyright matters to be gone into; and both may have been making tentative feelers towards returning to Naulakha. Kipling was tired of, and disappointed in, England: 'grey skies and boiled potatoes'. They sailed on 25 January 1899, and were in New York on 2 February. The reporters, eager to make whatever they could out of this return, were unable to draw from him more than a cliché about the necessity of sincerity in writers ('There is no surer guide, I am sure, than the determination to tell the truth that one feels'). One of the reporters expressed his frustration in awful verses which are quoted in a gossipy memoir and 'appreciation' of that year:

> We've met many men from overseas,
> An' some of 'em was shy and some was not.
> The Frenchmen and the Germans and Chinese,
> But Kipling was the hardest of the lot.
> Some of 'em talked in English an' the rest
> Would talk from early winter to the fall,
> But the Mowgli-man we found the greatest pest,
> For the bloomin' sod 'e wouldn't talk at all.

The newspapers 'reported' that Kipling intended to reopen his home 'in the spring'. Possibly he and Carrie really would have liked to. Kipling had written not long before, to Conland, that although he had put the place on the market, he had 'taken care' to put a prohibitive price on it. In the same letter he also told Conland that he often felt like coming along to see him. And had he not said to the reporters upon leaving America: 'I expect to come back, when I get ready. I haven't the least idea when that will be'? Clearly one part of him wished heartily to be back. Carrie, too, must have had strong wishes in that direction. Both had suffered a humiliation at the 'diabolical' hands of Beatty, and Kipling had certainly felt himself to be a coward. After all, whatever his apologists like to say, he *had* run away, and had been mocked for it in verse and in caricature.

To be prevented from dwelling in one's own house and kept from one's own community by the will of one's manly brother-in-law and fear of reporters and gossip! The people of Brattleboro (those of them that liked Kipling) 'set out preparing a round robin . . . urging him to come and live among them once more'. But Kipling must have known what the farmers and ordinary folk said about him, the husband of his wife: 'too peculiar a critter for anyone to want as friend'. He was also told that, despite the 'state dinner' offered him by his old friends, Beatty was proposing to sue him for fifty thousand dollars – for 'malicious persecution, false arrest and defamation of character'. He had matters of barefaced piracy to deal with, too.

'By God!' Beatty said to Van de Water in 1936, 'I wasn't going to let him come back into my country again. It would have blackened my face. I'd have had to get out myself.' Van de Water tells us that the 'fiendish expedient still had a pleasant flavour' for him, almost forty years after: 'He didn't come back,' added Beatty, 'because I scared him off again. I knew Rud's weakness. He'd had a hell of a time on the witness stand. I knew he'd run if he thought he'd have to appear in court again.'

Birkenhead here makes an apt observation: all this was a Kipling story that never got written. Upstart comes to territory strange to him. Gets his comeuppance from man whose own country it is. But did the story remain unwritten? One explanation of his increasingly enigmatic tales may be that Kipling was conducting a one-man campaign against his own behaviour, even his own nature – a campaign which he had to keep secret from his uncomprehending wife above all? Beatty was his daimon's hero!

He was at the Hotel Grenoble, wondering what to do, reading in one newspaper of how Beatty had already arrived in New York and had served the writ, in another of how he was expected any day in Manhattan, and in most of the rest inspiring discussions of 'The White Man's Burden'. Kipling occupied this frightened, innerly uncertain and confused time by writing to every one of his schoolmates he could trace. Perhaps, having by now invented a childhood he had never had, feeling afraid of Beatty ('the man of action'), he was nervous of the truth coming home to roost. He wrote to 'Stalky' (not knowing how much the book would embarrass him):

> ... I saw the balance sheet of the old Coll. the other day. It's in an awful condition – only 70 or 80 boys and the bulk of 'em day boarders ... We are the original OUSCS but remember, we don't know anything of the Coll. since Price left ... in 1894 ... I made a speech to the Coll. You ought to have heard the boys cheer. It was in the old Gym, and I nearly broke down.
>
> We came over here for a few weeks a fortnight ago ... so as to enable the wife (I married an American) to see her mother. It's a great nuisance to be a notorious and celebrated literary man ... I got a note in from White (he had the study below us and we poured fried bacon fat on his head); as soon as I can turn round I shall go and have a Coll. bukh with him ...
>
> All this time I haven't congratulated you on your marriage. I can only hope that you'll be as happy as I've been in that relation, old man. It's a good and honourable position and it makes a man's character ... I've a small son a year old who is all the world to me ...

Nothing about his daughters: he was writing to a college man who would only be interested in boys, or so he thought. Nor did he entirely mean that it was a 'great nuisance to be ... notorious': he had needed to be so, and now, when communing with his inner self, he felt that he was punished just for that.

He posted this letter before 8 February. On 8 February Carrie became badly ill with what was then called *grippe* (one or another of the many forms of virulent influenza) and took to her bed. Josephine and Elsie had already caught colds. Dr Dunham, now married to Josephine Balestier, was on hand: he diagnosed 'whooping-cough with complications'. Carrie developed a high temperature, but was up and about by 12 February. She and Kipling were leading, between 12 and 20 February, an active social life. Kipling was fighting for his copyrights, and in fact beginning what was eventually to be a losing battle with Putnams, whom he took to court over a collected edition of his works ('The Brushwood Boy' edition) which they proposed to put out.

The children had been well enough to visit Central Park, but then, on 20 February, Kipling himself fell ill, and so again did Josephine. Carrie now came into her own: her character was, indeed, constructed in order to meet disaster. On 22 February she wrote in her diary:

> An anxious day and night. Rud so good and patient – sleeps much – good friends and helping hands, and I feel how everyone Rud has ever spoken to has loved him, and is glad and happy to help do for him.

Kipling's illness developed into what the doctors called 'acute lobar pneumonia'. It was not at all true that everyone to whom Rud had spoken 'loved him': the contrary was more near the case. But Carrie felt that his illness was compensating for this. One can feel her acceptance of his moral 'evil' – that 'evil' which justified her existence as it was – in her new feelings as he lay ill. He might have this secret blight, she doubtless told herself – but had not everyone loved him?

He meanwhile, in high delirium, dreamed. In the dream he was in the hotel in which he actually was, the Grenoble. He later described this dream: it was of a series of *public disgraces*. Before his illness he had been seeing hundreds of newspaper clippings about himself. But in the dream he saw newspaper clippings about his sexual behaviour: a New York girl 'called Bailey or Brady' (a reflection of *Beatty*, pronounced '*Bayty*', brother of his dead lover, and exposer of his 'cowardice'?) had written letters to him 'couched in the vilest personal style. I was much moved by these. They were calculated to make harm between my wife and myself' (did Beatty ever make nasty suggestions?). They accused him of 'having larked around with a great many girls both before and after marriage'. The dream continued: on the hotel's rooftop he took some fruit and drink, having just characterised Miss Bailey or Brady as 'an unclean-minded person' (swinish?), and Theodore Roosevelt appeared. He was in Miss Bailey's pay (did this express a fear that such a man of action as Roosevelt might learn his 'secret'?). Miss Bailey owned a submarine which could take him to Samoa to see Stevenson, a project with which his offended wife, 'in the interests of our own happiness', fully endorsed (the threatener in possession of submerged truth?). A submarine is something that travels unseen, is, like a guilty secret, unknown.

And so the dream went on, its main and only significant theme (apart from his obsession with 'uncleanliness') being Kipling's imminent humiliation. What was he anxious should not be 'found out'? Possibly the project to go to visit Stevenson is significant, since the first time he had decided not to do that was at a crisis-point in his life. His doctors told Carrie, who told Norton, that his 'simple life and habits would count in his favour': perhaps hearing of this made him dream about Miss Bailey's 'false' accusations, although he never in his dictated account of his dream (which he made immediately after recovery) actually says that they *were* false. He also dreamed of being put on trial in New York with no bail allowed – a recollection of his part in Beatty's trial.

Enquiries and get-well messages flowed in from all over the world. Even the Kaiser, not Kipling's favourite monarch, caused one of his clerks to send an anxious telegram. Carrie, eating well and keeping calm and paradoxically enjoying being the necessary centre of attention (in the absence of Kipling) began to worry less about her husband and more about the older of her two daughters. Dr MacDonald, one of the doctors who was treating the cases – although Dunham was in charge – himself became anxious on behalf of his younger patient, and suggested that she be sent to the house of some old friends of the Kiplings, the de Forests, who lived on Long Island. Carrie, in what she called 'a moment of conscious agony to stand out from the average', agreed. On 27 February she wired Norton, on the subject of Rudyard, 'NO MATERIAL CHANGE. WE ARE MAKING A STRONG FIGHT AND MAY WIN OR LOSE AT ANY HOUR. CAROLINE KIPLING. 1.35 PM.' Telegrams continued to pour in. That same public that was so anxious for his survival, and would very soon thrill to his activities in the Boer War, would soon turn against him on that very account. This was the very apogee of his fame; not long afterwards his long decline would begin.

At 6.30 a.m. on 6 March 1899, while he was still recovering, Josephine
died. Sallie, Norton's daughter, wrote to her father from New York, on 25
March:

> She told me a great deal about Ruddy's illness but she said very little about
> little Josephine . . . She said the days between little Josephine's death and
> Ruddy's knowing of it, were 'dreadful', and that at last she *had* to tell him
> though the doctors . . . 'he was too ill to realise it quite, but now every
> day he feels it more.'

The composure of both Kipling and Carrie impressed everyone, although
it was not perhaps so out of the ordinary. Miss Norton was led to wonder
'which at its best is the best . . . the nature which is unconsciously steady,
or the highly organised nature which keeps its balance by conscious
effort'. Carrie, she thought, was 'splendidly restrained and controlled, but
vibrating with sensitiveness'. It was, and very genuinely, her finest hour,
her one vibrating act on the world scene. It is bad taste not to celebrate it,
and even Angus Wilson calls it heroic. No doubt it was; but it should be
remembered that she merely acted with the dignity and control of which
most women are capable. On one occasion, while she still could not tell
Kipling of Josephine's death, she hastily caught up a scarlet shawl, instead
of a black one, as she walked into his room. Henry James wrote two excited
and emotional letters in quick succession. First, to Kipling, calling him a
'Daemonic Indestructible Youth': 'I fold you both in my arms . . . What
you must have got out of it!' Then, learning about Josephine, to Carrie:
'My letter will have had the effect of a jubilation so mistimed . . . dear
little surrendered, sacrificed soul!' Kipling's old friend from Brattleboro
the Rev. Day lied: 'I know too well the profound faith of Mr Kipling . . . A
new wonder will arise in his soul.' By Easter, mentally unrelieved, Kipling
was able to express his thanks to the world through Reuter's. Lockwood
could say no more than that he couldn't help believing that all 'the weight
of love' 'may count for something'.

When Kipling fully recovered he (or Carrie) got Conland to 'forbid'
him to winter in England. When in June they returned to Rottingdean
they were minus Josephine but plus the future of a South Africa teeming
with violence – and England given 'no end of a lesson' an army betrayed.
Kipling may have known this already, and even been looking forward to
it. They went to a house in the Highlands made available to them by the
millionaire Andrew Carnegie, where Kipling doubtless studied the news.
Soon after that, a master of how machines work, he got very early into the
new world of motoring – a pioneer in a hired and chauffeured car.

South Africa

The side of Kipling that feared and hated came out uppermost during the Boer War, although he saw little of the fighting. Yet his being able to give full rein to this fear and hate, to popular approval and applause, may be well be responsible for *Kim* – inasmuch as it cleared the decks for the operation of its author's imaginative faculties. After the Boer War was ended, won, and then lost without fighting, Kipling's polemic went right out of fashion. Never again would he have so wide an audience to which to preach.

Rudyard and Carrie arrived at Cape Town on 5 February 1900, and left in May. They returned on Christmas Day of the same year, but spent the following summer and the first months of the winter in England; they were back again in South Africa on 7 January 1902, and left on 16 April. Thereafter, up to and including 1907, they wintered in South Africa. They decided to go there no more after 1907 because Rhodes's dream of a united Africa south of the Zambezi was fast beginning to fade; and perhaps because Milner had been forced to resign in 1905: his bid to encourage British immigration to South Africa had failed, and then a vote of censure upon him was passed in the Commons because it was discovered that Chinese labourers were, despite Cabinet policy, being flogged. The Boers were going to have their day after all. At that time Kipling wrote:

> I do hope you'll be able to make the people down your way realise that this silent capable man worrying out his path alone, down south, in the face of all conceivable discouragements, is not a steward to be got rid of on the threats or wire-pulling of a rebel commando.

More or less everything Kipling said about the Boer War was wrong; what was right, or, rather, turned out to be right, was accidental: it did not arise from humane or sensible considerations. These, apparently, were working in a part of Kipling that the public, until he published *Kim*, were not permitted to view.

It is hard to say whether he would have reacted differently had he known of the full facts. Certainly he would never have been able to see it as a notable South African, William Plomer, much later saw it: 'Out of that bungled, unwise war/An alp of unforgiveness grew'. Yet that sentence sums it up. It is true that Kipling was always against military incompetence, and that he shared Baden-Powell's horror of the fact that of volunteers for the Boer and then for the 1914–18 wars, only some four out of ten were even fit for service. But whereas Baden-Powell was at least a soldier (if a very odd one), Kipling was himself a bungling and unfit incompetent. His obsession with the fitness of others (he was after all not yet forty), and with the desirability of conscription, during this period, might have incurred extremely rude and derisive comment had he not been so famous a man. Furthermore, he was so anxious to be 'in' with those in charge on the spot that he failed to blame them, or refused to acknowledge that they were to blame, for what went wrong. He visited his wrath on the clerks in London. They were to blame – but so were the majority of the commanding officers in the field, not least Roberts.

But what would he have said if he had been present before, during and after the Jameson Raid, which, as Smuts later wrote, was the real beginning, the 'declaration' on the part of the imperialists – of the Second Boer War? Of course, it was Kipling above all who, in his juvenile way, helped create the legend that crack troops enjoyed fighting. In fact, only psychopaths enjoy fighting. So the truly humiliating and almost comic circumstances that constituted the Jameson Raid would probably have bounced off a deaf ear: this was the laureate of false, not real, war – and such legends are the stuff of dreams. Thus, Jameson was the man Kipling had in mind when he wrote 'If'. It is often objected that this poem is specious. So it is: it appeals to a set of ideals, all expressed as unironic clichés, that have no existence outside the vulgar rhetoric that it generates. It is (as almost always with Kipling) able; otherwise it is not a good poem, or even a good set of verses, under any circumstances. But there is another way into its essential speciousness, which is to look into the truth about Dr Jameson and his Raid.

The legend that swept across England a few weeks after the Raid (29 December 1895 – 2 January 1896), largely because the Kaiser made the mistake of sending Kruger a telegram congratulating him on his escape, was that Jameson was a daring hero who had acted wisely, bravely and well. The truth was that he had acted with the reckless bravery of an adolescent, against advice, and badly. He had just received a coded wire from his fellow conspirator, Rhodes (who was wily enough not to sign it): 'DEAD AGAINST IT . . . FIASCO . . . YOU MUST NOT MOVE . . . TOO AWFUL . . . VERY SORRY . . . ICHABOD.' Although the Raid was supposed to take the Boers in the Transvaal by surprise, rumours had already reached the press. The telegraph wire was cut too late (some said owing to drunkenness). Jameson had wanted to avenge the white flag of Majuba, but on 2 January someone in his own party raised the white apron of an African servant girl: Rhodes and his fellow conspirators had done a deal, not a single person had ridden out to join the band of 600, and Jameson's humiliation was complete. He was led off to Pretoria jail in tears. It was a gamble that had not come off – unlike Rhodes's youthful venture to make a fortune. It never stood a chance of doing so. Back at home the equivocal rogue Chamberlain, half in the know and half deliberately not, could only look forward to smoothing things over.

So the Raid was in no way an immediate success; Jameson had behaved like an over-precipitate little boy (although socially he was a self-possessed and even witty companion). But what ought to have been a 'squalid little episode' became a paper triumph. Meanwhile, that complex man Sir Alfred Milner, not privately under many illusions, himself saw the Raid as a fiasco. What interested him, however, was how quickly it became successful in the popular British imagination. Lest an unsuspecting reader should regard Milner as any sort of paragon, I should remind people that his previous apogee – before being sent to South Africa as High Commissioner – had been at Somerset House, as Chairman of the Inland Revenue.

It is unlikely that Milner would have told Kipling, when he saw him (as he did, in South Africa – they all had to see the bustling and enthusiastic little man, however they may have felt about it: he had the ear of the public, and could be useful to them, so better be polite), that he had remarked (1897), of Rhodes's plan for invading the Transvaal, that it was 'idiotic' and 'unscrupulous', and that Rhodes and his fellow-conspirators were 'money-grubbers' and 'potential rebels'; 'Rhodes is thoroughly untrustworthy,' he declared, although he confusedly admitted to a personal admiration. He believed the truth about Rhodes to be one of the 'arcana imperii', and did not want it passed on to imperial enthusiasts other than 'fully initiated augurs'. He regarded the former as 'excellent, simple-minded' fellows. As I have suggested, although Kipling reserved to himself all the 'cynical' rites of 'those in the know', the 'inner ring', he did not share in the cynicism of the Boer War gang about each other and almost everything else.

Chamberlain might not have got away with it had it not been for the Kaiser, whose wire to Kruger angered, as well it might, the British people. The Fleet was mobilised, and Jameson, though in durance vile, found himself the hero of the hour: 'Then, over the Transvaal border,/ And gallop for life or death,' wrote the Poet Laureate Alfred Austin. This helped Chamberlain to survive, since his enemies dared not make an issue of his involvement; gratefully, he referred (if only in private) to Rhodes as a 'blunderer' and a 'blackmailer'.

These details are mentioned in passing only because they serve to demonstrate what Rudyard Kipling, the man in with the people who had the real power, did not know. I hardly think that it was a matter, even, of 'not wanting to know'. He kept the side of him that easily and naturally could have known right out of sight of himself. Lastly, though, whatever did he think, let alone know, of Milner, whom he never ceased to worship until the latter's death in 1925? Writers of Kipling's cunning and calibre ought to see through such interesting, violent and mixed rogues as Milner.

Milner, like many of his ilk of that age, began his adult life with a genuine interest in social reform. He became a friend of Asquith and Arnold Toynbee (uncle of the theorist of history), and did social work. He was Private Secretary to Goschen, both before and during the latter's occupation of the post of Chancellor of the Exchequer – and he was in on the founding of, and helped with, the Liberal Unionist Association. It was Goschen who gave him the job of Chairman of the Board of Inland Revenue in 1892. By the end of that decade no man high up in the corridors of power, not even Chamberlain himself, was master of a more intricate lattice of friendships. He knew where to drop a word for it to be spread. He knew where to speak in confidence. He had served Sir Evelyn Baring in Egypt and had justified the Egyptian administration in a book. He had friends in every party, and in every sub-section of any party. He was open to every kind of idea. He would tell his friends that things were hard for him: he saw too many sides to every question. Except for one: the matter of the British Empire. He saw no alternative to the imperialist solution, but was not in the least 'racist' beyond that. His position, like that of his fellow imperialists, was very close to those of the French who saw the supreme goal of the 'native' as an 'assimilated' Frenchman.

When Chamberlain sent Milner to South Africa he knew what he was doing. The two men did not trust each other, yet each had the same aim. Thomas Packenham states Milner's aims when he discusses the belief of the imperialists that war with Kruger was 'inevitable':

> Inevitable? It would have been easy, Milner later confessed to his intimates, to patch things up with Kruger, and settle those differences with the Uitlanders in a Great Deal that would have lasted five, ten or fifteen years. He had resisted the temptation, and 'precipitated' a war before it was too late. The truth was that Milner believed in 'the clean slate' and the 'Big Things in Life' . . . War . . . would finally 'knock the bottom out of "the Great Afrikaaner nation" for ever and ever Amen'. He would rule South Africa as Cromer ruled Egypt.

In private Milner called the Boer War 'his war'. He had been sent to South Africa by Chamberlain in the hope that he would work 'things up to a crisis', even though Chamberlain seemed to be against this . . . After all, when he sent Milner he knew very well that this was the view he took. Chamberlain may have been 'against' the War until after it started; but that suited his strategy – the self in him that enjoyed politics and hoodwinking public opinion (for which he had much less regard than he had for the working man) was almost as strong as the imperial self. No politician has been more adept at being all things to all men, and, in all probability, to himself. He was less keen on actual war than Milner, being a more imaginative man in such matters; but he was also less consistent. And even he could not know that Milner had made an unholy alliance with two Germans who had taken up British citizenship: the gold millionaires Beit and Wernher. For without these grotesque financiers Milner could not have gone ahead. (It is indeed at least ironic, since Kipling was the laureate of this war, that the millionaires were Germans and that its architect was British but had a German education: Kipling's hatred of the Germans was one of the overriding passions of his life.) He knew, however, that he could: they had at the very least agreed to take the enormous losses that they knew it would entail: to foot the bill for the war, as Packenham puts it.

Carrington's account of the War is different from Packenham's. He even says that the 'manifest destiny' of the *uitlanders* was to 'unite South Africa as a free and progressive country'. But although Milner made utterances about justice, and was sincere, he did nothing for them in his conduct of the War. Nor did anyone else – let alone, of course, the Boers. But the practice of giving Kipling and others credit for anticipating the Boers' cruel treatment of the 'kaffirs' is unjustified: the people who conducted the War, and those who supported it, had no true interest in the 'natives'. Carrington merely thinks that Kitchener's concentration camps were 'unfortunately named', and that the diseases which ravaged them (and the troops) were unavoidable; he thinks that Roberts, called out at the end of 1899, was a heroic and effective general – whereas he was barely competent.

It is clear enough that much of the disease that ravaged the inhabitants of the concentration camps was avoidable (not that this in itself did not shock Kipling; but he did not use his influence on the people who could have improved the conditions), and that inhumanity of an extreme kind – a dress rehearsal for the First World War, no doubt – was practised. Thus Baden-Powell – despite his extraordinary ingenuity and good spirits in holding out at Mafeking – had Africans deliberately starved and forced away at great danger to themselves ('by forcing natives away from Mafeking we can get their share of horseflesh for whites'), as well as flogged and executed. The future gentle philosopher of holism and co-architect of apartheid, Jan Smuts, oversaw the wholesale slaughter of 'kaffirs' on at least one occasion. All this was denounced at the time, even by *The Times* correspondent; somehow that particular copy did not get printed.

At the end of 1899 Kipling wrote in Carrie's diary that he owed his life to her, which was true in perhaps more ways than one. He was politically at odds with many of his friends, and with Aunt Georgie above all. But this could not prevent him from doing all he could, locally, to aid what Carrington calls 'the war for liberty'. He wrote the famous 'The Absent-Minded Beggar', in part a channel for his aggressive feelings ('But we do not want his kiddies to remind him/That we sent 'em to the workhouse while their daddy hammered Paul' – always, when one looks into Kipling's patriotic-imperialistic verse, one finds this vein somewhere: he is 'hammering' liberals), and published it in the *Daily Mail*, which would doubtless take it today if a few words were changed.

He also went hard to work with his influence and reputation to form a volunteer company in Rottingdean; he did not volunteer to join it himself, although he was only thirty-four. Since he knew nothing whatsoever about organising volunteers, he irritated the authorities considerably. Henry James ('nice man, much beloved' wrote Carrie in her diary) came to lunch on 17 October, and must have kept his thoughts to himself – for Kipling was just then working at his poem. Kipling did say of these verses that they 'lacked poetry', even if they had 'some elements of direct appeal'.

This may cast some light on his consistent refusal to accept public honours, which has often puzzled commentators, who usually accept the explanation he gave: that he felt he could do his work 'better without' them – this was what Carrie noted in her diary when Salisbury sent his secretary down to Rottingdean to see how the land lay on the matter of a knighthood, on 14 December 1899. Long before this, in 1896, after Tennyson had been dead for four years, Kipling had indicated that he didn't want the post of Poet Laureate, although Balfour, Salisbury's nephew, thought of him for the post. In part this was modesty arising from his sense of his calling. But it may have been a certain sense of conscience, too, arising from his misuse of his genius in the interests of rhetoric. He justified himself in the case of 'The Absent-Minded Beggar' by pointing out that all the funds earned by its performance (Sir Arthur Sullivan set it to music) went to the soldiers in South Africa – and, indeed, it earned a great deal for this cause.

But he was over-defensive, to the extent that he quoted 'friends' whenever he was attacked for writing bad poetry even of 'admirable' content. When Lord Newton did just this, in the course of a debate, Kipling wrote to him angrily saying that friends 'deplored' his remarks, since the poem had raised a quarter of a million. Newton replied reiterating what he had said: that he admired Kipling's patriotism but deplored his verse. Kipling replied that his 'friends' were still dissatisfied, but Newton refused to be cowed: 'There is no law written or unwritten which compels one to admire poetry which is distasteful.' Alas, Kipling commentators have tended to suppress most of the antipathy which Kipling aroused from early on – and that Birkenhead did not altogether suppress it was perhaps one of the keys to his misfortunes.

When Kipling arrived in South Africa on 5 February 1900 he went straight into the heart of imperial things: to the Mount Nelson Hotel, where he got in with the real correspondents – Perceval Landon, the *Times* man in the field, the ferocious H.T. Gwynne, then with Reuter's, future editor of the *Morning Post*, and Julian Ralph, an American after his own heart, who had become the African correspondent of the *Daily Mail*. The first two remained Kipling's lifelong friends; Ralph died young, but not before he had written a book with the title of *War's Brighter Side* (1901). Kipling, feeling good that he could meet on equal or even better terms with what Birkenhead calls the 'strange riff-raff' of millionaires and high officials, saw Lord Roberts before he went into the field, and doubtless offered his services – and his experiences – as a member of the editorial board of the newspaper Roberts intended to, and did, set up, *The Friend*. Ostensibly for the troops and their morale, this was bilingual, and was as much intended for the Boers. It was started up only two days after Bloemfontein was abandoned by the Boers. Roberts had given Kipling a pass to go wherever he wished in South Africa – and all the British congratulated those Boers at Bloemfontein who, strategically left at the posts they had occupied before their army abandoned it, ordered twenty-seven Africans to be given five lashes each for being without passes ('good work'). He thoroughly enjoyed his fortnight's stint at *The Friend*, and was able to take the opportunity, at a dinner, to propose, in the presence of Milner:

> the health of the man who has taught the British Empire its responsibilities, and the rest of the world its power, who has filled . . . the earth with the tramp of armed men . . . who has turned the loafer of the London streets into a man . . . I give you the name of the Empire-builder – Stephanus Paulus Kruger.

He also took the opportunity on this occasion to praise 'the men who wear the maple-leaf', the New Zealanders, all those colonials who wanted a bit of action and who had therefore come to South Africa to see Oum Paul destroyed (and, indeed, poor old Oum Paul did die in exile, in Switzerland).

Retrospectively, in a letter to Ted Hill of 1906, he described his times in South Africa as 'political'; he admitted that he 'enjoyed' these. Angus Wilson, quoting this, adds that his political views were 'intense, at times frenetic, ardent, subject to extremes of hope and despair and very muddled'. Wilson does not at all agree with these views, but respects them. I do not respect them, on the grounds that they express personal emotions in the guise of views, and that the views in themselves are highly dangerous and unpleasant. The emotions at this time had, I am sure, a great deal to do with the psychological instability of his wife – and I am equally sure that this instability was not much helped by her (and, indeed, his own) picture of his 'moral nature'.

He may have been driven to an extremity of excitement, or even been hypomanic, in these few weeks he spent in South Africa. Much of his attention was given to his old juvenile game of inventing high-up conspiracies of 'those in the know'. To his fellow editors of *The Friend* he suggested the formation of a Masonic-style club. Not only did he order an elaborate set of gold and enamel medals to be made for each of the editors, but he wrote down, in a one hundred-page notebook (it came into the possession of Gwynne), a sort of pastiche of Masonic ritual, itself childish enough. 'Never such fine larks,' he said of all this, and of his other activities.

On 29 March he witnessed a very minor action: Birkenhead calls this 'being under fire', but Carrington, more cautiously, calls it 'a day's holiday to watch a battle'. It does seem that he may have wished to avoid getting get too far into the thick of things, though less from cowardice than for fear he would in some way disgrace himself. In *Something of Myself* he speaks only of single bullets 'singing', which doubtless they did. Certainly he remembered the occasion, as his inclusion of it in his autobiography demonstrates.

He gained the most delight, however, by ministering to the needs of the soldiers, well and sick alike: he distributed plug tobacco amongst them, and was a frequent visitor to the wounded in hospital. Though always anxious to keep his 'name out of it' so far as tributes to his genius were concerned, he could be counted on to recite his stirring verses at hospital smoking-concerts. Then, when Ralph's son, Lester, fell dangerously ill with enteric fever, Kipling, said Julian Ralph afterwards, 'nursed him with consummate skill and the gentleness of a woman'. This tenderness lasted an hour or two: until Lester could be taken to hospital. But Kipling was deeply moved by what he saw, rather in the spirit of a poet whom he had learned to admire in his early youth, but about whom he was increasingly reticent as he grew older. Did he remember his reading of *Drum-Taps*, 'put together' (wrote Whitman) 'by fits and starts, on the field, in the hospitals, as I worked with the soldier boys' (but he was 'on the field' for longer than Kipling, and knew what he was talking about)? Had he not always approved, and even quite often almost echoed, these lines from 'Eighteen Sixty-One'?

> Arm'd year, year of the struggle,
> No dainty rhymes or sentimental love verses for you terrible year,
> Not you as some pale poetling seated at a desk lisping cadenzas piano,
> But as a strong man erect, clothed in blue clothes, advancing, carrying
> a rifle on your shoulder . . .

And did he perhaps, as he hung around the beds of the wounded, feel as Whitman had felt ('The Wound Dresser')?

> An old man bending I come among new faces . . .
> (Arous'd and angry, I'd thought to beat the alarum, and urge relentless
> war,
> But soon my fingers fail'd me, my face droop'd and I resign'd myself,
> To sit by the wounded and soothe them . . .)

> I am faithful, I do not give out,
> The fractur'd thigh, the knee, the wound in the abdomen,

These and more I dress with impassive hand (yet deep in my breast a fire,
a burning flame . . .

But once again, his pleasure and his pity, like his war feats, were
vicarious. He must return to England. His delight in being in the midst
of things was undoubted; why, then, did he have to return so soon? For
the Kiplings were in England, at Rottingdean, by May 1900. It was in
Rottingdean that he hired men to fire a cannon from the cliffs to welcome
three soldiers back from South Africa (to the disgust of Aunt Georgie), and
in Rottingdean that he celebrated the relief of Mafeking. He also founded
a shooting club, in whose competitions he took part; Birkenhead says
that his shooting was 'adequate' despite his poor eyesight, but none of
his efforts have survived. When he got back to South Africa he sent the
sergeant-instructor of the local preparatory school, who drilled Kipling's
recruits, a list of instructions which included the following:

> Men and boys' evenings to be kept separate.
> The Rifle Club may hold meetings and concerts in the shed under
> Sergeant's supervision.
> *No intoxicating drinks* allowed under any circumstances.
> The Sergeant to be the officer in charge until my return.

All this was playing at soldiers. But he seems to have been on the crest of
a mood. He took such a dislike to the local clergyman that, even after he
had left the parish, he refused to subscribe to a heater for the church that
had once been his.

They were not back in Cape Town until Christmas Day of that year. Was
Carrie always restless, complaining or ill? After they returned to England
in 1901, and after a lightning trip to Paris – in part because Carrie had been
ill – Kipling wrote to her mother:

> You have no notion what a sweet and winning little woman your
> Carrie has grown into. Her face gets more beautiful year by year
> and her character deepens and broadens with every demand upon
> it. She is near an angel, but her Puritan conscience she has inherited
> from her New England forbears still makes her take life too blame
> seriously.

Grown into? One might be excused for thinking that her mother had not
always thought her 'sweet and winning'. But more important is Kipling's
recognition of her fierce gloom.

During the winter previous to the writing of this letter, they had stayed
in Rhodes's house, the Woolsack, on his Groote Schuur estate. It had
been built in part for artists, and offered to the Kiplings whenever they
should want it. Carrington says that this was Carrie's 'ideal house' ('dear
Woolsack'). He says that it was she who persuaded Rhodes to increase
the money for the Rhodes scholarships from the planned £250 per annum
to £350 per annum.

But what did Kipling think about one of the qualifications for the scholarships: 'fondness for and success in manly outdoor sports such as cricket,
football and the like'? His poem 'The Islanders', published in *The Times* a
little over a year later, annoyed many by its reference to 'flannelled fools'
and 'muddied oafs': was its passion in this regard prompted by irritation at

Rhodes's over-valuation of the value of sport, from which, while at school, he had himself been excused? It seems so, for in this violent admonition to his countrymen to see to their preparedness for war, he warmed to the theme. Perhaps the combination of sport and Oxford was too much for him. Yet what would he have made of this passage (perhaps he read it) from the biography of Rhodes (1933) by Sarah Gertrude Millin, one of Rhodes's more enthusiastic, if not unshrewd, biographers? She wrote:

> The fact is that abnormal people are pathetically respectful of normality . . . Even Kipling, who dreamt as Rhodes dreamt . . . knew better than to make his heroes fit subjects for Rhodes Scholarships . . . he forgot that the Empire-makers have been, not the decent fellows, but men rather sickly, imaginative and artistic . . . not always very nice in their dealings.

Kipling did know about the 'dark' side of heroism, but not, it seems, so far as Rhodes was concerned. Did they all keep their conversation seemly that winter at the 'Woolsack' in order to make Carrie happy? She was usually the only lady at the table, and the talk would have been adjusted accordingly. Kipling must at times have cursed her presence. Did Rhodes admit that his private term for the quality that he described in his draft will as 'exhibition during school days of moral force of character' was 'unctuous rectitude'? Did Kipling hold forth about flannelled fools, muddied oafs and greasy idols? It is unlikely.

But would he have liked to share their cynicism, to have talked to Milner and Rhodes about the inside way of doing things? That does seem likely. Already, perhaps, he was beginning to feel stifled by his wife. Yet Rhodes idealised Kipling as a writer: himself a failure as a scholar with a deep-seated inferiority complex on the subject, he idolised 'great writers'; he would often expect Kipling to 'say' for him what he could not put into words. But he thought of literature not as the expression of truth but as rhetorical achievement, and so expected it to miss out on all the cynicism.

The Kiplings arrived in South Africa again on 7 January 1902, and within a month learned that Rhodes, after giving evidence at Princess Radziwill's trial for forgery (her influence over Rhodes much upset Kipling), was dying. But Rhodes had known for some months that his days were numbered, and that he could not take up the post of premier of Cape Colony which Milner now wished him to have. The air at Groote Schuur was oppressive to him, and he went to a little seaside cottage he had built at Muizenberg, near Cape Town. Kipling called on him every day there until 18 March, when he went into a coma (he died on 26 March). He wrote special funeral verses, but, very oddly, refused to accompany the executors (of which Jameson was one) to Bulawayo, where Rhodes had elected to be buried.

Carrington gives as the reason that these were Kipling's 'last days in Africa'; but when he adds that Jameson (and 'the pater') were his companions on the voyage home, this looks rather thin. Was Kipling afraid to pass again through hostile territory – the funeral train passed through a thousand miles of it? Carrie might easily have been concerned about it, and Kipling might have been relieved that she did. She was becoming increasingly neurotic (as Kipling more or less admitted in his letter to her mother of that epoch), and unfortunately she 'masked' it, as Birkenhead puts it, 'by a brisk managing exterior'. Such an exterior is not pleasant for others.

In the previous summer, while Kipling had been with his parents at Tisbury (always a difficult matter for Carrie, since she knew very well that they disliked her), and then with the Royal Navy on manoeuvres, she had confided hysterically to her diary:

> *July 13.* Wires from Rud. *14.* Two letters from Rud from Tisbury. *15.* Four wires from Rud. *16.* Four wires from Rud. He returns to Tisbury which appals me. My nurse comes. A night of agony. *17.* Rud goes to see Willoughby Manor. I sink down leagues in my declining stride to reach my actual physical state when not braced by necessity. An awful ghost to live with. *18.* Down and down I go. Rud writes from Tisbury. *20.* Still down. Rud joins his ship and gets into her this evening. *21.* Still more down in body my mind doing a series of acts in a circus beyond words to depict in its horrors. Rud writes from Sandown Bay at anchor. *22nd.* Dreary enough. Rud at anchor off Brighton. *26.* Rud at Shillington. I remain empty at the bottom of my collapse I think. *27.* I remain stationary at the bottom depth physically. *31.* The children return, very pleased to see me as I am to see them. *Aug 3rd.* Rud goes to Tisbury. I can not realise it – it has shocked me so. *4.* Dreadful night trying to think out the black future. *5.* Rud means to stop longer away. *6.* A night of mental agony leaves me down in the bottom of the pit and well nigh hopeless for the black future. *7.* Rud arrives at 6 p.m. Great rejoicings.

This was a private diary, of course, and it is clear from it that Carrie was given to bouts of depression when she was left alone for any substantial period of time. It is not clear, however, to what extent Carrie's account of her 'agony' is merely hysterical: Kipling used to write an 'end of the year' remark into the diary, and therefore must be supposed to have had access to it. It is, though, obvious that Carrie could be a pathological companion, jealous and possessive. The unmistakable message, since he would eventually, even if not immediately, read the diary, was: 'Don't dare go away again if you do not wish me to suffer the torments of the damned.' Birkenhead (who quotes this) brings it out more fully than Carrington, who seems to have been determined to leave the last word on Carrie's influence on Kipling to their daughter. Thus that baleful influence has been underestimated. Birkenhead, though he does not say much more (and certainly not enough), makes no bones about it: 'This strange passage is the first indication . . . of the emotional instability that was to grow upon her . . . and finally to cloud the relationship between her and Kipling.'

Could it be that, in the light of what I have suggested was their marriage bargain, Carrie worried about Kipling's moral as well as physical welfare when he was away (especially in the company of sailors)? This is possible, given her morbid and simple-minded temperament.

There is little to say about the stories Kipling wrote on the subject of the Boer War. 'A Sahib's War', written in the white heat of hatred and rage and published in December 1901 in *Windsor Magazine*, and in *Colliers*, is given in the brutal voice of an old Sikh who has accompanied his master, Captain Corbyn, to the War. The Captain is killed by treachery, so a nice piece of revenge is called for. But bad journalism is to the fore here. There is a trick reminiscent of 'The Brushwood Boy', when Corbyn contrives 'heroically' to get to South Africa by pretending to be sick – much is facetiously made of this.

Kurban Sahib, as his old servant calls him, says that 'They have taken men afoot to fight men ahorse, and they will foolishly show mercy to these Boer-log because it is believed they are white.'

Kipling does here criticise the conduct of the war, not only on the grounds of the mismanagement of horses, but also because 'no vengeance was taken'. When he was in this mood he could not control himself. He will only face this when he comes to write 'Dayspring Mishandled'. The Sikh narrator describes the Kaffirs as 'filth unspeakable', and the fact that the reader is supposed to make allowances for this bit of (splendid) Sikh racism by no means improves matters. Kipling's exercise of ambiguity does not improve matters, either: the ghost of the Captain appears to the uncomprehending Sikh, Umr, when he is about to hang the treacherous 'neutral' minister who has shot him in the liver, and forbids him to take vengeance.

He obeys this command without understanding it, and the phrase 'Sahibs' war' from then onwards takes on an ironic significance. But when Australian troops come, the 'mercy' they show to the Boers is not apparently, as Tompkins puts it, 'quite complete'. And, as she suggests, Kipling 'may be felt to have had it both ways at once'. Here it is reprehensible. The story fails because, being political, it is as artistically muddled as Kipling was politically. The fuel for it was hatred of 'neutral' Boers. Throughout his life Kipling hated non-participants in wars who were on 'the wrong side' (i.e. against the one he supported); he also hated people at home who 'knew nothing' ('what do they know of England who only England know'?). This means nothing in intellectual terms; but in personal terms it meant something to Kipling. The explanation for it is not hard to find: since he was inept at the very thing he would have liked to be brilliant at, namely fighting, he felt himself in all honesty to be a 'neutral'. Thus, as a 'neutral' (i.e. one unable to fight and be brilliantly brave and enjoy killing), he was at least bound to be 'right' in his attitudes.

Now, as Wilson (who does not like this story) claims, the plot is not particularly improbable. But what is improbable is the Sikh's attitude towards his officer as his 'baby' or 'child'. Nor is the tale free from bias. The implication here is that the Boer War was fought on the one hand by 'soft' Sahibs and on the other by treacherous and dishonest Boers. This was not the case. As we have seen, although the attitude of the British towards the Blacks was on the whole more humane, their actions towards them were careless and ruthless. That Smuts among others was not only a slaughterer of Kaffirs in the War, but also (ultimately) one of the architects of apartheid, does not change this in the least. As for the Boer 'neutrals': Kipling's attitude simply assumes that it is 'loyal' to back the British and 'disloyal' (notwithstanding one's race) to favour the Boers. That is as uncomprehending as the portrait of Umr which he gives us (and which is, incidentally, unconvincing).

'The Comprehension of Private Copper' appeared after the War. Once again the target is a 'traitor', and there is an effort to maintain an air of ambiguity. So muddled is this effort that one critic, C.A. Bodelsen, has tried to demonstrate that it is 'a daring piece of symbolisation', and that the real subject is the 'rights of the Uitlanders'. But this won't do. Private Copper, son of a 'Southdown shepherd', is taken prisoner by a rich young English-speaking farmer. But he turns the tables on him and takes him prisoner. The farmer, while he has the soldier in his power, expresses his hatred of the English. His much reiterated threat to the Sussex man is that he is going to give him a vengeful flogging, naked.

When, by a stratagem worthy of the *Boys' Own Paper*, Copper turns the tables, he says to the farmer, 'You ain't 'alf-caste, but you talk *chee-chee – pukka* bazar chee-chee.' His original idea about the farmer having been half-caste arises from listening to his enraged anti-British talk, which has seemed to some commentators to imply that he *is* half-caste. But the burden of the African's complaint seems to have been that his father, who believed in the British, found himself to be a 'prisoner of war'.

Far from there being any daring symbolisation here, there is confusion, and the reader can hardly make out whose grievance is what – only that Private Copper is heroic and resourceful and that any enemy of the English, once properly subdued, 'screams *like a woman*' (my italics). It is all strangely distasteful unless one understands that, yet again, Kipling was indulging his fascination with flogging and his hatred of himself as an inept and screaming 'feminine' 'neutral'. The story might have been better had its author made up his mind exactly who the South African was: a Boer, a half-caste, an Indian, an Etonian, or, somehow, all of these. All these are possible, but the shifting emphases have the effect of a demonic dream rather than of an exercised imagination. As Wilson points out, the relatively simple figure of Private Copper stands no chance against this confusion. Yet the business of Copper's understanding of what the farmer actually is might have been brilliant, and, although it is not, it bears the marks of a master.

The other stories with a Boer War background add nothing to Kipling's artistic achievements, but, again, rehearse various obsessions. In 'The Outsider' it is vainly demonstrated that upper-class people with private means make worse soldiers than vulgar tradesmen, an absurd generalisation. Only volunteers are really any good: to volunteer is the making of people. No wonder Kipling felt unworthy! 'The Captive' demonstrates how Americans can be wrong in siding with the Boers. Indeed, war, and Kipling's incapacity to fight in it, is responsible for much of his most irresponsible and silly writing. His partiality for other ranks over officers looks and is, in these tales, ingratiating: he did not have the courage to challenge the upper-class officers whom he despised on social occasions – yet when he felt like it, he could be rude and boorish (as in his remarks about 'yids'). The glory of being 'in' on the War proved too much for his convictions. Yet all this time, he was working at *Kim*.

No one can tell for certain just how much 'the pater' contributed to *Kim*, which is by common consent the most successful of Kipling's longer works. Kipling himself never sought to minimise his debt to his father. The origins of the book, which gave him as much trouble as anything he ever wrote, lie in the old *Mother Maturin* effort of his Indian days. His father had been against this, and so, when he visited his son in America, may well have taken pains to encourage him with *Kim*, which came into his mind again, in something like the form we know it, at that time. Certainly it is in this novel that Kipling pays his most eloquent and undistorted homage to the India that he remembered and loved – for the sake of its own virtues rather than for any putative political ones, imagined by him in the wrong way.

Kim is not, for me, quite the masterpiece that it is for many critics. That it is essentially a children's book hardly matters. But it falls between two stools: it is a book written for children *and* one written for adults, and its author can never make up his mind which. He could never have got it quite right unless he had made the painful return to India, to look at the past, irrevocably lost, in the light of the present. Understandably, he didn't have the courage to do this: he was not a man who liked to go back, and such an attitude is a part and parcel of his refusal ever to talk about people who had died, and could not be brought back into his life. Quite possibly, too, Carrie point-blank refused to go to India with him – a decision which in that case he could greet with relief. So *Kim* has a slightly laboured air as a narrative, although this is continually redeemed by its evocative descriptive touches, certainly arising from childhood memories.

Kipling fails to resolve the conflict he sets out to solve, between the Way and the Great Game; in that sense, although in that sense only, he ought not to have attempted it, since he was not capable of writing that kind of novel. Indeed, as it is, the book is more like a number of discrete episodes, or stories, than a continuous narrative. Its fault is that, paradoxically, it does successfully set up a conflict, between values material and immaterial; but it then fails to illuminate this conflict. The well-known criticism of the book, that at the end Kim has failed to choose between the Lama and government service, holds good. Yet, so far as the contrast between the characters of the Lama and Kim is concerned – the adult innocent and the precocious boy – it is brilliant, and promises so much; but it hardly delivers. Sandison claims that the end is 'absolutely proper'. Any reader can see what he means. But this verdict ignores the expectations that are set up by the book itself. We want to know what Kim will become when he is a man, and Kipling is not prepared to tell us: he does not know what he himself has become beyond childhood, and therefore he does not know what Kim will become. He cannot deal with him as a man at all. So far as the Lama is concerned: he is a mystic in any case, and mysticism, for the Western readers for whom *Kim* is intended, looks after itself.

Yet it must be conceded that Alan Sandison is right when, in his edition of the novel (1987), he asserts that it is a 'great and glowing exception' to its author's 'pathological' habit of savaging those 'whose ideas and conduct seem to him to threaten those structures which are all man has to protect his fragile identity'. That view is, of course, being charitable to Kipling, although essentially it is right: while it is true that Kipling's hatred of liberals or pro-Boers is partly explained by his conviction that they are 'subversives' who threaten what little order humanity can muster against chaos, it should not be forgotten that, first, he succumbed to hatred when he had no business to, and, secondly, that he regarded *himself*, above all, as the subversive one! Again, while Sandison is right to point out that the very first words of the novel, the heading to the first chapter, 'Oh ye who tread the Narrow Way/By Tophet-flare to Judgement Day,/Be gentle when the heathen pray/To Buddha at Kamkura', are an admonition to 'tolerance and respect', as well as 'ecumenical understanding', he forgets to add that this is very much a matter of following Kipling's mood in this instance. A writer is partly responsible for the expectations he creates in his readers, and it is hardly to be wondered at that some of the readers were unused to ideas of tolerance from this apostle of war and vengeance. Sandison writes: 'There were armies of Pharisees amongst the camp-followers of Victorian imperialism, so Kipling's plea for tolerance and respect were timely if not necessarily popular.' *Kim* for the most part does make a 'plea' for something like tolerance; but Sandison is disingenuous in failing to add that Kipling himself was one of the latter-day creators of just the Victorian imperialism that he is condemning! This is to pretend Kipling was consistent.

When writing *Kim* Kipling relaxed from a mood of rage and frus-tration – frustration that he could not be a man of action. Quoting Lockwood's remark on the 'kind of reviewer who finds fault' because there is 'no finale', Sandison says that those 'who expect Kim to make a choice' are 'wholly misguided': 'the book has never shown any signs of this sort of development'. This defence is justified: the book does end with Kim just still in childhood. But because it does so, it lacks a stature it might have had.

It is Angus Wilson who makes the most eloquent plea for *Kim*, finding the account of Kim's thirst for the new, 'magical'. Yet he unwittingly puts a finger on the main reason for its failure as a 'masterpiece':

> True, Kim will be serving British rule, but this must be read within the context of Kipling's belief that the two higher values in the book – the richness and variety of Indian life and the divine and spiritual idiocy of the Lama – can only be preserved from destruction by anarchic chaos or from despotic tyranny by that rule.

Kim finally depends – as Wilson has admitted – on a set of values (imperialist values) that exist wholly outside itself. How could the *survival* of such a man as the Lama, certainly presented as a sincere and devoted Buddhist, *depend* on any *rule*? His survival could not depend on native rule, on despotic rule, on democratic rule, or on any rule. If the Lama is credible – but is he, altogether, in the book? – then he must have a final contempt for all worldly things.

The truth is that *Kim*, fine though it is, and containing very beautiful and relaxed things, is episodic: its dependence upon 'a pictorial narrative structure' impoverishes it in the light of the expectations it is bound to create in the Western mind – and its ideology, when this does intervene, impoverishes it even more. We cannot say, 'a novel of this form *ought not* to generate a wish for a resolution' – if it does. And Kipling is not, here, clever or cunning enough to make sure that it does *not*.

That *Kim* fails to cohere as a whole, and that the Lama is hardly convincing does not, though, make it a poor book. It is still a remarkable one, shot through with a profound nostalgia for the past. It is a book that tends to lose its appeal – its magic, in Wilson's word – the more it is *thought* about. Wilson's own approach demonstrates this: he begins to try to explain his enchantment (all the more intense for his own knowledge of India), and, despite himself, draws our attention to the book's chief failing: For how can he marry his own enthusiasm and his expressed conviction that in reading *Kim* we touch 'literary heights', with his other view that, if his writing of his biography of him had been dependent upon his agreement with Kipling's views, then he could not have brought it off? For he here clearly shows that *Kim* does depend upon an agreement with Kipling's view, here not merely disagreeable and unrealistic, but plain nonsense in at least its assertion that immaterialism depends on materialism.

That is not to say that the problem of the conflict between the Way and the Great Game, how it looks to a Westerner, is not well and ably presented. It is; and, as Wilson rightly asserts, it is done magically. But despite the undoubted spell cast by the book, one may rather too easily see through it. *Kim* is the nostalgic history of Kipling's childhood, in which he makes himself out to have been more of a scamp, and more important (at one point Kim carries 'a few score thousand other folks' fates round his neck' – which simply does not bear much thinking about, being a sudden lapse into fantasy and polemic that is unworthy of its context), than he really was. That Kipling's proneness to fantasise is here under benign auspices, gives the novel a charm and kindly tone that is lacking in some contemporaneous work. But it does not make it into a novel proper, and I do not believe that the special pleading on its behalf is convincing. Kipling was a master of the short story, but never of the novel as a form. What operates more strongly than the Lama's mystical 'innocence', which is never really compulsive of belief (and is depicted with some patronisation), is the love he feels for Kim.

An almost paedophilic attractiveness is given to Kim himself. This may endow *Kim* with a special magic for those who like little boys. Such readers will appreciate the episode in Lurgan Sahib's shop when the Hindu boy, out of jealousy of Kim, tries to kill Lurgan. The last-named is an ambiguous figure. Indeed, had Kipling been permitted to be explicit about these overtones and undertones, he might have written an even more successful book. But he could only smuggle in such details; and in any case he was not consciously aware of what vein of feeling in himself he was exploring. Angus Wilson points out that, although Kim is successfully kept by Kipling from 'being fully sexual', he is nonetheless 'remarkably physically beautiful'; he is 'flirtatious with all and sundry'. His beauty is fully appreciated by Creighton, the Lama, Lurgan, and the other male characters in the book, and it is a tribute to Kipling's artistic cunning that this should be so. It explains Wilson's remark that none of the 'sensuality' is explicitly sexual.

But, if it is not explicitly sexual, the sexuality nonetheless is there – or no one would need to mention it at all. 'I do not believe that this is Victorian self-censorship upon the part of Kipling,' declares Wilson; but here he forgets that without such 'self-censorship' the book could not have been published . . . How could Kipling possibly have made Kim *explicitly* 'flirtatious' with the grown-up male characters?

But there is in fact no question of conscious motive: safe under the auspices of the pater, Kipling would never have suspected himself of paedophilic emotions. That he may later have been aware of himself, or suddenly realised of what he was 'guilty', is another matter altogether. The straightforward references to prostitutes in the book were perfectly acceptable to its readership, since, whether 'daring' or not, they do not touch upon the 'forbidden'. But what is truly appealing in this novel is

Kipling's reaping of the harvest of the Pre-Raphaelitism of his youth; and he was hardly ever, from the time he left school (if not earlier than that), prepared to acknowledge this even to himself. Even the raffish paedophilia of it all, so beautifully done perhaps because so unconsciously done, is at heart decadent Pre-Raphaelite. It is where the strength of the book lies.

Mrs Bathurst

Horse-bus loads of sightseers from nearby Brighton, and even farther afield, come to inspect one's property would be irritating for anyone; for Rudyard and Carrie at Rottingdean it was beyond endurance. They remembered with horror the attentions of the American journalists, both before and after the Beatty affair in Vermont. They also associated with Rottingdean what little of Josephine's childhood (by all accounts, she had been unusually lively, witty and enchanting) they had been vouchsafed to know. Again, and sadly, the increasing eccentricity and pathological bossiness of Carrie, together with his own political attitudes, were causing Kipling to become estranged from his relatives who lived on the green. There is much evidence that he grew morose and unhappy in his last two years there, although not as morose and unhappy as he became during the last seventeen years of his life.

Lockwood wrote to Susan Norton that Carrie and Rudyard had found their return there in 1899 'much harder and more painful than they had imagined', the house and garden seeming to them 'full of the lost child'; but Carrie, he continued, 'hitherto . . . stone-dumb', had 'to Mrs K . . . softened', and 'broke forth and they had long discourse, mingling their tears as women and mothers must'. Lockwood thought then that the loss would 'grow easier to bear with time'; but, for various reasons, it did not really, for either of them. Rudyard tried hard to pay tribute, and give expression to, Carrie's grief; and he himself (Lockwood told Susan Norton), saw Josephine 'when a door opened, when a space was vacant at table, coming out of every green dark corner of the garden'.

As most unhappy people are inclined to do, the Kiplings tended to put the blame for their unhappiness on their house, The Elms. Once Kipling may have liked it. Now it had too sad associations. He must, too, have given up any hope of leading a 'normal' life: the way Carrie's personality was developing, of which he had given her mother more than a hint, must have augmented his own almost morbid need for invisibility from the world.

The unhappiness they both felt at Rottingdean did not go unnoticed, and in all probability their neighbours and relatives put it down to their recent tragic loss, rather than to Kipling's enthusiasm for the British cause in South Africa. However much some may have shared this enthusiasm, in his case they more likely put it down to the eccentricity of a great man – or 'genius' – than to normal patriotic emotion: Kipling much strained his ideal, and a strained ideal is always obvious to beholders. But he was always, as a 'great man', in the position that he would be humoured, rather than challenged (although even the authorities became annoyed with his aggressive and ignorant recruiting activities).

He now quarrelled with the members of his own rifle club, and closed down the hall he had built for them. They were getting tired of him at the Plough, the local pub, and even started to challenge his unique authority. At his next abode he would make no visits to the local pub. Some good-hearted neighbours, however, tried to protect them from the worse excesses of the tourists and gawpers. One, a Mrs Ridsdale, used to refuse to guide these people if they answered her question, 'Have you read anything of his?' with a negative; most did. They had to have their gate boarded over with a hole left to put the hand through to open it from the inside – and the now majestic and broad-bodied Carrie on more than one occasion had to ask a crowd to disperse in order to make entrance to her own property.

The pressure increased their morbidity of outlook. They started to go house-hunting in their chauffeured motor-car – and money was no object. In *Something of Myself* Kipling recalls the moment he first saw Bateman's:

> We had seen an advertisement of her, and we reached her down an enlarged rabbit-hole of a lane. At first sight the Committee of Ways and Means said: 'That's her! The Only She! Make an honest woman of her – quick.' We entered and felt her Spirit – her Feng Shui – to be good. We went through every room and found no shadow of ancient regrets, stifled miseries, nor any menace though the 'new' end of her was three hundred years old! To our woe the Owner said: 'I've just let it for twelve months.' We withdrew, each repeatedly telling the other that no sensible person would be found dead in the stuffy little valley where she stood. We lied thus while we pretended to look at other houses till, a year later, we saw her advertised again, and got her.

His memory slightly failed him – or he condensed his account. This was their second visit: they saw it, dithered for three days, and then found to their consternation that someone else had rented it. Two years later, in 1902, they heard that it was vacant again, took the train to Etchingham (the nearest station), and then a hired fly. They took possession on 3 September. One can see why Kipling now felt (although he would not have put it like this) that he must hide Carrie from the public view, if not from that of his closer friends.

Carrie took the move hard. She confided her misery to her diary:

> *Sept. 3.* Go to Bateman's to meet chaos and black night. Hudson has not kept a single promise and foreman of removers is drunk. Labour and struggle to put things right. *4.* A hopeless day. *5.* Fought with workmen and cleaners all day long. A terrible day.

This 'running commentary of peevish complaint' might have been confined only to the diary, and one does note the vein of black humour in 'chaos and black night'; not a few people are like that. But in Carrie's case, as we have good reason to know, it was not confined to the diary. Those in the thrall of her employment were, with one or two exceptions, the victims of the malicious construction she put on the universe. When one remembers that she was supposed to have been in love with the new house, one begins to wonder what she was like when she *dis*liked anything. As Mr Walter Frizell, a former employee still alive today, puts it: 'Someone should have told her that she never had it so good.' (He was agreeing with Lord Stockton's candid remark, in one of the last interviews he gave to television, that Kipling 'married the wrong woman'.)

Kipling tended to express his official self, the self that felt how he thought it ought to feel, rather than how it did, to C.E. Norton, one of those many 'close acquaintances' who counted for him as close friends. Now at last really disposing of the American house – and for a poor price ($8000), because the relentless Beatty gave out that he was disputing the title, although of course he had no intention of doing that – Kipling told Norton on 30 November, when Carrie was recovering from the move, that they had left Rottingdean because it was 'getting too populated'. 'England is a wonderful land,' he said defiantly to Norton, 'the most marvellous of the foreign countries I have been in', 'and at last I'm one of the gentry'. He valued this greatly, and valued it at the expense of his contact with the common people. But it is only fair to add, here, that he may simply have abdicated to Carrie's snobbery and acute malice towards them.

The house, pure Jacobean, was completed in 1634, built (tradition insists, for its history is incomplete) for an ironmaster in those days when the Kent, Sussex and Surrey (Wealden) iron industry, which so caught Kipling's imagination, still prospered. This industry had been active in Roman times, but then fell into desuetude until early Tudor times, when it was revived. One of the biggest forges in the entire area was situated at the village of Burwash, to which the house lay less than a mile to the south.

The Kiplings, with the advice of Sir William Willcocks, who had installed the hydro-electrics at Aswan in Egypt not so long before, put electricity into the house in 1903: they harnessed the Dudwell at an old Mill, now famous, that lay at the bottom of the garden.

It is a lovely house in itself, but melancholy. It lies too low in the valley to be cheerful. Beautiful in the summer, when the sun is shining, it is grim, oppressive and very often misty in the winter, while the air above it is clear all over. Most are agreed that Kingsley Amis's description of it as an 'overground dungeon' is appropriate. What must have attracted the Kiplings, whatever they really said about it to each other, was that it was perfect for the preservation of privacy – too perfect. That they had earned the right to be fanatical about their privacy must be allowed; but neither learned to handle it graciously or well.

They decorated the house pleasantly, with a mixture of Pre-Raphaelite and Jacobean furniture, and some Indian items; on the whole the interior decoration shows the influence of the 'pater' more than that of his daughter-in-law.

After their purchase of this lonely house that was so gloomy in spite of itself, and of the undoubted beauty of its setting in the little valley of the River Dudwell, a not always insubstantial tributary of the Rother, their lives settled down into a routine. Until 1908, as has been noted, they went to South Africa for six months of the year. After that they were away elsewhere for that period of time in each year.

The only personal events that touched them deeply were: Kipling's slow but certain descent into illness, manifesting itself in increasing abdominal anguish and costiveness; Carrie's descent into even deeper depression and domineeringness (causing Walter Frizell to refer to her, in a moment of retrospective candour, as a 'wicked old bitch', and Bob Crouch, a former cowhand reminiscing on local radio, to burst out, having granted that Mr Kipling was 'always a gentleman', 'but Mrs Kipling, she was no lady!'); the First World War, and of course the death of young John Kipling in action at Loos. The marriage of their daughter Elsie to Captain Bambridge in October 1924 also caused them (as Elsie herself acknowledged) much jealous misery.

They added to the property as the years went by, thus rendering it even more stranger-proof. By 1905 they had Rye Green Dairy Farm, Mill Park Farm, and Dudwell Mill Farm. The property of thirty-three acres they had originally bought, for just under £10,000, was eventually extended to three hundred acres. Mrs Kipling insisted that everyone living on her land or in her houses should, without exception, be employed by her. This sometimes led to friction.

Kipling, the friend of the common soldier, made the initial mistake of regarding the quite large staff he employed as children. Apart from the chauffeur and the private secretary, who enjoyed higher status, there were eventually over a dozen labourers, a head gardener (always being changed), and a wily carter who eventually got the Kiplings' measure and refused to leave when dismissed. Kipling told one of his earlier private secretaries, Miss Dorothy Ponton, that she would 'get on all right with the farm-hands if you treat the men as boys of fourteen and the women as younger in intellect'. This is not a good way to get yourself liked, and the ordinary people of Burwash, while duly awed by Kipling's fame, disliked him and Carrie, and felt that they did no good for their village, described oddly by Carrington as 'unfrequented', despite its large number of pubs (relics of coaching days). Since they bought almost everything from the Army and Navy Stores, one can immediately see why at least the tradesmen were not enamoured of the strange couple.

They were, in most respects, though scrupulous about rates of pay, bad and uninterested employers. Carrie was worse, being positively malicious. Yet Kipling told Rider Haggard (22 December 1902): 'I *do* want to make it possible to rear clean and healthy men on my fraction of England.' (In this same letter he tells Haggard off for referring, in one of his books, to a 'Hornsley or Horley oil Engine' when it should be 'Hornsby-Ackroyd I fancy'. He added, 'I have one for my electric light and sawing.' But the generator was in fact by Compton and Co., and at that point was not yet even built! This suggests that Kipling could not resist correcting others, even at the expense of a little fiction).

Miss Ponton, who wrote not only *Rudyard Kipling at Home and at Work* (1953), but also *The Knowall Maths, The Wonderwhy Tales* and *How Numbers and Letters Began*, went there in 1911 as secretary, and found Kipling's advice to her 'invaluable' when 'petty feuds' sprang up amongst the employees. But they never agreed with her assessment of such feuds, and preferred her successor Miss Gardener-Smith.

It is not hard to see why Kipling has acquired such a deserved reputation for concealing everything. Such acute defensiveness raises a question in itself. But the ability in concealment that he displays in his personal life does pass over into the best of his fiction. I have not said, and shall not say, much about the public precepts he preached in his speeches and addresses, and which comprise the most boring and least read volumes of his collected works. They were like 'If', and like that poem original only in the intensity with which they gathered together and then drummed home the unoriginal, the stilted: that false but necessary cheer which is, precisely, the phenomenologically unreal.

Kipling was by now well into his marriage, and well into a private realisation that Carrie's gloom was not going to be dispelled by motherhood, as he must certainly, whatever his original guilt feelings, have hoped. He had also perfectly developed his public face; and that perfect development demanded that, along with all the other leading imperialists whose views he reflected – giving them an extra poetical glow – he become angrily disillusioned with the failure of successive governments to maintain the forces in a state of preparedness. It was made easier for him to attack the government, even before the defeat of the Tories in 1906, when Chamberlain resigned in October 1903 on the issue of colonial preference. The resignation was felt to be a blight on imperialist prospects, and Kipling chose to register it with a sense of personal bitterness. With *The Five Nations* he, as Carrington puts it, 'put South African affairs behind him'. But not imperialism. He became more obsessed with this as soon as he did give up South African affairs in disgust: in Angus Wilson's words, the 'court poet of a dynasty that was at its end'. This gave him something other than Carrie to complain at in the privacy of his mind. And it was all the more effective a safety-valve because he believed in it. It is fortunate for us that his qualms should have taken so thoroughly underground a form: his best writings. Wilson continues:

> Increasingly in his correspondence, even from 1903 onwards, there comes a kind of shrill, hysterical, gossipy note whenever South African politics are being discussed, a note of the supporter in the grandstand who sees his team steadily losing and yet cannot admit to himself that they are playing a losing game from the start – it is a reflection in little of the world view that he was proclaiming back in England.

Kipling was particularly vehement in his condemnation of the man who took Milner's place in 1905, Sir Walter Hely-Hutchinson, whom, characteristically, he saw as a kind of spy determined to subvert the Empire so far as he could. But all that hysteria was largely a matter of habit – fame, and the approval that it can gather, makes bad habits easier to maintain – and, as I have suggested, a safety-valve for the release of personal emotions of a negative sort. Kipling's public face did not allow, so to say, for an 'inner tension' (as Wilson rightly terms it) between the desire for the new, which excited him just as machines did, and which was inspired by the radicalism of his heroes – and his more buried but more certain love for the old, the traditional, the Indian, the 'native'. In South Africa he went awry because he had no feeling at all for the Boers (and don't let us fail to grant him, or at least his daimon, a certain intuitive foresight, for in the mass they are a cruel people), or for the indigenous population (any pleas on their behalf were, alas, strictly temporary grist for his colonial mill). But underneath all this bluster, unavoidable in a man of such high energy as Kipling, something very different was going on. The daimon was not going to allow such outlets unhindered.

In the years between 1902 and 1914 Kipling published, after *Just So Stories for Little Children* (1902), five books (and the *Definitive Edition*): *The Five Nations* (1903), *Traffics and Discoveries* (1904), *Puck of Pook's Hill* (1906), *Actions and Reactions* (1909) and *Rewards and Fairies* (1910). He published only three more story collections.

Traffics and Discoveries is one of his weaker collections. Certainly it marks, as Edmund Wilson noted, 'the beginning of the more sombre Kipling'. Here he began his regular later practice of interspersing stories with poems (he had done it earlier, but intermittently: it was doubtless a means of lending the reader a helping hand in making out his meaning, which he started to realise he had deliberately withheld to what was an unreasonable degree), although he does not here usually bring it to the fine cryptic art of the later stories. Of the eleven stories the volume contains, only three are really memorable: 'They', 'Wireless' and 'Mrs Bathurst'. It is significant that these three most notable tales are all, to a certain degree, personal in a sense that the others are not; this is to say, they clearly draw their power from personal experience.

'Wireless' and 'Mrs Bathurst' are about obsessive love and the suffering it entails. 'Mrs Bathurst' was greatly admired, although not always for explicit reasons; then a reaction set in, and Angus Wilson and Kingsley Amis attacked it as pretentious, over-revised, over-complex, over-compressed and lacking in intelligibility. Norman Page (*A Kipling Companion*, 1984) was nearer the mark in drawing attention to the manner in which its 'obscure power' exercises 'a perennial fascination'. Eliot Gilbert has devoted an essay to it (*The Good Kipling*, 1972). One or two 'solutions' to the tale (these tend to treat it as if it were a kind of superior crossword puzzle) are patently impossible or else over-ingenious, yet – and here again we must pay tribute to Kipling's cunning and skill – irresistible. The 'meaning' of the story, as dense as that of a Shakespeare play or a Hardy novel, lies in how we try to answer the questions set by the text: we need to understand, if not at the outset, that there is no single meaning, no single 'explanation'. Or *is* that what we should understand?

'Mrs Bathurst' comes into the category of supreme literature, leading such critics as Walter Allen to put Kipling at the top of their lists of short-story writers in the English language. It is always hard to give the exact reasons why writing does come into this category; but one of them must be that it has the thrilling ambiguity of that kind of experience which touches the heart, which, to adapt what Wordsworth said of poetry, is recollected in a tranquillity redolent with colloquial exactitude. One of the story's most powerful features – though to draw attention to this is to isolate it artificially – is to make use of the novelty of the influence (then) of the new technique of moving pictures. Its influence on movies must have been as incalculable as it is unacknowledged. The wary reader must here be alive to, and perpetually on the lookout for, what has become known as 'synchronicity'. Joyce's name for this was an 'epiphany': moments of significant and breathtaking coincidence. The sense of aptness perhaps derives from the Heraclitan realisation that 'character is fate', that the state of a person's being attracts the circumstances of his life: suddenly, here, this is clarified. Then such moments are lost to us, and banality (here presented in the form of the facetious reminiscences of Pyecroft and his acquaintances: the frame of the story) returns; but nothing is ever quite the same again – and no one is ever quite the same again, after reading this tale.

It was distilled by extreme suffering. Yeats spoke of perfection of the life *or* of the art, and nowhere is this better illustrated than in 'Mrs Bathurst'. Kipling's life had become imperfect and unhappy: morose, disappointed, crude, false. Yet his daimon, using him like a telephone wire (for years he would not have the actual instrument put into Bateman's, and when he did it was in the sole control of Carrie), produced this in defiance of it all. No wonder he felt unworthy when he considered his life by the side of it. It is the same with any successful creative artist.

When in 1914 or late 1913 Rider Haggard sent him what was probably the manuscript of his play *The Wanderer's Necklace* (published in January 1914), based on a Norse tale of reincarnation, Kipling reacted by saying that he was an 'envious dramatist'. The two men did not (unfortunately) write much on the subject in their letters; but they must have talked a great deal about it. Both were interested in all aspects of reincarnation.

Kipling was unlucky with stage adaptations of his books and stories, and *The Harbour Watch*, a play he wrote with Elsie, although performed once or twice, was not a success. He also wrote fragments of a strange pastiche of Jacobean drama, which he called either *Gow's Watch*, or 'Lyden's *Irenius*'. Some passages are extant, and appear 'enlarged from various sources' in the *Definitive Edition* as *Gow's Watch* – but not 'Act III, Scene II' which prefaces 'Mrs Bathurst'.

Both 'They' and 'Wireless' deal with the reincarnation theme, or some aspect of it; whether 'Mrs Bathurst' does is more problematical. Few if any commentators apart from Tompkins have given attention to Kipling's unprecedented experiments in verse drama – for the very good reason that, on the face of it, they are scarcely intelligible. But, while I will not pretend to offer the key to this mystery, the bit from the *Gow* tragedy that precedes 'Mrs Bathurst' is worth looking at, and particularly so because, although occasionally mentioned, it is never discussed, and, I suspect, very seldom read.

> *Gow.* – Had it been your Prince instead of a groom caught of this noose there's not an astrologer of the city –
> *Prince.* – Sacked! Sacked! We were a city yesterday.
> *Gow.* – So be, but I was not governor. Not an astrologer, but would ha' sworn he's foreseen it at the last versary of Venus, when Vulcan caught her with Mars in the house of stinking Capricorn. But since 'tis Jack of the Straw that hangs, the forgetful stars had it not on their tablets.
> *Prince.* – Another life! Were there any left to die? How did the poor fool come by it?
> *Gow.* – *Simpliciter* thus. She that damned him to death knew not that she did it, or would have died ere she had done it. For she loved him. He that hangs him does so in obedience to the Duke, and asks no more than 'Where is the rope?' The Duke, very exactly he hath told us, works God's will, in which holy employ he's not to be questioned. We have then left upon this finger, only Jack whose soul now plucks the left

sleeve of Destiny in Hell to overtake why she clapped him up like a fly
`on a sunny wall. Whuff! Soh!
Prince. – Your cloak, Ferdinand. I'll sleep now.
Ferdinand. – Sleep, then . . . He too, loved his life?
Gow. – He was born of woman . . . but at the end threw life from him,
like your Prince, for a little sleep . . . 'Have I any look of a King?' said
he, clanking his chain – 'so to be baited on all sides by Fortune, that I
must e'en now die to live with myself one day longer.' I left him railing
at Fortune and woman's love.
Ferdinand. – Ah, woman's love!
(Aside) Who knows not Fortune, glutted on easy thrones,
Stealing from feasts as rare to coneycatch,
Privily in the hedgerows for a clown
With that same cruel-lustful hand and eye,
Those nails and wedges, that one hammer and lead,
Are the very gerb of long-stored lightnings loosed
Yesterday 'gainst some King.

Either this is a piece of fun, with no relation to what follows it; or it
has a partial (casual) relation to it; or it offers the key to it. I have met
no reader who can say exactly what it means; and many who believe
'Lyden's *Irenius*' to be a real play . . . Let us, for the time being, leave it
aside; but keep it in mind.

The frame, a device developed and elaborated by Kipling from very old
practice, is provided here by a convivial meeting between the narrator
and three others in a 'brake-van chalked for repair'. It all comes about
because the narrator's visit to a ship has been frustrated by its absence
up the coast. His friend Inspector Hooper, a detective on the Cape
Government Railways, runs them down line to a place that is cool. They
are soon joined by Second-Class Petty Officer Emanuel Pyecroft – in other
stories a facetious bore – and his friend Pritchard, an enormous Marine
Sergeant with a black moustache, Pyecroft's old shipmate. They begin to
reminisce, over bottles of Bass, and the conversation drifts to deserters, of
whom the most remarkable, according to Pyecroft, has a name beginning
with 'V'. They are not altogether happy with the subject, and qualify 'desertion' (as service people always do) by saying, 'only permanent absence
up-country'. We learn the deserter's nickname before we learn his name:
'Click.' He was sent to Bloemfontein to take over some navy ammunition
left in the fort there, took it, but disappeared. This has been the talk of the
fleet. Hooper, the inspector, is interested; but we do not know why. The
talk gets a little heated, and the narrator, in order to 'tide over the uneasy
little break', asks why he was called Click. Because, explains Pyecroft,

an ammunition hoist broke away and knocked out four of his teeth:
'The substitutes which he bought weren't screwed home, in a manner
of sayin'. When he talked fast they used to lift a little on the bed-plate.
'Ence, 'Click'. They called 'im a superior man, which is what we'd call
a long, black-'aired, genteely speakin', 'alf-bred beggar on the lower
deck.

It becomes clear that Hooper knows something about a man answering
to the description, and the marine, Pritchard, tries to leave – he thinks
Hooper is after Vickery; but the narrator 'takes responsibility' for Hooper.
Then Mrs Bathurst is introduced:

'Why did Vickery run?' I began, but Pyecroft's smile made me turn my question to 'Who was she?'

'She kep' a little hotel at Hauraki – near Auckland,' said Pyecroft.

'By Gawd!' roared Pritchard, slapping his hand on his leg. 'Not Mrs Bathurst!'

Pyecroft nodded slowly, and the Sergeant called all the powers of darkness to witness his bewilderment.

Pritchard, who has not before heard of this, protests that 'you don't make me believe that was any of 'er fault. She wasn't *that*!' It also emerges that Vickery has been married, and has a fifteen-year-old daughter. Some care is taken to establish the personality of Mrs Bathurst, who is described as a 'Queen of air and darkness' figure, but in a more plebeian context. The 'Queen of air and darkness' is, of course, Housman's enigmatic poem: an expression of both the 'romantic agony' in general, and his own homosexual predicament. I do not want to try to draw too close a parallel between it and 'Mrs Bathurst' – but it does have the same enigmatic air, and in both the lyric and in the tale there is a 'fatal' female figure:

Her strong enchantments failing,
  Her towers of fear in wreck,
Her limbecks dried of poisons
  And the knife at her neck.

The Queen of air and darkness
  Begins to shrill and cry,
'O young man, O my slayer,
  Tomorrow you shall die.'

O Queen of air and darkness,
  I think 'tis truth you say,
And I shall die tomorrow;
  But you will die today.

Mrs Bathurst is not so aggressive; yet here are these two men discussing just how she could bring such a man as 'Click' to defeat and despair. 'She – she never scrupled to feed a lame duck or set 'er foot on a scorpion at any time of 'er life.' Even this magnificent piece of information fails to satisfy Pyecroft, who says it 'don't help him . . . My mother's like that for one'. Clearly Mrs Bathurst is in some indefinable way, to these two men (who have seen her only a few times), *different* from other women. Pyecroft says:

. . . I've only been to Auckland twice – how she stood an' what she was sayin' an' what she looked like. That's the secret. 'Tisn't beauty, so to speak, nor good talk necessarily. It's just It. Some women'll stay in a man's memory if they once walk down the street, but most of 'em you can live with a month on end, an' next commission you'd be put to it to certify whether they talked in their sleep or not, as one might say.

To this Hooper says that he has known a couple of women 'of that nature', and Pritchard, trying to get his (and Pyecroft's) sense of Mrs Bathurst across, immediately asks, 'An it was no fault of theirs'. Does this imply that, as in the Housman poem, such women are *doomed*? There follows a key piece of dialogue:

> 'None whatever, I know *that*!'
> 'An' if a man gets struck with that kind o' woman, Mr Hooper?' Pritchard went on.
> 'He goes crazy – or just saves himself,' was the answer.
> 'You've hit it,' said the Sergeant. 'You've seen and known somethin' in the course o' your life, Mr Hooper. I'm lookin' at you!' He set down his bottle.
> 'And how often had Vickery seen her?' I asked.
> 'That's the dark and bloody mystery,' Pyecroft answered. 'I'd never come across him till I came out in the *Hierophant* just now, an' there wasn't any one in the ship who knew much about him. You see, he was what you call a superior man. 'E spoke to me once or twice about Auckland and Mrs B on the voyage out. I called that to mind subsequently. There must 'ave been a good deal between 'em, to my way o' thinkin'. Mind you, I'm only givin' you my *resumé* of it all, because all I know is second-hand, so to speak, or rather I should say more than second-hand.'

The reader has to be attentive to everything here. Note, for instance, the name of the ship on which Pyecroft sailed with Vickery (the Hierophant – or Pope – is one of the Greater Arcana of the Tarot pack; possibly Kipling followed Mathers, and saw it as representing 'Mercy' or 'Beneficence', although its original significance seems to have been 'religion').

Pyecroft now goes on to give his account of Vickery's extraordinary behaviour when he and Pyecroft went to 'Home and Friends for a Tickey'. This was the cinematograph or biograph given during the performance at Phyllis' Circus in Cape Town (a tickey is a threepenny-bit). Vickery has desired him to accompany him, while sober – even to the extent of paying for his ticket. The sight of Vickery's face, Pyecroft says, 'quite cured me of my thirsts': 'Don't mistake. It didn't frighten me. It made me anxious . . . If you want to know, it reminded me of those things in bottles in those herbalistic shops in Plymouth – preserved in spirits of wine. White an' crumply things – previous to birth as you might say.' There is certainly something ineffably sinister and unpleasant about a white and crumply thing *previous* to birth, and even the Sergeant comments that Pyecroft has a 'beastial mind'.

At the show Vickery asks him to note 'anything that strikes him'. They watch 'London Bridge an' so forth an' so on, an' it was very interestin'' – Hooper points out that, 'you see', 'they are taken from the very thing itself', an observation that may certainly be made of stories in general. Then the Western Mail coming into Paddington is shown,

> Then the doors opened and the passengers came out and the porters got the luggage – just like life. Only – only when any one came down too far towards us that was watchin', they walked right out o' the picture, so to speak. I was 'ighly interested, I can tell you. So were all of us. I watched an old man with a rug 'oo'd dropped a book an' was tryin' to pick it up, when quite slowly, from be'ind two porters – carryin' a little reticule an' looking from side to side – comes out Mrs Bathurst. There was no mistakin' the walk in a hundred thousand. She came forward – right forward – she looked out straight at us with that blindish look which

Pritchard alluded to. She walked on and on till she melted out of the picture – like – like a shadow jumpin' over a candle, an' as she went I 'eard Dawson in the tickey seats be'ind sing out: 'Christ! there's Mrs B!'

Vickery, Pyecroft reports, 'clickin' his four false teeth with his jaw down like an enteric at his last kick' – like a dying man, be it noted – wants to be sure, and even asks Pyecroft to come again the next day to make doubly sure.

We have experienced three things (at least) here. First, our own growing attention to the story. What *is* happening? Secondly, the account of the cinematograph show. Thirdly, Mrs Bathurst herself twice over (so, as Pyecroft would say, to speak): as herself reanimated in the memories of the sailor spectators, and as an image on film, then so much of a novelty as to shock deeply anybody who recognised someone they knew on it, coming (threateningly, like Nemesis?) towards them, and towards the terrified Vickery most of all.

They go to the show four more times, simply for the forty-five seconds of Mrs Bathurst's appearance, interspersing their attendance with heavy drinking. Vickery becomes increasingly disturbed, murderous in mood, even suicidal, and when Pyecroft says to him, 'I wonder what she's doin' in England . . . Don't it seem to you she's lookin' for somebody?' answers, 'She's lookin' for me . . . Yes, lookin' for me . . . *But* . . . in future, Mr Pyecroft, I should take it kindly of you if you'd confine your remarks to the drinks set before you. Otherwise . . . with the best will in the world towards you, I may find myself guilty of murder!'

He visits the captain of the ship. What transpires is not known – only that the captain is angry, and that Vickery is detailed to go up-country.

Pyecroft, with his innate shrewdness and his own recognition of the power of Mrs Bathurst, so ubiquitous in the memories of sailors, doesn't want to know any more, and tells Vickery, 'Consume your own smoke.' Vickery answers:

> You! . . . What have you got to complain of? – you've only 'ad to watch. I'm *it* . . . but that's neither here nor there . . . I've only one thing to say before shakin' 'ands. Remember . . . remember, that I'm *not* a murderer, because my lawful wife died in childbed six weeks after I came out. That much at least I'm clear of.

He will say no more, but, as a 'superior man' might, quotes *Hamlet*: 'the rest is silence'. Then, having seen the guns into the trucks, he disappears, 'within eighteen months of his pension'.

One more detail remains: when Pyecroft remarks how, in the kind of south-east wind in which he walked around with the half-crazed Vickery (it is blowing even now, outside the carriage where they sit), he can 'hear those teeth click, so to say', Hooper, fingering his waistcoat pocket, says, 'Permanent things false teeth are. You read about 'em in all the murder trials.' Does he have the teeth in this pocket? We do not know for certain; only that Hooper simply returns to a question he had asked of the narrator, just as they were interrupted by Pyecroft and Pritchard, as to whether he knew Wankies 'on the way to the Zambezi – beyond Bulawayo'. He then told the narrator, feeling in the waistcoat pocket, that he had a 'curiosity' for him, or 'more of a souvenir perhaps than . . .' Now, could false teeth possibly be a 'souvenir', under any circumstances, and especially to a totally ignorant narrator? Would not four false teeth on a small plate be a somewhat grotesque gift from anyone? Be that as it may, he now takes this up again and tells the company, 'There's a curious bit o' line there, you see. It runs through solid teak forest . . . seventy-two miles without a curve . . . I was up there a month ago relievin' a sick inspector . . . He told me to look out for a couple of tramps in the teak.'

Pyecroft catches on very quickly indeed: 'Two? . . . I don't envy that other man . . .' Hooper finishes his account: they often get tramps there, he saw these two . . . looking up at him; they were 'stone dead', struck by lightning, 'as black as charcoal'. He buried them, since there was nothing else he could do. 'They fell to bits when we tried to shift 'em. The man who was standin' up had the false teeth. I saw 'em shinin' up against the black.' He had asked about marks because Vickery had a tattoo on his arms and chest, 'a crown and foul anchor with M.V. above'. How could he have seen that when they were burned black? 'You know how writing shows up white on a burned letter. Well, it was like that, you see. And I buried 'em in the teak and I kept . . . But he was a friend of you two gentlemen, you see.' He puts his hand to his waistcoat pocket, but draws it away – empty.

Irritated critics of this story tend to misjudge it by grasping after 'evidence'. But this is a story, prompted by the then very new technique of movie-making, about the telling of stories; actually about – one might say – why we are so often irritated by life itself: it consists of various almost random features, such as might very well entertain a crowd at a circus. The teeth themselves, so much at the centre of it, are *false*. It is, like the very best stories (for example, *Don Quixote*), incidentally the most precious of all sorts of literary criticism.

Four people are thrown gratuitously together, through an initial error on the part of the narrator, and their talk over beer settles gradually into the pursuit of what is *to them* a mystery. The story is not, at its first level, about the nature of the precise connection between Vickery and Mrs Bathurst at all: that intriguing matter only comes into it by chance. It is about stories themselves, and how they arise: about reality. We are not 'taking up a book' here, but getting a story in a different way. At the second level 'Mrs Bathurst' is, clearly, about 'significant coincidence', or 'synchronicity'. At the third level it is 'about' Mrs Bathurst and Vickery; and our curiosity is, indeed, aroused. We are bound to ask the questions that have so often been asked. What do we really know about Vickery? But – perhaps an even more germane question – what do we know about *Hooper*?

This story has provoked so many fantastic questions, to which so many fantastic answers have been given, that there is nothing incongruous about the suggestion that all might not be as it seems, that someone may not be acting, or speaking, in good faith. After all, Pyecroft's own initial tale about the sailor Boy Niven, who lured eight sailors away with a lie – he had been *reading books*, and wanted a day ashore and to 'have himself talked of' – is about a kind of bad faith: when Pyecroft and Pritchard, as both remember without rancour, get back to their ship, they are accused of leading Niven astray. Gilbert has pointed this out in his essay on the story, in which he ably argues the case for its being 'about' 'the fortuitousness of life', 'the intransigence of the universe'. But he insists that 'inability to apportion blame correctly follows necessarily from the fortuitousness of life'. He feels that the indignation of Pyecroft and Pritchard about Boy Niven's unfairness entails a reversal of values when they come to speak of Vickery, in their 'vehement' exoneration of Mrs Bathurst. But they don't exonerate Mrs Bathurst at all. They simply state that they *can't believe* that any of Vickery's sufferings *could* be her fault! Gilbert goes on to suggest, rightly I think, that Mrs Bathurst is, by her capacity to arouse love in men, an unwilling agent of disaster for them – but this misses the point of Pyecroft's and Pritchard's confidence in her innocence of wrongdoing: being men, and having seen and been struck by her, they would be thus confident! Mrs Bathurst's emphasised 'blindish' way of looking tells us that she was short-sighted but too vain, as a popular landlady, to wear glasses. Perhaps she was *not* so innocent, even in her consciousness . . . But that is only a suggestion, to open up the field of enquiry at the point where commentators, for some reason, feel they want to close it up. Why? We know about Mrs Bathurst from what a couple of sailors say about her, and from what Pyecroft reports of the state Vickery is in because of her. They say she has 'It' (Kipling anticipated Elinor Glyn by some years in the use of this term for 'sex appeal'), and later Vickery says that he himself 'is' '*it*', which is emphasised. As in a newsreel – Gilbert is right in drawing attention to this – the tale consists of discreet bits of 'clips', each clip seen through the eye, not of a camera, but of a sensibility, truthful or untruthful, prejudiced or unprejudiced, honest or misleading, shrewd or dense, subtle or coarse, sensitive or insensitive . . . The exception, if Pyecroft is telling the truth, is what the camera shows us of Mrs Bathurst: to the newsman, the cameraman making up his reel, she is just a striking woman getting off a train; but in the sensibility of Click Vickery she is coming towards and after him . . .

But let us play the game – it is only a game, like the cinema, or reading – of looking at this story with the intention of testing Inspector Hooper's role in it. The narrator meets Hooper, whom he knows, after discovering that the ship he wanted to visit has just steamed away. What is he going to find out about Hooper? A few lines on, he speaks of his 'prophetic soul' in buying extra beer from the Greeks, thinking of what the newly arrived Pyecroft and Pritchard are going to consume.

Hooper, a detective, has just come back from an investigative trip up-country. The two others soon turn up, and he takes no particular interest in them, though he responds civilly enough to their services banter ('an' I assure you, Mr Hooper, even a sailor-man has a heart to break'). But the story they tell of Boy Niven's exploit might (or might not) alert him (as a detective) to the fact that they are *gullible*. For Boy Niven led them a merry dance, and what is emphasised in their recounting of this is just how tall the story was. Perhaps, then, Pyecroft is *still as stupid and liable to misunderstand as he was then* (perhaps, though, he is not: we are in life here, not fiction). What they got for their gullibility was thunder and 'continuous lightning'. The subject of Vickery comes up when the desertion of a man, one of the eight misled by Boy Niven, is being discussed. This man, Moon (another suggestion of *lunacy* in connection with *running off with women*?), who 'always showed signs o' bein' a Mormonistic beggar', 'slipped off quietly' while his ship was cruising among the South Seas.

They hadn't the time to chase him even, says Pritchard, if the navigation officer had been up to his job. Wasn't he, Hooper asks? Pyecroft explains that he was not, and ends, 'They *do* do strange things at sea, Mr Hooper', and Mr Hooper comments, 'Ah! I'm not a taxpayer'. Then, the narrator adds, Pritchard 'seemed to be one who had a difficulty dropping subjects', for he persists in comments about Moon, and these lead Pyecroft into the subject of Vickery: 'It takes them at all ages. Look at – you know?' When Pritchard alludes to his absence without leave up-country, Hooper takes an interest. (He has seen the 'M.V.' on the charred chest.) But when he asks, 'Did they circulate his description?' Pritchard becomes suspicious that this detective is trying to capture his service colleague for a reward, and he gets up as if to leave: 'per'aps we may 'ave made an error in . . .' (the tale is redolent with error) he begins; Hooper crimsons 'rapidly', and the narrator – perhaps he is Kipling – has to turn to Pyecroft to cool things down. Pritchard, appealed to, comments that he only wishes to observe that Hooper takes 'a *bloomin'* curiosity' in the matter. We cannot say that the matter of his embarrassment is not emphasised. The narrator, who *may* be Kipling himself after a story at all costs (even if it is hardly a story), smooths things over by explaining to Hooper that while Pritchard regards him as 'the Law', he will 'vouch' for him: the storyteller will '*take all the responsibility for Mr Hooper*'. When asked facetiously by Pyecroft to apologise 'all round' for his rudeness, Pritchard cannot understand quite why his behaviour has been unreasonable, and, so far as Pyecroft is concerned, it is merely a matter of politeness because Mr Hooper has been offended and Mr Hooper has been vouched for by his friend, the narrator.

At this point Hooper says something that can hardly be an error, since Kipling so carefully went over all his writings. (He did talk about a certain error he had made which no reader had ever noticed, but he might have made that up to tease; if he didn't, then he probably meant some technical error. Kipling readers have delighted to try to find it. This can hardly be it, though.)

Hooper says, 'You did quite right to look out for your own end o' the line . . . I'd ha' done the same with a gentleman I didn't know, you see.' (In this tale Pyecroft is always saying, 'so to speak', 'so to say', and Hooper is always saying 'you see' – both these tricks of speech drawing our attention to the nature of reality, which is never what it seems to be.) Then he asks, 'If you don't mind I'd like to hear a little more o' your Mr Vickery. It's safe with me, you see?'

Now how can he possibly have known Vickery's full name? It has not yet been mentioned, by anyone. He has seen the tattooed 'M.V.', and they have spoken of him as 'V'. The narrator has never heard the name or the story. Hooper was merely told by the sick inspector whom he relieved that he should look out for two tramps in the teak; he does find them, but they have been struck by lightning and there are no means of identification beyond the teeth and the tattoo . . . In so careful a writer, and in so deliberately obscure a story, this must give rise to enquiry. Kipling so cunningly links up details in the story itself with ones in the epigraph that he must have been perfectly aware of what he was doing.

So far as that is concerned, there is the matter of lightning, which is mentioned three times. There is hell: the fool, the groom, Jack Straw, waiting to be *hanged* (murder comes into this when Vickery denies it), 'plucks the left sleeve of Destiny in Hell to overtake why she clapped him up like a fly on a sunny wall' – and then the Sergeant 'called all the powers of darkness to witness his bewilderment' when Pyecroft suddenly brings in Mrs Bathurst, whom he, Pritchard, has known, too, and whom he remembers so well. *Vulcan*, who in the epigraph caught Venus with Mars in the 'house of stinking Capricorn' (Kipling's joke about his, his wife's and one of his children's sun-sign), is of course the God of thunder and *lightning*. The epigraph, a mere fragment from a play, is as obscure as the tale. Three men, Gow, a prince, Ferdinand, speak: of the sacking of a city and of a man, Jack of the Straw, about to be hanged. There is also a Duke who works God's will 'very exactly' in the hanging. Jack is condemned because of some actions of a woman who loved him, and never knew what she did to him (or would not have done it). Yet Jack may in a sense have had some control since he 'threw life from him' for 'a little sleep'. Gow says that the astrologers would have predicted his fate had he been a King; and he is reported by him as asking, 'Have I any look of a King . . . to be so baited on all sides by Fortune . . .?'

To return to Hooper. When he sits down with the narrator, it is to 'a tray of spiked documents'. Since Pritchard must see these (Hooper has been at work on these before he came, while the narrator fell into sleep), he has every reason to be suspicious. And are they not indeed likely to be documents relating not only to the damage to rolling stock, which Hooper went up country to investigate, but also to the two lightning-struck corpses which he says he found? The two visitors cannot know Hooper, or he would recognise them. But do they already know *of* him? The conversation jovially turns to beer, and Pyecroft makes a joke about Pritchard's having obtained the Bass through being so attractive to women. 'It was all a mistake,' he protests, and insists that the maid who gave them the beer had *mistaken* him for Maclean, 'we're about of a size'. Countering Pyecroft's fun, he begins, 'Why – why – to listen to him you wouldn't think that only yesterday –', and Pyecroft interrupts, 'be warned in time. If we began tellin' what we know about each other we'll be turned out . . .'

It is worth repeating that everything, from the epigraph onwards, has been about error and things not being what they seem. The clown Jack of the Straw was hanged for some random reason not even predicted by the astrologers: something has happened to a clown that might more fittingly have happened to a prince, perhaps. If 'Fortune' here be a women, then, in the last recondite lines of the epigraph, perhaps she went out secretly, a great lady (as she would be) from some feast to steal for herself, in lust, a clown (*coneycatch* has strong sexual implications), and somehow punished him by putting him in a situation (once again that seems to be the implication) more fitting to a King, more fitting to the predictions of an astrologer (who did, indeed, in such times as these, predict only for 'important' people – whose fates involved everyone else). (In 'gerb of long-stored lightnings' Kipling really is chancing his arm: 'gerb' is a very rare word meaning 'ear of wheat', and then, by extension, a fountain or firework shaped like one; presumably he is here using it in the third sense.)

Pritchard's belief in the essential moral goodness of Mrs Bathurst is absolutely sincere, but is based on no more than that she attracted him greatly, and that she rememberd him and kept his beer for him. Again, when Pyecroft states that she was a widow, left 'so very young and never re-spliced', that is only hearsay, or, maybe, what she told inquisitive or over-familiar sailors. Why should it be true?

Hooper shows at least understanding of what the two men are telling him about the nature of Mrs Bathurst: when Pyecroft tries to convey her uniqueness, he replies: 'Ah! . . . That's more the idea. I've known just two women of that nature.' Eagerly Pritchard asks, 'An' it was no fault o' theirs?' and Hooper is quick to agree: 'None whatever. I know *that*!'

What if one of the two women he knows 'like that' has been Mrs Bathurst? He is easily able to answer, although he talks slowly, Pritchard's question, what do you do if you 'get struck with that kind o' woman': go crazy or just save yourself. 'You've seen and known something in the course o' your life, Mr Hooper. I'm lookin' at you!' responds Pritchard, now quite satisfied about the *bona fides* of the detective.

We are exercising, here, just the state of inquisitiveness that the writer has set up in us – and so, in that state, we ask, 'would, in such an economical story, such a writer not attach to each tiny detail a special significance?' Hooper, in view of his slip (in knowing Vickery's name before it has been mentioned), must have something he wishes to conceal. Pyecroft, dwelling on the 'dark and bloody mystery' of how well Vickery knew Mrs Bathurst, admits that 'all I know is second-hand so to speak, or rather I should say more than second-'and'. Hooper is 'peremptory' in his sharp response: 'How? . . . You must have seen it or heard it?' And Pyecroft warns him, or the reader, or both: 'Ye-es . . . I used to think seein' and hearin' was the only regulation aids to ascertainin' facts, but as we get older we get more accomodatin'. The cylinders work easier, I suppose . . .' He asks Hooper if he was in Cape Town last December, when the Circus came; Hooper is rattled by this, and we are told he was not. But he admits that he has seen 'Home and Friends' there when he was 'up country' – and, indeed, Vickery himself appears to have deserted in pursuit of the show, to Worcester ('Did he stop to see Mrs Bathurst at Worcester?' the narrator asks, later, and Pyecroft answers. 'It's not known'). The implication is that he has therefore himself seen Mrs Bathurst, or perhaps it is; but he does not elaborate, or say that he has seen *her*. He does exclaim, 'impatiently', 'Seen 'em all. Seen 'em all.' The reader must make of this what he will: the implication is surely that he does not want to go further into the matter of what he has seen. But since Pyecroft specifically mentions 'the Plymouth express arrivin' at Paddin'ton', we must suppose that Hooper almost slips up once again.

Commentators have felt that the other corpse reported by Hooper would not have been included by Kipling unless there was a special point to it, and they have therefore concluded that it must be that of Mrs Bathurst herself, one going so far as to suggest that it is her *ghost*! But, if Mrs Bathurst is not the other charred corpse, then whose is this corpse, and what significance can it possibly have that properly arises from the information presented by the story?

The common interpretation that Vickery went crazy for love after seeing Mrs Bathurst in a moving picture show does not do credit to the facts presented: namely that he believes that she is looking for him in England, and that he is at least clear of the murder of his wife. Something has happened beyond his mere feelings, however intense these may have been. But we are of course playing the writer's game exactly in all this, which is right, and is what he wants us to do: to look at the very nature of the connection between reality and various sorts of purported narratives of it. The epigraph plainly emphasises that stories of common people are just as important as those of notable people. And as we search for the exact meaning we are reminded, by our own curiosity, that this is the nature of stories, that in this lies their appeal. Therefore (such is Kipling's skill and power here) we do have faith in the existence of a meaning in 'Mrs Bathurst', and we go on searching. (In such tales as 'The Dog Hervey', where the language is less intense and the whole less tense, that faith tends to fade.) We therefore go on asking, alluding to various possibilities intrinsic in the text.

This is Kipling's first story to be written in a 'modernistic' idiom, similar, as Walter Allen suggests, to the poetry that Eliot and Pound were to write in a few years time. To anticipate modernism is no artistic feat in itself, although it is a technical one. But the elliptical technique here is demanded by the nature of the tale: here is one of the earliest examples of the demonstrated necessity of such a technique. Belief collapses, and so coherence, if it exists, needs to be questioned and rediscovered. We have become familiar (over-familiar by now) with the comparison of the storyteller with God; in 1904 it was novel, and this story reads the better if we see its writer as a God in command of his characters withholding, from his expectant bourgeois audience, the resolution they demand.

Certainly Gilbert puts his finger on it when he says that the narrator in the story represents 'man's eternal quest for the meaning concealed in random events. And the art of the story is aposiopesis, the device of classical rhetoric which seeks, on every level of the narrative, to withhold the ultimate secret.'

Ah: the ultimate secret! That is what Gilbert omits to mention, as I also do. Yet there is no point in the practice of aposiopesis if there is *no* meaning, no 'ultimate secret' . . . That is what lies behind this masterpiece: the secret that has not yet been discovered. There is something factual here, a circumstantial truth, which is so terrifying that we should be unable to bear it if we knew. If it does not exist then it is some tribute to Kipling's achievement in this tale that he creates the eternal illusion of it. For such a terror lies behind every half-grasped situation.

An illuminating parallel may be drawn between this famous tale and a piece of English music belonging to almost the same time (1899), and written by a man who had much in common with Kipling: he achieved enormous popularity which he lost after the First World War; he was 'right-wing', although not as right-wing as Kipling; his music was inextricably linked with imperial splendour; he was a gloomy and often morose man; he held something like the same view of inspiration; he even had an excessively difficult and snobbish wife . . . I am speaking of course of Sir Edward Elgar, and, in particular, of the *Enigma Variations*. What a lot of happy ink has been spilled about the theme of those? Yet how many will claim that the music itself is diminished? Enigma was in the air just then, but grasped only by a few.

'Wireless' was written in August 1902 and first published in *Traffics and*

Discoveries. In this story a deliberate experiment with radio transmission (Marconi had transmitted signals across the Channel in 1898) becomes mixed up with an involuntary reception of something else. There is an echo of Keats's poem 'The Eve of St Agnes': a consumptive chemist's assistant, who is in love with a girl called Fanny Brand, is in a drugged trance induced by a fortuitous mixture of spirits prepared for him by the narrator. Keats was an apothecary (once) in love with a girl called Fanny Brawne. But Shaynor, the assistant, has neither heard of, nor read, Keats . . .

Kipling had been haunted by 'The Eve of St Agnes' since early youth, and in particular, we know, by the first stanza, of which he wrote a facetious parody. But Keats is not the only romantic poet alluded to in this tale. The epigraph purports to be 'From the Swedish of Stagnelius'. In the *Definitive Edition* this is reprinted as 'Butterflies'; Stagnelius is not mentioned. That Erik Johan Stagnelius (1793–1823), not much heeded in his own lifetime but afterwards thought of as being Sweden's first romantic poet, was an alcoholic and drug addict (he is said to have turned to drugs for relief from a painful heart affliction), is probably all that is significant here. He died young, was solitary, and was torn between ascetiscism and eroticism. Whether Kipling knew that he was attracted to and influenced by gnostic literature is open to doubt; but such is the case. The poem is given at the head of 'Wireless' as 'Kaspar's Song in Varda', and the only difference between the *Definitive Edition* version and the 1904 one is that Butterflies are substituted for Psyche, which must imply a link with Keats's 'Ode to Psyche'.

'Wireless' has been called 'over-ingenious', but those who so call it seem not to have taken its close-knit imagery – clustered around the details in 'The Eve of St Agnes' and in Keats's life – into account. The creation of atmosphere is extraordinary in its power: the chilly night, the brutal east wind that clears the street of most people (compare 'Mrs Bathurst'), the shop with its many-coloured jars, the sickness that is prevalent in the town, the eerieness produced by the strange experiment . . . The setting is in Brighton (one assumes – but it could be Newhaven or Seaford), where, in the back-room of a chemist's shop, an experiment in radio transmission is about to take place. For anyone who lives on the Sussex coast the evocative power is uncanny. The pharmacist, Mr Cashell, is in bed with influenza; his nephew is in the back getting things ready for his experiment. Last time he performed it in a hotel, and the batteries electrified the water-supply, with the result that the ladies got a shock when they took a bath. This instantly creates an image of 'electrified' naked women. Shaynor is presented as a zealous fellow, romantically interested in medicines, without 'polish', excessively commercial, in thrall to a determined young lady who excites him and makes him flush. He does resemble Keats, but there is something missing somewhere.

Young Mr Cashell, the experimenter, is as romantic about radio as Shaynor is about drugs and their prices: he is about, he feels, to test the 'Powers'. Asked what exactly the power is, he answers, in a word of which Kipling was fond, 'It's just It'. The powers all depend, he explains, on a thin glass tube which he picks up, and which he calls the 'coherer'.

When Shaynor goes off into his drugged trance, young Cashell tries to explain to the narrator how radio works. His explanation is a metaphor, too, for how Kipling wants us to consider 'inspiration':

> 'The Hertzian waves, you see, come out of space from the station that despatches 'em, and all these little particles are attracted together – cohere, we call it – for just so long as the current passes through them . . . Now, it's important to remember that the current is an induced current. There are many kinds of induction –'
> 'Yes, but what *is* induction?'
> 'That's rather hard to explain untechnically. But the long and short of it is that when a current of electricity passes through a wire there's a lot of magnetism present round that wire; and if you put another wire parallel to, and within what we call its magnetic field – why then, the second wire will also become charged with electricity.'
> 'On its own account?'
> 'On its own account.'

Cashell goes on to explain that it is not the 'Hertzian waves' that 'set the coherer at work'. That, he says, is a mistake made by many people. No, they 'can only just make that dust cohere, and while it coheres . . . the current from this battery – the home battery . . . can get through to the Morse printing-machine to record the dot or the dash.' And he calls the Hertzian wave 'the child's hand'. Poole, west along the coast, from which the message is being sent, is late. But there is a 'rending crackle' as Cashell sends them a call, and excitedly he speaks of 'our unknown Power – kicking and fighting to let loose . . .' And just at that moment Shaynor seems to awaken, to begin speaking words from 'The Eve of St Agnes', 'his face all sharp with some inexplicable agony'. Then he starts to write, not always getting it quite correctly; the narrator's first impression is of 'some vile chromo' recalling 'some incomparable canvas'.

Something does start to come through to Cashell, 'but not from Poole'; the narrator, however, to whom the Keatsian development is entirely unexpected, and who has come solely to witness the radio experiment, has to shut Cashell up when he indignantly remonstrates with 'I thought you'd come to see this wonderful thing – Sir': 'Leave me alone till I tell you. Be quiet.' Witnessing the reconstruction of the poem the narrator feels divided: 'there is no escape from this law', 'the result is logical and inevitable'; but 'the other half of my soul refused to be comforted. It was cowering in some minute and inadequate corner – at an immense distance.'

The tale is scarcely over-ingenious or over-contrived, as has been charged, because its writer does not shrink from speculation or, indeed, explanation. If we may sometimes complain that 'Mrs Bathurst' contains evasive techniques, we cannot make that complaint here.

It is really very bold, as an attempt to explain the mystery of creation – and Kipling has chosen an example that hardly anyone would dismiss as unworthy. Indeed, his choice of this rich and lovely poem is uncanny in its exact appropriateness. I suspect that the tale has attracted criticism and irritation, despite Kipling's newly won critical status, because the whole idea of 'inspiration' is at present unfashionable. Inspiration, like any other word, can be misused, and often is; but there is such a process. Nor is there any reason, allowing that such explanations are necessarily metaphorical, why this one should not be as near the

truth as any critic has ever got. But readers, or those of them who are
critics and feel the need to keep up with fashion, may all too easily treat
the tale as simply ingenious fantasy run riot: a bit of fun not to be taken
seriously. They hardly realise that it is a very serious – I should call it
a majestic – treatment of this mystery. For it is a mystery, and to try
to explain it is therefore irresistible. Stravinsky said that he was merely
the 'vessel' through which his music passed; Elgar spoke of 'plucking
music from the air' – and there are countless other examples. It must be
acknowledged as something artists do feel. Few writers or poets capable
of the heights achieved in 'The Eve of St Agnes' have tried to attribute their
powers to something wholly inside themselves, and few can explain what
happens. The reader who has responded to such art knows this very well,
in the feeling that he and the writer share an insight that is in some way
universally true, beyond materialism; beyond here and now.

Kipling also connects the process with a feeling of 'over-mastering
fear'. There is, to him, something supernatural about it. He makes it into
something highly dramatic – and who, reflecting upon it, is to say that it
is not? He also connects it with the gross, for Shaynor writes out some ten
or fifteen lines of 'bald prose – the naked soul's confession of its physical
yearning for its beloved – unclean as we count uncleanliness; unwholesome, but human exceedingly . . . Shame I had none in overseeing this
revelation . . .'

Cashell has been at pains to insist that the 'coherer' needs the power of
the 'home battery'. So Kipling, while he is certainly agreeing with his (also
melancholy) contemporary Elgar that art (we have been calling it simply
that, to avoid complications) is something that is there, free, powerful,
to be 'plucked out of the air', is trying to say something about the artist,
too. It is not an accident that Shaynor is rather a mean, small-minded
person – hardly a Keats. His commercialism is emphasised. To obtain
the word he wants, already held by the power, he turns to Christie's
New Commercial Plants, with a 'clerkly air'. The contrast between what he
has just written, and this, is unmistakable, and reminds us at once of the
wretched bank-clerk, Charlie Mears, and the grand power that was wasted
through his small mind. The 'home battery' in Shaynor is supplied by his
desire for Fanny Brand, so that he writes (and this is his own), 'I wish we
could run away like two lovers into the storm and get that little cottage
by the sea which we are always thinking about, my own dear darling.'
Commonplace stuff, yes, but . . . It does enable him to 'pick up the signal'.
He is even able to achieve what the narrator feels is supreme poetry; but
the effort causes him great anguish, and he awakes from his trance, not
knowing at all what he has done. When the narrator reads him what he
has just written his comment is, 'Ah! Anybody could see that he was a
druggist from that line about the tinctures and syrups. It's a fine tribute to
our profession'!

Now young Mr Cashell is allowed a word. Something peculiar is going
on.

> The Morse instrument was ticking furiously. Mr Cashell interpreted:
> '"K.K.V. Can make nothing of your signals."' A pause. '"M.M.V. M.M.V.
> Signals unintelligible. Purpose anchor Sandown Bay. Examine instruments
> tomorrow."* Do you know what that means? It's a couple of men-o'-war
> working Marconi signals off the Isle of Wight. They are trying to talk to

each other. Neither can read the other's messages, but all their messages are being taken in by our receiver here . . .'

The ships' transmitters were in good order, explains Cashell, but their receivers were not. The narrator asks why that was, and Cashell can only say that there is no explanation, but that 'Science will know tomorrow'. The induction, he surmises, is faulty: not 'tuned to receive just the number of vibrations per second that the transmitter sends'. In a master stroke, the Morse at just that moment springs to life: '*Disheartening. Most disheartening.*' 'It's quite pathetic,' comments Cashell, 'Have you ever seen a spiritualistic seance? It reminds me of that sometimes – no end of messages coming out of nowhere – a word here and there – no good at all.'

This is what Shaynor has produced: pathetic and disheartening. But his own comment, ignorant as he is of the force of his passion and of his imminent death, is 'But mediums are all imposters . . . They only do it for the money they can make. I've seen 'em.'

Supreme poetry such as the (surely heart-rendingly beautiful and poignant!) 'Eve of St Agnes', is something that can't be done for money or for fame; and the power in it to move and excite (and exhaust and terrify) is altogether higher – or perhaps 'other' is the better word – than the worth of a mere human personality. Yet it is not enough that the conditions be right. Although the artist must always remain humble, yet he must in some way try to be worthy of the power he plucks (to use Elgar's phrase) from the air. He must have 'home batteries' strong enough, without even being clear about how he can maintain them, to pluck successfully (worthily).

As for the 'vibrations' . . . These, too, are unfashionable amongst hard-headed literary critics. We cannot but sympathise. But, alas, what is known of 'the laws of physics' can be explained as well (by hard-headed scientists) as a series of differing vibrations as by anything else. Perhaps Kipling, in telling this tale, was as 'scientific' as he could well be. The difficulty with inner experiences as of such external power as Kipling so persuasively alleges here, is that little concerned with them can be measured in the accepted scientific manner; there are limits to the method. Perhaps that is at least one of the corollaries of the tale.

Bateman's

J.M.S. Tompkins long ago established that the theme of healing in Kipling's work first appeared in the eight stories collected in *Actions and Reactions* (1909). The dog tale 'Garm – a Hostage' had appeared as long ago as January 1900, in *Pearson's*, and, since, though light, its theme is one of healing (master ceases to pine when reunited with dog), it seems certain that Kipling was well aware of his subject, which is, specifically, psychological healing. Why should he have been so concerned with this? The question is usually answered by references to the relatively large number of stories of revenge in his work. He was obsessed with revenge, and it is a truism that his desire for it originated – so far as it was not already in his nature – in his unhappy experiences at Southsea. However, he must have known – as I have tried to show earlier in this book – that there was a fraudulent element in his complaints: to say the least, he had been unfair in his portrait of Mrs Holloway; more seriously, for so emotionally a conscientious man as he certainly was, he carried the burden of his revengeful anger towards her, in his mind, and knew very well that it was largely unjustified. We must pause and consider the effect upon *her* of 'Baa, Baa, Black Sheep' – for he undoubtedly did. This event had established the habit of angry and revengeful thinking in him. He never lost it, as the late and lamentable tale 'The Tie' (*Limits and Renewals*, 1932) demonstrates. But he was able to cast it righteously away from himself in the form of 'political belief', which was, alas, little more than an excuse for hatred and denunciation.

Only his daimon was undeceived. Kipling's daimon, as we know from the manner in which he could, almost to the painful end of his life, pluck its powers from the air, was never inactive for long. At the beginning of the century he had much behind him. He had been married under what were very peculiar – and unhappy – circumstances, just after he had suddenly and without warning lost the love of his life. He had lost a much loved daughter. He had discovered that his wife's temperament was depressive, difficult, and over-serious. She must, despite her devotion to him, have been a leaden weight. On that last point, though: it is clear that he had decided, with a nobility that stands in striking contrast to his political hooliganism, to make the best of that, to love as much as he could love, and to discover and bring out in Carrie all the goodness of heart he could. Considering that, by every account, she could not understand his stories except at a very elementary level (that doesn't mean that she didn't understand *him* at a deep, intuitive, level at which she was unable to articulate) and that her sullen and tyrannical behaviour, as well as her simplicity of intellect, must have frequently embarrassed him, there was something heroic in the course he took: a humane direction, as cannot be over-emphasised, in very sharp contrast to his public mask. So it is not surprising that during the first decade of the century, considering the private turn he took, he should devote himself not only to Carrie, but to the theme of healing. It first became apparent in *Actions and Reactions*. But, although imaginative writing is not (primarily) undertaken as a matter of self-therapy, it may – for a writer – function as such. And Kipling, soon after he was settled in at Bateman's, was in an unhappy and wounded state. Not all his work could prevent his stomach ailment from troubling him increasingly. But he could heal his own heart of its disappointments: Carrie above all, the guilt-inducing ambiguities of his sexual nature (what lusts assailed him?), the slow but sure defeat of his political ideals (as he saw them). The way he healed himself, and kept despair at bay, was through *Puck of Pook's Hill* (1906) and its successor, *Rewards and Fairies* (1910).

Not much more need be said about the Kiplings' lives at Bateman's – and the few but decisive events that took place during it – in the last thirty-six years of their lives together. Kipling became noticeably more morose in his behaviour to strangers after the death of his son. But that kind of disappointment was already second nature to him, and he was never really sweet in his disposition except to his well-off neighbours. He was, as he called himself, costive towards them. He was never, to the ordinary local people, more than a patronising great author – and he was never even as friendly as he had been to the soldiers when he first went to the Boer War. He appreciated working men more as soldiers than as working men, by whom he felt threatened. Yet *Puck* is, among other things, a celebration of countrymen, and in particular of the figure of Ralph Hobden, the typical son of the soil through countless Sussex generations.

To read most accounts of Kipling's life at Burwash one might be excused for assuming that he had a good relationship with such men. My enquiries (and I have lived only a few miles away for over thirty years) do not bear this out; indeed, I can find no evidence of it. True, the well-off neighbours – Colonel H.W. Feilden, Lady Edward Cecil (who bought a house near Burwash while Cecil was serving in Egypt, which she did not like), Sir George Allen (his old employer in India), and a few others – were unanimous in their praise of Kipling's warm attitude towards the peasantry; but the views of the peasantry need at least to be taken into account, without such a filter – and some biographers of Kipling don't seem to have known how to talk to them. In his autobiography Kipling treats them as a kind of foreign race – 'Labour', he gloomily calls them; 'we only knew that' the inhabitants of Burwash 'came of a smuggling, sheep-stealing stock, brought more or less into civilisation within the past three generations'. He could be jocular towards and about them. But imagine Hardy writing like that! Carrington writes approvingly, of this passage, that Carrie and Rudyard had 'no romantic illusions about the peasantry'. But, nor did Hardy! We shall examine this apparent paradox in due course.

In considering Kipling's behaviour one has to allow for how far, if he was going to be loyal (so to say) to Carrie, he could go in fraternising with the working people. He always spent a certain amount of time at the village school, where he was an honoured guest, and to which he was a benefactor (in keeping with his calling as a children's writer) – but then children, as Carrie would have said, are different. They have not learned the cunning and cheating ways of the proletariat, always (as Kipling makes clear he thinks in *Something of Myself*), happy to ask for more if they think they can get it (unlike Colonel Fielden, Milner, Rhodes or the more honest upper classes in general). He always managed to get on with children, although it should be noted that it was from the lofty position of great-uncle: he did not unbend. He talked *to* children but he never talked *with* them.

However, just as he felt frustrated that he could not drive a car, fish very well, or fight at all, so, I am sure, he felt frustrated that he could not relate as man-to-man with the ordinary, 'unimportant' people all around him. He had visited the pub (where he argued with the landlord) at Rottingdean; at Burwash he became a recluse. Carrington has tried to defend Kipling from the charge – if indeed it is a charge – of being a recluse by pointing out, correctly, that he received many guests, and that he made many visits. In some years, in the 1920s, there were as many as one hundred and fifty guests. However, as Carrington proudly says, these visitors were 'half the people in England who were eminent in the world of action, not merely the fashionable or the literary'. Kipling was able to have these people because Carrie was a snob – let us make no bones about that. He liked having them, too; but his own motivation was not snobbery – he did not much care for that, for he had too much of the rebel about him. Carrington, explaining Carrie's point of view as his notoriously over-fierce guardian, writes that when she had married him he had been 'a young man with precocious talents and Bohemian habits' – if only he had elaborated a little more about those 'Bohemian habits' he might have got nearer to the psychological truth of things.

No, Kipling's enjoyment of such guests was based upon the opportunity it gave him to indulge his love of being 'at the centre of things'. There were more visitors in the 1920s because by then Kipling's politics had gone entirely out of fashion except amongst those normally termed reactionary. There were few writers, because most of these doubtless felt that it would be unfashionable to visit him. His popularity was at that time right out of the hands of established critics (and, of the early capable ones who did – to their credit – dare to take him up, it is significant that it was an ex-military man, and a right-winger, Bonamy Dobreé, who did).

What Carrington calls the 'protective crust' with which Carrie surrounded Kipling grew ever harder with time. He encouraged this by meekly submitting to it; but he had to if he was to love her. She followed him with devoted but jealous eyes wherever he went – as even their closer friends noticed – and she not only opened all his letters but replied to them, as well. She was so parsimonious a housekeeper, so mean with her employees, that they used to say that she would have squeezed more out of her property if she had put more into it. Although Kipling was a heavy smoker of anything smokable (pipe, cigars, cigarettes – I suspect that when in 'Wireless' he describes the nicotine-stained fingers of the temporarily inspired Shaynor he was wryly thinking of himself), she was down like a ton of bricks on any of her employees who smoked. If they were caught, she told them, they would have *one minute's notice*. She spied on them from the bedroom window, to try to catch them out. On one occasion she walked into a hut: a farm-worker had just rolled a cigarette, but had not had the chance to light it. 'Well,' she said, 'I haven't caught you smoking, so I won't dismiss you instantly. You can go after one week.'

She was nothing if not just. She wore a red cloak, and Bill Crouch recalls how useful that was: 'When you saw that red cloak,' he says, 'you knew you had to look out.' Her head, remembers Walter Frizell, nodded back and forth always: a nervous habit that grew more pronounced with time. They didn't like her as a human being, and her strictness won her no respect. She liked to make people unhappy.

Kipling had always had two sides to his head, as he said; he must have felt this all the more keenly for the silence in which he had to feel it. How hurt and devastated he would have been to hear Bill Crouch say, today, how he was a gentleman, but that Carrie was *no lady*. Yet at times he would imitate her, as men often do their wives. He would greet his workers when he felt like it. At other times and especially after 1918, he would not even nod. But if they didn't doff their caps to him, they would receive a note from the secretary – 'she didn't like handing them out,' recalls Walter Frizell.

But they did respect Kipling because they knew that he had other things than tyranny and unpleasantness on his mind. When wrapped up with his writing, as his daughter wrote, 'he was utterly absorbed in it and quite oblivious to anything else.' Almost all his employees, although not readers, noticed how frequently, when he was out walking around his property, he would 'think of something to do with his books and rush back full pelt to his study', as one of them put it. Later, either during the war or in any case by the early 1920s, he became rather more eccentric in this respect (I owe the observation to Mr Frizell, but others were aware of it): he acquired a boy's gun with a cork on a piece of string. One works ('fires') these dreadful objects, if they still exist, by cranking them, thus compressing the air; and then pulling a trigger. But because the 'bullet' is on a string, it never goes very far, and may thus without inconvenience be expelled again with the utmost speed. Kipling acquired one of these – it might have been a relic of John's extreme youth, although given his dislike of reminders of the irretrievable past, this seems unlikely – and would go about with it at his shoulder, accompanied by his Yorkshire terrier. Suddenly, says Mr Frizell, he would shoulder it, fire it, and 'rush back into the house' followed by the excited dog. It was always thought that this was the signal for an 'inspiration', but whether the daimon really sometimes spoke to him in that way I cannot tell.

In 1910 and 1911 Kipling's parents both died, in rapid succession; first Alice, then Lockwood. He felt this deeply, perhaps more deeply even than most men do. That might very well be an ill-advised thing to say; but it must be appreciated that Kipling had by now decided, to the extent that he admitted it to himself and confided it to others, that his wife could not be exactly the companion he had hoped for. He did not love her less because of that, and possibly he loved her the more; but the lacuna within what may be called normal expectations was nonetheless there. He was an intuitive, and he must have seen, with the death of both parents, shades of the prison house closing in. Of the two deaths, it was that of his father which he felt the most deeply; but the loss of his mother shook him badly, too.

He cannot have found relations with Alice, in her difficult old age, as easy as they had once been – if, indeed, they ever had been, beneath the surface, easy at all. Both had pretended from time to time that it was easy, or even that it was perfect; but it never was. The side of him that was averse to women may well have been initially inspired, if only at an unconscious level, not only by his fear of his own nature and what society would expect of it, but also by his reservations about her (and the betrayal he had to pretend to forgive her for, and yet simultaneously to punish her for, too).

Alice Kipling did not take kindly to old age. She felt it brought out the worst in her; it was by no means suited to the best in her. She had been vivacious, even flirtatious in manner, as Trix had rather resentfully noted all those years ago, back in India. She liked the limelight, or at least she liked attention; she liked to be the centre of the social stage – although she was not in any way a raging egoist: she was far too witty, too sophisticated, for that. Unlike the raging egoist, she had plenty of consideration for the feelings of others, and in social contexts was always better able than her son to understand how they felt. She had very largely determined Kipling's ambivalent attitude towards women; in that respect she was more influential than Carrie. Although the famous remark which he uses about Mrs Bathurst in the tale of that name was picked up while he was in New Zealand ('never scrupled to help a lame duck or put her foot on a scorpion'), there may be something of his mother in Mrs Bathurst's subtly hinted at, but unmistakable, flirtatiousness; her 'blindish' look.

But now Alice had grown brittle. She was 'too bright': her vivacity seemed false because it did not hide her resentment of the toll taken upon her by the years. She found looking after Trix an immense burden, and it was this that many said had caused her to age prematurely. Her insistence upon continuing to write verse and sketches seemed more an act of defiance than the fulfilment of a need. She wore a ginger wig, and it made people feel uncomfortable. Despite their temporary reconciliation after the death of Josephine, she and Carrie never got on, and she must at times, given her wit and speed, have made acid remarks. Both John and Elsie found her a difficult and trying old lady, which must have made Rudyard very sad.

When she died on 22 November 1910 he had to make all the arrangements. Lockwood, a shadow of his former self, bitter over reforms in India, and no longer able to 'smoke things over', as his son used to say, with real enthusiasm, followed her within two months, after a sudden heart attack. Kipling took this opportunity to 'destroy the evidence' (for that was surely the unconscious rationale behind his bitter love of destroying all relics) by burning every letter that either parent had ever sent him. Trix said: 'If Rud had been a criminal, he could not have been fonder of destroying any family papers that came his way – especially after the parents died.' Kipling wrote to Ted Hill that although his mother had been dear to him, 'my father was more to me than most men are to their sons.' (There were bitter rows about Kipling's correspondence with Mrs Hill, and the final result was that after his death Carrie destroyed all the letters.) Alice had been the more sensitive of his parents, and it is possible that she had been the more sensible, too – at least until they came back to England permanently. But the relationship was perhaps spoiled by her (understandable) jealousy of her son; it would be hard to imagine a mother who wrote at all without such jealousy – doubtless she coped with it as valiantly as such feelings can be coped with.

Rather more should now be said about Trix, the states into which she got, and the effect they had on Kipling. In *Something of Myself* he speaks,

glancingly and amusedly, of Madame Blavatsky, whom he came across
while he was a newspaperman in India. She was by then in the last decade
of her life.

> At one time our little world was full of the aftermaths of Theosophy as
> taught by Madame Blavatsky to her devotees. My Father knew the lady,
> and, with her, would discuss wholly secular subjects; she being, he told
> me, one of the most interesting and unscrupulous imposters he had ever
> met. This, with his experience, was a high compliment. I was not so
> fortunate, but came across queer, bewildered, old people, who lived in an
> atmosphere of 'manifestations' running about their houses. But the earliest
> days of Theosophy devastated the *Pioneer*, whose Editor became a devout
> believer, and used the paper for propaganda to an extent which got on the
> nerves not only of the public but of a proof-reader . . .

This passage can't have tripped quite so easily from Kipling's pen as
it seems to. For Trix – and Alice – took Theosophy more seriously than
Lockwood did. Madame Blavatsky, originally Russian, was a woman
of small intellect but great charisma, shrewdness and, above all,
chutzpah – she had been a pianist and circus performer, then a successful
medium in America – whose *Secret Doctrine* (1888) had a very wide
influence. Blavatsky was certainly a charlatan, but her works, although
shot through and through with spurious learning, and vilely written, deal
with things that interest every man and woman, whether they choose to
hate and deny them, or to over-embrace them. Blavatsky drew, in her
uneducated but ebullient way, mainly on Hinduism and its offshoot
Buddhism, both of which, as we know, fascinated Kipling. He was not,
beside such men as Henry James, an educated man or a discriminating
critic (in an intellectual sense, anyhow), but he had quite enough nous
to realise that there was something wrong with Blavatsky. At the same
time, he was drawn by her subject matter, which embraced not only
reincarnation and religious belief, but also ghosts and the occult. It would
be very unfair indeed to state that Theosophy in itself influenced Kipling's
works. But it made an impact upon him, and I think that he searched the
theosophical books – *Isis Unveiled* (1873) was another – in order to satisfy
his curiosity. That this is likely, and that the matter was more discussed
than he let on in his autobiography, is suggested by the fact that Trix,
when she went mad (although whether it really amounted to that seems
unlikely), not only became averse to her good but unimaginative husband
(he was a military surveyor, 'a model of patience' and totally bewildered;
spirits to him meant a stiff whisky) but also saw an alarming number of
ghosts, including some of famous personages of the past. It was all kept
decently dark. She had had breakdowns in India in the 1890s, but had got
over them; in the new century she seemed to have collapsed altogether,
although on occasion she would return to India and rejoin her husband.

Trix's mental and emotional difficulties, of which few details are
available, took a distinctly theosophical form, but on the whole involved its
occult rather than its religious features. The advent of Madame Blavatsky
at Simla had caught hold of her imagination. Unfortunately Alice, while
she found Trix's instability a great burden, could not help half-encouraging
her daughter. It is an error into which those who care for such people have
frequently fallen. Although Alice rejected the existence of the powers of

time-transportation, telekinesis and so forth, that Trix from time to time would manically claim, she did not actively discourage her, since she too claimed what Wilson calls 'psychic vibrations', and she too speculated on notions of reincarnation (influenced here, there is no doubt, by the theosophical theology).

It must be understood that in the theosophical context these things were commonplace, as was personal communication with the 'masters' (all, curiously enough, male) who lived on in frail bodies at various locations in the East (although they could also be seen strolling in Rome). Madame Blavatsky, her successor Mrs Besant – in no way a contemptible or dishonest person – and countless other initiates were in contact, getting instructions, all the time. Once someone announced that a certain cat, which was offered the best seats, was in its last animal incarnation: next time it would be a person of importance. A lady was embarrassed, when it strayed into her bedroom, to undress in front of it. Since people who thought and felt like this were not counted 'mad', why should Trix be counted as such?

She later recovered. A sneering journalist, recounting this, adds the comment that she used to talk to the animals in Edinburgh Zoo (as if to say that she had no mentality to speak of). But lots of people talk to animals, and not only in zoos. Trix's mind was certainly battered by its descents into incoherence, but she may have been undervalued: written off as 'Kipling's eccentric sister'. She had been an enormous social success in India, praised by Kitchener and by many others, and her literary hopes must have seemed to her to have been submerged by Kipling's success. He must himself have felt this keenly on her behalf. He knew his ego was destructive, and that it had been more so in the past.

Trix, like the rest of her family, did not like Carrie ('a true business Yankee', she called her in 1945). This, too, like the finer points of his art, he had to keep to himself.

But be all this as it may, Trix's illness affected him deeply. Cancer was only one of his dreads; the other was madness. And here was she, his sister, 'mad'. This fear is hardly surprising, given the prevailing attitudes about art and homosexuality, which, in combination, added up to something too fearful even to contemplate. Fascinated by notions of reincarnation (as his stories, and his affection for Haggard, who was convinced of it beyond a doubt, very plainly show), he was both decently sceptical of vulgar speculation and terrified for his own sanity. If he was not aware of the fashionable Dr Forbes Winslow's pronouncements, to the effect that 'insanity commences with lewd and impure thoughts', and that 'ten thousand unfortunate people are at present confined in lunatic asylums on account of having tampered with the supernatural', then he agreed with them – such pronouncements were on the lips of everyone who did not toy with ouija boards. Whenever the conversation with Haggard turned to these matters he would become nervous. Haggard recounted in a diary entry for 23 May 1918 how Kipling had told him that he felt that only a 'glimpse' of God was allowed for human beings, 'because otherwise we should become unfitted for our work in the world'. Haggard also recounted how he and Kipling had agreed on the 'probability' of reincarnation ('every year which passes draws back a curtain as it were, and shews us to ourselves in yet completer nakedness').

Such ideas as Winslow's were common amongst those who opposed becoming involved with spiritualism and theosophy – and hardly surprisingly, since 'tampering with the supernatural' does tend to make people hysterical; at the very least it causes upset. Getting in touch with the dead, which Trix did all the time and as a matter of course when she was unwell, and in which her mother also indulged to a less unlimited degree, was a common practice. These were the days that produced, when tragedy struck, such books as Sir Oliver Lodge's *Raymond*. Even Carrie, desperate with grief, wanted to try to 'contact' John after his death. Kipling would have nothing to do with it, feeling that it was wrong as well as dangerous. However, when he was asked if he thought that there was 'anything in' spiritualism, he replied that he knew for certain that there was – and that it should be avoided like the plague:

> Whispers shall comfort us out of the dark –
> Hands – ah, God! – that we knew!
> Visions and voices – look and hark! –
> Shall prove that the tale is true,
> And that those who have passed to the further shore
> May be hailed – at a price – on the road to En-dor.
>
> But they are so deep in their new eclipse
> Nothing they say can reach,
> Unless it be uttered by alien lips
> And framed in a stranger's speech . . .
>
> *Oh, the road to En-dor is the oldest road*
> *And the craziest road of all!*
> *Straight it runs to the Witch's abode,*
> *As it did in the days of Saul,*
> *And nothing has changed of the sorrow in store*
> *For such as go down on the road to En-dor!*

But there was, for him, a worse association so far as Trix's theosophical inclinations were concerned. When Kipling agreed with Rider Haggard that the many temptations to which men were subject in this world made it into 'one of the hells', he probably did not know that the latter's main anxiety was that while in Africa as a very young man he had enjoyed a black girl more than (he felt) he had ever enjoyed his wife. (True, Kipling had told him, Haggard writes in his diary, that he thought 'imagination such as mine is the sign and expression of unusual virility', to which he modestly appended, 'a queer theory which may have something in it'.) I don't think, from indications in the Haggard-Kipling correspondence, and in Haggard's diary, that he ever did confide in Haggard or in anyone else about what the 'temptations' were for him. Yet Carrie, as I have speculated, did know. So he cannot have liked the Leadbeater scandal, which was widely used to discredit theosophy.

The theosophist C.W. Leadbeater did not care what anyone thought of him. But the theosophists, even for a time Mrs Besant, did care when he was accused of paedophilic practices by some of the boys he had had in his charge, and when a note allegedly typed by him and addressed to one of them (he said it was a forgery, and it may have been) was found, reading 'Glad sensation is so pleasant. Thousand kisses darling'. Everyone knew about this 1906 scandal. Kipling's ostensible views of this kind of 'swinishness' have already been discussed, and we can only wonder at his reactions. How funny he may have found it is a matter for our speculation, although he must have laughed when he later read that a Dr Nair had accused Leadbeater, in a journal called the *Antiseptic*, of being, in a previous incarnation, Onan (on 2 June 1913 the 'semi-divine' Mrs Besant wrote to *The Times* defending Leadbeater's 'academical view' that masturbation should be undertaken once-weekly on the grounds that it was 'based on the desire to shield women from ruin by a sin which destroys the woman for life while the man goes scot free'). Had Kipling known that Leadbeater, in opposition to Mrs Besant, who now believed in Indian Home Rule, was a 'staunch British Imperialist' who believed, at the age of sixty-eight, that it was 'a great blessing to be killed in the War, for it was helping the plans of the occult hierarchy to draw old egos from the West for speedy rebirth to Theosophical families in bodies of the new race' (Mary Lutyens, *Krishnamurti*, 1975) it would only have added to his confusion, as would the Australian headline, after Leadbeater had been created 'Bishop' in the 'New Catholic Church', LEADBEATER SWISH BISH WITH BOYS. It was all dangerously unpleasant ground for Kipling, and the grafting upon it of a form of Masonry must have exercised him greatly, too.

The duties of caring for Trix devolved upon him after the death of his parents, and the effect of her, as of her condition, upon him, can hardly be underestimated. The first signs of Trix's illness had broken out just before Kipling's last visit to America – and on that occasion Josephine had died. Her presence at Tisbury, and his duties there, could not have made him happy.

The worst blow to both Carrie and Rudyard, though, was the death of John in action at Loos in 1916. The boy, very much loved by Carrie (and by his father, too), had not turned out altogether well, and there are some hints that he gave cause for anxiety. He was bumptious, cared nothing for literature, and gave every sign of wanting to be his own man. Although he may have given little serious concern in respect of character (but I am not sure even of this), he did not do well at school. Most of Kipling's letters to John escaped the destructive hand of Carrie, but she seems to have destroyed nearly all the ones he wrote to Elsie, whom she never really forgave for marrying; probably she could not bear to destroy the letters written by Kipling to his son and now collected by Elliot Gilbert in *O Beloved Kids* (1983), although she got rid of all the evidence pertaining to Kipling's efforts to get John into the army, just as she got rid of whatever 'secrets' there may have been. The letters do not show Kipling in a distinguished light, and no one would guess from them that he could write as he did for children. They are just letters from a father to his son (there are a few to Elsie), marked by the style of their period. The amount of material about paedophilia is, as has already been remarked, inordinate. This, of 1 May 1912, is typical:

> What really bothered me most was not being able to have a last jaw with you. I wanted to tell you a lot of things about keeping clear of any chap who is even suspected of beastliness. There is no limit to the trouble possible if one goes about (however innocently) with swine of that type. Give them the widest of wide berths. Whatever their merits may be in the athletic line they are at heart only sweeps and scum and *all* friendship

or acquaintance with them ends in sorrow and disgrace. More on this subject when we meet.

The next-but-one letter, written in June, bids him 'flee from contaminating swine'. Since, as we have seen from what he said to Walpole, he was fairly tolerant on this subject, it is hard to see why he was so obsessed with it.

John certainly meant much more to Kipling than the honours with which he was loaded in the middle of the decade: honorary degrees from universities (accepted because they carried no strings), and the Nobel Prize for Literature (1907) – until Camus, he was the youngest man to receive it, and he was the first Englishman. The loss of Josephine swiftly followed by the final realisation that he could never regard Carrie as less than a difficult companion must have made his affections for and hopes in the boy even stronger. Alas, he hoped for him to fulfil himself in a manner in which he himself could not, and this must inevitably have led to much choked-back, agonised guilt.

In September 1907, having previously had a governess, John was enrolled at a boarding-school, St Aubyns at Rottingdean, which had been founded in 1895. He went on to Wellington in Berkshire in 1911, but left there two years later for an army crammer at Bournemouth, as it seemed unlikely that he could pass his examinations for Sandhurst. He was quite good at games but indifferent (despite private coaching by Elsie's teacher in the vacations) at school work. It is improbable that John ever really wanted to join the regular army; but all that was in any case changed in late 1914. In 1904 he was still destined for the navy, and had been given a plaited lanyard. But his eyesight was not good enough. He got himself baptised into the Church of England in early 1914, and this seems to have been entirely on his own initiative, although his parents did not oppose the move. Carrington thinks that Kipling was moving nearer to what he calls 'the Christian revelation' in these years – but the correspondence with Haggard shows that this is not so; Carrington confuses Christianity with a religious sense, which, as he rightly says, was always there.

John went up to London just before his seventeenth birthday and tried to enlist, first as an officer, then, when that failed, as a private. It seems that his father accompanied him, at least on the occasions when he tried to join up at Maidstone and Hastings (both recruiting centres). But his eyesight was very poor, and he was rejected every time he tried. There is no doubt that he wanted to go to France, as almost every young man did, and that it would have been impossible to stop him. Kipling appealed to Lord Roberts, who, although really too old for it, had been given the command of the British Expeditionary Force. He got John a commission in the Irish Guards, his own regiment. When people asked the Kiplings why he had joined up when, with such poor eyesight, he need not have done, they answered that indeed he did not have to. But Kipling must have asked himself what *he* really ought to have done.

Rudyard and Carrie billeted officers at Bateman's, and even offered the house for use as a hospital (this was turned down). He went to France before John was sent there, to report for newspapers at first hand. His attacks of gastritis, as they called it, began just before John went missing, and must have been caused at least in part by anxiety about how John was managing. When Haggard saw him in March 1915 he wrote that Kipling did not look well, and that this was clearly because of their worry about John: 'not yet 18 . . . one can see that they are terrified lest he should be sent to the front and killed . . . He does not take a cheerful view of things . . .'

John was managing very well, and there is a new laconic note towards the understandable fussings of his mother and father over him, and the various things they sent him that were of no practical use to him, in the few letters he had time to write from France. Then, on 2 October 1915 he was reported missing. The Kiplings hoped without hope, as did so many others. Haggard's diaries tell the rest of the tragic story, including the harrowing details of John's death, which, we must hope, were never related to this parents. (It is possible that they were, as the son of Stanley Baldwin, Oliver, found a Sergeant Farrell who may have been the last to see John alive.) On 22 December 1915 Haggard related how he saw Kipling in town, and he had 'practically lost hope'. Haggard kindly went into the matter on Kipling's behalf, and was able to interview a Guardsman called Bowe just after Christmas. Bowe told him that the boy had been much praised by his platoon, and that so far as he knew he had been 'blown absolutely to bits' by a shell. He sent a signed statement from Bowe, but omitted the horrible details. But Bowe had been nervous, and the soldier who accompanied him to Haggard's house wrote to tell the Haggards that he had been able to get more details out of him:

> The Irish Guards had dug themselves in on the edge of the wood when they heard a loud shouting from a body of men in their rear. The Sergeant in charge thinking the Germans were making a flank or rear attack ordered them to retire from the wood. This they did and found the noise to be the cheers of the Grenadier Guards who had come up to support the Irish. Bowe now says that as they left this wood he saw an officer, who *he could swear* was Mr Kipling, leaving the wood on his way to the rear and trying to fasten a field dressing round his mouth which was badly shattered by a piece of shell. Bowe would have helped him but for the fact the officer was crying with the pain of the wound and he did not want to humiliate him by offering him assistance.

Haggard added that he would not send this on to Kipling. John's body was never found, and the likelihood is that he was buried by a shell. He had been the apple of Carrie's eye, the only human being who could make her laugh. Kipling knew this, and must have wondered whether he should have intervened when John wanted to join up, on grounds of the boy's bad eyesight. He did occasionally burst out about it in a manner which he would normally have found distasteful, but no one should blame him. It did not help him to become more reasonable in his attitude to individual Germans. And it finished him, as it did Carrie, so far as health was concerned. The sense of the importance of healing was deepened in him, though: he never ceased to be war-like in his utterances, and could not help himself; but he questioned it, and his questionings emerge in a few stories. The poignancy of the loss is only increased by the facts that John was so absurdly young – a schoolboy still except in courage – and that humanity, including Kipling himself, learned nothing from such sacrifices. And yet in what counted of himself, and what he left behind that was imaginative, he did.

Later Writings

As I have suggested, *Puck of Pook's Hill* and *Rewards and Fairies*, tales written for Elsie and John, and so much better than the letters written to them, were undertaken by Kipling at least in part for the purpose of healing himself. These stories are not amongst the very best of his work. But they are superior to anything else he wrote for children, perhaps because they were also, as he said, for adults. He tells of the genesis of this series of tales in *Something of Myself*: how Ambrose Poynter suggested he wrote something about the Romans in Britain, and thought up the name Parnesius for him; how he 'smoked it over' with 'the Father', and above all, how

> since the tales had to be read by children, before people realised that they were meant for grown-ups ... I worked the material in three or four overlaid tints and textures, which might or might not reveal themselves ...

These tales meant a great deal to the generation of Ms Tompkins, who wrote well on them. If they mean less to us, this is because they are dated: the various philosophies behind them, especially that of Empire, are obtrusive. There is just a smell of 'If' about them that disallows them from the timeless. It is only a whiff, but it is there, as is the just too obvious delight in telling allegorical tales to children: 'Now little ones, come unto your uncle and he will tell you a tale, isn't it all wonderful and magical?'

But they have validity as a kind of dream of health, a refuge in child-like fantasy, which Kipling must have found healing to himself. That they are not wholly successful (good critics such as Wilson and Gilbert tend to fight a little shy of them) is owing, I think, to their being engineered to a theory in which Kipling did not really fully believe, but rather hoped might be the case. They are thus too much of a pageant; and the children's comments, although delightful, are not delightful enough to have lasted well. The theory behind them has been well described by Wilson:

> During the late nineteenth century, men, who had lost faith in a benevolent ordering of the universe and could see nothing but chance where once had been the Divine plan, felt that their pessimism could be limited ... by a picture of historical civilisations rising and falling and being replaced by others ...

We must remember that Kipling had just about convinced himself, after seeing the Boer War, that the British Empire was on the way out. Even many of those he loved – I think chiefly of Aunt Georgie – thought that this was a good development. So there is a didacticism in the books: Kipling is telling children (and warning 'grown-ups') what *ought* to happen. Although he diligently researched in Doomsday Book and in Theodore Mommsen's *History of Rome*, the book does not stand up as history. But one would not want that. Unfortunately it does not really stand up as anthropology, and the descriptions of how gods become assimilated and transformed in the course of time are often rather laboured: nice ways to teach lessons.

But where the books succeed is in their evocation of English – and of course in particular, East Sussex landscape. You don't have to have lived in that part of the world to feel this, for it is based upon a love that is never gloating, but truly grateful. Long even before John was taken from him, perhaps when Wolcott died, Kipling had gone to ground. When Carrie turned out sour and difficult, and, except for her son, incapable of much except taking life 'so blamed seriously', it confirmed him in his reclusehood. But, having few people to talk to, save his own children and political men who knew nothing of the daimon, he had to find something to attach himself to, or go under. The evocation of the district immediately around him – he does not often venture very far from it, except to go to places like Pevensea, which is in any case but a few miles down the road – rings out true and clear. The series does not have the quality of a vision of life; but it does have a dream-like quality when it escapes from the shadow of didacticism. Old Hobden's continual reappearances were once applauded as a supreme instance of the survival of the wise common man. But Hobden is seen through falsely aristocratic and patronising eyes: aristocrats usually treat their employees better than Kipling treated his (or allowed them to be treated), and this aspect of the books reads as falsely as his own boasts to his friends of being a good farmer. He did not understand farming, and those who tended his cattle tell me that his notions about breeding them were all from books, and simply a nuisance to their work. He wasn't respected for that. Had he been aware of the power and potency of his dream, and concentrated upon the poetic expression of that, instead of linking it all with children's talk of Latin and tea and homework and being kept in, and with the sadly declining Empire, then he could have achieved much more than he did: two timeless books. As it is, only the dream really stands out and endures. He is able, as he always is; and Tompkins' claim for the language, while not in my view justified, is by no means empty. But, to me at least, it smells even at its best of the schoolroom: 'children, this is the best prose,' it seems to say. I suspect that praise of these books is frequently too awed and half-false praise; it seldom rings true, and is seldom justified by example. Tompkins is quite different: she gives her reasons, and they are sincere. But I think they have dated.

She instances two examples which are impressive, but also may, for some readers, illustrate what I mean. Parnesius, describing his home in Vectis, says, 'Red-hot in summer, freezing in winter, is that big, purple heather country of broken stone.' This is good purple prose rather than good prose. It is a little too like an adaptation from Shakespeare. The inversion spoils it. It is 'for children' – and to impress 'grown-ups'. Equally lucubrated, and not in fact as impressive, is 'a dark stain on the outer roll that my heavy heart perceived was the valiant blood of Maximus'. This is wooden, stilted, over-literary, and, while the words may – Tompkins' words – 'commend themselves to the hearer as what the event requires' – they do so in a schoolroom manner.

The passages about the local weather read less forcedly and much more naturally. But one can seldom feel other than that these books, for all their sweetness, represent an over-self-conscious antithesis to the self-destructive political ferocity and negativity of those years. All the violence, after all, was to culminate in the death of John in violent circumstances. The poetry prompted by the war has occasionally been compared to that of Wilfred Owen in its bitterness, but this is an exaggeration. Owen, Sassoon, Sorley and the other war poets – if not Brooke, earlier – were unequivocally against all war. There is an element, in Owen, of ugly and terrible brooding over the injustice caused by war, but his own bad feelings – his 'injustice collecting' – is explored in his most powerful poetry. Kipling's poems do not achieve such complexity – yet their simplicity is often specious. In them his prosodic ability is misused to revert to primitive emotions, with lines such as '. . . the mirth of a seaport dies/When our blow gets home'. It is appalling to see ability such as this wasted in the exercise of such emotions. We know that Kipling had earned no right to bitterness, either by having to fight, or by having opposed or really thought about the consequences of war; that hardly matters – what does is that his war poems demonstrate his insensitivity, because they are in the main entirely personal. Either they skilfully glorify the British effort – which is all right in its place, but not in itself poetry – or they dwell on death without illuminating it. An exception is 'My Boy Jack', which, while not profound, spoke for thousands in their pain, and has some lyric force:

'Have you news of my boy Jack?'
  Not this tide.
'When d'you think that he'll come back?'
  Not with this wind blowing, and this tide.

'Has any one else had word of him?'
  Not this tide.
For what is sunk will hardly swim,
  Not with this wind blowing, and this tide.

'Oh, dear, what comfort can I find?'
  None this tide,
  Nor any tide,
Except he did not shame his kind –
  Not even with that wind blowing, and that tide.

Then hold your head up all the more,
  This tide,
  And every tide;
Because he was the son you bore
  And gave to that wind blowing and that tide!

So venomous, indeed, had Kipling become in his feelings about the war, that when a rumour (probably unfounded) spread about to the effect that he intended to visit the United States with a view to getting it to join in, Sir Edward Grey wrote to C.F.G. Masterman:

I hear Rudyard Kipling is going to the United States. This is to give notice that unless I am in a position to say that his visit has no official character, is not authorised or in any way countenanced by H.M. Government, I shall resign.

Grey was Foreign Secretary, and his vehemence – whilst only a rush of blood to the head – does make clear the impact made by Kipling's tendency to interfere in matters of which he knew very little. He did take these things at an self-importantly personal level. He felt that all *his* warnings had gone unheeded, but did not stop to consider that element in himself that so wanted war. Only when John died could he have become aware of his own frustration and violence. Yet 'Mrs Postgate', certainly a masterpiece, was written before John was killed (at least, he had started it before his death). Thus his daimon was always at work at the deepest levels of his being: there is hardly a clearer example in literature of a text that does not so thoroughly undermine itself. This exists alongside the silly, revengeful, rambling and needlessly obscure 'Sea Constables' (1915), which he did not print in *A Diversity of Creatures* but unfortunately did include in his penultimate, 1926, collection, *Debits and Credits*. That story is yet another of his tedious attacks on 'neutrals'.

Birkenhead comments on the 'distastefulness' of the letter he wrote to John, soon enough to see it all for himself, from near the Front, in which he says, 'It's a grand life though and does not give you a dull minute.' The point, though, is that while he was indulging himself in these insensitivities and rages, something else, running entirely counter to all this, was working in him.

The first sign of this process in him, very different from the necessary exercises of *Puck* and *Rewards*, and intimately connected with his views of women, is to be seen in the strange story 'The Dog Hervey'. Not reckoned by most critics as a success, this is at least one of the most fascinating of his tales. It was written in early 1914, published first in *Century Magazine* in April, and then in *A Diversity of Creatures*.

It may be seen to develop, in certain important features, out of the last tale in *Actions and Reactions*, 'The House Surgeon' (1909). This is less a tale of healing than one of exorcism, of a hideous burden lifted. It is relatively straightforward, lightly told tale, with a joke about the Sherlock-Holmes-like capacities of the narrator running through it. What is interesting in it is, once again, the theme of *error*. This is highlighted, before the denouement, when Baxter, the solicitor, expresses himself on the subject of circumstantial evidence:

> 'Why, have you seen men hanged on it?'
> 'Hanged? People have been supposed to be eternally lost on it,' his face turned grey again. 'I don't know how it is with you, but my consolation is that God must know. He *must*! Things that seem on the face of 'em like murder, or say suicide, may appear different to God. Heh?'
> 'That's what the murderer and the suicide can always hope – I suppose.'
> 'I have expressed myself clumsily as usual. The facts as God knows 'em – may *be* different – even after the most clinching evidence. I've always said that – both as a lawyer and a man, but some people won't – I don't want to judge 'em – we'll say they can't – believe it; whereas *I* say there's always a working chance – a certainty – that the worst hasn't happened.'

This says no less than that there is an entirely different view to be taken of all wrong-doing and sin: Baxter modifies his 'working chance' to a 'certainty'. The matter in 'The House Surgeon' turns out to be no more than a mean, hateful, wilful and ultimately malicious misbelief. But the implications are wider, and invite to a mercy hardly familiar to those who still respond fervently to Kipling's polemic. It should not only cause readers of 'Mrs Bathurst' to beware of too easy assumptions, but also to consider all that he wrote about the evil that men do, with the utmost care.

The tale deals with a common theme in Kipling: *Feng Shui*, the spirit of a place or house. Could it be that by then he was worried about the *feng shui* of Bateman's itself, and was anxious to discover some spiritual means, some healing mercy, of exorcising a badness that had come into the atmosphere? And could, further, a sense of his early 'sins' have started to re-infect him? This story has an epigraph from 2 *Samuel*, ending 'God . . . doth devise means whereby his banished are not expelled by him', and a poem, 'The Rabbi's Song', which is about the power of thought to reach to heaven or to hell, and which entreats to let it dwell on heaven, since otherwise it can reach hell; essentially it is a gloss on the 2 *Samuel* quotation. It is likely that Kipling was just then trying to banish bad thoughts from his own mind.

The spirit of Carrie might well have caused him anxiety, for he could hardly have remained unaware – whatever he chose not to say – of her malicious habits and her brooding on the imaginary wrongs done to her by her employees. Nor can we ever know what (if anything) she may have said to him, in her wildest ill humours, in the way of blame. It is likely, given her temperament, that she did on occasions turn against him. He could use the children and their fun to escape her main furies – he would celebrate not having to dress for dinner by waving his gaitered legs in the air – but then John went off to school, and, after that, death; and Elsie grew up. The main reason why 'The House Surgeon' leads into the almost murderously recondite 'The Dog Hervey' is that the two tales have in common a malevolent woman (but we have to bear in mind the views he had developed, and expressed through Baxter, about the appearance of evil or malice). By concentrating upon mercy he may well have found matters to forgive himself both for his 'temptations' and his wife's nastiness.

'In the Same Boat' (1911) is a highly professional, but more artificial, story which is associated by Tompkins with both 'The House Surgeon' and 'The Dog Hervey' for its dwelling upon horrific experiences. But the horrors are not at all as well done here as in 'The House Surgeon', in the course of which is a truly profound account of a feeling of oppression; the interest lies in the dwelling at all upon them, and in the fact that they are found to originate in women.

The ingredients of 'The Dog Hervey' are in themselves highly promising and unusual. Who can forget the malice of Moira Sichliffe's father, the retired doctor who, in his 'mid-Victorian house of peculiar villainy even for its period', would 'pick up stormy young men in the repentant stage, take them home, and patch them up till they were sound enough to be insured'? Then Dr Sichliffe 'insured them heavily, and let them out into the world again – with an appetite . . . no one knew him when he was alive, but he left pots of money to his daughter'.

Moira, described as a 'she-dromedary', 'sallow-skinned, slack-mouthed', is awkward and disliked (reminiscent of Carrie); but kindly people explain it by 'what she suffered' from her father. She is a witch, but does not seem to know it. Her misery at living on the ill-gotten gains of her father is powerfully conveyed, as is the sickeningly involuntary need she has to hand out, to all and sundry, 'gifts' of orchids and goldfish – clearly curses. She loves the evil she feels in herself – but hardly does more than feel it. She wants her 'victims' to contemplate the fishy nature of her sexuality flaunting itself – as 'pretty-tailed goldfish' – unhappily behind thick glass. When they cannot understand they go down with violent illness. Once again we encounter narrowness and need in a woman – this is going to culminate in the horrifying tale of Miss Postgate. The only creature Moira loves is a sickly dog, Hervey, picked by her from a litter but loathed by everyone else. This dog is seen in what J.I.M. Stewart well calls, after Blake, its 'Spiritual Form', first by the narrator – who has had it passed to him to care for, when his friend Will Attley can no longer bear it – and then by Shend, a former 'patient' of her father's. Thus the theme of healing is brought in.

While on board ship, where he has been caring for two of Moira's victims (though this isn't explicit), the narrator meets Shend, a son of 'some merchant-prince in the oil and colour line'. Shend is mysterious but, apparently, good: he likes to make others happy. But it transpires, first, that he suffers from episodes of severe drunkenness, although he is 'ever so much better about liquor' than he used to be, and secondly, that he is haunted by a dog, who turns out to be, of course, Hervey. He is a man, one of Miss Sichliffe's father's old 'patients', who once saved her from the usual insults with which (presumably) she had to bear. The narrator takes him home and the two are reunited, and marry.

Tompkins thought this the most difficult of all Kipling's stories; although it is difficult, it does not seem to me to be quite that. In the first place, it seems that the evil in the story – it takes the form of illness, as so often in Kipling – does not stem from Moira; rather, she is a victim of it. Her father's malevolence is responsible; but so also may be the uncharitable view taken of her by her neighbours, including the narrator. Kipling must have had somewhere in his mind Carrie's bad reputation, her awkwardness, the impression she made upon others. We know that it got to the point where he had to discuss her with old friends, although that may not have happened until the 1920s. It is not as if we are dealing with a man who was unaware of the kind of woman he was married to. Yet although Moira Sichliffe is presented rather obviously as a victim, there is some ambiguity, since the narrator's comment about its all being frightening woman's work seems to imply that in his view, anyhow, Miss Sichliffe in some way caused the dog, which she had after all herself selected (the worst one in a litter of six) to appear to Shend. In that case her use of everyone has involved witchcraft. *Moira* does after all mean *fate*. Her mother (she tells the narrator) calls her Marjorie 'because it's more refined'; she makes a point of his knowing her real name. *Shend*, it should here be added, means *disgrace*, or *ruin*. The poem, 'The Comforters', which follows the 'The Dog Hervey' is obscure in its relation to it. One stanza echoes, or is at least on the same lines as, the words of Baxter in 'The House Surgeon': 'Only the Lord can understand/When these first pangs begin/How much is reflex action and/How much is really sin.'

'The Dog Hervey' is not as powerful or compelling as 'Mrs Bathurst', but it is still rich in suggestiveness. It may be that the evil or the healing, or both, stems from the Mrs Godfrey who, with her daughter, is infected with enteric fever – that is an interpretation to which the cryptic conclusion lends itself; nothing, certainly, is what it seems here, and we may legitimately suspect both the narrator and his friends the Attleys in their motivations. The dog, though, is restored to normal doghood.

'Swept and Garnished', the penultimate story in A Diversity of Creatures, has attracted a good deal of disapproving attention, and is not generally liked even by ardent Kiplingites. It was initially generated by that primitive hatred of the Germans that, in Kipling, is almost all his own – and has little relationship to the Germans or to their nature. At the time he wrote it he was displaying almost uncontainable rage about the rumours of their atrocities in Belgium. There was some basis for these rumours, but nevertheless there was enormous exaggeration of the true facts. Kipling did not stop to consider the matter temperately: as so often in his life so far as violence was concerned, he *wanted* the results he would then enjoy deploring.

But in 'Swept and Garnished', although a comparatively slight work, he reverses his rage. It is not, as even Carrington believes, 'rather horrid' – or not as a story, anyway, even if the subject-matter is horrible. It is framed around a sincere belief that the Germans were as guilty of atrocities as rumour said they were. As I have suggested, Kipling knew in his heart, very well, that the side of him that needed to pursue feelings of hatred and revenge also needed its fuel. Therefore anyone who questioned the accuracy of the rumours (Germans cutting off the arms of boys so that they could never fight) was a flabby liberal who did not understand the Germans in their true monstrosity. Such feeling masquerading as thinking – intelligent people did not fall victim to the rumours so easily, although they were anxious – was one (only one) of the factors that led to the manifestation of Nazidom: give a dog a bad name. Yet here Kipling, despite himself, humanises a German.

'Mary Postgate' is a story on an altogether higher level, and little or nothing in it is not the product of conscious art. It may well have started life as a blatant revenge piece, although not one arising from the death of John in action, as used to be supposed, for, according to Carrington, there is an entry in Carrie's diary for 15 March 1915 saying that Kipling is at work on it. However, since we are already aware of Kipling's immature propensity towards revenge-taking, it is in fact irrelevant when he wrote the story – and he might easily in any case not have finished it until after he heard that John was missing.

What, again, may have begun – it probably did – as an expression of hatred of Germans turned into something entirely different. On the surface the tale is without complications. Regarded as irritating and 'deadly mechanical' even by Miss Fowler, whose paid companion she is, Mary Postgate is 'a treasure at domestic accounts', whose mind does not allow itself to dwell on unpleasant things. The only evident light in her life has been her relationship with Miss Fowler's nephew, a bantering orphan called Wyndham (Wynn) who horse-played with her, thumped 'her narrow shoulders', and chased her 'bleating, round the garden'. She attended to his school affairs, and stood in as mother to him. He reduced her to 'tears of physical fatigue', and 'helpless laughter'. It mirrors exactly the relationship between young John and his otherwise gloomy mother,

Carrie Kipling, who has been described as clay in his hands. The 'joking relationship' between them continues when Wyndham starts to study to be a solicitor.

When war comes Miss Postgate regards it as 'most vexatious'. Wynn joins the Royal Flying Corps, continues to insult her affectionately ('A sheep would know more than you do, Postey. You're lamentable. You are less use than an old tin can, you dowey old cassowary'), and his exploits in the air hold her attention: 'mere land and sea battles' pass her 'like idle breath', whereas her 'heart and interest' are 'high in the air with Wynn'. He tells her that flying is much safer than the trenches, but Miss Fowler – who has 'no large sympathy with the young' – is sceptical and realistic. Miss Postgate is oblivious to the danger, and, when asked by Miss Fowler, 'Would you *ever* have been anything except a companion?', answers, 'I've no imagination, I'm afraid.' She sees Wynn's plane overhead, or what she takes to be it; then in the evening a telegram arrives, stating that he has been killed in a trial flight.

The room whirls around Miss Postgate, and whereas Miss Fowler's verbal reaction is that it is a comfort that he was killed instantly, hers is: 'It's a great pity he didn't die in action after he had killed somebody.'

This alone should have alerted those readers convinced of Kipling's bestial revengefulness in this tale. There is no mistaking the contrast between the two reactions: Miss Fowler's – fairly casual though it is – concerned for the boy, Miss Postgate's concerned with murder. Nor can there be any question of the writer's moral awareness of the contrast. It is indicated that Miss Postgate is less interested in the death of the boy than in the idea of killing. She hardly registers the fact of his death, and, in reply to Miss Fowler's comment that he did not suffer, replies, as though he were still alive, 'But Wynn says the shock of a fall kills a man at once – whatever happens to the tanks.' She is caught up in violence and the technicalities of war. Earlier she has been shown as fascinated with types of aircraft.

Then, having found the tears of another bereaved woman somewhat comic, Miss Postgate tidies up Wynn's things and prepares to burn them. Both Miss Fowler's and her own urge to have a 'general tidy' remind us of Frau Ebermann's similar meticulousness – for those who believe Kipling the artist to have a bias against the Germans.

She goes to the village for paraffin, and as it mists over (one is reminded of the mists of the hollow where Kipling wrote the story), can 'almost hear the beat' of Wynn's propellers overhead, 'but there was nothing to see'. Does this imply that what follows is the beginning of the bloody revenge fantasy, or series of misinterpretations, leading to orgasm? I think not, though it hardly matters, since what we are witnessing is her state of mind. She is with the village nurse when they hear 'a gun, they fancied . . . fired immediately behind' the Royal Oak. As Miss Postgate sees it, 'little Edna Gerritt', the publicans' child, dies in the nurse's arms, and Mary sees the 'ripped and torn body'. 'What in God's name was it?' asks the nurse. Miss Postgate herself replies: 'A bomb'. She says that it came from an aeroplane – but we have just read that she could *almost* hear the beat of Wynn's propellers . . . Her belief is an assumption that she, like Kipling himself in certain of his own violent assumptions (and it does not matter whether they are correct or not in this context) *needs* to make. So, after Miss Postgate has seen the village doctor (he was needed to attend the girl's stricken mother), she is able to say to herself: 'Bloody pagans! They are *all* bloody pagans.' But we know that her evidence is based on an assumption – if, indeed, the whole thing is not a fantasy. Having delivered herself of this, she adds, 'one mustn't let one's mind dwell on these things'. It is quite clear that this exercise, of not allowing the mind to dwell on such things, can lead to undesirable results.

The doctor comes across her again, and tells her, unequivocally:

> Oh, Miss Postgate . . . I wanted to tell you that the accident at the 'Royal Oak' was due to Gerritt's stable tumbling down. It's been dangerous for a long time. It ought to have been condemned.

Miss Postgate registers this, and says that she thought she heard an explosion, to which the doctor replies that she had been 'misled by the beams snapping . . . Of course, as they broke, they would make a noise just like a gun.' 'Yes,' she answers, 'politely.' There follows some further business which makes the death ambiguous again: the doctor might, it is implied, wish to keep the matter dark for fear of stirring people up . . . The point is that it *is* ambiguous, and not definite. There is a curious incident when Miss Fowler points out to Miss Postgate that her boots are 'soaking'. She changes them and wraps them up to burn them. The clear implication is that they are wet with the child's blood (one feature of the description of her death), and that she is preparing for some sexual ritual involving blood. The place where she is performing the burning she describes as a 'sanctuary', which she does not wish to be 'profaned'. As she throws the match into the 'pyre' she says 'Sheep' (who, Wynn used to tell her, knew more than she did – it has a certain grim truth). This 'Sheep' is an echo, in her sexual delirium (for that is real, whatever else may not be), of the name of the chauffeur, Cheape, whose name she has anxiously called in case he were 'profaning' the 'sanctuary'. As she is thinking, 'How Wynn would have loved this!', 'stepping back from the blaze', she sees a 'bareheaded man sitting very stiffly at the foot of one of the oaks'.

It is almost always assumed that this is a German airman, simply because Mary Postgate has no doubt of it. But enough clues have been left, in the confused situation, to allow of no certainty. She has herself said to the nurse that the plane she 'heard' might have been 'one of ours'. She makes sure that he is German because, whereas the English airmens' heads are 'dark and glossy', his is 'as pale as a baby's, and so closely cropped that she could see the disgusting pinky skin beneath'. Did she perhaps mistake Wynn himself for a German, projecting her needs onto reality?

She refuses to find the doctor, for whom the airman asks in both French and English, but not in German (she speaks in the small German she can muster). She fetches a revolver from the house and points it at him. Then, thinking that this is 'woman's work', she watches him die, in a climax that is all the more horrible for not quite reaching the explicit:

> A woman who had missed these things could still be useful – more useful than a man in certain respects. She thumped like a pavior through the settling ashes at the secret thrill of it all. The rain was damping the fire, but she could feel – it was too dark to see – that her work was done. There was a dull red glow at the bottom of the destructor, not enough to char the wooden lid if she slipped it half over the driving wet. This arranged,

she leaned on the poker and waited, while an increasing rapture laid hold
on her. She ceased to think. She gave herself up to feel. Her long pleasure
was broken by a sound that she had waited for in agony several times in her
life. She leaned forward and listened, smiling. There could be no mistake.
She closed her eyes and drank it in. Once it ceased abruptly.

'Go on,' she murmured, half aloud. 'That isn't the end.'

Then the end came very distinctly in a lull between two rain-gusts. Mary
Postgate drew her breath short between her teeth and shivered from head
to foot. '*That's* all right,' said she contentedly, and went up to the house,
where she scandalised the whole routine by taking a luxurious bath before
tea, and came down looking, as Miss Fowler said when she saw her lying
all relaxed on the other sofa, 'quite handsome!'

It seems amazing that this story should have been misunderstood in
the sense that anyone has been able to think that Kipling regarded Mary
Postgate with approval or sympathy. She had waited for the sound of a
man's death in agony *several* times in her life. Whose? When she says to
the airman 'Stop that you bloody pagan!' the words 'come smoothly and
naturally' because they 'were Wynn's own words': 'Wynn was a gentleman
who for no consideration on earth would have torn little Edna into those
vividly coloured strips and strings.'

Her years of humiliation and class envy climax in an orgy of sexual rage,
and her suppressed fury at Wynn's jokes, at her expense, are revenged.
But her mind, such as it is, will not allow her to see it in that way. The
airman is German and 'did this' to little Edna Gerritt . . . But we know
that it is unlikely, or at least uncertain. It is most likely that he is Belgian or
French, 'one of ours'. It does not matter, though, and we should not here
irritably reach after facts and certainties. The text makes it crystal clear
that neither we nor, more importantly, Mary Postgate, could be certain.
One must again draw attention to letters Kipling wrote to various people
about the Germans almost contemporaneously with this tale, for their
revengeful hatred – he is guilty of what he so stridently says the Germans
are guilty of – is exactly what he shows Miss Postgate to be the victim of.
He must have known that the German atrocities in Belgium had been vastly
exaggerated, and yet justified his belief in them to himself in precisely the
same way that Miss Postgate justified her beliefs about the Germans, Edna
Gerritt, and the airman. The story demonstrates, with a brilliant finesse,
exactly why it is wrong to act as Miss Postgate did – whether the pilot was
German or not.

But from whom did Kipling get the inspiration to create this revengeful
and, indeed, as Tompkins writes, unendurable figure of a woman? There
can be little doubt. It may not be strictly true of Carrie – although it is clear
that she could be exceedingly ferocious – and he would certainly never
have admitted it, even to himself. No man not a misogynist at heart could
have written it, perhaps: its rendering of Miss Postgate's cruelty and lust
is so merciless that it shows no more pity than she shows to the wounded
and dying human being she refuses to help. Yet it is so precise in its
delineation and its understanding that it has much pity in it. It is hardly,
in itself, a document in the chronicles of misogyny, simply because it is so
convincing as a portrait, not at all of *women*, but of a particular *woman* who
has been made to become like that. It is a masterly study in the mechanics
of repression, suppression and self-deceit. That is its justification. That it

should represent the dark side of his devotion to Carrie is an irrelevance in the terms of his art.

'Friendly Brook', written in March 1914, is Kipling's wry tribute to his beloved little local river, really a brook, the Dudwell. Since with the best conscience in the world one cannot say that Kipling's 'responsibilities as a landowner', as one commentator puts it, were fulfilled except in the most vicarious way, the fidelity of this tale to Sussex mores (if not individuals) is quite remarkable. The people with whom he did not truly get on are nonetheless rendered with freshness and accuracy. It must have hurt him that he could not behave towards them in a natural way. Alas, not many of them could appreciate how he felt in his heart, for this depends upon reading such stories.

Consider the opening, as perfect a piece of writing as anything in Kipling:

> The valley was so choked with fog that one could scarcely see a cow's length across a field. Every blade, twig, bracken-frond, and hoof-print carried water, and the air was filled with the noise of rushing ditches and field-drains, all delivering to the brook below. A week's November rain in water-logged land had gorged her to full flood, and she proclaimed it aloud.

The tale has been misunderstood (except by Tompkins, as so often), if only slightly. Wilson says that Rudyard and Carrie were 'wise' in their dealings with the local people: that they 'wisely saw them as they were'. Since he also says that Kipling expressed 'conventional dislike' of 'peasant society', in his letters and his autobiography, one must assume that for once Wilson agrees with the conventional view . . . But does he? This is, I think, a little lazy of him: he too easily assumes that 'peasant communities' are simply out to make the most they can out of 'toffs' such as the Kiplings were. That is the easy, cynical view of these communities which we do indeed gather from *Something of Myself*.

It just isn't true, and it just isn't as simple. Local people's expectations change, as the attitudes of outsiders towards them change – the attitude of the Kiplings, considered socially, was wanting in understanding. Wilson then states that in this particular story Kipling 'expresses sympathy' with peasants. I think this is all wrong, or at the least confused. Firstly, as I have tried to show, Rudyard and Carrie did not see the local people 'as they were' at all, and they were not 'wise' (unless, of course, they actually wanted to be disliked – but this need not be taken seriously). 'Friendly Brook' owes much to Zola (as Wilson sees, drawing our attention to the crib from *Thérèse Raquin* of the detail of the dumb woman forced to communicate by writing on a slate), in particular to *La Terre*, with its Bosch-like celebrations of the sheer vitality of peasant life. Wilson goes on to assert that Kipling here has none of Zola's 'savagely comic horror' of the peasantry.

Not perhaps 'savagely comic horror'; but there is horror, all right. The operative word ought not to be *'sympathy'* with peasant cunning or hardness, but 'empathy'. That is a very different thing.

'Friendly Brook' seems to me to be quite as shocking, in its deliberately understated way, as anything by Zola. There is irony in the title: the brook

is friendly to Jim, but also murderous and convenient. It is relentless life
with its demands, for once doing something to Jim's advantage, instead
of to his disadvantage; it has stood in, so to say, for his violence, rescuing
him from his inhibition, obtained from prison in Lewes for six months
when he was a young man. The poem 'The Land', tacked on the end,
asserts that Hobden, no matter who pays the taxes, is the real owner of the
land; it has no organic relationship with the story, which is really a piece
of thoroughgoing naturalism manifesting itself late in Kipling.

'Friendly Brook', like Frost's poem, 'Mending Wall', is concerned with
barriers. It begins in the dense fog of loneliness. Essentially the theme is
isolation, barren loneliness, ingratitude and pointlessness, and so the tale
is closed in upon itself, by the mist with which it begins and by the
unintelligible soft mumbling of the brook with which it ends.

By the time he came to publish *Debits and Credits* in 1926 Kipling had
completed and published *The Irish Guards in the Great War* (1923, two
volumes). He had set himself this penal task in 1917, perhaps as some
secret self-punishment for whatever part he had played in sending his
weak-eyed son to his death, or, rather (as he would have felt it – and what
father would not?) in failing to save him by drawing attention to his bad
eyesight. Few have read the military work, and it is not distinguished even
among its kind – the laureate of force did not understand much about its
practical application. But it is conscientiously done.

In the same year as he received the Nobel Prize Kipling had been
awarded an honorary degree from Oxford, Cambridge following the next
year. Since John's death more honours had been piled upon him: honorary
degrees from Edinburgh (1920), Paris, Strasbourg (1921) . . . The Rector-
ship of St Andrew's (1922) . . . Athens (1924) . . . He would accept these
because, reasonably enough, he felt that they were rewards for services
rendered, and involved him in no unsigned contracts. But in 1921 and 1924
he declined the Order of Merit.

Kipling felt exceedingly lonely, for these (1917–26) were the years of
now ever-deepening estrangement from Carrie, inconsolable over the loss
of John. His bouts of pain came more often and were increasingly intense.
He was being driven in upon himself, and saw not a highly successful and
happy writer, but an increasingly hurt, puzzled and frightened old man.
He had always had to manipulate any world in which he had been in any
manner humiliated; at the very least he had had to find means of bringing
it back under his own control. Forty and more years back at Southsea he
had endured Mrs Holloway, and later had had to invent a narrative about
it: in a narrative of it, he could control it, and thus master his fear of
finding himself back in a similar, abandoned situation. He also had to have
his revenge, by making Mrs Holloway's behaviour *unforgivable*, in as many
people's eye as possible. It was different, now, only inasmuch as he was
intuitively aware of the damage that he done to himself: his bad stories are
not usually as crude as they once had been, although he persisted until the
end with such nonsense as 'The Tie'. But he still could not contain himself
in society or upon paper. Reports on his crude anti-semitic and racist talk
become much more frequent from the period after John's death. When
Lord Lansdowne wrote a letter to the *Telegraph* (1917) talking of peace, he
declared that it had been published because the owner 'is a Hebrew, and

. . . suffering from cold feet'. As for his Lordship, a 'female' must have been getting at him, 'in the Liberal interest'. Such behaviour was, he thought, 'doing our mental toilet in public'.

John's death did not deter him from expressing his obsessions with 'swinishness', and in a letter to Dunsterville (Stalky), acknowledging receipt of his memoirs (which he privately regarded as a betrayal of trust: taking money because his old friend was famous), he complained: 'Don't you think you might bring out the amazing "cleanness" of the Coll as compared to other seats of learning, which for ages have been full of accepted beastliness.' He felt estranged from Dunsterville, anyway, because since 1922 the latter had been helping with the creation of a Kipling Society, which he regarded with sincere loathing and distrust. He was over-influenced by Carrie, who, in her turn, was simply ill-natured and jealous. Her belief that everyone was out to make money from her husband's fame had become pathological, just like her parsimony, and she may have rationalised her keen envy of him by objecting to the Kipling Society, or whatever else it may have been, on the grounds that it would encourage people to research into his past, and therefore into his privacy: what might they not come up with? Let alone the opportunities it would create for making money out of him through the selling of signatures, letters, and so forth. How would he be able to refuse their reasonable requests? Since there is no direct evidence for this conjecture, however, it may be that Kipling declined these offers in order to get back at her. Their mutual devotion in the matter of emptying each other's slops, mentioned by Angus Wilson, is indeed genuinely touching. But as in all marriages, let alone ones of that close-knit sort, in which the two protagonists are as much unconscious antagonists, there is much savagery in everyday and habitual behaviour.

Kipling became increasingly to resemble Carrie. Georgie (who had noted the terrible change in him after John's death, and had said that he looked as though he held the keys of heaven and hell) died. Stanley Baldwin, although never openly repudiated, was regarded as a traitor ready to sell his country down the line. Beaverbrook he now distrusted, and would not see any more. He would brood over the fact that he did not know where John was buried, and make himself sick with anger at the Germans, resenting the fact that his hatred of them bored people, who could see that it was more obsessional than considered. He refused to drop the notion, formed during the war, that the Germans were in the regular habit of killing their wounded prisoners and then processing them for food.

Kipling worked long and hard for the Imperial War Graves Commission, but used even this as a stick with which to beat cowards, liberals and traitors. Naturally the literary establishment, such as it was, became bored with him: less on account of his views than because he had become a bore. He refused to meet Shaw. He tended to view everything in terms of what had happened in India in his own time, against which he had, he would tell everyone, warned. Those who admired him, such as Stanley Baldwin, put down the deterioration in his personality to his health but, most of all, to John's death. Apart from such people as the ferocious Gwynne, his Tory friends regarded him as an obsessed bore – but they did not like to say so. When Maurice Bowra met him, full of curiosity, in the summer of 1921, he found him to be, he implied to Birkenhead, a sick man: no one wanted to talk about the war (others having suffered in and from it, too), but Kipling, looking unwell and eating little, insisted on talking about it. Bowra suspected that he might have 'bitter regrets' at having got his boy into the army so early, by influence. Kipling showed off by his use of technical terms, but then his language started to become crude, as he turned to politics and the Germans: he slated Balfour (whom he had always hated) for his Jewish policy, and seemed to Bowra to be 'hysterical' and violent. His views about developments in Ireland were all too predictable. Very few, apart from Haggard (who was to die in 1925), could get him off these subjects. And if, in private, he complained about Carrie, she complained in her diary about him, stating that she could not get him to understand that everything connected with travel exhausted her.

Elsie, sick of the unhealthy atmosphere at Bateman's, must have been relieved to get married to Captain George Bambridge on 22 October 1924. 'We don't like the idea of losing her, and I am appalled at the change it will make,' wrote the inexorable Carrie. Kipling, described by Carrie herself as sometimes 'quite hopeless with depression', suddenly developed a jealousy of Bambridge – but the details of all this, perhaps quasi-pathological, have been suppressed.

The effort to finish the *Irish Guards* book in 1922 had already exhausted him, and he became seriously ill – as ill with his terrified anticipations of cancer, and madness, perhaps, as with anything else. The local doctor was at a loss, and he was subjected to exhaustive and painful examinations. He was suffering from one of the most terrible and misunderstood of illnesses, as well as (possibly) from the as yet undiagnosed ulcer: hypochondria. His symptoms were undoubtedly among those presented by cancer: loss of weight, loss of appetite, stomach pains. For a while he went into a nursing home in London, where he waited in agony for the results of a series of exhaustive X-ray examinations which he insisted on having. All of these were negative. Carrington says that he was so ill when he returned to Bateman's, a bed-ridden invalid on a strict diet, that he hardly noticed the end of the hated Lloyd-George's coalition government and the installation of one headed by a friend of his, Bonar-Law. He was almost submerged by depression. All that he hated existed most realistically in his own sickened mind.

Carrie, as always when under pressure, coped admirably. Then a bitter row broke out, which put her under pressure even more severe, since Kipling was not well enough to cope with it. Among those neighbours with whom the Kiplings did keep company was Moreton Frewen, who had married a sister of Lady Randolph Churchill (they lived at Brede in Kent). Their daughter Clare Consuelo, born in Madrid in 1885, had married a descendant of the playwright Sheridan; he had been killed in France in 1915. She turned to sculpting and journalism, and had upset the Americans with her sensationalist *My American Diary*. Now she was a correspondent of the isolationist New York *Evening World*, and went about interviewing (and sculpting when she could) such notables as Mussolini. She seems to have been an acid opportunist of some talent but no principles at all, after any story so long as it would make news and gain her attention. So she invited herself to tea with the Kiplings on false pretences – as the daughter of a neighbour. In the course of this Kipling undoubtedly held forth on the subject of America – corrupted by low-class immigrants, came into the war for money, and so forth – not knowing that he was going to be quoted. When all this appeared in the *World* the U.S. government protested (so big was Kipling's name, still) and the British issued what amounted to an apology. He was beside himself with grief and rage at this, and Carrie eventually got him to issue a disclaimer, in which he denied saying what Clare Sheridan had reported him as saying, and pointed out (rightly) that he had not granted her an interview. Carrie wrote: 'Rud concerned to save the position as much as possible, for after all, they, the Frewens, are old friends and she came to Bateman's first as a child herself . . . Never was hospitality so basely returned.' Clare Sheridan, who became a spiritualist and might thus have heard from Kipling after 1936, contented herself with saying, in one of her books, that this 'jolly little man' was 'wrung dry by domesticity'; she mistook his pathetic desire for poor Carrie to tell his best stories, and insisted that 'Mrs K intervened to tell it better'. Kipling collapsed after this – such events must have reminded him, and perhaps Carrie too, of the Beatty humiliations – and in November underwent an operation. This seems to have been merely exploratory, and was perhaps done more to satisfy him that he did not have cancer than anything else. 'The Wish House' was written at the beginning of 1924.

So when in May Elsie took the plunge and announced that she wished to marry Bambridge, it seemed to both of them that their world had ended. Kipling eventually reconciled himself to it, but Carrie never really did, and disgraced herself by interfering in her daughter's marriage in an unacceptable, and even pathological, manner. In 1925 Kipling resigned from the Rhodes Trust because someone appointed to it was a 'liberal' and an 'internationalist'. Carrie's entry for the last day of 1925, a year as full of honours (such as the freedom of the City of London) as any other, and as empty of pleasure or companionship as all the other post-war years, sums up the years until his death: 'Rud sits these last few days a little in the chair. So ends the year. A very sad year for me with nothing ahead for other years, but the job of living.'

Physical death did not come until early in the year 1936. He continued to rant and fulminate against socialists, liberals, Gandhi, and other enemies to those who would listen (chiefly Gwynne); he was still sought after by some. But to the young and even the middle-aged, he was yesterday's man, but still very famous. Travel continued to relieve his unhappiness and depression, and to add to those of Carrie; thus they struggled together. The hatred that he had long ago developed for America continued to deepen, although he maintained his friendship with Frank Doubleday: he must often have brooded on the malignant Beatty. His feelings cannot have been improved when in 1919 Mrs Balestier died, and it was found that she had spent money on Beatty. Hours must have been wasted by these two, Carrie and Rudyard, as they tore through their teeth the bestial ingratitude of this monster; in fact he was not unlike the two of them, but he had been less responsible, braver – and much more cheerful. Carrie's own health failed, and once when they were in the Bermudas she had to go to hospital with appendicitis. Now at long last release came for him. It was 9 January 1936, and they were at Brown's Hotel, their favourite since they were married, when Kipling was seized with sudden violent pain in the night. It was found that he was suffering from a perforated duodenum.

He did not long survive the necessary operation, and died on 18 January, which was, as Carrie noted, their wedding day. He was secretly cremated at Golders Green two days after that, and his ashes buried in Westminster Abbey. But the news of his death was entirely submerged by that of King George V.

We now know that the monarch, besides being one of the earliest unofficial beneficiaries of euthanasia, uttered last words which could not be quoted in the *Daily Telegraph* – 'Bugger Bognor!' he is supposed to have said, when consoled with the prospect of a visit to it on his recovery. The *Telegraph* did write that 'in the midst of her greater sorrow, England was not unmindful yesterday of the poet'. There are always public pomp, polite rhetoric and lies (as well as genuine semi-articulate public good will) on the one hand, and the truth behind them, on the other. In the case of George V, a good honest man of no great intelligence or culture, the truth was banal but at least human. The truth behind the fine phrases that accompanied Kipling to his grave, when he was lean, neglected and rusty, is more complicated. 'Ah! What avails the classic bent/And what the cultured word,/Against the undoctored incident/That actually occurred?'

It would be wrong to end with a solemn description of Kipling's obsequies. It is not so much that what he had by then become was seriously bad (except for his own conscience), as that it was either silly or irrelevant. A whole generation and more was to remain unpersuaded of his essential genius because they had been so bored by what they thought he stood for. This was not because they were liberals. It was because in his public life he became monotonous. After that his reputation was protected in a wrong, or at least misguided, spirit – although this is understandable.

Now the reputation is falling into the hands of academics; but not a few of these are so interested in seeing him as he was as in grabbing him and putting him into the mainstream of modernism. He was not part of it, although, like many writers good in spite of themselves, he found himself forced into an unobtrusive use of modernist (and post-modernist) techniques. Much contemporary commentary on his work is taken up with pointing out how near he really is to such writers as T.S. Eliot. This seems to me to be a little pointless, if not disingenuous. A writer is not made to be a good writer because, despite his 'old-fashioned' politics, he is like T.S. Eliot (whose politics were in fact even more insensitive than Kipling's). True, it can be shown that any good writer is a better literary critic than any mere prescriptive literary critic. True, the technique of 'Mrs Bathurst' (as Walter Allen pointed out before Kipling became fashionable among critics) is nearer to that of Ezra Pound in *The Cantos* than it is to that of (say) his younger contemporary H.E. Bates, who, in a survey of the short story he wrote, did not feel it necessary to put in more than a mention of Kipling. 'Mrs Bathurst' resembles Pound only, perhaps, in that it is elliptical – and in any case it preceded *The Cantos* by many years. Kipling is supremely good in perhaps a dozen tales (not much more) because he is like no one else, because he illuminates life as no one else does – not because he is modernist. Still, there has been much good new comment on him, especially when it has drawn attention to how his stories actually work.

But diligent enquiry reveals that he is not quite so much read today, and that even his children's books are in danger of falling into neglect (not unjustifiably, in my view). The undoctored incident that is of interest to us is the manner in which he undermined himself in just a few of his last stories.

Some of these stories, such as 'Beauty Spots' (except for its revealing epigraph), or, worse, 'The Tie', are bad, cruel, unfunny or all three. Others transcend the ugliness, anger and pain that now almost entirely filled their author's life. It may well be that critical neglect of him – his audience was now strictly 'non-literary' – helped spur him on.

In *Debits and Credits*, the earlier volume, the finest stories are 'The Wish House', 'A Madonna of the Trenches' and 'The Gardener'. 'The Wish House' has frequently been taken as a frankly supernatural story in which a woman is able to take on and experience, and thus relieve, the cancer of a man she loves. It may be just that. It might, however, quite as easily be taken as a study in misunderstanding – and belief that such a thing is possible. Certainly it has a powerful conviction: it points to a hardly known or understood law in life, by no means restricted to the educated or to the rich, by which love can be transformed into healing. It is a tale at once terrible and compassionate, and it contrasts very oddly with the Kipling creed – unless the daimon actively opposed such a creed, and was even conscious of its violence.

W.W. Robson, the critic who has done more to draw our attention to this story than any other, suggests that it is his most remarkable. There is no doubt that it is one of the most remarkable stories ever written: one does not have to write a huge number of stories if one is going to achieve this kind of economy. Nothing goes wrong in it. It cannot, as Robson writes, really be summarised: it tells itself by means of 'touches, implications, details'.

Mrs Ashcroft, it emerges from the affectionate conversation between her and her visitor, Mrs Fettley, has not always been a model of decorum. She suffers – is perhaps indeed dying – from an ulcer on her leg. 'An' you that *was* so able, too!' Mrs Fettley tells her, 'with real affection', 'It's all come on ye before your time, like. *I*'ve watched ye goin'.' Later Mrs Ashcroft recalls that her dying husband told her, 'You pray no man'll ever deal with you like you've dealt with some.' She then relates to Mrs Fettley, who hasn't known of it before, that she and Harry Mockler were in love (''E was me master'). Then he left her, and she suffered. A child who had become fond of her, and who is able to take pain from people, told her of a 'Wish House', where one can 'take trouble off of 'ooever 'tis you've chose for your love'. Mrs Ashcroft would not visit it until she saw Harry, who was wasting away. Then, 'nothin' front o' me but my own shame an' God's croolty', she went to the Wish House and said through the letter-slit, as she had been told, 'Let me take everythin' bad that's in store for my man, 'Arry Mockler, for love's sake.' And so it proves, for soon he is, in her description, 'wonnerful fleshed up an' restored back'. She says to herself, 'I've got ye now, my man . . . You'll take your good from me, 'thout knowin' it till my life's end. O God send me long to live for 'Arry's sake.' She tells Mrs Fettley that she now controls him, through 'regulatin' my own range'. There is an apparent reward, because Harry now doesn't look at another woman, except his mother.

'But – just for de sake o' sayin' somethin' – s'pose 'Arry *did* get married?' said Mrs Fettley.

Mrs Ashcroft drew her breath sharply between her still even and natural teeth. '*Dat* ain't been required of me,' she answered. 'I reckon my pains 'ull be counted again that. Don't *you*, Liz?'

'It ought to be, dearie. It ought to be.'

'It *do* 'urt sometimes. You shall see it when Nurse comes. She thinks I don't know it's turned.'

Mrs Fettley understood. Human nature seldom walks up to the word 'cancer'.

Saying that she will be gone within a year, commiserating with the other woman because of her oncoming blindness, Grace Ashcroft asks, 'But the pain *do* count, don't ye think, Liz? The pain *do* count to keep 'Arry – where I want 'im. Say it can't be wasted, like.'

It is a heart-rending tale, as beautifully and restrainedly told as anything in Kipling's work. The poem that accompanies it, too, announcing that God is nothing compared to a woman, is deeply felt and at times almost majestic in its language. Yet it is not quite without ambiguity. It seems impossible that Kipling could mean us to register Grace's sacrifice as a means of keeping Harry Mockler from other women . . . Yet what does she mean when she says to Liz, 'where I want 'im'? Is she asking for reassurance that he will be well – or that he will keep from other women? Or both? Is cancer homosexuality; is Grace Carrie?

Kipling did not, as we know, embrace Christianity. But the theme of taking others' pain for the sake of love for them is, most obviously, drawn from it. Sandra Kemp, in her edition of *Debits and Credits*, thinks that Kipling may have been influenced specifically by the Catholic tradition of the 'Way of Exchange', and I believe that this is an excellent suggestion: that reading something along these lines may have helped crystallise in his mind just how this could work outside the Gospels, and in a sense more immediate and personal. That he leaves it and Grace Ashcroft's motivations open, without seeking to dispel our belief in them as stemming from love, is proof of the mastery of his material he had by this time reached. It is possible that, alone able to judge of the quality of Carrie's real character (he must have been perfectly well aware of how others, including her much put-upon daughter, regarded her from the outside), he half-believed that she had drawn his own cancer from him – just as she had drawn what he saw as 'sin' from him so long ago. At the same time, she kept him where she wanted him, as he had good cause to know. Doubtless this is not important in comparison with the power of the story; but the story would certainly have been a marvellously apt objective correlative for just such a situation. Mrs Ashcroft's first name was no accident.

The Christ motif is again rampant, and even more obviously so, in 'The Gardener', a more subtle tale than it was once given credit for being. Helen Turrell is rescued by Christ, the gardener, not only from ignorance of the place where her 'nephew' is buried, but also from a gentility so crippling that it denies her acknowledgment of her maternal feelings. Edmund Wilson, although he admired this story, thought it almost too brilliant, technically, to work. Angus Wilson, again admiring, thinks the tale marred by 'such a cliché'. It is a 'misjudgement of taste'. In a critic whom I admire I find this (for once) astonishing, although I do note that Wilson insists that the cliché is not a bad one just because it is Christian.

I don't think it matters if it is Christian or not. It makes use of myth which happens to be Christian. Robson writes, 'Helen can be left to assume that the gardener was mistaken', and points out that there is no 'explicit assurance' that this was a 'religious experience'. That is true. But there is no doubt of the direction in which Kipling was going – and I certainly do not mean that it was one of Christian dogma. It is the writer of this narrative who has chosen to tell it like that, with its allusion to the gardener. The writer has pointed out that the gardener, whether a Belgian or not, was just then a Christ (not necessarily *the* Christ), for Helen in her need of truthful maternal grief. If he did not believe it, at least up to the point that he evidently does (it is, I repeat, entirely undogmatic in its implications), then he would not say it: *supposing him to be the gardener* means, almost unequivocally, that he was not the gardener. Moreover, the woman in *John* is Mary Magdalene, and she is looking for Jesus, her Lord, because she does not know where he is laid. She is looking for a tomb. So those commentators who maintain that the gardener actually is Michael are in one sense right: love lives, and love resurrects. This is indeed secularising a pious Victorian notion – and with a vengeance! I can see why Angus Wilson feels so angry about Kipling's 'taste', since there has been a bad habit, persisting over some centuries, of opportunistically sentimentalising Jesus Christ. But this is surely tactful and beautiful. Of course, one may easily and fairly say, Helen resembles Mary in that she mistakes Christ for a gardener, but otherwise she is not thus mistaken: Christ could not have been in that cemetery, and so all we know is that he was posing as a gardener. The point, though, even in face of humanist rejection of the miraculous, is that the man not the gardener, but only supposed to be, was like Christ in that he compassionately acknowledged a mother's pain. Thus even the sceptic Kipling is denied, as one might put it, the grim consolation of his logic. There *is* such a thing as the miraculous, and the tale resolutely demonstrates it.

In 'A Madonna of the Trenches' some small time is wasted in the Masonic business which serves as an unworthy frame for what must be one of the supreme ghost-stories. Kipling may originally only have shown such an interest as he did in Mithraism because he took it as a kind of Masonry (and he seems to have misunderstood the nature of the sacrifice of the bull that was at the centre of it). Yet his intuitions were uncannily right inasmuch as it has connections with the gnosticism that may well be (as I have suggested) at the heart of his vision. In the case of the Masonic element running through the late stories, however, he added nothing. There is again here a religious element, and love – love, be it noted, that is illicit in the eyes of society, if not actually the love that (then) dared not speak its name – is yet again shown to exercise an uncanny power, and to be connected in some uncertain manner with resurrection. It was written at a time when Kipling was insisting, against all his doctors' reassurances, that he had cancer, which he may indeed have felt – in a deep-down superstitious way that he couldn't get rid of – was a retributive disease. He was feeling towards the kind of mercy he had casually shown when he spoke to Walpole about Radclyffe Hall (whom one would have thought he would have loathed at sight).

Strangwick's aunt has died of cancer, and has sent a message to her sergeant lover, Godsoe, that she is 'dying to see him'. Strangwick does see her ghost in the trenches – and the sergeant kills himself to be with her. The language in this story shows a return to that of *The Disturber of Traffic* in its poetic power – and the narrator is again an 'imperfect' one. But now the sense has deepened, for the matter of the tale is not only the power of love, whether forbidden or not, but also the way in which a complex and elaborate idea, that of the resurrection of the dead, supposed by most of us for most of the time to be abstract, difficult and remote, may inform our language when this is heightened by fear.

Kipling is feeling towards a reconciliation between scepticism and faith in at least such supernaturalism as may be revealed by love and mercy of the sort preached in the Christian texts, but never (as he unforgettably demonstrates here) well understood. The notion, he shows us, although frozen in dogma for most of our lives, can suddenly become as alive as Strangwick's aunt seemed to him. Thus, Strangwick, sent half mad by his experiences of frozen creaking bodies in the trenches, by seeing his aunt's ghost, and by new knowledge of an affair between her and Godsoe, is bewildered and resentful, but he quotes with involuntary rapture from the scriptures: 'Whatever a man may say in his heart unto the Lord, yea verily I say unto you – Gawd hath shown man, again and again, marvellous mercy an' - an' somethin' or other love' (this is confused with a bit out of Swinburne's 'Les Noyades', which Kipling quoted from at the top of the story, and which we must understand Strangwick to have heard from Godsoe). He is quoting Godsoe, but he too has been enraptured by the magic of the words. Like Helen Turrell, he does not understand what grace he is receiving, but he does feel the grace. Kipling was daringly trying to equate the real mysteries of the Christian religion with the sayings of the folk. It is a very far cry from the artificialities he had perpetrated in *Puck* and its successor. 'What a bloody mix-up things are, when one's as young as me,' wails Strangwick, and we feel with him. The figure of Auntie Armine, Bella, although we only glimpse it, comes over with immense power: 'like somethin' movin' slow, in armour' – the comparison with Carrie, of the slowly and unhappily nodding head, is hardly resistible.

Remembering her, shocked by his knowledge of her affair with the man he called uncle, Strangwick bursts out: "Tisn't fair of 'em to 'ave unloaded it all on me, because – because – if the dead *do* rise, why, what in 'ell becomes of me an' all I've believed in my life? I want to know *that*! I – I –' Thus Kipling expresses, as memorably perhaps as it has been expressed in our times, the dilemma of men and women caught between reason and certain knowledge. 'If the dead *do* rise,' he explains later on, 'and I saw 'em – why – why *anything* can happen'. But the apparent message would have discomforted any lip-serving Christian who happened to stumble upon it, for Strangwick adds: 'I saw 'im an' 'er – she dead since mornin' time, an' he killin' 'imself before my livin' eyes so's to carry on with 'er for all Eternity – an' she 'oldin' out 'er arms for it! I want to know where I'm *at*! Look 'ere, you two – why stand *we* in jeopardy every hour?'

This story ends with a shock, inasmuch as we learn that Strangwick is not only affected by shell-shock and his experiences with Godsoe, but also because he has been sued for breach of promise. All we

learn of that is from the last incoherent phrases in his long outburst:

> Not twice in the world shall the Gods do thus ... And I'm damned if
> it's goin' to be even once for me! ... *I* don't care whether we *'ave* been
> pricin' things in the windows ... *Let* 'er sue if she likes! She don't know
> what reel things mean. *I* do – I've 'ad occasion to notice 'em ... *No,* I
> tell you, I'll 'ave 'em when I want 'em, an' be done with 'em, but not till
> I see that look on a face ... that look ... I'm not takin' any. The reel
> thing's life an' death. It *begins* at death, d'ye see. *She* can't understand
> ... Oh, go on an' push off to Hell, you an' your lawyers. I'm fed up with
> it – fed up!

We learn immediately after this outburst, from his uncle-by-marriage,
that although 'she'd make him a good little wife', he 'says she ain't his
ideal or something'. Given the unmistakably erotic nature of the words
young Clem Strangwick has used to describe the reunion of Godsoe and
his aunt in eternity – 'an' she holdin' out 'er arms for it!' – what has
happened to him as a result of his breakdown is that he cannot go through
with sexual love with the girl he was going to marry, is afraid to do it
without seeing 'that look'; and there is a terrible acknowledgement here
of the time-honoured equation between physical love (and reproduction)
and death.

Kipling here becomes one of his century's most powerful religious
writers – and much more 'modern', if we must have that word, and for
what it is really worth – than Eliot, who could only utilise the symbols of
an outworn creed. 'Modern' implies no more than that Kipling adumbrated
here a viable kind of religious feeling, based on some kind of 'scientific'
certainty (where the old was based, or seemed in an age of science to be
based, on what was uncertain, from that point of view). The liturgical is
given new life by being seen as based so firmly in immediate experience
that it even embraces the erotic, and the uninnocently erotic at that.
Godsoe, perhaps a 'superior' sort of man, like Vickery (it is hinted), quotes
from *Corinthians*: 'If, after the manner of men, I have fought with beasts at
Ephesus, what advantageth it me if the dead rise not?' Strangwick does
not understand this, and so hears it, in the trenches, as 'to fight beasts
of officers'. But it is the reality ('she don't know what reel things mean'!)
buried in these and the other words (mainly from the Burial Service) that
he hears that brings him to a crisis of nerves. This is the religious element
in mankind that is neither 'binding together' nor crass superstition: it is
seen and heard where it must matter, in life and death. This is therefore,
as is 'The Gardener' in its more carefully limited way, a profoundly
religious story.

Limits and Renewals is the book of a tired and sick man, and it is
weaker as a whole. There are stories in it with wonderful touches, none
more wonderful perhaps than the detail of the dog John Marden believes
he sees in 'The Woman in his Life'. The epigraph is, once again, the verse
from *Corinthians*: 'If after the manner of men I have fought with beasts'.
But here Kipling adds a new gloss to it. John Marden is an ex-sapper who
suddenly suffers from a nervous breakdown, although he has built up a
good business. He begins to drink. The tale deals with his redemption
through a dog – through his saving of, and love for, a dog. 'The Woman

in his Life' fails because it is too engineered. The manservant Shingle, to be exact, is the one who does the engineering: he effects the cure. It is as if Kipling had determined to avoid the very difficult matter of the supernatural or the religious, and so contrived to create the phenomenon of healing through funny-peculiar causes. The story does not live up to its promise. Its author was perhaps no longer strong enough, or determined enough, to wait for the kind of revelation he experienced – through, as he would have put it, his daimon – in 'A Madonna of the Trenches'. The bones of the ideas in 'The Woman in his Life' stick out far too much, and his attempts to conceal them are ineffective by his own highest standards: the repetition of the phrase 'repetition work', to emphasise his realisation that traumas can be resolved by re-enacting them, is too self-conscious. But the initial hallucination from which a different tale might have been built is vintage Kipling.

'The Church that was at Antioch' is again too contrived. Here he goes back to Mithraism in order to try to demonstrate that this religion was really 'as good as' Christianity, that all religions are really one. But it is too self-conscious, its language is dead, and it does not work.

But *Limits and Renewals* contains one masterpiece, at a level with anything that Kipling ever wrote: 'Dayspring Mishandled'. The story of a revenge that was never taken, but actually worked against by its progenitor, it reflects Kipling's disenchantment with the current literary scene, and with his own banishment from it; but it does not do so in a bitter or revengeful manner. This is the author at the top of his stride, his confidence in himself absolute. It would not have succeeded otherwise, because the theme, at the first level anyway, is the pointlessness of revenge and hatred. But there are other levels: the nature of power when it is held; the nature of creation; the nature of dawn (dayspring) in its various meanings. It is an exception amongst Kipling's stories, in that character, or at least the characters of the protagonists, are revealed in some detail. It is also like a Chinese box: each time it is read, some entirely new theme emerges – and this process is inexhaustible.

There is the tale of two men's hatred for each other. There is the tale of Castorley's early injury to Manallace in the matter of an odiously sly and 'unclean' review of one of his books: what is behind that, what did he say there, was it true, does it have anything to do with Manallace's love for the mother of Vidal? There is the tale of Manallace and the mother of Vidal. There is the more cryptic tale of Castorley and the mother of Vidal: what did he do to her (if anything), what did he eventually (or always, at the bottom of his mind) think there was that he ought to 'put right', what did he say to Manallace about her that changes Manallace's life, and leads him to plan the revenge that brings him fame? Castorley proposed marriage to the mother of Vidal at the time of the beginning of the story (1891–2 – Kipling's own time in London?), but was refused. But did he subsequently marry and leave her? There is the tale of Manallace's corruption – the poet turned hack – of his revenge, of its slow building-up. There is the tale of how Castorley carefully and evilly built up his reputation. There is the tale of how he (he never knows of Manallace's role) confirms that reputation by the 'discovery' of a Chaucer manuscript, and thus gains a knighthood. Then there is the tale of how Manallace changes direction and wants to save Castorley from the trap he has set for him, and from his wife: of how his revenge turns to dust in his hands. There is even the tale within the tale, contained in the forged manuscript itself, of the old knight who wants his daughter to marry someone she doesn't love. There is, too, amongst the hundreds of other discrete possibilities of tales to be extracted from this text (surely the equivalent of a score of novels?), an account of the state of literature. But all these separate themes, separate tales, might be stated in different terms. As could be said of certain other stories, there is a resemblance here to a Dutch 'story picture'. Any number of interpretations may be put upon what is there, but not one that denies the picture as a whole, or any detail in it. One could carry out the exercise on any picture – or story; one is *impelled* to do so, however, by the quality of the painting, or in the case of stories, the writing.

In the case of 'Dayspring Mishandled' one might rather use the metaphor of a series of pictures of the same object: such a series, after all, serves as the beginning of the tale. Or almost. For the opening paragraph, although apparently set in the literary London of 1891–2, the one Kipling knew so well, is prophetic:

> In the days beyond compare and before the Judgements, a genius called Graydon foresaw that the advance of education and the standard of living would submerge all mind-marks in one mudrush of standardised reading-matter, and so created the Fictional Supply Syndicate to meet the demand.

He might here have been suffering, initially, from a sudden revival of the early scorn he affected to feel for the Pre-Raphaelitism to which he owed so much; but there is no sign of anger. I think that in the process of editing his best stories he succeeded in cutting this out entirely. What we have is a picture of the modern pseudo-literary scene. It sets the tone for what is in fact, in one of its many aspects, a tale of corruption. For Manallace (who might originally have been suggested to Kipling by the supercilious romancer Maurice Hewlett, who wrote *The Forest Lovers*), a type who 'does not ignite', but has to be 'detonated' (this stresses the enormity of Castorley's offence, whatever it is), has genuine gifts. But he finds a line in historical romances which provides him with a reputation, and, when asked to write a 'real book', replies that 'if you save people thinking, you can do anything with them'. This becomes a key motif. But a set of 'cuts' from a child's book sets Manallace off into real poetry, and in one night of drunkenness he composes what will one day be his means to destroy Castorley. The 'mannered, bellied' Castorley, when we first meet him at a café supper, is merely another hack, jealous of Manallace: when Graydon gives the latter two guineas, he is shrill with rage, but this is suppressed only to emerge years later in a scream. However, he announces that on account of a legacy he will in the future devote himself to 'Literature'. He is subsequently presented, with consummate mastery, as an insufferable snob and fake, but one who possesses, despite this, genuine knowledge of his subject, which is Chaucer. It is, though, a dead knowledge. There are few such deadly portraits.

However, we must beware of identifying too closely with Manallace, who is himself a fake who produces stuff that 'exactly met, but never exceeded, every expectation'. He is, adds the narrator with laconic justice, 'genuinely a man of letters,' 'his output apart'. He has thus denied the daimon which we, the readers, have seen him obeying, and all too easily and all too irresolutely. A set of cuts from an 'extinct children's book' speak to him, and he recites the poetry he has made out of them when drunk; but then he deplores 'the Upas-tree influence of Gilbert and Sullivan', goes with a whore (appropriately, a 'negress in yellow satin' whom he tells he has been 'faithful to in his fashion' – quoting Dowson's best-known poem), and abandons his project for what he calls 'his label', which he is not going 'to chew off' in pursuit of any serious nonsense, any 'real book'. 'Dayspring Mishandled', the title of the story, has many meanings here, but one is certainly Manallace's inertia and failure to handle the dawn of inspiration in him. For his life is doomed, ironically, to turn into one long work of art, and that work malicious and evil. You don't, Kipling is telling us, escape the daimon so easily. Thus, although Manallace is set up by the narrator of the story as so genial and pleasant a chap that he can agree with his revenge on the dastardly Castorley, the narrator (who is he, or she, by the way?) also knows enough to condemn him, on account of the thing he said about Vidal's mother, in a couple of acid remarks.

The narrative is extremely elliptical. Tompkins wrote, in what must be one of the finest pieces of constructive criticism of our times (in her comments on 'Dayspring Mishandled' she surpasses even herself), 'every sentence tells and matters. The writing is of that "infolded" sort which, at first reading, may seem to present a crumpled mass, but which gradually fills and spreads and tightens with the fullness and tension of its meanings, until it is a House of Life itself, a tent covering the erring and suffering spirit of men.' This is eloquent indeed, and 'Dayspring Mishandled' is of that quality that does draw such responses.

The jealous Castorley leaves the gathering, and, while Manallace is getting drunk and saying farewell to poetry (the 'reel thing' as Kipling called it elsewhere, dealing with the non-literary Strangwick in 'A Madonna of the Trenches'), proposes to Vidal Benzaguen's mother, and is refused. Since he is both painted by the narrator, and revealed through his conversation and actions, as being a petty and small-minded soul, the clear implication is that the refusal fills him with spite. All we are told, though, is that Manallace devoted himself to Vidal's mother when she became paralysed after her husband left her, and nursed her until she died in the April of 1915 (Kipling says 1914, but this must be a mistake, for he also says the 'first year of the war'). Castorley, too, saves people the trouble of thinking, even if he is not an imposter in the matter of his knowledge of Chaucer.

> He also, 'for old sake's sake', as he wrote to a friend, went out of his way to review one of Manallace's books with an intimacy of unclean deduction (this was before the days of Freud) which long stood as a record. Some member of the extinct Syndicate took occasion to ask him if he would – for old sake's sake – help Vidal's mother to a new treatment. He replied that he had 'known the lady very slightly and the calls on his purse were so heavy that', etc. The writer showed the letter to Manallace, who said he was glad that Castorley hadn't interfered.

But Manallace is not started off on his quest for revenge until he talks with Castorley while they are working together as civil servants in the war. They talk 'humanly', Manallace 'spoke of Vidal's mother', and

'Castorley said something in reply'. Angus Wilson is irritated that we are never told what this is; but I think therein lies the clue – for it does not really matter. Revenge is an inner process, and one which rots the soul. Whatever actuates it, be it ever so 'justified', it destroys or turns against itself. In Manallace's case it turns into a work of art in its own right (but a work directed in an evil direction), so that it becomes even more important to him to set Castorley up for his knighthood than to destroy him. Taking as his basis the poem he wrote inspired by the pictures he got from the worthless populariser Graydon (who says that if they have turned to poetry, then they are no use to him), Manallace now constructs an elaborate forgery of a Chaucer manuscript, getting at least half of his information from Castorley, by encouraging him to show off his knowledge.

Wilson thinks that all Castorley says to Manallace is that 'her paralysis was syphilis contracted by whoring', and that Kipling was unable to say this because of censorship. But he is altogether too cavalier about this story. He asserts that it is about 'a Stalky joke that misfires', and says that Castorley tried and failed to 'get her to bed'! That is not necessarily so at all: trying to get a woman to bed is by no means the same as proposing. He might have taken her to bed and then proposed – and *then* been rebuffed, thus gaining real reason for hate. There is something altogether darker and fouler behind this than a mere dirty gibe. Again, Wilson assumes that Kipling himself knew exactly what Castorley said to Manallace. I am not sure that he did. But I think that we are entitled, in view of the theme of syphilis that surfaces in Kipling's work from time to time (it was a great ravager of literary men in those days), to speculate that Castorley, who doesn't mind being unpleasant, may well have said to Manallace: 'Ah yes, that whore, I infected her', or something on those lines. It is always assumed that Gleeag, the doctor and the lover of Castorley's wife, is telling the truth to the narrator when he tells him on the telephone that Castorley died of 'malignant kidney trouble – generalised at the end'. But, since there is a deliberate confusion about his illness, couldn't it have been syphilis (if he wasn't poisoned by Gleeag, or Lady Castorley, or both)?

Even before he learns of the attitude of Castorley's 'unappetizing, ash-coloured', 'infernally plain' wife, Manallace's plan is taking a wrong turn: he has become zealous on Castorley's behalf, showing him off, sitting at his feet, forgetting about how he is going to humiliate and destroy him. When the wife, a mysterious figure who is said to hate her husband, guesses the nature of Manallace's plan, and turns out to be having an affair with Gleeag, he becomes his enemy's defender. His life has meaning only in the terms of the course his revenge has taken, and he has had little control over that. He has been as much of a fake as Castorley, and is now responsible for the perpetuation of a fake.

When Castorley – manipulated into 'sacred hours' of collaboration with Manallace during which Lady Castorley is enjoyed by the demonic Gleeag – breaks down, he half goes back into the remote past, voices his old hatred and envy of Manallace, and wants to set 'an urgent matter' right; his life has 'been one long innuendo', his wife is disturbing him, especially when she says that 'a man could do anything with anyone if he saved him the trouble of thinking'.

Now Manallace himself has saved Castorley the trouble of thinking (for himself) by quite literally inventing his triumph for him, and putting it in his way. But his own life and success at literary potboilers has been based on just that. And where did Lady Castorley discover that turn of phrase? What and who is she?

Kipling prefaces this story with a quotation from Charles Nodier: 'C'est moi, c'est moi, c'est moi!/Je suis la Mandagore!/La fille des beaux jours qui s'éveille à l'aurore/Et qui chante pour toi!'

Mandragora is a narcotic love-philtre, but Tompkins followed the quotation to its source in Nodier's tale 'La Fée aux miettes', and found that it is told by a lunatic to a melancholic. The melancholic takes it because he seeks forgetfulness (compare Manallace in his 'death' at the death of Vidal's mother). 'This,' comments Tompkins, 'is the narcotic that Manallace finds for his empty and aching life. Since its origin is in the 'dayspring' and good days of his youth, it is indeed 'la fille des beaux jours' . . . It cradles him in delusions for a while . . . Revengeful hatred is a powerful cathartic that can empty the mind of other pains, but is more often deadly than sanative to the mind that entertains it.' This is right, for Manallace has merely disliked Castorley before the latter gave him the excuse he needed, to replace his numb grief by hatred: when Castorley played a characteristically dirty trick on a typist, he merely 'possessed himself of every detail of the affair, as compensation for the review of his book'. That is nothing by the side of a plan to destroy him. But was that review, however foul, true in its 'unclean' deductions, and, since Freud is mentioned as well, so that we may assume these were sexual, must they not have had to do with Vidal's mother? Did he care for her because, or in part because, *he* had infected her with syphilis, and felt responsible? We know that he has been with Kentucky Kate (the negress), and that he has been faithful to her 'in his fashion'. This seems perhaps more likely than Castorley's having infected her (if she has been infected at all) – but in that case whatever 'urgent' matter was there that, for the whole of his life thereafter, he wanted to set right?

The darker and more mysterious side of the tale lies in the function played by Castorley's apparently hideously ugly wife. When Manallace begins to suspect her and Gleeag, her lack of attractiveness puts him off the scent for 'weeks'. What are we told about her? She is unattractive, makes no secret of the fact that her husband's friends weary her, and that she has the effect on Manallace of being able to 'hear' him think (but she doesn't strike the narrator in that way). Manallace, as soon as he sees that she is a factor in the matter, regards himself as 'playing against her'. We know, too, that Lady Castorley is the possessor of a cruelly ironic tongue: nothing she says is without malice, and when she insists that Castorley should not 'be over-taxed in . . . the sacred hours' she is of course malevolent in the extreme. Is all this yet another example of what Kipling darkly called 'woman's work'? Manallace, even in his black gloves, is going to be no match for her.

Almost all commentators say that Castorley's illness is cancer. But the details of it are very confused. Since Gleeag is having an affair with his wife, he can hardly be counted as in the least truthful. I think that there is enough evidence to suggest that Castorley may be being poisoned; and, since Gleeag is a surgeon, that he might even have been manipulated during his operation. Indeed, Gleeag and his lover may well be demons ± very slightly reminiscent, perhaps, of Peter Quint – who are punishing both

Castorley and Manallace for their betrayal of the 'reel thing', which is after all apparent in this story, standing as it does as a silent contrast to all that is done against it. The ending is quite as authentically terrifying as anything Henry James, himself a master of the sinister and the evil, wrote:

> As, on the appointed words, the coffin crawled sideways, through the noiselessly-closing doorflaps, I saw Lady Castorley's eyes turn toward Gleeag.

But the victims here, Castorley and Manallace – now set for a losing battle-royal with a woman who can hear him think – have not been good people, and are neither innocent nor children. Manallace has been more genial, has been more able to get opinion on his side – but nothing we hear of him has been good. He has, true, cared for a sick woman, but we have no details and so cannot know his motives. The wife of Castorley never believed a word he said (so she tells him) since before she married him. Why did she marry him? The questions this tale seeks to draw from us cannot, perhaps, ever be answered. But by posing themselves as insistently as they do, they draw attention to their universality: they are all connected with forces that rule men (not, perhaps, in this context, women – or there is no certainty of it), love, devotion, self-esteem both sexual and professional, envy, revenge, hate . . .

Kipling had desired fame, and had found even more than he bargained for. He spent the rest of his life not only in having revenge for the intrusion into his privacy that it entailed, but also in examining, however reluctantly, the mainsprings of his angry feelings. From being the most talked-of author in the world, he declined to a – in the eyes of the establishment – has-been. He felt that deeply, too. He liked the company of George V, but even so complained to Haggard of how boring it was at Buckingham Palace. He lost the respect of well-disposed people by his extremism – simply, really, through being unable to control his emotions. He belonged, in politics, to an area that contributes nothing to rational or civilised behaviour. That made him irresponsible, for he had influence.

But in his art he so thoroughly undermined himself that he had to attribute it to an external daimon of which he was simply the instrument. If Lady Castorley is indeed an instrument of fate, determined to take Manallace to terrible task for his betrayal of art, and for his professed wish to free people from the burden of thought, then we may wish to think of Carrie as in some way Kipling's muse. She did not understand much of his work, certainly at a critical level, and she was by no means a literary lady; she made his day-to-day life increasingly difficult and unhappy. She was 'infernally plain'. But she was also Vidal's mother.

Select Bibliography

Martindell, E.W., *Bibliography of the Works of Rudyard Kipling*,
   London, Bodley Head, 1922, rev. 1923.
Livingstone, Flora V., *Bibliography of the Works of Rudyard Kipling*,
   Cambridge, Mass., Harvard University Press, 1927, and *Supplement*, 1938.
Stewart, J.McG., *Rudyard Kipling: A Bibliographical Catalogue*, London,
   Oxford University Press, 1959.

Brown, H., *Rudyard Kipling*, London, Hamish Hamilton, 1945.
Carrington, C., *Rudyard Kipling: His Life and Work*, London, Macmillan,
   1955, rev. 1978.
Mason, P., *Kipling: The Glass, the Shadow and the Fire*, London, Jonathan
   Cape, 1975.
Wilson, A., *The Strange Ride of Rudyard Kipling*, London, Secker & Warburg,
   1977.
Birkenhead, Lord, *Rudyard Kipling*, London, Weidenfeld & Nicolson, 1978.

Tompkins, J.M.S., *The Art of Rudyard Kipling*, Cambridge, Cambridge
   University Press, 1959.

Rutherford, A. (ed.), *Kipling's Mind and Art*, Edinburgh and London, Oliver
   and Boyd, 1964.
Gilbert, E. (ed.), *Kipling and the Critics*, London, Owen, 1965.
Gross, J. (ed.), *Rudyard Kipling: The Man, His Work and His World*, London,
   Weidenfeld & Nicolson, 1972.

Page, N., *A Kipling Companion*, London, Macmillan, 1984.

Index